The
American
Spirit

Selected and Edited with
Introductions and Commentary by

Thomas A. Bailey
David M. Kennedy

Stanford University

D. C. Heath and Company
Lexington, Massachusetts Toronto

The American Spirit

UNITED STATES HISTORY AS SEEN BY CONTEMPORARIES

Volume II

FIFTH EDITION

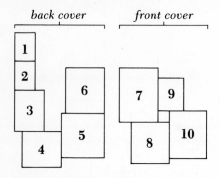

back cover | front cover

COVER ILLUSTRATIONS:

1. and 2. The drawings of the authors are by Robert Rose.
3. This 1926 magazine cover features jazz, "flappers," and Prohibition—three distinctive developments in the Delirious Decade of the 1920's. (Courtesy of the New York Historical Society, New York City)
4. Franklin Roosevelt, who liked to refer to himself as "Doctor New Deal," experimented with all kinds of remedies for the sick American economy in the Depression Decade of the 1930's. (Library of Congress)
5. America finally exited from the frustrating maze of Vietnam with unseemly haste in April 1975, when the pro–U.S. regime in Saigon collapsed. (Swann Collection of Carica-tures and Cartoons, Library of Congress)
6. The Emergency Quota Act of 1921 imposed quotas on immigration for the first time in American history. The immigrant flood thereafter slowed to a trickle. (Library of Congress)
7. Millions of women went to work in factories during World War II. The war marked the beginning of a major shift in the roles of American women—out of the house and into the workplace. (State Historical Society of Wisconsin)
8. Theodore Roosevelt, who believed America should "speak softly and carry a big stick," practiced what he preached when he aided a Panamanian rebellion against Colombia in 1903, paving the way for construction of the Panama Canal. (The New York *Globe*, ca. 1903)
9. Reminiscent of the ill-starred Ancient Mariner in Samuel Taylor Coleridge's epic poem, Richard Nixon was cursed with the "albatross" of the Watergate scandal in the early 1970's. Fallout from the scandal eventually forced his resignation from the Presidency in 1974. (Courtesy Scrawls and the Palm Beach *Post*)
10. This World War I–era cartoon, showing the winged goddess of Victory shepherding an American soldier into battle, illustrates the romantic and heroic attitude toward war felt by many Americans of the time. (The Bettmann Archive)

International Standard Book Number: 0-669-05381-3

Library of Congress Catalog Card Number: 83-80924

Preface

The American Spirit attempts to recapture the spirit of the American past as expressed by the men and women who lived it. Movers and shakers who shaped events share the spotlight with humble folk whose lives were touched by them. In all cases we have tried to find clear and pungent documents that combine intrinsic human interest with significant historical perspectives. Students in American history courses will discover in these selections the satisfactions of working with "primary" documents—the "raw material" from which coherent historical accounts are crafted.

Our objective is to convey a sense of the wonder and the woe, the passion and the perplexity, with which Americans have confronted their lives and their times. We seek especially to stimulate reflection on the richness, variety, and complexity of American history, and an appreciation of the problems and prejudices of people in the past. We consequently devote much attention to the unpopular or unsuccessful side of controversial issues, to the plight of minorities, and to the criticisms of foreigners. A number of these selections will also introduce the reader to the techniques of historical analysis and criticism.

This edition of *The American Spirit* has been revised to make it fully compatible with the Seventh Edition of our textbook *The American Pageant*. For each chapter in the *Pageant* there is now a corresponding chapter in the *Spirit*. If they choose, instructors may use the two books together; but we have also maintained the chronological framework and enriched the explanatory materials of the *Spirit*, so that it can be used with virtually any conventional text, or on its own. Prologues for each chapter, headnotes for each document, and occasional explanatory inserts provide continuity. Selections relating to the same topic are grouped together in sections within chapters. Questions at the end of each headnote and Thought Provokers at the end of each chapter stimulate students to think critically. Several specially drawn maps and numerous cartoons add visual interest and perspective.

Like the revised *Pageant*, this new *Spirit* contains more material than previous editions about native Americans, blacks, women, family history, and economic history. We have also added several "landmark" documents, such as James Madison's *Federalist No. 10*, John Marshall's Supreme Court decision in the case of *Marbury* v. *Madison*, Martin Luther King's *Letter From a Birmingham Jail*, and Dwight D. Eisenhower's *Farewell Address*. The result, we hope, is a more balanced and much improved *Spirit* that will enable readers to savor the taste and feel the texture of the American past.

T.A.B.
D.M.K.
Stanford University

Contents

24. **THE ORDEAL OF RECONSTRUCTION**   447

A. THE STATUS OF THE SOUTH: *Schurz Reports Southern Defiance. General Grant Is Optimistic. The Ex-Slaves Confront Freedom. Emancipation Violence in Texas.* B. IMPEACHING THE PRESIDENT: *Johnson's Cleveland Speech. Senator Trumbull Defends Johnson.* C. "BLACK RECONSTRUCTION": *Stevens Demands Black Suffrage. Black-and-White Legislatures. Du Bois Justifies Black Legislators. Tillman's Anti-Black Tirade.* D. THE LEGACY OF RECONSTRUCTION: *Editor Godkin Grieves. Frederick Douglass Complains. Booker T. Washington Reflects.*

25. **POLITICS IN THE GILDED AGE, 1869–1889**   469

A. THE LIBERAL REPUBLICAN REVOLT: *Schurz Exposes the Spoilsmen. Greeley Praises Greeley. The Democrats Arraign Grant. Grant's Farewell Apology.* B. HAYES AND THE SOUTHERN PROBLEM: *Hayes Believes Himself Defrauded. Chandler Assails the Solid South.* C. THE BEGINNINGS OF CIVIL SERVICE REFORM: *Morton Praises the Spoils System.* Harper's Weekly *Hails a New Era. Schurz Applauds Partial Gains.* D. THE BLAINE-CLEVELAND MUDSLINGERS: *The Moralists Condemn Cleveland. The Mugwumps Condone Cleveland.* E. CLEVELAND TAKES COMMAND: *Cleveland Pleads for Tariff Reduction. Philadelphians Criticize Cleveland. The New York* Times *Acclaims Courage.*

26. **INDUSTRY COMES OF AGE, 1865–1900**   490

A. THE PROBLEM OF THE RAILROADS: *A Defense of Long-Haul Rates. President Dillon Supports Stock Watering. General Weaver Deplores Stock Watering.* B. THE TRUSTS AND MONOPOLY: *Rockefeller Justifies Rebates. An Oil Man Goes Bankrupt. Weaver Attacks the Trusts.* C. THE RISE OF THE NEW SOUTH: *Grady Issues a Challenge. A Yankee Visits the New South.* D. THE KNIGHTS OF LABOR: *Powderly Battles for Larger Goals. Gompers Condemns the Knights. Chicago Anarchists Demand Blood. Powderly Denies a Breakup.*

27. **NEW SOCIAL AND CULTURAL HORIZONS, 1865–1900**   506

A. IMMIGRATION AND URBANIZATION: *Mary Antin Praises America. Jacob Riis Goes Slumming. The A.P.A. Hates Catholics. Lodge Urges a Literacy Test. Cleveland Vetoes a Literacy Test.* B. THE CHURCH ON THE DEFENSIVE: *The Shock of Dar-*

winism. Beecher Accepts Evolution. C. THE NEW MATERI-
ALISM: *Carnegie's Gospel of Wealth.* The Nation *Challenges
Carnegie. Conwell Deifies the Dollar.* D. THE ANTI-SALOON
CRUSADE: *Frances Willard Prays in a Saloon. Gompers Defends
the Saloon.* E. THE CHANGING ROLE OF WOMEN: *Victoria
Woodhull Advocates "Free Love." The Life of a Working Girl.
An Italian Immigrant Woman Faces Life Alone in the Big City.*

28. THE GREAT WEST AND THE AGRICULTURAL
    REVOLUTION, 1865–1890   533
    A. THE PLIGHT OF THE INDIAN: *Custer's Last Stand. Chief
    Joseph's Lament. Roosevelt Downgrades the Indians.* B. THE
    CRUSADE FOR FREE HOMESTEADS: *"Vote Yourself a Farm." A
    Texan Scorns Futile Charity. Buchanan Kills a Homestead
    Bill.* C. THE HOMESTEAD HOAX: *Pre-emption Grafters. Going
    Broke in Kansas. Wheat Bowls Become Dust Bowls.* D. THE
    FARMERS' PROTEST MOVEMENT: *An Iowan Assesses Discontent.
    Mrs. Lease Raises More Hell. Godkin Sneers at the Populists.*

29. THE REVOLT OF THE DEBTOR, 1889–1900   550
    A. THE TARIFF ISSUE: *McKinley Pleads for Protection. Mills
    Challenges McKinley. The Sugar Trust Lobby.* B. THE PULL-
    MAN STRIKE: *A Populist Condemns Pullman. Pullman Defends
    His Company. Starvation at Pullman.* C. THE FREE-SILVER MIR-
    AGE: *Coin's Financial School. A "Gold Bug" Defends Britain.*
    D. THE FREE-SILVER CONVENTION: *Tillman Repudiates Cleve-
    land. Senator Hill Urges Sanity. Bryan's Cross of Gold.* E. THE
    TRIUMPH OF MCKINLEY: *The "Anarchists" Lose Out. Bryan's Af-
    terthoughts. The London* Standard *Rejoices.*

30. THE PATH OF EMPIRE   569
    A. YELLOW JOURNALISM IN FLOWER: *Pulitzer Demands Interven-
    tion. Hearst Stages a Rescue.* B. THE DECLARATION OF WAR:
    Madrid's Diplomatic Concessions. Spain Regrets the Maine.
    *McKinley Submits a War Message. Professor Norton's Patriotic
    Protest.* C. THE SORDID LITTLE WAR: *Rough Times for Rough
    Riders. Disillusionment over the Cubans.* D. THE SIREN SONG
    OF IMPERIALISM: *McKinley Prays for Guidance. Professor Sum-
    ner Spurns Empire. Beveridge Trumpets Imperialism.*

31. AMERICA ON THE WORLD STAGE, 1899–1909   584
    A. THE BITTER FRUITS OF IMPERIALISM: *Beveridge Deplores Un-
    patriotic Talk. Bryan Vents His Bitterness.* The Nation *De-
    nounces Atrocities. A San Francisco Weekly Defends the Ar-
    my.* B. THE PANAMA REVOLUTION: *Hay Twists Colombia's Arm.
    Roosevelt Hopes for Revolt. Official Connivance in Washing-*

ton.   D. THE MONROE DOCTRINE IN THE CARIBBEAN: *Roosevelt Launches a Corollary. A Latin American Protests.* E. ROOSEVELT AND JAPAN: *The President Anticipates Trouble. Japan Resents Discrimination. The Gentlemen's Agreement.*

32. PROGRESSIVISM AND THE REPUBLICAN ROOSEVELT   598

A. THE HEYDAY OF MUCKRAKING: *Exposing the Meat Packers. Roosevelt Roasts Muckrakers.*   B. CORRUPTION IN THE CITIES: *Steffens Bares Philadelphia Bossism. Plunkitt Defends "Honest Graft".*   C. THE PLIGHT OF LABOR: *Baer's Divine Right of Plutocrats. Child Labor in the Coal Mines. Sweatshop Hours for Bakers.*   D. THE ERA OF TRUST BUSTING: *Roosevelt Attacks the Anti-Trust Act. LaFollette Exposes Roosevelt.*   E. THE CONSERVATION CRUSADE: *Roosevelt Saves the Forests. The West Protests Conservation.*

33. WILLIAM HOWARD TAFT AND THE PROGRESSIVE REVOLT   616

A. THE CRUSADE FOR WOMAN SUFFRAGE: *Senator Owen Supports Women. A Woman Assails Woman Suffrage.*   B. THE POPULAR ELECTION OF SENATORS: *Woodrow Wilson Favors Reform. Senator Root Opposes Change.*   C. THE INITIATIVE AND THE REFERENDUM: *Wilson Urges Popular Control. Taft Scorns the Initiative and Referendum.*   D. POPULAR CONTROL OF THE JUDICIARY: *Taft Lambasts the Recall of Judges. Roosevelt and Judicial Decisions.*

34. WOODROW WILSON AND THE NEW FREEDOM   631

A. BATTLING FOR TARIFF REFORM: *A President Appears before Congress. Wilson Tackles the Tariff Lobby. Senator Cummins Defends Lobbying.*   B. CAMPAIGNING FOR MONETARY REFORM: *Brandeis Indicts Interlocking Directorates. Morgan Denies a Money Trust. McAdoo Exposes the Bankers.*   C. MORAL MEDDLING IN MEXICO: *Wilson Asks for War on Huerta. A Republican Assails "Watchful Waiting."*

35. THE ROAD TO WORLD WAR I   645

A. ACQUIESCING IN THE BRITISH BLOCKADE: *Lord Bryce's Propaganda Report. Page Plays Britain's Game. Lansing's Pro-Ally Tactics.*   B. MERCHANTS OF DEATH: *Bryan Backs the Munitions Business. Berlin Condemns the Munitions Traffic.*   C. THE SINKING OF THE "LUSITANIA": *Wilson Demands Muzzled U-Boats. Germany Justifies the Sinking. Viereck Upholds the Torpedoing.*   D. WAR WITH GERMANY: *Wilson Breaks Diplomatic Relations. Representative Kitchin Assails the War Resolution.*

36. THE WAR TO END WAR, 1917–1918   661

A. THE RAISING OF ARMIES: *Houston Urges a Draft. T.R. Lambasts Broomstick Preparedness.* B. WARTIME HYSTERIA: *UnChristlike Preachers. Abusing the Pro-Germans.* C. FREE SPEECH IN WARTIME: *La Follette Demands His Rights. Chafee Upholds Free Speech.* D. THE PROPAGANDA FRONT: *Creel Spreads Fear Propaganda. Wilson Unveils His Fourteen Points. Roosevelt Blunts Wilson's Points.* E. THE FACE OF WAR: *General Pershing Defines American Fighting Tactics. A "Doughboy" Describes the Fighting Front.*

37. MAKING AND UNMAKING THE PEACE   681

A. THE OCTOBER APPEAL: *Wilson Asks for a Democratic Congress. Roosevelt Assails Wilson's Appeal.* B. THE TREATY OF VERSAILLES: *General Smuts Lectures Wilson. Colonel House Appraises the Conference. Editor Villard Reproaches Wilson.* C. THE ISSUE OF ARTICLE X: *The Text of Article X. Editor Harvey Belittles Article X. Wilson Testifies for Article X. The LodgeHitchcock Reservations.* D. THE DEFEAT OF THE TREATY: *Mrs. Wilson as Assistant President. The Aborted Lodge Compromise. Wilson Defeats Lodge's Reservations. Lodge Blames Wilson.* E. THE PRESIDENTIAL CAMPAIGN OF 1920: *Wilson Suggests a "Solemn Referendum." Harding Sidetracks the League. An Editor Dissects the "Referendum."*

38. AMERICAN LIFE IN THE "ROARING
     TWENTIES"   700

A. THE REVIVAL OF ANTI-FOREIGNISM: *William A. White Condemns Deportations. Vanzetti Condemns Judge Thayer. Lippmann Pleads for Sacco and Vanzetti.* B. THE RECONSTITUTED KU KLUX KLAN: *Tar-Bucket Terror in Texas. A Methodist Editor Clears the Klan.* C. THE WETS VERSUS THE DRYS: *A German Observes Bootlegging. La Guardia Pillories Prohibition. The W.C.T.U. Upholds Prohibition.* D. THE AUTOMOBILE AGE DAWNS: *Henry Ford Discusses Manufacturing and Marketing. Labor Policies at the Ford Motor Company.* E. NEW GOALS FOR WOMEN: *Margaret Sanger Campaigns for Birth Congrol. The Lynds Discover Changes in the Middle American Home.*

39. THE POLITICS OF BOOM AND BUST, 1920–1932   728

A. HARDING AND THE WASHINGTON CONFERENCE: *Harding Hates His Job. Hearst Blasts Disarmament at Washington. Japan Resents the Washington Setback.* B. DUNNING THE DEBTORS: *Hoover Opposes Cancellation. Baker Urges Cancellation. Lippmann Foresees Default.* C. THE DEPRESSION DESCENDS: *The Plague of Plenty. Distress in the South. Rumbles of Revolution.* D. HOOVER CLASHES WITH ROOSEVELT: *Hoover Upholds Free Enterprise. Roosevelt Pushes Public Power. Hoover Assails*

Federal Intervention. Roosevelt Attacks Business in Government. Hoover Stresses Economy. Roosevelt Stresses Humanity. Roosevelt Urges Welfare Statism. Hoover Calls for New Frontiers. E. AN APPRAISAL OF HOOVER: *Hoover Defends His Record. Roosevelt Indicts Hoover.*

40. THE GREAT DEPRESSION AND THE NEW DEAL   751

A. AN ENIGMA IN THE WHITE HOUSE: *The Agreeable F.D.R. Coffee for the Veterans. F.D.R. the Administrative "Artist."* B. PLOWING THE SURPLUSES UNDER: *The Planned-Scarcity Scandal. Wallace Puts People above Pigs.* C. THE TENNESSEE VALLEY AUTHORITY (TVA): *Norris Plays Down Electric Power. Willkie Exposes the Rubber Yardstick. Displaced Tennesseans.* D. LITTLE STEEL VERSUS THE C.I.O.: *Tom Girdler Girds for Battle. Lewis Lambasts Girdler.* E. THE SUPREME COURT FIGHT AND AFTER: *Ickes Defends His Chief. Dorothy Thompson Dissents. Republicans Roast Roosevelt.*

41. FRANKLIN D. ROOSEVELT AND THE SHADOW OF WAR   770

A. THE ARMS EMBARGO DEBATE: *Senator Connally Rejects Rigidity. Roosevelt Pleads for Repeal. Senator Vandenberg Fights Repeal.* B. THE INTERVENTION ISSUE: *Lindbergh Argues for Isolation. The New York* Times *Rejects Insulationism. F.D.R. Pledges No Foreign War.* C. THE LEND-LEASE CONTROVERSY: *F.D.R. Drops the Dollar Sign. Senator Wheeler Assails Lend-Lease. Hearst Denounces Aid to Russia.* D. WAR IN THE ATLANTIC: *Framing the Atlantic Charter. The Chicago* Tribune *Is Outraged. F.D.R. Proclaims Shoot-at-Sight.* E. BLOWUP IN THE PACIFIC: *Ickes Prepares to "Raise Hell." Tōgō Blames the United States. Hull Justifies His Stand.*

42. AMERICA IN WORLD WAR II   791

A. THE BLAME FOR PEARL HARBOR: *War Warnings from Washington. Admiral Kimmel Defends Himself. Secretary Stimson Charges Negligence. Roosevelt Awaits the Blow.* B. SOVIET-AMERICAN FRICTION: *Communists Distrust Capitalists. Stalin Resents Second-Front Delays. Roosevelt Manages "Uncle Joe."* C. THE "UNCONDITIONAL SURRENDER" CONTROVERSY: *Sherwood Defends F.D.R. Hull Opposes "Unconditional Surrender."* D. DROPPING THE ATOMIC BOMB: *Japan's Horrified Reaction. The* Christian Century *Deplores the Bombing. Truman Justifies the Bombing.*

43. HARRY S TRUMAN AND THE COLD WAR   808

A. THE YALTA AGREEMENTS: *Roosevelt "Betrays" China and Japan. The Freeman's Bill of Indictment. Secretary Stettinius De-*

fends Yalta. B. THE TRUMAN DOCTRINE: *Kennan Proposes Containment. Truman Appeals to Congress. The Chicago* Tribune *Dissents.* C. THE MARSHALL PLAN: *Secretary Marshall Speaks at Harvard. Senator Vandenberg Is Favorable. Moscow's Misrepresentations.* D. THE NORTH ATLANTIC PACT: *Senator Connally Pleads for Support. Senator Taft Spurns Entanglements.* E. THE CHINA TANGLE: *Senator Acheson Drops Chiang. Senator McCarthy Blasts "Traitors".*

44. KOREA AND THE EISENHOWER ERA   834

A. THE KOREAN CRISIS: *Senator Connally Writes Off Korea. Truman Accepts the Korean Challenge.* B. THE SACKING OF GENERAL MACARTHUR: *Truman Asserts Civil Supremacy. MacArthur Calls for Victory. Truman Looks Beyond Victory.* C. THE MCCARTHY HYSTERIA: *McCarthy Upholds Guilt by Association. A Senator Speaks Up. McCarthy Inspires Fear at Harvard.* D. THE SUPREME COURT AND THE BLACK REVOLUTION: *The Court Rejects Segregation. One Hundred Congressmen Dissent. Eisenhower Sends Federal Troops. The* Arkansas Democrat *Protests. A Black Newspaper Praises Courage.* E. EISENHOWER SAYS FAREWELL.

45. THE STORMY SIXTIES   857

A. THE CUBAN MISSILE CRISIS: *Kennedy Proclaims a "Quarantine". Kruschev Proposes a Swap. Kennedy Advances a Solution. The Russians Save Face.* B. THE "GREAT SOCIETY": *President Johnson Declares War on Poverty. War on the Anti-Poverty War.* C. THE BLACK REVOLUTION ERUPTS: *Martin Luther King Writes from a Birmingham Jail. President Johnson Supports Civil Rights. A Conservative Denounces Black Rioters. A Christian Journal Takes the Long View.* D. VIETNAM TROUBLES: *The Joint Chiefs of Staff Propose a Wider War. President Johnson Asserts His War Aims. British Prime Minister Criticizes American Bombing. Defense Secretary McNamara Foresees a Stalemate. Secretary McNamara Opposes Further Escalation. The Soldiers' War.* E. THE POLITICS OF PROTEST IN THE 1960'S: *Students for a Democratic Society Issues a Manifesto. A War Protester Decides to Resist the Draft. George Kennan Chastises the Student Left.*

46. THE RISE AND FALL OF RICHARD NIXON   900

A. THE SUPREME COURT "CODDLES" CRIMINALS: *The Outlawing of Third-Degree Confessions. The Minority Supports the Police. A Green Light for Criminals. President Nixon Outlines His Judicial Philosophy.* B. NIXON'S CAMBODIAN COUP: *The President Defends His Incursion. The St. Louis* Post-Dispatch *Dissents. Kissinger Dissects the Dissenters.* C. WINDING DOWN THE VIETNAM WAR: *Nixon's Grand Plan in Foreign Policy. Nixon's Ad-*

dress to the Nation. Canadians See Neither Peace Nor Honor. The Expulsion from Vietnam. D. THE MOVE TO IMPEACH NIXON: *The First Article of Impeachment. Impeachment as a Partisan Issue. Nixon Incriminates Himself. A Critical Canadian Viewpoint. Nixon Accepts a Presidential Pardon.*

47.   THE CARTER INTERLUDE AND THE REAGAN
      REVOLUTION   935
      A. RELINQUISHING CONTROL OF THE PANAMA CANAL: *Secretary of State Vance Favors Letting Go of the Canal. Ronald Reagan Denounces the Panama "Giveaway".*   B. COPING WITH THE ENERGY CRISIS: *Carter Calls For "The Moral Equivalent Of War".* The Houston Chronicle *Blasts Carter's Energy Program.*   C. CARTER'S TROUBLED PRESIDENCY: *Carter Diagnoses The National Mood. Carter Agonizes Over the Iranian Hostages. Hugh Sidey Assesses the Carter Presidency.*   D. THE REAGAN "REVOLUTION": *President Reagan Asks For A Tax Cut.* The New York Times *Attacks Reagan's Policies.*

48.   THE AMERICAN PEOPLE SINCE WORLD WAR II   970
      A. THE CHANGING AMERICAN FAMILY: *Dr. Spock Advises Parents. Betty Friedan Strikes a Blow for Women's Freedom. Margaret Mead Assesses the Modern Family. A Bill of Rights for Modern Women.*   B. ECONOMIC CONTRADICTIONS: *John Kenneth Galbraith Criticizes the Affluent Society. Michael Harrington Discovers Another America. Working for a Living.*   C. HEATING UP THE MELTING POT: Black Enterprise *Champions Affirmative Action. George Will Blasts Reverse Discrimination. Robert Coles Examines the White American Mind. Chicanos on the Move.*   D. ASSESSING MODERN AMERICA: *A Russian Journalist Looks at American Violence. A Frenchman Praises the American Example.*

CONSTITUTION OF THE UNITED STATES   i

INDEX   xix

Maps

INDIAN WARS, 1876–1877   534

U.S. ARMY IN CUBA, 1898   577

ROOSEVELT AND THE CARIBBEAN   592

BRITISH MINED AREA; GERMAN SUBMARINE ZONE   652

TVA WATER CONTROL SYSTEM   758

THE NORTH ATLANTIC, 1941   785

THE FAR EAST, 1945   809

THE NEW POLAND, 1945   812

U.S. DEFENSE PERIMETER, JANUARY, 1950   836

THE KOREAN WAR   837

VIETNAM AND SOUTHEAST ASIA   891

The American Spirit

24 · The Ordeal of Reconstruction

The years of war tried our devotion to the Union; the time of peace may test the sincerity of our faith in democracy.

HERMAN MELVILLE, *c.* 1866

PROLOGUE: President Johnson, a rough-hewn Tennessean, favored reconstruction of the seceded states on a "soft" basis. But he soon ran afoul of the Radical Republicans, who would not readmit the wayward sisters until they had adopted the 14th Amendment. This amendment (ratified in 1868) would guarantee civil rights to the blacks while reducing Congressional representation in states where the ex-slave was denied a vote. But such terms were spurned by ten of the eleven high-spirited Southern states. The Radical-dominated Congress thereupon passed the drastic military reconstruction acts of 1867, under which black suffrage was forced upon the white South. The Radicals also came within a hairsbreadth, in 1868, of removing the obstructive President Johnson by impeachment. Meanwhile the part-black Southern legislatures, despite grievous excesses, passed stacks of long-overdue social and economic legislation. The whites struck back through secret terrorist organizations, and ultimately secured control of their state governments by fraud, fright, and force.

A. THE STATUS OF THE SOUTH

1. Schurz Reports Southern Defiance (1865)

President Johnson sent Carl Schurz—the lanky, bewhiskered, and bespectacled German-American reformer—into the devastated South to report objectively on conditions there. But Schurz was predisposed to see continued defiance. He was on intimate terms with the Radical Republican leaders, who favored a severe reconstruction of the South, and in addition he was financially obligated to the Radical Charles Sumner. President Johnson, evidently hoping for evidence that would support his lenient policies, brushed aside Schurz's elaborate report with ill-concealed annoyance. Schurz partially financed his trip by selling a series of letters under an assumed name to the Boston *Advertiser*, which presumably welcomed his pro-Radical bias. In the following letter, which he wrote from Savannah to the newspaper, what class of people does he deem responsible for the trouble? What motivated them? Why were their outbursts not more serious?

But there is another class of people here [in Savannah], mostly younger men, who are still in the swearing mood. You can overhear their conversations as you pass them on the streets or even sit near them on the stoop of a hotel. They are "not conquered but only overpowered." They are only smothered for a time. They want to fight the war over again, and they

1. *Georgia Historical Quarterly,* XXXV (1951), 244–47 (July 31, 1865). Reprinted by permission.

are sure in five years they are going to have a war bigger than any we have seen yet. They are meaning to get rid of this d——d military despotism. They will show us what stuff Southern men are made of. They will send their own men to Congress and show us that we cannot violate the Constitution with impunity.

They have a rope ready for this and that Union man when the Yankee bayonets are gone. They will show the Northern interlopers that have settled down here to live on their substance the way home. They will deal largely in tar and feathers. They have been in the country and visited this and that place where a fine business is done in the way of killing Negroes. They will let the Negro know what freedom is, only let the Yankee soldiers be withdrawn.

Such is their talk. You can hear it every day, if you have your ears open. You see their sullen, frowning faces at every street corner. Now, there may be much of the old Southern braggadocio in this, and I do not believe that such men will again resort to open insurrection. But they will practice private vengeance whenever they can do it with impunity, and I have heard sober-minded Union people express their apprehension of it. This spirit is certainly no evidence of true loyalty.

It was this spirit which was active in an occurrence which disgraced this city on the Fourth of July. Perhaps you have heard of it. The colored firemen of this city desired to parade their engine on the anniversary of our independence. If nobody else would, they felt like celebrating that day. A number will deny that it was a legitimate desire. At first the engineer of the fire department, who is a citizen of this town, refused his permission. Finally, by an interposition of an officer of the "Freedmen's Bureau,"* he was prevailed upon to give his consent, and the parade took place. In the principal street of the city the procession was attacked with clubs and stones by a mob opposed to the element above described, and by a crowd of boys all swearing at the d——d niggers. The colored firemen were knocked down, some of them severely injured, their engine was taken away from them, and the peaceable procession dispersed. Down with the d——d niggers. A Northern gentleman who loudly expressed his indignation at the proceeding was in danger of being mobbed, and had to seek safety in a house. . . .

To return to the "unconquered" in Savannah—the occurrence of the Fourth of July shows what they are capable of doing even while the Yankee bayonets are still here. If from this we infer what they will be capable of doing when the Yankee bayonets are withdrawn, the prospect is not altogether pleasant, and Union people, white and black, in this city and neighborhood may well entertain serious apprehensions. . . .

Unfortunately, this spirit receives much encouragement from the fair sex. We have heard so much of the bitter resentment of the Southern ladies that the tale becomes stale by frequent repetition, but when inquiring into the feelings of the people, this element must not be omitted. There are certainly

* A federal agency designed to help the ex-slaves adjust to freedom.

PRIMARY SCHOOL FOR FREEDMEN IN VICKSBURG, MISSISSIPPI
Note the wide range of ages. *Harper's Weekly,* 1866.

a good many sensible women in the South who have arrived at a just appreciation of the circumstances with which they are surrounded. But there is a large number of Southern women who are as vindictive and defiant as ever, and whose temper does not permit them to lay their tongues under any restraint. You can see them in every hotel, and they will treat you to the most ridiculous exhibitions whenever an occasion offers.

A day or two ago a Union officer, yielding to an impulse of politeness, handed a dish of pickles to a Southern lady at the dinner-table of a hotel in this city. A look of unspeakable scorn and indignation met him. "So you think," said the lady, "a Southern woman will take a dish of pickles from a hand that is dripping with the blood of her countrymen?"

It is remarkable upon what trifling material this female wrath is feeding and growing fat. In a certain district in South Carolina, the ladies were some time ago, and perhaps are now, dreadfully exercised about the veil question. You may ask me what the veil question is. Formerly, under the old order of things, Negro women were not permitted to wear veils. Now, under the new order of things, a great many are wearing veils. This is an outrage which cannot be submitted to; the white ladies of the neighborhood agree in being indignant beyond measure. Some of them declare that whenever they meet a colored woman wearing a veil they will tear the veil from her face. Others, mindful of the consequences which such an act of violence might draw after it, under this same new order of things, declare their resolve never to wear veils themselves as long as colored women wear veils. This is the veil question, and this is the way it stands at present.

Such things may seem trifling and ridiculous. But it is a well-known fact that a silly woman is sometimes able to exercise a powerful influence over a man not half as silly, and the class of "unconquered" above described is undoubtedly in a great measure composed of individuals that are apt to be influenced by silly women. It has frequently been said that had it not been for the spirit of the Southern women, the rebellion would have broken down long ago, and there is, no doubt, a grain of truth in it.

2. General Grant Is Optimistic (1865)

President Johnson, hoping to capitalize on Grant's enormous prestige, also sent the General on a fact-finding trip to the South. Grant spent less than a week hurriedly visiting leading cities in four states. Schurz had ranged far more widely over a longer period, from July to September, 1865. But just as Schurz was predisposed to see defiance, Grant was predisposed to see compliance. Bear in mind also that Schurz was an idealist, strongly pro-black, and a leading Republican politician closely in touch with the Radicals. Grant was none of these. Which of their reports is more credible?

I am satisfied that the mass of thinking men of the South accept the present situation of affairs in good faith. The questions which have heretofore divided the sentiment of the people of the two sections—slavery and state rights, or the right of a state to secede from the Union—they regard as having been settled forever by the highest tribunal—arms—that man can resort to. I was pleased to learn from the leading men whom I met that they not only accepted the decision arrived at as final, but, now that the smoke of battle has cleared away and time has been given for reflection, that this decision has been a fortunate one for the whole country, they receiving like benefits from it with those who opposed them in the field and in council.

Four years of war, during which law was executed only at the point of the bayonet throughout the states in rebellion, have left the people possibly in a condition not to yield that ready obedience to civil authority the American people have generally been in the habit of yielding. This would render the presence of small garrisons throughout those states necessary until such time as labor returns to its proper channel, and civil authority is fully established. I did not meet anyone, either those holding places under the government or citizens of the Southern states, who think it practicable to withdraw the military from the South at present. The white and the black mutually require the protection of the general government.

There is such universal acquiescence in the authority of the general government throughout the portions of country visited by me that the mere presence of a military force, without regard to numbers, is sufficient to maintain order. . . .

My observations lead me to the conclusion that the citizens of the Southern states are anxious to return to self-government, within the Union, as

2. *Senate Executive Documents*, 39 Cong., 1 sess., I, No. 2, pp. 106–07.

soon as possible; that whilst reconstructing they want and require protection from the government; that they are in earnest in wishing to do what they think is required by the government, not humiliating to them as citizens, and that if such a course were pointed out they would pursue it in good faith.

3. The Ex-slaves Confront Freedom

The reactions of the freed slaves to their new liberty ran the gamut of human emotions from jubilation to anxiety. Attitudes toward former masters—and toward whites generally—ranged from resentment and fear to pity. Booker T. Washington was a young boy no more than eight years of age when the day of freedom came. What was his response? From what he describes as the first reactions of his family members and other freed slaves, what might one conclude were the worst deprivations suffered in slavery?

Finally the war closed, and the day of freedom came. It was a momentous and eventful day to all upon our plantation. We had been expecting it. Freedom was in the air, and had been for months. Deserting soldiers returning to their homes were to be seen every day. Others who had been discharged, or whose regiments had been paroled, were constantly passing near our place. The "grape-vine telegraph" was kept busy night and day. The news and mutterings of great events were swiftly carried from one plantation to another. In the fear of "Yankee" invasions, the silverware and other valuables were taken from the "big house," buried in the woods, and guarded by trusted slaves. Woe be to any one who would have attempted to disturb the buried treasure. The slaves would give the Yankee soldiers food, drink, clothing—anything but that which had been specifically intrusted to their care and honour. As the great day drew nearer, there was more singing in the slave quarters than usual. It was bolder, had more ring, and lasted later into the night. Most of the verses of the plantation songs had some reference to freedom. True, they had sung those same verses before, but they had been careful to explain that the "freedom" in these songs referred to the next world, and had no connection with life in this world. Now they gradually threw off the mask, and were not afraid to let it be known that the "freedom" in their songs meant freedom of the body in this world. The night before the eventful day, word was sent to the slave quarters to the effect that something unusual was going to take place at the "big house" the next morning. There was little, if any, sleep that night. All was excitement and expectancy. Early the next morning word was sent to all the slaves, old and young, to gather at the house. In company with my mother, brother, and sister, and a large number of other slaves, I went to the master's house. All of our master's family were either standing or seated on the veranda of the house, where they could see what was to take place and hear what was said. There was a feeling of deep interest, or perhaps sadness, on their faces, but not bitterness. As I now recall the impression they made upon me, they did not at the moment seem to be sad

3. Booker T. Washington, *Up From Slavery* (1901), pp. 224–27.

because of the loss of property, but rather because of parting with those whom they had reared and who were in many ways very close to them. The most distinct thing that I now recall in connection with the scene was that some man who seemed to be a stranger (a United States officer, I presume) made a little speech and then read a rather long paper—the Emancipation Proclamation, I think. After the reading we were told that we were all free, and could go when and where we pleased. My mother, who was standing by my side, leaned over and kissed her children, while tears of joy ran down her cheeks. She explained to us what it all meant, that this was the day for which she had been so long praying, but fearing that she would never live to see.

For some minutes there was great rejoicing, and thanksgiving, and wild scenes of ecstasy. But there was no feeling of bitterness. In fact, there was pity among the slaves for our former owners. The wild rejoicing on the part of the emancipated coloured people lasted but for a brief period, for I noticed that by the time they returned to their cabins there was a change in their feelings. The great responsibility of being free, of having charge of themselves, of having to think and plan for themselves and their children, seemed to take possession of them. It was very much like suddenly turning a youth of ten or twelve years out into the world to provide for himself. In a few hours the great questions with which the Anglo-Saxon race had been grappling for centuries had been thrown upon these people to be solved. These were the questions of a home, a living, the rearing of children, education, citizenship, and the establishment and support of churches. Was it any wonder that within a few hours the wild rejoicing ceased and a feeling of deep gloom seemed to pervade the slave quarters? To some it seemed that, now that they were in actual possession of it, freedom was a more serious thing than they had expected to find it. Some of the slaves were seventy or eighty years old; their best days were gone. They had no strength with which to earn a living in a strange place and among strange people, even if they had been sure where to find a new place of abode. To this class the problem seemed especially hard. Besides, deep down in their hearts there was a strange and peculiar attachment to "old Marster" and "old Missus," and to their children, which they found it hard to think of breaking off. With these they had spent in some cases nearly a half-century, and it was no light thing to think of parting. Gradually, one by one, stealthily at first, the older slaves began to wander from the slave quarters back to the "big house" to have a whispered conversation with their former owners as to the future. . . .

After the coming of freedom there were two points upon which practically all the people on our place were agreed, and I find that this was generally true throughout the South: that they must change their names, and that they must leave the old plantation for a least a few days or weeks in order that they might really feel sure that they were free.

In some way a feeling got among the coloured people that it was far from proper for them to bear the surname of their former owners, and a great many of them took other surnames. This was one of the first signs of freedom. When they were slaves, a coloured person was simply called "John" or "Susan." There was seldom occasion for more than the use of the one name. If "John" or "Susan" belonged to a white man by the name of "Hatcher," sometimes he was called "John Hatcher," or as often "Hatcher's John." But there was a feeling that "John Hatcher" or "Hatcher's John" was not the proper title by which to denote a freeman; and so in many cases "John Hatcher" was changed to "John S. Lincoln" or "John S. Sherman," the initial "S" standing for no name, it being simply a part of what the coloured man proudly called his "entitles."

As I have stated, most of the coloured people left the old plantation for a short while at least, so as to be sure, it seemed, that they could leave and try their freedom on to see how it felt. After they had remained away for a time, many of the older slaves, especially, returned to their old homes and made some kind of contract with their former owners by which they remained on the estate.

My mother's husband, who was the stepfather of my brother John and myself, did not belong to the same owners as did my mother. In fact, he seldom came to our plantation. I remember seeing him there perhaps once a year, that being about Christmas time. In some way, during the war, by running away and following the Federal soldiers, it seems, he found his way into the new state of West Virginia. As soon as freedom was declared, he sent for my mother to come to the Kanawha Valley, in West Virginia. At that time a journey from Virginia over the mountains to West Virginia was rather a tedious and in some cases a painful undertaking. What little clothing and few household goods we had were placed in a cart, but the children walked the greater portion of the distance, which was several hundred miles.

4. Emancipation Violence in Texas

In the following recollection by a former slave woman in Texas, what is revealed about the response of some slave-owners to Emancipation? What implications did such responses have for the future of the freed slaves? for federal policy during Reconstruction?

I heard about freedom in September and they were picking cotton and a white man rode up to master's house on a big, white horse and the house-boy told master a man wanted to see him and he hollered, "Light, stranger." It was a government man and he had the big book and a bunch of papers and said why hadn't master turned the niggers loose. Master said he was trying to get the crop out and he told master to have the slaves in. Uncle

4. George P. Rawick, editor, *The American Slave: A Composite Autobiography*, (Westport, Conn.: Greenwood Publishing Company, 1972), volume 5, Texas Narratives, part 3, p. 78.

Steven blew the cow horn that they used to call to eat and all the niggers came running, because that horn meant, "Come to the big house, quick." The man read the paper telling us we were free, but master made us work several months after that. He said we would get 20 acres of land and a mule but we didn't get it.

Lots of niggers were killed after freedom, because the slaves in Harrison County were turned loose right at freedom and those in Rusk County weren't. But they heard about it and ran away to freedom in Harrison County and their owners had them bushwhacked, then shot down. You could see lots of niggers hanging from trees in Sabine bottom right after freedom, because they caught them swimming across Sabine River and shot them. There sure are going to be lots of souls crying against them in judgment!

B. IMPEACHING THE PRESIDENT

1. Johnson's Cleveland Speech (1866)

A tactless and stubborn President Johnson clashed openly with the Radical Republicans in Congress, including embittered Thaddeus Stevens, when he vetoed a series of Radical-sponsored bills. Two of the measures designed to help the ex-slaves—the Civil Rights Bill and the New Freedman's Bureau Bill—were speedily repassed over his veto. Nothing daunted, Johnson embarked upon a speech-making tour to urge the election of anti-Radical Congressmen favorable to his policies. But the public was in an ugly mood. Ex-President Jefferson Davis, though still in prison, was untried and unhanged, as were other ex-Confederates. A recent anti-black riot in New Orleans had resulted in some two hundred casualties. Johnson had earlier distinguished himself as a rough-and-ready stump speaker in Tennessee, but, as Secretary Seward remarked, the President of the United States should not be a stump speaker. His undignified harangue in Cleveland contained passages (here italicized) which formed the basis of some of the impeachment charges later brought by the House. What criticisms can be leveled against this speech? Which one is the most serious?

Notwithstanding the subsidized gang of hirelings and traducers [in Congress?], I have discharged all my duties and fulfilled all my pledges, and I say here tonight that if my predecessor had lived, the vials of wrath would have been poured out upon him. [Cries of "Never!" "Three cheers for the Congress of the United States!"]

. . . Where is the man or woman who can place his finger upon one single act of mine deviating from any pledge of mine or in violation of the Constitution of the country? [Cheers.] . . . Who can come and place his finger on one pledge I ever violated, or one principle I ever proved false to? [A voice, "How about New Orleans?" Another voice, "Hang Jeff Davis."] Hang Jeff Davis, he says. [Cries of "No," and "Down with him!"] . . . Hang Jeff Davis. Why don't you hang him? [Cries of "Give us the opportunity."] Have not you got the court? Have not you got the Attorney General? . . .

1. Edward McPherson, *The Political History of the United States of America during the Period of Reconstruction* (3rd ed., 1880), pp. 134–36.

I will tell you what I did do. I called upon your Congress that is trying to break up the government. [Cries, "You be d——d!" and cheers mingled with hisses. Great confusion. "Don't get mad, Andy!"] Well, I will tell you who is mad. "Whom the gods wish to destroy, they first make mad." Did your Congress order any of them to be tried? [Three cheers for Congress.] . . .

You pretend now to have great respect and sympathy for the poor brave fellow who has left an arm on the battlefield. [Cries, "Is this dignified?"] I understand you. . . . I care not for dignity. . . . [A voice, "Traitor!"] I wish I could see that man. I would bet you now that if the light fell on your face, cowardice and treachery would be seen in it. Show yourself. Come out here where I can see you. [Shouts of laughter.] If you ever shoot a man you will do it in the dark, and pull the trigger when no one is by to see you. [Cheers.]

("HANG JEFF DAVIS.") "THEN I WOULD ASK YOU WHY NOT HANG THAD STEVENS AND WENDELL PHILLIPS?"

Thomas Nast represents Johnson's remarks to a heckler to mean that he would pardon Jeff Davis (imprisoned at Fortress Monroe) and hang the abolitionists Stevens and Phillips. *Harper's Weekly,* 1866.

I understand traitors. I have been fighting them at the south end of the line, and we are now fighting them in the other direction. [Laughter and cheers.] I come here neither to criminate or recriminate, but when attacked, my plan is to defend myself. [Cheers.] . . . As Chief Magistrate, I felt so after taking the oath to support the Constitution, and when I saw encroachments upon your Constitution and rights, as an honest man I dared to sound the tocsin of alarm. [Three cheers for Andrew Johnson.] . . .

I love my country. Every public act of my life testifies that is so. Where is the man that can put his finger upon any one act of mine that goes to prove the contrary? And what is my offending? [A voice, "Because you are not a Radical," and cry of "Veto."] Somebody says veto. Veto of what? What is called the Freedmen's Bureau Bill? . . . I might refer to the Civil Rights Bill, the results of which are very similar. I tell you, my countrymen, that though the powers of hell and Thad Stevens and his gang were by, they could not turn me from my purpose. . . .

In conclusion, beside that, Congress had taken such pains to poison their constituents against him.* But what had Congress done? Had they done anything to restore the Union of these states? No; on the contrary, they had done everything to prevent it; and because he stood now where he did when the rebellion commenced, he had been denounced as a traitor. Who had run greater risks or made greater sacrifices than himself? But Congress, factious and domineering, had [under]taken to poison the minds of the American people.

2. Senator Trumbull Defends Johnson (1868)

Johnson's unrestrained oratory backfired, and at the polls in November the Radicals won control of a two-thirds majority in both Houses of Congress. They proceeded to pass the Tenure of Office Act, which was designed to entrap Johnson. Doubting its constitutionality (by indirection it was later judged unconstitutional) and seeking to bring a test case, he deliberately challenged it by removing Secretary Stanton. The House thereupon impeached Johnson for "high crimes and misdemeanors." Most of its indictment related to Johnson's alleged violation of the Tenure of Office Act; other charges related to his "scandalous harangues." Particularly objectionable was a speech at the White House in which the President had declared that acts of Congress were not binding upon him because the South did not enjoy proper representation in it. One of the ablest of those who spoke for Johnson was Senator Lyman Trumbull of Illinois, a brilliant constitutional lawyer and a former associate of Lincoln. As one who followed principle rather than partisanship, he changed parties three times during his career. In the following speech, what is his main reason for thinking that Johnson's removal would be unfortunate?

In coming to the conclusion that the President is not guilty of any of the high crimes and misdemeanors with which he stands charged, I have endeavored to be governed by the case made, without reference to other acts of his not contained in the record, and without giving the least heed to the clamor of intemperate zealots who demand the conviction of Andrew Johnson as a test of party faith, or seek to identify with and make responsible for his acts those who from convictions of duty feel compelled, on the case made, to vote for his acquittal.

His speeches and the general course of his administration have been as distasteful to me as to anyone, and I should consider it the great calamity of the age if the disloyal element, so often encouraged by his measures, should gain political ascendancy. If the question was, Is Andrew Johnson a fit person for President? I should answer, no; but it is not a party question, nor upon Andrew Johnson's deeds and acts, except so far as they are made to appear in the record, that I am to decide.

Painful as it is to disagree with so many political associates and friends whose conscientious convictions have led them to a different result, I must,

---

* The reporter now lapses into the third person.

2. *Congressional Globe,* 40 Cong., 2 sess., Supplement, p. 420 (May 7, 1868).

nevertheless, in the discharge of the high responsibility under which I act, be governed by what my reason and judgment tell me is the truth, and the justice and law of this case. . . .

Once set the example of impeaching a President for what, when the excitement of the hour shall have subsided, will be regarded as insufficient causes, as several of those now alleged against the President were decided to be by the House of Representatives only a few months since, and no future President will be safe who happens to differ with a majority of the House and two-thirds of the Senate on any measure deemed by them important, particularly if of a political character. Blinded by partisan zeal, with such an example before them, they will not scruple to remove out of the way any obstacle to the accomplishment of their purposes, and what then becomes of the checks and balances of the Constitution, so carefully devised and so vital to its perpetuity? They are all gone.

In view of the consequences likely to flow from this day's proceedings, should they result in conviction on what my judgment tells me are insufficient charges and proofs, I tremble for the future of my country. I cannot be an instrument to produce such a result; and at the hazard of the ties even of friendship and affection, till calmer times shall do justice to my motives, no alternative is left me but the inflexible discharge of duty.

[*President Johnson escaped removal by the margin of a single vote, and only because seven conscientious Republican Senators, including Trumbull, risked political suicide by refusing to go along with the Radical majority.*]

C. "BLACK RECONSTRUCTION"

1. Stevens Demands Black Suffrage (1867)

The most influential Radical Republican in the House, crippled and vindictive Thaddeus Stevens of Pennsylvania, loathed slavery, slaveholders, and slave-breeders. He felt a deep compassion for blacks, and arranged to be buried in a black cemetery. But in his demands for black suffrage he was motivated, like many other Radicals, by a mixture of idealism and realism. Of the arguments for black voting that he set forth in the following speech in the House, which ones were the most selfish? the most idealistic?

There are several good reasons for the passage of this bill [for reconstructing the South].

In the first place, it is just. I am now confining my argument to Negro suffrage in the rebel states. Have not loyal blacks quite as good a right to choose rulers and make laws as rebel whites?

In the second place, it is a necessity in order to protect the loyal white men in the seceded states. The white Union men are in a great minority in each of those states. With them the blacks would act in a body; and it is believed that in each of said states, except one, the two united would form a majority, control the states, and protect themselves. Now they are the

1. *Congressional Globe,* 39 Cong., 2 sess., p. 252 (Jan. 3, 1867).

victims of daily murder. They must suffer constant persecution, or be exiled. . . .

Another good reason is, it would insure the ascendancy of the Union [Republican] Party. "Do you avow the party purpose?" exclaims some horror-stricken demagogue. I do. For I believe, on my conscience, that on the continued ascendancy of that party depends the safety of this great nation.

If impartial suffrage is excluded in the rebel states, then every one of them is sure to send a solid rebel representative delegation to Congress, and cast a solid rebel electoral vote. They, with their kindred Copperheads of the North, would always elect the President and control Congress. While Slavery sat upon her defiant throne, and insulted and intimidated the trembling North, the South frequently divided on questions of policy between Whigs and Democrats, and gave victory alternately to the sections. Now, you must divide them between loyalists, without regard to color, and disloyalists, or you will be the perpetual vassals of the free-trade, irritated, revengeful South.

For these, among other reasons, I am for Negro suffrage in every rebel state. If it be just, it should not be denied; if it be necessary, it should be adopted; if it be a punishment to traitors, they deserve it.

2. Black-and-White Legislatures (*c.* 1876)

Black suffrage was finally forced upon the Southern whites by their new state constitutions and by the 15th Amendment to the federal Constitution (1870). Tension grew worse as designing Northern "carpetbaggers" and Unionist Southern whites ("scalawags") moved in to exploit the inexperienced ex-slaves. J. W. Leigh, an English clergyman turned Georgia rice planter, recorded the following observations in a personal letter. What conditions were most galling to the ex-Confederates?

The fact is, the poor Negro has since the war been placed in an entirely false position, and is therefore not to be blamed for many of the absurdities he has committed, seeing that he has been urged on by Northern "carpetbaggers" and Southern "scalawags," who have used him as a tool to further their own nefarious ends.

The great mistake committed by the North was giving the Negroes the franchise so soon after their emancipation, when they were not the least prepared for it. In 1865 slavery was abolished, and no one even among the Southerners, I venture to say, would wish it back. In 1868 they [Negroes] were declared citizens of the United States, and in 1870 they had the right of voting given them, and at the same time persons concerned in the rebellion were excluded from public trusts by what was called the "iron-clad" oath. And as if this was not enough, last year [1875] the Civil Rights Bill was passed, by which Negroes were to be placed on a perfect equality with whites, who were to be compelled to travel in the same cars with

2. Frances B. Leigh, *Ten Years on a Georgia Plantation since the War* (1883), pp. 268–92 (Appendix).

them, and to send their children to the same schools.

The consequence of all this is that where there is a majority of Negroes, as is the case in the states of Louisiana, Mississippi, and South Carolina, these states are placed completely under Negro rule, and scenes occur in the state legislatures which baffle description.

I recollect at the beginning of 1870 being at Montgomery, the capital of Alabama, and paying a visit to the State House there, when a discussion was going on with respect to a large grant which was to be made for the building of the Alabama and Chattanooga Railway, the real object of which was to put money into the pockets of certain carpetbaggers, who, in order to gain their object, had bribed all the Negroes to vote for the passing of the bill.

The scene was an exciting one. Several Negro members were present, with their legs stuck up on the desks in front of them, and spitting all about them in free and independent fashion. One gentleman having spoken for some time against the bill, and having reiterated his condemnation of it as a fraudulent speculation, a stout Negro member from Mobile sprung up and said, "Mister Speaker, when yesterday I spoke, I was not allowed to go on because you said I spoke twice on the same subject. Now what is sauce for the goose is sauce for the gander. Dis Member is saying over and over again de same thing; why don't you tell him to sit down? for what is sauce for," etc. To which the Speaker said, "Sit down yourself, sir." Another member (a carpetbagger) jumped up and shook his fist in the speaking member's face, and told him he was a liar, and if he would come outside he would give him satisfaction.

This is nothing, however, to what has been going on in South Carolina this last session. Poor South Carolina, formerly the proudest state in America, boasting of her ancient families, remarkable for her wealth, culture, and refinement, now prostrate in the dust, ruled over by her former slaves, an old aristocratic society replaced by the most ignorant democracy that mankind ever saw invested with the functions of government. Of the 124 representatives, there are but 23 representatives of her old civilization, and these few can only look on at the squabbling crowd amongst whom they sit as silent enforced auditors. Of the 101 remaining, 94 are colored, and 7 their white allies. The few honest amongst them see plundering and corruption going on on all sides, and can do nothing. . . .

The Negroes have it all their own way, and rob and plunder as they please. The Governor of South Carolina lives in luxury, and treats his soldiers to champagne, while the miserable planters have to pay taxes amounting to half their income, and if they fail to pay, their property is confiscated.

Louisiana and Mississippi are not much better off. The former has a Negro barber for its Lieutenant-Governor, and the latter has just selected a Negro steamboat porter as its United States Senator, filling the place once occupied by Jefferson Davis.

3. Du Bois Justifies Black Legislators (1910)

W. E. B. Du Bois, a Massachusetts-born black of French Huguenot extraction, received his Ph.D. from Harvard University in 1895. Distinguished as a teacher, lecturer,
historian, economist, sociologist, novelist, poet, and propagandist, he became a militant
advocate of equal rights. A founder of the National Association for the Advancement
of Colored People, he served for twenty-four years as editor of its chief organ. Du Bois,
who was born the day before the House impeached Johnson, here writes as a scholar.
In what important respects does he argue that Reconstruction legislatures have been
unfairly represented? In what ways were these bodies responsible for significant achievements?

Undoubtedly there were many ridiculous things connected with Reconstruction governments: the placing of ignorant field-hands who could neither
read nor write in the legislature, the gold spittoons of South Carolina, the
enormous public printing bill of Mississippi—all these were extravagant
and funny; and yet somehow, to one who sees, beneath all that is bizarre,
the real human tragedy of the upward striving of downtrodden men, the
groping for light among people born in darkness, there is less tendency to
laugh and jibe than among shallower minds and easier consciences. All that
is funny is not bad.

Then, too, a careful examination of the alleged stealing in the South
reveals much. First, there is repeated exaggeration. For instance, it is said
that the taxation in Mississippi was fourteen times as great in 1874 as in
1869. This sounds staggering until we learn that the state taxation in 1869
was only ten cents on one hundred dollars, and that the expenses of government in 1874 were only twice as great as in 1860, and that too with a
depreciated currency. . . .

The character of the real thieving shows that white men must have been
the chief beneficiaries. . . . The frauds through the manipulation of state
and railway bonds and of banknotes must have inured chiefly to the benefit
of experienced white men, and this must have been largely the case in the
furnishing and printing frauds. . . .

That the Negroes, led by astute thieves, became tools and received a small
share of the spoils is true. But . . . much of the legislation which resulted in
fraud was represented to the Negroes as good legislation, and thus their
votes were secured by deliberate misrepresentation. . . .

Granted, then, that the Negroes were to some extent venal but to a much
larger extent ignorant and deceived, the question is: Did they show any
signs of a disposition to learn better things? The theory of democratic
governments is not that the will of the people is always right, but rather
that normal human beings of average intelligence will, if given a chance,
learn the right and best course by bitter experience. This is precisely what
Negro voters showed indubitable signs of doing. First, they strove for
schools to abolish ignorance, and, second, a large and growing number of
them revolted against the carnival of extravagance and stealing that marred

the beginning of Reconstruction, and joined with the best elements to institute reform. . . .

We may recognize three things which Negro rule gave to the South:

1. Democratic government.
2. Free public schools.
3. New social legislation. . . .

In South Carolina there was before the war a property qualification for officeholders, and, in part, for voters. The [Reconstruction] constitution of 1868, on the other hand, was a modern democratic document . . . preceded by a broad Declaration of Rights which did away with property qualifications and based representation directly on population instead of property. It especially took up new subjects of social legislation, declaring navigable rivers free public highways, instituting homestead exemptions, establishing boards of county commissioners, providing for a new penal code of laws, establishing universal manhood suffrage "without distinction of race or color," devoting six sections to charitable and penal institutions and six to corporations, providing separate property for married women, etc. Above all, eleven sections of the Tenth Article were devoted to the establishment of a complete public-school system.

So satisfactory was the constitution thus adopted by Negro suffrage and by a convention composed of a majority of blacks that the state lived twenty-seven years under it without essential change. And when the constitution was revised in 1895, the revision was practically nothing more than an amplification of the constitution of 1868. No essential advance step of the former document was changed except the suffrage article. . . .

There is no doubt but that the thirst of the black man for knowledge—a thirst which has been too persistent and durable to be mere curiosity or whim—gave birth to the public free-school system of the South. It was the question upon which black voters and legislators insisted more than anything else, and while it is possible to find some vestiges of free schools in some of the Southern states before the war, yet a universal, well-established system dates from the day that the black man got political power. . . .

Finally, in legislation covering property, the wider functions of the state, the punishment of crime, and the like, it is sufficient to say that the laws on these points established by Reconstruction legislatures were not only different from and even revolutionary to the laws in the older South, but they were so wise and so well suited to the needs of the new South that in spite of a retrogressive movement following the overthrow of Negro governments, the mass of this legislation, with elaboration and development, still stands on the statute books of the South.

4. Tillman's Anti-Black Tirade (1907)

Reared in a slaveowning family, Senator Benjamin R. Tillman of South Carolina had participated in anti-black outrages during Reconstruction days. His face contorted, his

4. *Congressional Record,* 59 Cong., 2 sess., p. 1440 (Jan. 21, 1907).

one good eye glowing like a live coal, and his voice rising to a whine, "Tillman the Terrible" shocked the Senate and the nation with wild speeches in which he boasted that "we took the government away [from blacks]," we "stuffed the ballot boxes," we used "tissue ballots," "we shot them," "we are not ashamed of it," and "we will do it again." Whom does he blame most for the alleged conditions to which he refers?

It was in 1876, thirty years ago, and the people of South Carolina had been living under Negro rule for eight years. There was a condition bordering upon anarchy. Misrule, robbery, and murder were holding high carnival. The people's substance was being stolen, and there was no incentive to labor. Our legislature was composed of a majority of Negroes, most of whom could neither read nor write. They were the easy dupes and tools of as dirty a band of vampires and robbers as ever preyed upon a prostrate people. . . . Life ceased to be worth having on the terms under which we were living, and in desperation we determined to take the government away from the Negroes.

We reorganized the Democratic Party [of South Carolina] with one plank, and only one plank, namely, that "this is a white man's country, and white men must govern it." Under that banner we went to battle.

We had 8000 Negro militia organized by carpetbaggers. . . . They used to drum up and down the roads with their fifes and their gleaming bayonets, equipped with new Springfield rifles and dressed in the regulation uniform. It was lawful, I suppose, but these Negro soldiers—or this Negro militia, for they were never soldiers—growing more and more bold, let drop talk among themselves where the white children might hear their purpose, and it came to our ears. This is what they said: "The President [Grant] is our friend. The North is with us. We intend to kill all the white men, take the land, marry the white women, and then these white children will wait on us." . . .

We knew—who knew better?—that the North then was a unit in its opposition to Southern ideas, and that it was their purpose to perpetuate Negro governments in those states where it could be done by reason of there being a Negro majority. Having made up our minds, we set about it as practical men. . . .

Clashes came. The Negro militia grew unbearable and more and more insolent. I am not speaking of what I have read; I am speaking of what I know, of what I saw. There were two militia companies in my township and a regiment in my county. We had clashes with these Negro militiamen. The Hamburg riot was one clash, in which seven Negroes and one white man were killed. A month later we had the Ellenton riot, in which no one ever knew how many Negroes were killed, but there were forty or fifty or a hundred. It was a fight between barbarism and civilization, between the African and the Caucasian, for mastery.

It was then that "we shot them"; it was then that "we killed them"; it was then that "we stuffed ballot boxes." After the [federal] troops came and told us, "You must stop this rioting," we had decided to take the government away from men so debased as were the Negroes. . . .

IN SELF-DEFENSE

Southern Chiv. [Chivalrous gentleman] "Ef I hadn't-er killed
you, you would hev growd up to rule me."
A brutal Northern reference to the fact that some blacks were
killed during the Hayes-Tilden Presidential campaign. *Harper's
Weekly*, 1876.

[President] Grant sent troops to maintain the carpetbag government in
power and to protect the Negroes in the right to vote. He merely obeyed the
law. . . . Then it was that "we stuffed ballot boxes," because desperate
diseases require desperate remedies, and having resolved to take the state
away, we hesitated at nothing. . . .

I want to say now that we have not shot any Negroes in South Carolina
on account of politics since 1876. We have not found it necessary. Eighteen
hundred and seventy-six happened to be the hundredth anniversary of the
Declaration of Independence, and the action of the white men of South
Carolina in taking the state away from the Negroes we regard as a second
declaration of independence by the Caucasian from African barbarism.

D. THE LEGACY OF RECONSTRUCTION

1. Editor Godkin Grieves (1871)

Irish-born E. L. Godkin, a fearless liberal, founded the distinguished and long-lived
New York *Nation* in 1865. So biting were his criticisms that the magazine was dubbed

1. *The Nation* (New York), XIII, 364 (Dec. 7, 1871).

"the weekly day of judgment." His views on the blunders of Reconstruction were aired with incisiveness. He argued that there were two ways of dealing with the post-war South: (1) reorganize the section "from top to bottom"; (2) treat the whole community as made up of "unfortunate Americans, equally entitled to care and protection, demoralized by an accursed institution for which the whole Union was responsible, and which the whole Union had connived at, and, down to 1860, had profited by. . . ." But the North, wrote Godkin, followed neither course. Which aspects of Reconstruction does he regard as the most regrettable?

The condition of the Negro after emancipation . . . attracted the carpet-bagger as naturally as a dead ox attracts the buzzard. The lower class of demagogue scents an unenlightened constituency at an almost incredible distance, and travels towards it over mountain, valley, and river with the certainty of the mariner's compass.

But then we hastened his coming by our legislation. We deliberately, and for an indefinite period, excluded all the leading Southern men from active participation in the management of their local affairs, by a discrimination not unlike that which would be worked in this city [New York], but very much worse, if every man who had not at some time belonged to the Tammany Society were declared incapable of holding office.

It was before the war the time-honored custom of the Southern states, and a very good custom too, to put their ablest men, and men of the highest social standing and character, in office. The consequence was that it was these men who figured most prominently in the steps which led to the rebellion, and in the rebellion itself. When the war was over, we singled these men out, and not unnaturally, for punishment by the 14th Amendment and other legislation.

But we forgot that, as the President points out, they were no worse, so far as disloyalty went, than the rest of the community. They broke their oaths of allegiance to the United States, but the other white men of the South would have done the same thing if they had got the chance of doing it by being elevated to office, either under the United States or under the Confederacy. We forgot, too, that when putting a mutinous crew in irons, the most justly indignant captain leaves at liberty enough able-bodied seamen to work the ship. . . .

The results . . . have been positively infernal. In the idea that we were befriending the Negroes, we gave them possession of the government, and deprived them of the aid of all the local capacity and experience in the management of it, thus offering the states as a prey to Northern adventurers, and thus inflicting on the freedmen the very worst calamity which could befall a race newly emerged from barbarism—that is, familiarity, in the very first moments of enfranchisement, with the processes of a corrupt administration, carried on by gangs of depraved vagabonds, in which the public money was stolen, the public faith made an article of traffic, the legislature openly corrupted, and all that the community contained of talent, probity, and social respectability put under a legal ban as something worthless and disreputable.

We do not hesitate to say that a better mode of debauching the freedmen, and making them permanently unfit for civil government, could hardly have been hit on had the North had such an object deliberately in view Instead of establishing equal rights for all, we set up the government of a class, and this class the least competent, the most ignorant and inexperienced, and a class, too, whose history and antecedents made its rule peculiarly obnoxious to the rest of the community.

Out of this state of things Ku-Kluxing has grown . . . naturally. . . . We cannot gainsay anything anybody says of the atrocity of riding about the country at night with one's face blackened, murdering and whipping people. But we confess we condemn Ku-Kluxing very much as we condemn the cholera. . . . There is no more use in getting in a rage with Ku-Kluxery, and sending cavalry and artillery after it, than of legislating against pestilence, as long as nothing is done to remove the causes.

2. Frederiek Douglass Complains (1882)

The incredible ex-slave Frederick Douglass (see earlier, p. 340) raised two famous black regiments in Massachusetts during the Civil War. Among the first recruits were his own sons. Continuing his campaign for civil rights and suffrage for the freedmen, he wrote the following bitter commentary in his autobiography. One of his keenest regrets was that the federal government, despite the urgings of Thaddeus Stevens and others, failed to provide land for the freed slaves. In the light of his observations, how would free land have alleviated the conditions he describes? Why did the former slaveowners make life extremely difficult for the ex-slaves?

Though slavery was abolished, the wrongs of my people were not ended. Though they were not slaves, they were not yet quite free. No man can be truly free whose liberty is dependent upon the thought, feeling, and action of others, and who has himself no means in his own hands for guarding, protecting, defending, and maintaining that liberty. Yet the Negro after his emancipation was precisely in this state of destitution.

The law on the side of freedom is of great advantage only where there is power to make that law respected. I know no class of my fellow men, however just, enlightened, and humane, which can be wisely and safely trusted absolutely with the liberties of any other class. Protestants are excellent people, but it would not be wise for Catholics to depend entirely upon them to look after their rights and interests. Catholics are a pretty good sort of people (though there is a soul-shuddering history behind them); yet no enlightened Protestants would commit their liberty to their care and keeping.

And yet the government had left the freedmen in a worse condition than either of these. It felt that it had done enough for him. It had made him free, and henceforth he must make his own way in the world, or, as the slang phrase has it, "root, pig, or die." Yet he had none of the conditions for self-preservation or self-protection.

2. *Life and Times of Frederick Douglass* (1882), pp. 458–59.

He was free from the individual master, but the slave of society. He had neither money, property, nor friends. He was free from the old plantation, but he had nothing but the dusty road under his feet. He was free from the old quarter that once gave him shelter, but a slave to the rains of summer and the frosts of winter. He was, in a word, literally turned loose, naked, hungry, and destitute, to the open sky.

The first feeling toward him by the old master classes was full of bitterness and wrath. They resented his emancipation as an act of hostility toward them, and, since they could not punish the emancipator, they felt like punishing the object which that act had emancipated. Hence they drove him off the old plantation, and told him he was no longer wanted there. They not only hated him because he had been freed as a punishment to them, but because they felt that they had been robbed of his labor.

An element of greater bitterness still came into their hearts: the freedman had been the friend of the government, and many of his class had borne arms against them during the war. The thought of paying cash for labor that they could formerly extort by the lash did not in any wise improve their disposition to the emancipated slave, or improve his own condition.

Now, since poverty has, and can have, no chance against wealth, the landless against the landowner, the ignorant against the intelligent, the freedman was powerless. He had nothing left him but a slavery-distorted and diseased body, and lame and twisted limbs, with which to fight the battle of life.

3. Booker T. Washington Reflects (1901)

Booker T. Washington was reared in a one-room, dirt-floored shanty, and never slept on a bed until after Emancipation. Obtaining an education under grave hardships, he ultimately became the head of the famed industrial institute at Tuskegee, Alabama. The acknowledged leader of his race after Frederick Douglass died in 1895, he won additional fame as an orator and as an apostle of "gradualism" in achieving equality with the whites. He believed that blacks should acquire manual skills and otherwise prove themselves worthy of a place beside whites. Black intellectuals like Du Bois (see earlier, p. 460) criticied this conservative "Uncle Tomism" as condemning the race to permanent inferiority. In the following selection from Washington's justly famous autobiography, what does the author regard as the chief mistakes made by both whites and blacks in Reconstruction?

Though I was but little more than a youth during the period of Reconstruction, I had the feeling that mistakes were being made, and that things could not remain in the condition that they were in then very long. I felt that the Reconstruction policy, so far as it related to my race, was in a large measure on a false foundation, was artificial and forced. In many cases it seemed to me that the ignorance of my race was being used as a tool with which to help white men into office, and that there was an element in the North which wanted to punish the Southern white men by forcing

3. B. T. Washington, *Up from Slavery* (1901), pp. 83–86.

the Negro into positions over the heads of the Southern whites. I felt that the Negro would be the one to suffer for this in the end. Besides, the general political agitation drew the attention of our people away from the more fundamental matters of perfecting themselves in the industries at their doors and in securing property.

The temptations to enter political life were so alluring that I came very near yielding to them at one time, but I was kept from doing so by the feeling that I would be helping in a more substantial way by assisting in the laying of the foundation of the race through a generous education of the hand, head, and heart. I saw colored men who were members of the state legislatures, and county officers, who, in some cases, could not read or write, and whose morals were as weak as their education.

Not long ago, when passing through the streets of a certain city in the South, I heard some brick-masons calling out, from the top of a two-story brick building on which they were working, for the "Governor" to "hurry up and bring up some more bricks." Several times I heard the command, "Hurry up, Governor!" "Hurry up, Governor!" My curiosity was aroused to such an extent that I made inquiry as to who the "Governor" was, and soon found that he was a colored man who at one time had held the position of Lieutenant-Governor of his state.

But not all the colored people who were in office during Reconstruction were unworthy of their positions, by any means. Some of them, like the late Senator B. K. Bruce, Governor Pinchback, and many others, were strong, upright, useful men. Neither were all the class designated as carpetbaggers dishonorable men. Some of them, like ex-Governor Bullock of Georgia, were men of high character and usefulness.

Of course the colored people, so largely without education, and wholly without experience in government, made tremendous mistakes, just as any people similarly situated would have done. Many of the Southern whites have a feeling that, if the Negro is permitted to exercise his political rights now to any degree, the mistakes of the Reconstruction period will repeat themselves. I do not think this would be true, because the Negro is a much stronger and wiser man than he was thirty-five years ago, and he is fast learning the lesson that he cannot afford to act in a manner that will alienate his Southern white neighbors from him. . . .

During the whole of the Reconstruction period our people throughout the South looked to the federal government for everything, very much as a child looks to its mother. This was not unnatural. The central government gave them freedom, and the whole nation had been enriched for more than two centuries by the labor of the Negro. Even as a youth, and later in manhood, I had the feeling that it was cruelly wrong in the central government, at the beginning of our freedom, to fail to make some provision for the general education of our people in addition to what the states might do, so that the people would be the better prepared for the duties of citizenship.

It is easy to find fault, to remark what might have been done, and perhaps, after all, and under all the circumstances, those in charge of the conduct of affairs did the only thing that could be done at the time. Still, as I look back now over the entire period of our freedom, I cannot help feeling that it would have been wiser if some plan could have been put in operation which would have made the possession of a certain amount of education or property, or both, a test for the exercise of the franchise, and a way provided by which this test should be made to apply honestly and squarely to both the white and black races.

THOUGHT PROVOKERS

1. Was the white South ever really defeated in spirit? Would the results have been more satisfactory from its point of view if it had accepted the rule of the conqueror with better grace?

2. It has been said that Johnson was his own worst enemy, and that the white Southerners were damaged by his determination to befriend them with a "soft" policy. Comment critically.

3. Present the cases for and against *immediate* and *gradual* black suffrage. Form conclusions. Why have the excesses of the black-white legislatures been overplayed and their achievements downgraded?

4. Why did organizations like the Ku Klux Klan flourish in the Reconstruction South? In what ways did the KKK resemble a modern "terrorist" group?

5. What was the most serious long-run mistake made in Reconstruction?

25 · Politics in the Gilded Age, 1869-1889

The lessons of paternalism ought to be unlearned and the better lesson taught that while the people should patriotically and cheerfully support their government, its functions do not include the support of the people.

GROVER CLEVELAND, *Inaugural Address*, 1893

PROLOGUE: War hero Ulysses S. Grant came to the White House in 1869, when corruption abounded at many levels of government. A great general, the politically infantile Grant proved to be a great disappointment as President. Disaffected Republicans, unable to stomach Grant for a second term, organized the Liberal Republican Party in 1872, and together with the Democrats, chose the outspoken and outrageous Horace Greeley as their presidential standard-bearer. Greeley went down to inglorious defeat. Politics at the national level turned into a petty and highly partisan stalemate, as the delicately balanced major parties hesitated to upset the shaky electoral stand-off by emphasizing controversial issues. Rutherford B. Hayes narrowly triumphed over Democrat Samuel Tilden in 1877. As part of the arrangements that eventually secured his election, Hayes effectively ended Reconstruction in the South. The assassination of newly elected President Garfield in 1881 dramatized the need for civil service reform. The ex-spoilsman President Arthur, unexpectedly elevated to the highest office in the land after Garfield's death, cooperated with reformers in launching the Pendleton Act, which brought badly needed changes to the civil service. The widening reform movement was further strengthened by the outcome of the gutter-low presidential contest of 1884, from which Grover Cleveland emerged triumphant. Cleveland, the first Democratic president since 1861, displayed a fierce commitment to fiscal orthodoxy and to lowering sky-high Republican-passed tariffs.

A. THE LIBERAL REPUBLICAN REVOLT

1. Schurz Exposes the Spoilsmen (1871)

The whiteness of the White House was blackened by the scramble for offices under the gullible Grant. Cigar-chomping politicians, like hogs at the swill-box, grunted and shoved for soft jobs. The reformers, soon to organize the Liberal Republican Party, were prodded into protest. Conspicuous among them was the angular gadfly Carl Schurz (see earlier p. 447), who had grown up under the efficient German civil service. Now a liberal Senator from Missouri, he delivered the following indictment in the Senate. What evils does he find in the existing spoils system? Which one does he regard as the most serious?

After the incoming of this administration, a gentleman of my acquaintance who had strong "claims" desired to be appointed postmaster in a

1. *Congressional Globe*, 41 Cong., 3 sess., Appendix, p. 70.

Western city. But the President happened to put one of his own friends into that office; and so the man to be provided for could not be postmaster. Then the [Congressional] delegation of his state agreed to make him pension agent at the same place; but an influential member of that delegation opposed it, and so he could not be pension agent.

Then he took his case into his own hands, for he knew that he was a man to be provided for, and the President nominated him as minister resident to a South American republic. Having obtained that, he thought he could obtain more. He saw a chance to be appointed minister plenipotentiary to another government, and, sure enough, he received the nomination for that also. Then his nomination came into the Senate, and was rejected. There was a terrible disappointment! And yet the man to be provided for was provided for. He was finally sent as a governor to a territory.

Thus, sir, under the present intelligent system of making appointments, the same man aspired to a post office, a pension agency, a minister resident-ship, a full mission, and finally landed in the governorship of a territory. And the appointing power, yielding to the peculiar pressure characteristic of the existing system, declared him fit for all these places consecutively. And all this in seven days, save the territorial governorship, which was discovered for him afterward.

And with him there were a multitude of men to be provided for at the same time; there always are a good many more than places to put them in. Do you complain of the unnecessary multiplication of offices? That evil is unavoidable as long as we suffer under the system which recognizes men to be provided for.

Must it not be clear to every observing mind that our present mode of making appointments is a blindfold game, a mere haphazard proceeding? Was Mr. Lincoln very wrong when once, in a moment of despair, he said with grim humor: "I have discovered a good way of providing officers for the government: put all the names of the applicants into one pepper-box and all the offices into another, and then shake the two, and make appointments just as the names and the offices happen to drop out together."

2. Greeley Praises Greeley (1872)

The voices of the liberals, including that of Carl Schurz, swelled to a roar. With scandals bursting like popcorn, the reformers clamored for a renovation of the civil service. With the most difficult phase of Reconstruction going forward, they demanded more lenient treatment of the vanquished. When the spoilsmen and regulars of the Republican Party insisted on renominating the "old man" Grant, the reformers bolted and formed the short-lived Liberal Republican Party. Meeting in a chaotic convention in Cincinnati, they emerged with a most unlikely nominee in the erratic and politically inept editor Horace Greeley. His own influential paper published the following appeal on the eve of the election. In reading this statement, note the extent to which the Southern question was involved. What did the slogan "Reunion and Reform" mean?

2. New York *Tribune*, Nov. 5, 1872.

**"WHOEVER SAYS THIS ISN'T A REAL ELEPHANT
IS 'A LIAR'"**

Greeley tries to make a Republican elephant of states'
righters, Northern Tammany Democrats, and Southern
Ku Kluxers. *Harper's Weekly,* 1872.

We ask those who are accustomed to read and trust the *Tribune* to vote
today for Horace Greeley for President of the United States—

Because he is the best man for the place. He is incomparably abler, better
informed, safer than his antagonist.

Because his election would mean reconciliation with the South, an end
of the war, a revival of Southern industry, increased markets for Northern
products, a homogeneous country, with consequent safety and prosperity.

Because his election would mean reform at the North—an end of government patronage in elections, an end of administering the civil service
not to do the government work but to defeat one party and help another—
an investigation of the corruptions which have seemed to pervade all
branches of the national government, and have made the rule at Washington as much worse than Tweed's* rule as its scope was wider and its power
more resistless.

Because his election would mean an end of carpetbag governments at
the South, propped up by Washington interference for yet longer robbery
of already bankrupt communities.

Because, in a word, it would secure those great ends of Reunion and
Reform for which the Cincinnati [Liberal Republican] movement was
begun, and the triumph of which, whether today hastened or delayed, is as
sure to come as the Republic is to endure.

* Tweed was the corrupt "boss" of New York City who filched millions of dollars.

3. The Democrats Arraign Grant (1876)

"Eight long years of scandal" was the tag that the Democrats tellingly attached to
the Grant era. Meeting in their national convention in St. Louis and nominating the
reformer Samuel J. Tilden, they flayed the Republican regime as follows in their
platform. How realistic is the assumption that a change of administration will eliminate
the evils described?

Reform is necessary in the civil service. Experience proves that efficient,
economical conduct of the government is not possible if its civil service be
subject to change at every election, be a prize fought for at the ballot-box,
be an approved reward of party zeal instead of posts of honor assigned for
proved competency and held for fidelity in the public employ; that the
dispensing of patronage should neither be a tax upon the time of our public
men nor an instrument of their ambition. Here, again, profession falsified
in the performance attest that the party in power can work out no practical
or salutary reform.

Reform is necessary even more in the higher grades of the public service.
President, Vice-President, judges, Senators, Representatives, Cabinet officers
—these and all others in authority are the people's servants. Their offices
are not a private perquisite; they are a public trust. When the annals of
this Republic show disgrace and censure of a Vice-President [Schuyler
Colfax]; a late Speaker of the House of Representatives [James G. Blaine]
marketing his rulings as a presiding officer; three Senators profiting secretly
by their votes as law-makers; five chairmen of the leading committees of
the late House of Representatives exposed in jobbery; a late Secretary of
the Treasury [W. A. Richardson] forcing balances in the public accounts;
a late Attorney-General [G. H. Williams] misappropriating public funds;
a Secretary of the Navy [G. M. Robeson] enriched and enriching friends
by a percentage levied off the profits of contractors with his department;
an Ambassador to England [R. C. Schenck] censured in a dishonorable
speculation; the President's Private Secretary [O. E. Babcock] barely
escaping conviction upon trial for guilty complicity in frauds upon the
revenue; a Secretary of War [W. W. Belknap] impeached for high crimes
and misdemeanors—the demonstration is complete that the first step in
reform must be the people's choice of honest men from another party, lest
the disease of one political organization infect the body politic, and lest by
making no change of men or parties we get no change of measures and
no real reform.

All these abuses, wrongs, and crimes, the product of sixteen years' ascendancy of the Republican Party, create a necessity for reform, confessed by
Republicans themselves; but their reformers are voted down in convention
and displaced from the Cabinet. The party's mass of honest voters is powerless to resist the eighty thousand office-holders, its leaders and guides.
Reform can only be had by a peaceful civic revolution. We demand a

3. K. H. Porter, comp., *National Party Platforms* (1924), pp. 89–90.

change of system, a change of administration, a change of parties, that we may have a change of measures and of men.

[*The Republican platform of 1876 naturally praised Grant's "honorable work" as President, while stressing the rebellion-stained record of the Democrats. The scandals were dismissed in one brief paragraph: "We rejoice in the quickened conscience of the people concerning political affairs. We will hold all public officers to a rigid responsibility, and engage that the prosecution and punishment of all who betray official trusts shall be speedy, thorough, and unsparing." Yet precisely here Grant had failed tragically. In 1876 he had shielded his private secretary, Babcock (when tried for graft involving the whiskey revenue frauds), and also his Secretary of War, Belknap (when involved in graft regarding Indian supplies). But Grant had nothing whatever to do with the scandals besmirching Speaker Blaine and Vice-President Colfax. Cabinet members Richardson, Williams, and Robeson were all his appointees, and to that extent he was responsible for their shortcomings. Minister Schenck in London, who used his popularity as the "high priest of draw poker" to sell bogus mining stock, also falls into this category.*]

4. Grant's Farewell Apology (1876)

Grant had voted only once for a President prior to his own nomination (though a Republican, he had backed the Democrat Buchanan in the hope of averting secession). A regimented military life had not fitted him for civilian administration, and his blind loyalty to his thieving appointees was carried to an incredible point. Into his last annual message to Congress he inserted a farewell apology which indicated that he was becoming aware of his own shortcomings. This remarkable statement has been called both naïve and lacking in manliness. Where does he lay the blame for his failures?

It was my fortune, or misfortune, to be called to the office of Chief Executive without any previous political training. From the age of seventeen, I had never even witnessed the excitement attending a presidential campaign but twice antecedent to my own candidacy, and at but one of them was I eligible as a voter.

Under such circumstances, it is but reasonable to suppose that errors of judgment must have occurred. Even had they not, differences of opinion between the Executive, bound by an oath to the strict performance of his duties, and writers and debaters must have arisen. It is not necessarily evidence of blunder on the part of the Executive because there are these differences of views. Mistakes have been made, as all can see and I admit, but it seems to me oftener in the selections made of the assistants appointed to aid in carrying out the various duties of administering the government—in nearly every case selected without a personal acquaintance with the appointee, but upon recommendations of the representatives chosen directly by the people.

It is impossible, where so many trusts are to be allotted, that the right

4. J. D. Richardson, ed., *Messages and Papers of the Presidents* (1897), VII, 399–401.

parties should be chosen in every instance. History shows that no administration from the time of Washington to the present has been free from these mistakes. But I leave comparisons to history, claiming only that I have acted in every instance from a conscientious desire to do what was right, constitutional, within the law, and for the very best interests of the whole people. Failures have been errors in judgment, not of intent.

My civil career commenced, too, at a most critical and difficult time. Less than

IN FOR IT

U. S. [Grant]: "I hope I shall get to the bottom soon." Grant, after promising a probe, has not reached bottom yet. *Harper's Weekly,* 1876.

four years before, the country had emerged from a conflict such as no other had ever survived. . . . Immediately on the cessation of hostilities the then noble President, who had carried the country so far through its perils, fell a martyr to his patriotism at the hands of an assassin.

The intervening time of my first inauguration was filled up with wrangling between Congress and the new Executive [Johnson] as to the best mode of "reconstruction," or, to speak plainly, as to whether the control of the government should be thrown immediately into the hands of those who had so recently and persistently tried to destroy it, or whether the victors should continue to have an equal voice with them in this control. Reconstruction, as finally agreed upon, means this and only this, except that the late slave was enfranchised, giving an increase, as was supposed, to the Union-loving and Union-supporting votes. If *free* in the full sense of the word, they would not disappoint this expectation.

Hence, at the beginning of my first administration, the work of Reconstruction, much embarrassed by the long delay, virtually commenced. It was the work of the legislative branch of the government. My province was wholly in approving their acts, which I did most heartily, urging the legislatures of states that had not yet done so to ratify the 15th Amendment [Negro vote] to the Constitution.

The country was laboring under an enormous debt, contracted in the suppression of rebellion, and taxation was so oppressive as to discourage production. Another danger also threatened us—a foreign war. The last difficulty had to be adjusted, and was adjusted without a war and in a manner highly honorable to all parties concerned.

B. HAYES AND THE SOUTHERN PROBLEM

1. Hayes Believes Himself Defrauded (1876)

In 1876 the Republicans nominated, as Grant's successor, Governor Rutherford B. Hayes of Ohio. Hayes was a political Puritan so serious-minded that at the age of twelve he had written in his diary of the necessity of reading law books rather than the frivolous newspapers. The Democrats nominated a multimillionaire bachelor, Governor Samuel J. Tilden of New York, a prominent corporation lawyer and a noted but overrated reformer. The first electoral returns, although not the later ones, indicated a Democratic landslide, and Hayes privately conceded defeat in his diary. Why does he feel that he would have won in a fair election?

Sunday, November 12.—The news this morning is not conclusive. The headlines of the morning papers are as follows: the *News,* "Nip and Tuck"; "Tuck has it"; "The Mammoth National Doubt"; and the *Herald* heads its news column, "Which?" But to my mind the figures indicate that Florida has been carried by the Democrats. No doubt both fraud and violence intervened to produce the result. But the same is true in many Southern states.

We shall, the fair-minded men of the country will, history will hold that the Republicans were by fraud, violence, and intimidation, by a nullification of the 15th Amendment, deprived of the victory which they fairly won. But we must, I now think, prepare ourselves to accept the inevitable. I do it with composure and cheerfulness. To me the result is no personal calamity.

I would like the opportunity to improve the civil service. It seems to me I could do more than any Democrat to put Southern affairs on a sound basis. I do not apprehend any great or permanent injury to the financial affairs of the country by the victory of the Democrats. The hard-money wing of the party is at the helm. . . .

We are in a minority in the electoral colleges; we lose the administration. But in the former free states—the states that were always loyal—we are still in a majority. We carry eighteen of the twenty-two and have two hundred thousand majority of the popular vote. In the old slave states, if the recent Amendments were cheerfully obeyed, if there had been neither violence nor intimidation nor other improper interference with the rights of the colored people, we should have carried enough Southern states to have held the country and to have secured a decided popular majority in the nation.

1. C. R. Williams, ed., *Diary and Letters of Rutherford Birchard Hayes* (1924), III, 377–78. By permission of the Ohio Historical Society.

Our adversaries are in power, but they are supported by a minority only of the lawful voters of the country. A fair election in the South would undoubtedly have given us a large majority of the electoral votes, and a decided preponderance of the popular vote.

2. Chandler Assails the Solid South (1879)

With the electoral vote of three Southern states in hot dispute, the Hayes-Tilden deadlock of 1876 was broken in 1877 by the specially constituted Electoral Commission of fifteen men. Its questionable decision for Hayes was grudgingly accepted by the Democrats. But they did not yield until they had received assurances that federal bayonets would no longer prop up Republican regimes in Louisiana and South Carolina—the last of the states under military reconstruction. Hayes honored this pledge and withdrew the troops, despite Republican outcries. The two states then went over to the Democratic Solid South. Senator Zachariah Chandler of Michigan, who had been an outspoken anti-slaveryite, deplored these developments in a fiery speech in Chicago. (He died the next day.) The Democrats at that time controlled both Houses of Congress. Why does Chandler regard the Southern states as grossly overrepresented?

They [the Confederates] have forfeited all their property—we gave it back to them. We found them naked, and we clothed them. They were without the rights of citizenship, and we restored to them those rights. We took them to our bosoms as brethren, believing that they had repented of their sins. We killed for them the fatted calf and invited them to the feast, and they gravely informed us that they had always owned that animal, and were not grateful for the invitation.

By the laws of war, and by the laws of nations, they were bound to pay every dollar of the expense incurred in putting down that rebellion. But we forgave them that debt, and today you are being taxed heavily to pay the interest on the debt that they ought to have paid. Such magnanimity as was exhibited by this nation to these rebels has never been witnessed on the earth since God made it, and, in my humble judgment, it will never be witnessed again.

Mistakes we undoubtedly made, errors we committed, but, in my judgment, the greatest mistake we made, and the gravest error we committed, was in not hanging enough of these rebels to make treason forever odious.

Today, in Congress, the men have changed but not the measures. Twenty years ago they said: "Do this, or fail to do that, and we will shoot your government to death." If I am to die, I would rather be shot to death with musketry than starved to death. These rebels (for they are just as rebellious now as they were twenty years ago; there is not a particle of difference— I know them better than any other living mortal man; I have summered and wintered with them)—these rebels today have thirty-six members on the floor of the House of Representatives. Without one single constituent, and in violation of law, those thirty-six members represent 4,000,000 people, lately slaves, who are as absolutely disfranchised as if they lived in another

2. C. M. Depew, ed., *The Library of Oratory* (1902), VIII, 448–51 (Oct. 31, 1879).

"OF COURSE HE WANTS TO VOTE THE DEMOCRATIC TICKET!"

Democratic "Reformer": "You're free as air, ain't you? Say you are, or I'll blow yer black head off!"

A satire on the Southern claim that the former slaves of the South were "free as air" in the Hayes-Tilden campaign. *Harper's Weekly,* 1876.

sphere, through shotguns, and whips, and tissue-ballots. For the law [14th Amendment] expressly says that wherever a race or class is disfranchised, they shall not be represented upon the floor of the House. And these thirty-six members thus elected constitute three times the whole of their majority upon the floor.*

This is not only a violation of the law, but it is an outrage upon all the loyal men of the United States. It ought not to be. It must not be. And it shall not be. Twelve members of the Senate—more than their whole majority—occupy their seats upon the floor by fraud and violence; and I am saying no more to you than I said to those rebel generals. With majorities thus obtained by fraud and violence in both Houses, they dared to dictate terms to the loyal men of these United States. . . .

What they want is not free elections, but free fraud at elections. They

---

* The House numbered 149 Democrats and 130 Republicans; the Senate, 42 Democrats and 33 Republicans.

have got a Solid South by fraud and violence. Give them permission to perpetrate the same fraud and violence in New York City and Cincinnati, and New York and Ohio, with the Solid South, will give them the Presidency, and that once obtained by fraud and violence, they would hold it for a generation. Today 8,000,000 of people in the Southern states control the legislation of the country through caucus dictation, as they controlled their slaves when slavery existed.

[*Chandler was partially correct. The Democratic Party that finally won the White House under Cleveland, Wilson, and Franklin Roosevelt was basically the Solid South plus the Democratic machines of the large Northeastern and Middle Western cities.*]

C. THE BEGINNINGS OF CIVIL SERVICE REFORM

1. Morton Praises the Spoils System (1871)

Oliver P. Morton, Indiana's able war governor, had labored so zealously against hostile Copperhead Democrats that his exertions were blamed for the paralytic stroke that crippled him in 1865. As a devoted Republican, he could see little good in the Democrats, and consequently favored appointing fellow partisans to office. His speech in the United States Senate in 1871 against the proposed civil service reform is a classic argument for the spoils system. How does he defend it?

The Senator [Trumbull of Illinois] says that he is in favor of organizing the civil service so that officers shall be appointed without regard to politics. . . . Now, sir, to have appointments made without regard to politics will suit our Democratic friends remarkably well while they are not in power, but it would not suit them one moment after they came into power. . . .

The Senator from Illinois praises the civil service system of Great Britain. A system that might be appropriate to Great Britain would not be appropriate here; our institutions are different. In England the tenure of office in the civil service is for life. They hold their offices during good behavior; that is to say, during life. Can we adopt the life tenure here?

Why, sir, ten thousand men in this city [Washington] holding office for life would form a privileged class that would revolutionize the very foundation principle of this government. We have but one life tenure under our Constitution, and if we had it to make over again we would not have that. I refer to the Supreme Court of the United States. . . . If a man has an office for life, it takes a very serious cause to get him out. An ordinary delinquency, an ordinary neglect or abuse or failure, is never sufficient to oust a man who holds an office for life.

No, sir, we cannot afford to adopt the English system under any circumstances; it is anti-republican; it is contrary to the fundamental principles of this government; and yet the Senator held up to us the beauties of

1. *Congressional Globe,* 41 Cong., 3 sess., Pt. I, pp. 458, 460–61 (Jan. 12, 1871).

CAN A MAN BE A NURSE?

U. S. Grant holds the baby as he finds neither party
wanting it. *Harper's Weekly*, 1875.

the English system!

Sir, what is the fact there? Are the English clerks better qualified than those in our departments are? From the evidence I have, they are not. But they have one quality that our clerks have not got: that is, they have "the insolence of office" that results from a life tenure. I could refer to the facts on this point. You have all read *Little Dorrit*, by Charles Dickens, where he described the Circumlocution Office and the Somerset House. . . .

I am not arguing against competitive examinations. I am in favor of them; but they are not infallible by any means. Men may pass an examination, and a first-rate examination, and yet be utterly unqualified for the position. How does it happen so often that the young men who graduate at law schools and carry off the first prizes fail in the practice of the law? So in regard to medicine. And how often does it happen that those who take the honors of the class at West Point do not succeed upon the field of battle or in the Army? You can adopt no system that will guard against exceptional cases. . . .

But the Senator says that officers ought to be appointed without regard to politics. Whenever you can carry on this government without regard to politics, that doctrine will do. But this is a government of the people and a government of public opinion, in which the mass of the people take a deep interest, as they do not in England and in countries on the continent of Europe. Just so long as the character of this government continues as it is, appointments will continue to be made with reference to politics; and no system can be devised that will prevent it. I do not care how many competitive examinations you institute, or whether you make the tenure for life or a tenure for ten years, you cannot change that thing unless you change the character of the government.

But what propriety is there in it? A man high in office, who has climbed up the political ladder, may then turn around and slap the faces of his friends who helped him up, if they should want appointments, and call that virtue! Would it make it a virtue? . . .

I have been in the Senate now nearly four years, and, so far as I know, there have been but three clerks appointed upon my recommendation. . . . As far as I am personally concerned, I would be glad to be relieved of all this labor. But what right have I to be relieved? My friends have the same right to call upon me that I have had in times past to call upon them, and, if they are respectable, and capable, and honest, why should I refuse to give them that legitimate aid which may be within my power? Why, sir, men act upon this principle in all conditions of life, whether in regard to politics or in regard to business; and you cannot change it by any enactment which you can make.

2. *Harper's Weekly* Hails a New Era (1883)

The Pendleton Civil Service Reform Act finally passed Congress in 1883. Most of the opposition came from spoils-hungry Democrats, who now resented the death-bed repentance of the Republicans. The new law forbade obligatory political contributions from officeholders, and authorized competitive examinations to ascertain fitness. But the act was initially applied to only about 10,000 officials in the "classified service," out of some 130,000 federal employees. The passage of the measure was unwittingly assisted by Congressman J. A. Hubbell, chairman of the Republican Congressional Committee, who had given ammunition to the reformers by brazenly demanding contributions from federal officers as office insurance. *Harper's Weekly*, whose editor (George W. Curtis) was a leading civil service reformer, here comments on the passage of the bill by the Senate, before its approval by the House. Why was the measure enacted at this particular time?

The passage of the Pendleton bill by the Senate is an important event in our political history. It is the first practical legislative step toward the correction of abuses of administration involving dangerous consequences which are plainly perceived and universally acknowledged. It is a measure which, should it become law, will overthrow the aristocracy of patronage and spoils, and open the public service to all the people.

It will not, indeed, purify politics at a blow. There will still be corruption and demagogism, and no good citizen can put off his armor of diligent watchfulness and effort. But it is not an argument against sanitary regulations that they do not abolish disease, nor against penal laws that crime still continues. It is no reason for refusing to try to improve a situation that still further improvement may be possible.

The passage of this bill by the Senate is a prompt response to a public demand unmistakably expressed at the autumn election, and it is a significant sign of the immediate influence of sound public opinion upon legislation. . . .

The awakening of public sentiment which has produced this great result is largely due to two very different events—the murder of Garfield and the assessments of Hubbell. Last spring Mr. Hubbell issued his circulars as a matter of course. The storm that followed showed how truly the public mind attributed the murder of Garfield to the spoils system. The result was impressive. Before the year ended, the action of Hubbell had been condemned by the Supreme Court, and the Senate of the United States had unanimously made it a penal offense.

The history of the year upon this subject exhorts every friend of wise progress to trust the people, and never to despair.

3. Schurz Applauds Partial Gains (1893)

The liberal German-American reformer and orator Carl Schurz (see earlier, p. 469) was regarded by spoilsmen as a foreign busybody trying to "Prussianize" the civil service. Here he speaks eloquently in New York City as president of the Civil-Service Reform League. Ten years after the much-heralded birth of the Pendleton Act, he finds much to deplore and something to praise. Does he feel that the gains outweigh the drawbacks?

The Fourth of March last [1893] a new administration went into power. Untold thousands of men poured into the national capital clamoring for office; not for offices that were vacant, but to be vacated in order to make room for the clamorers. No matter whether he was ever so good a public servant, the man who was in was to be kicked out, to let him in who was out, no matter whether he would be not half so good a public servant.

The office-hunting throng swept into the White House and into the departments like a cloud of locusts. . . . The Cabinet ministers, all new men in their places, who felt the urgent need of studying somewhat their departmental duties, were hunted down so that they had hardly time to eat and to sleep, much less to study. When their cry for pity availed nothing, they at last barricaded their doors with strict regulations. They went into hiding in order to save some hours for the business of the government.

The Post Office Department was not only overrun by the crowd, but snowed under with written applications and recommendations for office, which in huge heaps covered the floors of the rooms, and the whole force of the department had to work after business hours merely to open and assort them. Senators and members of the House of Representatives ran wildly about like whipped errand boys to press the claims of greedy constituents or mercenary henchmen. . . .

But there is one part of the public service which now remains untouched by the tumultuous debauch of the spoils carnival. It is like a quiet, peaceable island, with a civilized, industrious population, surrounded by the howling sea. The President and the chiefs of the government departments contemplate this part of the service with calmness and contentment, for it gives them no trouble while the turmoil of the office hunt rages all around it.

3. National Civil-Service Reform League, *Proceedings* (1893), pp. 7–8, 10, 11–12, 16–17.

The good citizen, anxious for the honor of his country, beholds it with relief and satisfaction, for here he finds nothing to be ashamed of, and much that is worthy of this free and great nation. This is the "classified service," covered by the Civil Service Law, the creation of Civil Service Reform. On the portals the words are written: "Nobody enters here who has not proved his fitness for the duties to be performed." The office-hunting mob reads this and recoils. The public servant within it calmly walks the paths of his duty, undisturbed by the thought of the greedy cormorant hungering for his place. He depends upon his merit for his security and advancement, and this consciousness inspires his work. This is the application of common sense and common honesty to the public service. It is Civil Service Reform. . . .

At the close of President Arthur's administration in 1885 the number of places classified—that is, covered by the Civil Service Law—was about 15,500. At the close of President Cleveland's administration in 1889, it was about 27,300. At the close of President Harrison's administration in 1893 it was about 43,400, to which should be added several thousand laboring men in the navy yards placed under similar rules by the voluntary and most laudable act of Secretary Tracy.

As the whole number of places under the national government amounts to about 180,000, we may say that more than one-fourth of the service of the national government has ceased to be treated as mere spoils of party warfare. In one-fourth the party boss has lost his power. One-fourth is secure from the quadrennial loot. In one-fourth influence and favoritism go for nothing. One-fourth has been rescued from barbarism. One-fourth is worthy of a civilized country. So much, Civil Service Reform has accomplished in the time of three presidential terms.

But great and encouraging as its progress has been, Civil Service Reform, having conquered only one-fourth of the service, has done only one-fourth of its work. . . . Civil Service Reform has undertaken to open the offices to all according to their ability to serve the people.

The spoils system asks the candidate for office: "Does your member of Congress recommend you, or does the party boss in your state or your county ask for your appointment? Or are you backed by a man who gives much money to our campaign fund? What men of influence have you behind you? If you have none, you can have no place." Civil Service Reform asks the candidate: "Are you a man of good character, and what can you show to prove it? What do you know? What can you do? What qualifications have you for serving the people? Have you more than other candidates for the place?"

On the one side, under the spoils system, the aristocracy of influence—and a very vulgar aristocracy it is—robbing the man who has only merit, unbacked by power, of his rightful chance. On the other hand, Civil Service Reform, inviting all freely to compete, and then giving the best chance to the best man, be that man ever so lowly, and be his competitor ever so great a favorite of wealth and power. On that side the aristocracy of "pull"; on this the democracy of merit. . . .

The spoils politician is fond of objecting that civil service examinations do not always point out the fittest man for the place. Perhaps not always. The best marksman does not hit the bull's-eye every time; but he misses it rarely. The civil service examinations may have a small record of failures. But what the system, fairly conducted, *always* does is to snatch public office from the undemocratic control of influence and favoritism. And there is the point which stings the spoils politician.

D. THE BLAINE-CLEVELAND MUDSLINGERS

1. The Moralists Condemn Cleveland (1884)

The Republicans nominated for the Presidency in 1884 their premier personality and orator, James G. Blaine of Maine. In so doing they brushed aside suspicions that he had prostituted the Speakership of the House for private gain. Republican reformers, sneeringly dubbed "Mugwumps," turned their backs on the nominee. The Democrats gleefully nominated their reformist New York governor, bachelor Grover Cleveland. The crusade of the Clevelandites against immorality in public life faltered badly when Republican scandal-seekers revealed that Cleveland had fathered an illegitimate son eight years earlier in Buffalo. The accused candidate, courageously confessing his guilt, responded, "Tell the truth." The burning issue then became one of alleged public immorality versus private immorality. A leading Republican religious journal, *The Independent*, righteously turned its back on both candidates, especially Cleveland. **What force is there in the argument that weakness of character in private life indicates weakness in public life, and that the Democrats, in their own interests and in the interests of the high office, should have replaced Cleveland as soon as the scandal broke?**

Some of Mr. Cleveland's supporters try to comfort themselves with the idea that the offense charged against him, being a delinquency in his private life, has nothing to do with the question of his fitness or unfitness for the Presidency. Though his morals in this respect may be bad, he may, nevertheless, be trusted with the duties of the office. . . .

The plain truth is that licentiousness is one of the very worst of vices, that a man's real character is the one shown by his private life, and that this is the character which he will carry with him into his public life, if elected thereto. The connection between the two lives is direct and intimate; and, hence, no one who is bad in his private character is fit to be trusted with public duties.

No decent man surely would think of voting for a horse-thief; and, for an equally good reason, no one should vote for the lecherous corrupter of womanhood. Both are essentially rotten at the seat of moral life. It is bad enough to have them in private life, and will be much worse to have them in public life, especially when the latter would carry with it the virtual acceptance and indorsement of a gross immorality. A nation that, with its

1. *The Independent*, XXXVI, 16 (Oct. 30, 1884).

eyes open, will select a libertine for its chief magistrate must be in the worst stage of moral decay.

It is, however, urged by some of the Cleveland supporters, who find it difficult to adopt this new philosophy, that he has sincerely repented of what the law of God makes a grievous sin, and the law of man in some states makes a crime.

The first answer is that there is no evidence before the public to show the fact of such repentance, and that, in the absence of such evidence, the presumption is exactly the reverse. It will be time enough to reason from Mr. Cleveland's assumed repentance when the fact itself is established.

A s·cond answer is that, if we admit the repentance alleged, this would not cancel the wrong to such an extent as to render him a fit candidate for President. We take it that repentant debauchees, though they may be forgiven by both God and man, are not, any more than repentant thieves and robbers, to be deemed morally eligible to the supreme magistracy of this great nation. Their past record is a fatal objection to them. The people can and should do better with the office than to burlesque it with such a palpable incongruity. The interests of sound morality sternly demand that this office should not be associated with an admitted bastardy on the part of its incumbent.

It was, hence, the duty of the Democratic Party, the moment the uncleanness in Mr. Cleveland's private character was made known, to withdraw him from the field, and put a decent, pure, and competent candidate in his place. The continuance of his candidacy with this knowledge is a disgrace to the party; and his election would be a burning disgrace to the whole country. The example of his success would be a moral calamity. His defeat is an imperative duty.

2. The Mugwumps Condone Cleveland (1884)

Blaine, in sharp contrast to bachelor Cleveland, appears to have been a model husband and father. A Democratic orator, noting that the allegedly dishonest Blaine was a splendid family man and that the once-immoral Cleveland was a spotless public servant, proposed that "we should elect Cleveland to the public office which he is so admirably qualified to fill and remand Mr. Blaine to the private life which he is so eminently fitted to adorn." *Harper's Weekly*, a leading Mugwump journal, here puts the best face it can on the dilemma. Evaluate its most convincing argument in support of Cleveland. Would a throw-away vote for a third-party candidate have been the proper course?

Undoubtedly every good citizen would prefer a choice between two candidates absolutely irreproachable in every respect, and there are many honest persons who will prefer not to vote for a candidate of whom any kind of irregularity at any time can be justly alleged. Such voters, however, if they cannot support Mr. Cleveland, who said at once, "Tell the truth,"

2. *Harper's Weekly*, XXVIII, 528 (Aug. 16, 1884).

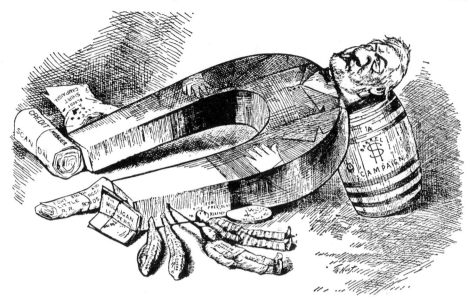

THE "MAGNETIC" BLAINE: OR, A VERY HEAVY "LOAD"-STONE
[MAGNET] FOR THE REPUBLICAN PARTY TO CARRY

Blaine's personal magnetism, which was famous, here attracts to himself assorted scandals of the Grant era, including his own involvement in the railroad bonds and the Mulligan letters. *Harper's Weekly,* 1880.

can still less support Mr. Blaine, who said, "Let my private [financial] affairs alone," and tried in vain to deceive the country.*

In the actual situation the practical alternative seems to us to lie between a candidate whose offense is wholly in the past, and was of a kind which does not necessarily disqualify him for the highest public trusts, and a candidate who deliberately prostituted public office to private gain. No such man . . . has ever been nominated or elected to a great office in this country. But Franklin and Hamilton and Jefferson and Webster and Clay, and other eminent men still nearer our own time, were held by their fellow citizens to be worthy of the highest public responsibilities, although it was known that their private lives had not been always without stain. It was not that the people were indifferent to morality, but that they wisely discriminated between conduct which justly and necessarily unfits a man for public trusts, and that which experience and the general consciousness prove to be compatible with the utmost personal honesty and official fidelity.

---

* Blaine had acquired wealth out of all proportion to his known salaries, and had resisted all attempts "to expose his private business." A decision that he had rendered as Speaker of the House in 1869 had saved a grant of land for the Little Rock and Fort Smith Railroad. He subsequently sought and secured a financial favor from the company. The accusation was that he had made his ruling *after* entering into the secret deal. Proof of his guilt or innocence presumably lay in a packet of letters ("Mulligan letters") which he had written, but which he refused to make public in their entirety.

The allegation that Mr. Cleveland is at this time a libertine and a drunkard is unquestionably, upon any kind of evidence known to us, false. His official career has been open to the eyes of all men, and if during the time that he has faithfully executed great public trusts his private life has disgraced his public office, the fact is wholly unknown to us, and certainly no evidence of it has been submitted to the public.

No honest man will mistake us as defending moral irregularities of any kind, nor, on the other hand, will he doubt our hearty contempt of those who affect horror at private immorality in order to divert public attention from official corruption. . . . The supporters of Mr. Blaine have chosen by his nomination to raise the question of official integrity as an indispensable qualification for the chief office in the government. Such an issue cannot be evaded, and it is the paramount issue of this election. But if those who are utterly unable to impeach Mr. Cleveland's official integrity, or to establish that of Mr. Blaine, should invite a contest of the comparative decency of their past and private lives, the contest must be declined for the honor of the American name. A controversy for the Presidency which should turn upon such a discussion would be the most disgusting and degrading in our history.

[*The hope expressed by this journal proved futile. Panicky Democrats, with no encouragement from Cleveland, discovered a disconcerting date on the headstone over the grave of the first-born Blaine child. It indicated that the baby had arrived within three months of the marriage. Blaine hastened to explain this irregularity by pointing to two wedding ceremonies several months apart. He also brought a libel suit against an Indiana newspaper, but subsequently dropped it. Someone—presumably a Republican—thoughtfully and surreptitiously destroyed the evidence by chiseling away the offensive date.*]

E. CLEVELAND TAKES COMMAND

1. Cleveland Pleads for Tariff Reduction (1885)

The financial embarrassments of Cleveland's first administration, oddly enough, stemmed from too much money in the Treasury. The great bulk of federal revenue then came from tariff duties, which the consumer repaid as a hidden tax in the increased price of the import. The only feasible way to reduce the unnecessarily large inflow to the Treasury was to reduce the tariff, and such a reduction was bound to arouse the high-protectionists, mostly Republicans but some Democrats. Cleveland, never one to shrink from disagreeable duty, courageously recommended such a remedy in his first annual message to Congress. Is he really hostile to protection? Why does he single out a certain class of items for reduction?

The fact that our revenues are in excess of the actual needs of an economical administration of the government justifies a reduction in the amount exacted from the people for its support. Our government is

1. J. D. Richardson, ed., *Messages and Papers of the Presidents* (1897), VIII, 341.

THE NATIONS NEEDS. A TARIFF FOR REVENUE. A REDUCTION OF TARIFF DUTIES BUT NO TARIFF FOR SURPLUS. AND NO TARIFF FOR MONOPOLISTS ONLY.

U.S. CONGRESS.

CLEVELAND DEMANDS TARIFF REDUCTION
Thomas Nast cartoon. Roger Butterfield, *The American Past,* 1947.

but the means established by the will of a free people, by which certain principles are applied which they have adopted for their benefit and protection. And it is never better administered, and its true spirit is never better observed, than when the people's taxation for its support is scrupulously limited to the actual necessity of expenditure, and distributed according to a just and equitable plan.

The proposition with which we have to deal is the reduction of the revenue received by the government, and indirectly paid by the people, from customs duties. The question of free trade is not involved, nor is there now any occasion for the general discussion of the wisdom or expediency of a protective system.

Justice and fairness dictate that, in any modification of our present laws relating to revenue, the industries and interests which have been encouraged by such laws, and in which our citizens have large investments, should not be ruthlessly injured or destroyed.

We should also deal with the subject in such manner as to protect the interests of American labor, which is the capital of our workingmen. Its stability and proper remuneration furnish the most justifiable pretext for a protective policy.

Within these limitations a certain reduction should be made in our customs revenue. The amount of such reduction having been determined, the inquiry follows: Where can it best be remitted and what articles can best be released from duty in the interest of our citizens?

I think the reductions should be made in the revenue derived from a tax upon the imported necessaries of life. We thus directly lessen the cost of living in every family of the land, and release to the people in every humble home a larger measure of the rewards of frugal industry.

2. Philadelphians Criticize Cleveland (1887)

To Cleveland's repeated pleas for tariff reduction, the protectionists, both Republicans and Democrats, turned a deaf ear. The President finally decided to arouse the country by taking the unprecedented step of devoting his entire annual message to one subject—the tariff and its implications. Old-line Democratic politicians, fearful that such boat-rocking tactics would lose the next presidential election, vainly urged him to reconsider. But, one of his critics remarked, he would rather be wrong than President. In his sensational tariff message of 1887, he declared that the surplus confronted the nation with a "condition," and "not a theory." He called for a "slight reduction" of the tariff, and branded as "irrelevant" and "mischievous" Republican charges of "free trade." In what particular is the following reaction of the Philadelphia *Press* (Republican) most unfair?

A thousand thanks to President Cleveland for the bold, manly, and unequivocal avowal of his extreme free-trade purposes! And a thousand rebukes and defeats for the false, dangerous, and destructive policy which he thus frankly and unreservedly proclaims!

The message deserves all the glory of courage, all the praise of high public issue, all the condemnation of utter, ruinous heresy.

It is a surprise in its method and a still greater surprise in its matter. It comes like the sudden, echoing boom of a great gun signaling a crucial fight on unexpected ground. In its immediate flash of light and in its broad bearings it looms up as one of the most momentous political events since the war.

It plants the President and his party squarely on free trade; it clarifies the next presidential battle as by a lightning stroke; it makes free trade *vs.* protection the overshadowing issue; it dwarfs and dismisses all other questions; it clears away all cowardly evasions and juggling subterfuges; it ends all pitiful personal bespattering; and it summons the American people to decide the supreme question whether the grand protective system which has built up our splendid industries shall be overthrown or not!

For the distinct and emphatic manner in which the President has faced and forced this paramount issue he deserves all credit; for the wrongs, the perils, and the inevitable disasters of his policy he must be crushed unless the people would have their own vital interests crushed.

3. The New York *Times* Acclaims Courage (1887)

The New York *Times*, an independent newspaper with Democratic leanings, regarded Cleveland's tariff message as statesmanlike but politically unwise. Explain why, in the light of this editorial.

2. Quoted in *Public Opinion*, IV, 193 (Dec. 10, 1887).

3. New York *Times*, Dec. 7, 1887.

Mr. Cleveland has done an act of statesmanship in the best sense. Recognizing a great duty, he has performed it with courage, with firmness, and at the right time. And he has performed it so that every honest man must see that it is an honest act—disinterested, faithful to the requirements of conscience, without hope or purpose of personal or party advantage except such as comes from the public recognition of public service.

Judged by an ordinary standard of political expediency, the President's act is inexpedient. He has forced upon his party an issue as to which the party is divided, and so divided that unless the minority yield, it can defeat the will of the majority. He has done this on the eve of a national contest in which a considerable number of men of influence in the party have been urging him to avoid this issue, and threatening him and the party with disaster if he did not avoid it.

On the other hand, there is nothing in this issue, thus presented, by which Mr. Cleveland could hope to draw from the Republican Party any votes to compensate those he is in danger of losing, and which he has been warned over and again by leaders of his own party that he would lose.

Nor this alone, for if the protectionist faction in the Democratic Party carry out their own desires, or do what they have continually declared that they would do, Mr. Cleveland has done the one thing by which he could imperil the prospect of his own renomination. From the point of view of the politician, he has shown a courage that is temerity in the pursuit of an end of no value to himself.

[*The Cleveland-Harrison presidential canvass of 1888 hinged on the tariff, not the private morals of the candidates, and the Republican Harrison won. The tariff message of 1887 is commonly blamed for the Democratic defeat. But Cleveland actually polled in excess of 100,000 more popular votes than his opponent, and he showed increased strength in states like New Jersey and Rhode Island, where manufacturing was strong. Other factors were no doubt important in tipping the scales, notably the blundering interference of the British minister in Washington, Sackville-West. He declared in effect that a vote for Cleveland was a vote for England.*]

THOUGHT PROVOKERS

1. How might one explain the fact that Grant was a success as a general but an embarassment as a President?
2. Could a better case be made for the spoils system in 1883 than now? What can be said for and against partisanship in public life? What major changes did civil service reform effect?
3. What might have been the consequences for whites and blacks in the South if the election of 1876 had gone to Tilden?
4. Many Republicans who supported the Civil Service Reform Act were accused of hypocrisy. Explain. Is it desirable to have public officials, including Supreme Court Justices, hold office for life?
5. With reference to the tariff-surplus problem, what did Cleveland mean when he said that "unnecessary taxation is unjust taxation"? In what ways might the "surplus" have been legitimately spent?

26 · *Industry Comes of Age, 1865-1900*

> *That is the most perfect government in which an injury to one is the concern of all.*
>
> MOTTO OF THE KNIGHTS OF LABOR

PROLOGUE: A few of the railroad companies after 1865 had more employees than a number of the state governments—and more power to inflict harm. When cutthroat competition failed to eliminate abuses, Congress finally passed the precedent-shattering Interstate Commerce Act of 1887. But this pioneer measure fell far short of providing adequate safeguards. Competing industries had meanwhile been merging as monopolistic trusts, notably Rockefeller's Standard Oil Company. Congress belatedly tried to restrain these monsters with the rather toothless Sherman Anti-Trust Act of 1890. As the new industrial giants grew, their power over their unorganized employees increased. The Knights of Labor, who in the 1870's and 1880's made the most successful attempt until then to organize the nation's army of toilers, amassed considerable numerical strength. But they overreached themselves in the 1880's, and the wage-conscious American Federation of Labor, with its component skilled unions, forged to the front.

A. THE PROBLEM OF THE RAILROADS

1. A Defense of Long-Haul Rates (1885)

A serious grievance against the "railroad rascals" was discrimination. Their rates would often be lower where a line had competition, and higher elsewhere. Charges were sometimes heavier for a short haul than for a long haul over the same track. At one time the freight rate on cotton goods shipped from Boston to Denver was $1.79 a hundredweight; if the shipment went 1400 miles farther to San Francisco, the total charge was only $1.50. Is the following justification of this practice by a Southern railroad manager (H. S. Haines) convincing? Why did certain farmers favor this type of discrimination?

If it costs $600,000 per annum to keep up a [rail]road, then the money must come out of the freight and passengers that are obliged to pass over it. Whether the amount of business be small or large, the money to keep up the road must be forthcoming, or it will go to decay.

If 100,000 bales of cotton were the only freight that passed over a road which carried no passengers, that cotton would have to pay a freight of $6 per bale if it cost $600,000 per annum to maintain the road, and no legislation could make it otherwise. But if the quantity of cotton to be transported could be increased to 200,000 bales, then the cost of transportation could be fixed at $3 per bale, to the great joy and relief of the

1. Report of the Senate Select Committee on Interstate Commerce, 49 Cong., 1 sess., *Senate Reports*, No. 46, II, pt. 1, Appendix, pp. 130-31.

shippers of the first 100,000 bales; and yet the $600,000 required to operate the road would be forthcoming.

Now, suppose that the community which raised this second 100,000 bales had a water route to market and said to the railroad company, "It only costs a dollar per bale to ship our cotton by water, but we prefer to ship it by rail at the same price." Who would be benefited if the company took the cotton at a dollar per bale? Who but the local shippers themselves, for without this addition to the business of the road they would have to pay $600,000 per year, or $6 per bale, to keep up the road, while with the $100,000 obtained from the other 100,000 bales of competitive or through cotton they would have to pay but $500,000 or $5 per bale on their own cotton. Should they turn around upon the managers of the railroad and say that it was unjust to the local shippers to charge only a dollar per bale on the through cotton?

No, it is not only just, but to the benefit of the local shippers, that the railroad which they are obliged to use should get all the business it can from those who are not obliged to use it, and at any rate the latter choose to pay, provided—and it is a very important provision—that such competitive business adds something to the net revenue of the road; or, in other words, if it be carried at anything above the actual cost of transportation.

2. President Dillon Supports Stock Watering (1891)

Critics of the railroads especially condemned "stock watering"—the practice of issuing stocks and bonds grossly in excess of the value of the property. The more the stock was "watered," the higher the freight and passenger rates would have to be to ensure a normal return on the investment. Sidney Dillon, a later president of the Union Pacific Railroad, stoutly defended stock watering. Beginning his career at the age of seven as a "water boy"—appropriately enough—on a New York railway, he ultimately amassed a fortune by building railroads, including the Union Pacific. Present at the "wedding of the rails" in Utah in 1869, he retained one of the final silver spikes until his death. He here attacks regulatory legislation in an article for a popular magazine. What is his social philosophy? Why does he place his faith in competition and the courts?

Statutory enactments interfere with the business of the railway, even to the minutest details, and always to its detriment. This sort of legislation proceeds on the theory that the railroad is a public enemy; that it has its origin in the selfish desire of a company of men to make money out of the public; that it will destroy the public unless it is kept within bounds; and that it is impossible to enact too many laws tending to restrain the monster. The advocates of these statutes may not state their theory in these exact words. But these words certainly embody their theory, if they have any theory at all beyond such prejudices as are born of the marriage between ignorance and demagogism.

2. Sidney Dillon, "The West and the Railroads," *North American Review*, CLII, 445–48, *passim* (April, 1891).

Many of the grievances that are urged against railways are too puerile to be seriously noticed, but the reader will pardon a few words as to "overcapitalization". . . .

Now, it is impossible to estimate in advance the productive power of this useful and untiring servant. Sometimes a railway is capitalized too largely, and then it pays smaller dividends; sometimes not largely enough, and then the dividends are much in excess of the usual interest of money. In the former case stockholders are willing to reduce the face of their shares, or wait until increase of population increases revenue; in the latter they accept an enlarged issue. But, as a matter of reason and principle, the question of capitalization concerns the stockholders, and the stockholders only. A citizen, simply as a citizen, commits an impertinence when he questions the right of any corporation to capitalize its properties at any sum whatever. . . .

THE SENATORIAL ROUND-HOUSE

Railroad attorneys in Senate let off steam against a bill to prevent members of Congress from accepting fees from government-subsidized railroads. *Harper's Weekly,* 1886.

Then as to prices, these will always be taken care of by the great law of competition, which obtains wherever any human service is to be performed for a pecuniary consideration. That any railway, anywhere in a republic, should be a monopoly is not a supposable case. If between two points, A and B, a railway is constructed, and its charges for fares and freight are burdensome to the public and unduly profitable to itself, it will not be a long time before another railway will be laid between these points, and then competition may be safely trusted to reduce prices. We may state it as an axiom that no common carrier can ever maintain burdensome and oppressive rates of service permanently or for a long period. . . .

Given a company of men pursuing a lawful and useful occupation,—why interfere with them? Why empower a body of other men, fortuitously assembled, not possessing superior knowledge, and accessible often to unworthy influences, to dictate to these citizens how they shall manage their private affairs? Wherever such management conflicts with public policy or private rights, there are district attorneys and competent lawyers and upright courts to take care that the commonwealth or the citizen shall receive no detriment. . . .

3. General Weaver Deplores Stock Watering (1892)

General James B. Weaver, a walrus-mustached veteran of the Civil War, had early experienced extortion when he had to borrow $100 at 33⅓% interest to finish law school. Fiery orator and relentless foe of the railroads and other "predatory" corporations, he won the presidential nomination of the People's Party (Populists) in 1892. (See p. 548.) His book entitled *A Call to Action,* published during the campaign, condemned stock waterers. To what extent does the following excerpt from it cast doubts on the testimony of President Dillon, whose article, presented in the previous selection, he sharply attacks? What is Weaver's view of the citizens' "impertinence?"

In their delirium of greed the managers of our transportation systems disregard both private right and the public welfare. Today they will combine and bankrupt their weak rivals, and by the expenditure of a trifling sum possess themselves of properties which cost the outlay of millions. Tomorrow they will capitalize their booty for five times the cost, issue their bonds, and proceed to levy tariffs upon the people to pay dividends upon the fraud.

Take for example the Kansas Midland. It cost $10,200 per mile. It is capitalized at $53,024 per mile. How are the plain plodding people to defend themselves against such flagrant injustice?

Mr. Sidney Dillon, president of the Union Pacific, . . . is many times a millionaire, and the road over which he presides was built wholly by public funds and by appropriations of the public domain. The road never cost Mr. Dillon nor his associates a single penny. It is now capitalized at $106,000 per mile! This company owes the government $50,000,000 with accruing interest which is destined to accumulate for many years. The public lien exceeds the entire cost of the road, and yet this government, which Mr. Dillon defies, meekly holds a second mortgage to secure its claim. . . .

It is pretty clear that it would not be safe for the public to take the advice of either Mr. Dillon or Mr. Gould [railroad promoter] as to the best method of dealing with the transportation problem.

[*Responding to a mounting public outcry, Congress passed the Interstate Commerce Act in 1887—the first regulatory legislation of its kind in American history. Among various reforms it forbade unreasonable or unjust rates, discriminatory rates or practices, the payment of rebates, the pooling of profits among competing lines, and a higher charge for a short haul than for a long haul. In practice, the law proved to be riddled with loopholes, and subsequent legislation was required to provide adequate safeguards.*]

3. J. B. Weaver, *A Call to Action* (1892), pp. 412–13.

B. THE TRUSTS AND MONOPOLY

1. Rockefeller Justifies Rebates (1909)

John D. Rockefeller, who amassed a fortune of nearly one billion dollars, lived to give away more than half of his "oil-gotten gains" in philanthropy. A prominent lay Baptist, he early donated a tenth of his income to charities, and in 1859 helped a Cincinnati black man to buy his slave wife. As a founding father of the mighty Standard Oil Company, he here puts the best possible face on railroad rebates, which were finally banned by the Interstate Commerce Act. He tactfully neglects to add that at one time his company also extorted secret payments ("drawbacks") from the railways on shipments by his competitors. What were the advantages to the railroads of the rebate system? To what extent did they, rather than Standard Oil, profit from these under-the-counter deals?

Of all the subjects which seem to have attracted the attention of the public to the affairs of the Standard Oil Company, the matter of rebate from railroads has perhaps been uppermost. The Standard Oil Company of Ohio, of which I was president, did receive rebates from the railroads prior to 1880, but received no advantages for which it did not give full compensation.

The reason for rebates was that such was the railroads' method of business. A public rate was made and collected by the railroad companies, but, so far as my knowledge extends, was seldom retained in full; a portion of it was repaid to the shippers as a rebate.

By this method the real rate of freight which any shipper paid was not known by his competitors nor by other railroad companies, the amount being a matter of bargain with the carrying company. Each shipper made the best bargain that he could, but whether he was doing better than his competitor was only a matter of conjecture. Much depended upon whether the shipper had the advantage of competition of carriers.

The Standard Oil Company of Ohio, being situated at Cleveland, had the advantage of different carrying lines, as well as of water transportation in the summer. Taking advantage of those facilities, it made the best bargains possible for its freights. Other companies sought to do the same.

The Standard gave advantages to the railroads for the purpose of reducing the cost of transportation of freight. It offered freights in large quantity, carloads and trainloads. It furnished loading facilities and discharging facilities at great cost. It provided regular traffic, so that a railroad could conduct its transportation to the best advantage and use its equipment to the full extent of its hauling capacity without waiting for the refiner's convenience. It exempted railroads from liability for fire and carried its own insurance. It provided at its own expense terminal facilities which permitted economies in handling. For these services it obtained contracts for special allowances on freights. But notwithstanding these special allowances, this traffic

1. J. D. Rockefeller, *Random Reminiscences of Men and Events* (1909), pp. 107–09, 111–12. Copyright 1909, Doubleday & Company, Inc.; copyright renewed 1936, John D. Rockefeller. By permission of the Executors of the Estate of John D. Rockefeller, Jr.

THE SANCTIFICATION OF ROCKEFELLER

A muckraking satire on Rockefeller's donating
part of his rebate-swollen oil fortune for religious and educational purposes. *Collier's,* 1905.

from the Standard Oil Company was far more profitable to the railroad
companies than the smaller and irregular traffic, which might have paid a
higher rate.

To understand the situation which affected the giving and taking of
rebates, it must be remembered that the railroads were all eager to enlarge
their freight traffic. They were competing with the facilities and rates
offered by the boats on lake and canal and by the pipe lines. All these
means of transporting oil cut into the business of the railroads, and they
were desperately anxious to successfully meet this competition. . . .

The profits of the Standard Oil Company did not come from advantages
given by railroads. The railroads, rather, were the ones who profited by the
traffic of the Standard Oil Company, and whatever advantage it received
in its constant efforts to reduce rates of freight was only one of the many
elements of lessening cost to the consumer which enabled us to increase
our volume of business the world over because we could reduce the selling
price.

How general was the complicated bargaining for rates can hardly be
imagined; everyone got the best rate that he could. After the passage of

the Interstate Commerce Act, it was learned that many small companies which shipped limited quantities had received lower rates than we had been able to secure, notwithstanding the fact that we had made large investments to provide for terminal facilities, regular shipments, and other economies.

I well remember a bright man from Boston who had much to say about rebates and drawbacks. He was an old and experienced merchant, and looked after his affairs with a cautious and watchful eye. He feared that some of his competitors were doing better than he in bargaining for rates, and he delivered himself of this conviction:

"I am opposed on principle to the whole system of rebates and drawbacks —unless I am in it."

2. An Oil Man Goes Bankrupt (1899)

Rockefeller's great passion was not so much love of power or money as a dislike of waste and inefficiency. Having begun as a $3.50-a-week employee, he ultimately moved into the chaotically competitive oil business with a vision that enabled him to see far ahead, and then "around the corner." Overlooking no detail, he insisted that every drop of solder used on his oil cans be counted. By acquiring or controlling warehouses, pipe lines, tankers, railroads, oil fields, and refineries, he helped forge America's first great trust in 1882. He produced a superior product at a lowered price but, in line with existing ethics, resorted to such "refined robbery" as ruthless price cutting, dictation to dealers, deception, espionage, and rebates. George Rice, one of his ill-starred competitors, here complains to the United States Industrial Commission. What are his principal grievances?

I am a citizen of the United States, born in the state of Vermont. Producer of petroleum for more than thirty years, and a refiner of same for twenty years. But my refinery has been shut down during the past three years, owing to the powerful and all-prevailing machinations of the Standard Oil Trust, in criminal collusion and conspiracy with the railroads to destroy my business of twenty years of patient industry, toil, and money in building up, wholly by and through unlawful freight discriminations.

I have been driven from pillar to post, from one railway line to another, for twenty years, in the absolutely vain endeavor to get equal and just freight rates with the Standard Oil Trust, so as to be able to run my refinery at anything approaching a profit, but which I have been utterly unable to do. I have had to consequently shut down, with my business absolutely ruined and my refinery idle.

This has been a very sad, bitter, and ruinous experience for me to endure, but I have endeavored to the best of my circumstances and ability to combat it the utmost I could for many a long waiting year, expecting relief through the honest and proper execution of our laws, which have [has] as yet, however, never come. But I am still living in hopes, though I may die in despair. . . .

2. *Report of the U. S. Industrial Commission,* I (1899), 687, 704.

Outside of rebates or freight discriminations, I had no show with the Standard Oil Trust, because of their unlawfully acquired monopoly, by which they could temporarily cut only my customers' prices, and below cost, leaving the balance of the town, nine-tenths, uncut. This they can easily do without any appreciable harm to their general trade, and thus effectually wipe out all competition, as fully set forth. Standard Oil prices generally were so high that I could sell my goods 2 to 3 cents a gallon below their prices and make a nice profit, but these savage attacks and [price] cuts upon my customers' goods . . . plainly showed . . . their power for evil, and the uselessness to contend against such odds. . . .

3. Weaver Attacks the Trusts (1892)

Rockefeller's Standard Oil of Ohio was not authorized to operate outside the state, so in 1882 the Standard Oil Trust, the first of its kind, was born. "A corporation of corporations," it secretly merged forty-one different concerns. In 1892 the courts held this trust to be illegally in restraint of trade, but Rockefeller and his associates were able to achieve their semi-monopolistic ends by less formal agreements. General Weaver, the fiery Populist candidate for President in 1892 (see later, p. 548), here assails the trusts, whose unwritten motto was said to be "Let us prey." Note his enumeration of the evils of the trusts. What does he make of the monopolists' claim that the elimination of wasteful competition is advantageous to the consumer?

The trust is organized commerce with the Golden Rule excluded and the trustees exempted from the restraints of conscience.

They argue that competition means war and is therefore destructive. The trust is eminently docile and hence seeks to destroy competition in order that we may have peace. But the peace which they give us is like that which exists after the leopard has devoured the kid. This professed desire for peace is a false pretense. They dread the war of competition because the people share in the spoils. When rid of that, they always turn their guns upon the masses and depredate without limit or mercy.

The main weapons of the trust are threats, intimidation, bribery, fraud, wreck, and pillage. Take one well-authenticated instance in the history of the Oat Meal Trust as an example. In 1887 this trust decided that part of their mills should stand idle. They were accordingly closed. This resulted in the discharge of a large number of laborers who had to suffer in consequence. The mills which were continued in operation would produce seven million barrels of meal during the year. Shortly after shutting down, the trust advanced the price of meal one dollar per barrel, and the public was forced to stand the assessment. The mills were more profitable when idle than when in operation.

The Sugar Trust has it within its power to levy a tribute of $30,000,000 upon the people of the United States by simply advancing the price of

3. J. B. Weaver, *A Call to Action* (1892), pp. 392–93.

sugar one cent per pound for one year. If popular tumult breaks out and legislation in restraint of these depredations is threatened, they can advance prices, extort campaign expenses and corruption funds from the people, and force the disgruntled multitude to furnish the sinews of war for their own destruction. They not only have the power to do these things, but it is their known mode of warfare, and they actually practice it from year to year.

The most distressing feature of this war of the trusts is the fact that they control the articles which the plain people consume in their daily life. It cuts off their accumulations and deprives them of the staff upon which they fain would lean in their old age.

C. THE RISE OF THE NEW SOUTH

1. Grady Issues a Challenge (1889)

The industrialized South—the New South—was slow to rise from the ashes of civil conflict. A kind of inferiority complex settled over the area. Henry W. Grady, eloquent editor of the Atlanta *Constitution*, did more than anyone else to break the spell. With Irish wit he preached the need for diversified crops, a readjustment of the freed slaves, the encouragement of manufacturing, and the development of local resources. In demand as a speaker, he broadcast his message widely and with demonstrable effect. The South of the 1880's was experiencing a marvelous economic boom, and new industries were spreading like its own honeysuckle. The following is a selection from a speech in Boston in which Grady contrasted the broken-down South of Reconstruction days with the new industrialized South. What major lesson must this passage have impressed upon his Northern listeners?

I attended a funeral once in Pickens county in my state [Georgia]. A funeral is not usually a cheerful object to me unless I could select the subject. I think I could, perhaps, without going a hundred miles from here, find the material for one or two cheerful funerals. Still, this funeral was peculiarly sad. It was a poor "one-gallus" fellow, whose breeches struck him under the armpits and hit him at the other end about the knee—he didn't believe in décolleté clothes.

They buried him in the midst of a marble quarry—they cut through solid marble to make his grave—and yet a little tombstone they put above him was from Vermont. They buried him in the heart of a pine forest, and yet the pine coffin was imported from Cincinnati. They buried him within the touch of an iron mine, and yet the nails in his coffin and the iron in the shovel that dug his grave were imported from Pittsburgh. They buried him by the side of the best sheep-grazing country on earth, and yet the wool in the coffin bands and the coffin bands themselves were brought from the North. The South didn't furnish a thing on earth for that funeral but the corpse and the hole in the ground.

1. Joel C. Harris, *Life of Henry W. Grady* (1890), pp. 204–05. Shortly after delivering this speech, Grady contracted pneumonia and died.

There they put him away and the clods rattled down on his coffin, and they buried him in a New York coat and a Boston pair of shoes and a pair of breeches from Chicago and a shirt from Cincinnati, leaving him nothing to carry into the next world with him to remind him of the country in which he lived, and for which he fought for four years, but the chill of blood in his veins and the marrow in his bones.

Now we have improved on that. We have got the biggest marble-cutting establishment on earth within a hundred yards of that grave. We have got a half-dozen woolen mills right around it, and iron mines, and iron furnaces, and iron factories. We are coming to meet you. We are going to take a noble revenge, as my friend Mr. Carnegie said last night, by invading every inch of your territory with iron, as you invaded ours [in the Civil War] twenty-nine years ago.

2. A Yankee Visits the New South (1887)

New England-born Charles Dudley Warner—lecturer, newspaper editor, essayist, and novelist—shone as one of the literary lights of the post–Civil War years. World traveler and humorist, he collaborated with his friend and neighbor Mark Twain in writing a satirical novel that gave a name to an era, *The Gilded Age* (1873). He revisited the South, after a two-year absence, on an extensive six-week tour. The result was the charming magazine article from which the following section is excerpted. What is most remarkable about the industrial flowering of the South, and who or what was primarily responsible for it?

When we come to the New Industrial South, the change is marvelous. . . . Instead of a South devoted to agriculture and politics, we find a South wide awake to business, excited and even astonished at the development of its own immense resources in metals, marbles, coal, timber, fertilizers, eagerly laying lines of communication, rapidly opening mines, building furnaces, founderies, and all sorts of shops for utilizing the native riches.

It is like the discovery of a new world. When the Northerner finds great founderies in Virginia using only (with slight exceptions) the products of Virginia iron and coal mines; when he finds Alabama and Tennessee making iron so good and so cheap that it finds ready market in Pennsylvania, and founderies multiplying near the great furnaces for supplying Northern markets; when he finds cotton mills running to full capacity on grades of cheap cottons universally in demand throughout the South and Southwest; when he finds small industries, such as paper box factories and wooden bucket and tub factories, sending all they can make into the North and widely over the West; when he sees the loads of most beautiful marbles shipped North; when he learns that some of the largest and most important engines and mill machinery were made in Southern shops; when he finds in Richmond a "pole locomotive," made to run on logs laid end to end, and

2. C. D. Warner, "The South Revisited," *Harper's New Monthly Magazine*, LXXIV, 638–39 (March, 1887).

drag out from Michigan forests and Southern swamps lumber hitherto inaccessible; when he sees worn-out highlands in Georgia and Carolina bear more cotton than ever before by help of a fertilizer the base of which is the cotton seed itself (worth more as a fertilizer than it was before the oil was extracted from it); when he sees a multitude of small shops giving employment to men, women, and children who never had any work of that sort to do before; and when he sees Roanoke iron cast in Richmond into car irons, and returned to a car factory in Roanoke which last year sold three hundred cars to the New York and New England Railroad—he begins to open his eyes.

The South is manufacturing a great variety of things needed in the house, on the farm, and in the shops, for home consumption, and already sends to the North and West several manufactured products. With iron, coal, timber contiguous and easily obtained, the amount sent out is certain to increase as the labor becomes more skillful. The most striking industrial development today is in iron, coal, lumber, and marbles; the more encouraging for the self-sustaining life of the Southern people is the multiplication of small industries in nearly every city I visited.

When I have been asked what impressed me most in this hasty tour, I have always said that the most notable thing was that everybody was at work. In many cities this was literally true: every man, woman, and child was actively employed, and in most there were fewer idlers than in many Northern towns. There are, of course, slow places, antiquated methods, easygoing ways, a-hundred-years-behind-the-time makeshifts, but the spirit in all the centers, and leavening the whole country, is work. Perhaps the greatest revolution of all in Southern sentiment is in regard to the dignity of labor. Labor is honorable, made so by the example of the best in the land. There are, no doubt, fossils or Bourbons, sitting in the midst of the ruins of their estates, martyrs to an ancient pride; but usually the leaders in business and enterprise bear names well known in politics and society. The nonsense that it is beneath the dignity of any man or woman to work for a living is pretty much eliminated from the Southern mind. It still remains true that the purely American type is prevalent in the South, but in all the cities the business signboards show that the enterprising Hebrew is increasingly prominent as merchant and trader, and he is becoming a plantation owner as well.

It cannot be too strongly impressed upon the public mind that the South, to use a comprehensible phrase, "has joined the procession." Its mind is turned to the development of its resources, to business, to enterprise, to education, to economic problems; it is marching with the North in the same purpose of wealth by industry. It is true that the railways, mines, and furnaces could not have been without enormous investments of Northern capital, but I was continually surprised to find so many and important local industries the result solely of home capital, made and saved since the war.

D. THE KNIGHTS OF LABOR

1. Powderly Battles for Larger Goals (1893)

The blue-eyed and ruddy-complexioned Terence V. Powderly, a nimble-witted son of Irish immigrants, became a machinist and joined the secret order of the all-embracing Knights of Labor. He ultimately rose to be its influential head as Grand Master Workman, and saw the organization attain a maximum strength of some 700,000 members—skilled and unskilled, white and colored. But lawyers, bankers, gamblers, and liquor dealers were barred. The Knights strove primarily for social and economic reform on a broad front, rather than the piecemeal raising of wages that was the chief concern of the skilled-crafts unions. Powderly favored the substitution of arbitration for strikes, the regulation of trusts and monopolies, and the replacement of the wage system with producers' cooperatives. Shot at from the front by conservatives, who accused him of communism, he was sniped at from the rear by some of his own following. From this account in his autobiography, ascertain why.

I have held a most anomalous position before the public for the last twenty years. All of this time I have opposed strikes and boycotts. I have contended that the wage question was of secondary consideration; I have contended that the short-hour question was not the end but merely the means to an end; I have endeavored to direct the eyes of our members to the principal parts of the preamble of our Order—government ownership of land, of railroads, or regulation of railroads, telegraphs, and money. But all of this time I have been fighting for a raise in wages, a reduction in the hours of labor, or some demand of the trade element in our Order, to the exclusion of the very work that I have constantly advocated and which the General Assembly of the Order commanded me to advocate.

Just think of it! Opposing strikes and always striking; battling for short hours for others, obliged to work long hours myself, lacking time to devote to anything else. Battling with my pen in the leading journals and magazines of the day for the great things we are educating the people on, and fighting with might and main for the little things.

Our Order has held me in my present position because of the reputation I have won in the nation at large by taking high ground on important national questions, yet the trade element in our Order has always kept me busy at the base of the breastworks throwing up earth which they trample down.

2. Gompers Condemns the Knights (*c*. 1886)

Samuel Gompers, a stocky Jewish cigarmaker who had been born in a London tenement, emerged as the potent leader of the skilled-crafts American Federation of Labor. Once asked what organized labor wanted, he is said to have replied, "More"—

1. T. V. Powderly, *The Path I Trod* (1940), p. 401. By permission of the Columbia University Press.
2. From *Seventy Years of Life and Labor: An Autobiography* by Samuel Gompers. Copyright 1925 by E. P. Dutton. Copyright renewal 1953 by Gertrude Gleaves Gompers. Reprinted by permission of the publisher, E. P. Dutton, Inc.

by which he meant more wages, more power, more liberty, more leisure, more benefits. He and his skilled crafts battled the unskilled of the Knights of Labor against revolutionary schemes for remaking American society. What are the principal weaknesses of the Knights of Labor from the skilled-union point of view? Which one is the most serious in the eyes of Gompers?

In 1886 a definite order went out from D. A. [District Assembly No.] 49 [of the Knights of Labor] to make war on the International Cigarmakers' Unions. It was the culmination of years of friction developing over Knights of Labor encroachments on trade union functions.

The two movements were inherently different. Trade unions endeavored to organize for collective responsibility persons with common trade problems. They sought economic betterment in order to place in the hands of wage-earners the means to wider opportunities.

The Knights of Labor was a social or fraternal organization. It was based upon a principle of cooperation, and its purpose was reform. The Knights of Labor prided itself upon being something higher and grander than a trade union or political party. Unfortunately, its purposes were not always exemplified through the declarations and the acts of its members.

The order admitted to membership any person, excluding only lawyers and saloonkeepers. This policy included employers among those eligible. Larger employers gradually withdrew

BETWEEN TWO FIRES

Employer: "If you don't go to work, I must fill your place."
Anarchist: "If you go to work, I'll make it hot for you." *Harper's Weekly*, 1886.

from the order, but the small employers and small businessmen and politicians remained.

The order was a hodgepodge with no basis for solidarity, with the exception of a comparatively few trade assemblies. The aggressive policy inaugurated in 1886 [against the Cigarmakers' Unions] was not due to any change of heart or program, but solely to the great increase in the membership of the Knights of Labor that made it seem safe to put declarations into effect.

When the order began to encroach upon the economic field, trouble was inevitable, for such invasion was equivalent to setting up a dual organization to perform a task for which they were entirely unfitted. It was particularly unfortunate when it endeavored to conduct strikes. The Knights of Labor was a highly centralized organization, and this often placed decision upon essential trade policies in the hands of officers outside the trade concerned. Strikes are essentially an expression of collective purpose of workers who perform related services and who have the spirit of union growing out of joint employment. . . .

Talk of harmony with the Knights of Labor is bosh. They are just as great enemies of trade unions as any employer can be, only more vindictive. I tell you they will give us no quarter, and I would give them their own medicine. It is no use trying to placate them or even to be friendly. They will not cooperate with a mere trades union, as they call our organization. The time will come, however, when the workingmen of the country will see and distinguish between a natural and an artificial organization.

3. Chicago Anarchists Demand Blood (1886)

The rank and file of the Knights of Labor favored an eight-hour day, and their agitation for this goal came to a boil in Chicago on May Day, 1886. The McCormick Harvesting Machine Company, involved with strikers on other issues, had hired strikebreakers. These "scabs" were attacked by the displaced men, whereupon the police killed or injured several of the aroused strikers. August Spies, a German-born anarchist and newspaper editor, angrily issued a circular containing the following appeal in German and English. How does Spies describe the condition of working people? How accurate is his description?

REVENGE!

WORKINGMEN, TO ARMS!!!

Your masters sent out their bloodhounds—the police; they killed six of your brothers at McCormick's this afternoon. They killed the poor wretches, because they, like you, had the courage to disobey the supreme will of your bosses. They killed them, because they dared ask for the shortening of the hours of toil. They killed them to show you, "Free American Citizens," that you must be satisfied and contented with whatever your bosses condescend to allow you, or you will get killed!

You have for years endured the most abject humiliations; you have for years suffered unmeasurable iniquities; you have worked yourself to death; you have endured the pangs of want and hunger; your children you have sacrificed to the factory-lords. In short, you have been miserable and obedient slave[s] all these years. Why? To satisfy the insatiable greed, to fill the coffers of your lazy thieving master! When you ask them now to

3. B. R. Kogan, *The Chicago Haymarket Riot* (1959), p. 9 (reproduction of a copy of the circular in the Chicago Historical Society collection).

lessen your burden, he sends his bloodhounds out to shoot you, kill you!

If you are men, if you are the sons of your grand sires, who have shed their blood to free you, then you will rise in your might, Hercules, and destroy the hideous monster that seeks to destroy you. To arms we call you, to arms!

YOUR BROTHERS

[*Responding to such inflammatory appeals, a protest meeting against police brutality assembled at Haymarket Square in Chicago, May 4, 1886. It was about to break up peaceably when some 180 policemen advanced, to be met by an exploding bomb which killed several persons (including a policeman) and injured many others. To this day no one has revealed who threw the bomb, but eight alleged anarchists, accused of preaching incendiary doctrines, were tried and found guilty. Four of them, including August Spies, were hanged.*]

4. Powderly Denies a Breakup (1887)

The Knights of Labor suffered a lasting black eye when the public erroneously associated them with the Chicago anarchists and the "Haymarket Massacre." In addition, many of the May Day strikes of 1887 had failed, internal friction was multiplying, and unwise producers' cooperatives were draining away union funds. Visionary schemes, rather than down-to-earth projects, preoccupied the leaders. Powderly's own denial of a decline was whistling in the dark, but the following statement by him is highly revealing of the broad social objectives of the Knights. How many of these objectives would the hardheaded Samuel Gompers and his skilled-crafts unions have approved?

This prophecy, so long deferred of fulfillment, approaches its realization: "The Knights are breaking up" at last. The Philadelphia *Chronicle,* in a late issue, notes the approach of their dissolution without one word of sympathy or regret. Others of our esteemed contemporaries seem just as callous to our approaching dissolution, and watch the coming of the fatal moment of the fleeting breath with the same degree of insensibility.

It is true, the Knights are breaking up. We are at last forced to acknowledge the truth so long, so stubbornly, resisted. We are breaking up— breaking up as the plowman breaks up the soil for the sowing of new seed. We are breaking up old traditions. We are breaking up hereditary rights, and planting everywhere the seed of universal rights. We are breaking up the idea that money makes the man and not moral worth. We are breaking up the idea that might makes right. We are breaking up the idea that legislation is alone for the rich. We are breaking up the idea that the Congress of the United States must be run by millionaires for the benefit of millionaires. We are breaking up the idea that a few men may hold millions of acres of untilled land while other men starve for the want of one acre. We are breaking up the practice of putting the labor of criminals [convict labor] into competition with honest, industrious labor and starving it to death. We are breaking up the practice of importing [European] ignorance, bred of monarchies and dynamite, in order to depreciate intelligent, skilled labor at home. We are breaking up the practice of employing little children in factories, thus breeding a race of deformed, ignorant, and profligate. We are breaking up the idea that a man who works with his hands has need neither of education nor of civilized refinements. We are breaking up the idea that the accident of sex puts one-half of the human race beyond the pale of constitutional rights. We are breaking up the practice of paying woman one-third the wages paid man simply because she is a woman. We are breaking up the idea that a man may debauch an infant [minor] girl and shield himself from the penalty behind a law he himself has made. We are breaking up ignorance and intemperance, crime and oppression, of whatever character and wherever found.

Yes, the Knights of Labor are breaking up, and they will continue their appointed work of breaking up until universal rights shall prevail; and while they may not bring in the millennium, they will do their part in the evolution of moral forces that are working for the emancipation of the race.

[*With Samuel Gompers at the helm, the skilled-crafts American Federation of Labor emerged in 1886. By 1890 it had overshadowed the fast-fading Knights of Labor. Skilled carpenters, striking for their own narrow objectives, could not easily be replaced by strikebreakers. Unskilled workers could be. The skilled crafts became weary of sacrificing themselves on the altar of large social objectives. This, in brief, was the epitaph of the Knights of Labor.*]

THOUGHT PROVOKERS

1. Which of the so-called railroad abuses of the post-Civil War are the easiest to justify and which are the hardest? In view of the fact that the railway rates were becoming progressively lower when the Interstate Commerce Act was passed in 1887, why should the public have complained?
2. Comment critically on the advantages and disadvantages of the monopolistic trust from the standpoint of the consumer. Was the attempted distinction between "good" and "bad" trusts a valid one?
3. Why was the South, which has many natural resources and is being rapidly industrialized today, so slow to be industrialized after the Civil War?
4. Is organized labor today tending toward the Gompers or the Powderly approach? Explain. Why does the United States not have a Labor Party?

27. New Social and Cultural Horizons, 1865-1900

Th' worst thing ye can do f'r anny man is to do him good.
F. P. DUNNE ("MR. DOOLEY"), PARAPHRASING ANDREW CARNEGIE, 1906

PROLOGUE: The inpouring of the New Immigration from southern and eastern Europe, beginning conspicuously in the 1880's, aggravated existing social ills. It further crowded the melting pot, worsened slum conditions, stimulated agitation to halt cheap foreign labor, and revived anti-Catholic outcries. Protestant denominations, already disturbed by the numerical primacy of the Roman Catholic Church in America, were alarmed by its hundreds of thousands of new communicants. At the same time Protestantism was profoundly shaken by the impact of Darwinism. One manifestation was a heated debate between the rock-ribbed Fundamentalists and the more adaptable Modernists, who came to see in evolution a more glorious revelation of a wonder-working God. Private philanthropy was flourishing, particularly when conscience-pricked millionaires like Rockefeller and Carnegie donated unprecedented sums to worthy causes. White reformers now largely left the recently freed blacks to their own devices. The temperance crusade intensified, as did the still-frustrated campaign for women's suffrage. Meanwhile, new work patterns in the booming cities provided new opportunities and challenges for women, which in turn sparked fresh debate on women's role, marital relations, and sexual morality.

A. IMMIGRATION AND URBANIZATION

1. Mary Antin Praises America (1894)

The bomb-assassination of Czar Alexander II in 1881 touched off an outburst of anti-Semitism in Russia that resulted in countless riots, burnings, pillagings, rapings, and murders. Tens of thousands of Jewish refugees fled to America then and later. Mary Antin, a Polish Jew thirteen years of age, joined her father in Boston in 1894. She later distinguished herself as an author and a welfare worker. In her autobiographical account, excerpted herewith, what did these Jewish immigrants find most gratifying in America?

In our flat we did not think of such a thing as storing the coal in the bathtub. There was no bathtub. So in the evening of the first day my father conducted us to the public baths. As we moved along in a little procession, I was delighted with the illumination of the streets. So many lamps, and they burned until morning, my father said, and so people did not need to carry lanterns.

---

1. From *The Promised Land* by Mary Antin. Copyright 1912 by Houghton Mifflin Company. Reprinted by permission of Houghton Mifflin Company.

In America, then, everything was free, as we had heard in Russia; the streets were as bright as a synagogue on a holy day. Music was free; we had been serenaded, to our gaping delight, by a brass band of many pieces, soon after our installation on Union Place.

Education was free. That subject my father had written about repeatedly, as comprising his chief hope for us children, the essence of American opportunity, the treasure that no thief could touch, not even misfortune or poverty. It was the one thing that he was able to promise us when he sent for us; surer, safer, than bread or shelter.

On our second day I was thrilled with the realization of what this freedom of education meant. A little girl from across the alley came and offered to conduct us to school. My father was out, but we five between us had a few words of English by this time. We knew the word *school*. We understood. This child, who had never seen us till yesterday, who could not pronounce our names, who was not much better dressed than we, was able to offer us the freedom of the schools of Boston! No application made, no questions asked, no examinations, rulings, exclusions; no machinations, no fees. The doors stood open for every one of us. The smallest child could show us the way.

This incident impressed me more than anything I had heard in advance of the freedom of education in America. It was a concrete proof—almost the thing itself. One had to experience it to understand it.

[*Distressingly common was the experience of Anzia Yezierska, whose impoverished family came from Russia to New York City in 1901. Buoyed up by the hope of finding green fields and open places, she found herself in a smelly, crowded slum. God's blue sky was not visible; the landscape was the brick wall of the next building; and there was no place for the pasty-faced children to play. One of her despairing companions said, "In Russia, you could hope to run away from your troubles to America. But from America where can you go?"*]

2. Jacob Riis Goes Slumming (1890)

Police reporter Jacob A. Riis, a Danish-born immigrant who had known rat-infested tenements in Denmark, aimed his talented pen at the scandalous slums of New York. He was shocked by the absence of privacy, sanitation, and playgrounds, and by the presence of dirt, stench, and vermin. One tenement area in New York was known as the "Lung Block" because of the prevalence of tuberculosis. Despite the opposition of heartless landlords, who worked hand-in-glove with corrupt politicians, Riis helped to eliminate some of these foul firetraps, especially the dark "rear tenements." What does he regard as the chief obstacles to good health and good morals in these slums?

Suppose we look into one? No. — Cherry Street. Be a little careful, please! The hall is dark and you might stumble over the children pitching pennies back there. Not that it would hurt them; kicks and cuffs are their daily diet. They have little else.

2. J. A. Riis, *How the Other Half Lives* (1890), pp. 43–44.

Here where the hall turns and dives into utter darkness is a step, and another, another. A flight of stairs. You can feel your way, if you cannot see it. Close? Yes! What would you have? All the fresh air that ever enters these stairs comes from the hall-door that is forever slamming, and from the windows of dark bedrooms that in turn receive from the stairs their sole supply of the elements God meant to be free, but man deals out with such niggardly hand.

That was a woman filling her pail by the hydrant you just bumped against. The sinks are in the hallway, that all the tenants may have access—and all to be poisoned alike by their summer stenches.

Hear the pump squeak! It is the lullaby of tenement-house babes. In summer, when a thousand thirsty throats pant for a cooling drink in this block, it is worked in vain. But the saloon, whose open door you passed in the hall, is always there. The smell of it has followed you up.

Here is a door. Listen! That short hacking cough, that tiny, helpless wail —what do they mean? They mean that the soiled bow of white you saw on the door downstairs will have another story to tell—oh! a sadly familiar story—before the day is at an end. The child is dying with measles. With half a chance it might have lived; but it had none. The dark bedroom killed it.

"It was took all of a suddint," says the mother, smoothing the throbbing little body with trembling hands. There is no unkindness in the rough voice of the man in the jumper, who sits by the window grimly smoking a clay pipe, with the little life ebbing out in his sight, bitter as his words sound: "Hush, Mary! If we cannot keep the baby, need we complain—such as we?"

Such as we! What if the words ring in your ears as we grope our way up the stairs and down from floor to floor, listening to the sounds behind the closed doors—some of quarreling, some of coarse songs, more of profanity. They are true. When the summer heats come with their suffering, they have meaning more terrible than words can tell.

Come over here. Step carefully over this baby—it is a baby, spite of its rags and dirt—under these iron bridges called fire-escapes, but loaded down, despite the incessant watchfulness of the firemen, with broken household goods, with washtubs and barrels, over which no man could climb from a fire.

This gap between dingy brick walls is the yard. That strip of smoke-colored sky up there is the heaven of these people. Do you wonder the name does not attract them to the churches?

That baby's parents live in the rear tenement here. She is at least as clean as the steps we are now climbing. There are plenty of houses with half a hundred such in. The tenement is much like the one in front we just left, only fouler, closer, darker—we will not say more cheerless. The word is a mockery. A hundred thousand people lived in rear tenements in New York last year.

3. The A.P.A. Hates Catholics (1893)

The flood of cheap South European labor in the 1880's, predominantly Roman Catholic, rearoused nativist bigots. The most powerful group, the secretive American Protective Association (A.P.A.), claimed a million members by 1896. Among various activities, it circulated forged documents revealing alleged papal orders to "exterminate" non-Catholics. In Toledo, Ohio, the local branch gathered Winchester rifles for defense. The A.P.A. was especially alarmed by the Irish-Catholic political machines, which in cities like New York and Chicago had secured a semi-monopoly of public offices, including the fire department and the police department. In the following secret oath of the A.P.A. are the economic or the political prohibitions more damaging?

I do most solemnly promise and swear that I will always, to the utmost of my ability, labor, plead, and wage a continuous warfare against ignorance and fanaticism; that I will use my utmost power to strike the shackles and chains of blind obedience to the Roman Catholic Church from the hampered and bound consciences of a priest-ridden and church-oppressed people; that I will never allow anyone, a member of the Roman Catholic

THE UNSEEN SIGNAL OF THE JESUITS

Anti-Catholic cartoon showing a government official at confession betraying state secrets that are being relayed to Rome by secret wire. New York Public Library.

3. Reprinted with permission of Macmillan Publishing Company from *Documents of American Catholic History*, edited by John Tracy Ellis. © John Tracy Ellis, 1956.

Church, to become a member of this order, I knowing him to be such; that I will use my influence to promote the interest of all Protestants everywhere in the world that I may be; that I will not employ a Roman Catholic in any capacity, if I can procure the services of a Protestant.

I furthermore promise and swear that I will not aid in building or maintaining, by my resources, any Roman Catholic church or institution of their sect or creed whatsoever, but will do all in my power to retard and break down the power of the Pope, in this country or any other; that I will not enter into any controversy with a Roman Catholic upon the subject of this order, nor will I enter into any agreement with a Roman Catholic to strike or create a disturbance whereby the Catholic employees may undermine and substitute their Protestant co-workers; that in all grievances I will seek only Protestants, and counsel with them to the exclusion of all Roman Catholics, and will not make known to them anything of any nature matured at such conferences.

I furthermore promise and swear that I will not countenance the nomination, in any caucus or convention, of a Roman Catholic for any office in the gift of the American people, and that I will not vote for, or counsel others to vote for, any Roman Catholic, but will vote only for a Protestant, so far as may lie in my power (should there be two Roman Catholics in opposite tickets, I will erase the name on the ticket I vote); that I will at all times endeavor to place the political positions of this government in the hands of Protestants, to the entire exclusion of the Roman Catholic Church, of the members thereof, and the mandate of the Pope.

To all of which I do most solemnly promise and swear, so help me God. Amen.

4. Lodge Urges a Literacy Test (1896)

The continued influx of hordes of impoverished and illiterate South Europeans during the depression of the 1890's intensified outcries for their exclusion. Organized labor objected to their low wages; religious bigots, to their Catholicism; city planners, to their slum residence; racial purists, to their "degenerate" stock. Senator Henry Cabot Lodge, a Massachusetts blue blood and later the arch-foe of Woodrow Wilson, here argues for a bill that would establish a literacy test. Which group was he trying to exclude? Would the best interests of the nation have been served by his proposal?

It is found, in the first place, that the illiteracy test will bear most heavily upon the Italians, Russians, Poles, Hungarians, Greeks, and Asiatics, and very lightly, or not at all, upon English-speaking emigrants or Germans, Scandinavians, and French.

In other words, the races most affected by the illiteracy test are those whose emigration to this country has begun within the last twenty years and swelled rapidly to enormous proportions, races with which the English-speaking people have never hitherto assimilated, and who are most alien to the great body of the people of the United States.

4. *Congressional Record,* 54 Cong., 1 sess., p. 2817 (March 16, 1896).

On the other hand, emigrants from the United Kingdom and of those races which are most closely related to the English-speaking people, and who with the English-speaking people themselves founded the American colonies and built up the United States, are affected but little by the proposed test. These races would not be prevented by this law from coming to this country in practically undiminished numbers.

These kindred races also are those who alone go to the Western and Southern states, where immigrants are desired, and take up our unoccupied lands. The races which would suffer most seriously by exclusion under the proposed bill furnish the immigrants who do not go to the West or South, where immigration is needed, but who remain on the Atlantic seaboard, where immigration is not needed and where their presence is most injurious and undesirable.

The statistics prepared by the committee show further that the immigrants excluded by the illiteracy test are those who remain for the most part in congested masses in our great cities. They furnish, as other tables show, a large proportion of the population of the slums. The committee's report proves that illiteracy runs parallel with the slum population, with criminals, paupers, and juvenile delinquents of foreign birth, or parentage, whose percentage is out of all proportion to their share of the total population when compared with the percentage of the same classes among the native-born.

It also appears from investigations which have been made that the immigrants who would be shut out by the illiteracy test are those who bring least money to the country, and come most quickly upon private or public charity for support.

5. Cleveland Vetoes a Literacy Test (1897)

In 1897 Congress finally passed a bill excluding all prospective immigrants who could not read or write twenty-five words of the Constitution of the United States in some language. One of the several goals of the exclusionists was to bar anarchists and other radical labor agitators. Cleveland, ever ruggedly independent, vetoed the bill. What is his most effective argument against it?

It is not claimed, I believe, that the time has come for the further restriction of immigration on the ground that an excess of population overcrowds our land.

It is said, however, that the quality of recent immigration is undesirable. The time is quite within recent memory when the same thing was said of immigrants who, with their descendants, are now numbered among our best citizens.

It is said that too many immigrants settle in our cities, thus dangerously increasing their idle and vicious population. This is certainly a disadvantage. It cannot be shown, however, that it affects all our cities, nor that it is

5. J. D. Richardson, ed., *Messages and Papers of the Presidents* (1897), IX, 758–59.

permanent; nor does it appear that this condition, where it exists, demands as its remedy the reversal of our present immigration policy.

The claim is also made that the influx of foreign laborers deprives of the opportunity to work those who are better entitled than they to the privilege of earning their livelihood by daily toil. An unfortunate condition is certainly presented when any who are willing to labor are unemployed, but so far as this condition now exists among our people, it must be conceded to be a result of phenomenal business depression and the stagnation of all enterprises in which labor is a factor. With the advent of settled and wholesome financial and economic governmental policies, and consequent encouragement to the activity of capital, the misfortunes of unemployed labor should, to a great extent at least, be remedied. If it continues, its natural consequences must be to check the further immigration to our cities of foreign laborers and to deplete the ranks of those already there. In the meantime those most willing and best entitled ought to be able to secure the advantages of such work as there is to do. . . .

The best reason that could be given for this radical restriction of immigration is the necessity of protecting our population against degeneration and saving our national peace and quiet from imported turbulence and disorder.

I cannot believe that we would be protected against these evils by limiting immigration to those who can read and write in any language twenty-five words of our Constitution. In my opinion, it is infinitely more safe to admit a hundred thousand immigrants who, though unable to read and write, seek among us only a home and opportunity to work than to admit one of those unruly agitators and enemies of governmental control who can not only read and write, but delight in arousing by inflammatory speech the illiterate and peacefully inclined to discontent and tumult.

Violence and disorder do not originate with illiterate laborers. They are, rather, the victims of the educated agitator. The ability to read and write, as required in this bill, in and of itself affords, in my opinion, a misleading test of contented industry and supplies unsatisfactory evidence of desirable citizenship or a proper apprehension of the benefits of our institutions.

If any particular element of our illiterate immigration is to be feared for other causes than illiteracy, these causes should be dealt with directly, instead of making illiteracy the pretext for exclusion, to the detriment of other illiterate immigrants against whom the real cause of complaint cannot be alleged.

[*President Taft, following Cleveland's example of 1897, successfully vetoed a literacy test in 1913, as did President Wilson in 1915. Finally, in 1917, such a restriction was passed over Wilson's veto. Wilson had declared that the prohibition was "not a test of character, of quality, or of personal fitness." In fact, a literacy test denied further opportunity to those who had already been denied opportunity.*]

B. THE CHURCH ON THE DEFENSIVE

1. The Shock of Darwinism (1896)

The theory of evolution, popularized by Charles Darwin's *On the Origin of Species* (1859), directly challenged the Biblical story of creation. (In 1654 a distinguished English scholar had declared the date of creation to be "the 26th of October, 4004 B.C. at 9 o'clock in the morning.") Orthodox religionists flooded the New York publishers of Darwin's volume with letters demanding its suppression. Andrew D. White, a prominent American educator, scholar, and diplomat, here describes in a famous book some of the reactions in the United States. How might one explain the violence of these comments?

Darwin's *Origin of Species* had come into the theological world like a plough into an anthill. Everywhere those thus rudely awakened from their old comfort and repose had swarmed forth angry and confused. Reviews, sermons, books light and heavy, came flying at the new thinker from all sides. . . .

Echoes came from America. One review, the organ of the most widespread of American religious sects, declared that Darwin was "attempting to befog and to pettifog the whole question"; another denounced Darwin's views as "infidelity"; another, representing the American branch of the Anglican Church, poured contempt over Darwin as "sophistical and illogical," and then plunged into an exceedingly dangerous line of argument in the following words: "If this hypothesis be true, then is the Bible an unbearable fiction; . . . then have Christians for nearly two thousand years been duped by a monstrous lie. . . . Darwin requires us to disbelieve the authoritative word of the Creator."

A leading journal representing the same church took pains to show the evolution theory to be as contrary to the explicit declarations of the New Testament as to those of the Old, and said: "If we have all, men and monkeys, oysters and eagles, developed from an original germ, then is St. Paul's grand deliverance—'All flesh is not the same flesh; there is one kind of flesh of men, another of beasts, another of fishes, and another of birds'—untrue." . . .

But a far more determined opponent was the Rev. Dr. Hodge, of Princeton. His anger toward the evolution doctrine was bitter: he denounced it as thoroughly "atheistic"; he insisted that Christians "have a right to protest against the arraying of probabilities against the clear evidence of the Scriptures"; he even censured so orthodox a writer as the Duke of Argyll, and declared that the Darwinian theory of natural selection is "utterly inconsistent with the Scriptures," and that "an absent God, who does nothing, is to us no God"; that "to ignore design as manifested in God's creation is to dethrone God"; that "a denial of design in Nature is virtually a denial of God"; and that "no teleologist can be a Darwinian."

1. A. D. White, *A History of the Warfare of Science with Theology in Christendom* (1896), I, 70, 71–72, 79–80.

Even more uncompromising was another of the leading authorities at the same university—the Rev. Dr. Duffield. He declared war not only against Darwin but even against men like Asa Gray, Le Conte, and others, who attempted to reconcile the new theory with the Bible. He insisted that "evolutionism and the Scriptural account of the origin of men are irreconcilable"—that the Darwinian theory is "in direct conflict with the teaching of the apostle, 'All Scripture is given by inspiration of God.'" He pointed out, in his opposition to Darwin's *Descent of Man* and Lyell's *Antiquity of Man,* that in the Bible "the genealogical links which connect the Israelites in Egypt with Adam and Eve in Eden are explicitly given."

These utterances of Prof. Duffield culminated in a declaration which deserves to be cited as showing that a Presbyterian minister can "deal damnation round the land" *ex cathedra* in a fashion quite equal to that of popes and bishops. It is as follows: "If the development theory of the origin of man," wrote Dr. Duffield in the *Princeton Review,* "shall in a little while take its place—as doubtless it will—with other exploded scientific speculations, then they who accept it with its proper logical consequences will in the life to come have their portion with those who in this life 'know not God and obey not the gospel of His Son.'"

2. Beecher Accepts Evolution (1886)

The Reverend Henry Ward Beecher, a famed Congregational minister, was the most popular and influential preacher of his day. Like his sister, Harriet Beecher Stowe, he crusaded against slavery, and in a mock auction in his Brooklyn church raised money to redeem a black girl from slavery. Although besmirched by a notorious adultery trial which ended in a hung jury, he continued to preach religion and discuss public issues with eloquence and boldness. His disbelief in a literal hell, combined with his belief in evolution, generated friction with orthodox clergymen and led to his withdrawal from the Association of Congregational Ministers. He customarily preached to 2500 people; after he died, 40,000 viewed his body. Why does he accept Darwin's views, and why does he believe that evolution will help true religion?

As thus set forth, it may be said that Evolution is accepted as the method of creation by the whole scientific world, and that the period of controversy is passed and closed. A few venerable men yet live with many doubts; but it may be said that 99 percent—as has been declared by an eminent physicist—99 percent of scientific men and working scientists of the world are using this theory without any doubt of its validity. . . .

This science of Evolution is taught in all advanced academies, in all colleges and universities, in all medical and surgical schools, and our children are receiving it as they are the elements of astronomy or botany or chemistry. That in another generation Evolution will be regarded as uncontradictable as the Copernican system of astronomy, or the Newtonian doctrine of gravitation, can scarcely be doubted. Each of these passed through the same contradiction by theologians. They were charged by the

2. H. W. Beecher, *Evolution and Religion* (1886), pp. 50–54.

Church, as is Evolution now, with fostering materialism, infidelity, and atheism.

We know what befell Galileo for telling the truth of God's primitive revelation. We know, or do not know, at least, how Newton stood charged with infidelity and with atheism when he announced the doctrine of gravitation.

Who doubts the heliocentric theory [of Copernicus] today? Who doubts whether it is the sun which is moving round the earth or the earth round the sun? Who doubts that the law of attraction, as developed by Newton, is God's material law universally? The time is coming when the doctrine of Evolution, or the method of God in the creation of the world, will be just as universally accepted as either of these great physical doctrines. The whole Church fought them; yet they stand, conquerors. . . .

Evolution is substantially held by men of profound Christian faith: by the now venerable and universally honored scientific teacher, Professor Dana of Yale College, a devout Christian and communicant of a Congregational Church; by Professor Le Conte of the University of California, an elder in the Presbyterian Church; by President McCosh of Princeton College, a Presbyterian of the Presbyterians, and a Scotch Presbyterian at that; by Professor Asa Gray of Harvard University, a communicant of the Christian Church; by increasing numbers of Christian preachers in America; by Catholics like Mivart, in England. . . .

To the fearful and the timid let me say that while Evolution is certain to oblige theology to reconstruct its system, it will take nothing away from the grounds of true religion. It will strip off Saul's unmanageable armor from David, to give him greater power over the giant. Simple religion is the unfolding of the best nature of man towards God, and man has been hindered and embittered by the outrageous complexity of unbearable systems of theology that have existed. If you can change theology, you will emancipate religion; yet men are continually confounding the two terms, religion and theology. . . .

Evolution, applied to religion, will influence it only as the hidden temples are restored, by removing the sands which have drifted in from the arid deserts of scholastic and medieval theologies. It will change theology, but only to bring out the simple temple of God in clearer and more beautiful lines and proportions. . . .

In every view, then, it is the duty of the friends of simple and unadulterated Christianity to hail the rising light and to uncover every element of religious teaching to its wholesome beams. Old men may be charitably permitted to die in peace, but young men and men in their prime are by God's providence laid under the most solemn obligations to thus discern the signs of the times, and to make themselves acquainted with the knowledge which science is laying before them. And above all, those zealots of the pulpit who make faces at a science which they do not understand, and who reason from prejudice to ignorance; who not only will not lead their people, but hold up to scorn those who strive to take off the burden of ignorance from their shoulders—these men are bound to open their eyes and see God's sun shining in the heavens.

C. THE NEW MATERIALISM

1. Carnegie's Gospel of Wealth (1889)

Andrew Carnegie, the ambitious little Scottish steel magnate, spent the first part of his life in America making a half-billion or so dollars, and the rest of it giving his fortune away. Not a gambler or speculator at heart, he gambled everything on the future prosperity of America. His social conscience led him to preach "The Gospel of Wealth," notably in the following magazine article. Why does he believe that the millionaire is a trustee for the poor, and that direct charity is an evil?

This, then, is held to be the duty of the man of wealth: first, to set an example of modest, unostentatious living, shunning display or extravagance; to provide moderately for the legitimate wants of those dependent upon him; and after doing so to consider all surplus revenues which come to him simply as trust funds, which he is called upon to administer, and strictly bound as a matter of duty to administer in the manner which, in his judgment, is best calculated to produce the most beneficial results for the community—the man of wealth thus becoming the mere agent and trustee for his poorer brethren, bringing to their service his superior wisdom, experience, and ability to administer, doing for them better than they would or could do for themselves. . . .

Those who would administer wisely must, indeed, be wise, for one of the serious obstacles to the improvement of our race is indiscriminate charity. It were better for mankind that the millions of the rich were thrown into the sea than so spent as to encourage the slothful, the drunken, the unworthy. Of every thousand dollars spent in so-called charity today, it is probable that $950 is unwisely spent; so spent, indeed, as to produce the very evils which it proposes to mitigate or cure.

A well-known writer of philosophic books admitted the other day that he had given a quarter of a dollar to a man who approached him as he was coming to visit the house of his friend. He knew nothing of the habits of this beggar; knew not the use that would be made of this money, although he had every reason to suspect that it would be spent improperly. This man professed to be a disciple of Herbert Spencer; yet the quarter-dollar given that night will probably work more injury than all the money which its thoughtless donor will ever be able to give in true charity will do good. He only gratified his own feelings, saved himself from annoyance —and this was probably one of the most selfish and very worst actions of his life, for in all respects he is most worthy.

In bestowing charity, the main consideration should be to help those who will help themselves; to provide part of the means by which those who

1. Andrew Carnegie, "Wealth," *North American Review,* CXLVIII, 661–64 (June, 1889).

THE MACMILLION

The Scotsman Carnegie in 1901 provided £2,000,000
for establishing free education at four Scottish universities, each of which is represented by an up-
turned hat. *Punch* (London), 1901.

desire to improve may do so; to give those who desire to rise the aids by
which they may rise; to assist, but rarely or never to do all. Neither the
individual nor the race is improved by almsgiving. Those worthy of
assistance, except in rare cases, seldom require assistance. The really valuable men of the race never do, except in cases of accident or sudden
change. Everyone has, of course, cases of individuals brought to his own
knowledge where temporary assistance can do genuine good, and these he
will not overlook.

But the amount which can be wisely given by the individual for individuals is necessarily limited by his lack of knowledge of the circumstances
connected with each. He is the only true reformer who is as careful and
as anxious not to aid the unworthy as he is to aid the worthy, and, perhaps,
even more so, for in almsgiving more injury is probably done by rewarding
vice than by relieving virtue.

The rich man is thus almost restricted to following the examples of
Peter Cooper, Enoch Pratt of Baltimore, Mr. Pratt of Brooklyn, Senator

Stanford,* and others, who know that the best means of benefiting the community is to place within its reach the ladders upon which the aspiring can rise—parks, and means of recreation, by which men are helped in body and mind; works of art, certain to give pleasure and improve the public taste; and public institutions of various kinds, which will improve the general condition of the people;—in this manner returning their surplus wealth to the mass of their fellows in the forms best calculated to do them lasting good. . . .

The man who dies leaving behind him millions of available wealth, which was his to administer during life, will pass away "unwept, unhonored, and unsung," no matter to what uses he leaves the dross which he cannot take with him. Of such as these the public verdict will then be: "The man who dies thus rich dies disgraced."

Such, in my opinion, is the true Gospel concerning Wealth, obedience to which is destined some day to solve the problem of the Rich and the Poor, and to bring "Peace on earth, among men good will."

2. *The Nation* Challenges Carnegie (1901)

Carnegie died "disgraced" by dying rich. He managed to give away only $350,000,-000, from both income and principal. A total of $60,000,000 went to public municipal libraries, many named after himself. Finley Peter Dunne ("Mr. Dooley") poked fun at this immodest arrangement, especially the feature that required the community to provide the site, the books, the upkeep: "Ivry time he [Carnegie] dhrops a dollar, it makes a noise like a waither [waiter] fallin' downstairs with a tray iv dishes." The New York *Nation* reviewed rather critically Carnegie's essay on the Gospel of Wealth when it was published in book form. Does Carnegie or *The Nation* have the better of the argument as to the baleful effects of inherited riches? How have these issues changed since Carnegie's day?

Mr. Carnegie's philosophy is perfectly simple, and it is stated clearly and forcibly. He holds, first, that the present competitive system, which necessarily creates millionaires, or allows men to get rich, is essential to progress, and should not be altered. Secondly, rich men should not leave their fortunes to their children, because their children will be demoralized by having money to spend which they have not earned. Thirdly, rich men should not indulge in luxury. Fourthly, they should dispose of their fortunes while living, or the government should confiscate them at their death. Fifthly, the only practical way of disposing of them is to found libraries and other public institutions, requiring the public to contribute to their support.

Evidently, this system assumes that millionaires are sinners above other

---

* Cooper founded an institute in New York City for educating the working classes; Enoch Pratt established a free library in Baltimore; Charles Pratt created an institute in Brooklyn for training skilled workers; and Leland Stanford endowed Stanford University.
2. *The Nation* (New York), LXII, 55 (Jan. 17, 1901).

men. The number of persons who have wealth sufficient to maintain their children in idleness is very large, and such persons are able to indulge in many luxuries. We cannot concede that the children of millionaires will go straight to perdition if they inherit their parents' wealth, while those who get but a hundred thousand shall be immune. Everyone familiar with the life of the common people knows that an inheritance of a very few thousand dollars may demoralize a young man, and this principle has been illustrated on a prodigious scale in our pension largesses.

On the other hand, virtue among the children of millionaires is not quite so rare as Mr. Carnegie intimates. Instances are known where inherited wealth has been wisely administered by men of respectable and even irreproachable habits. Mr. Carnegie's dictum, "I would as soon leave to my son a curse as the almighty dollar," is too sweeping. Millions of people who are not millionaires desire to give their children the advantages of wealth, and this desire is one of the greatest incentives to accumulation. Provided they educate their children wisely, it is impossible to maintain that the gift of these advantages is necessarily injurious.

On this point Mr. Carnegie and Mr. Gladstone [British statesman] had some debate; the latter contending that "the hereditary transmission of wealth and position, in conjunction with the calls of occupation and of responsibility, is a good and not an evil thing." Of course, this is nothing but the old conflict between the ideals of democracy and aristocracy, and we need not restate it. . . .

Probably we shall see the experiment of confiscating large fortunes at the death of their owners tried on an increasing scale, together with progressive taxes on incomes.

3. Conwell Deifies the Dollar (c. 1900)

The Reverend Russell H. Conwell was a remarkable Baptist preacher of Philadelphia who founded Temple University and had a large hand in establishing three hospitals. He delivered his famous lecture, *Acres of Diamonds*, more than six thousand times. The proceeds went to the educating of some ten thousand young men. His basic theme was that in seeking riches people were apt to overlook the opportunities in their own backyards (acres of diamonds). Critics charged that Conwell was merely throwing the cloak of religion about the materialistic ideals of his time, especially since he combined philanthropy with dollar-chasing. In the following excerpt from his famous lecture, what is his attitude toward the poor? How might one reconcile this brand of Christianity with the teachings of Christ, who said to the young man, "Go and sell that thou hast, and give to the poor . . ." (Matthew 19:21)?

You have no right to be poor. It is your duty to be rich.

Oh, I know well that there are some things higher, sublimer than money! Ah, yes, there are some things sweeter, holier than gold! Yet I also know

3. R. H. Conwell, *Acres of Diamonds* (1901), pp. 145–47, 151. Reprinted from *Modern Eloquence.*

that there is not one of those things but is greatly enhanced by the use of money.

"Oh," you will say, "Mr. Conwell, can you, as a Christian teacher, tell the young people to spend their lives making money?"

Yes, I do. Three times I say, I do, I do, I do. You ought to make money. Money is power. Think how much good you could do if you had money now. Money is power, and it ought to be in the hands of good men. It would be in the hands of good men if we comply with the Scripture teachings, where God promises prosperity to the righteous man. That means more than being goody-good—it means the all-round righteous man. You should be a righteous man. If you were, you would be rich.

I need to guard myself right here. Because one of my theological students came to me once to labor with me, for heresy, inasmuch as I had said that money was power.

He said: "Mr. Conwell, I feel it my duty to tell you that the Scriptures say that money 'is the root of all evil.' ". . .

So he read: "The *love* of money is the root of all evil." Indeed it is. The *love* of money is the root of all evil. The love of money, rather than the love of the good it secures, is a dangerous evil in the community. The desire to get hold of money, and to hold on to it, "hugging the dollar until the eagle squeals," is the root of all evil. But it is a grand ambition for men to have the desire to gain money, that they may use it for the benefit of their fellow men.

Young man! you may never have the opportunity to charge at the head of your nation's troops on some Santiago's heights. Young woman! you may never be called on to go out in the seas like Grace Darling to save suffering humanity. But every one of you can earn money honestly, and with that money you can fight the battles of peace; and the victories of peace are always grander than those of war. I say then to you that you ought to be rich. . . .

No man has a right to go into business and not make money. It is a crime to go into business and lose money, because it is a curse to the rest of the community. No man has a moral right to transact business unless he makes something out of it. He has also no right to transact business unless the man he deals with has an opportunity also to make something. Unless he lives and lets live, he is not an honest man in business. There are no exceptions to this great rule. . . .

It is cruel to slander the rich because they have been successful. It is a shame to "look down" upon the rich the way we do. They are not scoundrels because they have gotten money. They have blessed the world. They have gone into great enterprises that have enriched the nation and the nation has enriched them. It is all wrong for us to accuse a rich man of dishonesty simply because he secured money. Go through this city and your very best people are among your richest people. Owners of property are always the best citizens. It is all wrong to say they are not good.

D. THE ANTI-SALOON CRUSADE

1. Frances Willard Prays in a Saloon (1874)

An independent girl, Frances E. Willard defied her novel-hating father by openly reading Scott's *Ivanhoe* on her eighteenth birthday. At first an educator of females, she gained fame as an advocate of temperance and woman suffrage. She was one of the founders of the Woman's Christian Temperance Union, which grew out of the praying-in-saloons crusade of 1873–1874. Miss Willard stressed not so much the social and economic evils of drinking as the need for protecting the home and the Christian way of life. The saloon, often in league with gambling and prostitution, was riding high from 1870 to 1900. Some towns had one for every two hundred inhabitants; and the swinging doors, the heavy brass rails, and the nude Venus over the huge gilded mirror were all familiar sights. Miss Willard here describes her experiences in Pittsburgh. How effective is this approach, and how would it be received today?

We paused in front of the saloon that I have mentioned. The ladies ranged themselves along the curbstone, for they had been forbidden in any wise to incommode the passers-by, being dealt with much more strictly than a drunken man or a heap of dry-goods boxes would be.

At a signal from our gray-haired leader, a sweet-voiced woman began to sing, "Jesus the water of life will give," all our voices soon blending in that sweet song. I think it was the most novel spectacle that I recall. There stood women of undoubted religious devotion and the highest character, most of them crowned with the glory of gray hairs. Along the stony pavement of that stoniest of cities rumbled the heavy wagons, many of them carriers of beer; between us and the saloon in front of which we were drawn up in line, passed the motley throng, almost every man lifting his hat and even the little newsboys doing the same. It was American manhood's tribute to Christianity and to womanhood, and it was significant and full of pathos.

The leader had already asked the saloonkeeper if we might enter, and he had declined, else the prayer meeting would have occurred inside his door. A sorrowful old lady, whose only son had gone to ruin through that very death-trap, knelt on the cold, moist pavement and offered a broken-hearted prayer, while all our heads were bowed.

At a signal we moved on and the next saloonkeeper permitted us to enter. I had no more idea of the inward appearance of a saloon than if there had been no such place on earth. I knew nothing of its high, heavily corniced bar, its barrels with the ends all pointed towards the looker-on, each barrel being furnished with a faucet, its shelves glittering with decanters and cut glass, its floors thickly strewn with sawdust, and here and there a round table with chairs—nor of its abundant fumes, sickening to healthful nostrils.

The tall, stately lady who led us placed her Bible on the bar and read a psalm, whether hortatory or imprecatory I do not remember, but the spirit of these crusaders was so gentle, I think it must have been the former.

1. Frances E. Willard, *Glimpses of Fifty Years* (1880), pp. 340–41.

HERE THEY COME

Praying ladies about to descend on a saloon. *Harper's Weekly*, 1874.

Then we sang "Rock of Ages" as I thought I had never heard it sung before, with a tender confidence to the height of which one does not rise in the easy-going, regulation prayer meeting, and then one of the older women whispered to me softly that the leader wished to know if I would pray. It was strange, perhaps, but I felt not the least reluctance, and kneeling on that sawdust floor, with a group of earnest hearts around me, and behind them, filling every corner and extending out into the street, a crowd of unwashed, unkempt, hard-looking drinking men, I was conscious that perhaps never in my life, save beside my sister Mary's dying bed, had I prayed as truly as I did then. This was my Crusade baptism. The next day I went on to the West and within a week had been made president of the Chicago W.C.T.U.

2. Gompers Defends the Saloon (*c.* 1886)

The Knights of Labor, joining the foes of the saloon, refused to admit liquor sellers to their membership. Their leader, Terence V. Powderly, even accused certain employers of encouraging drink so that the employees would become more content with their underpaid lot. (This argument assumes that docility is preferable to efficiency.) But Samuel Gompers of the American Federation of Labor had a good word to say for the attractively lighted "poor man's club," even though it drained away the family's grocery money. Did the advantages offset the disadvantages?

The saloon was the only club the workingmen had then. For a few cents we could buy a glass of beer and hours of congenial society. Talk in these meeting places had a peculiar freedom from formality that engendered good-fellowship and exchange of genuine intimacies.

The saloon rendered a variety of industrial services. Frequently, wages were paid there—in checks which the saloonkeeper cashed. Of course, it was embarrassing to accept that service without spending money with him.

All too frequently the saloonkeeper also served as an employment agent. But on the other hand the saloonkeeper was often a friend in time of strikes and the free lunch [salty foods to stimulate thirst] he served was a boon to many a hungry striker.

Nearly every saloon had a room or a hall back of it or over it that could be rented for a nominal sum. Of course, the saloon was counting on increased receipts due to gatherings held in the hall. These rooms were practically the only meeting places available to unions, which were poor and small in numbers.

[*The continued callousness of "booze barons" resulted in the launching of the Anti-Saloon League in 1893. It supplemented the efforts of the Prohibition Party, organized in 1869, and the Woman's Christian Temperance Union, organized in 1874. With mounting zeal the reformers harped on the following arguments: (1) Alcohol was a debauching force in American politics. (2) The rapid mechanization of industry required sobriety for safety and efficiency. (3) The liquor sellers were saddling the taxpayers with the occupants of prisons and poorhouses. But prohibition in the localities and the states was slow in coming. By 1905 only four states had entered the "dry" column: Kansas, Maine, Nebraska, and North Dakota. Success was slowest in the large urban areas, where huge colonies of undigested immigrants had brought with them Old World drinking habits.*]

E. THE CHANGING ROLE OF WOMEN

1. Victoria Woodhull Advocates "Free Love" (1871)

Victoria Woodhull, a brilliant, beautiful, and erratic woman, arrived in New York in 1868 with her sister, Tennessee Celeste Claflin. They quickly emerged as outspoken champions of women's suffrage, and of a new egalitarian standard of sexual morality. Woodhull gained wide support from leaders of the suffrage movement when she persuaded the House Judiciary Committee in 1871 to hold hearings on a suffrage amendment. But many of her fellow feminists began to wonder about Woodhull's usefulness to their cause when she accused Horace Greeley, who favored women's suffrage but opposed "free love," of ruining his wife's health and causing the deaths of five of his seven children. She also denounced Catherine Beecher (see Vol. I, p. 315) as among those "who now clog the wheels of progress, and stand forth as the enemies of their

1. Victoria C. Woodhull, *The Scarecrows of Sexual Slavery* (1874), pp. 19–22.

sex . . . doing their utmost to cement the chains of their degradation, giving to man the same power over them as he possesses over his horses and dogs. . . ." Finally, in 1872, Woodhull accused Henry Ward Beecher, probably the most famous American preacher of his day and another friend of women's suffrage, of carrying on an adulterous relationship—an accusation that resulted in a sensational trial that eventually acquitted Beecher. In the article excerpted below, what are Woodhull's views of marriage? How do they differ from those of Catherine Beecher and other traditional women of the day? What might have been the relationship between these views and Woodhull's advocacy of women's suffrage?

Many are the tales of horror and brutal violence that have been related of negro slavery, where the lash of the driver was depicted until their hearers almost felt its stings in their own flesh, and almost the red streams flowing down their own backs, and these appealed to the souls of men and women until they were ready to do whatever was needed to destroy a monster that could cause such suffering to a single human being. But I am fully convinced that all the suffering of all the negro slaves combined, is as nothing in comparison to that which women, as a whole, suffer. There were several millions of negro slaves. There are twenty millions of women slaves. The negroes were dependent upon their masters for all the comforts of life they enjoyed; but it was to the interest of their masters to give them all of these that health demanded. Women are as much dependent upon men for their sustenance as were the negroes upon their masters, lacking the interest that they had in the negroes as personal property.

It is an unpleasant thing to say that women, in many senses, are as much slaves as were the negroes, but if it be true, ought it not to be said? I say, a thousand times, yes! And when the slavery to which they are subjected is compared to that which the negro endured, the demand for its consideration increases again, still a thousand times more.

Perhaps it may be denied that women are slaves, sexually, sold and delivered to man. But I tell you, as a class, that they are, and the conclusion cannot be escaped. Let me convince all doubters of this. Stand before me, all ye married women, and tell me how many of you would remain mistresses of your husbands' homes if you should refuse to cohabit sexually with them? Answer ye this, and then tell me that ye are free, if ye can! I tell ye that you are the sexual slaves of your husbands, bound by as terrible bonds to serve them sexually as ever a negro was bound to serve his owner, physically; and if you don't quite believe it, go home and endeavor to assert your freedom, and see to what it will lead! You may not be made to feel the inevitable lash that followed rebellion on the part of the negro, but even this is not certain; yet lashes of some sort will surely be dealt. Refuse to yield to the sexual demands of your legal master, and ten to one he will turn you into the street, or in lieu of this, perhaps, give you personal violence, even to compelling you to submit by force. Tell me that wives are not slaves! As well might you have done the same of the negroes, who, as the women do not, did not realize their condition!

I offer it as a well-grounded conclusion that I have come to, after years of inquiry and observation, that nine of every ten wives, at some time during their marriage, are compelled, according to the injunction of St. Paul, to submit themselves to their husbands, when every sentiment of their souls revolts to the act; and I feel an answering response coming up to me from many sick souls among you, that shrink in horror from the contemplation of the terrible scenes to which they have been compelled.

Remember, I do not say this is universally true; I do not say that all wives, at all times, are thus situated. Neither were all negro slaves at all times subjected to the lash or to other brutal treatment. The large majority of negroes were well treated and comparatively happy; but they were slaves, nevertheless. The cases of extreme cruelty were really rarer than is generally believed, but they were enough to condemn the system and to cause its terrible washing out by the blood of hundreds of thousands of the brightest souls of the country. So, also, are the cases of extreme cruelty on the part of husbands not exceedingly common, but they are sufficiently so to condemn the whole system, and to demand, if need be, that it, too, be washed out by the blood, if necessary, of millions of human beings.

For my part I would rather be the labor slave of a master, with his whip cracking continually about my ears, my whole life, than the forced sexual slave of any man a single hour; and I know that every woman who has freedom born in her soul will shout in deepest and earnest response to this —Amen! I know what it is to be both these. I have traveled the city pavements of New York in mid-winter, seeking employment, with nothing on my feet except an old pair of india-rubber shoes, and a common calico dress only to cover my body, while the man who called me wife and who made me his sexual slave, spent his money upon other women. I am not speaking whereof I know not. My case may be thought an extreme one, but I know of thousands even worse. Then tell me I shall not have the right to denounce this damned system! Tell me I shall be sent to Sing Sing if I dare expose these things! Open your Sing Sings a thousand times, but none of their terrors shall stop a single word. I will tell the world, so long as I have a tongue and the strength to move it, of all the infernal misery hidden behind this horrible thing called marriage, though the Young Men's Christian Association sentence me to prison a year for every word. I have seen horrors beside which stone walls and iron bars are heaven, and I will not hold my peace so long as a system, that can produce such damnation and by which, as its author, heaven is blasphemed, exists.

Would to Heaven I could thunder these facts forth until women should be moved by a comprehension of the low degradation to which they have fallen, to open rebellion; until they should rise *en masse* and declare themselves free, resisting all sexual subjection, and utterly refusing to yield their bodies up to man, until they shall grant them perfect freedom. It was not the slaves themselves who obtained their own freedom. It was their noble white brothers of the North, who, seeing their condition, and realizing that though they were black, still that they were brothers, sacrificed themselves for the time to emancipate them. So it will not be the most suffering slaves of this horrible slavery who will accomplish its abolition; but it must be those who know and appreciate the terrible condition, who must, for the time, sacrifice ourselves, that their sisters may come to themselves and to own themselves.

Go preach this doctrine, then, ye who have the strength and the moral courage: No more sexual intercourse for men who do not fully consent that all women shall be free, and who do not besides this, also join the standard of the rebellion. It matters not if you be wife or not, raise your voice for your suffering sex, let the consequences to yourself be what they may. They say I have come to break up the family; I say amen to that with all my heart. I hope I may break up every family in the world that exists by virtue of sexual slavery, and I feel that the smiles of angels, the smiles of those who have gone on before, who suffered here what I have suffered and what thousands are suffering, will give me strength to brave all opposition, and to stand even upon the scaffold, if need be, that my sisters all over the world may be emancipated, may rise from slavery to the full dignity of womanhood.

2. The Life of a Working Girl (1905)

Dorothy Richardson, a fairly well-educated, obviously middle-class young woman, was compelled by necessity to seek employment in a New York "sweatshop" around the turn of the century. She recorded her experiences in a remarkable book, *The Long Day*, excerpted below. What is her attitude toward the immigrant, working-class girls who became her companions and work-mates? Why did these young women work? How were their working conditions different from those of today? Elsewhere in her book, Richardson quoted one of her fellow-workers who spoke of "long ago, when they used to treat the girls so bad. Things is ever so much better now." How might the conditions here described have been worse in an earlier day?

Bessie met Eunice and me at the lower right-hand corner of Broadway and Grand Street, and together we applied for work at the R—— Underwear Company, which had advertised that morning for twenty operators.

"Ever run a power Singer?" queried the foreman.

"No, but we can learn. We're all quick," answered Bessie, who had volunteered to act as spokesman.

"Yes, I guess you can learn all right, but you won't make very much at first. All come together? . . . So! Well, then, I guess you'll want to work in the same room," and with that he ushered us into a very inferno of sound, a great, yawning chaos of terrific noise. The girls, who sat in long rows up and down the length of the great room, did not raise their eyes to the newcomers, as is the rule in less strenuous workrooms. Every pair of eyes seemed to be held in fascination upon the flying and endless strip of white

2. From Dorothy Richardson, *The Long Day: The Story of a New York Working Girl as Told by Herself* (Century Company, 1905), as it appears in William L. O'Neill, *Women at Work* (Quadrangle, 1972).

that raced through a pair of hands to feed itself into the insatiable maw of the electric sewing-machine. Every face, tense and stony, bespoke a superb effort to concentrate mind and body, and soul itself, literally upon the point of a needle. Every form was crouched in the effort to guide the seam through the presser-foot. And piled between the opposing phalanxes of set faces were billows upon billows of foamy white muslin and lace—the finished garments wrought by the so-many dozen per hour, for the so-many cents per day,—and wrought, too, in this terrific, nerve-racking noise.

The foreman led us into the middle of the room, which was lighted by gas-jets that hung directly over the girls' heads, although the ends of the shop had bright sunshine from the windows. He seemed a good-natured, respectable sort of man, of about forty, and was a Jew. Bessie and me he placed at machines side by side, and Eunice a little farther down the line. Then my first lesson began. He showed me how to thread bobbin and needle, how to operate ruffler and tucker, and also how to turn off and on the electric current which operated the machinery. My first attempt to do the latter was productive of a shock to the nerves that could not have been greater if, instead of pressing the harmless little lever under the machine with my knee, I had accidently exploded a bomb. The foreman laughed good-naturedly at my fright.

"You'll get used to it by and by," he shouted above the noise; "but like as not for a while you won't sleep very good nights—kind of nervous; but you'll get over that in a week or so," and he ducked his head under the machine to adjust the belt. . . .

I leaned over the machine and practised at running a straight seam. Ah, the skill of these women and girls, and of the strange creature opposite, who can make a living at this torturing labor! How very different, how infinitely harder it is, as compared with running an ordinary sewing-machine. The goods that my nervous fingers tried to guide ran every wrong way. I had no control whatever over the fearful velocity with which the needle danced along the seam. In utter discouragement, I stopped trying for a moment, and watched the girl at my right. She was a swarthy, thick-lipped Jewess, of the type most common in such places, but I looked at her with awe and admiration. In Rachel Goldberg's case the making of muslin, lace-trimmed corset-covers was an art rather than a craft. She was a remarkable operator even among scores of experts at the R——. Under her stubby, ill-kept hands ruffles and tucks and insertion bands and lace frills were wrought with a beauty and softness of finish, and a speed and precision of workmanship, that made her the wonder and envy of the shop. . . .

Result of my first hour's work: I had spoiled a dozen garments. Try as I would, I invariably lost all control of my materials, and the needle plunged right and left—everywhere, in fact, except along the straight and narrow way laid out for it. . . .

As I spoiled each garment I thrust it into the bottom of a green paste-board box under the table, which held my allotment of work, and from the top of the box grabbed up a fresh piece. I glanced over my shoulder and saw that Bessie was doing the same thing, although what we were going to do with them, or how account for such wholesale devastation of goods, we were too perturbed to consider. At last, however, after repeated trials, and by guiding the seam with laborious care, I succeeded in completing one garment without disaster; and I had just started another, when—crash!— flying shuttles and spinning bobbins and swirling wheels came to a standstill. My sewing-machine was silent, as were all the others in the great workroom. Something had happened to the dynamo.

There was a howl of disappointment. . . .

Rachel Goldberg had finished four dozen of extrafine garments, which meant seventy-five cents, and it was not yet eleven o'clock. She would make at least one dollar and sixty cents before the day was over, provided we did not have any serious breakdowns. She watched the clock impatiently,— every minute she was idle meant a certain fraction of a penny lost,—and crouched sullenly over her machine for the signal. . . .

In half an hour we had resumed work, and at half-past twelve we stopped for another half-hour and ate luncheon—Bessie, Eunice, and I in a corner by ourselves.

We held a conference, and compared notes of the morning's progress, which had been even more discouraging to poor Eunice than to us; for to her it had brought the added misfortune of a row of stitches in her right forefinger. We counted up our profits for the morning, and the aggregate earnings of the three of us did not amount to ten cents. Of course we would learn to do better, but it would take a long, long time, Bessie was firmly convinced, before we could even make enough to buy our lunches. It was decided that one of us should resign the job that night, and the other two keep at it until the delegate found something better for us all and had tested the new job to her satisfaction. Bessie was of course appointed, and the next morning Eunice and I went alone, with plausible excuses for the absent Bessie, for we had a certain delicacy about telling the real facts to so kind a foreman as "Abe."

The second day we had no better luck, and the pain between the shoulderblades was unceasing. All night long I had tossed on my narrow cot, with aching back and nerves wrought up to such a tension that the moment I began to doze off I was wakened by a spasmodic jerk of the right arm as it reached forward to grasp a visionary strip of lace. That evening, as we filed out at six o'clock, Bessie was waiting for us, her gentle face full of radiance and good news. Even the miserable Eunice was affected by her hopefulness.

"Oh, girls, I've got something that's really good—three dollars a week while you're learning, and an awful nice shop; and just think, girls!—the hours—I never had anything like it before, and I've knocked around at eighteen different jobs—half-past eight to five, and—" she paused for breath to announce the glorious fact—"Girls, just think of it!—*Saturday afternoons off,* all the year round."

3. An Italian Immigrant Woman Faces Life Alone
in the Big City (*c.* 1896)

Rosa Cavalleri came from her native Lombardy, in Italy, to Chicago in 1884. Though she never knew her exact birth-date, she was probably about eighteen years of age when she arrived in America. In later years, she recounted her life story to Marie Hall Ets, a social worker at the Chicago Commons, a settlement house founded in 1894 by Dr. Graham Taylor, an associate of the pioneering urban reformer, Jane Addams. What might have been Rosa Cavalleri's response to Victoria Woodhull's call for "free love"? What were the most important concerns in Cavalleri's life? Who helped her? What evidence does this account provide of the existence of an immigrant "community"? What was the role of the municipal government in Rosa Cavalleri's life?

The year my Leo was born I was home alone and struggled along with my children. My husband went away because he was sick—he went by a doctor in St. Louis to get cured. That doctor said he must stay away from his home one year and gave him a job to do all the janitor work around his house for five dollars a month and his board. So me, I used to go all around to find the clothes to wash and the scrubbing. The city hall was helping me again in that time—they gave me a little coal and sometimes the basket of food. Bob, the sign painter downstairs, he helped me the most. He was such a good young man. He used to bring a big chunk of coal and chop it up right in my kitchen and fix the stove.

I was to the end of my nine months, but the baby never came. So I went by one woman, Mis' Thomas, and I got part of the clothes washed. Then I said, "Oh, Mis' Thomas, I've got to go. I've got the terrible pains!"

She said, "You can go when you finish. You've got to finish first."

"No, I go. Otherwise I'll have to stay in your bed." When I said that she got scared I would have the baby there, so she let me go.

I went by the midwife, Mis' Marino, and told her to come; then I went home. When I saw it was my time, I told Domenico something and sent him with all the children to the wife of Tomaso. I told those people before, when they see the children come they must keep them all night—it's my time. It was really, really my time, and I had such a scare that I would be alone a second time. So when I heard a lady come in the building—she lived downstairs—I called to her. She said, "I have no time." And she didn't come up.

I was on my bed all alone by myself and then I prayed Sant' Antoni with all my heart. I don't know why I prayed Sant' Antoni—the Madonna put it in my mind. And then, just when the baby was born, I saw Sant' Antoni right there! He appeared in the room by me! I don't think it was really Sant' Antoni there, but in my imagination I saw him—all light like the sun. I saw Sant' Antoni there by my bed, and right then the door opened and the midwife came in to take care of the baby! It was February seventh and

3. Marie Hall Ets, *Rosa: The Life of an Italian Immigrant* (1970), pp. 228–231. University of Minnesota Press, Minneapolis. Copyright © 1970 by the University of Minnesota. Reprinted by permission of the publisher.

six below zero. There I had him born all alone, but Mis' Marino came when I prayed Sant' Antoni. She washed the baby and put him by me, but then she ran away. She didn't light the fire or nothing.

Oh, that night it was *so* cold! And me in my little wooden house in the alley with the walls all frosting—thick white frosting. I was crying and praying, "How am I going to live?" I said. "Oh, Sant' Antoni, I'll never live till tomorrow morning! I'll never live till the morning!"

And just as I prayed my door opened and a lady came in. She had a black shawl twice round her neck and head and that shawl came down to her nose. All I could see was half the nose and the mouth. She came in and lighted both the stoves. Then she came and looked at me, but I couldn't see her face. I said, "God bless you!"

She just nodded her head up and down and all the time she said not one word, only "Sh, sh."

Then she went down in the basement herself, nobody telling her nothing, and she got the coal and fixed the fire. Pretty soon she found that little package of camomile tea I had there on the dresser and she made a little tea with the hot water. And that woman stayed by me almost till daylight. But all the time she put her finger to her mouth to tell me to keep still when I tried to thank her. And I never knew where that lady came from! I don't know yet! Maybe she was the spirit of that kind girl, Annina, in *Canaletto*? I don't know. I really don't know! I was *so* sick and I didn't hear her voice or see her face. All the time she put her finger on her mouth and said, "Sh, sh." And when the daylight came she was gone.

About seven o'clock morning my children came home. And Mis' Marino, that midwife, she came at eight o'clock and said, "It's so cold I thought I'd find you dead!"

Then here came the city hall, or somebody, with a wagon. They wanted to take me and my new baby to the hospital. But how could I leave all my children? I started to cry—I didn't want to go. And my children cried too—they didn't want me to leave them. So then they didn't make me. They pulled my bed away from the frosting on the wall and put it in the front room by the stove. And my baby, I had him wrapped up in a pad I made from the underskirt like we do in *Italia*. But that baby froze when he was born; he couldn't cry like other babies—he was crying weak, weak.

My Visella was bringing up the wood and the coal and trying to make that room warm. But she was only a little girl, she didn't know, and she filled that stove so full that all the pipes on the ceiling caught fire. I had to jump up from the bed and throw the pails of water so the house wouldn't burn down. Then God sent me help again. He sent that Miss Mildred from the settlement house. She didn't know about me and my Leo born; she was looking for some other lady and she came to my door and saw me. She said, "Oh, I have the wrong place."

"I said, "No, lady, you find the right place."

So she came in and found out all. Then she ran away and brought back all those little things the babies in America have. She felt sorry to see my baby banded up like I had him. She didn't know then, Miss Mildred, that the women in *Italia* always band their babies that way. And she brought me something to eat too—for me and for my children. That night another young lady from the Commons, Miss May, she came and slept in my house to take care of the fire. She was afraid for the children—maybe they would burn themselves and the house. Oh, that Miss Mildred and Miss May, they were angels to come and help me like that! Four nights Miss May stayed there and kept the fire going. They were high-up educated girls—they were used to sleeping in the warm house with the plumbing—and there they came and slept in my wooden house in the alley, and for a toilet they had to go down to that shed under the sidewalk. They were really, really friends! That time I had my Leo nobody knew I was going to have the baby—I looked kind of fat, that's all. These women in the settlement house were so surprised. They said, "Why you didn't tell us before, Mis' Cavalleri, so we can help you?"

You know that Mis' Thomas—I was washing her clothes when the baby started to come—she wanted a boy and she got a baby girl right after my baby was born. When I went there the next week to do the washing I had to carry my baby with me. When she saw him she said, "Well better I have a girl than I have a boy that looks like your baby! He looks for sure like a monkey!"

In the first beginning he did look like a monkey, but in a few weeks he got pretty. He got so pretty all the people from the settlement house came to see him. After two or three months there was no baby in Chicago prettier than that baby.

When the year was over for him, my husband came home from St. Louis. He didn't sent me the money when he was there—just two times the five dollars—so he brought twenty-five dollars when he came back. Oh, he was so happy when he saw that baby with exactly, exactly his face and everything—the same dark gold hair and everything—and so beautiful. But he saw that baby was so thin and pale and couldn't cry like the other babies. "Better I go by a good doctor and see," he said. "I've got twenty-five dollars—I'm going to get a good doctor." So he did.

But the doctor said, "That baby can't live. He was touched in the lungs with the cold. Both lungs got froze when he was born."

And sure enough he was all the time sick and when it was nine months he died. My first Leo and my second Leo I lose them both. Oh, I was brokenhearted to lose such a beautiful baby! . . .

THOUGHT PROVOKERS

1. If the New Immigrants were disillusioned by America, why did more of them not return to the Old Country? Why did they congregate in slums?
2. Was a literacy test fairer than restricting immigrants by quota? Why was the immigrant less welcome in the 1890's than in the 1790's?

3. It has been said that Darwin jolted orthodox Christianity more severely than Copernicus did three hundred years earlier with his discoveries regarding the solar system. Explain. Why was it so difficult to reconcile evolution with a literal reading of the Bible?

4. To what extent was Carnegie selfish in his Gospel of Wealth? Is it better to have large private benefactions or to have the government tax wealth and engage in benefactions itself? Why is it difficult to give away large sums of money intelligently?

5. Critics have charged that one reason why the saloon prospered was that the churches and the community failed to provide wholesome alternatives. Discuss.

6. What was "new" about the "New Woman" at the end of the nineteenth century? Why did women in growing numbers work for wages? Did women workers deserve special protection?

28 · The Great West and the Agricultural Revolution, 1865-1890

Many, if not most, of our Indian wars have had their origin in broken promises and acts of injustice upon our part. . . .

PRESIDENT HAYES, 1877

PROLOGUE: The fence-erecting white men inevitably clashed with the wide-roaming Indians of the plains. As land-greed undermined ethical standards, many settlers acted as though the Indians had no more rights than the buffalo, which were also ruthlessly slaughtered. The seemingly endless frontier wars ended finally when the native Americans, cooped up in "human zoos" called reservations, were forced to adopt in part the economic life of their conquerors. The honest farmer and the fraudulent speculator were now free to open the Far West under the Homestead Act of 1862—America's first big give-away program. Much of the settlement occurred in areas with only scanty rainfall; and when crops failed, or when over-production came, the farmer was trapped. Agitation for relief vented itself most spectacularly in 1892, when the Populist Party waged a colorful campaign for the Presidency under General James B. Weaver. Although he carried six Western states, he ran well behind the second-place Republicans as the Democrats again swept Grover Cleveland to victory.

A. THE PLIGHT OF THE INDIAN

1. Custer's Last Stand (1876)

As the white men closed in, the Western Indians were forced to make numerous treaties with Washington which confined them to reservations and guaranteed needed supplies. But rascally government contractors cheated them with moldy flour, rotten beef, and moth-eaten blankets. In 1875 the discovery of gold on the Sioux reservation in the Dakotas brought stampeding thousands of miners, who brutally ignored treaty guarantees. The Indians took to the warpath, and the dashing General George Custer with only 264 men rashly attacked a hostile force that turned out to number several thousand braves. Custer and his entire command were wiped out near the Little Big Horn River (Montana), in what the white men call a "massacre" and the Indians a "battle." What does this account in the reformist *Harper's Weekly* see as the principal mistakes in dealing with the Indians? Who was basically responsible for the situation that had developed?

The fate of the brave and gallant Custer has deeply touched the public heart, which sees only a fearless soldier leading a charge against an ambushed [lurking] foe, and falling at the head of his men and in the thick of the fray. A monument is proposed, and subscriptions have been made.

1. *Harper's Weekly*, XX, 630–31 (Aug. 5, 1876).

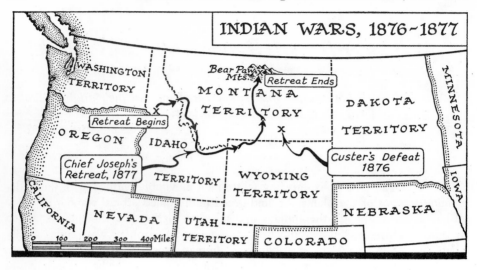

But a truer monument, more enduring than brass or marble, would be an Indian policy intelligent, moral, and efficient. Custer would not have fallen in vain if such a policy should be the result of his death.

It is a permanent accusation of our humanity and ability that over the Canadian line the relations between Indians and whites are so tranquil, while upon our side they are summed up in perpetual treachery, waste, and war. When he was a young lieutenant on the frontier, General Grant saw this, and watching attentively, he came to the conclusion that the reason of the difference was that the English respected the rights of the Indians and kept faith with them, while we make solemn treaties with them as if they were civilized and powerful nations, and then practically regard them as vermin to be exterminated.

The folly of making treaties with the Indian tribes may be as great as treating with a herd of buffaloes. But the infamy of violating treaties when we have made them is undeniable, and we are guilty both of the folly and the infamy.

We make treaties—that is, we pledge our faith—and then leave swindlers and knaves of all kinds to execute them. We maintain and breed pauper colonies. The savages, who know us, and who will neither be pauperized nor trust our word, we pursue, and slay if we can, at an incredible expense. The flower of our young officers is lost in inglorious forays, and one of the intelligent students of the whole subject rises in Congress and says, "The fact is that these Indians, with whom we have made a solemn treaty that their territory should not be invaded, and that they should receive supplies upon their reservations, have seen from one thousand to fifteen hundred [gold] miners during the present season entering and occupying their territory, while the Indians, owing to the failure of this and the last Congress to make adequate appropriations for their subsistence, instead of being fattened, as the gentleman says, by the support of this government, have simply been starved." . . .

It is plain that so long as we undertake to support the Indians as paupers, and then fail to supply the food; to respect their rights to reservations, and then permit the reservations to be overrun; to give them the best weapons and ammunition, and then furnish the pretense of their using them against us; to treat with them as men, and then hunt them like skunks—so long we shall have the most costly and bloody Indian wars, and the most tragical ambuscades, slaughters, and assassinations.

The Indian is undoubtedly a savage, and a savage greatly spoiled by the kind of contact with civilization which he gets at the West. There is no romance, there is generally no interest whatever, in him or his fate. But there should be some interest in our own good faith and humanity, in the lives of our soldiers and frontier settlers, and in the taxation to support our Indian policy. All this should certainly be enough to arouse a public demand for a thorough consideration of the subject, and the adoption of a system which should neither be puerile nor disgraceful, and which would tend to spare us the constant repetition of such sorrowful events as the slaughter of Custer and his brave men.

2. Chief Joseph's Lament (1879)

Chief Joseph, a noble-featured and humane Nez Percé (Pierced Nose) Indian, refused to be removed from his ancestral lands in Oregon and penned up on a reservation in Idaho. After an amazing strategic retreat of about 1000 miles, he was finally captured in 1877 near the Canadian border. The miserable remnants of his band were deported to Indian Territory (now Oklahoma), where many died of malaria and other afflictions. Chief Joseph appealed personally to the President, and subsequently the Nez Percés were returned to the Pacific Northwest. In the following narrative, what formula does he offer for ending white-Indian wars?

At last I was granted permission to come to Washington and bring my friend Yellow Bull and our interpreter with me. I am glad I came. I have shaken hands with a good many friends, but there are some things I want to know which no one seems able to explain. I cannot understand how the government sends a man out to fight us, as it did General Miles, and then breaks his word. Such a government has something wrong about it. . . .

I have heard talk and talk, but nothing is done. Good words do not last long unless they amount to something. Words do not pay for my dead people. They do not pay for my country, now overrun by white men. They do not protect my father's grave. They do not pay for my horses and cattle.

Good words do not give me back my children. Good words will not make good the promise of your war chief, General Miles. Good words will not give my people good health and stop them from dying. Good words will not get my people a home where they can live in peace and take care of themselves.

2. *North American Review*, CXXVIII, 431–32 (April, 1879).

I am tired of talk that comes to nothing. It makes my heart sick when I remember all the good words and all the broken promises. There has been too much talking by men who had no right to talk. Too many misinterpretations have been made; too many misunderstandings have come up between the white men and the Indians.

If the white man wants to live in peace with the Indian, he can live in peace. There need be no trouble. Treat all men alike. Give them the same laws. Give them all an even chance to live and grow.

All men are made by the same Great Spirit Chief. They are all brothers. The earth is the mother of all people, and all people should have equal rights upon it. You might as well expect all rivers to run backward as that any man who was born a free man should be contented penned up and denied liberty to go where he pleases. If you tie a horse to a stake, do you expect he will grow fat? If you pen an Indian up on a small spot of earth and compel him to stay there, he will not be contented nor will he grow and prosper.

I have asked some of the Great White Chiefs where they get their authority to say to the Indian that he shall stay in one place, while he sees white men going where they please. They cannot tell me.

I only ask of the government to be treated as all other men are treated. If I cannot go to my own home, let me have a home in a country where my people will not die so fast. I would like to go to Bitter Root Valley [western Montana]. There my people would be healthy; where they are now, they are dying. Three have died since I left my camp to come to Washington. When I think of our condition, my heart is heavy. I see men of my own race treated as outlaws and driven from country to country, or shot down like animals.

I know that my race must change. We cannot hold our own with the white men as we are. We only ask an even chance to live as other men live. We ask to be recognized as men. We ask that the same law shall work alike on all men. If an Indian breaks the law, punish him by the law. If a white man breaks the law, punish him also.

Let me be a free man—free to travel, free to stop, free to work, free to trade where I choose, free to choose my own teachers, free to follow the religion of my fathers, free to think and talk and act for myself—and I will obey every law or submit to the penalty.

Whenever the white man treats the Indian as they treat each other, then we shall have no more wars. We shall all be alike—brothers of one father and mother, with one sky above us and one country around us and one government for all. Then the Great Spirit Chief who rules above will smile upon this land and send rain to wash out the bloody spots made by brothers' hands upon the face of the earth. For this time the Indian race are waiting and praying. I hope no more groans of wounded men and women will ever go to the ear of the Great Spirit Chief above, and that all people may be one people.

3. Roosevelt Downgrades the Indians (1885)

Sickly and bespectacled young Theodore Roosevelt, the future President, invested more than $50,000 of his patrimony in ranch lands in Dakota Territory. He lost most of his investment, but gained robust health and valuable experience. Wasting little sympathy on the Indians, he felt that the government had "erred quite as often on the side of too much leniency as on the side of too much severity." The following account, based in part on firsthand observations, appears in one of his earliest books. What light do his observations cast on the allegation that the white man robbed the Indian of his lands? What is his proposed solution of the problem?

There are now no Indians left in my immediate neighborhood, though a small party of harmless Grosventres occasionally passes through. Yet it is but six years since the Sioux surprised and killed five men in a log station just south of me, where the Fort Keogh trail crosses the river; and, two years ago, when I went down on the prairies toward the Black Hills, there was still danger from Indians. That summer the buffalo hunters had killed a couple of Crows, and while we were on the prairie a long-range skirmish occurred near us between some Cheyennes and a number of cowboys. In fact, we ourselves were one day scared by what we thought to be a party of Sioux; but on riding toward them they proved to be half-breed Crees, who were more afraid of us than we were of them.

During the past century a good deal of sentimental nonsense has been talked about our taking the Indians' land. Now, I do not mean to say for a moment that gross wrong has not been done the Indians, both by government and individuals, again and again. The government makes promises impossible to perform, and then fails to do even what it might toward their fulfilment; and where brutal and reckless frontiersmen are brought into contact with a set of treacherous, revengeful, and fiendishly cruel savages a long series of outrages by both sides is sure to follow.

But as regards taking the land, at least from the Western Indians, the simple truth is that the latter never had any real ownership in it at all. Where the game was plenty, there they hunted; they followed it when it moved away to new hunting-grounds, unless they were prevented by stronger rivals; and to most of the land on which we found them they had no stronger claim than that of having a few years previously butchered the original occupants.

When my cattle came to the Little Missouri the region was only inhabited by a score or so of white hunters; their title to it was quite as good as that of most Indian tribes to the lands they claim; yet nobody dreamed of saying that these hunters owned the country. Each could eventually have kept his own claim of 160 acres, and no more.

The Indians should be treated in just the same way that we treat the white settlers. Give each his little claim; if, as would generally happen, he

---

3. Theodore Roosevelt, *Hunting Trips of a Ranchman* (1885), pp. 17–19. In the Dawes Act of 1887, Congress made provision for granting the Indians individual allotments, as Roosevelt here suggests.

THE INDIAN'S PORTION
Puck, 1880.

declined this, why then let him share the fate of the thousands of white hunters and trappers who have lived on the game that the settlement of the country has exterminated, and let him, like these whites, who will not work, perish from the face of the earth which he cumbers.

The doctrine seems merciless, and so it is; but it is just and rational for all that. It does not do to be merciful to a few, at the cost of justice to the many. The cattlemen at least keep herds and build houses on the land; yet I would not for a moment debar settlers from the right of entry to the cattle country, though their coming in means in the end the destruction of us and our industry.

B. THE CRUSADE FOR FREE HOMESTEADS

1. "Vote Yourself a Farm" (1846)

Free homesteads from the public domain found a powerful champion in George H. Evans, an immigrant from England who became a pioneer editor of American labor journals. A confirmed atheist, he was preoccupied with "natural rights" to the soil. He hoped particularly to increase the wages of Eastern laborers by luring surplus workers onto free lands in the West. On what grounds does he base the following appeal?

Are you an American citizen? Then you are a joint-owner of the public lands. Why not take enough of your property to provide yourself a home? Why not vote yourself a farm?

Remember Poor Richard's saying: "Now I have a sheep and a cow, every

1. J. R. Commons *et al.*, eds., *A Documentary History of American Industrial Society* (1910), VII, 305–07. "Vote Yourself a Farm" was a Republican slogan in the Lincoln campaign of 1860.

one bids me 'good morrow.'" If a man have a house and a home of his own, though it be a thousand miles off, he is well received in other people's houses; while the homeless wretch is turned away. The bare right to a farm, though you should never go near it, would save you from many an insult. Therefore, Vote yourself a farm.

Are you a party follower? Then you have long enough employed your vote to benefit scheming office-seekers; use it for once to benefit yourself— Vote yourself a farm.

Are you tired of slavery—of drudging for others—of poverty and its attendant miseries? Then, Vote yourself a farm.

Are you endowed with reason? Then you must know that your right to life hereby includes the right to a place to live in—the right to a home. Assert this right, so long denied mankind by feudal robbers and their attorneys. Vote yourself a farm.

Are you a believer in the Scriptures? Then assert that the land is the Lord's, because He made it. Resist then the blasphemers who exact money for His work, even as you would resist them should they claim to be worshiped for His holiness. Emancipate the poor from the necessity of encouraging such blasphemy—Vote the freedom of the public lands.

Are you a man? Then assert the sacred rights of man—especially your right to stand upon God's earth, and to till it for your own profit. Vote yourself a farm.

Would you free your country, and the sons of toil everywhere, from the heartless, irresponsible mastery of the aristocracy of avarice? Would you disarm this aristocracy of its chief weapon, the fearful power of banishment from God's earth? . . . Therefore forget not to Vote yourself a farm.

2. A Texan Scorns Futile Charity (1852)

Agitation for free land continued to mount, and a homestead bill was introduced in Congress designed to donate 160 acres of land to every landless head of a family needing it. Easterners objected that this was a give-away scheme to benefit a few new Western states at the expense of the old states. It would drain off factory workers and hence push up wages and jeopardize prosperity. Critics further argued that the public domain, which was then being sold to replenish the Treasury, was the property of all the taxpayers and should not be given away to a favored few. Representative Howard of Texas aired additional objections in Congress. What light do his remarks cast on the "safety-valve theory": that is, that impoverished Eastern families could reduce economic distress and relieve class conflict by moving West and taking up cheap land?

But, sir, I deny the constitutional power of Congress to grant away the public property in donations to the poor. This government is not a national almshouse. We have no right to collect money by taxation and then divide

2. *Congressional Globe*, 32 Cong., 1 sess., Appendix, pp. 583–84. The safety-valve theory, popularly attributed to the historian Frederick J. Turner, antedated him by many years. As early as 1843 a British journal referred to "the safety-valve of western emigration" in America (*Quarterly Review*, LXXI, 522). Only a few Eastern mechanics moved to the West, but many incoming immigrants were attracted there who otherwise would have further congested the seaboard cities.

the proceeds among the people generally, or those who are destitute of land, food, or raiment. . . .

There is no sound distinction between giving money by direct appropriations from the Treasury, and land, in the purchase of which [*e.g.*, Louisiana Purchase] that money has been invested. It is no more the property of the nation in one case than in the other, nor less an appropriation. What right have we to tax the property and industry of all classes of society to purchase homesteads, and enrich those who may not be the possessors of the soil? . . .

It is a great mistake to suppose that you will materially better the condition of the man in the old states, or the Atlantic cities, by giving him 160 acres of land in the Far West. The difficulty with him is not that of procuring the land, but to emigrate himself and family to the country where it is, and to obtain the means of cultivating it. Without this the grant is useless to the poor man.

The gift, to make it efficient, should be followed up by a further donation to enable the beneficiary to stock and cultivate it. It would be a far greater boon to all our citizens, of native and foreign origin, to furnish them, for a few dollars, a rapid means of reaching the land states in the West; and this, in my opinion, may be accomplished by exercising the legitimate powers of the government, and without drawing upon the Treasury, or diminishing the value of the public domain as a source of revenue.

3. Buchanan Kills a Homestead Bill (1860)

Free-soilers continued to argue that settlers not only had a "natural right" to Western land but that they should receive it as recompense for their own expense and sweat in taming the wilderness. In the 1850's homestead bills thrice passed the House, where the North was dominant, but all met defeat in the Senate, where the South was entrenched. Senator Wade of Ohio cried inelegantly in 1859 that it was "a question of land to the landless" while the Southern-sponsored bill to buy Cuba was "a question of niggers to the niggerless." Finally, in 1860, a compromise measure staggered through both Houses of Congress. It granted 160 acres of land to bona fide settlers who would pay the nominal sum of 25 cents an acre at the end of five years. President Buchanan, a Pennsylvanian under Southern influence, vetoed the measure. Comment critically on his views regarding unfairness to non-farmers and to the older states. Was he correct in arguing that such a law would undermine the nation's moral fiber?

4. This bill will prove unequal and unjust in its operation, because from its nature it is confined to one class of our people. It is a boon exclusively conferred upon the cultivators of the soil. Whilst it is cheerfully admitted that these are the most numerous and useful class of our fellow citizens, and eminently deserve all the advantages which our laws have already extended to them, yet there should be no new legislation which would

3. J. D. Richardson, ed., *Messages and Papers of the Presidents* (1897), V, 611–14, *passim*.

operate to the injury or embarrassment of the large body of respectable artisans and laborers. The mechanic who emigrates to the West and pursues his calling must labor long before he can purchase a quarter section of land, whilst the tiller of the soil obtains a farm at once by the bounty of the government. The numerous body of mechanics in our large cities cannot, even by emigrating to the West, take advantage of the provisions of this bill without entering upon a new occupation for which their habits of life have rendered them unfit.

5. This bill is unjust to the old states of the Union in many respects; and amongst these states, so far as the public lands are concerned, we may enumerate every state east of the Mississippi, with the exception of Wisconsin and a portion of Minnesota.

It is a common belief within their limits that the older states of the confederacy [Union] do not derive their proportionate benefit from the public lands. This is not a just opinion. It is doubtful whether they could be rendered more beneficial to these states under any other system than that which at present exists. Their proceeds go into the common Treasury to accomplish the objects of the government, and in this manner all of the states are benefited in just proportion. But to give this common inheritance away would deprive the old states of their just proportion of this revenue without holding out any, the least, corresponding advantage. Whilst it is our common glory that the new states have become so prosperous and populous, there is no good reason why the old states should offer premiums to their own citizens to emigrate from them to the West. That land of promise presents in itself sufficient allurements to our young and enterprising citizens without any adventitious aid.

The offer of free farms would probably have a powerful effect in encouraging emigration, especially from states like Illinois, Tennessee, and Kentucky, to the west of the Mississippi, and could not fail to reduce the price of property within their limits. An individual in states thus situated would not pay its fair value for land when, by crossing the Mississippi, he could go upon the public lands and obtain a farm almost without money and without price.

6. This bill will open one vast field for speculation. . . . Large numbers of actual settlers will be carried out by capitalists upon agreements to give them half of the land for the improvement of the other half. This cannot be avoided. Secret agreements of this kind will be numerous.* In the entry of graduated lands the experience of the Land Office justifies this objection. . . .

10. The honest poor man, by frugality and industry, can in any part of our country acquire a competence for himself and his family, and in doing this he feels that he eats the bread of independence. He desires no charity,

---

* Buchanan was right. Under the Homestead Act as finally passed, about ten acres were secured by speculators for every acre secured by a bona fide settler.

either from the government or from his neighbors. This bill, which proposes to give him land at an almost nominal price out of the property of the government, will go far to demoralize the people and repress this noble spirit of independence. It may introduce among us those pernicious social theories which have proved so disastrous in other countries.

C. THE HOMESTEAD HOAX

1. Pre-emption Grafters (1858)

The Homestead Act at last passed in 1862, after Southern obstructionists had left Congress—and the Union. Actual settlers might obtain 160 acres of land free, if they lived on it for five years, cultivated it, and paid a fee of $10. They could also continue to pre-empt 160 acres by paying $1.25 an acre, and by swearing that the land was for their exclusive use and cultivation. After the required five years the settler would have to prove "by two credible witnesses" that he had lived on and cultivated the grant, and he would have to swear that he had not alienated it to others by secret sale or other collusion. This open invitation to fraud led to grave abuses of the type that A. D. Richardson had discovered in Kansas in 1858. Why was so much perjury tolerated on the frontier among presumably law-respecting people?

During this fall many residents were pre-empting their claims. The law contemplates a homestead of 160 acres at a nominal price for each actual settler and no one else; but land is plenty and everybody pre-empts. A young merchant, lawyer, or speculator rides into the interior, to the un-occupied public lands, pays some settler five dollars to show him the vacant claims, and selects one upon which he places four little poles around a hollow square upon the ground, as children commence a cob house. Then he files a notice in the land office that he has laid the foundation of a house upon this claim and begun a settlement for actual residence. He does not see the land again until ready to "prove up," which he may do after thirty days. Then he revisits his claim, possibly erects a house of rough slabs, costing from ten to twenty dollars, eats one meal, and sleeps for a single night under its roof. More frequently, however, his improvements consist solely of a foundation of four logs. . . .

In three cases out of four, after "proving up," the pre-emptor never visits his land again unless for the purpose of selling it. Says the Spanish proverb, "Oaths are words, and words are wind." Thus this unequivocal perjury is regarded upon the frontier. The general feeling is that it wrongs no one, and that the settlers have a right to the land.

Hundreds of men whose families are still in the East find witnesses to testify that their wives and children are residing upon the land. I have known men to pre-empt who had never been within twenty miles of their claims, facile witnesses swearing with the utmost indifference that they were residing upon them.

The pre-emptors must state under oath that they have made no agree-

1. A. D. Richardson, *Beyond the Mississippi* (1866), pp. 137–38, 140–41.

A BONA FIDE RESIDENCE

A removable house for fraudulent purposes. Illustration in A. B.
Richardson's *Beyond the Mississippi,* 1866.

ment, direct or indirect, for selling any part of the land. But in numberless
instances these statements are falsehoods, connived at by the officers.

In most land offices a man cannot pre-empt unless he has a house at least
twelve feet square. I have known a witness to swear that the house in
question was twelve by fourteen when actually the only building upon the
claim was one whittled out with a penknife, twelve inches by fourteen.

Some officers require that the house must have a glass window. While
traveling in the interior I stopped at a little slab cabin where I noticed a
window sash without lights hanging upon a nail. As I had seen similar
frames in other cabins, I asked the owner what it was for.

"To pre-empt with," was the reply.

"How?"

"Why, don't you understand? To enable my witness to swear that there
is a window in my house!"

Sometimes the same cabin is moved from claim to claim until half a
dozen different persons have pre-empted with it. In Nebraska a little frame
house . . . was built for this purpose on wheels and drawn by oxen.
It enabled the pre-emptor to swear that he had a bona fide residence upon
his claim. It was let at five dollars a day, and scores of claims were proved
up and pre-empted with it. The discovery of any such malpractice and
perjury would invalidate the title. But I never knew of an instance where
the pre-emptor was deprived of his land after once receiving his title.

No woman can pre-empt unless she is a widow or the "head of a family."
But sometimes an ambitious maiden who wishes to secure 160 acres of land
borrows a child, signs papers of adoption, swears that she is the head of a
family, and pre-empts her claim, then annuls the papers and returns her
temporary offspring to its parents with an appropriate gift.

2. Going Broke in Kansas (1895)

The Homestead Act proved to be a bitter trap for thousands of honest settlers who pushed West to their "ultimate destitution." A farm of 160 acres could support a family in well-watered Illinois, but often not in the semi-arid West. A common saying on the frontier was that homesteading was a gamble: the government was "betting you 160 acres of land that you can't live on it five years." William Allen White, then twenty-seven years of age and just entering upon a distinguished journalistic career in Kansas, here describes a tragic scene. In light of his observations, how "free" were the 160 acres?

There came through Emporia yesterday two old-fashioned "mover wagons," headed east. The stock in the caravan would invoice four horses, very poor and very tired; one mule, more disheartened than the horses; and one sad-eyed dog, that had probably been compelled to rustle his own precarious living for many a long and weary day.

A few farm implements of the simpler sort were in the wagon, but nothing that had wheels was moving except the two wagons. All the rest of the impedimenta had been left upon the battlefield, and these poor stragglers, defeated but not conquered, were fleeing to another field, to try the fight again.

These movers were from western Kansas—from Gray County, a county which holds a charter from the state to officiate as the very worst, most desolate, God-forsaken, man-deserted spot on the sad old earth. They had come from that wilderness only after a ten years' hard, vicious fight, a fight which had left its scars on their faces, had beat their bodies, had taken the elasticity from their steps, and left them crippled to enter the battle anew.

For ten years they had been fighting the elements. They had seen it stop raining for months at a time. They had heard the fury of the winter wind as it came whining across the short burned grass, and their children huddling in the corner. They have strained their eyes watching through the long summer days for the rain that never came. They have seen that big cloud roll up from the southwest about one o'clock in the afternoon, hover over the land, and stumble away with a few thumps of thunder as the sun went down. They have tossed through hot nights wild with worry, and have arisen only to find their worst nightmares grazing in reality on the brown stubble in front of their sun-warped doors.

They had such high hopes when they went out there; they are so desolate now—no, not now, for now they are in the land of corn and honey. They have come out of the wilderness, back to the land of promise. They are now in God's own country down on the Neosho, with their wife's folks, and the taste of apple butter and good cornbread and fresh meat and pie—pieplant pie like mother used to make—gladdened their shrunken palates last night. And real cream, curdling on their coffee saucers last night for supper, was a sight so rich and strange that it lingered in their dreams, wherein they walked beside the still water, and lay down in green pastures.

2. Emporia (Kansas) *Gazette*, June 15, 1895.

3. Wheat Bowls Become Dust Bowls (1883)

The topsoil of the semi-arid great plains, especially beyond the 100th meridian, was held down by tough prairie grass. Gradually much of this protective covering was eroded by overgrazing cattle and by the plainsman's plow. In periods of drought, dust storms blew up with increasing intensity. They culminated in the 1930's in the great dust-bowl tragedy, which ruined vast areas in a half-dozen or so states. A Western journalist here reconstructs the details of a scene which has long been legendary in the West.

One day in the spring of 1883 as a Scandinavian farmer, John Christiansen, plowed his fields in Montana's neighbor state of North Dakota, he looked up to find that he was being watched . . . by an old and solemn Sioux Indian.

Silently the old Indian watched as the dark soil curled up and the prairie grass was turned under. Christiansen stopped, leaned against the plow handle, pushed his black Stetson back on his head, rolled a cigarette. He watched amusedly as the old Indian knelt, thrust his fingers into the plow furrow, measured its depth, fingered the sod and the buried grass.

Then the old Indian straightened up, looked at the farmer.

"Wrong side up," he said, and went away.

For a number of years that was regarded as a very amusing story indeed, betraying the ignorance of the poor Indian. Now there's a marker on Highway No. 10 in North Dakota on the spot where the words were spoken—a little reminder to the white man that his red brother was not so dumb.

D. THE FARMERS' PROTEST MOVEMENT

1. An Iowan Assesses Discontent (1893)

Farm distress increased during the 1890's, to a large extent in the South but more spectacularly on the Western plains. The four "d's"—drought, debt, deflation, and depression—played their dismal role, but the basic trouble was overproduction of grain. The farmer simply could not control prices that were determined by the world supply, and he vented his spleen on whipping boys nearer at hand, notably the railroads. Freight rates had fallen substantially since the Civil War, but no rates seemed fair to a farmer whose grain prices were so low that he could not make a profit. And inequities persisted, despite the Interstate Commerce Act of 1887. A prominent Iowa journalist here analyzes some of the grievances which caused these hardy sons of the soil to beat their Farmers Alliances into a political plowshare. In the following essay, what are the farmers' most pressing complaints?

Nothing has done more to injure the [Western] region than these freight rates. The railroads have retarded its growth as much as they first hastened it. The rates are often four times as large as Eastern rates. . . . The extortionate character of the freight rates has been recognized by all parties, and all have pledged themselves to lower them, but no state west of the Missouri has been able to do so.

3. J. K. Howard, *Montana: High, Wide, and Handsome* (1943), p. 14. By permission of the Yale University Press.
1. F. B. Tracy, "Why the Farmers Revolted," *The Forum*, XVI, 242–43 (Oct., 1893).

In the early days, people were so anxious to secure railways that they would grant any sort of concession which the companies asked. There were counties in Iowa and other Western states struggling under heavy loads of bond-taxes, levied twenty-five years ago, to aid railways of which not one foot has been built. Perhaps a little grading would be done, and then the project would be abandoned, the bonds transferred, and the county called upon by the "innocent purchaser" to pay the debt incurred by blind credulity. I have known men to sacrifice fortunes, brains, and lives in fighting vainly this iniquitous bond-swindle.

Railways have often acquired mines and other properties by placing such high freight rates upon their products that the owner was compelled to sell at the railroad company's own terms. These freight rates have been especially burdensome to the farmers, who are far from their selling and buying markets, thus robbing them in both directions.

Another fact which has incited the farmer against corporations is the bold and unblushing participation of the railways in politics. At every political convention their emissaries are present with blandishments and passes and other practical arguments to secure the nomination of their friends. The sessions of these legislatures are disgusting scenes of bribery and debauchery. There is not an attorney of prominence in Western towns who does not carry a pass or has not had the opportunity to do so. The passes, of course, compass the end sought. By these means, the railroads have secured an iron grip upon legislatures and officers, while no redress has been given to the farmer.

The land question, also, is a source of righteous complaint. Much of the land of the West, instead of being held for actual settlers, has been bought up by speculators and Eastern syndicates in large tracts. They have done nothing to improve the land and have simply waited for the inevitable settler who bought cheaply a small "patch" and proceeded to cultivate it. When he had prospered so that he needed more land, he found that his own labor had increased tremendously the value of the adjacent land. . . .

Closely connected with the land abuse are the money grievances. As his pecuniary condition grew more serious, the farmer could not make payments on his land. Or he found that, with the ruling prices, he could not sell his produce at a profit. In either case he needed money, to make the payment or maintain himself until prices should rise. When he went to the moneylenders, these men, often dishonest usurers, told him that money was very scarce, that the rate of interest was rapidly rising, etc., so that in the end the farmer paid as much interest a month as the moneylender was paying a year for the same money. In this transaction, the farmer obtained his first glimpse of the idea of "the contraction of the currency at the hands of Eastern money sharks."

Disaster always follows the exaction of such exorbitant rates of interest, and want or eviction quickly came. Consequently, when demagogues went among the farmers to utter their calamitous cries, the scales seemed to drop from the farmer's eyes, and he saw gold bugs, Shylocks, conspiracies, and criminal legislation *ad infinitum.* Like a lightning flash, the idea of political action ran through the Alliances. A few farmers' victories in county campaigns the previous year became a promise of broader conquest, and with one bound the Farmers' Alliance went into politics all over the West.

2. Mrs. Lease Raises More Hell (*c.* 1890)

As the plains seethed with protest, the Populist Party emerged from the Farmers' Alliance. Kansas spawned the most picturesque and vocal group of orators. A flaming speaker in great demand was the Irish-born Mrs. Mary E. Lease, a tall, magnetic lawyer known as a "Patrick Henry in Petticoats." Noting that corn was so cheap that it was being burned as fuel, she demanded the raising of less corn and "more hell." Noting also the disparity between the wealthy families and the people allegedly living out of garbage cans, she insisted on drastic measures. In the following selection, which are substantial grievances and which are demagogic outpourings? Which of her complaints seem to be the most serious?

This is a nation of inconsistencies. The Puritans fleeing from oppression became oppressors. We fought England for our liberty and put chains on four million of blacks. We wiped out slavery and by our tariff laws and national banks began a system of white wage slavery worse than the first.

Wall Street owns the country. It is no longer a government of the people, by the people, and for the people, but a government of Wall Street, by Wall Street, and for Wall Street.

The great common people of this country are slaves, and monopoly is the master. The West and South are bound and prostrate before the manufacturing East.

Money rules, and our Vice-President is a London banker. Our laws are the output of a system which clothes rascals in robes and honesty in rags.

The parties lie to us and the political speakers mislead us. We were told two years ago to go to work and raise a big crop, that was all we needed. We went to work and plowed and planted; the rains fell, the sun shone, nature smiled, and we raised the big crop that they told us to; and what came of it? Eight-cent corn, ten-cent oats, two-cent beef, and no price at all for butter and eggs—that's what came of it.

Then the politicians said we suffered from overproduction. Overproduction, when 10,000 little children, so statistics tell us, starve to death every year in the United States, and over 100,000 shopgirls in New York are forced to sell their virtue for the bread their niggardly wages deny them.

Tariff is not the paramount question. The main question is the money question. . . . Kansas suffers from two great robbers, the Santa Fe Railroad and the loan companies. The common people are robbed to enrich their masters. . . .

We want money, land, and transportation. We want the abolition of the

2. Elizabeth N. Barr, "The Populist Uprising," in W. E. Connelley, ed., *History of Kansas, State and People* (1928), II, 1167. By permission of the Lewis Historical Publishing Company.

national banks, and we want the power to make loans direct from the government. We want the accursed foreclosure system wiped out. Land equal to a tract thirty miles wide and ninety miles long has been foreclosed and bought in by loan companies of Kansas in a year.

We will stand by our homes and stay by our fireside by force if necessary, and we will not pay our debts to the loan-shark companies until the government pays its debts to us. The people are at bay; let the bloodhounds of money who have dogged us thus far beware.

3. Godkin Sneers at the Populists (1892)

The embittered farmers and laborites, organized into the People's (Populist) Party, met in a frenzied convention in Omaha, Nebraska, in July, 1892. They nominated General James B. Weaver for President and adopted a scorching platform. In addition to other grievances, they pilloried corruption among politicians and judges, the subsidized and "muzzled" press, the impoverishment of labor, the shooting of strikers, and the hypocrisy of the two major parties. More specifically, the platform demanded distribution of monopolized land to actual settlers; government ownership of the telegraphs, telephones, and railroads ("the railroad corporations will either own the people or the people must own the railroads"); reduction of bloated fortunes by a graduated income tax; and inflation of the currency by issuing more paper money and coining all silver produced. Editor Godkin of the New York *Nation* viewed many of these schemes with the intolerant eye of a smug Easterner. How does his basic philosophy regarding the government square with that in vogue today?

The People's Party convention, which has just completed its sessions at Omaha, was the most largely attended and most thoroughly representative national gathering which any third party has ever got together. All sections of the country sent delegates, and the delegates were full of enthusiasm.

The dominant tone of the assembly was discontent with existing conditions. A large part of this discontent was the vague dissatisfaction which is always felt by the incompetent and lazy and "shiftless" when they contemplate those who have got on better in the world. But there was also manifested that spirit of doubt as to the tendencies of our social development of late years which is shared by many thoughtful and philosophic observers, and which causes such observers to question whether something should not be done to check these tendencies.

Practically the platform declares that everybody could be made happy if the government would print a vast quantity of paper currency, allow free coinage and foist light-weight silver dollars upon the country, establish an immense loaning agency, and take control of the railroads. In other words, the fundamental theory of the party is that the federal government is an institution of such omniscience and omnipotence, such a repository of wealth and wisdom, that it can be trusted with limitless power. In short, the theory holds that a paternal government can make all its children "healthy, wealthy, and wise."

3. *The Nation* (New York), LV, 1 (July 7, 1892).

General Weaver is the proper candidate for President of such a party. He is a demagogue who came to the surface in the Greenback period, and was nominated for President by that element in 1880. He is the sort of man who is always ready to take up with any new organization which can give him either office or prominence, and no platform could be constructed so ridiculous that he would not gladly stand upon it.

[*In the presidential election of 1892 General Weaver suffered the fate of all third-party candidates in American history—overwhelming defeat at the hands of the old-line parties.*]

THOUGHT PROVOKERS

1. It has been said that there was no Indian problem, but a white problem; no black problem, but a white problem. Comment critically. Why did Canada have less trouble with the Indians than the United States?
2. Did the American settlers have a "natural right" to the free lands? Was selling the public land to replenish the Treasury sound in principle?
3. Would you agree that the Homestead Act was class legislation? How can you account for the wholesale fraud in connection with the Western lands? Why was the Homestead Act so long delayed? Did the East and South both have legitimate objections to it?
4. Farmers, to be successful, had to be good businessmen, and many failed because they were not. It was charged that they illogically put the blame for their failures on other factors. Comment. Other critics accused them of not doing well because they had fallen into habits of indolence. Would greater energy and larger harvests have cured the basic ills?

29 · *The Revolt of the Debtor, 1889-1900*

Bryan . . . has every crank, fool, and putative criminal in the country behind him, and a large proportion of the ignorant and honest class.

THEODORE ROOSEVELT, 1896

PROLOGUE: The Big Business Republicans, capitalizing on President Harrison's victory over Cleveland in 1888, passed the highly protective McKinley Tariff in 1890. It wiped out the troublesome surplus by putting sugar on the free list. It also supplemented Harrison's lavish pension program, which further depleted dwindling Treasury reserves. Reacting unfavorably to these extravagant Republican policies, the voters reinstated Cleveland in 1893. The panic which burst that year led to violent labor disturbances, notably the Pullman strike centering in Chicago. Cleveland incurred much abuse by sending federal troops there to restore order, and by making a secret bond deal with Wall Street to stem the alarming leakage of gold from the Treasury. To his unconcealed annoyance, all attempts at genuine tariff reform were frustrated by entrenched lobbyists in 1894. As the depression deepened, the underprivileged clutched desperately at the cure-all of free silver. It became the overshadowing issue in the class-struggle presidential campaign of 1896, in which the Republican McKinley emerged victorious over the Democratic (and allegedly demagogic) Bryan.

A. THE TARIFF ISSUE

1. McKinley Pleads for Protection (1890)

The amiable Republican Congressman McKinley, chairman of the House Ways and Means Committee, sponsored the tariff bill that bears his name. It carried protection to a new extreme. It not only protected "infant" industries but, in the case of tinplate, it extended protection to an industry yet unborn. The free list was delusively large, for it contained such inconsequential items as arsenic, stuffed birds, bladders, fossils, broken glass, salted guts, orchids, turtles, and manufactured teeth. As a sop to the farmer, new duties—largely unneeded—were levied on agricultural products. It has been said that for McKinley the tariff was a religious rather than an economic issue. Comment in the light of this excerpt from his speech in the House. What is the fallacy in his argument in behalf of a tariff for American grain producers?

It has been asserted in the views of the [Democratic] minority that the duty put upon wheat and other agricultural products would be of no value to the agriculturists of the United States. The committee, believing differently, have advanced the duty upon these products.

As we are the greatest wheat-producing country of the world, it is

1. *Congressional Record*, 51 Cong., 1 sess., pp. 4249, 4255 (May 7, 1890).

habitually asserted and believed by many that this product is safe from foreign competition. We do not appreciate that while the United States last year raised 490,000,000 bushels of wheat, France raised 316,000,000 bushels, Italy raised 103,000,000 bushels, Russia 189,000,000 bushels, and India 243,000,000 bushels. . . . Our sharpest competition [in the world market] comes from Russia and India . . . and if we will only reflect on the difference between the cost of labor in producing wheat in the United States and in competing countries, we will readily perceive how near we are, if we have not quite reached, the danger line so far even as our own markets are concerned. . . .

It is also to be noted, Mr. Chairman, that having increased the duties on wools we have also increased the duties on the product—the manufactures of wool—to compensate for the increased duty on the raw product. . . .

If our trade and commerce are increasing and profitable within our own borders, what advantage can come from passing it by, confessedly the best market, that we may reach the poorest by distant seas? In the foreign market the profit is divided between our own citizen and the foreigner, while with the trade and commerce among ourselves the profit is kept in our own family and increases our national wealth and promotes the welfare of the individual citizen. Yet in spite of all the croaking about foreign trade, our exports were never so great as they are today. We send abroad what is not consumed at home, and we could do no more under any system. . . .

Experience has demonstrated that for us and ours, and for the present and the future, the protective system meets our wants, our conditions, promotes the national design, and will work out our destiny better than any other.

With me this position is a deep conviction, not a theory. I believe in it, and thus warmly advocate it because enveloped in it are my country's highest development and greatest prosperity. Out of it come the greatest gains to the people, the greatest comforts to the masses, the widest encouragement for manly aspirations, with the largest rewards, dignifying and elevating our citizenship, upon which the safety, and purity, and permanency of our political system depend.

2. Mills Challenges McKinley (1890)

Colonel Roger Q. Mills of Texas, twice severely wounded during his service in the Confederate army, had recently been chairman of the House Ways and Means Committee. A lawyer, a Democrat, and long an earnest advocate of a lowered tariff, he here contradicts the Republican McKinley in the simple yet eloquent style for which he was famous. What are his arguments against higher duties on agricultural products? How convincingly does he meet McKinley's allegation that a higher duty was needed to protect American grain?

The [Republican members of the] committee are greatly alarmed about our wheat-growers. That great industry is imperiled by "a most damaging

2. *Ibid.*, pp. 4260–61 (May 7, 1890).

competition". . . . They have increased the duty on wheat and that great product is safe.

How many bushels of wheat are imported into this country? We exported last year 90,000,000 bushels in wheat and flour . . . and last year . . . imported the inconsiderable amount of 1,946 bushels of wheat. And that duty has been put on to protect America's farmers against the damaging foreign competition from India and Russia.

What did that 1,946 bushels of wheat cost? Our wheat was at an average price of 89 cents per bushel, and the average price of the 1,946 bushels which we imported was $2.05. . . . What do you suppose that wheat was imported for? Do not all speak at once, please.

It was seed wheat, imported by the wheat-grower of the West to improve his seed. Does not every man know that? And you have made it cost him that much more to improve his agricultural product so that he can raise a better character of wheat and better compete in the markets of the world, where he has to meet all comers in free competition. . . .

We exported 69,000,000 bushels of corn last year and we imported into this country 2,388 bushels, an amount, we are told, that imperils the market of those who raise 2,000,000,000 bushels. . . .

How much rye did we import last year? Sixteen bushels! It could all have been raised on a turnip patch. . . .

The Germans, French, English, Spaniards, Austrians, and others with whom we are trading are dissatisfied with our discriminations against their products, and they have been taking steps to retaliate upon us. They have increased the duty on wheat in Germany two or three times since 1880. . . .

Why have we not the prices of 1881? Because we have cut off importation from our European customers, and they have cut off importation from us. Our surplus is increasing with our population, and we have no markets to consume it. What ought we to do?

We should reduce the duties on imports, put all raw materials on the free list, increase our importation four or five hundred millions more if we could, and thus increase our exports to that extent. That would raise the prices of agricultural products and the aggregate value of our annual crops $1,500,000,000 or $2,000,000,000 per year. That would distribute a large amount of wealth that would be expended in the employment of labor, and thus unbounded prosperity would be brought to the whole country.

Instead of this the committee have prepared a bill increasing taxes, raising duties, restricting importations, shutting in our farm products, and decreasing prices. They are going in the opposite direction and struggling to intensify the distress of the country.

3. The Sugar Trust Lobby (1894)

The high-duty McKinley Tariff of 1890 boomeranged against the Republicans, and the Democrat Grover Cleveland returned triumphantly to the White House in 1893.

3. _Senate Reports,_ 53 Cong., 2 sess., X, pp. 656–57 (June 13, 1894).

An attempt to put sugar on the free list provoked powerful opposition from the lobby of the so-called Sugar Trust, and the "sugar Senators" succeeded in forcing a protective duty into the new Wilson-Gorman Tariff Bill of August, 1894. Ugly charges that the giant American Sugar Refining Company was exerting improper influence to secure tariff changes led to a grilling, by a Senate committee, of its president, the multimillionaire Henry O. Havemeyer. What is surprising about his revelations?

Senator ALLEN. I do understand you, however, to say and repeat that in states where you have a financial interest, at least where the sugar refining company has an interest as refiners, you do contribute to either the Democratic or Republican Party as one or the other may be in the ascendancy in that state?

Mr. HAVEMEYER. We do for local and state purposes, but not national.

Senator ALLEN. You never contribute to the campaign fund of a party in the minority?

Mr. HAVEMEYER. We may; I will not say we do not.

Senator ALLEN. Your policy, however, is to stand in with the ruling power?

Mr. HAVEMEYER. Not to "stand in" but to contribute to the campaign expenses of that party, for the reason that, they being in power and control, it could give us the protection we should have.

Senator ALLEN. And by that means you placate—

Mr. HAVEMEYER. Oh, no; there is no placation or obligation at all; nothing more than we consider the proper thing to do; everybody does it.

THE SOW THAT BREEDS THE LITTER

In Populist eyes the Wall Street Money Trust bred and fattened the other trusts, while the little pig representing the people lay dead. W. H. Harvey, *Coin's Financial School up to Date,* 1895.

Senator ALLEN. Does any other corporation in these same states do the same thing, that you know?

Mr. HAVEMEYER. I understand every individual, corporation, and firm in existence does it in their respective states.

Senator ALLEN. So the American Sugar Refining Company's politics, so far as its contributions to the campaign fund are concerned, is controlled by the political complexion of the state in which it happens to have a particular refinery?

Mr. HAVEMEYER. The American Sugar Refining Company has no politics of any kind.

Senator ALLEN. Only the politics of business?

Mr. HAVEMEYER. Only the politics of business.

Senator LINDSAY. You say the company is separate and distinct from the officers and stockholders; each man has his own politics?

Mr. HAVEMEYER. We have nothing to do with politics in any shape or manner. Our business is the refining of sugar at a slight profit that is consistent with a reasonable return on the industry.

[*The scandalous pressures of the various lobbies ("the third house of Congress") became so notorious that President Cleveland refused to sign the new Wilson-Gorman Tariff Bill. Additional scandals were aired in response to rumors that certain United States Senators had speculated in sugar stocks while the duty on sugar was under consideration. After an investigation, Senators McPherson of New Jersey and Quay of Pennsylvania admitted the charge. Senator Quay, a powerful and unsavory political boss, declared defiantly: "I do not feel that there is anything in my connection with the Senate to interfere with my buying or selling the stock when I please; and I propose to do so." Contrast this with present-day conflict-of-interest practices.*]

B. THE PULLMAN STRIKE

1. A Populist Condemns Pullman (1894)

George M. Pullman, who invented the popular upper-and-lower-berth Pullman Palace Car, made a fortune in manufacturing and controlling his brain child. A generous philanthropist with his millions, he built for his employees the model town of Pullman (now in Chicago). But when the depression came and the company slashed wages about 25 percent, the workers struck. They were joined by Eugene V. Debs' powerful American Railway Union. According to Debs, the management had said, "There is nothing to arbitrate." Senator Peffer, a Populist from Kansas who combed his long whiskers with his fingers while delivering even longer speeches, here presents his views. What are the two main grievances of the Pullman workers? How legitimate are they?

Without going into all the details, I will state by way of preface that the Pullman Company established what most people in this world believed to be an ideal community, in which all the citizens should have equal rights, in which none should have special privileges. The object was to build a

1. *Congressional Record*, 53 Cong., 2 sess., p. 7231 (July 10, 1894).

community where the best modern scientific principles of hygiene, drainage, sewerage, grading, lighting, watering, and every other convenience should abound.

But while the company was doing that, while the world was looking on applauding, the company, like every other corporation of which I have ever known anything, held all of the power, all of the reins within its own grasp. That is to say, while there was sewerage, while there was light, while there was water, while there were parks, and all those desirable things, at the end of every month or of every week, as the case might be, when pay day came around, the charges that were set up against the residents of the town of Pullman for their lots and for their conveniences were deducted from their pay (just as the clothing of a soldier or extra rations or a lost gun were deducted from his pay) and the balance found to be due was paid to these people. Among these charges were rents and stated dues for the purchase of property.

After a while hard times began to pinch the company as it did everybody else, and it began to reduce the pay of the men. The men submitted patiently. Another reduction came and the men again submitted, only asking, however, that their rent charges should be reduced, that their taxes should be reduced, to correspond to the amount of reduction in their wages.

Then it was found that these poor people were absolutely defenseless, absolutely powerless in the hands of a corporation that had no soul. They asked to have a reduction of their rent charges and of other charges; they asked for a little time to turn around.

All these things were denied them. Finally, the Pullman citizens came to the conclusion that they might as well starve in defense of their rights as to starve while the proprietors of the town, the organizers and controllers of the corporation, were feasting on the fat things that these men had made for them. Now the trouble is on hand, and the leader of this great corporation [George M. Pullman] is off at the seashore, or on a lake, or on an island, or somewhere, refusing to entertain even a newspaper man, except to say, "I have nothing to say; the company at Chicago will look after the company's interest there"—heartless, soulless, conscienceless, Mr. President, this tyrant of tyrants.

2. Pullman Defends His Company (1894)

The bloody disorders attending the Pullman strike led to an investigation by the United States Strike Commission. George M. Pullman took the stand and testified that his company had undertaken to manufacture cars at a loss so as to keep his men employed. But he conceded that it was better to operate at a slight loss than to incur the larger losses resulting from idle factories. He also testified that the salaries of management (including his own) had not been cut; that the Pullman Company still had about $25,000,000 in undivided profits; and that the dividends paid to stockholders had ranged from 12% to the current 8%. United States Commissioner Worthington extracted the following information from Pullman. How sound is Pullman's position on arbitration? How does his general business philosophy square with that prevalent today in America?

Commissioner WORTHINGTON. Now, let me ask you right there, Mr. Pullman, what do you see that is objectionable, in a business point of view, under the existing state of affairs, . . . in submitting to disinterested persons the question as to whether under all the circumstances wages might not be increased somewhat of your employees?

Mr. PULLMAN. I think I have made that as plain in this [written] statement as I can make it if I should repeat it a thousand times.

Commissioner WORTHINGTON. Is that the only reason you can give?

Mr. PULLMAN. What do you mean by that, "The only reason"?

Commissioner WORTHINGTON. The reason you give here (in the statement), "It must be clear to every businessman and to every thinking workman that no prudent employer could submit to arbitration the question whether he should commit such a piece of business folly." Is that the only answer to it?

Mr. PULLMAN. Well, now, I have a little memorandum here which is practically the same thing on the question of arbitration. Of course there are matters which are proper subjects of arbitration—matters of opinion.

Commissioner WORTHINGTON. What are those matters that are proper subjects for arbitration?

Mr. PULLMAN. A matter of opinion would be a proper subject of arbitration, as, for instance, a question of title, or a disagreement on a matter of opinion. . . . But as to whether a fact that I know to be true is true or not, I could not agree to submit to arbitration. Take the case in hand: the question as to whether the shops at Pullman shall be continuously operated at a loss or not is one which it was impossible for the company, as a matter of principle, to submit to the opinion of any third party; and as to whether they were running at a loss on contract work in general, as explained to the committee of the men in my interview with them—that was a simple fact that I knew to be true, and which could not be made otherwise by the opinion of any third party.

Commissioner WORTHINGTON. You use the expression, "Impossible to be submitted." Why is it impossible?

Mr. PULLMAN. Because it would violate a principle.

Commissioner WORTHINGTON. What principle?

Mr. PULLMAN. The principle that a man should have the right to manage his own property.

Commissioner WORTHINGTON. The decision of arbitrators would not be compulsory, would it?

Mr. PULLMAN. I still think, having managed the property of the Pullman Company for twenty-seven years, that I am perhaps as well calculated to manage it for the interests of its stockholders and for the interests of the public—for the general interest—as some man who is not interested, who comes in to arbitrate certain points.

3. Starvation at Pullman (1894)

The Pullman strike was finally broken by federal bayonets, and the Company allegedly imported more docile workers to replace those who had struck. A group signing themselves "The Starving Citizens of Pullman" appealed to Governor Altgeld of Illinois for relief. After examining conditions personally, the Governor wrote the following letter to George M. Pullman. Does the evidence here given support the charge of discrimination?

Sir: I examined the conditions at Pullman yesterday, visited even the kitchens and bedrooms of many of the people. Two representatives of your company were with me and we found the distress as great as it was represented. The men are hungry and the women and children are actually suffering. They have been living on charity for a number of months and it is exhausted. Men who had worked for your company for more than ten years had to apply to the relief society in two weeks after the work stopped.

I learn from your manager that last spring there were 3,260 people on the payroll; yesterday there were 2,220 at work, but over 600 of these are new men, so that only about 1,600 of the old employees have been taken back, thus leaving over 1,600 of the old employees who have not been taken back. A few hundred have left, the remainder have nearly all applied for work, but were told that they were not needed. These are utterly destitute. The relief committee on last Saturday gave out two pounds of oatmeal and two pounds of cornmeal to each family. But even the relief committee has exhausted its resources.

Something must be done and at once. The case differs from instances of destitution found elsewhere, for generally there is somebody in the neighborhood able to give relief; this is not the case at Pullman. Even those who have gone to work are so exhausted that they cannot help their neighbors if they would. I repeat now that it seems to me your company cannot afford to have me appeal to the charity and humanity of the state to save the lives of your old employees. Four-fifths of those people are women and children. No matter what caused this distress, it must be met.

[Mr. Pullman turned a deaf ear to appeals for relief, and humane citizens were forced to help the destitute. "Mr. Dooley" (F. P. Dunne) referred to the time "whin God quarried his heart. . . ." Reconcile Pullman's attitude in this instance with his large private philanthropies, including a bequest of $1,200,000 for a free manual training school in Pullman.]

C. THE FREE-SILVER MIRAGE

1. Coin's Financial School (1894)

By the 1880's and 1890's indebted Americans, especially the farmers, were caught in a deflationary pinch. A cry arose for inflating the currency by abandoning the

3. John P. Altgeld, *Live Questions* (1899), pp. 422–23 (Aug. 21, 1894).
1. W. H. Harvey, *Coin's Financial School* (1894), pp. 130–33, *passim.*

single gold standard and restoring the bimetallic gold-silver standard, dropped by Congress in 1873 ("the Crime of '73"). The silverites specifically demanded the free and unlimited coinage of silver in the ratio of sixteen ounces of silver to one ounce of gold, despite Britain's adherence to the gold standard. William Hope Harvey, a frustrated silver-mine operator from Colorado, came to Chicago and in 1894 published his best-selling tract *Coin's Financial School*. His fictional account tells how Coin, the boy wizard of Chicago, conducted a six-day financial school attended by many leading figures, whom he converted to the gospel of free silver. The 174-page booklet, cleverly but deceptively illustrated, sold upwards of a million copies and was a major propaganda weapon in the free-silver crusade. Why was Harvey bitter against England? Why did the proposed international agreement on bimetallism have little prospect of realization?

His [Coin's] appearance upon the platform was the signal for an ovation. He had grown immensely popular in those last five days.

He laid his silk hat on the table, and at once stepped to the middle of the platform. He raised his eyes to the audience, slowly turned his head to the right and left, and looked into the sea of faces that confronted him.

"In the midst of plenty, we are in want," he began. "Helpless children and the best womanhood and manhood of America appeal to us for release from a bondage that is destructive of life and liberty. All the nations of the Western Hemisphere turn to their great sister republic for assistance in the emancipation of the people of at least one-half the world.

"The Orient, with its teeming millions of people, and France, the cradle of science and liberty in Europe, look to the United States to lead in the struggle to roll back the accumulated disasters of the last twenty-one years [since "the Crime of '73"]. What shall our answer be? [Applause.]

"If it is claimed we must adopt for our money the metal England selects [gold], and can have no independent choice in the matter, let us make the test and find out if it is true. It is not American to give up without trying. If it is true, let us attach England to the United States and blot her name out from among the nations of the earth. [Applause.]

"A war with England would be the most popular ever waged on the face of the earth. [Applause.] If it is true that she can dictate the money of the world, and thereby create world-wide misery, it would be the most just war ever waged by man. [Applause.]

"But fortunately this is not necessary. Those who would have you think that we must wait for England, either have not studied this subject, or have the same interest in continuing the present conditions as England. It is a vain hope to expect her voluntarily to consent. England is the creditor nation of the globe, and collects hundreds of millions of dollars in interest annually in gold from the rest of the world. We are paying her two hundred millions yearly in interest. She demands it in gold; the contracts call for it in gold. Do you expect her to voluntarily release any part of it? It has a purchasing power twice what a bimetallic currency would have. She knows it. . . .

"Whenever property interests and humanity have come in conflict,

UNCLE SAM: "IT WON'T WORK WITHOUT
A NEW WHEEL."

A specious argument for bimetallism. W. H. Harvey, *Coin's Financial School Up to Date*, 1895.

England has ever been the enemy of human liberty. All reforms with those so unfortunate as to be in her power have been won with the sword. She yields only to force. [Applause.]

"The moneylenders in the United States, who own substantially all of our money, have a selfish interest in maintaining the gold standard. They, too, will not yield. They believe that if the gold standard can survive for a few years longer, the people will get used to it—get used to their poverty—and quietly submit.

"To that end they organize international bimetallic committees and say, 'Wait on England, she will be forced to give us bimetallism.' Vain hope! Deception on this subject has been practiced long enough upon a patient and outraged people."

2. A "Gold Bug" Defends Britain (1895)

"Coin" Harvey's pamphlets inspired both imitations and rebuttals. Among the more prominent critics was a New York international lawyer, Everett P. Wheeler, who, despite an interest in a silver mine, attacked Harvey. He had served as counsel for a company doing business in Central America, where the silver standard had caused his clients inconvenience and loss. How convincing is his argument that the ruin of England would not operate to the benefit of America?

Coin [Harvey] resorts to the familiar and well-worn appeal to the prejudice which some people in this country are supposed to feel against England.

The people of that country have the same religion, the same laws, and the same language as ourselves. We did fight in years gone by, but we are now united by the close ties of business and friendship. The English octopus, as Coin calls it, is really a country that is our best customer for wheat, for cotton, for beef, for petroleum, and for Yankee notions.

He says it "feeds on nothing but gold." In fact, however, it feeds on the wheat, the coffee, the sugar of South America, the tea of China; in short,

2. E. P. Wheeler, *Real Bi-Metallism or True Coin versus False Coin* (1895), pp. 69–70, 73.

the natural or manufactured products of every part of the world, all of which it pays for. Along its arms, steamers ply, freighted with the merchandise which is the subject of this mutual trade, which benefits both parties. Telegraphic cables thread the bottom of the sea to its head, carrying messages of business and of friendship. American investors draw great sums in royalties from this "octopus". . . .

In short, the whole octopus business, like the other delectable illustrations in Coin's school, is a delusion and a snare. The worst thing that could happen to this country would be the ruin of England. No merchant would look with satisfaction on the ruin of his best customer or want to quarrel with him.

Another favorite argument of the free-silver advocates is that England first adopted the gold standard and has grown rich by it, and that therefore it must be bad for other countries.

Let us note two things in this connection.

1. England first adopted trial by jury, and the writ of *habeas corpus*. She first enforced the principle of freedom that no man should be deprived of life, liberty, or property but by the judgment of his peers, or the law of the land. Shall we discard these sacred muniments of liberty because they are of English origin?

2. If England has prospered under the gold standard, why not the United States? Certainly no country ever became really prosperous by the ruin of its neighbors. In the great commonwealth of nations, the prosperity of one makes trade with all, and helps to enrich all.

D. THE FREE-SILVER CONVENTION

1. Tillman Repudiates Cleveland (1896)

Negro-baiting Benjamin R. Tillman (see p. 461) had recently emerged as the demagogic champion of the poor white farmers of South Carolina. Rabidly opposed to President Cleveland's conservative gold policy, he had run successfully for the United States Senate in 1894, shouting, "Send me to Washington and I'll stick my pitchfork into his [Cleveland's] old ribs!" He was vehement in denouncing Cleveland's secret bond deal with the Wall Street bankers. Aspiring to the Democratic presidential nomination as a silverite, he ruined his chances at the Chicago convention by the following violent speech attacking the Cleveland administration. During this harangue he paced the platform like a madman. What are his grievances against Cleveland, and which one seems to rankle the deepest?

When this convention disperses, I hope my fellow citizens will have a different opinion of the man with the pitchfork from South Carolina. I am from South Carolina, which was the home of secession. [Great hissing.] Oh, hiss if you like. There are only three things on earth which can hiss— a goose, a serpent, and a man, and the man who hisses the name of South Carolina has no knowledge whatever of its grand history.

But I tell you I do not come from the South Carolina of 1860, which you

1. *Public Opinion*, XXI, 69–70 (July 16, 1896). The speech was delivered on July 9.

charge brought about the disruption of the Democratic Party. The war there declared was for the emancipation of the black slaves. I come now from a South Carolina which demands the emancipation of the white slaves. You charge that in 1860 South Carolina brought about the disruption of the Democratic Party. I say to you now that I am willing to see the Democratic Party disrupted again to accomplish the emancipation of the white slaves.

New York for twenty years or more has been the one dominant factor and dictator of the National Democratic Party. While we want to thank New York and Connecticut and New Jersey for the aid extended to us in the past, I want to say to you here that we have at last recognized in the South that we are mere hewers of wood and drawers of water, while the great states I have named have eaten up our substance. My friends say this is not a sectional issue. I say it is. . . .

[*Great scenes of disorder then ensued, and quiet was restored with difficulty. Many times the Senator was interrupted, but he went on:*]

As Grover Cleveland stands for gold monometallism, we have repudiated him. We are diametrically opposed to his policy, and why should we write ourselves down as asses and liars? They ask us to say that he is honest. Well, in reply I say he signed a contract for bonds in secret, with one of his partners as a witness. Nobody disputes his boldness or obstinacy. He had the courage to overthrow the Constitution of the United States when he overrode the rights of the citizens of Illinois [during the Pullman strike] and sent federal troops into this state. You ask us to indorse his fidelity. In reply, I say he has been faithful unto death—the death of the Democratic Party. We have denounced him in South Carolina as a tool of Wall Street, and what was prophecy then is history now. . . .

I tell you that the Democratic Party of the United States will turn out the party in this fall's election if it dares indorse Grover Cleveland here. I tell you you dare not go before this country after indorsing the Cleveland administration. We of the South have burned our bridges behind us so far as the Eastern Democrats are concerned. We have turned our faces to the West and they have responded.

2. Senator Hill Urges Sanity (1896)

The gold-standard Democrats, supporting Cleveland, were clearly outnumbered in the wildly shouting Chicago convention. The ranks of the silverite majority were swelled by Populists and by free-silver delegates who had deserted the gold-standard Republican Party. The Chicago "assembly of lunatics"—so called by the Republican New York *Tribune*—uproariously endorsed the platform reported by a majority of the resolutions committee. It endorsed the well-known Populist scheme of freely coining, at the ratio of 16 to 1, all silver mined. Dissenting Senator David B. Hill of New York, an adroit machine politician bitten by the presidential bug, here speaks logically but vainly for the gold-standard minority on the resolutions committee. After

2. *Ibid.*, XXI, 70 (July 16, 1896). The speech was delivered on July 9.

the convention, he reputedly said, "I am a Democrat still—very still." What is his solution of the problem and why does he propose it?

I am a Democrat, but I am not a revolutionist. My mission here today is to unite, not to divide—to build up, not to destroy—to plan for victory, not to plot for defeat. The question which this convention is to decide is: What is the best position to take at this time on the financial question? In a word, the question presented is between international bimetallism and local bimetallism. If there are any different points in it, they are not represented either in the majority or in the minority report.

I therefore start out with this proposition, that the Democratic Party stands today in favor of gold and silver as the money of the country; that it stands in favor neither of a silver standard nor of a gold standard, but that we differ as to the means to bring about the result.

Those whom I represent and for whom I speak—the sixteen minority members of the committee—insist that we should not attempt the experiment of the free and unlimited coinage of silver without cooperation of other great nations. It is not a question of patriotism, it is not a question of courage, it is not a question of loyalty, as the majority platform speaks of it. The minority has thought it was simply a question as to whether we were able to enter on this experiment. It is a question of business. It is a question of finance. . . .

I think, Mr. President, that the safest and best course for this convention to have pursued was to take the first step forward in the great cause of monetary reform by declaring in favor of international bimetallism. I know that it is said by enthusiastic friends that America can mark out a course for herself. I know that that idea appeals to the pride of the average American, but I beg to remind you that if that suggestion be carried out to its legitimate conclusion, you might as well do away with our international treaties. . . .

Be not deceived. Do not attempt to drive those Democrats out of the party who have grown gray in its service, in order to make room for a lot of Republicans and Populists who will not vote your ticket at all. My friends, I speak more in sorrow than in anger.

[*A resolution backed by Hill and approving the Democratic administration of President Cleveland was voted down by a face-slapping vote of 564 to 357.*]

3. Bryan's Cross of Gold (1896)

The dramatic assignment of replying to Senator Hill and closing the debate on the platform fell to William Jennings Bryan of Nebraska. Although a well-known ex-Congressman and free-silver orator, he was not then regarded as one of the front runners for the presidential nomination. Tall, lean, smooth-shaven, hawk-nosed, and wide-mouthed, "the Boy Orator of the Platte" hushed the vast assemblage of some 15,000 with his masterful presence. The "cross of gold" analogy to the crucifixion of

3. C. M. Depew, ed., *The Library of Oratory* (1902), XIV, 415, 418, 420–25, *passim*.

Christ he had already used a number of times, but never so effectively. Projecting his organ-like voice to the outer reaches of the vast hall, he had the frenzied crowd cheering his every sentence as he neared the end. The climax swept the delegates off their feet and won Byran the presidential nomination the next day. How do you account for the success of his memorable speech? To what different kinds of prejudice does Bryan appeal?

I would be presumptuous, indeed, to present myself against the distinguished gentlemen to whom you have listened if this were a mere measuring of abilities. But this is not a contest between persons. The humblest citizen in all the land, when clad in the armor of a righteous cause, is stronger than all the hosts of error. I come to speak to you in defense of a cause as holy as the cause of liberty—the cause of humanity. . . .

We [silverites] do not come as aggressors. Our war is not a war of conquest. We are fighting in the defense of our homes, our families, and posterity. We have petitioned, and our petitions have been scorned. We have entreated, and our entreaties have been disregarded. We have begged, _nd they have mocked when our calamity came. We beg no longer; we entreat no more; we petition no more. We defy them! . . .

The gentleman from New York [Senator Hill] . . . says he wants this country to try to secure an international agreement. Why does he not tell us what he is going to do if he fails to secure an international agreement? . . . Our opponents have tried for twenty years to secure an international agreement, and those are waiting for it most patiently who do not want it at all. . . .

We go forth confident that we shall win. Why? Because upon the paramount issue of this campaign there is not a spot of ground upon which the enemy will dare to challenge battle. If they [the Republicans] tell us that the gold standard is a good thing, we shall point to their platform and tell them that their platform pledges the party to get rid of the gold standard and substitute bimetallism. If the gold standard is a good thing, why try to get rid of it? . . .

Mr. Carlisle* said in 1878 that this was a struggle between "the idle holders of idle capital" and "the struggling masses, who produce the wealth and pay the taxes of the country"; and, my friends, the question we are to decide is: upon which side will the Democratic Party fight—upon the side of "the idle holders of idle capital" or upon the side of "the struggling masses"? That is the question which the party must answer first, and then it must be answered by each individual hereafter. The sympathies of the Democratic Party, as shown by the platform, are on the side of the struggling masses who have ever been the foundation of the Democratic Party.

There are two ideas of government. There are those who believe that, if you will only legislate to make the well-to-do prosperous, their prosperity will leak through on those below. The Democratic idea, however, has been

* John G. Carlisle of Kentucky, formerly a distinguished member of Congress, was Cleveland's Secretary of the Treasury in 1896.

that if you legislate to make the masses prosperous, their prosperity will find its way up through every class which rests upon them.

You come to us and tell us that the great cities are in favor of the gold standard. We reply that the great cities rest upon our broad and fertile prairies. Burn down your cities and leave our farms, and your cities will spring up again as if by magic. But destroy our farms, and the grass will grow in the streets of every city in the country.

My friends, we declare that this nation is able to legislate for its own people on every question, with-

"YOU SHALL NOT PRESS DOWN UPON THE BROW OF LABOR *this* CROWN"

A parody of Bryan's famous crown-of-thorns speech, with Bryan pressing down the fifty-cent "bunco dollar." *Harper's Weekly,* 1896.

out waiting for the aid or consent of any other nation on earth; and upon that issue we expect to carry every state in the Union. I shall not slander the inhabitants of the fair state of Massachusetts nor the inhabitants of the state of New York by saying that, when they are confronted with the proposition, they will declare that this nation is not able to attend to its own business. It is the issue of 1776 over again. Our ancestors, when but three millions in number, had the courage to declare their political independence of every other nation. Shall we, their descendants, when we have grown to seventy millions, declare that we are less independent than our forefathers?

No, my friends, that will never be the verdict of our people. Therefore, we care not upon what lines the battle is fought. If they say bimetallism is good but that we cannot have it until other nations help us, we reply that, instead of having a gold standard because England has, we will restore bimetallism, and then let England have bimetallism because the United States has it. If they dare to come out in the open field and defend the gold standard as a good thing, we will fight them to the uttermost.

Having behind us the producing masses of this nation and the world, supported by the commercial interests, the laboring interests, and the toilers everywhere, we will answer their demand for a gold standard by saying to them: You shall not press down upon the brow of labor this crown of thorns; you shall not crucify mankind upon a cross of gold.

[*The Cleveland Democrats, with their devotion to the gold standard, were appalled by the nomination of Bryan. "What a burlesque on a Democratic convention," wrote Postmaster General Wilson in his diary. "May God help the country!" He stressed the youth, ambition, and Populist leanings of the candidate, while noting that Bryan's "utter ignorance of the great diplomatic, financial, and other questions a President has constantly to dispose of, will be lost sight of in the fanaticism of the one idea he represents." (F. P. Summers,* The Cabinet Diary of William L. Wilson, 1896–1897 *[1957], p. 116.) Conservatives, then and later, generally agreed that Bryan was strong on sound but weak on substance.*]

E. THE TRIUMPH OF McKINLEY

1. The "Anarchists" Lose Out (1896)

Bryan's whirlwind campaign for free silver gained such momentum in the early stages that he might have won if the election had been held two months earlier. But frightened "gold-bug" Republicans opened wide their purses, and the subsequent deluge of propaganda helped bring victory to William McKinley, the Republican candidate. Many of the gold-standard Cleveland Democrats spurned Bryan and contributed actively to McKinley's victory. The "gold-bug" East stressed the presence in Bryan's camp of such radicals as Eugene V. Debs, who had headed the Pullman strike of 1894, and Governor Altgeld of Illinois, who had pardoned the three surviving Haymarket Riot anarchists. In what respects is this editorial in the New York *Nation* least fair?

We have escaped from what a large number of people supposed was an immense danger, the danger of having our currency adulterated and our form of government changed, and a band of ignoramuses and anarchists put at the head of what remained of the great American republic. Probably no man in civil life has succeeded in inspiring so much terror, without taking life, as Bryan. Attila and Tamerlane frightened more people, but they killed or threatened to kill them; they hardly destroyed more property.

Bryan succeeded in persuading hundreds of thousands that the great fabric of government which was built up by the wisdom of experience of a thousand years, and cemented by hundreds of thousands of lives, was, almost in the first century of its existence, about to be handed over by the vote of its own people to a knot of silly, half-taught adventurers and anarchists. We were to exchange the Constitution and the Supreme Court for the decrees of Altgeld and Debs and Bryan and Teller, whose principal occupation was to be striking off "cheap money for the poor man."

The whole episode has been utterly discreditable to our politics, as conducted by politicians. Could anything better reveal the character of our

1. *The Nation* (New York), LXIII, 337 (Nov. 5, 1896).

nominating system than the fact that the nominating convention of one of our two great parties could be taken possession of by a few adventurers, that the platform could be drawn, in the main, by a noted anarchist [Altgeld], and an unknown young man nominated on it simply because the audience was pleased with one of his metaphors, and that it should drive away from it all the party's men of light and leading before going to the country?

2. Bryan's Afterthoughts (1896)

While his memory of the campaign was still fresh, Bryan recorded his impressions. His then unprecedented 600 speeches and his 18,000 miles of sweaty travel must have left him in something of a daze. What does his account suggest about the ethics of the opposition, the intellectual level of the campaign, and the assumption that the canvass was a crusade rather than a campaign?

The reminiscences of the campaign of 1896 form such a delightful chapter in memory's book that I am constrained to paraphrase a familiar line and say that it is better to have run and lost than never to have run at all. . . .

Unless I am mistaken, the deep awakening among the people during the campaign just closed will result in a more careful study of political questions by both men and women, and in a more rigid scrutiny of the conduct of public officials by those whom they serve. No matter what may be the ultimate outcome of the struggle over the financial question, better government will result from the political interest which has been aroused. . . .

During the campaign I ran across various evidences of coercion, direct and indirect. One of the most common means of influencing voters was the advertising of orders placed with manufacturers, conditioned upon Republican success at the polls. The following is an illustration. Tuesday morning, November 3rd, there appeared at the head of the last column of the first page of the *Morning News,* of Wilmington, Del.:

CONTINGENT ORDERS.
The Harlan and Hollingsworth Company, of this city, have received a contract for a boat costing $300,000. One clause in the contract provides that in the event of Bryan's election the contract shall be canceled. If the boat is built here, $160,000 of its cost would be paid to Wilmington workmen for wages. The corporation wanting the boat feel that it would not be justified in having it constructed if Bryan should become President. . . .

2. W. J. Bryan, *The First Battle* (1896), pp. 612–24, *passim.*

I may mention a still more forcible means adopted by many employers. The workingmen were paid off Saturday night before election and notified that they might expect work Wednesday morning in case of Mr. McKinley's election, but that they need not return if I was elected. Whether the employers themselves were actually afraid or whether they merely intended to frighten their employees, the plan worked admirably and exerted a most potent influence on election day. . . .

MONEY TALKS

"No, Mr. McKinley will not make any campaign speeches, but there will be other eloquent speakers in the field." Mark Hanna [Republican National Chairman]. A reference to the common assumption that Hanna's lavish use of money swung the election. Buffalo *Times,* 1896.

The ratio of 16 to 1 was scrupulously adhered to during the campaign, and illustrated with infinite variety. At one place our carriage was drawn by sixteen white horses and one yellow horse; at any number of places we were greeted by sixteen young ladies dressed in white and one dressed in yellow, or by sixteen young men dressed in white and one dressed in yellow. But the ratio was most frequently represented in flowers, sixteen white chrysanthemums and one yellow one being the favorite combination. . . .

It is impossible to chronicle all the evidences of kindly feeling given during the campaign; in fact the good will manifested and the intense feeling shown impressed me more than any other feature of the campaign. When the result was announced my composure was more endangered by the sorrow exhibited by friends than it was during all the excitement of the struggle. Men broke down and cried as they expressed their regret, and there rises before me now the face of a laboring man of Lincoln, who, after he dried his tears, held out his hand from which three fingers were missing, and said: "I did not shed a tear when those were taken off."

People have often lightly said that they would die for a cause, but it may be asserted in all truthfulness that during the campaign just closed there were thousands of bimetallists who would have given their lives, had their lives been demanded, in order to secure success to the principles which they advocated. Surely, greater love hath no man than this. . . .

I am proud of the character of my support. Those who voted for me did so of their own volition; neither coercion nor purchase secured their suffrages; their confidence and good will robbed defeat of all its pangs.

3. The London *Standard* Rejoices (1896)

William McKinley, the high priest of high protection, had expected to emphasize the tariff in the campaign, but Bryan took the play away from him with free silver.

3. Quoted in *Public Opinion,* XXI, 623 (Nov. 12, 1896).

The business world on both sides of the Atlantic, unwilling to be paid off in fifty-cent silver dollars, rejoiced over the Republican triumph. London reported that millions of dollars' worth of orders from the United States had been placed in England contingent on Bryan's defeat. Why is the London *Standard*, in the following article not altogether happy?

The complete rejection of Bryan's tempting program, addressed to indolence, incapacity, and cupidity, shows that these qualities are less widely distributed in the United States than Bryan would have us believe. There has been a revolt of the honest and loyal citizens, who are solicitous for the fair name and fame of the Republic, and the Bryanites astonished the world by the comparative paucity of their numbers. The hopelessly ignorant and savagely covetous waifs and strays of American civilization voted for Bryan, but the bulk of the solid sense, business integrity, and social stability sided with McKinley. The nation is to be heartily congratulated. The victory has drawbacks for Englishmen, and, indeed, for every country in Europe engaged in manufacturing industries. It is a triumph of good faith, but also a triumph of [tariff] protection.

THOUGHT PROVOKERS

1. Was it improper for the Sugar Trust to lobby for a tariff on sugar?
2. Is a company like Pullman's justified in cutting wages when it has a large surplus of money? Does management have a higher obligation to the investor than to the laborer? Is the businessman the best interpreter of the public interest? Is a large-scale business a purely private matter?
3. Explain how the money question increased anti-British bitterness. Was this feeling rational? irrational? To what extent is the United States today the object of such envy?
4. Explain why the free-silver craze developed the momentum that it did. Comment on the common assumption that the silverites were all ignorant, poor, and basically dishonest.
5. Would disaster have befallen America if Bryan had been elected and the Treasury had coined many dollars with the purchasing power of fifty cents each? Did Bryan's defeat help improve or worsen British-American relations?

30 · *The Path of Empire*

It has been a splendid little war [with Spain]; begun with the highest motives, carried on with magnificent intelligence and spirit, favored by that fortune which loves the brave.

JOHN HAY, 1898

PROLOGUE: As the century neared its sunset, the American people felt a strange restlessness. The frontier was filling up; factories and farms were pouring out exportable surpluses; the nation had not had a rousing war for a generation. Spain, trying desperately to crush a rebellion in Cuba with brutal measures, proved to be the whipping boy. The Big Business administration of McKinley did not want war; but public opinion, inflamed by the racy new yellow journalism, did. Spain made important eleventh-hour diplomatic concessions, but an impatient and outraged Congress declared hostilities. The United States navy was ready, and smashed two badly outmatched Spanish fleets, one at Manila, the other off Cuba. But the army was most unready. After some sharp and confused fighting in Cuba, the Spaniards hoisted the white flag. The imperialistic virus had meanwhile attacked the American people, and McKinley, their ever-obedient servant, demanded and obtained all of the Philippines in the treaty of peace signed at Paris in December, 1898.

A. YELLOW JOURNALISM IN FLOWER

1. Pulitzer Demands Intervention (1897)

The oppressed Cubans revolted in 1895, and the Spanish commander, General ("Butcher") Weyler, tried to crush them by herding them into pesthole concentration camps. Atrocities on both sides were inevitable, but the United States heard little of Cuban misdeeds. The American yellow press, with Joseph Pulitzer's New York *World* and William Randolph Hearst's New York *Journal* competing in sensationalism, headlined lurid horror tales. The basic principle of the "new journalism" seemed to be "Anything to Sell a Paper," regardless of the truth. A *World* reporter wrote from Cuba that slaughtered rebels were fed to dogs, and that children of high-ranking Spanish families clamored for Cuban ears as playthings. The following editorial in Pulitzer's *World* demanded action. What point or points probably made the heaviest impact on the American public?

How long are the Spaniards to drench Cuba with the blood and tears of her people?

How long is the peasantry of Spain to be drafted away to Cuba to die miserably in a hopeless war, that Spanish nobles and Spanish officers may get medals and honors?

1. New York *World*, Feb. 13, 1897.

How long shall old [Cuban] men and women and children be murdered by the score, the innocent victims of Spanish rage against the patriot armies they cannot conquer?

How long shall the sound of rifles in Castle Morro at sunrise proclaim that bound and helpless prisoners of war have been murdered in cold blood?

How long shall Cuban women be the victims of Spanish outrages and lie sobbing and bruised in loathsome prisons?

How long shall women passengers on vessels flying the American flag be unlawfully seized and stripped and searched by brutal, jeering Spanish officers, in violation of the laws of nations and of the honor of the United States?*

How long shall American citizens, arbitrarily arrested while on peaceful and legitimate errands, be immured in foul Spanish prisons without trial?†

How long shall the navy of the United States be used as the sea police of barbarous Spain?

How long shall the United States sit idle and indifferent within sound and hearing of rapine and murder?

How long?

2. Hearst Stages a Rescue (1897)

William R. Hearst, the irresponsible California playboy who had inherited some $20,000,000 from his father, was even more ingenious than his arch-rival Joseph Pulitzer. He is said to have boasted (with undue credit to himself) that it cost him $3,000,000 to bring on the Spanish-American War. He outdid himself in the case of Evangelina Cisneros, a "tenderly nurtured" Cuban girl of eighteen imprisoned in Havana on charges of rebellion, and reportedly facing a twenty-year incarceration with depraved fellow inmates. The yellow press pictured her as a beautiful young woman whose only crime had been to preserve her virtue against the lustful advances of a "lecherous" Spanish officer. Hearst's New York *Journal* whipped up a storm of sympathy for the girl, and inspired appeals to the Spanish Queen and to the Pope. All else failing, a *Journal* reporter rented a house next to the prison, drugged the inmates, sawed through the cell bars, and, using a forged visa, escaped with Señorita Cisneros disguised as a boy. What does this account in the *Journal* reveal about the character and the techniques of the new yellow journalism?

EVANGELINA CISNEROS RESCUED BY THE JOURNAL

AN AMERICAN NEWSPAPER ACCOMPLISHES AT A SINGLE
STROKE WHAT THE RED TAPE OF DIPLOMACY
FAILED UTTERLY TO BRING ABOUT IN
MANY MONTHS

By Charles Duval
(Copyright, 1897, by W. R. Hearst)

* The most highly publicized case actually involved an examination by a police matron.
† By 1897 there were few, if any, American citizens in Cuban prisons, even naturalized Americans of Cuban birth.
2. New York *Journal*, Oct. 10, 1897.

Havana, Oct. 7, via Key West, Fla., Oct. 9.—Evangelina Cosio y Cisneros is at liberty, and the *Journal* can place to its credit the greatest journalistic coup of this age. It is an illustration of the methods of new journalism and it will find an indorsement in the heart of every woman who has read of the horrible sufferings of the poor girl who has been confined for fifteen long months in Recojidas Prison.

The *Journal*, finding that all other methods were unavailing, decided to secure her liberation through force, and this, as the specially selected commissioner of the *Journal*, I have succeeded in doing.

I have broken the bars of Recojidas and have set free the beautiful captive of monster Weyler, restoring her to her friends and relatives, and doing by strength, skill, and strategy what could not be accomplished by petition and urgent request of the Pope.

Weyler could blind the Queen to [the] real character of Evangelina, but he could not build a jail that would hold against *Journal* enterprise when properly set to work.

Tonight all Havana rings with the story. It is the one topic of conversation; everything else pales into insignificance.

B. THE DECLARATION OF WAR

1. Madrid's Diplomatic Concessions (1898)

General Stewart L. Woodford, a New Yorker of distinguished bearing and ingratiating manner, had served as a Civil War officer, a lawyer, and a Congressman. Although an amateur diplomat, he revealed surprising skill as the American minister in Madrid. He was under instructions from the State Department to secure from Spain (a) an immediate end to the (modified) reconcentration policy, (b) the granting of an armistice to the insurgents, and (c) acknowledgment of Cuba's independence if the President deemed it necessary. After long haggling, the Madrid government ordered an end to reconcentration, March 30, 1898. Two of Woodford's subsequent cablegrams to Washington, reprinted herewith, reveal his further progress. What pressures were being exerted for peace in Madrid? Did Spain's concessions offer hope of an amicable adjustment in Cuba?

Madrid, April 9, 1898

Assistant Secretary Day, Washington:

Spanish minister for foreign affairs has just sent for me. The representatives of the European powers called upon him this morning and advised acquiescence in Pope's request for an armistice [in Cuba]. Armistice has been granted. Spanish minister in Washington instructed to notify our Department of State and yourself. Authority has been cabled to General Blanco [in Cuba] to proclaim armistice. I send verbatim memorandum just handed me by Spanish minister for foreign affairs, as follows:

"In view of the earnest and repeated request of His Holiness [the Pope], supported resolutely by declarations and friendly counsels of the repre-

1. *Foreign Relations of the United States, 1898,* p. 746.

sentatives of the six great European powers, who formulated them this morning in a collective visit to the minister of state, as corollary of the efforts of their Governments in Washington, the Spanish Government has resolved to inform the Holy Father that on this date it directs the general-in-chief [Blanco] of the army in Cuba to grant immediately a suspension of hostilities for such length of time as he may think prudent to prepare and facilitate the peace earnestly desired by all."

I hope that this dispatch may reach you before the President's message goes to Congress.

Woodford

Madrid, April 10, 1898

President McKinley, Washington:

[Referring to] My personal [dispatch] No. 66. In view of action of Spanish Government, as cabled Saturday, April 9, I hope that you can obtain full authority from Congress to do whatever you shall deem necessary to secure immediate and permanent peace in Cuba by negotiations, including the full power to employ the Army and Navy, according to your own judgment, to aid and enforce your action. If this be secured, I believe you will get final settlement before August 1 on one of the following bases: either such autonomy as the insurgents may agree to accept, or recognition by Spain of the independence of the island, or cession of the island to the United States.

I hope that nothing will now be done to humiliate Spain, as I am satisfied that the present Government is going, and is loyally ready to go, as fast and as far as it can. With your power of action sufficiently free you will win the fight on your own lines. I do not expect immediate reply, but will be glad to have an early acknowledgment of receipt.

Woodford

2. Spain Regrets the *Maine* (1898)

The American commission investigating the *Maine* had not permitted Spanish officials to examine the wreck, no doubt out of fear that the evidence might be tampered with. The Spaniards nevertheless ran their own inquiry, and concluded that the explosion was internal. (In 1976, a U.S. Navy investigation conducted by Admiral Hyman G. Rickover came to a nearly identical conclusion.) When the Spanish minister in Washington reported to the State Department his nation's recent concessions regarding Cuba, he added the following plea regarding the *Maine*. What light does it cast on the theory of Spanish official culpability, and what is the most convincing evidence of Spain's good faith?

The Government of Her Majesty doubts not that this [granting of concessions to Cuba] will be recognized by the United States Government, even as it must recognize the manifest injustice with which a portion of the public opinion of this country [U.S.] claims to discover responsibilities on

2. *Ibid.*, pp. 748–49 (April 10, 1898).

the part of Spain for the horrible catastrophe which took place on the calamitous night of the 15th of February last. Her Majesty the Queen Regent, her responsible government, the Governor-General of Cuba, the insular government, and all the higher authorities of Habana displayed from the first moment the profound sorrow and sentiments of horror which that measureless misfortune caused to them, as well as the sympathy which on that melancholy occasion linked them to the American Government and people.

Proof of this is found in the visits of Her Majesty's chargé d'affaires to the illustrious President of the United States, the visits made by the highest officers of the Spanish State to Mr. Woodford, the assistance unsparingly given to the victims, the funeral obsequies which were provided for them by the municipal council of Habana, and the notes addressed to the Department of State by this legation. . . .

The officers and crews of Her Majesty's war vessels lying near the *Maine,* heedless of the evident peril that menaced them, as is testified by the officers of that American ironclad, immediately lowered their boats, saving a large number of the wrecked ship's men, who alone owe their lives to the instant and efficient aid of the Spanish sailors.

It is singular that these well-known facts and impressive declarations seem to have been forgotten by [American] public opinion, which instead lends credence to the most absurd and offensive conjectures.

The Government of Her Majesty would very greatly esteem the sense of justice and the courtesy of the United States Government were an official statement to set the facts in their true light, for it would seem that they are ignored, and the failure to appreciate them is potentially contributing to keep up an abnormal excitement in the minds of the people that imperils, causelessly and most irrationally, the friendly relations of the two countries.

As for the question of fact which springs from the diversity of views between the reports of the Spanish and American boards, the Government of Her Majesty, although not yet possessed of the official text of the two reports, has hastened to declare itself ready to submit to the judgment of impartial and disinterested experts, accepting in advance the decision of the arbitrators named by the two parties, which is obvious proof of the frankness and good faith which marks the course of Spain on this as on all occasions.

[*The United States government failed to accept Spain's offer of arbitration.*]

3. McKinley Submits a War Message (1898)

Despite the belated concessions of Spain, McKinley sent his war message to Congress on April 11, 1898. His nerves were giving way under the constant clamor for war; his heart went out to the mistreated Cubans. (He had anonymously contributed $5000 for their relief.) He realized that Spain's offer of an armistice, at

---

3. J. D. Richardson, ed., *Messages and Papers of the Presidents* (1899), X, 147–50, *passim*.

the discretion of her commander, did not guarantee peace. The rebels had to agree on terms; and Spain had shown a talent for breaking promises and protracting negotiations. Further delay would only worsen the terrible conditions. Among the reasons that McKinley here gives Congress for intervention, which ones are the soundest and which the weakest? Was there danger in intervening for humanitarian reasons?

The grounds for such intervention may be briefly summarized as follows:

First. In the cause of humanity and to put an end to the barbarities, bloodshed, starvation, and horrible miseries now existing there, and which the parties to the conflict are either unable or unwilling to stop or mitigate. It is no answer to say this is all in another country, belonging to another nation, and is therefore none of our business. It is specially our duty, for it is right at our door.

Second. We owe it to our citizens in Cuba to afford them that protection and indemnity for life and property which no government there can or will afford, and to that end to terminate the conditions that deprive them of legal protection.

Third. The right to intervene may be justified by the very serious injury to the commerce, trade, and business of our people and by the wanton destruction of property and devastation of the island.

Fourth, and which is of the utmost importance. The present condition of affairs in Cuba is a constant menace to our peace, and entails upon this government an enormous expense. With such a conflict waged for years in an island so near us and with which our people have such trade and business relations; when the lives and liberty of our citizens are in constant danger and their property destroyed and themselves ruined; where our trading vessels are liable to seizure and are seized at our very door by warships of a foreign nation; the expeditions of filibustering [freebooting] that we are powerless to prevent altogether, and the irritating questions and entanglements thus arising—all these and others that I need not mention, with the resulting strained relations, are a constant menace to our peace and compel us to keep on a semi-war footing with a nation with which we are at peace.

These elements of danger and disorder already pointed out have been strikingly illustrated by a tragic event which has deeply and justly moved the American people. I have already transmitted to Congress the report of the Naval Court of Inquiry on the destruction of the battleship *Maine* in the harbor of Havana during the night of the 15th of February. The destruction of that noble vessel has filled the national heart with inexpressible horror. Two hundred and fifty-eight brave sailors and marines and two officers of our Navy, reposing in the fancied security of a friendly harbor, have been hurled to death, [and] grief and want brought to their homes and sorrow to the nation.

The Naval Court of Inquiry, which, it is needless to say, commands the unqualified confidence of the government, was unanimous in its conclusion that the destruction of the *Maine* was caused by an exterior explosion—that of a submarine mine.* It did not assume to place the responsibility. That remains to be fixed.

In any event, the destruction of the *Maine*, by whatever exterior cause, is a patent and impressive proof of a state of things in Cuba that is intolerable. That condition is thus shown to be such that the Spanish government cannot assure safety and security to a vessel of the American Navy in the harbor of Havana on a mission of peace, and rightfully there. . . .

[*McKinley here refers to the offer by the Spanish minister to arbitrate the* Maine, *and simply adds, "To this I have made no reply."*]

The long trial has proved that the object for which Spain has waged the war cannot be attained. The fire of insurrection may flame or may smolder with varying seasons, but it has not been, and it is plain that it cannot be, extinguished by present methods. The only hope of relief and repose from a condition which can no longer be endured is the enforced pacification of Cuba. In the name of humanity, in the name of civilization, in behalf of endangered American interests which give us the right and the duty to speak and to act, the war in Cuba must stop. . . .

The issue is now with the Congress. It is a solemn responsibility. I have exhausted every effort to relieve the intolerable condition of affairs which is at our doors. Prepared to execute every obligation imposed upon me by the Constitution and the law, I await your action.

Yesterday, and since the preparation of the foregoing message, official information was received by me that the latest decree of the Queen Regent of Spain directs General Blanco, in order to prepare and facilitate peace, to proclaim a suspension of hostilities, the duration and details of which have not yet been communicated to me.

This fact, with every other pertinent consideration, will, I am sure, have your just and careful attention in the solemn deliberations upon which you are about to enter. If this measure attains a successful result, then our aspirations as a Christian, peace-loving people will be realized. If it fails, it will be only another justification for our contemplated action.

[*The President had prepared the foregoing war message a week or so before he submitted it; the delay was primarily to permit American citizens to flee Cuba. A few hours before McKinley finally moved, the cablegrams on pp. 597– 598, above, arrived from Minister Woodford in Madrid. They brought the news that Spain, having already revoked reconcentration, had met the rest of the President's demands by authorizing an armistice. So, at the end of a message that urged war, McKinley casually tacked on the two foregoing paragraphs hinting that hostilities might be avoided. Eight days later a bellicose Congress overwhelmingly passed what was in effect a declaration of war. Several years after*

---

* Assuming that the outside-explosion theory is correct—and it has been seriously challenged —the *Maine* might have been blown up by Cuban insurgents seeking to involve the United States in the war.

the event General Woodford told O. G. Villard, "When I sent that last cable to McKinley, I thought I should wake up the next morning to find myself acclaimed all over the United States for having achieved the greatest diplomatic victory in our history. . . ." Instead, he learned of the war message. (O. G. Villard, Fighting Years *[1939], p. 136.)]*

4. Professor Norton's Patriotic Protest (1898)

Lovable and immensely popular, Charles Eliot Norton served for many years at Harvard as professor of the history of the fine arts. After war broke out, he shocked public opinion with a speech in Cambridge urging young men not to enlist. The press denounced him as one of the "intellectual copperheads." McKinley had recommended war in the interests of civilization; Norton here urges an opposite course. Who had the sounder arguments? Was it more patriotic to protest than to acquiesce?

And now of a sudden, without cool deliberation, without prudent preparation, the nation is hurried into war, and America, she who more than any other land was pledged to peace and good will on earth, unsheathes her sword, compels a weak and unwilling nation to a fight, rejecting without due consideration her [Spain's] earnest and repeated offers to meet every legitimate demand of the United States. It is a bitter disappointment to the lover of his country; it is a turning back from the path of civilization to that of barbarism.

"There never was a good war," said Franklin. There have indeed been many wars in which a good man must take part. . . . But if a war be undertaken for the most righteous end, before the resources of peace have been tried and proved vain to secure it, that war has no defense. It is a national crime. The plea that the better government of Cuba, and the relief of the *reconcentrados,* could only be secured by war is the plea either of ignorance or of hypocrisy.

But the war is declared; and on all hands we hear the cry that he is no patriot who fails to shout for it, and to urge the youth of the country to enlist, and to rejoice that they are called to the service of their native land. The sober counsels that were appropriate before the war was entered upon must give way to blind enthusiasm, and the voice of condemnation must be silenced by the thunders of the guns and the hurrahs of the crowd.

Stop! A declaration of war does not change the moral law. "The Ten Commandments will not budge" at a joint resolve of Congress. . . . No! the voice of protest, of warning, of appeal is never more needed than when the clamor of fife and drum, echoed by the press and too often by the pulpit, is bidding all men fall in and keep step and obey in silence the tyrannous word of command. Then, more than ever, it is the duty of the good citizen not to be silent, and spite of obliquity, misrepresentation, and abuse, to insist on being heard, and with sober counsel to maintain the everlasting validity of the principles of the moral law.

4. *Public Opinion,* XXIV, 775–76 (June 23, 1898).

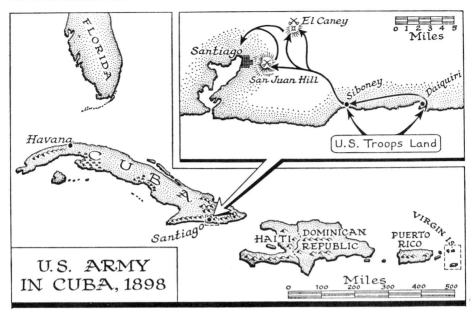

U.S. ARMY IN CUBA, 1898

C. THE SORDID LITTLE WAR

1. Rough Times for Rough Riders (1898)

Fight-thirsty Theodore Roosevelt was so determined to get into action that he resigned his post as Assistant Secretary of the Navy. He hastily raised a volunteer cavalry outfit and, as lieutenant colonel of these Rough Riders, managed to reach Cuba—without the horses. Exposing himself with reckless courage, he got into the thick of the fray and won renown near Santiago. But commanding General Shafter was too fat for active duty, the "embalmed beef" was vomit-inducing, and most of the volunteers were poorly trained and equipped. They betrayed their position with old-fashioned, smoke-emitting powder; and one outfit dragged around a captive balloon, thereby revealing its movements. The easy naval victories, combined with the nation's holiday mood and John Hay's reference to the "splendid little war," left a false impression of glamour. What does Roosevelt's letter to his close friend, Senator Henry Cabot Lodge, suggest about this romantic image of the war? About Roosevelt's character?

Outside Santiago, July 3, 1898

Dear Cabot: Tell the President for Heaven's sake to send us every regiment and, above all, every battery possible. We have won so far at a heavy cost; but the Spaniards fight very hard, and charging these intrenchments against modern rifles is terrible. We are within measurable distance of a terrible military disaster; we *must* have help—thousands of men, batteries, and *food* and ammunition. The other volunteers are at a hideous disadvantage owing to their not having smokeless powder. Our General [Shafter] is poor; he is too unwieldy to get to the front. I commanded my regiment, I think I may say, with honor. We lost a quarter of our men. For three days I have been at the extreme front of the firing line; how I have escaped I know not; I have not blanket or coat; I have not taken off my shoes even; I sleep in the drenching rain, and drink putrid water. Best love to Nannie.

2. Disillusionment over the Cubans (1898)

The American press, in playing up Spanish atrocities, had idealized the nondescript Cuban insurgents and their shadowy government. The liberating United States troops were speedily disillusioned. They had to restrain their ragged allies from pillaging towns, shooting Spanish prisoners, and butchering the wounded. The insurgents flatly refused to help their deliverers with such menial tasks as building roads and carrying American wounded from the battlefield. American anger and contempt naturally bred Cuban resentment. In the Teller Amendment, passed by Congress in 1898, the United States had pledged itself to free Cuba; in the Platt Amendment, passed by Congress in 1902, Washington reserved the right to intervene to preserve order. What was the relationship between the Platt Amendment and the views expressed in the following Virginia editorial?

Day by day the news from Santiago brings out more clearly the real character of the majority of the Cuban insurgents. Men who have to be prevented by force from killing prisoners and plundering surrendered cities are not likely to make admirable citizens of an independent country. Liberty, according to their conception of it, would truly be synonymous with many crimes.

In the meanwhile, let us be thankful that the President [McKinley] stood so strongly against the recognition of the alleged insurgent government—a step which was urged with cease-

PEACE! — AND AFTER?

Spain (to Uncle Sam): "Well, you wanted him! You've got him! And I wish you joy of him!!" *Punch* (London), 1898.

2. Norfolk (Va.) *Landmark,* in *Public Opinion,* XXV, 104 (July 28, 1898).

less vehemence by many influential members of Congress, and by innumerable orators and periodicals. Wouldn't we have been in a pretty predicament if we had found ourselves obliged at every point to bow to the wishes of the undisciplined, bloodthirsty guerrillas who seem to compose the majority of the insurgent forces?

Of course, we believe that Cuba will rise from her ruin and show herself fully worthy of the attempt that has been made to save her, but a good many years will pass before it will be safe for the United States to withdraw their troops and leave the island to her own devices. Even then, it is a question whether Cuban independence outside of the Union will be a success or a failure.

D. THE SIREN SONG OF IMPERIALISM

1. McKinley Prays for Guidance (1898)

What to do with the conquered Philippines? At first McKinley considered taking only a foothold at Manila, on the main island of Luzon. But this would be rendered militarily untenable if the remaining islands should fall into the hands of an unfriendly power, possibly Germany. The decision then lay between all or nothing. To hand back the islands to Spain was unthinkable. After fighting a war to free Cuba from Spanish misrule, America could hardly return the Filipinos, who had likewise risen in revolt, to Spanish misrule. To cut them completely loose might result in a mad scramble among the powers that would touch off a world war into which America might be drawn. McKinley had to make the decision while badly upset by the murder of his brother-in-law at the hands of a betrayed woman. He later told a group of fellow Methodists how he sought divine guidance, presumably late in October, 1898. How sound is McKinley's reasoning? Are there elements of racism in his thinking?

When next I realized that the Philippines had dropped into our laps, I confess I did not know what to do with them. I sought counsel from all sides—Democrats as well as Republicans—but got little help. I thought first we would take only Manila; then Luzon; then other islands, perhaps, also.

I walked the floor of the White House night after night until midnight; and I am not ashamed to tell you, gentlemen, that I went down on my knees and prayed Almighty God for light and guidance more than one night. And one night late it came to me this way—I dont know how it was, but it came:

(1) That we could not give them back to Spain—that would be cowardly and dishonorable;

(2) That we could not turn them over to France or Germany, our commercial rivals in the Orient—that would be bad business and discreditable;

---

1. This document is a report of an interview with McKinley at the White House, November 21, 1899, written by one of the interviewers and confirmed by others present. Published in *The Christian Advocate,* Jan. 22, 1903, it is here reprinted from C. S. Olcott, *The Life of William McKinley* (1916), II, 110–11.

(3) That we could not leave them to themselves—they were unfit for self-government, and they would soon have anarchy and misrule worse than Spain's was; and

(4) That there was nothing left for us to do but to take them all, and to educate the Filipinos, and uplift and civilize and Christianize them and by God's grace do the very best we could by them, as our fellow men, for whom Christ also died.

And then I went to bed and went to sleep, and slept soundly, and the next morning I sent for the chief engineer of the War Department (our map-maker), and I told him to put the Philippines on the map of the United States (pointing to a large map on the wall of his office), and there they are and there they will stay while I am President!

2. Professor Sumner Spurns Empire (1898)

The "magnificently bald" and "iron-voiced" Professor William G. Sumner, of Yale, was an immensely popular lecturer and a leading anti-imperialist. Fearlessly outspoken, he offended influential alumni by opposing tariff protection and by turning a cynical eye on America's "civilizing mission" in the Philippines. The truth is that the more obvious the natural resources of the islands became, the less capable the inhabitants seemed of self-rule. The moral obligation of the "White Man's Burden," which the British poet Kipling urged the United States to shoulder, had many of the earmarks of the loot sack. The British welcomed Americans as fellow civilizers, no doubt in part because imperialistic misery loved company. Why does Sumner believe that the conquered peoples would be unlikely to accept American rule, and that such rule was a perversion of American principles?

There is not a civilized nation which does not talk about its civilizing mission just as grandly as we do. The English, who really have more to boast of in this respect than anybody else, talk least about it, but the Phariseeism with which they correct and instruct other people has made them hated all over the globe. The French believe themselves the guardians of the highest and purest culture, and that the eyes of all mankind are fixed on Paris, whence they expect oracles of thought and taste. The Germans regard themselves as charged with a mission, especially to us Americans, to save us from egoism and materialism. The Russians, in their books and newspapers, talk about the civilizing mission of Russia in language that might be translated from some of the finest paragraphs in our imperialistic newspapers.

The first principle of Mohammedanism is that we Christians are dogs and infidels, fit only to be enslaved or butchered by Moslems. It is a corollary that wherever Mohammedanism extends it carries, in the belief of its votaries, the highest blessings, and that the whole human race would be enormously elevated if Mohammedanism should supplant Christianity everywhere.

2. W. G. Sumner, *War and Other Essays* (1919), pp. 303–05. By permission of the Yale University Press.

To come, last, to Spain, the Spaniards have, for centuries, considered themselves the most zealous and self-sacrificing Christians, especially charged by the Almighty, on this account, to spread true religion and civilization over the globe. They think themselves free and noble, leaders in refinement and the sentiments of personal honor, and they despise us as sordid money-grabbers and heretics. I could bring you passages from peninsular authors of the first rank about the grand rôle of Spain and Portugal in spreading freedom and truth.

Now each nation laughs at all the others when it observes these manifestations of national vanity. You may rely upon it that they are all ridiculous by virtue of these pretensions, including ourselves. The point is that each of them repudiates the standards of the others, and the outlying nations, which are to be civilized, hate all the standards of civilized men.

We assume that what we like and practice, and what we think better, must come as a welcome blessing to Spanish-Americans and Filipinos. This is grossly and obviously untrue. They hate our ways. They are hostile to our ideas. Our religion, language, institutions, and manners offend them. They like their own ways, and if we appear amongst them as rulers, there will be social discord in all the great departments of social interest. The most important thing which we shall inherit from the Spaniards will be the task of suppressing rebellions.

If the United States takes out of the hands of Spain her mission, on the ground that Spain is not executing it well, and if this nation in its turn attempts to be schoolmistress to others, it will shrivel up into the same vanity and self-conceit of which Spain now presents an example. To read our current literature one would think that we were already well on the way to it.

Now, the great reason why all these enterprises which begin by saying to somebody else, "We know what is good for you better than you know yourself and we are going to make you do it," are false and wrong is that they violate liberty; or, to turn the same statement into other words, the reason why liberty, of which we Americans talk so much, is a good thing is that it means leaving people to live out their own lives in their own way, while we do the same.

If we believe in liberty, as an American principle, why do we not stand by it? Why are we going to throw it away to enter upon a Spanish policy of dominion and regulation?

3. Beveridge Trumpets Imperialism (1898)

Albert J. Beveridge delivered this famous speech, "The March of the Flag," at Indianapolis, Indiana, on September 16, 1898, before McKinley had decided to keep the Philippines. Born to an impoverished family, Beveridge had spent his youth at hard manual labor, but ultimately secured a college education with prizes won in oratorical contests. The cadences of his spellbinding oratory were such that

3. C. M. Depew, ed., *The Library of Oratory* (1902), XIV, 438–40.

"Mr. Dooley" (F. P. Dunne) said you could waltz to them. The year after making this address Beveridge was elected to the United States Senate from Indiana at the remarkably youthful age of thirty-six. How convincing is his reply to the anti-imperialists' warnings against the annexation of non-contiguous territory and to their argument that no more land was needed? What were his powers as a prophet?

Distance and oceans are no arguments. The fact that all the territory our fathers bought and seized is contiguous is no argument. In 1819 Florida was further from New York than Porto Rico is from Chicago today; Texas, further from Washington in 1845 than Hawaii is from Boston in 1898; California, more inaccessible in 1847 than the Philippines are now. . . . The ocean does not separate us from lands of our duty and desire—the oceans join us, a river never to be dredged, a canal never to be repaired.

Steam joins us; electricity joins us—the very elements are in league with our destiny. Cuba not contiguous! Porto Rico not contiguous! Hawaii and the Philippines not contiguous! Our navy will make them contiguous. [Admirals] Dewey and Sampson and Schley have made them contiguous, and American speed, American guns, American heart and brain and nerve will keep them contiguous forever.

But the Opposition is right—there is a difference. We did not need the western Mississippi Valley when we acquired it, nor Florida, nor Texas, nor California, nor the royal provinces of the far Northwest. We had no emigrants to people this imperial wilderness, no money to develop it, even no highways to cover it. No trade awaited us in its savage fastnesses. Our productions were not greater than our trade. There was not one reason for the land-lust of our statesmen from Jefferson to Grant, other than the prophet and the Saxon within them.

But today we are raising more than we can consume. Today we are making more than we can use. Today our industrial society is congested; there are more workers than there is work; there is more capital than there is investment. We do not need more money—we need more circulation, more employment. Therefore we must find new markets for our produce, new occupation for our capital, new work for our labor. And so, while we did not need the territory taken during the past century at the time it was acquired, we do need what we have taken in 1898, and we need it now.

Think of the thousands of Americans who will pour into Hawaii and Porto Rico when the republic's laws cover those islands with justice and safety! Think of the tens of thousands of Americans who will invade mine and field and forest in the Philippines when a liberal government, protected and controlled by this republic, if not the government of the republic itself, shall establish order and equity there! Think of the hundreds of thousands of Americans who will build a soap-and-water, common-school civilization of energy and industry in Cuba, when a government of law replaces the double reign of anarchy and tyranny!—think of the prosperous millions that Empress of Islands will support when, obedient to the law of political gravitation, her people ask for the highest honor liberty can bestow, the sacred Order of the Stars and Stripes, the citizenship of the Great Republic!

What does all this mean for every one of us? It means opportunity for all the glorious young manhood of the republic—the most virile, ambitious, impatient, militant manhood the world has ever seen. It means that the resources and the commerce of these immensely rich dominions will be increased as much as American energy is greater than Spanish sloth; for Americans henceforth will monopolize those resources and that commerce.

[*The Treaty of Paris, by which the United States acquired the Philippines, received Senate approval by a close vote on February 6, 1899. The imperialists had little to add to the materialistic-humanitarian arguments herein presented by McKinley and Beveridge. The anti-imperialists stressed the unwisdom of annexing non-contiguous areas in the tropics thickly populated by alien peoples. They also harped on the folly of departing from the principles of freedom and non-intervention as set forth in the Declaration of Independence, Washington's Farewell Address, the Monroe Doctrine, and the Emancipation Proclamation. Senator Hoar of Massachusetts assailed the imperialists with these words: "If you ask them what they want, you are answered with a shout: 'Three cheers for the flag! Who will dare to haul it down? Hold on to everything you can get. The United States is strong enough to do what it likes. The Declaration of Independence and the counsel of Washington and the Constitution of the United States have grown rusty and musty. They are for little countries and not for great ones. There is no moral law for strong nations. America has outgrown Americanism.'"* (Congressional Record, 55 Cong., 3 sess., p. 495.)]

THOUGHT PROVOKERS

1. Have the newspapers in a democracy an ethical responsibility to pursue sober policies, even though such tactics hurt circulation? Has the press shown more responsibility in recent years than in 1898?

2. Should a diplomat be dismissed because of a *private* letter stolen from the mails? Were patriotic Spaniards justified in resenting American attitudes and accusations in 1897–1898? Should the United States have accepted arbitration of the *Maine* dispute?

3. It has been said that a joint-power intervention in Cuba for humanitarian reasons would have been on sounder ground than America's unilateral intervention. Explain. Using McKinley's reasoning, would Spain have been justified in intervening in the American Civil War to prevent continued bloodshed off Cuba's shores? Would a grant of autonomy have solved the Cuban problem?

4. To what extent were the anti-imperialists idealists? Was there anything morally objectionable in their attitude?

5. In the long run would the United States have been better off if it had kept Cuba and relinquished the Philippines? Did intervention solve the Cuban problem? Has the White Man's Burden proved to be unselfish or a cover for selfishness?

The mission of the United States is one of benevolent assimilation.

PRESIDENT MC KINLEY, 1898

PROLOGUE: The resentful Filipinos, unwilling to be caged by American overlords, revolted in 1899. The insurrection dragged on scandalously for seven years. In 1900 the Democratic Bryan, trumpeting anti-imperialism as the "paramount issue," again ran unsuccessfully against the prosperity President, William McKinley. The victor was fatally shot late in 1901 after serving only six months of his second term. Theodore Roosevelt, moving up from the Vice-Presidency, promptly launched a two-fisted, Big Stick foreign policy. By strong-arm methods, he secured a canal zone at Panama, and then "made the dirt fly." By devising the Roosevelt corollary to the Monroe Doctrine, he intervened in the bankrupt Dominican Republic to prevent other powers from intervening. By mediating a settlement at the end of the Russo-Japanese War in 1905, he won the Nobel Peace Prize. And by interceding in the quarrel between California and Japan over Japanese immigrants, he worked out the "Gentlemen's Agreement" for amicably halting the inflow.

A. THE BITTER FRUITS OF IMPERIALISM

1. Beveridge Deplores Unpatriotic Talk (1900)

The Filipino troops, under their leader Emilio Aguinaldo, had cooperated loyally with the Americans in capturing Manila. They had received informal promises of freedom, but when these were not honored, they rose in revolt. The fighting between Filipinos and Americans rapidly degenerated into brutal guerrilla warfare. Albert J. Beveridge of Indiana (see p. 581), recently elected to the United States Senate, went to the Philippines on a personal tour of inspection and reported his findings in an impressive Senate speech. Should the anti-imperialists have been silenced by his argument?

It has been charged that our conduct of the war has been cruel. Senators, it has been the reverse. I have been in our hospitals and seen the Filipino wounded as carefully, tenderly cared for as our own. Within our lines they may plow and sow and reap and go about the affairs of peace with absolute liberty. And yet all this kindness was misunderstood, or rather not understood. Senators must remember that we are not dealing with Americans or Europeans. We are dealing with Orientals. We are dealing with Orientals who are Malays. We are dealing with Malays instructed in Spanish methods. They mistake kindness for weakness, forbearance for fear. . . .

---

1. *Congressional Record*, 56 Cong., 1 sess., p. 708 (Jan. 9, 1900).

SENATOR BEVERIDGE URGES PHILIPPINE IMPERIALISM
America ignores Puerto Rico bound hand and foot with tariffs.
Brooklyn *Daily Eagle*, 1900.

Mr. President, reluctantly and only from a sense of duty am I forced to say that American opposition to the war has been the chief factor in prolonging it. Had Aguinaldo not understood that in America, even in the American Congress, even here in the Senate, he and his cause were supported; had he not known that it was proclaimed on the stump and in the press of a faction in the United States that every shot his misguided followers fired into the breasts of American soldiers was like the volleys fired by Washington's men against the soldiers of King George, his insurrection would have dissolved before it entirely crystallized.

The utterances of American opponents of the war are read to the ignorant soldiers of Aguinaldo, and repeated in exaggerated form among the common people. Attempts have been made by wretches claiming American citizenship to ship arms and ammunition from Asiatic ports to the Filipinos, and these acts of infamy were coupled by the Malays with American assaults on our government at home.

The Filipinos do not understand free speech, and therefore our tolerance of American assaults on the American President and the American government means to them that our President is in the minority or he would not permit what appears to them such treasonable criticism. It is believed and stated in [the islands of] Luzon, Panay, and Cebu that the Filipinos have only to fight, harass, retreat, break up into small parties, if necessary, as they are doing now, but by any means hold out until the next presidential election, and our forces will be withdrawn.

All this has aided the enemy more than climate, arms, and battle. Senators, I have heard these reports myself; I have talked with the people; I have seen our mangled boys in the hospital and field; I have stood on the firing line and beheld our dead soldiers, their faces turned to the pitiless southern sky, and in sorrow rather than anger I say to those whose voices in America have cheered those misguided natives on to shoot our soldiers down, that the blood of those dead and wounded boys of ours is on their hands, and the flood of all the years can never wash that stain away. In sorrow rather than anger I say these words, for I earnestly believe that our brothers knew not what they did.

2. Bryan Vents His Bitterness (1901)

In 1900 the Republican President McKinley, who favored keeping the Philippines, again ran against the Democrat William J. Bryan, who favored giving them independence. Republicans accused Bryan of prolonging the insurrection by holding out false hopes. One popular magazine published a picture of the Filipino leader on its front cover, with the query, "Who is behind Aguinaldo?" The curious reader lifted a flap and saw the hawklike features of Bryan. McKinley triumphed by a handsome margin, and Republicans misleadingly hailed the results as a national mandate to retain the islands. The next year Bryan expressed his bitterness as follows, several months after the Americans had captured Aguinaldo. What is his strongest rebuttal to Republican charges that the Democrats were responsible for prolonging the insurrection? How good a prophet was Bryan?

In the campaign of 1900 the Republican leaders denied that their party contemplated a permanent increase in the standing army. They asserted that a large army was only necessary because of the insurrection in the Philippines, and they boldly declared that the insurrection would cease immediately if the Republican ticket was successful. The Democratic platform and Democratic speakers were blamed for the prolongation of the war. "Just re-elect President McKinley," they said, "and let the Filipinos know they are not to have independence, and they will lay down their arms and our soldiers can come home."

Well, the Republican ticket was elected, and the Filipinos were notified that they were not to have independence. But a month after the election the Republicans rushed through Congress a bill authorizing the President to raise the regular army to 100,000, and now, after a year has elapsed, the insurrection is still in progress and the end is not yet. Some of the worst losses of the year have been suffered by our troops within two months. . . .

After the Republican victory made it impossible for the imperialists to blame the anti-imperialists for the continuation of hostilities, the Republican leaders declared that Aguinaldo, actuated by selfish ambition, was compelling his countrymen to continue the war. But even after his capture and imprisonment—yes, even after his captors had secured from him an address advising his comrades to surrender—the insurrection continued.

How long will it take the imperialists to learn that we can never have peace in the Philippine Islands? That we can suppress open resistance is certain, although the cost may be far beyond any gain that can be derived from a colonial government, but that we can ever make the Filipinos love us or trust us while we rule them through a carpetbag government is absurd.

2. *The Commoner*, Nov. 22, 1901.

If the Republicans had read the speeches of Abraham Lincoln as much recently as they did in former years, they would have known that hatred of an alien government is a natural thing and a thing to be expected everywhere. Lincoln said that it was God himself who placed in every human heart the love of liberty. . . .

3. *The Nation* Denounces Atrocities (1902)

Many of the Filipino tribesmen were simple peoples who knew little of so-called "civilized warfare." Some of them would horribly mutilate and torture American captives, sometimes fastening them down to be eaten alive by insects. The infuriated white soldiers retaliated by shooting a few prisoners and by administering the "water cure"—that is, forcing buckets of dirty water into Filipinos, deflating them with rifle butts, and repeating the painful process. In certain areas, the Americans herded the populace into reconcentration camps, somewhat after the manner of "Butcher" Weyler in Cuba. General Jacob ("Hell Roaring Jake") Smith was "admonished" by the War Department for an order (not carried out) to kill all males over ten years of age on the island of Samar. How sound is the parallel that the New York *Nation* here draws between Spanish behavior in Cuba and American behavior in the Philippines?

Even if the condemnation of barbarous warfare in the Philippines by the imperialist press is somewhat belated, we welcome it, as we welcome everything that compels Americans to give attention to a subject to which too many of them have become increasingly indifferent. Silence, we know, is consistent with shame, and may be one of the signs of its existence; and the fact that only a few of the more unblushing or foolish newspapers have defended Gen. Smith's policy of extermination shows what the general sentiment is.

To allege the provocation which our soldiers had is to set up a defense which President Roosevelt brushed aside in advance. To fall back on the miserable sophistry that "war is hell" is only another way of making out those who engage in that kind of war to be fiends. It is, besides, to offer an excuse for ourselves which we did not tolerate for an instant in the case of Spanish atrocities. That is our present moral humiliation in the eyes of the world.

We made war on Spain four years ago for doing the very things of which we are now guilty ourselves. As the Chicago *News* pointedly observes, we are giving Spain as good reason to interfere with us on the ground of humanity as we had to interfere with her. Doubtless she would interfere if she were strong enough and thought she could acquire some islands in the virtuous act.

4. A San Francisco Weekly Defends the Army (1902)

Moderate defenders of the Republican administration replied that the charges of cruelty were grossly exaggerated, that atrocity stories were being used by Democrats

3. *The Nation* (New York), LXXIV, 357 (May 8, 1902).
4. San Francisco *Argonaut*, L, 342 (May 26, 1902).

for partisan advantage, and that in any event such tales did not affect the question of America's duty in the Philippines. The *Outlook* (April 26, 1902) concluded: "The humanity of the army as a whole cannot be discredited by single acts of cruelty, no matter how abhorrent these may be in their character." The extreme imperialists openly avowed a policy of brutality. Shockingly frank was the San Francisco *Argonaut*, a respectable and long-lived weekly magazine. How does it apportion the blame for the existing situation, between Republicans and Democrats? What force is there in its case for the army?

There has been too much hypocrisy about this Philippine business—too much snivel—too much cant. Let us all be frank.

WE DO NOT WANT THE FILIPINOS.

WE WANT THE PHILIPPINES.

All of our troubles in this annexation matter have been caused by the presence in the Philippine Islands of the Filipinos. Were it not for them, the Treaty of Paris would have been an excellent thing; the purchase of the archipelago for twenty millions of dollars would have been cheap. The islands are enormously rich; they abound in dense forests of valuable hardwood timber; they contain mines of the precious metals; their fertile lands will produce immense crops of sugar cane, rice, and tobacco. Touched by the wand of American enterprise, fertilized with American capital, these islands would speedily become richer than Golconda was of old.

But, unfortunately, they are infested by Filipinos. There are many millions of them there, and it is to be feared that their extinction will be slow. Still, every man who believes in developing the islands must admit that it cannot be done successfully while the Filipinos are there. They are indolent. They raise only enough food to live on; they don't care to make money; and they occupy land which might be utilized to much better advantage by Americans. Therefore the more of them killed, the better.

It seems harsh. But they must yield before the superior race, and the American syndicate. How shortsighted, then, to check the army in its warfare upon these savages; particularly when the army is merely carrying out its orders and the duly expressed wishes of the American people, as shown through their elections and their representatives.

Doubtless, many of the excellent gentlemen now in Congress would repudiate these sentiments as brutal. But we are only saying what they are doing. We believe in stripping all hypocritical verbiage from national declarations, and telling the truth simply and boldly. We repeat—the American people, after thought and deliberation, have shown their wishes. THEY DO NOT WANT THE FILIPINOS. THEY WANT THE PHILIPPINES.

It is no one party, no one class, that is responsible for our Philippine policy. It is the people of the United States. The Democratic Party shares equally the responsibility with the Republican Party. The Democratic Party voted for the war with Spain. Had it opposed the fifty-million [arms] appropriation, the war could not have taken place. The Democrats advocated the purchase of the Philippines. For a time the confirmation of the Philippine treaty was in doubt. It was the direct personal lobbying of William J. Bryan with the Democratic Senators which led to the confirmation of the Philippine purchase, and which also led to the present bloody war. Mr. Bryan said at the time that he advocated the confirmation of the treaty in order to put "the Republicans into a hole." He has certainly put his country into a hole. Is he proud of his work?

We are all responsible. You, reader, are responsible. If you are a Republican, your party has made this action part of its national policy. If you are a Democrat, your party, by its vote in the House of Representatives, made the war possible, and by its vote in the Senate turned the scales for the purchase of the Philippines.

But if we, the people of the United States, are responsible for the Philippine campaign, the American army is not. The army is only seventy thousand out of seventy millions. The army did not ask to go there. It was sent. It has fought for four years under tropic suns and torrential rains, in pestilential jungles and miasmatic swamps, patiently bearing the burdens placed upon it by the home country, and with few laurels to be gained as a result of hard and dangerous duty. Nearly every general officer returning from the Philippines has returned to either a wrecked reputation, newspaper odium, or public depreciation. Look at Merritt, Otis, Merriam, MacArthur, Funston. The best treatment that any of them has received is not to be abused. And yet, with these melancholy examples before them, our army toils on uncomplainingly doing its duty.

The army did not bring on the war. We civilians did it. The army is only doing our bidding as faithful servants of their country. And now that they have shown a perfectly human tendency to fight the devil with fire, we must not repudiate their actions, for their actions are our own. They are receiving the fire of the enemy from the front. It is shameful that there should be a fire upon them from the rear.

B. THE PANAMA REVOLUTION

1. Hay Twists Colombia's Arm (1903)

The Spanish-American War, which netted a far-flung empire, increased public pressure for an isthmian canal. Nicaragua had long been the favored route, but in 1902 Congress approved Colombia's Isthmus of Panama. Secretary of State Hay, by threatening to revert to the Nicaragua route, finally secured a treaty from the reluctant Colombian envoy in Washington. But the Senate of Colombia delayed ratification, for it was dissatisfied with the rather niggardly financial terms offered for this priceless asset—$10,000,000 plus an annual payment of $250,000. Secretary Hay thereupon sent the following telegram to the American minister in Bogotá, the capital of Colombia. Critics have contended that this statement contains an intolerable threat to a sovereign republic. Does it?

1. *Foreign Relations of the United States, 1903*, p. 146.

Department of State
Washington, June 9, 1903

The Colombian Government apparently does not appreciate the gravity of the situation. The canal negotiations were initiated by Colombia, and were energetically pressed upon this Government for several years. The propositions presented by Colombia, with slight modifications, were finally accepted by us. In virtue of this agreement our Congress reversed its previous judgment [favoring Nicaragua] and decided upon the Panama route. If Colombia should now reject the treaty or unduly delay its ratification, the friendly understanding between the two countries would be so seriously compromised that action might be taken by the Congress next winter which every friend of Colombia would regret. Confidential. Communicate substance of this verbally to the minister of foreign affairs. If he desires it, give him a copy in form of memorandum.

Hay

[*When the American envoy in Bogotá conveyed this stern message to the foreign minister, the latter asked whether the threat meant hostile measures against Colombia or the adoption of the Nicaragua route. The American was unable to answer. Actually, Secretary Hay took liberties with the truth when he stated that Colombia had "energetically pressed" canal negotiations for several years. Washington had done the pressing.*]

2. Roosevelt Hopes for Revolt (1903)

The Colombian Senate unanimously rejected the canal-zone treaty on August 12, 1903. Among other motives, it hoped to secure for Colombia an additional $40,000,-000—the sum that Washington was proposing to pay the heirs of the French company that had started the canal in the 1870's. The Panamanians feared that the United States would now turn to Nicaragua, as the law required Roosevelt to do if blocked, and thus deprive the Panamanians of the anticipated prosperity that the canal would bring. They had revolted against Colombia's misrule fifty-three times in the past fifty-seven years (by Roosevelt's count), and they were now riper than ever for rebellion. The following letter that Roosevelt sent to Dr. Albert Shaw, editor of the *Review of Reviews*, is often cited as evidence that he connived at the revolt. Does it provide good supporting evidence for that conclusion?

My dear Dr. Shaw: I enclose you, purely for your own information, a copy of a letter of September 5th from our Minister to Colombia. I think it might interest you to see that there was absolutely not the slightest chance of securing by treaty any more than we endeavored to secure. The alternatives were to go to Nicaragua, against the advice of the great majority of competent engineers—some of the most competent saying that we

2. Reprinted by permission of the publishers from *The Letters of Theodore Roosevelt,* edited by E. E. Morison (Cambridge, Mass.: Harvard University Press), copyright © 1951, 1952 by the President and Fellows of Harvard College, © 1979, 1980 by E. E. Morison.

had better have no canal at this time than go there—or else to take the territory by force without any attempt at getting a treaty.

I cast aside the proposition made at this time to foment the secession of Panama. Whatever other governments can do, the United States cannot go into the securing by such underhand means, the secession. Privately, I freely say to you that I should be delighted if Panama were an independent State, or if it made itself so at this moment; but for me to say so publicly would amount to an instigation of revolt, and therefore I cannot say it.

3. Official Connivance in Washington (1903)

The rebels in Panama, encouraged by Roosevelt's ill-concealed anger, revolted on November 3, 1903. Under the ancient treaty of 1846 with Colombia, the United States had guaranteed the neutrality of the Isthmus, obviously against *foreign invaders*. In this case Roosevelt guaranteed the neutrality of the Isthmus by having orders issued to the *Nashville* and other United States naval units to prevent Colombian troops from landing and crossing from the Atlantic port of Colón to Panama City and crushing the rebellion. On November 4, 1903, Panama proclaimed her independence. A little more than an hour after receiving the news, Roosevelt hastily authorized *de facto* recognition, which was extended on November 6, 1903. This unseemly haste suggested improper connivance by Washington, and in response to a public demand Roosevelt sent the following official documents to Congress. They consist of interchanges between Acting Secretary of State Loomis (Hay was then absent) and the American Vice Consul General at Panama City, Felix Ehrman. What do these documents suggest about American complicity in the Panamanian revolution?

Mr. Loomis to Mr. Ehrman
Department of State
Washington, November 3, 1903
(Sent 3:40 P.M.)

Uprising on Isthmus reported. Keep Department promptly and fully informed.

Loomis, Acting

Mr. Ehrman to Mr. Hay
Panama, November 3, 1903
(Received 8:15 P.M.)

No uprising yet. Reported will be in the night. Situation is critical.

Ehrman

Mr. Ehrman to Mr. Hay
Panama, November 3, 1903
(Received 9:50 P.M.)

Uprising occurred [at Panama City] tonight, 6; no bloodshed. [Colombian] Army and navy officials taken prisoners. Government will be organ-

---

3. Senate Documents, 58 Cong., 2 sess., No. 51, p. 104.

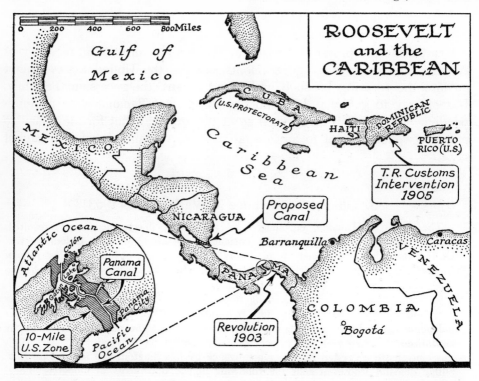

ized tonight, consisting three consuls, also cabinet. Soldiers changed. Supposed same movement will be effected in Colón. Order prevails so far. Situation serious. Four hundred [Colombian] soldiers landed Colón today [from] Barranquilla.

Ehrman

Mr. Loomis to Mr. Ehrman
Department of State
Washington, November 3, 1903
(Sent 11:18 P.M.)

Message sent to *Nashville* to Colón may not have been delivered. Accordingly see that following message is sent to *Nashville* immediately: *Nashville*, Colón:

In the interests of peace make every effort to prevent [Colombian] Government troops at Colón from proceeding to Panama. The transit of the Isthmus must be kept open and order maintained. Acknowledge.

(signed) Darling, Acting [Secretary of Navy]

Secure special train [to deliver message], if necessary. Act promptly.

Loomis, Acting

[*Resolute action by Commander Hubbard of the* Nashville, *in response to his instructions from Washington, forced the Colombian troops to sail away from Colón on November 5, two days after the revolutionists had seized Panama City.*]

C. THE MONROE DOCTRINE IN THE CARIBBEAN

1. Roosevelt Launches a Corollary (1904)

The corrupt and bankrupt "banana republics" of the Caribbean were inclined to overborrow, and Roosevelt believed that they could properly be "spanked" by European creditors. But the British-German "spanking" of Venezuela in 1902 resulted in the sinking of two Venezuelan gunboats and the bombardment of a fort and village. Such interventions foreshadowed a possibly permanent foothold and a consequent violation of the Monroe Doctrine. Sensing this danger, Roosevelt, in his annual message to Congress of 1904, sketched out his famous corollary to the Monroe Doctrine. Monroe had in effect warned the European powers in 1823, "Hands Off." Roosevelt was now saying that since the United States would not permit the powers to lay their hands on, he had an obligation to do so himself. In short, he would intervene to keep them from intervening. In the statement embodied in his annual message, how does he justify this newly announced American role, and what assurances does he give to the Latin American countries?

It is not true that the United States feels any land hunger or entertains any projects as regards the other nations of the Western Hemisphere, save such as are for their welfare. All that this country desires is to see the neighboring countries stable, orderly, and prosperous. Any country whose people conduct themselves well can count upon our hearty friendship. If a nation shows that it knows how to act with reasonable efficiency and decency in social and political matters, if it keeps order and pays its obligations, it need fear no interference from the United States.

Chronic wrongdoing, or an impotence which results in a general loosening of the ties of civilized society, may in America, as elsewhere, ultimately require intervention by some civilized nation, and in the Western Hemisphere the adherence of the United States to the Monroe Doctrine may force the United States, however reluctantly, in flagrant cases of such wrongdoing or impotence, to the exercise of an international police power. If every country washed by the Caribbean Sea would show the progress in stable and just civilization which, with the aid of the Platt amendment, Cuba has shown since our troops left the island, and which so many of the republics in both Americas are constantly and brilliantly showing, all question of interference by this Nation with their affairs would be at an end.

Our interests and those of our southern neighbors are in reality identical. They have great natural riches, and if within their borders the reign of law and justice obtains, prosperity is sure to come to them. While they thus obey the primary laws of civilized society, they may rest assured that they will be treated by us in a spirit of cordial and helpful sympathy. We would interfere with them only in the last resort, and then only if it became evident that their inability or unwillingness to do justice at home and abroad had violated the rights of the United States or had invited foreign aggression to the detriment of the entire body of American nations. It is a mere truism

1. *A Compilation of the Messages and Papers of the Presidents* (n.d.), XVI, 7053–54 (Dec. 6, 1904).

to say that every nation, whether in America or anywhere else, which desires to maintain its freedom, its independence, must ultimately realize that the right of such independence cannot be separated from the responsibility of making good use of it.

2. A Latin American Protests (1943)

Following up his new corollary to the Monroe Doctrine, Roosevelt arranged with the local authorities to take over and administer the customhouses of the bankrupt Santo Domingo. The European creditors then had no real excuse for interfering, for they received their regular payments. In his annual message of 1905, Roosevelt added a refinement to his corollary to the Monroe Doctrine: to prevent European creditors from taking over customhouses (and perhaps staying), the United States had an obligation to take over the customhouses itself. In subsequent years, and pursuant to the Roosevelt corollary to the Monroe Doctrine, the marines landed and acted as international policemen, notably in Haiti, Santo Domingo, and Nicaragua. The Latin Americans, cherishing their sovereign right to revolution and disorder, bitterly resented this bayonet-enforced twisting of Monroe's protective dictum. Below, an outspoken Mexican diplomat, with a Ph.D. from Johns Hopkins University, expresses his wrath. It has been said that the Roosevelt corollary was so radically different from the original Monroe Doctrine (see Vol. I, p. 213) that the two should never have been associated. Was Roosevelt's corollary a logical extension or a radical revision of the Monroe Doctrine?

No document has proved more harmful to the prestige of the United States in the Western Hemisphere [than the Roosevelt corollary]. No White House policy could be more distasteful to Latin Americans—not even, perhaps, outspoken imperialism. Latin Americans are usually inclined to admire strength, force, a nation *muy hombre* [very manly]. This was imperialism without military glamour. . . . Moreover, it was a total distortion of the original Message. Monroe's Doctrine was defensive and negative: defensive, in that it was essentially an opposition to eventual aggression from Europe; negative, in that it simply told Europe what it should not do—not what the United States should do.

The Monroe Doctrine of later corollaries became aggressive and positive: aggressive, because, even without actual European attack, it urged United States "protection" of Latin America—and that was outright intervention; positive, because instead of telling Europe what not to do, it told the United States what it should do in the Western Hemisphere. From a case of America vs. Europe, the corollaries made of the Doctrine a case of the United States vs. America.

President Monroe had merely shaken his head, brandished his finger, and said to Europe, "Now, now, gentlemen, if you meddle with us, we will not love you any more," while Teddy Roosevelt, brandishing a big stick, had shouted, "Listen, you guys, don't muscle in—this territory is ours."

In still another corollary, enunciated to justify United States intervention [in Santo Domingo], the same Roosevelt said: "It is far better that this

2. Luis Quintanilla, *A Latin American Speaks* (1943), pp. 125–26. By permission of the author.

country should put through such an arrangement [enforcing fulfillment of financial obligations contracted by Latin American states] rather than to allow any foreign country to undertake it." To intervene in order to protect: to intervene in order to prevent others from so doing. It is the "Invasion for Protection" corollary, so much in the limelight recently, in other parts of the world.

[*Latin American bitterness against this perversion of the Monroe Doctrine festered for nearly three decades. A sharp turn for the better came in 1933. President Franklin D. Roosevelt, implementing a policy initiated by President Hoover, formally renounced the doctrine of intervention in Latin America. Thus what the first Roosevelt gave, the second Roosevelt took away.*]

D. ROOSEVELT AND JAPAN

1. The President Anticipates Trouble (1905)

Secretary of State John Hay, attempting to halt European land-grabbing in China, had induced the reluctant powers to accept his famed Open Door policy in 1899–1900. But Russia's continued encroachments on China's Manchuria led to the exhausting Russo-Japanese War of 1904–1905, during which the underdog Japanese soundly thrashed the Russian army and navy. President Roosevelt, who was finally drafted as peace mediator, wrote the following letter to his close friend Senator Henry Cabot Lodge. Victory-drunk, Japan was becoming understandably cocky, while the race-conscious California legislature was preparing to erect barriers against Japanese immigrants. Why does Roosevelt regard the attitude of Californians as bigoted, foolish, and dangerous?

That Japan will have her head turned to some extent I do not in the least doubt, and I see clear symptoms of it in many ways. We should certainly as a nation have ours turned if we had performed such feats as the Japanese have in the past sixteen months; and the same is true of any European nation. Moreover, I have no doubt that some Japanese, and perhaps a great many of them, will behave badly to foreigners. They cannot behave worse than the State of California, through its Legislature, is now behaving toward the Japanese.

The feeling on the Pacific slope, taking it from several different standpoints, is as foolish as if conceived by the mind of a Hottentot. These Pacific Coast people wish grossly to insult the Japanese and to keep out the Japanese immigrants on the ground that they are an immoral, degraded, and worthless race; and at the same time that they desire to do this for the Japanese, and are already doing it for the Chinese, they expect to be given advantages in Oriental markets; and with besotted folly are indifferent to building up the navy while provoking this formidable new power— a power jealous, sensitive, and warlike, and which if irritated could at once take both the Philippines and Hawaii from us if she obtained the upper hand on the seas.

Most certainly the Japanese soldiers and sailors have shown themselves to be terrible foes. There can be none more dangerous in all the world. But our own navy, ship for ship, is I believe at least as efficient as theirs, although I am not certain that our torpedo boats would be handled as well as theirs. At present we are superior to them in number of ships, and this superiority will last for some time. It will of course come to an end if [Senator] Hale has his way, but not otherwise.

I hope that we can persuade our people on the one hand to act in a spirit of generous justice and genuine courtesy toward Japan, and on the other hand to keep the navy respectable in numbers and more than respectable in the efficiency of its units. If we act thus we need not fear the Japanese. But if, as Brooks Adams says, we show ourselves "opulent, aggressive, and unarmed," the Japanese may sometime work us an injury.

2. Japan Resents Discrimination (1906)

The San Francisco Board of Education precipitated a crisis in 1906 by ordering all Oriental students to attend a specially segregated school. The sensitive Japanese rose in instant resentment against what they regarded as a deliberate and insulting act of discrimination. The Tokyo *Mainichi Shimbun*, a reputable journal, reacted as follows. Where was Japanese national pride most deeply wounded?

The whole world knows that the poorly equipped army and navy of the United States are no match for our efficient army and navy. It will be an easy work to awake the United States from her dream of obstinacy when one of our great admirals appears on the other side of the Pacific. . . . The present situation is such that the Japanese nation cannot rest easy by relying only upon the wisdom and statesmanship of President Roosevelt. The Japanese nation must have a firm determination to chastise at any time the obstinate Americans.

Stand up, Japanese nation! Our countrymen have been HUMILIATED on the other side of the Pacific. Our poor boys and girls have been expelled from the public schools by the rascals of the United States, cruel and merciless like demons.

At this time we should be ready to give a blow to the United States. Yes, we should be ready to strike the Devil's head with an iron hammer for the sake of the world's civilization. . . . Why do we not insist on sending [war]ships?

3. The Gentlemen's Agreement (1908)

The San Francisco school incident revealed anew that a municipality or a state could take perfectly legal action that might involve the entire nation in war. Roosevelt soothed the Japanese, but not the Californians, by adopting the Oriental side of the

2. Oct. 22, 1906, in T. A. Bailey, *Theodore Roosevelt and the Japanese-American Crises* (1934), p. 50. By permission of the Stanford University Press.
3. *Annual Report of the Secretary of Commerce and Labor, 1908* (1908), pp. 221–22.

dispute. He publicly branded the action of the School Board as a "wicked absurdity," and he brought that entire body to Washington, where he persuaded the members to come to terms. The San Franciscans agreed to readmit Japanese children to the public schools, on condition that Roosevelt would arrange to shut off the influx of Japanese immigrants. This he did in the famous Gentlemen's Agreement, which consisted of an understanding growing out of an extensive exchange of diplomatic notes. These were officially summarized as follows in the annual report of the United States Commissioner-General of Immigration. In what ways did these agreements leave the fundamental issues unresolved?

In order that the best results might follow from an enforcement of the regulations, an understanding was reached with Japan that the existing policy of discouraging the emigration of its subjects of the laboring classes to continental United States should be continued and should, by cooperation of the governments, be made as effective as possible.

This understanding contemplates that the Japanese Government shall issue passports to continental United States only to such of its subjects as are non-laborers or are laborers who, in coming to the continent, seek to resume a formerly acquired domicile, to join a parent, wife, or children residing there, or to assume active control of an already possessed interest in a farming enterprise in this country; so that the three classes of laborers entitled to receive passports have come to be designated "former residents," "parents, wives, or children of residents," and "settled agriculturists."

With respect to Hawaii, the Japanese Government stated that, experimentally at least, the issuance of passports to members of the laboring classes proceeding thence would be limited to "former residents" and "parents, wives, or children of residents." The said government has also been exercising a careful supervision over the subject of the emigration of its laboring class to foreign contiguous territory [Mexico, Canada].

[*The honor-system Gentlemen's Agreement worked reasonably well until 1924, when Congress in a fit of pique slammed the door completely in the faces of the Japanese. The resulting harvest of ill will had much to do with the tragic events that led to Pearl Harbor and World War II.*]

THOUGHT PROVOKERS

1. Critics said that while the Filipinos might not have been able to govern themselves, Americans were incapable of governing them if true to the "consent of the governed" philosophy of the Declaration of Independence. Comment.
2. Would it have been better to delay construction of the Panama Canal for ten or so years rather than have the scandal that attended the Panama coup? Was the scandal really necessary?
3. With reference to Roosevelt's corollary to the Monroe Doctrine, are nations entitled to complete sovereignty if they fail to exercise it properly? When certain states of the United States defaulted on their debts to British creditors in the 1830's, Britain did not attempt to take over American custom-houses. Why not? Are there different rules of international behavior for small nations and large nations?
4. Why did Japan especially resent California's discrimination in 1906, and why was the Gentlemen's Agreement better than exclusion by act of Congress?

Men with the muckrake are often indispensable to the well-being of society, but only if they know when to stop raking the muck.

THEODORE ROOSEVELT, 1906

PROLOGUE: The wholesale exposure of iniquities during the Roosevelt years led to a wave of reform in the Progressive era, which crested about 1908. A group of professional writers (muckrakers) pilloried sweatshop conditions, municipal graft, adulterated food and drugs, and other kinds of skulduggery. At first Roosevelt was not hostile to the revelations of the muckrakers. But he finally came to believe that they were corrupting public taste by overstressing the bad to the exclusion of the good. His own major contribution as a reformer was to reinvigorate the movement for conserving the nation's fast-melting natural resources, especially the forests. As brandisher of the Big Stick, he won a great reputation for trust busting. But the truth is that he regarded the Sherman Anti-Trust Act as ineffective, and he did not bestir himself as mightily as all the uproar indicated.

A. THE HEYDAY OF MUCKRAKING

1. Exposing the Meat Packers (1906)

Upton Sinclair, the youthful and prolific Socialist writer, published his novel *The Jungle* in 1906. It was a damning exposure of conditions in the Chicago meat-packing plants. Seeking to turn people to socialism, he turned their stomachs. The uproar that followed publication of his novel caused President Roosevelt to initiate an official investigation, and the following sober report was hardly less shocking than *The Jungle.* It confirmed the essential truth of Sinclair's exposé, except for such lurid scenes as men falling into vats and emerging as lard. **Which aspect of this official investigation revealed conditions most detrimental to the public health?**

. . . Meat scraps were also found being shoveled into receptacles from dirty floors, where they were left to lie until again shoveled into barrels or into machines for chopping. These floors, it must be noted, were in most cases damp and soggy, in dark, ill-ventilated rooms, and the employees in utter ignorance of cleanliness or danger to health expectorated at will upon them. In a word, we saw meat shoveled from filthy wooden floors, piled on tables rarely washed, pushed from room to room in rotten box carts, in all of which processes it was in the way of gathering dirt, splinters, floor filth, and the expectoration of tuberculous and other diseased workers. Where comment was made to floor superintendents about these matters,

---

1. *Congressional Record,* 59 Cong., 1 sess., p. 7801 (June 4, 1906).

it was always the reply that this meat would afterwards be cooked, and that this sterilization would prevent any danger from its use. Even this, it may be pointed out in passing, is not wholly true. A very considerable portion of the meat so handled is sent out as smoked products and in the form of sausages, which are prepared to be eaten without being cooked. . . .

As an extreme example of the entire disregard on the part of employees of any notion of cleanliness in handling dressed meat, we saw a hog that had just been killed, cleaned, washed, and started on its way to the cooling room fall from the sliding rail to a dirty wooden floor and slide part way into a filthy men's privy. It was picked up by two employees, placed upon a truck, carried into the cooling room and hung up with other carcasses, no effort being made to clean it. . . .

In one well-known establishment we came upon fresh meat being shoveled into barrels, and a regular proportion being added of stale scraps that had lain on a dirty floor in the corner of a room for some days previous. In another establishment, equally well known, a long table was noted covered with several hundred pounds of cooked scraps of beef and other meats. Some of these meat scraps were dry, leathery, and unfit to be eaten; and in the heap were found pieces of pigskin, and even some bits of rope strands and other rubbish. Inquiry evoked the frank admission from the man in charge that this was to be ground up and used in making "potted ham."

All of these canned products bear labels, of which the following is a sample:

ABATTOIR NO. —

THE CONTENTS OF THIS PACKAGE HAVE BEEN
INSPECTED ACCORDING TO THE ACT OF
CONGRESS OF MARCH 3, 1891.

[*The agitation and investigation inspired by Sinclair's* The Jungle *had much to do with bringing about the passage by Congress of the Meat Inspection Act and the Pure Food and Drug Act of 1906.*]

2. Roosevelt Roasts Muckrakers (1906)

President Roosevelt, though recognizing some unpalatable truth in Upton Sinclair's *The Jungle,* was critical. He wrote the author bluntly that he had said things which should not have been written unless backed up "with testimony that would satisfy an honest man of reasonable intelligence." Privately he declared that Sinclair had reflected unfairly on both honest and dishonest capitalism in Chicago. Finally nauseated by excessive sensationalism, Roosevelt made the following famous attack (which gave rise to the term "muckraker") in a Washington speech. What are the strengths and weaknesses of his argument that hysterical and indiscriminate muckraking was doing more harm than good?

In Bunyan's *Pilgrim's Progress* you may recall the description of the Man with the Muck-rake [manure rake], the man who could look no way

2. Theodore Roosevelt, "The Man with the Muck-Rake," *Putnam's Monthly and The Critic,* I, 42–43 (October, 1906).

but downward, with the muck-rake in his hand; who was offered a celestial crown for his muck-rake, but who would neither look up nor regard the crown he was offered, but continued to rake to himself the filth of the floor.

In *Pilgrim's Progress* the Man with the Muck-rake is set forth as the example of him whose vision is fixed on carnal instead of on spiritual things. Yet he also typifies the man who in this life consistently refuses to see aught that is lofty, and fixes his eyes with solemn intentness only on that which is vile and debasing.

Now it is very necessary that we should not flinch from seeing what is vile and debasing. There is filth on the floor, and it must be scraped up with the muck-rake: and there are times and places where this service is the most needed of all the services that can be performed. But the man who never does anything else, who never thinks or speaks or writes save of his feats with the muck-rake, speedily becomes, not a help to society, not an incitement to good, but one of the most potent forces for evil.

There are—in the body politic, economic, and social—many and grave evils, and there is urgent necessity for the sternest war upon them. There should be relentless exposure of and attack upon every evil man, whether politician or businessman; every evil practice, whether in politics, in business, or in social life. I hail as a benefactor every writer or speaker, every man who, on the platform, or in book, magazine, or newspaper, with merciless severity makes such attack, provided always that he in his turn remembers that the attack is of use only if it is absolutely truthful. The liar is no whit better than the thief, and if his mendacity takes the form of slander, he may be worse than most thieves. It puts a premium upon knavery untruthfully to attack an honest man, or even with hysterical exaggeration to assail a bad man with untruth. An epidemic of indiscriminate assault upon character does no good, but very great harm. The soul of every scoundrel is gladdened whenever an honest man is assailed, or even when a scoundrel is untruthfully assailed.

Now, it is easy to twist out of shape what I have just said. . . . Some persons are sincerely incapable of understanding that to denounce mudslinging does not mean the indorsement of whitewashing, and both the interested individuals who need whitewashing and those others who practice mudslinging like to encourage such confusion of ideas. One of the chief counts against those who make indiscriminate assault upon men in business or men in public life is that they invite a reaction which is sure to tell powerfully in favor of the unscrupulous scoundrel who really ought to be attacked, who ought to be exposed, who ought, if possible, to be put in the penitentiary. If Aristides is praised overmuch as just, people get tired of hearing it;* and overcensure of the unjust finally and from similar reasons results in their favor.

* An allusion to Plutarch's story of the Athenian who voted for the banishment of Aristides (called "The Just") because he was tired of hearing everyone call him just.

Any excess is almost sure to invite a reaction; and, unfortunately, the reaction, instead of taking the form of punishment of those guilty of the excess, is very apt to take the form either of punishment of the unoffending or of giving immunity, and even strength, to offenders. The effort to make financial or political profit out of the destruction of character can only result in public calamity. Gross and reckless assaults on character, whether on the stump or in newspaper, magazine, or book, create a morbid and vicious public sentiment, and at the same time act as a profound deterrent to able men of normal sensitiveness and tend to prevent them from entering the public service at any price.

[*Roosevelt thus threw muck at the muckrakers. They resented his attack, claiming that even if they exaggerated they were exposing evil conditions and promoting desired legislation. (At the same time, they made money selling their magazine articles and books.) But Roosevelt was unconvinced. In 1911 he went so far as to write privately: ". . . I think the muckrakers stand on a level of infamy with the corruptionists in politics. After all, there is no great difference between violation of the eighth [no stealing] and the ninth [no lying] commandments; and to sell one's vote for money is morally, I believe, hardly as reprehensible as to practice slanderous mendacity for hire." (Roosevelt Letters, VII, 447.) The truth is that he continued with intemperate muckraking himself, attacking "malefactors of great wealth," "nature fakers," and others. "You're the chief muckraker," Speaker Cannon told him flatly in 1906.*]*

B. CORRUPTION IN THE CITIES

1. Steffens Bares Philadelphia Bossism (1904)

A California-born journalist, (Joseph) Lincoln Steffens, after serving as a "gentleman reporter" in New York, emerged as one of the first and most influential of the reforming muckrakers. Associated with *McClure's Magazine*, the leading muckraking journal, he published a sensational series of articles on municipal graft, later collected in book form as *The Shame of the Cities* (1904). After the muckraking craze ended, Steffens became disillusioned, visited Russia, interviewed Lenin, and developed a warm admiration for the Soviet Union. In reading his famous exposé about conditions in Philadelphia, what is most ironical? What is most shocking? Who was responsible for the existence and continuation of these irregularities?

Other American cities, no matter how bad their own condition may be, all point with scorn to Philadelphia as worse—"the worst-governed city in the country." St. Louis, Minneapolis, Pittsburgh submit with some patience to the jibes of any other community; the most friendly suggestion from Philadelphia is rejected with contempt. The Philadelphians are "supine," "asleep"; hopelessly ring-ruled, they are "complacent." "Politically benighted," Philadelphia is supposed to have no light to throw upon a state of things that is almost universal.

This is not fair. Philadelphia is, indeed, corrupt; but it is not without

1. Lincoln Steffens, *The Shame of the Cities* (1904), pp. 193–201, *passim*.

significance. Every city and town in the country can learn something from the typical political experience of this great representative city. New York is excused for many of its ills because it is the metropolis; Chicago, because of its forced development; Philadelphia is our "third largest" city and its growth has been gradual and natural.

Immigration has been blamed for our municipal conditions. Philadelphia, with 47 percent of its population native-born of native-born parents, is the most American of our greater cities.

It is "good," too, and intelligent. I don't know just how to measure the intelligence of a community, but a Pennsylvania college professor who declared to me his belief in education for the masses as a way out of political corruption, himself justified the "rake-off" of preferred contractors on public works on the ground of a "fair business profit."

Another plea we [Americans] have made is that we are too busy to attend to public business, and we have promised, when we come to wealth and leisure, to do better. Philadelphia has long enjoyed great and widely distributed prosperity. It is the city of homes. There is a dwelling house for every five persons—men, women, and children—of the population; and the people give one a sense of more leisure and repose than any community I ever dwelt in. Some Philadelphians account for their political state on the ground of their ease and comfort. . . .

Then we hear that we are a young people and that when we are older and "have traditions," like some of the old countries, we also will be honest. Philadelphia is one of the oldest of our cities and treasures for us scenes and relics of some of the noblest traditions of "our fair land." Yet I was told once, "for a joke," a party of boodlers [grafters] counted out the "divvy" [division] of their graft in unison with the ancient chime of Independence Hall. . . .

Philadelphia is proud; good people there defend corruption and boast of their machine. My college professor, with his philosophic view of "rake-offs," is one Philadelphia type. Another is the man who, driven to bay with his local pride, says: "At least you must admit that our machine is the best you have ever seen." . . .

Disgraceful? Other cities say so. But I say that if Philadelphia is a disgrace, it is a disgrace not to itself alone, nor to Pennsylvania, but to the United States and to American character. For this great city, so highly representative in other respects, is not behind in political experience, but ahead, with New York.

Philadelphia is a city that has had its reforms. . . . The present condition of Philadelphia, therefore, is not that which precedes, but that which follows reform, and in this distinction lies its startling gen-

PHILADELPHIA REFORM BUTTON

An uprising of honest voters blocked a scheme to lease the municipal gas plant for seventy-five years. *Literary Digest,* 1905.

eral significance. What has happened . . . in Philadelphia may happen in any American city "after the reform is over."

For reform with us is usually revolt, not government, and is soon over. Our people do not seek, they avoid self-rule, and "reforms" are spasmodic efforts to punish bad rulers and get somebody that will give us good government or something that will make it. A self-acting form of government is an ancient superstition. We are an inventive people, and we all think that we shall devise some day a legal machine that will turn out good government automatically. The Philadelphians have treasured this belief longer than the rest of us and have tried it more often. . . .

The Philadelphia machine isn't the best. It isn't sound, and I doubt if it would stand in New York or Chicago. The enduring strength of the typical American political machine is that it is a natural growth—a sucker, but deep-rooted in the people. The New Yorkers vote for Tammany Hall. The Philadelphians do not vote; they are disfranchised, and their disfranchisement is one anchor of the foundation of the Philadelphia organization.

This is no figure of speech. The honest citizens of Philadelphia have no more rights at the polls than the Negroes down South. Nor do they fight very hard for this basic privilege. You can arouse their Republican ire by talking about the black Republican votes lost in the Southern states by white Democratic intimidation, but if you remind the average Philadelphian that he is in the same position, he will look startled, then say, "That's so, that's literally true, only I never thought of it in just that way." And it is literally true.

The machine controls the whole process of voting, and practices fraud at every stage. The [tax] assessor's list is the voting list, and the assessor is the machine's man. . . . The assessor pads the list with the names of dead dogs, children, and non-existent persons. One newspaper printed the picture of a dog, another that of a little four-year-old Negro boy, down on such a list. A "ring" orator, in a speech resenting sneers at his ward as "low down," reminded his hearers that that was the ward of Independence Hall, and, naming over the signers of the Declaration of Independence, he closed his highest flight of eloquence with the statement that "these men, the fathers of American liberty, voted down here once. And," he added with a catching grin, "they vote here yet."

Rudolph Blankenburg, a persistent fighter for the right and the use of the right to vote (and, by the way, an immigrant), sent out just before one election a registered letter to each voter on the rolls of a certain selected division. Sixty-three percent were returned marked "not at," "removed," "deceased," etc. . . .

The repeating [voting more than once] is done boldly, for the machine controls the election officers, often choosing them from among the fraudulent names; and when no one appears to serve, assigning the heeler [political hanger-on] ready for the expected vacancy. The police are forbidden by law to stand within thirty feet of the polls, but they are at the [ballot] box and they are there to see that the machine's orders are obeyed and that repeaters whom they help to furnish are permitted to vote without "intimidation" on the names they, the police, have supplied. . . .

The business proceeds with very few hitches; there is more jesting than fighting. Violence in the past has had its effect; and is not often necessary nowadays, but if it is needed the police are there to apply it. Several citizens told me that they had seen the police help to beat citizens or election officers who were trying to do their duty, then arrest the victim. . . .

2. Plunkitt Defends "Honest Graft" (1905)

Tammany Hall was the powerful and corrupt Democratic political machine that dominated New York City politics for many years. One of its cleverest officials, who became a millionaire through "honest graft," was George Washington (!) Plunkitt. According to his account as here recorded by a newspaper reporter, he was above such dirty work as "shaking down" houses of prostitution ("disorderly houses"). Is his distinction between two kinds of graft legitimate? How did Tammany Hall sustain its power? Did it provide any valuable service?

"Everybody is talkin' these days about Tammany men growin' rich on graft, but nobody thinks of drawin' the distinction between honest graft and dishonest graft. There's all the difference in the world between the two. Yes, many of our men have grown rich in politics. I have myself. I've made a big fortune out of the game, and I'm gettin' richer every day, but I've not gone in for dishonest graft—blackmailin' gamblers, saloon-keepers, disorderly people, etc.—and neither has any of the men who have made big fortunes in politics.

"There's an honest graft, and I'm an example of how it works. I might sum up the whole thing by sayin': 'I seen my opportunities and I took 'em.'

"Just let me explain by examples. My party's in power in the city, and it's goin' to undertake a lot of public improvements. Well, I'm tipped off, say, that they're goin' to lay out a new park at a certain place.

"I see my opportunity and I take it. I go to that place and I buy up all the land I can in the neighborhood. Then the board of this or that makes its plan public, and there is a rush to get my land, which nobody cared particular for before.

"Ain't it perfectly honest to charge a good price and make a profit on my investment and foresight? Of course it is. Well, that's honest graft.

"Or, supposin' it's a new bridge they're goin' to build. I get tipped off and I buy as much property as I can that has to be taken for approaches. I sell at my own price later on and drop some more money in the bank.

"Wouldn't you? It's just like lookin' ahead in Wall Street or in the coffee or cotton market. It's honest graft, and I'm lookin' for it every day in the year. I will tell you frankly that I've got a good lot of it, too.

2. William L. Riordan, *Plunkitt of Tammany Hall* (1948 ed.), pp. 3–8. By permission of Alfred A. Knopf, Inc.

"I'll tell you of one case. They were goin' to fix up a big park, no matter where. I got on to it, and went lookin' about for land in that neighborhood.

"I could get nothin' at a bargain but a big piece of swamp, but I took it fast enough and held on to it. What turned out was just what I counted on. They couldn't make the park complete without Plunkitt's swamp, and they had to pay a good price for it. Anything dishonest in that?

"Up in the watershed I made some money, too. I bought up several bits of land there some years ago and made a pretty good guess that they would be bought up for water purposes later by the city.

"Somehow, I always guessed about right, and shouldn't I enjoy the profit of my foresight? It was rather amusin' when the condemnation commissioners came along and found piece after piece of the land in the name of George Plunkitt of the Fifteenth Assembly District, New York City. They wondered how I knew just what to buy. The answer is—I seen my opportunity and I took it. I haven't confined myself to land; anything that pays is in my line. . . .

"I've told you how I got rich by honest graft. Now, let me tell you that most politicians who are accused of robbin' the city get rich the same way.

"They didn't steal a dollar from the city treasury. They just seen their opportunities and took them. That is why, when a reform administration comes in and spends a half million dollars in tryin' to find the public robberies they talked about in the campaign, they don't find them.

"The books are always all right. The money in the city treasury is all right. Everything is all right. All they can show is that the Tammany heads of departments looked after their friends, within the law, and gave them what opportunities they could to make honest graft. Now, let me tell you that's never goin' to hurt Tammany with the people. Every good man looks after his friends, and any man who doesn't isn't likely to be popular. If I have a good thing to hand out in private life, I give it to a friend. Why shouldn't I do the same in public life? . . .

"Tammany was beat in 1901 because the people were deceived into believin' that it worked dishonest graft. They didn't draw a distinction between dishonest and honest graft, but they saw that some Tammany men grew rich, and supposed they had been robbin' the city treasury or levyin' blackmail on disorderly houses, or workin' in with the gamblers and lawbreakers.

"As a matter of policy, if nothing else, why should the Tammany leaders go into such dirty business when there is so much honest graft lyin' around when they are in power? Did you ever consider that?

"Now, in conclusion, I want to say that I don't own a dishonest dollar. If my worst enemy was given the job of writin' my epitaph when I'm gone, he couldn't do more than write:

" 'George W. Plunkitt.
He Seen His Opportunities and He Took 'Em.' "

C. THE PLIGHT OF LABOR

1. Baer's Divine Right of Plutocrats (1902)

The anthracite coal miners of Pennsylvania, who were frightfully exploited and accident-cursed, struck for higher wages in 1902. About 140,000 men were idled, and the chilled East was threatened with paralysis. George F. Baer, the multi-millionaire spokesman for the owners, refused to permit intervention, arbitration, or even negotiation. He believed that mining was a "business," not a "religious, senti-mental, or academic proposition." In response to a complaining letter from a Mr. W. F. Clark, he sent the following reply. What is the social philosophy of Big Business as here revealed?

My dear Mr. Clark:—   17th July 1902

I have your letter of the 16th instant.

I do not know who you are. I see that you are a religious man; but you are evidently biased in favor of the right of the working man to control a business in which he has no other interest than to secure fair wages for the work he does.

I beg of you not to be discouraged. The rights and interests of the laboring man will be protected and cared for—not by the labor agitators, but by the Christian men to whom God in His infinite wisdom has given the control of the property interests of the country, and upon the successful management of which so much depends.

Do not be discouraged. Pray earnestly that right may triumph, always remembering that the Lord God Omnipotent still reigns, and that His reign is one of law and order, and not of violence and crime.

Yours truly,

Geo. F. Baer

President

[*When the Baer letter was published, the press assailed its "arrant hypocrisy," "egregious vanity," and "ghastly blasphemy." Roosevelt nevertheless finally brought the disputants together late in 1902. Although he admittedly lost his temper and did not behave "like a gentleman," he had a large hand in working out the resulting compromise wage increase.*]

2. Child Labor in the Coal Mines (1906)

The arrogant attitude of the coal operators seems even less excusable in the light of John Spargo's book *The Bitter Cry of the Children*—another significant contribu-tion to the "muckraking" movement. An English-born Socialist, Spargo had come to America in 1901 at the age of twenty-five. He was especially stirred by the rickety children of the New York tenement districts. Their mothers had no time to prepare proper meals; needlework labor in the sweatshops ran from twelve to twenty hours

1. *Literary Digest*, XXV, 258 (Aug. 30, 1902). A photostatic copy of the letter is in Caro Lloyd, *Henry Demarest Lloyd* (1912), II, 190.
2. From *The Bitter Cry of the Children* by John Spargo (New York: Macmillan, 1906), pp. 163–65.

a day, at a wage ranging from ten cents to a cent and a half an hour. In Spargo's description of work in the coal mines, what were the various kinds of hazards involved?

Work in the coal breakers is exceedingly hard and dangerous. Crouched over the chutes, the boys sit hour after hour, picking out the pieces of slate and other refuse from the coal as it rushes past to the washers. From the cramped position they have to assume, most of them become more or less deformed and bent-backed like old men. When a boy has been working for some time and begins to get round-shouldered, his fellows say that "He's got his boy to carry round wherever he goes."

The coal is hard, and accidents to the hands, such as cut, broken, or crushed fingers, are common among the boys. Sometimes there is a worse accident: a terrified shriek is heard, and a boy is mangled and torn in the machinery, or disappears in the chute to be picked out later smothered and dead. Clouds of dust fill the breakers and are inhaled by the boys, laying the foundations for asthma and miners' consumption.

I once stood in a breaker for half an hour and tried to do the work a twelve-year-old boy was doing day after day, for ten hours at a stretch, for sixty cents a day. The gloom of the breaker appalled me. Outside the sun shone brightly, the air was pellucid, and the birds sang in chorus with the trees and the rivers. Within the breaker there was blackness, clouds of deadly dust enfolded everything, the harsh, grinding roar of the machinery and the ceaseless rushing of coal through the chutes filled the ears. I tried to pick out the pieces of slate from the hurrying stream of coal, often missing them; my hands were bruised and cut in a few minutes; I was covered from head to foot with coal dust, and for many hours afterwards I was expectorating some of the small particles of anthracite I had swallowed.

I could not do that work and live, but there were boys of ten and twelve years of age doing it for fifty and sixty cents a day. Some of them had never been inside of a school; few of them could read a child's primer. True, some of them attended the night schools, but after working ten hours in the breaker the educational results from attending school were practically nil. "We goes fer a good time, an' we keeps de guys wot's dere hoppin' all de time," said little Owen Jones, whose work I had been trying to do. . . .

As I stood in that breaker I thought of the reply of the small boy to Robert Owen [British social reformer]. Visiting an English coal mine one day, Owen asked a twelve-year-old lad if he knew God. The boy stared vacantly at his questioner: "God?" he said, "God? No, I don't. He must work in some other mine." It was hard to realize amid the danger and din and blackness of that Pennsylvania breaker that such a thing as belief in a great All-good God existed.

From the breakers the boys graduate to the mine depths, where they become door tenders, switch boys, or mule drivers. Here, far below the surface, work is still more dangerous. At fourteen or fifteen the boys assume the same risks as the men, and are surrounded by the same perils. Nor is it in Pennsylvania only that these conditions exist. In the bituminous mines of West Virginia, boys of nine or ten are frequently employed. I met one little fellow ten years old in Mt. Carbon, W. Va., last year, who was employed as a "trap boy." Think of what it means to be a trap boy at ten years

UNCLE SAM: "HE'S GOOD ENOUGH FOR ME."
Millions of copies of this pro-Roosevelt cartoon by Davenport were circulated during the presidential campaign of 1904. New York *Evening Mail*, 1904.

of age. It means to sit alone in a dark mine passage hour after hour, with no human soul near; to see no living creature except the mules as they pass with their loads, or a rat or two seeking to share one's meal; to stand in water or mud that covers the ankles, chilled to the marrow by the cold draughts that rush in when you open the trap door for the mules to pass through; to work for fourteen hours—waiting—opening and shutting a door—then waiting again—for sixty cents; to reach the surface when all is wrapped in the mantle of night, and to fall to the earth exhausted and have to be carried away to the nearest "shack" to be revived before it is possible to walk to the farther shack called "home."

Boys twelve years of age may be *legally* employed in the mines of West Virginia, by day or by night, and for as many hours as the employers care to make them toil or their bodies will stand the strain. Where the disregard of child life is such that this may be done openly and with legal sanction, it is easy to believe what miners have again and again told me—that there are hundreds of little boys of nine and ten years of age employed in the coal mines of this state.

3. Sweatshop Hours for Bakers (1905)

The abuse of labor in dangerous or unhealthful occupations prompted an increasing number of state legislatures, exercising so-called "police powers," to pass

3. 198 *U.S. Reports* 57, 59, 61.

regulatory laws. In 1898 the Supreme Court upheld a Utah statute prohibiting miners from working more than eight hours a day, except in emergencies. But in 1905 the Court, by a 5-to-4 decision in the case of Lochner *vs.* New York, overthrew a state law forbidding bakers to work more than ten hours a day. The majority held that the right of both employers and employees to make labor contracts was protected by the 14th Amendment. How might one describe the social conscience of the majority of the Supreme Court in the light of this memorable decision written by Mr. Justice Peckham?

The question whether this act is valid as a labor law, pure and simple, may be dismissed in a few words. There is no reasonable ground for interfering with the liberty of person or the right of free contract, by determining the hours of labor, in the occupation of a baker. There is no contention that bakers as a class are not equal in intelligence and capacity to men in other trades or manual occupations, or that they are not able to assert their rights and care for themselves without the protecting arm of the state interfering with their independence of judgment and of action. They are in no sense wards of the state.

Viewed in the light of a purely labor law, with no reference whatever to the question of health, we think that a law like the one before us involves neither the safety, the morals, nor the welfare of the public, and that the interest of the public is not in the slightest degree affected by such an act. The law must be upheld, if at all, as a law pertaining to the health of the individual engaged in the occupation of a baker. It does not affect any other portion of the public than those who are engaged in that occupation. Clean and wholesome bread does not depend upon whether the baker works but ten hours per day or only sixty hours a week. The limitation of the hours of labor does not come within the police power on that ground. . . .

We think that there can be no fair doubt that the trade of a baker, in and of itself, is not an unhealthy one to that degree which would authorize the legislature to interfere with the right to labor, and with the right of free contract on the part of the individual, either as employer or employee.

In looking through statistics regarding all trades and occupations, it may be true that the trade of baker does not appear to be as healthy as some other trades, and is also vastly more healthy than still others. To the common understanding the trade of a baker has never been regarded as an unhealthy one. Very likely physicians would not recommend the exercise of that or of any other trade as a remedy for ill health. Some occupations are more healthy than others, but we think there are none which might not come under the power of the legislature to supervise and control the hours of working therein, if the mere fact that the occupation is not absolutely and perfectly healthy is to confer that right upon the legislative department of the government. . . .

. . . We do not believe in the soundness of the views which uphold this law. On the contrary, we think that such a law as this, although passed in the assumed exercise of the police power, and as relating to the public health, or the health of the employees named, is not within that power, and is invalid. The act is not, within any fair meaning of the term, a health law, but is an illegal interference with the rights of individuals, both employers and employees, to make contracts regarding labor upon such terms as they may think best, or which they may agree upon with the other parties to such contracts.

Statutes of the nature of that under review, limiting the hours in which grown and intelligent men may labor to earn their living, are mere meddlesome interferences with the rights of the individual, and they are not saved from condemnation by the claim that they are passed in the exercise of the police power and upon the subject of the health of the individual whose rights are interfered with, unless there be some fair ground, reasonable in and of itself, to say that there is material danger to the public health, or to the health of the employees, if the hours of labor are not curtailed.

[*Mr. Justice Holmes, the great dissenter, filed a famous protest in the bakers' case. He argued that a majority of the people of New York State evidently wanted the law, and that the Court ought not to impose its own social philosophy. "The 14th Amendment," he solemnly declared, referring to a famous work by an arch-conservative British social theorist, "does not enact Mr. Herbert Spencer's Social Statics." As for the right to work more than ten hours, Mayor Gaynor of New York remarked, "There were no journeymen bakers that I know of clamoring for any such liberty." Possibly chastened by Holmes' vigorous views, the Court relented and in 1908 unanimously approved an Oregon statute prohibiting the employment of women in factories, laundries, and other establishments more than ten hours in one day. In 1917 the Court upheld an Oregon ten-hour law for both men and women.*]

D. THE ERA OF TRUST BUSTING

1. Roosevelt Attacks the Anti-Trust Act (1908)

Early in his thinking about trusts, Roosevelt concluded that bigness was not necessarily badness. He favored destroying the evils in trusts rather than the trusts themselves, and he had no sympathy with the "utter folly" of the "quacks" who cried, "Destroy the Trusts." Corporate organizations that used their power with a proper regard for the public welfare were necessary for the nation's prosperity, he believed, and should not be harassed; those that were guilty of malpractices should be curbed or broken up. Roosevelt instituted proceedings under the Sherman Act against the giant Standard Oil Company, and in 1911 the Supreme Court ordered it dissolved. But the pro rata distribution of stock among the new components left the combined power equal to what it had previously been, with stock values much higher. Why does Roosevelt, in this message to Congress, want a drastic revision of the Sherman Act? Is his position sound?

1. *A Compilation of the Messages and Papers of the Presidents* (n.d.), XVII, 7511 (Jan. 31, 1908).

In reference to the Sherman anti-trust law, I repeat the recommendations made in my message at the opening of the present Congress, as well as in my message to the previous Congress. The attempt in this law to provide in sweeping terms against all combinations of whatever character, if technically in restraint of trade as such restraint has been defined by the courts, must necessarily be either futile or mischievous, and sometimes both.

The present law makes some combinations illegal, although they may be useful to the country. On the other hand, as to some huge combinations which are both noxious and illegal, even if the action

THE TRUSTS: "HE'S GOOD ENOUGH FOR ME."

A famous anti-Roosevelt parody of the original Davenport cartoon (see p. 608) by Opper in the Hearst press.

undertaken against them under the law by the Government is successful, the result may be to work but a minimum benefit to the public. Even though the combination be broken up and a small measure of reform thereby produced, the real good aimed at cannot be obtained, for such real good can come only by a thorough and continuing supervision over the acts of the combination in all its parts, so as to prevent stock watering, improper forms of competition, and, in short, wrongdoing generally.

The law should correct that portion of the Sherman Act which prohibits all combinations of the character above described, whether they be reasonable or unreasonable. But this should be done only as a part of a general scheme to provide for this effective and thoroughgoing supervision by the National Government of all the operations of the big interstate business concerns.

2. La Follette Exposes Roosevelt (1912)

Prior to Roosevelt's day the trusts had flourished, in part because successive Attorneys General were friendly to Big Business. Roosevelt noisily inaugurated a new

2. R. M. La Follette, *Autobiography* (1960 ed.), pp. 296–97. By permission of the University of Wisconsin Press. The tabular data are from Eliot Jones, *The Trust Problem in the United States* (1928), pp. 441–45.

era of "trust busting." The relative results are revealed by this seventeen-year table of federal prosecutions against Big Business under the Sherman Anti-Trust Act of 1890:

PRESIDENTIAL ADMINISTRATION	BILLS IN EQUITY	INDICTMENTS	CONTEMPT PROCEEDINGS	FORFEITURE PROCEEDINGS	TOTAL ACTIONS
Harrison (1890–1893)	4	3	0	0	7
Cleveland (1893–1897)	4	2	2	0	8
McKinley (1897–1901)	3	0	0	0	3
Roosevelt (1901–1909)	18	25	0	1	44
Taft (1909–1913)	46	43	1	0	90
Wilson (1913–1920)	35	45	0	0	80

The fiery Progressive Robert M. La Follette, United States Senator from Wisconsin, took sharp exception to Roosevelt's view that the Sherman Act ought to be modified so as to differentiate more sharply between "good" and "bad" trusts. La Follette believed that the Sherman Act was quite adequate if the administration would only bestir itself properly. How should one appraise Roosevelt's reputation as a "trust buster" in the light of the above table and La Follette's following criticism?

Thus it was that Roosevelt put the Sherman Anti-Trust Law under the ban of executive disapproval. It was the only federal statute for the protection of the public against these plundering combinations. His denunciation of the law was an executive sanction to violate the law. It opened the floodgates for trust organization, and upon Theodore Roosevelt, more than any other man, must rest the responsibility for the gravest problem which ever menaced the industrial freedom of the American people. He prosecuted on an average six cases a year against a carefully selected list of these combinations. He went just far enough to give color to the claim that he was upholding the law, but not far enough seriously to injure those prosecuted or deter in the slightest degree the hundreds that were organizing every month throughout his entire administration.

A study of the more important of these cases against combinations under the Sherman Act shows that the actions were so brought that the government would, at best, win only a nominal victory; and that the decree of the court would be so limited by the allegation of the complaint as to leave the defendant combination in a position, under its existing form or by an easy shift, to continue its wrongdoing.

. . . When Roosevelt became President there were 149 combinations and trusts, including railways, the entire 149 having a total stock and bond issue of only $3,784,000,000. When he left the White House there were 10,020 of these monster plants in combination, including, with the combined railroads, a total capitalization amounting to the enormous sum of $31,672,-000,000—more than 70 percent of which was water. The power of these combinations was so extensive, and so completely did they suppress competition, that they were able to advance prices on transportation, and on the products of the mines and factories, to enable them to pay dividends on this fictitious and fraudulent overcapitalization.

[*The accusation by Senator La Follette and others that Roosevelt, the Trust Buster, merely flourished a padded stick is not altogether fair. He inaugurated a significant movement, and some of his most important prosecutions, notably the Standard Oil case, were not concluded until the days of his successor, President Taft.*]

E. THE CONSERVATION CRUSADE

1. Roosevelt Saves the Forests (1907)

Greedy or shortsighted Americans had plundered their forests and mineral resources with incredible rapacity. President Roosevelt, one-time Dakota cattle rancher, provided the lagging conservation movement with dynamic leadership. Under the Forest Reserve Act of 1891, he set aside about 150,000,000 acres of government timberland as national forest reserves—more than three times as much as his three predecessors had saved. The "predatory interests" complained bitterly, and in this private letter Roosevelt took them to task. Actually the worst offenders among the "skinners" were the small-fry lumbermen. The big trusts, though grasping, were in some degree governed by the reforestation needs of long-range lumbering. What advantages would result from Roosevelt's policy, as he describes it in the following letter?

As to the forest reserves, their creation has damaged just one class, that is, the great lumber barons: the managers and owners of those lumber companies which by illegal, fraudulent, or unfair methods have desired to get possession of the valuable timber of the public domain, to skin the land, and to abandon it when impoverished well-nigh to the point of worthlessness.

There are some small men who have wanted to get hold of this lumber land for improper purposes, but they are not powerful or influential, and though they have sometimes been put forward to cause an agitation, the real beneficiaries of the destruction of the forest reserves would be the great lumber companies, which would speedily monopolize them.

If it had not been for the creation of the present system of forest reserves, practically every acre of timberland in the West would now be controlled or be on the point of being controlled by one huge lumber trust. The object of the beneficiaries of this trust would be to exhaust the resources of the country for their own immediate pecuniary benefit, and then when they had rendered it well-nigh worthless to turn it contemptuously over to settlers, who would find too late that those responsible for such conditions had betrayed them and had been false to the public.

The policy of the Government is to put actual settlers on every plot of agricultural ground within the forest reserves, and then, instead of turning these forests over to great corporations or standing by with supine indifference while they are raided by timber thieves, to enforce the law with strict honesty against all men, big or little, who try to rob the public domain;

1. Reprinted by permission of the publishers from *The Letters of Theodore Roosevelt*, edited by E. E. Morison (Cambridge, Mass.: Harvard University Press), copyright © 1951, 1952 by the President and Fellows of Harvard College, © 1979, 1980 by E. E. Morison.

and all the time to permit the freest use of the timber, consistent with preserving the forests for the benefit of the next generation. . . .

It is absolutely necessary to ascertain in practical fashion the best methods of reforestation, and only the National Government can do this successfully.

In the East, the states are now painfully, and at great expense, endeavoring to undo the effects of their former shortsighted policy in throwing away their forest lands. Congress has before it bills to establish by purchase great forest reserves in the White Mountains and the Southern Appalachians, and the only argument against the bills is that of their great expense. New York and Pennsylvania are now, late in the day, endeavoring themselves to protect the forests which guard the headwaters of their streams. Michigan and Wisconsin have already had their good timber stripped from their forests by the great lumber companies. But the Western states, far more fortunate than their Eastern sisters in this regard, can now reserve their forests for the good of all their citizens, without expense, if they choose to show the requisite foresight.

2. The West Protests Conservation (1907)

The new forest-reserve policies often worked a hardship on honest Western settlers, who sometimes had to get permission from a federal official before they could lawfully cut a stick of firewood. The government, they charged, was more concerned with preserving trees than people. The Governor of Colorado, disturbed by the large-scale withdrawals of Western timber and coal lands by Washington, summoned a Public Lands Convention to meet in Denver in 1907. The deliberations of this body inspired the following editorial in a San Francisco newspaper. Did the West really oppose conservation? Was the East unfair in its demands?

The convention which has just adjourned at Denver is the first body of importance that has dealt with the subject of the disposal of the public lands of the United States. Considering the fact that the country has been in the real estate business for more than a century, and that during that period it has, by hook and crook, chiefly by crook, disposed of the major part of its holdings, it seems like a case of locking the stable door after nearly all of the horses have been stolen. The only question left to determine is whether the people who have permitted the theft of the horses, and who lent a hand in the stealing, shall be allowed to enjoy the most of the benefits which may accrue from taking good care of the steeds which still remain in the stalls.

The Far West, in which all the lands—coal-bearing, forest, pasture, and agricultural—still remaining in the possession of the government are to be found, has formally gone on record in this matter, and demands that the new states be treated with the same consideration as those commonwealths which have already divided their patrimony among their individual citizens. The Denver Convention in its resolutions recognizes the wisdom of treating

2. San Francisco *Chronicle*, June 22, 1907.

the lands of the nation as a public trust, but it insisted that this trust should be administered for the benefit of the states wherein the lands still remaining are situated and not for the benefit of the people of the older states of the Union, who have no lands, forests, mines, or pastures that are not in the possession of private individuals.

Congress will be unable to resist the justice of this contention. As a rule, that body is not overswift to recognize the rights of those sections of the Union with a small representation in the Lower House, but the American people, when they understand the matter thoroughly, may be depended upon to prevent an injustice. Just now the popular impression at the East is that the Far West is opposed to the conservation of its forests, and that it supports the efforts of unscrupulous grabbers to steal the public domain. But the campaign of education inaugurated by the Public Lands Convention will soon convince it that all that is asked for is even justice for the new states, and that demands that the profits arising from the eleventh-hour reform shall not be absorbed by the states that have eaten their cake and now wish to share with those who have scarcely had a chance to nibble theirs.

THOUGHT PROVOKERS

1. Vested interests opposed the Pure Food and Drug Law of 1906 on the ground that one of our basic freedoms is the freedom to eat what we want to. Comment. Does overemphasis on the seamy side of life develop a depraved taste or callousness or both? Which reaction is the more dangerous?

2. It has been said that no community has any better government than it deserves. Comment. Account for the failure of honest citizens to participate more actively in city government.

3. What would be the attitude of organized labor today toward George F. Baer's view that the only interest of the workingman in a business is to secure "fair wages for the work he does"?

4. Would there be fewer or more trusts today if Theodore Roosevelt had never been President?

5. The federal government owns over 20 percent of the land surface of the country today (exclusive of Alaska), chiefly in the West. Is this situation healthy or unhealthy?

33 · *William Howard Taft and the Progressive Revolt*

> *Taft is utterly hopeless. . . . It would be a misfortune to have him in the presidential chair for another term, for he has shown himself an entirely unfit President. . . .*
>
> THEODORE ROOSEVELT, 1911

PROLOGUE: President Taft, the hard-luck conservative, early floundered into hot water. Honestly attempting to revise the tariff, he had to accept a bill (Payne-Aldrich) clearly shaped by the "predatory interests." Seeking to conserve natural resources, he was forced to end a bureaucratic quarrel by dismissing the Chief Forester, Gifford Pinchot, a leading conservationist. He might have weathered such setbacks if the country had not been agitated by the reformist Progressive movement, which attained irresistible momentum between 1908 and 1912. The Progressives strove to achieve overdue reforms by instituting such innovations as woman suffrage, the direct election of United States Senators, and the initiative, the referendum, and the recall. The Progressive crusade reached a crescendo in 1912, when ex-President Roosevelt broke with President Taft, split the Republican Party, and headed a new ("Bull Moose") Progressive ticket. His rebellion insured victory for the Democrat Woodrow Wilson, who carried forward the Progressive tradition under the banner of the New Freedom.

A. THE CRUSADE FOR WOMAN SUFFRAGE

1. Senator Owen Supports Women (1910)

Wedded to the tried and true, President Taft was no enthusiast for woman suffrage. He believed that the issue was one which should be handled by the individual states. As late as 1912 he wrote privately, "I cannot change my view . . . just to suit the exigencies of the campaign, and if it is going to hurt me, I think it will have to hurt me." But the embattled females now had an increasingly strong argument. The rapid industrialization after the Civil War had lured millions of women from the home into the office and the factory, where they were competing with men. By 1910 four states—Wyoming, Colorado, Utah, and Idaho—had granted unrestricted suffrage to women, and the Progressive upheaval of the era added great impetus to the reform. Senator Robert L. Owen, of Oklahoma, who had earlier demanded citizenship for Indians, here makes a speech to a learned society favoring woman suffrage. What ideas about the nature of womanhood underlie his argument? What changes in society does he think woman suffrage will entail?

Women compose one-half of the human race. In the last forty years, women in gradually increasing numbers have been compelled to leave the

---

1. *Annals of the American Academy of Political and Social Science,* Supplement, XXXV (May, 1910), pp. 6–9, *passim.*

home and enter the factory and workshop. Over seven million women are so employed, and the remainder of the sex are employed largely in domestic services. A full half of the work of the world is done by women. A careful study of the matter has demonstrated the vital fact that these working women receive a smaller wage for equal work than men do, and that the smaller wage and harder conditions imposed on the woman worker are due to the lack of the ballot.

Many women have a very hard time, and if the ballot would help them, even a little, I should like to see them have it. . . . Equal pay for equal work is the first great reason justifying this change of governmental policy.

There are other reasons which are persuasive: First, women, take it all in all, are the equals of men in intelligence, and no man has the hardihood to assert the contrary. . . .

The man is usually better informed with regard to state government, but women are better informed about house government, and she can learn state government with as much facility as he can learn how to instruct children, properly feed and clothe the household, care for the sick, play on the piano, or make a house beautiful. . . .

The woman ballot will not revolutionize the world. Its results in Colorado, for example, might have been anticipated. First, it did give women better wages for equal work; second, it led immediately to a number of laws the women wanted, and the first laws they demanded were laws for the protection of the children of the state, making it a misdemeanor to contribute to the delinquency of a child; laws for the improved care of defective children; also, the Juvenile Court for the conservation of wayward boys and girls; the better care of the insane, the deaf, the dumb, the blind; the curfew bell to keep children off the streets at night; raising the age of consent for girls; improving the reformatories and prisons of the state; improving the hospital services of the state; improving the sanitary laws affecting the health of the homes of the state. Their [women's] interest in the public health is a matter of great importance. Above all, there resulted laws for improving the school system.

Several important results followed. Both political parties were induced to put up cleaner, better men, for the women would not stand a notoriously corrupt or unclean candidate. The headquarters of political parties became more decent, and the polling places became respectable. The bad women, enslaved by mercenary vice, do not vote, and good women do vote in as great proportion as men. Every evil prophecy against granting the suffrage has failed. The public men of Colorado, Wyoming, Utah, and Idaho give it a cordial support.

The testimony is universal:

First, it has not made women mannish; they still love their homes and children just the same as ever, and are better able to protect themselves and their children because of the ballot.

Second, they have not become office-seekers, nor pothouse politicians.

They have not become swaggerers and insolent on the streets. They still teach good manners to men, as they always have done. It [suffrage] has made women broader and greatly increased the understanding of the community at large of the problems of good government; of proper sanitation, of pure food, of clean water, and all such matters in which intelligent women would naturally take an interest.

It has not absolutely regenerated society, but it has improved it. It has raised the educational qualification of the suffrage, and has elevated the moral standard of the suffrage, because there are more criminal men than criminal women. . . .

The great doctrine of the American Republic that "all governments derive their just powers from the consent of the governed" justifies the plea of one-half of the people, the women, to exercise the suffrage. The doctrine of the American Revolutionary War that taxation without representation is unendurable justifies women in exercising the suffrage.

2. A Woman Assails Woman Suffrage (1910)

As late as 1910 many women plainly did not want to shoulder the heavy civic responsibilities that would come with the ballot. One argument was that each sex was superior in its own sphere—women in the home, men in the outside world— and that a separation was best for all concerned. Agitators for woman suffrage feared that if their cause were submitted to a vote by all women, it would be defeated. The suffragists argued that the women who wanted the vote ought to have it. Mrs. Gilbert E. Jones, an opponent of votes for women, here pleads her case before a scholarly group. How do her views differ from those of Senator Owen, just given? Which of them esteemed women more highly?

The anti-suffragists are not organizing or rushing into committees, societies, or associations, and their doings are not being cried out from the house-tops. Yet they show by undeniable facts, easily verified, that woman suffrage bills and proposals have been defeated and turned down at the rate of once in every twenty-seven days in the state legislatures for the last twelve years. . . .

A great many states have granted to women school suffrage, but only a partisan or sectarian issue will bring out the woman's vote. In Massachusetts women have voted on school boards, and after thirty years' training, only 2 or 3 percent of the women register to vote. This hardly can be pronounced "success," or worth while. . . .

Taxation without representation is tyranny, but we must be very careful to define what we mean by the phrase. If we adopt the suffrage attitude, "I pay taxes, therefore I should vote," the natural conclusion is that everybody who pays taxes should vote, or we have a tyrannical form of government. Remember that this argument is used in an unqualified way. We have a "tyranny" here, we are told, because some women pay taxes, yet do not vote. If this is true without any qualification, it must be true not only of

2. *Ibid.*, pp. 16–21, *passim.*

THE CHURCH VOTE DISFRANCHISED

Woman-suffrage propaganda issued by the National American Woman
Suffrage Association, *Headquarters News Letter*, October 25, 1916.

women, but of everybody. Accordingly, this government is tyrannical if
corporations pay taxes, but do not vote; if aliens pay taxes, but do not vote;
if minors pay taxes, but do not vote; if anybody pays taxes, but does not
vote. The only correct conclusion is, not that women should vote because
some of them pay taxes, but that every taxpayer should be given the
privilege of the ballot. . . .

A very conscientious investigation by this League cannot find that the
ballot will help the wage-earning woman. Women must resort to organization, association, and trade unions, and then they can command and maintain a standard wage. Supply and demand will do the rest. Women are not
well trained and often very deficient and unskilled in most of their occupations. They are generally only supplementary workers and drop their
work when they marry. When married, and home and children are to be
cared for, they are handicapped way beyond their strength. Married women
should be kept out of industry, rather than urged into it, as scientists, physicians, and sociologists all state that as women enter into competitive
industrial life with men, just so does the death rate of little children increase and the birth rate decrease.

Anti-suffragists deplore the fact that women are found in unsuitable
occupations. But the suffragists glory in the fact that there are women
blacksmiths, baggage masters, brakemen, undertakers, and women political
"bosses" in Colorado.

The suffragists call this progress, independence, and emancipation of women. "Anti's" ask for more discrimination and better selection of industrial occupations for wage-earning women. Knowing that the average woman has half of the physical strength of the average man, and the price she must pay when in competition with him is too great for her ultimate health and her hope of motherhood, the "Anti's" ask for caution and extreme consideration before new activities are entered upon. . . .

The suffrage leaders say that a woman without the vote has no self-respect. We must then look to the suffrage states to find the fulfillment of the woman's true position, complete—worthy, exalted, and respected. But what do we find when we look at Utah! Women have voted there for forty years. Mormonism and woman suffrage were coincident. By the very nature of its teachings, as indicated by Brigham Young, the basis of the Mormon Church is woman—and the Mormon Church is the greatest political machine in the four suffrage States. . . .

The question of woman suffrage should be summed up in this way: Has granting the ballot to women in the two suffrage states where they have had it for forty years brought about any great reforms or great results? No—Wyoming has many more men than women, so the results cannot be measured. The Mormon women of Utah are not free American citizens. They are under the Elder's supreme power, and vote accordingly, and polygamy has been maintained by the woman's vote, and is still to be found, although forbidden, because women have political power.

Have the saloons been abolished in any of the suffrage states? No.

Do men still drink and gamble? Yes, without a doubt.

Have the slums been done away with? Indeed no.

Are the streets better cleaned in the states where women vote? No, they are quite as bad as in New York City and elsewhere.

Have the red-light districts been cleared away? Decidedly not, and they can be reckoned upon as a political factor, when they are really needed.

Have women purified politics? No, not in the least.

Have women voted voluntarily? Some do; but thousands are carried to the polls in autos and carriages; otherwise they would not vote.

Has pure food and pure milk been established by the woman's vote? Not at all.

Have women's wages been increased because women vote? No, indeed.

Have women equal pay for equal work? Not any more than in New York City.

Are there laws on the statute books that would give women equal pay for equal work? No, and never will be.

Are women treated with more respect in the four suffrage states than elsewhere? Not at all—certainly not in Utah. . . .

[*The "Anti's" also argued that womenfolk were adequately represented by their menfolk; that women already exercised a strong influence indirectly ("harem government"); that suffrage would end chivalry; that women were already overburdened in the home; that family quarrels over partisan issues would increase*

the divorce rate; that females were too emotional; and that women, if allowed to
vote, would soon be serving on juries and forced to hear "indecent testimony."
Despite such objections, some of them frivolous, nationwide woman suffrage
finally triumphed with the 19th Amendment in 1920.]

B. THE POPULAR ELECTION OF SENATORS

1. Woodrow Wilson Favors Reform (1912)

The popular election of United States Senators was a favorite goal of the Progressives, and, somewhat surprisingly, President Taft did not come out publicly against it. Election by state legislatures, as required by the Constitution, had resulted in grave abuses. Some wealthy but unfit men were securing their seats by wirepulling and outright vote buying. At one time three Senators were under federal indictment for accepting bribes. Millionaires, like the powerful Senator Aldrich of Rhode Island, were more responsive to the demands of Big Business than to those of the people. Voting deadlocks in the legislatures over Senators often led to a paralysis of state business, to various unsavory "deals," and to a prolonged lack of representation in the Senate. For nearly two years, from 1895 to 1897, Delaware had only one Senator. Woodrow Wilson of New Jersey, the Democratic nominee for the Presidency in 1912, here delivers a "folksy" campaign speech for the direct election of Senators. Why, in his view, had the state legislatures not sent better men to the Senate?

Then there is another thing that the conservative people are concerned about: the direct election of United States Senators. I have seen some thoughtful men discuss that with a sort of shiver, as if to disturb the original constitution of the United States Senate was to do something touched with impiety, touched with irreverence for the Constitution itself. But the first thing necessary to reverence for the United States Senate is respect for United States Senators.

I am not one of those who condemn the United States Senate as a body; for, no matter what has happened there, no matter how questionable the practices or how corrupt the influences which have filled some of the seats in that high body, it must in fairness be said that the majority in it has all the years through been untouched by stain, and that there has always been there a sufficient number of men of integrity to vindicate the self-respect and the hopefulness of America with regard to her institutions.

But you need not be told, and it would be painful to repeat to you, how seats have been bought in the Senate; and you know that a little group of Senators holding the balance of power has again and again been able to defeat programs of reform upon which the whole country had set its heart; and that whenever you analyzed the power that was behind those little groups you have found that it was not the power of public opinion, but some private influence, hardly to be discerned by superficial scrutiny, that had put those men there to do that thing.

Now, returning to the original principles upon which we profess to stand,

1. Woodrow Wilson, *The New Freedom* (1913), pp. 231–34. By permission of Mrs. Edith Bolling Wilson.

have the people of the United States not the right to see to it that every seat in the Senate represents the unbought United States of America? Does the direct election of Senators touch anything except the private control of seats in the Senate?

We remember another thing: that we have not been without our suspicions concerning some of the legislatures which elect Senators. Some of the suspicions which we entertained in New Jersey about them turned out to be founded upon very solid facts indeed. Until two years ago New Jersey had not in half a generation been represented in the United States Senate by the men who would have been chosen if the process of selecting them had been free and based upon the popular will.

We are not to deceive ourselves by putting our heads into the sand and saying, "Everything is all right." Mr. Gladstone declared that the American Constitution was the most perfect instrument ever devised by the brain of man. We have been praised all over the world for our singular genius for setting up successful institutions, but a very thoughtful Englishman, and a very witty one, said a very instructive thing about that: he said that to show that the American Constitution had worked well was no proof that it is an excellent constitution, because Americans could run any constitution —a compliment which we laid like sweet unction to our soul; and yet a criticism which ought to set us thinking.

While it is true that when American forces are awake they can conduct American processes without serious departure from the ideals of the Constitution, it is nevertheless true that we have had many shameful instances of practices which we can absolutely remove by the direct election of Senators by the people themselves. And therefore I, for one, will not allow any man who knows his history to say to me that I am acting inconsistently with either the spirit or the essential form of the American government in advocating the direct election of United States Senators.

2. Senator Root Opposes Change (1911)

Senator Elihu Root of New York was probably the most influential conservative of his generation. Onetime Secretary of War and Secretary of State under Theodore Roosevelt, he shunned elective office, partly because public opinion was turning against wealthy corporation lawyers. Root instinctively took a strong position against the popular election of Senators. In the light of subsequent American history, how sound was his prediction that direct election would bring a different class of person to the Senate?

There are specific reasons against this change. The first great reason, in my mind, is that it is inconsistent with the fundamental design of the Senate. The purpose of the Constitution was to create in the Senate a body which would be as unlike as possible to the other House. It was to be a body more secure in tenure, different in the manner of its election, different in its responsibility, more conservative, more deliberate than the other

2. *The Independent*, LXX, 497–98, 500 (March 9, 1911).

House, which responds year by year to every movement of the public mind and the public feeling.

The Senate was established by the Constitution to protect the American democracy against itself. The framers of the Constitution realized that the weakness of democracy is the liability to continual change; they realized that there needed to be some guardian of the sober second thought, and so they created the Senate. This change is to decrease the difference between the two Houses; to make the two more alike; to make the function of the Senate less distinctive, and to reduce the benefit which the Senate can render to the public service. . . .

. . . By the change we should also prevent the Senate from having the benefit of the service of a large class of citizens who are specifically qualified by character and training to render a peculiar kind of service especially needed for the purposes of the Senate, men who by lives of experience and effort have attained the respect of their fellow citizens and who are willing to undertake the burdens of public office, but who are unwilling to seek it; men who will accept the burden as a patriotic duty, with mingled feelings of satisfaction at the honor and dissatisfaction with the burden, the disturbance of life, the abuse of the press, the controversies about performance of duty, but who never would subject themselves to the disagreeable incidents, the strife, the personalities of a political campaign. This change will exile from the floor of the Senate men who answer closely to many of the greatest names in the glorious history of this body.

It is wholly unnecessary to provide for or demand a reform in the constitution of the Senate upon the theory that the existing system has failed. It is true that occasionally bad men are sent to the Senate; occasionally a man is sent who would not have been chosen in a fair and honest election by the people of the State. But they find their level and they find it in innocuous insignificance. . . .

There is no weaker course for men to take than to endeavor to make up for failure to do their duty by changing the form of the duty. It is a proposition that the people who cannot elect honest men from their own neighbors to their state legislatures can elect honest men to the Senate of the United States. But how can men who are unable or unwilling to perform the duty of selecting an honest and faithful legislator from their own vicinage improve upon their performance in the selection of a candidate in a statewide election of candidates whom most of them know little or nothing about except what they get from the newspapers?

Why should we consent to any attempt at an evasion of duty? The pathway lies clear before us under the Constitution. If we will do our duty the Constitution needs no amendment. If we do not do our duty you can amend the Constitution a thousand times without any utility.

[*The direct election of Senators (17th Amendment) became a part of the Constitution on May 31, 1913, less than three months after Woodrow Wilson entered the White House.*]

C. THE INITIATIVE AND THE REFERENDUM

1. Wilson Urges Popular Control (1912)

President Taft was definitely unfriendly to the initiative and the referendum. But these devices were enthusiastically sponsored by the Progressives as means of coping with state legislatures that were failing to pass needed reform or were passing laws dictated by "the interests." Under the initiative, a stipulated percentage of the electorate (often 5 percent) could petition to have a proposed law placed on the ballot and then voted on at a general election. Under the referendum, a requisite percentage of the voters could petition to have a legislature-enacted law referred to the electorate for approval or disapproval. Candidate Woodrow Wilson, who as a professor of government at Princeton had long derided such schemes as "bosh," favored them in his down-to-earth speeches in the presidential campaign of 1912. How did he justify his reversal?

Why do you suppose that in the United States, the place in all the world where the people were invited to control their own government, we should set up such an agitation as that for the initiative and referendum and the recall? When did this thing begin?

I have been receiving circulars and documents from little societies of men all over the United States with regard to these matters for the last twenty-five years. But the circulars for a long time kindled no fire. Men felt that they had representative government and they were content. But about ten or fifteen years ago the fire began to burn—and it has been sweeping over wider and wider areas of the country—because of the growing consciousness that something intervenes between the people and the government, and that there must be some arm direct enough and strong enough to thrust aside the something that comes in the way.

I believe that we are upon the eve of recovering some of the most important prerogatives of a free people, and that the initiative and referendum are playing a great part in that recovery. I met a man the other day who thought that the referendum was some kind of an animal, because it had a Latin name; and there are still people in this country who have to have it explained to them. But most of us know and are deeply interested. Why? Because we have felt that in too many instances our government did not represent us, and we have said: "We have got to have a key to the door of our own house. The initiative and referendum and the recall afford such a key to our own premises. If the people inside the house will run the place as we want it run, they may stay inside and we will keep the latchkeys in our pockets. If they do not, we shall have to re-enter upon possession."

Let no man be deceived by the cry that somebody is proposing to substitute direct legislation by the people, or the direct reference of laws passed in the legislature to the vote of the people, for representative government. The advocates of these reforms have always declared, and declared in unmistakable terms, that they were intending to recover representative government, not supersede it; that the initiative and referendum would find

1. Woodrow Wilson, *The New Freedom* (1913), pp. 235–37. By permission of Mrs. Edith Bolling Wilson.

no use in places where legislatures were really representative of the people whom they were elected to serve. The initiative is a means of seeing to it that measures which the people want shall be passed—when legislatures defy or ignore public opinion. The referendum is a means of seeing to it that the unrepresentative measures which they do not want shall not be placed upon the statute book.

2. Taft Scorns the Initiative and Referendum (1915)

South Dakota blazed the trail in 1898 by adopting both the initiative and the referendum for ordinary state laws. A score or more of sister states ultimately followed in her footsteps. Several states, spurning the more dangerous initiative, espoused only the referendum, which the cynical Ambrose Bierce described as a means of determining "the nonsensus of public opinion." The radical West, more than the conservative East, embraced these Progressive schemes. Ex-President Taft spelled out his disapproval in a lecture at Yale University. Why does he regard these measures as threatening to American society?

Now what is the initiative? In practice, it means that if 5 percent of the electorate can get together and agree on a measure, they shall compel all the rest of the electorate to vote as to whether it shall become law or not. There is no opportunity for amendment, or for discussion. The whole legislative program is put into one act to be voted on by the people.

Speakers will get up and claim that the millennium will be brought about by some measure that they advocate. Suppose it is voted in? It never has had the test of discussion and amendment that every law ought to have. I am not complaining of the movement that brings about this initiative and referendum, for that is prompted by a desire to clinch the movement against corruption, on the theory that you cannot corrupt the whole people and that the initiative and referendum mean detailed and direct government by the whole people. But the theory is erroneous. The whole people will not vote at an election, much less at a primary. When the people are thus represented at the polls by a small minority, there is nothing that the politicians will not be able to do with that minority when they get their hands in. . . .

Now what is the referendum? It is a reference of the thing proposed by the initiative to the people who are to vote on it. . . .

What answer do the people themselves give with reference to the wisdom of the referendum? At many elections candidates run at the same time that questions are referred to the people, and what is the usual result of the vote? In Oregon, where they have tried it most, and where the people are best trained, they do sometimes get as much as 70 percent of those who vote on candidates to vote on the referendum. But generally, as in Colorado, the vote at the same election upon the referendum measures is not more than 50 percent—sometimes as low as 25 or 20 percent—of those who vote for candidates. . . .

2. W. H. Taft, *Ethics in Service* (1915), pp. 78–82. By permission of the Yale University Press.

They have tried it in Switzerland. We get a good many of these new nostrums from that country. They said in Switzerland, "These men vote for candidates, they shall vote on referendums." What was the result? The electors went up to the polls and solemnly put in tickets. When they opened the ballots, they were blanks. What does that mean? It means that the people themselves believe that they do not know how to vote on those issues, and that such issues ought to be left to the agents whom they select as competent persons to discuss and pass upon them in accordance with the general principles that they have laid down in party platforms.

In Oregon, at the last presidential election, the people were invited to vote on thirty-one statutes, long, complicated statutes, and in order to inform them, a book of two hundred and fifty closely printed pages was published to tell them what the statutes meant.

I ask you, my friends, you who are studious, you who are earnest men who would like to be a part of the people in determining what their policy should be, I ask you to search yourselves and confess whether you would have the patience to go through that book of two hundred and fifty closely printed pages to find out what those acts meant? You would be in active business, you would go down to the polls and say, "What is up today?" You would be told: "Here are thirty-one statutes. Here are two hundred and fifty pages that we would like to have you read in order that you may determine how you are to vote on them." You would not do it.

There was once a Senator from Oregon named Jonathan Bourne, who advocated all this system of more democracy. He served one term in the Senate, and then sent word back to his constituents that he was not coming home at the time of the primary. He said that he was not on trial, for a man who had worked as hard as he had for the people could not be on trial. Instead, he said, it was the people of Oregon who were on trial, to say whether they appreciated a service like this. They did not stand the test, and he was defeated at the primary. Then he concluded that after all he would have to forgive them and take pity on them in their blindness. So he went out to Oregon and ran on another ticket to give them the benefit of his service. But still they resisted the acid test. He himself went to the polls to vote at this election where there were thirty-one statutes to be approved or rejected. How many of the thirty-one submitted to him do you suppose he voted for? The newspapers reported him as admitting that he voted on just three, and the other twenty-eight he left to fate. Now, gentlemen, is not that a demonstration? Is not that a *reductio ad absurdum* for this system of pure and direct democracy?

D. POPULAR CONTROL OF THE JUDICIARY

1. Taft Lambasts the Recall of Judges (1911)

Hand in glove with the initiative and referendum went the recall of elected officials. The theory was that inept or corrupt public servants should be summarily

1. *Congressional Record*, 62 Cong., 1 sess., p. 3965 (Aug. 15, 1911).

removed by a special election. Oregon, the first state to adopt this scheme, was followed by about a dozen others. But several of the "recall" states specifically exempted elected judges. In 1911 the territory of Arizona applied for admission as a state with a constitution that provided for the recall of the judiciary. A scandalized President Taft, himself an ex-judge, sternly vetoed the resolution. Arizona removed the offensive provision and was admitted the next year. It thereupon defiantly restored the innovation, and the federal government was powerless to act. Why does Taft consider the recall of judges to be more dangerous than that of other elective officials?

By the recall in the Arizona constitution it is proposed to give to the majority power to remove arbitrarily, and without delay, any judge who may have the courage to render an unpopular decision. By the recall it is proposed to enable a minority of 25 percent of the voters of the district or state, for no prescribed cause, after the judge has been in office six months, to submit the question of his retention in office to the electorate.

The petitioning minority must say on the ballot what they can against him in two hundred words, and he must defend as best he can in the same ꞁpace. Other candidates are permitted to present themselves and have their names printed on the ballot, so that the recall is not based solely on the record or the acts of the judge, but also on the question whether some other more popular candidate has been found to unseat him.

Could there be a system more ingeniously devised to subject judges to momentary gusts of popular passion than this? We cannot be blind to the fact that often an intelligent and respectable electorate may be so roused upon an issue that it will visit with condemnation the decision of a just judge, though exactly in accord with the law governing the case, merely because it affects unfavorably their contest. Controversies over elections, labor troubles, racial or religious issues as to the construction or constitutionality of liquor laws, criminal trials of popular or unpopular defendants, the removal of county seats, suits by individuals to maintain their constitutional rights in obstruction of some popular improvement—these and many other cases could be cited in which a majority of a district electorate would be tempted by hasty anger to recall a conscientious judge if the opportunity were open all the time.

No period of delay is interposed for the abatement of popular feeling. The recall is devised to encourage quick action, and to lead the people to strike while the iron is hot. The judge is treated as the instrument and servant of a majority of the people and subject to their momentary will, not after a long term in which his qualities as a judge and his character as a man have been subjected to a test of all the varieties of judicial work and duty so as to furnish a proper means of measuring his fitness for continuance in another term. On the instant of an unpopular ruling, while the spirit of protest has not had time to cool and even while an appeal may be pending from his ruling in which he may be sustained, he is to be haled before the electorate as a tribunal, with no judicial hearing, evidence, or defense, and thrown out of office, and disgraced for life because he has failed, in a single decision, it may be, to satisfy the popular demand.

Think of the opportunity such a system would give to unscrupulous political bosses in control, as they have been in control, not only of conventions but elections! Think of the enormous power for evil given to the sensational, muckraking portion of the press in rousing prejudice against a just judge by false charges and insinuations, the effect of which in the short period of an election by recall it would be impossible for him to meet and offset!

Supporters of such a system seem to think that it will work only in the interest of the poor, the humble, the weak, and the oppressed; that it will strike down only the judge who is supposed to favor corporations and be affected by the corrupting influence of the rich.

Nothing could be further from the ultimate result. The motive it would offer to unscrupulous combinations to seek to control politics in order to control judges is clear. Those would profit by the recall who have the best opportunity of rousing the majority of the people to action on a sudden impulse. Are they likely to be the wisest or the best people in a community? Do they not include those who have money enough to employ the firebrands and slanderers in a community and the stirrers-up of social hate? Would not self-respecting men well hesitate to accept judicial office with such a sword of Damocles hanging over them? What kind of judgments might those on the unpopular side expect from courts whose judges must make their decisions under such legalized terrorism? The character of the judges would deteriorate to that of trimmers and time-servers, and independent judicial action would be a thing of the past.

As the possibilities of such a system pass in review, is it too much to characterize it as one which will destroy the judiciary, its standing, and its usefulness?

2. Roosevelt and Judicial Decisions (1912)

Ex-President Roosevelt, returning from shooting lions in Africa, became increasingly disturbed by President Taft's association with Old Guard reactionaries. Enthusiastically embracing the program of the Progressives, he went so far in a flaming speech at Columbus, Ohio, as to advocate the recall of judicial decisions at the state level. This extreme proposal shocked conservatives, and ultimately contributed to his defeat in the presidential race of 1912. In what ways are Roosevelt's views on this subject consistent or inconsistent with his general brand of Progressivism?

I do not believe in adopting the recall [of judges] save as a last resort, when it has become clearly evident that no other course will achieve the desired result. But either the recall will have to be adopted or else it will have to be made much easier than it now is to get rid, not merely of a bad judge, but of a judge who, however virtuous, has grown so out of touch with social needs and facts that he is unfit longer to render good service on the bench.

It is nonsense to say that impeachment meets the difficulty. In actual

2. *Senate Documents,* 62 Cong., 2 sess., No. 348, XXXVI, pp. 14–15 (Feb. 21, 1912).

practice we have found that impeachment does not work, that unfit judges stay on the bench in spite of it, and indeed because of the fact that impeachment is the only remedy that can be used against them. Where such is the actual fact it is idle to discuss the theory of the case. Impeachment as a remedy for the ills of which the people justly complain is a complete failure. . . .

A RADICAL ROOSEVELT DEMANDS A THIRD TERM
New York *World*, 1912.

But there is one kind of recall in which I very earnestly believe, and the immediate adoption of which I urge. There are sound reasons for being cautious about the recall of a good judge who has rendered an unwise and improper decision. Every public servant, no matter how valuable, and not omitting Washington or Lincoln or Marshall, at times makes mistakes. Therefore we should be cautious about recalling the judge, and we should be cautious about interfering in any way with the judge in decisions which he makes in the ordinary course as between individuals. But when a judge decides a constitutional question, when he decides what the people as a whole can or cannot do, the people should have the right to recall that decision if they think it wrong. We should hold the judiciary in all respect; but it is both absurd and degrading to make a fetish of a judge or of anyone else. . . .

When the supreme court of the state declares a given statute unconstitutional, because in conflict with the state or the national constitution, its opinion should be subject to revision by the people themselves. Such an opinion ought always to be treated with great respect by the people, and unquestionably in the majority of cases would be accepted and followed by them. But actual experience has shown the vital need of the people reserving to themselves the right to pass upon such opinion. If any considerable number of the people feel that the decision is in defiance of justice, they should be given the right by petition to bring before the voters at some subsequent election, special or otherwise, as might be decided, and after the fullest opportunity for deliberation and debate, the question whether or not the judges' interpretation of the Constitution is to be sustained. If it is sustained, well and good. If not, then the popular verdict is to be accepted as final, the decision is to be treated as reversed, and the construction of the Constitution definitely decided—subject only to action by the Supreme Court of the United States.

THOUGHT PROVOKERS

1. In what ways could women defend their rights before they received the ballot? Has woman suffrage improved conditions as much as anticipated? In what ways, if any, has the nation's political agenda changed as a result of woman suffrage?

2. Has the direct election of Senators achieved the changes that its most optimistic advocates predicted? Would we be better off under the old system?

3. Which is the least vulnerable to criticism: the initiative, the referendum, or the recall? Explain.

4. In the absence of recall, what means has the public to protect itself against incompetent, arbitrary, corrupt, or senile judges? Do greater evils flow from non-regulation than from popular regulation of the judiciary? Explain. Woodrow Wilson said: "Judges . . . determine not what the law should be, but what the law is." Comment.

5. In the light of our experience with third parties, including the Progressive, is it more effective to try to reform the party from within or to secede from the party?

34 · *Woodrow Wilson and the New Freedom*

> *We dare not turn from the principle that morality and not expediency is the thing that must guide us. . . .*
>
> PRESIDENT WILSON, 1913

PROLOGUE: Ex-Professor Wilson was spectacularly successful in inducing Congress to do the homework necessary to launch the New Freedom—that is, the economic freedom that would result from curbing monopoly and encouraging free competition. Legislative landmarks of 1913–1914 were the Underwood-Simmons Act (to lower the tariff), the Federal Reserve Act (to reform banking and currency), the Federal Trade Commission Act (to halt unfair practices), and the Clayton Anti-Trust Act (to restrain monopoly). Wilson's moralistic Mexican policy of "watchful waiting," despite the wholesale murder of Americans, evoked vehement demands for war. But Wilson, with the struggling masses of Mexico ever in mind, managed to avoid a full-dress intervention.

A. BATTLING FOR TARIFF REFORM

1. A President Appears before Congress (1913)

Woodrow Wilson, a lifelong foe of a highly protective tariff, had refused to uphold the "wrong side" of the question as a student debater at Princeton. As President, he was determined to redeem his campaign pledges and lower the existing Republican rates. Regarding himself as a colleague rather than a competitor of Congress, he decided to bridge the mile-long gap between Capitol Hill and the White House by presenting his messages in person. (President Jefferson, shy and weak-voiced, had discontinued personal appearances in 1801.) Wilson's shattering of precedent struck many Senators as effrontery. Secretary of Agriculture Houston, an ex-university president himself, here recaptures the tension in his diary entry. Note the distinction that Wilson makes between "protection" and "patronage." Why, basically, does he urge a lowering of the tariff?

The discussion [in the Cabinet] was interrupted because the President had to leave at twelve o'clock to go to the Capitol to read his Tariff Message. I had a distinct sensation when this departure was brought thus sharply to my mind. I recognized both its political and historical significance. Some members of the Cabinet seemed to be a trifle shaky about the venture. The President showed no sign that he was aware, as of course he was, that anything unusual was about to happen.

The President regards himself as the head of his party and its political leader. He believes that he can lead better, can get nearer to Congress, and

---

1. D. F. Houston, *Eight Years with Wilson's Cabinet* (1926), I, 52–55.

convey his message more impressively to the people by delivering his message in person. He is right; and his example will probably be followed till we get a President who is timid and a poor or indifferent speaker.

Most of the members of the Cabinet went to the Capitol to hear the President read his message. . . . There seemed to me to be a distinctly tense atmosphere, as if strange things were about to happen. Members of Congress appeared to be a trifle nervous, and something of a chill pervaded the air. Some members of Congress, I thought, had a sullen look. Suddenly the President of the United States was announced, and the Speaker rapped loudly with his gavel. The whole body stood up. . . .

The beauty of the President's English was instantly felt; and his first sentences relieved the strain and made for easier feeling. They were:

"I am very glad indeed to have this opportunity to address the two Houses directly and to verify for myself the impression that the President of the United States is a person, not a mere department of the government, hailing Congress from some isolated island of jealous power, sending messages, not speaking naturally and with his own voice—that he is a human being trying to cooperate with other human beings in a common service. After this pleasant experience I shall feel quite normal in all our dealings with one another."

The message was short. It pointed out that the tariff burden should be lightened; that, while the whole face of our commercial life had altered, tariff schedules had remained the same or had moved in the direction they had been given when no large circumstance of our industrial development was what it appeared today, and that our task was to square them with the facts. Tariff legislation had wandered very far afield. We had passed beyond the notion of protecting industry. We had come to hold that it was entitled to the direct patronage of the government. We were giving to each group of manufacturers what they thought they needed to maintain a closed market. We had built a set of privileges and fostered monopoly, "until at last nothing is normal, nothing is obliged to stand the test of efficiency and economy, in our world of big business, but everything thrives by concerted agreement.

"We must abolish everything that bears even the semblance of privilege or of any kind of artificial advantage, and put our businessmen and our producers under the stimulation of a constant necessity to be efficient, economical, and enterprising, masters of competitive supremacy, better merchants and better traders than any in the world." The object of duties henceforth must be to promote effective competition. We must accomplish our purpose without reckless haste. We must build up our foreign trade. We more than ever need an outlet for our energies. . . .

The next time I saw the President was at Cabinet meeting on Friday, April 11th. When he came in, I congratulated him on his address and on the success of his personally appearing before Congress. He thanked me and smilingly remarked: "Congress looked embarrassed. I did not feel so."

2. Wilson Tackles the Tariff Lobby (1913)

The new low-tariff Underwood Bill passed the Democratic House without undue difficulty, but when it reached the Senate the fast-talking lobbyists descended in droves. Buttonholing Senators, they resorted to high-pressure persuasion. The bill was in grave danger of being mutilated, as similar measures had been in the days of Presidents Cleveland and Taft. Wilson thereupon appealed over the heads of the lobbyists to the people in the following remarkable statement issued to the press. A snowstorm of approving telegrams and letters descended upon the White House and Congress. The lobbyists scurried for cover, and the Underwood-Simmons Bill passed in substantially its original form. Could the Senate properly regard this statement as a reflection on its integrity?

I think that the public ought to know the extraordinary exertions being made by the lobby in Washington to gain recognition for certain alterations of the Tariff bill. Washington has seldom seen so numerous, so industrious, or so insidious a lobby. The newspapers are being filled with paid advertisements calculated to mislead the judgment of public men not only, but also the public opinion of the country itself. There is every evidence that money without limit is being spent to sustain this lobby and to create an appearance of a pressure of opinion antagonistic to some of the chief items of the Tariff bill.

It is of serious interest to the country that the people at large should have no lobby and be voiceless in these matters, while great bodies of astute men seek to create an artificial opinion and to overcome the interests of the public for their private profit. It is thoroughly worth the while of the people of this country to take knowledge of this matter. Only public opinion can check and destroy it.

The Government in all its branches ought to be relieved from this intolerable burden and this constant interruption to the calm progress of debate. I know that in this I am speaking for the members of the two Houses, who would rejoice as much as I would to be released from this unbearable situation.

3. Senator Cummins Defends Lobbying (1913)

Wilson's routing of the lobbyists aroused the Senate to a four-hour debate, during which some Republicans professed to be insulted. Certain Senators attempted to draw a distinction between the professional lobbyist, who would espouse any cause for money, and the legitimate representatives of endangered interests. Senator Cummins of Iowa, a progressive Republican who had voted against the high Republican tariff of 1909, here recounts his own experience. Was the lobbying he describes legitimate or illegitimate?

. . . I represent a state that probably has as little direct concern in the tariff as any state in the Union. I represent a state that can probably care for itself without any assistance whatever from legislation as well or as completely as any state in the Union.

2. *Congressional Record*, 63 Cong., 1 sess., p. 1804 (statement of May 26, 1913).
3. *Ibid.*, pp. 1802–03 (May 29, 1913).

Yet this bill had barely reached the Senate until there came into my office a committee composed of three of the best-known and the most estimable men in my state. They constituted a committee raised by what is known as the Corn Belt Meat Producers' Association, an association made up of the farmers of my state, who would be horrified if from any source they were characterized as lobbyists attempting to improperly influence legislation. They came here to protest against admitting meat free and at the same time putting a duty on cattle.

I acted simply as their guide to the subcommittee room presided over so graciously and, I am sure, so fairly by my distinguished friend from Mississippi [Senator Williams]. They were received in a perfectly proper way; they were received kindly and decently, and they stated their case to the members of the subcommittee.

What impression they made I do not know, nor need I inquire. They did not confine the submission of their case to the subcommittee in formal session. They laid the facts, as they understood them, before every Senator with whom they could secure an audience; and having done so, like the good people they are, they went home.

I do not know whether their visit here accomplished anything or not; that is yet to be ascertained. But I do not want the people of this country to receive the impression that there was anything wrong in those men from my state coming to Washington for the purpose of putting before individual Senators or a committee of Senators their case as they understood it, and explaining how the proposed change in the tariff law would affect them.

[*The Democratic press generally acclaimed the new low-tariff Underwood-Simmons law. The New York* World *exulted: "It is the first tariff in fifty years which was passed by the representatives of the people, and not by the representatives of privilege and plutocracy." On the other hand, the Republican Boston* Evening Transcript *sourly remarked, "Framed unscientifically, and inspired by partisanship, the new tariff will of necessity encounter political and industrial opposition."*]

B. CAMPAIGNING FOR MONETARY REFORM

1. Brandeis Indicts Interlocking Directorates (1914)

Populists, muckrakers, Progressives, and Wilsonian Democrats alike had condemned the monopolistic "Money Trust." In 1912 the Democratic House of Representatives appointed the famed Pujo Committee, which launched a searching investigation. The next year it released a sensational report stating that 341 directorships in 112 corporations controlled resources amounting to $22,245,000,000. Many of these directorships, including the Wall Street House of Morgan, were interlocking. Louis D. Brandeis, a brilliant young liberal destined to be a Supreme Court justice, develops this aspect in the following partial summary of the Pujo Committee's findings. What is the most objectionable feature of interlocking directorates from the standpoint of the public?

1. L. D. Brandeis, *Other People's Money* (1914), pp. 51–53. By permission of Harper & Row, Publishers, Inc.

The practice of interlocking directorates is the root of many evils. It offends laws human and divine. Applied to rival corporations, it tends to the suppression of competition and to violation of the Sherman [anti-trust] law. Applied to corporations which deal with each other, it tends to disloyalty and to violation of the fundamental law that no man can serve two masters. In either event it tends to inefficiency; for it removes incentive and destroys soundness of judgment. It is undemocratic, for it rejects the platform: "A fair field and no favors," substituting the pull of privilege for the push of manhood. It is the most potent instrument of the Money Trust. Break the control so exercised by the investment bankers over railroads, public-service and industrial corporations, over banks, life-insurance and trust companies, and a long step will have been taken toward attainment of the New Freedom.

The term "interlocking directorates" is here used in a broad sense as including all intertwined conflicting interests, whatever the form, and by whatever device effected. The objection extends alike to contracts of a corporation, whether with one of its directors individually, or with a firm of which he is a member, or with another corporation in which he is interested as an officer or director or stockholder. The objection extends likewise to men holding the inconsistent position of director in two potentially competing corporations, even if those corporations do not actually deal with each other.

A single example will illustrate the vicious circle of control—the endless chain—through which our financial oligarchy now operates:

J. P. Morgan (or a partner), a director of the New York, New Haven & Hartford Railroad, causes that company to sell to J. P. Morgan & Co. an issue of bonds. J. P. Morgan & Co. borrow the money with which to pay for the bonds from the Guaranty Trust Company, of which Mr. Morgan (or a partner) is a director. J. P. Morgan & Co. sell the bonds to the Penn Mutual Life Insurance Company, of which Mr. Morgan (or a partner) is a director. The New Haven spends the proceeds of the bonds in purchasing steel rails from the United States Steel Corporation, of which Mr. Morgan (or a partner) is a director. The United States Steel Corporation spends the proceeds of the rails in purchasing electrical supplies from the General Electric Company, of which Mr. Morgan (or a partner) is a director. The General Electric Company sells supplies to the Western Union Telegraph Company, a subsidiary of the American Telephone and Telegraph Company; and in both Mr. Morgan (or a partner) is a director.

2. Morgan Denies a Money Trust (1913)

J. Pierpont Morgan, bulbous-nosed but august, appeared before the Pujo Committee with eight attorneys. (Their estimated fees for two days were $45,000.) He denied not only the existence of a "Money Trust" but the possibility of its existence. Less convincing was his claim that he neither possessed nor desired great financial

2. *Letter from Messrs. J. P. Morgan & Co.* . . . (privately printed, Feb. 25, 1913), pp. 8–9, 12, 17–18. Reproduced by permission.

power. A subsequent letter from the House of Morgan to the Pujo Committee summarized the influential financier's point of view. To what extent does this statement refute the charges against the bankers?

. . . There have been spread before your Committee elaborate tables of so-called interlocking directorates, from which exceedingly mistaken inferences have been publicly drawn. In these tables it is shown that 180 bankers and bank directors serve upon the boards of corporations having resources aggregating $25,000,000,000, and it is implied that this vast aggregate of the country's wealth is at the disposal of these 180 men.

But such an implication rests solely upon the untenable theory that these men, living in different parts of the country, in many cases personally unacquainted with each other, and in most cases associated only in occasional transactions, vote always for the same policies and control with united purpose the directorates of the 132 corporations on which they serve.

The testimony failed to establish any concerted policy or harmony of action binding these 180 men together, and, as a matter of fact, no such policy exists. The absurdity of the assumption of such control becomes more apparent when one considers that, on the average, these directors represent only one quarter of the memberships of their boards. It is preposterous to suppose that every "interlocking" director has full control in every organization with which he is connected, and that the majority of directors who are not "interlocking" are mere figureheads, subject to the will of a small minority of their boards.

Perhaps the greatest harm in the presentation referred to lay in the further unwarranted inference, to which has been given wide publicity, that the vast sum of $25,-000,000,000 was in cash or liquid form, subject to the selfish use or abuse of individuals. Such an idea excites the public mind to demand the correction of a fancied situation which does not and, in our belief, never can exist. . . .

Such growth in the size of banks in New York and Chicago has frequently been erroneously designated before your Committee as "concentration," whereas we have

HIS ALIBI
New York *World*, 1913.

hitherto pointed out [that] the growth of banking resources in New York City has been less rapid than that of the rest of the country. But increase of capital, and merger of two or more banks into one institution (with the same resources as the aggregate of the banks merging into it), has been frequent, especially since January 1, 1908.

These mergers, however, are a development due simply to the demand for larger banking facilities to care for the growth of the country's business. As our cities double and treble in size and importance, as railroads extend and industrial plants expand, not only is it natural, but it is necessary, that our banking institutions should grow in order to care for the increased demands put upon them. Perhaps it is not known as well as it should be that in New York City the largest banks are far inferior in size to banks in the commercial capitals of other and much smaller countries. . . .

For a private banker to sit upon . . . a directorate is in most instances a duty, not a privilege. Inquiry will readily develop the fact that the members of the leading banking houses in this country—and it was the leading houses only against which animadversions were directed—are besought continually to act as directors in various corporations, whose securities they may handle, and that in general they enter only those boards which the opinion of the investing public requires them to enter, as an evidence of good faith that they are willing to have their names publicly associated with the management.

Yet, before your Committee, this natural and eminently desirable relationship was made to appear almost sinister, and no testimony whatever was adduced to show the actual working of such relationships.

3. McAdoo Exposes the Bankers (*c.* 1913)

President Wilson, the foe of special privilege, was determined to break the so-called money monopoly. The need for a more flexible currency had been brought home to the nation by the disastrous "Bankers' Panic" of 1907. Wilson therefore threw the weight of his dynamic personality behind the Federal Reserve Bill introduced in Congress in 1913. The big bankers, mostly conservative Republicans, fought it passionately. They favored a huge new central bank with themselves in control; they were forced to accept a twelve-district Federal Reserve System, with a government-appointed Federal Reserve Board in control. Lanky, black-haired William G. McAdoo, Wilson's Secretary of the Treasury (and son-in-law), here describes the initial opposition of the bankers. In what respect are they most seriously wrong?

As time went by, we observed that the public generally—I mean the ordinary, average citizen—was in favor of the Federal Reserve Bill. The bankers in the larger money centers were almost to a man bitterly opposed to it, and many businessmen shared their views. Sentiment among the smaller banks was divided—those against the bill being largely in the majority.

At the national convention of the American Bankers' Association, held in Boston, October, 1913, only two delegates attempted to speak in favor of the legislation; each was howled down until the chairman managed to

3. From *Crowded Years* by W. G. McAdoo. Copyright 1931 by William G. McAdoo. Copyright © renewed 1959 by Eleanor McAdoo. Reprinted by permission of Houghton Mifflin Company.

make himself heard, and begged the convention to give them the courtesy of attention.

Dr. Joseph French Johnson, professor of political economy at New York University, said at a dinner of the Academy of Political Science that the bill, if passed, would bring on a dangerous credit expansion and that it would cause "a collapse of the banking system." He added that "blacksmiths could not be expected to produce a Swiss watch." The blacksmiths were, in this case, I suppose, the Democrats, and the Federal Reserve Bill was the Swiss watch. So I infer, and I fancy that another meaning, to the effect that Professor Johnson himself was an excellent watchmaker, lurked in the background.

And from Chicago came reports of a speech of Senator Lawrence Y. Sherman, Republican member of the Senate from Illinois. In addressing the Illinois Bankers' Association he said: "I would support a law to wind a watch with a crowbar as cheerfully as I will support any such bill."

But James B. Forgan, banking magnate of Chicago, was more direct in his expression of opinion. He said nothing about crowbars and blacksmiths and Swiss watches. He declared that the bill was "unworkable, impractical, and fundamentally bad." It would bring about, he said, "the most damnable contraction of currency ever seen in any country."

Forgan's idea that the currency would be damnably contracted was not shared by all the opponents of the Glass-Owen [Federal Reserve] Bill. Many bankers and economists proved, to their own satisfaction by figures and diagrams, that the Federal Reserve System would produce an extraordinary inflation. These vast and irreconcilable differences of opinion between the various groups of our adversaries had the effect of lessening my respect for so-called banking experts. I found that they could take the same set of facts and reach two diametrically opposite conclusions.

For example, Forgan estimated that the currency would be contracted to the extent of $1,800,000,000, while Senator Elihu Root, using the same data, predicted an inflation of at least $1,800,000,000.

President Arthur T. Hadley, of Yale, who had a high reputation as an economist, believed that the bill, if passed, would lead to inflation on an unparalleled scale, with a consequent depreciation. He was so deeply moved that he wrote a personal letter to President Wilson on July 1, 1913, for the purpose of pointing out to the President that the Act would "involve the country in grave financial danger." Practically all of our gold would leave for Europe, he thought. He was greatly mistaken. There is now in the United States about 45 percent of all the gold in the world.

Frank A. Vanderlip, president of the National City Bank of New York, declared that the notes of the Federal Reserve Banks would be "fiat money," and James J. Hill, the famous railroad builder and financier, said the plan was "socialistic." James R. Mann, Republican leader of the House, condemned the bill as all wrong, badly conceived, and impossible as a practical measure. However, he added bitterly, it did not matter; the national banks would not go into the system, anyway. Most of them would become state banks, and the Federal Reserve would just lie down and die for lack of support. Saying this, he washed his hands of the whole affair.

[*The Federal Reserve System, approved by Congress late in 1913, not only carried the nation triumphantly through World War I but remains the bulwark of the nation's financial structure. The sneers of the bankers gave way to cheers. Currency expansion to meet growing needs was abundantly provided by the issuance of Federal Reserve notes, backed in part by promissory notes and other assets held by the member banks. The national banks, authorized during the Civil War, were required to join the Federal Reserve System. The grip of Wall Street on money and credit was thus weakened, and interlocking directorates were curbed the next year (1914) by the Clayton Anti-Trust Act.*]

C. MORAL MEDDLING IN MEXICO

1. Wilson Asks for War on Huerta (1914)

The decade-long despotic rule of dictator Díaz in Mexico crumbled during the upheaval of 1910–1911. But the revolution took an ugly turn in 1913, when General Huerta—a full-blooded Indian who was an alcoholic and a drug addict—connived at the murder of the liberal President Madero and forthwith seized power. Wilson, whose heart went out to the oppressed masses of Mexico, refused to recognize this bloody-handed dictator, and thereby departed from the traditional American policy of recognizing established regimes. Pursuing a plan of "watchful waiting," he modified America's arms embargo to the advantage of Huerta's foes. The crisis came to a boil in April, 1914, when Mexican officials seized two men from a United States navy boat at Tampico. The local officials promptly tendered apologies. But Admiral Mayo, acting without specific authorization from Washington, demanded a twenty-one-gun salute to the American flag. When Huerta refused to comply, Wilson went before Congress to ask for authority (which he already had as Commander-in-Chief) to use force. How does he attempt to reconcile his friendship for the Mexican people with a request to fight them? What other inconsistencies emerge?

The [Tampico] incident cannot be regarded as a trivial one, especially as two of the men arrested were taken from the boat itself—that is to say, from the territory of the United States. But had it stood by itself, it might have been attributed to the ignorance or arrogance of a single officer. Unfortunately, it was not an isolated case. A series of incidents have recently occurred which cannot but create the impression that the representatives of General Huerta were willing to go out of their way to show disregard for the dignity and rights of this Government,* and felt perfectly safe in doing what they pleased, making free to show in many ways their irritation and contempt. . . . So far as I can learn, such wrong and annoyances have been suffered to occur only against representatives of the United States. . . .

1. *Ibid.*, pp. 6908–09 (April 20, 1914).
* Professor A. S. Link concludes that this statement misrepresents the facts; Huerta had shown "extraordinary concern" for American interests (*Wilson: The New Freedom* [1956], p. 398).

The manifest danger of such a situation was that such offenses might grow from bad to worse until something happened of so gross and intolerable a sort as to lead directly and inevitably to armed conflict. It was necessary that the apologies of General Huerta and his representatives should go much further; that they should be such as to attract the attention of the whole population to their significance, and such as to impress upon General Huerta himself the necessity of seeing to it that no further occasion for explanations and professed regrets should arise. I, therefore, felt it my duty to sustain Admiral Mayo in the whole of his demand, and to insist that the flag of the United States should be saluted in such a way as to indicate a new spirit and attitude on the part of the Huertistas.

Such a salute General Huerta has refused, and I have come to ask your approval and support in the course I now propose to pursue.

This Government can, I earnestly hope, in no circumstances be forced into war with the people of Mexico. Mexico is torn by civil strife. If we are to accept the tests of its own constitution, it has no government. General Huerta has set his power up in the City of Mexico, such as it is, without right and by methods for which there can be no justification. Only part of the country is under his control. If armed conflict should unhappily come as a result of his attitude of personal resentment toward this Government, we should be fighting only General Huerta and those who adhere to him and give him their support, and our object would be only to restore to the people of the distracted Republic the opportunity to set up again their own laws and their own government.

But I earnestly hope that war is not now in question. I believe that I speak for the American people when I say that we do not desire to control in any degree the affairs of our sister Republic. Our feeling for the people of Mexico is one of deep and genuine friendship, and everything that we have so far done or refrained from doing has proceeded from our desire to help them, not to hinder or embarrass them. We would not wish even to exercise the good offices of friendship without their welcome and consent. The people of Mexico are entitled to settle their own domestic affairs in their own way, and we sincerely desire to respect their right. The present situation need have none of the grave implications of interference if we deal with it promptly, firmly, and wisely.

No doubt I could do what is necessary in the circumstances to enforce respect for our Government without recourse to the Congress, and yet not exceed my constitutional powers as President. But I do not wish to act in a manner possibly of so grave consequence except in close conference and cooperation with both the Senate and House. I, therefore, come to ask your approval that I should use the armed forces of the United States in such ways and to such an extent as may be necessary to obtain from General Huerta and his adherents the fullest recognition of the rights and dignity of the United States, even amidst the distressing conditions now unhappily obtaining in Mexico.

There can in what we do be no thought of aggression or of selfish aggrandizement. We seek to maintain the dignity and authority of the United States, only because we wish always to keep our great influence unimpaired for the uses of liberty, both in the United States and wherever else it may be employed for the benefit of mankind.

2. A Republican Assails "Watchful Waiting" (1916)

A patriotic Congress promptly granted Wilson the authority to intervene. But a day earlier (April 21, 1914) American forces, under emergency orders from the White House, had bombarded and occupied Vera Cruz in a vain attempt to prevent a German ship from landing munitions that might be used against United States troops. With a Louisville paper crying "On to the Isthmus!" and with a full-blown war imminent, the ABC powers (Argentina, Brazil, and Chile) offered to mediate. Wilson gladly accepted this escape hatch, on April 25, 1914. Nearly three months later Huerta was forced to abdicate, but American businessmen clamored for full-dress intervention as United States citizens continued to lose both their property and their lives. The European war erupted later in 1914, and Republicans criticized Wilson for being "too proud to fight." They also condemned him for insisting that Americans leave the Mexican danger zone while he permitted others to sail through submarine-infested danger zones on the high seas. Here Representative William E. Humphrey, a prominent Congressman from Washington, voices typical Republican complaints. How effectively does he support his charges that Wilson's policy was meddling, vacillating, hypocritical, inconsistent, and futile?

The President's policy in Mexico is not based upon his party platform. It is characterized by weakness, uncertainty, vacillation, and uncontrollable desire to intermeddle in Mexican affairs. He has not had the courage to go into Mexico nor the courage to stay out.

The President has repeatedly declared that he would not interfere in Mexico nor permit others to do so. . . . At Columbus, Ohio, in his recent speech he said:

"The Mexicans may not know what to do with their government; but that is none of our business, and, so long as I have the power to prevent it, nobody shall 'butt in' to alter it for them."

At the notable talk in the White House not long ago to the Democratic National Committee, where he referred to other people "talking through their hat," if he is correctly reported, he declared "that the Mexicans can raise all the h - - - they please; it is none of our business." Remember, the language I am using is not mine but the reported language of the President. Certainly their ability to raise what he so delicately described ought to satisfy even the President and that wing of the Democratic Party that believes in "watchful waiting."

But if the President had followed these declarations, however un-American and indefensible they may be, it would have been far better for us and probably for Mexico. But his deeds have been strangers to his words.

2. *Congressional Record*, 64 Cong., 1 sess., pp. 1636–38, *passim* (Jan. 27, 1916).

Instead of a policy of "hands off," it has been a policy of constant interference in Mexican affairs.

The President told Huerta that he must not be a candidate; that he would not be recognized. He talked about fair elections and constitutional government, and showed a strong desire not only to control Mexican politics but to go into Mexico and regulate the land system of that country. He sent his secret special agents to Mexico City and became involved in a personal quarrel with Huerta. This controversy reached its climax in the most grotesque and stupendous piece of folly in the history of civilized nations when the President appeared here before Congress and virtually asked that the United States declare war against Huerta, the individual. And, what was even more ridiculous and absurd, it was done. And for what reason? Who today will tell us the cause of that action? Americans had been driven from Mexico; American property had been destroyed in Mexico; American men had been murdered in Mexico; American women had been outraged in Mexico. But all these did not disturb the serenity of "watchful waiting," or recall to the mind of the President the Democratic platform declarations about protecting life and property of American citizens along the border and on foreign soil.

We were told that Huerta was a murderer, an assassin, a usurper, and a traitor, and a man that we would never under any circumstances recognize. But Huerta, the individual, not representing Mexico but himself, had refused to salute the American flag on a gasoline launch in a place where it had no right to be; or, to be exact, for the sake of history, Huerta agreed to fire six guns in salute, while the President, as I recall, demanded twenty-one.*

This insult from an assassin and a murderer that we would not in any way recognize was more than this administration, too proud to fight, could endure. Our magnificent battleship squadron was hurried to Mexican waters, although at that time the Mexican Navy consisted of one old antiquated gunboat. The Army was sent to Mexico, and, after Vera Cruz was bombarded by our Navy, it was landed on Mexican soil. Seventeen [nineteen] of our own soldiers lost their lives and more than a hundred Mexicans were killed. We seized the customhouse and carried away more than a million dollars.

And all this for what purpose? Why did we go to Mexico and what did we accomplish and why did we return? We were told that a German vessel was about to land a cargo of guns and ammunition, and this was the reason for hurrying our Navy to Mexican waters. But that same German vessel landed its cargo in Mexico. We are told that our Army and Navy went to Mexico to make Huerta apologize. Has anyone read that apology? We are told that our Army and Navy went to Mexico to make Huerta salute the flag. Has anyone heard that salute? . . .

---

* Huerta had agreed to a twenty-one-gun salute if returned on a gun-for-gun basis, but this was unacceptable to Wilson.

A SORT OF WAR

President Wilson: "I hope you are not shooting at my
dear friends the Mexicans?"
U.S.A. Gunner: "Oh, no, sir. We have strict orders only
to aim at one Huerta." *Punch* (London), 1914.

Our policy in Mexico has earned us the contempt of the world, and
beyond question has greatly influenced the warring nations of Europe in
their present attitude toward us. . . .

We make a tremendous bluster about the killing of American citizens
upon the high seas and fill the air with the tumult and the noise of many
typewriters, although the killing is only accidental and undoubtedly really
regretted by those who did the act. But so far we have looked with
equanimity undisturbed while hundreds of Americans have been purposely
foully murdered in Mexico in a most cruel and fiendish manner. . . .

Speaking for myself, but believing that I voice the sentiment of the
American people, there are some things that I would do in regard to
Mexico if upon me rested the responsibility. I would either go into Mexico
and pacify the country or I would keep my hands entirely out of Mexico.
If we are too proud to fight, we should be too proud to quarrel. I would

not choose between murderers. I would not permit either side to procure guns or ammunition in this country that may hereafter be used to murder Americans. I would not depend upon secret personal agents for my information. I would deal openly and in the light of day with the Mexican situation. I would practice pitiless publicity as well as preach it. I would give the American people the facts. I would let them know the truth, and if that is done the American people will quickly decide what shall be done.

And, above all, I would do this—the thing that should have been done more than three years ago, and if it had been done, the letting of American blood in Mexico would not have occurred: I would serve notice upon all factions that no longer would any of them be permitted, under any pretense whatever, to destroy American property, or to murder American men, or to ravish American women, and back of that notice I would place the power of this great Republic.

THOUGHT PROVOKERS

1. Was the revival of personal appearances before Congress by the President desirable or undesirable? Argue both sides of the proposition that lobbies are useful and necessary. In what ways did a lower tariff benefit American producers? American consumers?

2. Are interlocking directorates of some kind inevitable in the American economy? Should the bankers have been permitted to write the Federal Reserve Act?

3. Why did Wilson ask Congress for authority to use the armed forces in Mexico when he already had that authority? Would the prestige of the United States have been better served by a disavowal of Admiral Mayo's unauthorized demand than by the bombardment of Vera Cruz? Should the President of the United States be the moral judge of foreign governments? Should Americans who live and invest in foreign countries be told that they do so purely at their own risk?

35 · *The Road to World War I*

We must be impartial in thought as well as in action.

WOODROW WILSON, 1914

PROLOGUE: When World War I erupted in 1914, the American people were overwhelmingly determined to stay out. But their Anglo-Saxon heritage on the one hand, and German aggressions on the other, caused their sympathies to go out to Britain, France, and their allies (the Allied Powers) against Germany, Austria-Hungary, and their allies (the Central Powers). In consequence, the United States acquiesced the more readily in the unorthodox British naval blockade of Germany, while protesting the more sternly against the irregular German submarine blockade of Britain. America further offended the Germans by immense sales of munitions to their enemies, and by insisting that American citizens should continue to have the right to travel on munitions-laden belligerent liners. Facing ultimate starvation, the Germans finally proclaimed a desperate all-out submarine campaign in January, 1917. When they sank four unarmed American merchant ships in mid-March, 1917, they were indubitably making war on the United States, and President Wilson reluctantly concluded that the nation had no choice but to fight back.

A. ACQUIESCING IN THE BRITISH BLOCKADE

1. Lord Bryce's Propaganda Report (1915)

The American people were so deeply shocked by Germany's brutal invasion of Belgium that they uncritically swallowed large doses of Allied propaganda. British propagandists stressed the medically preposterous stories of Belgian babies (still living) with their hands hacked off and the alleged German practice of converting battlefield corpses into fertilizer and soap. The Germans, with much less persuasiveness, charged that the Allies gouged out the eyes of prisoners, that French soldiers put cholera germs in wells used by Germans, and that a Belgian priest had placed a machine gun behind his altar and mowed down German Catholic soldiers who came to mass. Lord Bryce, admired in America for his sympathetic two-volume *The American Commonwealth,* served his country by lending his name to a sensational report on atrocities in Belgium. In the following account (one of many alleging German arson, rape, mayhem, and murder) what part is least worthy of belief? What was the probable effect of the Bryce report in predisposing the American people to accept British infractions of neutral rights?

The [German] officer spoke Flemish. He knocked at the door; the peasant did not come. The officer ordered the soldiers to break down the door,

1. Viscount Bryce, *Report of the Committee on Alleged German Outrages* (1915), p. 51. Many of the incidents in the Bryce report were later proved to have been grossly exaggerated or completely fabricated.

BABES ON BAYONETS

An exaggerated stereotype in America of German atrocities in Belgium. *Life,* 1915.

which two of them did. The peasant came and asked what they were doing. The officer said he did not come quickly enough, and that they had "trained up" [disciplined] plenty of others. His hands were tied behind his back, and he was shot at once without a moment's delay.

The wife came out with a little sucking child. She put the child down and sprang at the Germans like a lioness. She clawed their faces. One of the Germans took a rifle and struck her a tremendous blow with the butt on the head. Another took his bayonet and fixed it and thrust it through the child. He then put his rifle on his shoulder with the child up it, its little arms stretched out once or twice.

The officers ordered the houses to be set on fire, and straw was obtained, and it was done. The man and his wife and the child were thrown on the top of the straw. There were about forty other peasant prisoners there also, and the officer said: "I am doing this as a lesson and example to you. When a German tells you to do something next time you must move more quickly." The regiment of Germans was a regiment of Hussars, with crossbones and a death's-head on the cap.

2. Page Plays Britain's Game (*c.* 1915)

The British, with their powerful navy, undertook to starve Germany into submission with a blockade. But the ancient practice of stationing warships off the three-mile line proved hazardous, primarily because of new long-range guns and lurking submarines. The British therefore took "liberties" with international law. They mined the North Sea and forced neutral ships into their ports to be searched for munitions and other contraband of war. They arbitrarily broadened the normal contraband lists to include such necessities as food and cotton. They halted the slippage of supplies into Ger-

2. Viscount Grey, *Twenty-five Years* (1925), II, 109–10. By permission of Harper & Row, Publishers, Inc.

many through neighboring neutrals like Denmark by limiting these small countries to their pre-war imports. Even though London paid for many of the intercepted cargoes, Washington protested against these disagreeable practices as violations of international law. Foreign Secretary Grey here tells how he dealt with Ambassador Page, the ex-journalist who became Wilson's ardently pro-British representative in London. Did Page behave appropriately as the spokesman in London for the United States government?

We got a list of absolute contraband that was not seriously challenged. But there was much more difficulty to come. We were now entitled to seize such things as copper and rubber in any ship on the high seas, if they were consigned to a German port. This alone was of little use. Germany could import goods as easily through Dutch, Danish, or Swedish ports as through her own, and in Sweden especially there were people disposed to make Sweden a source of supply for Germany. It was therefore as essential to Britain and the Allies to seize copper or rubber going to a Swedish or neutral port as when going to a German port.

It was on this point that controversy arose with the United States. The very fact that the United States was, in a sense, the trustee for the right of weaker neutrals made its Government disposed to champion those rights. Was a peaceful Swede desiring copper for innocent purposes to have it stopped? On the other hand, was the British Navy to let copper pass under its very guns to a Swede who was importing it for the German Government, and going to send it straight to Germany to be made into munitions to kill British soldiers?

The argument between these two opposite points of view was long, voluminous, and extensive. It was published, and anyone who has enough curiosity and time may read it.

The Navy acted and the Foreign Office had to find the argument to support the action; it was anxious work. British action provoked American argument; that was met by British counter-argument. British action preceded British argument; the risk was that action might follow American argument. In all this [Ambassador] Page's advice and suggestion were of the greatest value in warning us when to be careful or encouraging us when we could safely be firm.

One incident in particular remains in my memory. Page came to see me at the Foreign Office one day, and produced a long despatch from Washington contesting our claim to act as we were doing in stopping contraband going to neutral ports. "I am instructed," he said, "to read this despatch to you." He read, and I listened. He then said: "I have now read the despatch, but I do not agree with it; let us consider how it should be answered!"

3. Lansing's Pro-Ally Tactics (*c.* 1916)

International law required a blockading power to stop and search all merchant ships before seizing or sinking them. If they were unresisting enemy merchantmen,

3. *War Memoirs of Robert Lansing* (1935), pp. 110–12. Copyright 1935 by the Bobbs-Merrill Company, Inc.; used by special permission of the publishers.

they could lawfully be destroyed only if proper provision was made for the safety of passengers and crew. The blockading British, because of the menace of new weapons, were taking "liberties" with the old rules. The Germans, unable to sustain an ortho-dox blockade of the British Isles with fragile submarines vulnerable to ramming or gunfire, began to sink enemy merchantmen without warning. Berlin argued that Ger-many was forced to take such "liberties" because Allied merchant ships had first sunk German submarines attempting to stop them. Secretary of State Lansing, a fussily precise legalist who was warmly pro-Ally at heart, here explains his reactions. Why did the United States turn against Germany rather than Britain?

Sifted down to the bare facts the position was this: Great Britain insisted that Germany should conform her conduct of naval [submarine] warfare to the strict letter of the rules of international law, and resented even a suggestion that there should be any variation of the rules to make them reasonably applicable to new conditions. On the other hand, Great Britain was herself repeatedly departing from the rules of international law, on the plea that new conditions compelled her to do so, and even showed resentment because the United States refused to recognize her right to ignore or modify the rules whenever she thought it necessary to do so.

Briefly, the British Government wished international law enforced when they believed that it worked to the advantage of Great Britain, and wished the law modified when the change would benefit Great Britain.

There is no doubt that the good relations between the United States and Great Britain would have been seriously jeopardized by this unreasonable attitude, which seems unworthy of British statesmanship, except for the fact that the British violations of law affected American property, while the German violations affected American lives. Nothing else saved our relations with Great Britain from becoming strained to the breaking point. Even as it was, there were many Americans, both in public and in private life, who considered that we were unjust, or at least unfair, because we differentiated between the illegal acts of the belligerents on the basis of their results.

These complaints against the conduct of the British were increasing in the United States, were gaining more and more converts in Congress, and were exerting more and more pressure upon the government to adopt vigorous measures to compel Great Britain to cease her illegal practices, when the Germans, with their genius for always doing the wrong thing in the wrong way and at the wrong time, perpetrated new crimes in their submarine campaign. These events made the complaints against the British seem insignificant and ill-timed, and aroused anew the indignation of the American people toward the ruthless commanders of Germany's undersea corsairs.

The British have only the stupidity of the Germans to thank for saving them from having a very serious situation develop in their relations with this country in the spring of 1916. It was luck on their part and nothing more. They had done everything that they could to make the position of this government difficult; and the worst of it was that they did not appear to realize it, for which our Embassy at London, it must be admitted, was by no means blameless.

Sympathetic as I felt toward the Allies and convinced that we would in the end join with them against the autocratic governments of the Central Empires, I saw with apprehension the tide of resentment against Great Britain rising higher and higher in this country. It was becoming increasingly difficult to avoid bringing the controversies between our two governments to a head, and to keep from assuming positions which went beyond the field of discussion.

I did all that I could to prolong the disputes by preparing, or having prepared, long and detailed replies, and introducing technical and controversial matters in the hope that, before the extended interchange of arguments came to an end, something would happen to change the current of American public opinion, or to make the American people perceive that German absolutism was a menace to their liberties and to democratic institutions everywhere.

Fortunately, this hope and effort were not in vain. Germany did the very thing which she should not have done. The tide of sentiment in the United States turned, and it was possible to prevent a widespread demand being made that the Allied Powers be "brought to book" without further delay for their illegal treatment of our commerce.

B. MERCHANTS OF DEATH

1. Bryan Backs the Munitions Business (1915)

Germany and Austria-Hungary, anticipating a blockade, had begun the war with adequate supplies of arms. Britain and her allies, counting on keeping the sea lanes open, were less well stocked. American factories soon began to provide the Allies with mountainous quantities of munitions. Meanwhile some of the small neutral countries, seeking to conserve their scanty supplies, had forbidden the export of arms. Berlin urged the United States to do likewise. Congress could have embargoed arms, as it later did in the neutrality laws of the 1930's. But taking such a step would have worked so greatly to the disadvantage of the Allies as to be virtually an unneutral act. Refusal to take such a step worked so heavily to the disadvantage of the Germans and their allies as to seem no less unneutral. Rather than slip back into the recent depression, the United States followed the profitable path of letting trade take its course. The silver-tongued orator William J. Bryan, Lansing's predecessor as Secretary of State, here defends official policy in a letter to Senator Stone. What is the weakest aspect of the German position? Was the obligation of the United States to stop the munitions traffic legal or moral?

There is no power in the Executive to prevent the sale of ammunition to the belligerents.

The duty of a neutral to restrict trade in munitions of war has never been imposed by international law or by municipal statute [domestic law]. It has never been the policy of this Government to prevent the shipment of arms

1. *Foreign Relations of the United States, 1914, Supplement*, pp. x, xiv (Jan. 20, 1915).

or ammunition into belligerent territory, except in the case of neighboring American Republics [*e.g.*, Mexico], and then only when civil strife prevailed. Even to this extent the belligerents in the present conflict, when they were neutrals, have never, so far as the records disclose, limited the sale of munitions of war. It is only necessary to point to the enormous quantities of arms and ammunition furnished by manufacturers in Germany to the belligerents in the Russo-Japanese war [1904–1905] and in the recent Balkan wars [1912–1913] to establish the general recognition of the propriety of the trade by a neutral nation. . . .

If any American citizens, partisans of Germany and Austria-Hungary, feel that this administration is acting in a way injurious to the cause of those countries, this feeling results from the fact that on the high seas the German and Austro-Hungarian naval power is thus far inferior to the British. It is the business of a belligerent operating on the high seas, not the duty of a neutral, to prevent contraband from reaching an enemy.

Those in this country who sympathize with Germany and Austria-Hungary appear to assume that some obligation rests upon this Government, in the performance of its neutral duty, to prevent all trade in contraband, and thus to equalize the difference due to the relative naval strength of the belligerents. No such obligation exists; it would be an unneutral act, an act of partiality on the part of this Government, to adopt such a policy if the Executive had the power to do so. If Germany and Austria-Hungary cannot import contraband from this country, it is not, because of that fact, the duty of the United States to close its markets to the Allies. The markets of this country are open upon equal terms to all the world, to every nation, belligerent or neutral.

2. Berlin Condemns the Munitions Traffic (1915)

The Germans were angered when America became a prime munitions factory of the Allies, all the more so when Wall Street bankers loaned hundreds of millions of dollars to finance the cargoes of death. The United States, on the other hand, stopped shipping foodstuffs and other commodities to the Germans. It was thwarted by the unconventional British blockade, in which the State Department protestingly acquiesced. Berlin, in this official protest in 1915, insisted that America was violating the true spirit of neutrality. Were the Germans reasonable in claiming that the unusual conditions of this war obligated Washington to embargo arms?

Then there is also the attitude of the United States in the question of the exportation of arms. The Imperial [German] Government feels sure that the United States Government will agree that, in questions of neutrality, it is necessary to take into consideration not only the formal aspect of the case, but also the spirit in which the neutrality is carried out.

The situation in the present war differs from that of any previous war. Therefore any reference to arms furnished by Germany in former wars is

2. *Ibid., 1915, Supplement*, pp. 157–58 (April 4, 1915).

not justified, for then it was not a question *whether* war material should be supplied to the belligerents, but *who* should supply it in competition with other nations. In the present war, all nations having a war material industry worth mentioning are either involved in the war themselves or are engaged in perfecting their own armaments, and have therefore laid an embargo against the exportation of war material.

The United States is accordingly the only neutral country in a position to furnish war materials. The conception of neutrality is thereby given a new purport, independently of the formal question of hitherto existing law. In contradiction thereto, the United States is building up a powerful arms industry in the broadest sense, the existing plants not only being worked but enlarged by all available means, and new ones built.

The international conventions [treaties] for the protection of the rights of neutral nations doubtless sprang from the necessity of protecting the existing industries of neutral nations as far as possible from injury in their business. But it can in no event be in accordance with the spirit of true neutrality if, under the protection of such international stipulations, an entirely new industry is created in a neutral state, such as is the development of the arms industry in the United States, the business whereof, under the present conditions, can benefit only the belligerent powers.

This industry is actually delivering goods only to the enemies of Germany. The theoretical willingness to supply Germany also, if shipments thither were possible, does not alter the case. If it is the will of the American people that there shall be a true neutrality, the United States will find means of preventing this one-sided supply of arms or at least of utilizing it to protect legitimate trade with Germany, especially that in foodstuffs.

This view of neutrality should all the more appeal to the United States Government because the latter enacted a similar [arms-embargo] policy toward Mexico. On February 4, 1914, President Wilson . . . declared that "we should stand for genuine neutrality. . . ." He then held that "in that case, because Carranza had no ports, while Huerta had them and was able to import these materials, that it was our duty as a nation to treat them [Carranza and Huerta] upon an equality. . . ." If this view were applied to the present case, it would lead to an embargo on the exportation of arms.

[*Representative Stephen G. Porter of Pennsylvania, pleading for true neutrality, added another argument to the German case in his speech of March 3, 1915:* "Our population is composed of former citizens of all the belligerent nations, and our position in the matter of these shipments is entirely different from that of any other country. They can sell these deadly materials to other nations without being a party to the death or wounding of those who are kin to their own people. Many a bullet made in an American factory, by an American workman, has found its deadly resting place in the body of that workman's brother, nephew, cousin, or even his father or son—the mere thought of which is horrible to contemplate." (Congressional Record, 63 Cong., 3 sess., Appendix, p. 585.)]

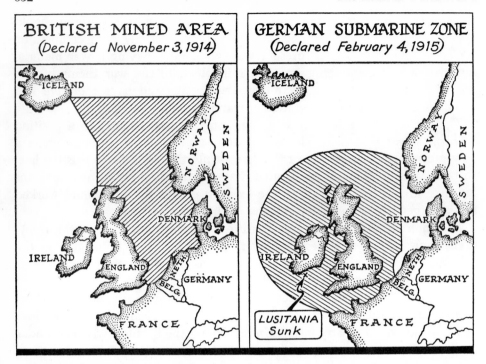

C. THE SINKING OF THE *LUSITANIA*

1. Wilson Demands Muzzled U-Boats (1915)

Late in 1914 the British, taking an unprecedented "liberty" with freedom of the seas, proclaimed the North Sea a military area and proceeded to mine it. (Washington did not protest, though more than two years later it formally declared that it had not abandoned its rights.) In retaliation, the Germans declared an unprecedented war zone around the British Isles, and announced that they would sink all enemy craft within those waters. Washington vigorously protested that it would hold Berlin to "strict accountability" if American ships were incidentally sunk and American lives were lost. But United States citizens continued to sail into the submarine-infested waters, as they had a perfect legal right to do. On May 1, 1915, the day the giant Cunard liner *Lusitania* left New York, an advertisement appeared in the local newspapers, over the name of the German Embassy, warning passengers of their danger. A week later the vessel was torpedoed without warning by a German submarine off the Irish coast and sank with the loss of 1198 persons, many of them women and children, and 128 of them Americans. Secretary Bryan signed the following stern protest. Was the United States fair to Germany in its position on the submarine?

The Government of the United States .·. . desires to call the attention of the Imperial German Government, with the utmost earnestness, to the fact that the objection to their present method of attack against the trade of their enemies lies in the practical impossibility of employing submarines

1. *Foreign Relations of the United States, 1915, Supplement,* pp. 394–95.

CUNARD

EUROPE VIA LIVERPOOL

LUSITANIA

Fastest and Largest Steamer
now in Atlantic Service Sails
SATURDAY, MAY 1, 10 A. M.
Transylvania - Fri, May 7, 5 P.M.
Orduna, - - - Tues., May 18, 10 A.M.
Tuscania, - - - Fri., May 21, 5 P.M.
LUSITANIA, - Sat., May 29, 10 A.M.
Transylvania, - Fri., June 4, 5 P.M.

Gibraltar—Genoa—Naples—Piraeus
S.S. Carpathia, Thur., May 13, Noon

ROUND THE WORLD TOURS
Through bookings to all principal Ports
of the World.
Company's Office, 21-24 State St., N. Y.

New York *World*, May 1, 1915.

in the destruction of commerce without disregarding those rules of fairness, reason, justice, and humanity which all modern opinion regards as imperative. It is practically impossible for the officers of a submarine to visit a merchantman at sea and examine her papers and cargo. It is practically impossible for them to make a prize of her; and, if they cannot put a prize crew on board of her, they cannot sink her without leaving her crew and all on board of her to the mercy of the sea in her small boats. These facts it is understood the Imperial German Government frankly admit. . . . Manifestly submarines cannot be used against merchantmen, as the last few weeks have shown, without an inevitable violation of many sacred principles of justice and humanity.

American citizens act within their indisputable rights in taking their ships and in traveling wherever their legitimate business calls them upon the high seas, and exercise those rights in what should be the well-justified confidence that their lives will not be endangered by acts done in clear violation of universally acknowledged international obligations, and certainly in the confidence that their own Government will sustain them in the exercise of their rights.

There was recently published in the newspapers of the United States, I regret to inform the Imperial German Government, a formal warning, purporting to come from the Imperial German Embassy at Washington, addressed to the people of the United States, and stating, in effect, that any citizen of the United States who exercised his right of free travel upon the seas would do so at his peril if his journey should take him within the zone of waters within which the Imperial German Navy was using submarines against the commerce of Great Britain and France, notwithstanding the respectful but very earnest protest of his Government, the Government of the United States.

I do not refer to this for the purpose of calling the attention of the Imperial German Government at this time to the surprising irregularity of a communication from the Imperial German Embassy at Washington addressed to the people of the United States through the newspapers, but only for the purpose of pointing out that no warning that an unlawful and inhumane act will be committed can possibly be accepted as an excuse or palliation for that act or as an abatement of the responsibility for its commission.

2. Germany Justifies the Sinking (1915)

Berlin, though regretting the loss of innocent life, stoutly defended the torpedoing of the *Lusitania*. But the German Foreign Office was mistaken on several counts. The Cunarder was not armed, as charged (though many British merchantmen were); it was not carrying an organized body of Canadian troops; and it had not demonstrably violated the American law which forbade carrying powerful explosives. The fact that the vessel was transporting 4200 (not 5400) cases of small-arms ammunition had no bearing on the time-honored rule that unarmed and unresisting passenger ships could not be sunk without warning and without proper provision for the safety of passengers and crew. Warships could lawfully be destroyed without warning, and in several respects, especially in secret orders to ram at sight, the *Lusitania* could technically be regarded as an offensively armed warship. In Berlin's official reply to Washington's protest, given below, do the Germans have a sound moral case, if not a legal one?

The Government of the United States proceeds on the assumption that the *Lusitania* is to be considered as an ordinary unarmed merchant vessel. The Imperial Government begs, in this connection, to point out that the *Lusitania* was one of the largest and fastest English commerce steamers, constructed with Government funds as auxiliary cruisers, and is expressly included in the navy list published by British Admiralty. It is moreover known to the Imperial Government, from reliable information furnished by its officials and neutral passengers, that for some time practically all the more valuable English merchant vessels have been provided with guns, ammunition, and other weapons, and reinforced with a crew specially practiced in manning guns. According to reports at hand here, the *Lusitania*, when she left New York, undoubtedly had guns on board which were mounted under decks and masked.

The Imperial Government further-

NOTICE!

TRAVELLERS intending to embark on the Atlantic voyage are reminded that a state of war exists between Germany and her allies and Great Britian and her allies; that the zone of war includes the waters adjacent to the British Isles; that, in accordance with formal notice given by the Imperial German Government, vessels flying the flag of Great Britian, or of any of her allies, are liable to destruction in those waters and that travellers sailing in the war zone on ships of Great Britian or her allies do so at their own risk.

IMPERIAL GERMAN EMBASSY,
WASHINGTON, D. C., APRIL 22, 1915.

When Washington refused to warn U.S. citizens to keep off belligerent ships, the German Embassy inserted the above notice in the leading New York papers. New York *World*, May 1, 1915.

2. *Ibid.*, p. 420 (May 28, 1915).

more has the honor to direct the particular attention of the American Government to the fact that the British Admiralty, by a secret instruction of February of this year, advised the British merchant marine not only to seek protection behind neutral flags and markings, but even, when so disguised, to attack German submarines by ramming them. High rewards have been offered by the British Government as a special incentive for the destruction of the submarines by merchant vessels, and such rewards have already been paid out.

In view of these facts, which are satisfactorily known to it, the Imperial Government is unable to consider English merchant vessels any longer as "undefended territory" in the zone of maritime war designated by the Admiralty Staff of the Imperial German Navy. The German commanders are consequently no longer in a position to observe the rules of capture otherwise usual, and with which they invariably complied before this.

Lastly, the Imperial Government must specially point out that on her last trip the *Lusitania,* as on earlier occasions, had Canadian troops and munitions on board, including no less than 5400 cases of ammunition destined for the destruction of brave German soldiers who are fulfilling with self-sacrifice and devotion their duty in the service of the Fatherland. The German Government believes that it acts in just self-defense when it seeks to protect the lives of its soldiers by destroying ammunition destined for the enemy with the means of war at its command.

The English steamship company must have been aware of the dangers to which passengers on board the *Lusitania* were exposed under the circumstances. In taking them on board in spite of this, the company quite deliberately tried to use the lives of American citizens as protection for the ammunition carried, and violated the clear provisions of American laws which expressly prohibit, and provide punishment for, the carrying of passengers on ships which have explosives on board. The company thereby wantonly caused the death of so many passengers. According to the express report of the submarine commander concerned, which is further confirmed by all other reports, there can be no doubt that the rapid sinking of the *Lusitania* was primarily due to the explosion of the cargo of ammunition caused by the torpedo. Otherwise, in all human probability, the passengers of the *Lusitania* would have been saved.[*]

3. Viereck Upholds the Torpedoing (1915)

America was shocked and outraged by the *Lusitania* slaughter. But many Germans, picturing the Cunarder as an arms-carrying warship, rejoiced when her lethal cargo sank. An unauthorized German struck off a medal showing the *Lusitania* bristling

---

[*] The *Lusitania* sank in eighteen minutes with unexpected rapidity, and there was a second explosion. American officials had interpreted the law against munitions on passenger vessels as not applying to small-arms ammunition, which it was believed could not be exploded en masse. Other munitions may have been smuggled aboard in small quantities, but the secondary explosion here referred to was almost certainly due to bursting steam boilers.

3. *The Fatherland*, II, 5 (June 9, 1915).

with guns. George S. Viereck, a German-born poet, playwright, and propagandist who had come to America at the age of eleven, here presents a German point of view in his outspoken propaganda magazine published in New York. Many Germans believed with Secretary Bryan that permitting civilians to sail on munitions-carrying passenger ships was like "putting women and children in front of an army." How credible is Viereck's view that the torpedoing of the *Lusitania* was really a humanitarian act?

In spite of heavy provocation on the part of the United States, Germany has kept her temper. Not content with furnishing implements of murder to Germany's enemies, we [Americans] actually ask Germany to commit suicide. For a modification of submarine warfare as suggested in Mr. Bryan's note would be tantamount to self-destruction on Germany's part. . . .

We prattle about humanity, while we manufacture poisoned shrapnel and picric acid for profit. Ten thousand German widows, ten thousand orphans, ten thousand graves bear the legend "Made in America." . . .

Perhaps the captain of the submarine that sank the *Lusitania* to the bottom had a vision of a thousand passengers drowned. But above that vision he must have seen another vision of German armies mowed down by the deadly cargo within her hold, and of ten times ten thousand widows and orphans pointing an accusing finger at him if he failed to destroy the ammunition on its passage to England. The dictates of humanity demanded the destruction of the death-carrying vessel.

However we may deplore the loss of innocent lives, the *Lusitania* deserved her doom. The Cunard Line deliberately inveigled American passengers to imperil their lives. . . .

D. WAR WITH GERMANY

1. Wilson Breaks Diplomatic Relations (1917)

After the *Lusitania* uproar, Germany generally avoided sinking unresisting passenger ships without warning. But in March, 1916, a German submarine torpedoed a French liner, the *Sussex*, and inflicted some eighty casualties, including injuries to several Americans. Wilson indignantly presented an ultimatum to Berlin threatening a severance of diplomatic relations—an almost certain prelude to war—unless Germany discontinued these inhumane tactics. The Germans reluctantly acquiesced. But finally driven to the wall by the British blockade, they dramatically announced, on January 31, 1917, the opening of an unrestricted submarine warfare on virtually all ships plying the war zone, including American vessels. Wilson, whose hand had now been called, went sorrowfully before Congress to deliver this speech. Was he naïve or idealistic? Was he hasty in accepting the German U-boat challenge?

I think that you will agree with me that, in view of this [submarine] declaration, . . . this Government has no alternative, consistent with the dignity and honor of the United States, but to take the course which . . . it announced that it would take. . . .

I have, therefore, directed the Secretary of State to announce to His

1. *Congressional Record*, 64 Cong., 2 sess., pp. 2578–79 (Feb. 3, 1917).

Excellency the German Ambassador that all diplomatic relations between the United States and the German Empire are severed. . . .

Notwithstanding this unexpected action of the German Government, this sudden and deeply deplorable renunciation of its assurances, given this Government at one of the most critical moments of tension in the relations of the two governments, I refuse to believe that it is the intention of the German authorities to do in fact what they have warned us they will feel at liberty to do. I cannot bring myself to believe that they will indeed pay no regard to the ancient friendship between their people and our own, or to the solemn obligations which have been exchanged between them, and destroy American ships and take the lives of American citizens in the willful prosecution of the ruthless naval program they have announced their intention to adopt. Only actual overt acts on their part can make me believe it even now.

If this inveterate confidence on my part in the sobriety and prudent foresight of their purpose should unhappily prove unfounded—if American ships and American lives should in fact be sacrificed by their naval commanders in heedless contravention of the just and reasonable understandings of international law and the obvious dictates of humanity—I shall take the liberty of coming again before the Congress, to ask that authority be given me to use any means that may be necessary for the protection of our seamen and our people in the prosecution of their peaceful and legitimate errands on the high seas. I can do nothing less. I take it for granted that all neutral governments will take the same course.

We do not desire any hostile conflict with the Imperial German Government. We are the sincere friends of the German people, and earnestly desire to remain at peace with the Government which speaks for them. We shall not believe that they are hostile to us unless and until we are obliged to believe it; and we purpose nothing more than the reasonable defense of the undoubted rights of our people.

We wish to serve no selfish ends. We seek merely to stand true alike in thought and in action to the immemorial principles of our people which I sought to express in my address to the Senate only two weeks ago—seek merely to vindicate our right to liberty and justice and an unmolested life. These are the bases of peace, not war. God grant we may not be challenged to defend them by acts of willful injustice on the part of the Government of Germany!

[*Wilson first undertook to arm American merchantmen ("armed neutrality") against the submarines. But when this tactic failed and German U-boats began to sink American vessels, he again went before Congress, on April 2, 1917. Referring principally to these sinkings, he asked for a formal resolution acknowledging the fact that Germany had "thrust" war on the United States. "We have no quarrel with the German people," he declared—only with their government. With militaristic forces rampant, "there can be no assured security for the democratic governments of the world." Hence "The world must be made safe for*

democracy." War is "terrible." "But the right is more precious than peace, and
we shall fight for the things which we have always carried nearest our hearts—
for democracy, for the right of those who submit to authority to have a voice in
their own governments, for the rights and liberties of small nations, for a universal dominion of right by such a concert of free peoples as shall bring peace
and safety to all nations and make the world itself at last free."]

2. Representative Kitchin Assails the War Resolution (1917)

Congress responded promptly to Wilson's request for a war resolution. But the
lopsided vote—82 to 6 in the Senate and 373 to 50 in the House—did not conceal
a widespread opposition to hostilities, especially in the German-American areas. A
flaming anti-war speech came from the lips of Representative Claude Kitchin of North
Carolina, an eloquent and beloved string-tie Congressman, whose outburst produced
a deluge of unflattering letters and telegrams. "Go to Germany," demanded one de-
tractor. "They need fertilizer!" Ascertain what truth there is in Kitchin's allegation
that Wilson's inconsistent and unneutral policies were taking the nation into war.
Did Kitchin deserve to be called a pro-German?

Great Britain every day, every hour, for two years has violated American
rights on the seas. We have persistently protested. She has denied us not
only entrance into the ports of the Central Powers but has closed to us by
force the ports of neutrals. She has unlawfully seized our ships and our
cargoes. She has rifled our mails. She has declared a war zone sufficiently
large to cover all the ports of her enemy. She made the entire North Sea a
military area—strewed it with hidden mines and told the neutral nations
of the world to stay out or be blown up. We protested.* No American ship
was sunk, no American life was destroyed, because we submitted and did
not go in. We kept out of war. We sacrificed no honor. We surrendered
permanently no essential rights. We knew that these acts of Great Britain,
though in plain violation of international law and of our rights on the
seas, were not aimed at us. They were directed at her enemy. They were
inspired by military necessity. Rather than plunge this country into war, we
were willing to forgo for the time our rights. I approved that course then;
I approve it now.

Germany declares a war zone sufficiently large to cover the ports of her
enemy. She infests it with submarines and warns the neutral world to stay
out, though in plain violation of our rights and of international law. We
know that these acts are aimed not directly at us but intended to injure
and cripple her enemy, with which she is in a death struggle.

We refuse to yield; we refuse to forgo our rights for the time. We insist
upon going in.

In my judgment, we could keep out of the war with Germany as we kept
out of the war with Great Britain, by keeping our ships and our citizens
out of the war zone of Germany as we did out of the war zone of Great

2. *Congressional Record*, 65 Cong., 1 sess., pp. 332–33 (April 5, 1917).
* Kitchin was mistaken. The United States did not formally protest against the British mined
zone; more than two years later it merely reserved its rights.

WAR AGAINST EVERYBODY

The German announcement of unrestricted submarine
warfare (January 31) was interpreted in America as war
on the entire civilized world by the Kaiser. New York
World, 1917.

Britain. And we would sacrifice no more honor, surrender no more rights,
in the one case than in the other. Or we could resort to armed neutrality,
which the President recently urged and for which I voted on March 1.

But we are told that Germany has destroyed American lives while Great
Britain destroyed only property. Great Britain destroyed no American lives
because this nation kept her ships and her citizens out of her war zone
which she sowed with hidden mines.

But are we quite sure that the real reason for war with Germany is the
destruction of lives as distinguished from property, that to avenge the killing of innocent Americans and to protect American lives war becomes a
duty?

Mexican bandits raided American towns, shot to death sleeping men,
women, and children in their own homes. We did not go to war* to avenge
these deaths. . . .

We were willing to forgo our rights rather than plunge this country into
war while half the world was in conflagration. I approved that course then;
I approve it now.

* Technically, the United States did not go to war, but Wilson sent General Pershing into
Mexico in 1916–1917 to pursue the bandit Villa.

Why can we not, why should we not, forgo for the time being the viola-tion of our rights by Germany, and do as we did with Great Britain, do as we did with Mexico, and thus save the universe from being wrapped in the flames of war?

I have hoped and prayed that God would forbid our country going into war with another for doing that which perhaps under the same circum-stances we ourselves would do.

THOUGHT PROVOKERS

1. It has been said that truth is the first casualty in any war. Explain. What would have happened if the United States had demanded, with arms, that both Britain and Germany conform to the conventional rules of war? Would such a course have been to America's advantage?

2. In what way did the American policy on loans and munitions finally involve the United States in the war? Explain why Congress refused to enact an em-bargo on arms in 1916 but did so in the 1930's.

3. Legalities aside, did self-interest alone justify the German sinking of the *Lusitania*? Why was the *Sussex* more important than the *Lusitania*?

4. Was there any real inconsistency between Wilson's warning Americans to get out of Mexico and his refusing to warn them to stay out of the European danger zone? Does a failure to exercise national rights mean that they are lost forever?

5. It has been said that the United States got involved in World War I because it was not truly neutral. Explain. How could America have kept out? If you had been a German, would you have been willing to lose the war rather than use the submarine inhumanely?

36 · *The War to End War, 1917-1918*

It is a fearful thing to lead this great peaceful people into war. . . .
WOODROW WILSON, WAR MESSAGE, APRIL 2, 1917

PROLOGUE: While the war-weary Allies held back the Germans, the United States belatedly, and with vast confusion, raised an army. More than a year passed before substantial forces under General Pershing got "over there" to France, where they helped turn the tide in the autumn of 1918. Back home, the current "Hang the Kaiser" hysteria had resulted in emotional crusades to raise money, produce food, build ships, conserve fuel, and silence dissent. The Espionage Act of 1917, stiffened by the Sedition Act of 1918, provided penalties up to $10,000 in fines and 20 years in prison for disloyal speech and writing. Especially noteworthy was the sensationally successful propaganda machine of George Creel, who featured Wilson's war aims as capsuled in the Fourteen Points. By November, 1918, the Germans were through. Their morale undermined by Allied propaganda, their belts tightened by the enemy blockade, and their armies reeling in the field, they sued for peace and were granted an armistice based on the Fourteen Points.

A. THE RAISING OF ARMIES

1. Houston Urges a Draft (1917)

The United States needed to create a huge army without delay, but the unhappy experience with conscription during the Civil War provided ready-made arguments against a draft. On the eve of the declaration of war, Secretary of Agriculture Houston met with the Council of National Defense, and then recorded his views. In the following excerpt, how sound is his reasoning that volunteering was actually less democratic than conscripting?

The majority of the members of the Council strongly objected to the volunteer idea and advocated the draft. One member questioned the wisdom of resorting to the draft, and another emphatically opposed it.

I advocated compulsory training. I strongly objected to volunteering on the ground that it was undemocratic and wasteful. It is unjust to allow those to fight our battles who have the vision to see and appreciate the issues, and the character and patriotism to offer their lives; and to permit those who are slow to remain in security. We cannot afford to have our most eager men swept away as England did. Volunteering is unjust. It is also inadequate and unsafe in modern war, especially where great numbers have to be raised and trained quickly. It has been ruinous in every other war in which we have engaged. It is likewise much more costly in dollars

1. D. F. Houston, *Eight Years with Wilson's Cabinet* (1926), I, 246.

and cents. Compulsion alone permits the requisite selection of men and their designation for tasks which are essential and for which they are best fitted.

2. T.R. Lambasts Broomstick Preparedness (1917)

Bitterly disappointed that his request to raise and lead a volunteer division was rejected, ex-President Theodore Roosevelt accepted an editorial post with the Kansas City *Star* (salary $25,000) and flailed away at lagging military preparations. His complaint was that if Wilson had earlier supported military preparedness and had created a Big Stick, the contemptuous German war lords would not have forced America into the conflict. He also attributed the confusion in raising an army to the President's ineptitude, and charged that shipments of coffins and clay pigeons were being sent to France instead of military supplies urgently needed by the troops. General Leonard Wood, a Republican who had pioneered with Roosevelt for preparedness, was not given command of the American expeditionary force although he was the senior general. But there were several reasons for such a snub: Wood, like T.R., was a notorious troublemaker, and like T.R. he was physically below par. What is the most incredible part of this blistering editorial by Roosevelt in the Kansas City *Star*?

It is earnestly to be hoped that the [current] Congressional investigation into the fruits of our military unpreparedness will keep two objects clearly in mind. First, the aim must be to speed up the work of efficient war preparation by doing away with all the present practices that are wrong. Second, the aim should be to make evident to all our people that our present shameful shortcomings are due to failure to prepare in advance, and that never again ought we to allow our governmental leaders to put us in such a humiliating and unworthy position.

It will be quite impossible to get at all the facts of our unpreparedness. Most officers will be very reluctant to testify to the whole truth. They know that they will suffer if they do so, because they have seen the punishment inflicted by the administration on Major General Wood for the sole reason that he dared to tell the truth about our shortcomings, and dared to advocate preparedness in advance. For this reason I am not at liberty to quote the generals, colonels, captains, and lieutenants of the artillery, infantry, medical corps, and quartermaster corps who have told me of their troubles with unheated hospitals, insufficient drugs, summer underclothes in winter weather, lack of overcoats, of shoes, of rifles, of ammunition, of cannon. But in the camps I visited I saw some things so evident that no harm can come to any officer from my speaking of them.

Last fall I saw thousands of men drilling with broomsticks. I have such a broomstick now before me. Last fall I saw thousands of men drilling with rudely whittled wooden guns. I have one such before me now. I saw them drilling with wooden machine guns as late as the beginning of December. I saw barrels mounted on sticks, on which zealous captains were endeavoring to teach their men how to ride a horse. I saw in the national army camps

2. Kansas City *Star*, Dec. 27, 1917. By permission of the Kansas City *Star*.

in Illinois and Ohio scores of wooden cannon. Doubtless any man can see them now if he goes there.

The excellent officers in the camps are as rapidly as possible remedying these deficiencies. I hope and believe that by spring they will all be remedied. But let our people not forget that for one year after Germany went to war with us, we were wholly unable to defend ourselves, and owed our safety only to the English and French ships and armies.

The cause was our refusal to prepare in advance. President Wilson's message of December, 1914, in which he ridiculed those who advocated preparedness, was part of the cause. His Presidential campaign [in 1916] on the "He kept us out of war" issue was part of the cause. We paid the price later with broomstick rifles, logwood cannon, soldiers without shoes, and epidemics of pneumonia in the camps. We are paying the price now. We pay the price in the doubled cost of necessary war supplies. We pay the price in shortage of coal and congested transportation. The refusal to prepare and the price we now pay because of the refusal stand in the relation of cause and effect.

B. WARTIME HYSTERIA

1. Un-Christlike Preachers (1918)

Ministers of the gospel, swallowing Allied propaganda and falling prey to the war-time hysteria, engaged in un-Christian excesses. "It is religious to hate the Kaiser," declared the Reverend James R. Day, Chancellor of Syracuse University, "because the Bible teaches us to hate the Devil and all his works." Less elegantly a prominent Baptist pastor in Cleveland cried, "To hell with the Kaiser!" Here a prominent Methodist bishop and author, Dr. William A. Quayle, pays his disrespects to Germany in a magazine article. Does he accept Wilson's view that America was fighting only Germany's rulers?

Let us set down sternly that we are at war with the Germans, not the Junkers [German aristocrats], not autocracy, not Prussianism, not the Kaiser. . . . The German people is what we war with. The German people is committing the unspeakable horrors which set the whole world aghast. The German people is not and has not been conducting war. It is and has been conducting murder. Hold fast to that. The Supreme Court of New York declared the sinking of the *Lusitania* an act of piracy. Piracy is not war. All decencies, honors, humanities, international agreements, and laws have been smashed by them day and night from the first rape of Belgium to now. The new atrocity which appeared this week was spraying prisoners with burning oil. This is Germany's most recent jest. It makes them laugh so!

They have violated every treaty with the United States; they have lied from start to finish and to everybody. A treaty was a scrap of paper.° . . .

---

1. *Northwestern Christian Advocate,* quoted in *Literary Digest,* LIX, 28 (Oct. 19, 1918).
° The phrase "scrap of paper" became one of the great propaganda weapons of the war. The German Chancellor, Bethmann-Hollweg, had defended Germany's invasion of Belgium in 1914 by referring to the treaty of 1839 guaranteeing her neutrality as a "scrap of paper."

EDITOR   CAPITALIST   POLITICIAN   MINISTER

HAVING THEIR FLING

In 1918 the editors of the anti-war Socialist journal, *The Masses*, were tried under the Espionage Act for obstructing the war. The above cartoon was Exhibit F for the prosecution. *The Masses* (New York), 1917.

Germany has ravished the women of Belgium, Servia, Roumania, Poland, Armenia. Germany murdered the passengers of the *Lusitania* and struck a medal to celebrate that German triumph, dating it two days before the horrible occurrence. Germany has ruined cathedrals and cities in sheer wanton fury, in such fashion as has not been done in all the wars waged in Europe since the days of the building of the cathedrals. Germany has poisoned wells, crucified inhabitants and soldiers, burned people in their houses, and this by system. Germany has denatured men and boys, has wantonly defaced the living and the dying and the dead. An eye-witness tells of seeing women dead at a table with their tongues nailed to the table and left to die.

Germany has stolen things little and big: playthings from children, finery from women, pictures of incalculable worth, bank-deposits, railroads, factories. Germany has sunk hospital-ships, has bombed hospitals and Red Cross camps. Germany has disclosed neither decency nor honor from the day it started war, nor has a single voice in Germany to date been lifted up against the orgies of ruthlessness which turn the soul sick and which constitute the chief barbarity of history. Germany remains unblushing and unconscious of its indecency. Germany's egotism still struts like a Kaiser. And to climax its horrid crimes, Germany has inflicted compulsory polygamy on the virgins of its own land.

[*If such tales were given currency by well-educated clergymen schooled in Christian forbearance, one can hardly blame rank-and-file Americans for believing the same accounts. Actually there were cases of rape and violence affecting civilians on both sides; the Germans were involved to a greater extent because they fought almost the entire war on enemy territory. The* Lusitania *medal was struck off after the sinking; the story of the "Crucified Canadian" was a complete hoax; the French cathedral at Rheims was damaged after the towers had been used for military observation. The rest of this account reflects an uncritical belief in the thoroughly unreliable stories in the Bryce report (see earlier, p. 645).*]

2. Abusing the Pro-Germans (1918)

The several million enemy aliens in the United States were under suspicion, especially those who did not buy Liberty Bonds. One of them was Robert Paul Prager, a young German residing in Illinois. He had tried to enlist in the Navy but was rejected because he had lost an eye. After he had spoken out for socialism, he was seized by a drunken mob in 1918, stripped of his clothes, wrapped in an American flag, and hanged. A patriotic jury acquitted the ringleaders. This was the worst outrage of its kind, but another almost occurred, as Secretary of War Baker related in the following letter. What does it reveal of the American state of mind at this time? Why was such an incident much less likely to occur in World War II?

The spirit of the country seems unsually good, but there is a growing frenzy of suspicion and hostility toward disloyalty. I am afraid we are going to have a good many instances of people roughly treated on very slight evidence of disloyalty. Already a number of men and some women have been "tarred and feathered," and a portion of the press is urging with great vehemence more strenuous efforts at detection and punishment. This usually takes the form of advocating "drum-head courts-martial"* and "being stood up against a wall and shot," which are perhaps none too bad for real traitors, but are very suggestive of summary discipline to arouse mob spirit, which unhappily does not take time to weigh evidence.

In Cleveland a few days ago a foreign-looking man got into a street car and, taking a seat, noticed pasted in the window next to him a Liberty Loan poster, which he immediately tore down, tore into small bits, and stamped under his feet. The people in the car surged around him with the demand that he be lynched, when a Secret Service man showed his badge and placed him under arrest, taking him in a car to the police station, where he was searched and found to have two Liberty Bonds in his pocket and

2. Frederick Palmer, *Newton D. Baker* (1931), II, 162–63. Copyright 1931 by Frederick D. Palmer. Reprinted by permission of Dodd, Mead and Company.
* Originally a hasty court-martial in the field, around a drum as a table.

to be a non-English-speaking Pole. When an interpreter was procured, it was discovered that the circular which he had destroyed had had on it a picture of the German Emperor, which had so infuriated the fellow that he destroyed the circular to show his vehement hatred of the common enemy. As he was unable to speak a single word of English, he would undoubtedly have been hanged but for the intervention and entirely accidental presence of the Secret Service agent.

I am afraid the grave danger in this sort of thing, apart from its injustice, is that the German Government will adopt retaliatory measures. While the Government of the United States is not only not responsible for these things, but very zealously trying to prevent them, the German Government draws no fine distinctions.

C. FREE SPEECH IN WARTIME

1. La Follette Demands His Rights (1917)

Senator Robert M. La Follette of Wisconsin—undersized, pompadoured, and fiery—was one of the most eloquent reformers of his generation. Representing a state with a heavy concentration of German-Americans, he had spoken out vehemently against war with Germany and had voted against it. He and his five dissenting colleagues were pilloried in the press as traitors for voting their consciences. On October 6, 1917, La Follette rose and quoted (from the press) a charge to a federal grand jury in Texas by a district judge. The jurist reportedly had said that these six Senators ought to be convicted of treason and shot. "I wish I could pay for the ammunition," he continued. "I would like to attend the execution, and if I were in the firing squad I would not want to be the marksman who had the blank shell." La Follette then went on to present this classic defense of free speech. Why was free speech so severely threatened in this particular war?

But, sir, it is not alone Members of Congress that the war party in this country has sought to intimidate. The mandate seems to have gone forth to the sovereign people of this country that they must be silent while those things are being done by their Government which most vitally concern their well-being, their happiness, and their lives.

Today—and for weeks past—honest and law-abiding citizens of this country are being terrorized and outraged in their rights by those sworn to uphold the laws and protect the rights of the people. I have in my possession numerous affidavits establishing the fact that people are being unlawfully arrested, thrown into jail, held incommunicado for days, only to be eventually discharged without ever having been taken into court, because they have committed no crime. Private residences are being invaded, loyal citizens of undoubted integrity and probity arrested, cross-examined, and the most sacred constitutional rights guaranteed to every American citizen are being violated.

---

1. *Congressional Record*, 65 Cong., 1 sess., pp. 7878–79.

It appears to be the purpose of those conducting this campaign to throw the country into a state of terror, to coerce public opinion, to stifle criticism, and suppress discussion of the great issues involved in this war.

I think all men recognize that in time of war the citizen must surrender some rights for the common good which he is entitled to enjoy in time of peace. *But, sir, the right to control their own Government, according to constitutional forms, is not one of the rights that the citizens of this country are called upon to surrender in time of war.*

Rather, in time of war, the citizen must be more alert to the preservation of his right to control his Government. He must be most watchful of the encroachment of the military upon the civil power. He must beware of those precedents in support of arbitrary action by administrative officials which, excused on the plea of necessity in wartime, become the fixed rule when the necessity has passed and normal conditions have been restored.

More than all, the citizen and his representative in Congress in time of war must maintain his right of free speech. More than in times of peace, it is necessary that the channels for free public discussion of governmental policies shall be open and unclogged.

I believe, Mr. President, that I am now touching upon the most important question in this country today—and that is the right of the citizens of this country and their representatives in Congress to discuss in an orderly way, frankly and publicly and without fear, from the platform and through the press, every important phase of this war; its causes, the manner in which it should be conducted, and the terms upon which peace should be made. . . .

I am contending for this right, because the exercise of it is necessary to the welfare, to the existence, of this Government, to the successful conduct of this war, and to a

FOR SERVICES RENDERED

German Kaiser hangs Iron Cross on Senator La Follette for speech opposing declaration of war. Los Angeles *Daily Times,* 1917.

peace which shall be enduring and for the best interest of this country. . . .

Mr. President, our Government, above all others, is founded on the right of the people freely to discuss all matters pertaining to their Government, in war not less than in peace. . . . How can that popular will express itself between elections except by meetings, by speeches, by publications, by petitions, and by addresses to the representatives of the people?

Any man who seeks to set a limit upon those rights, whether in war or peace, aims a blow at the most vital part of our Government. And then as the time for election approaches, and the official is called to account for his stewardship—not a day, not a week, not a month, before the election, but a year or more before it, if the people choose—they must have the right to the freest possible discussion of every question upon which their representative has acted, of the merits of every measure he has supported or opposed, of every vote he has cast and every speech that he has made. And before this great fundamental right every other must, if necessary, give way, for in no other manner can representative government be preserved.

2. Chafee Upholds Free Speech (1919)

The Socialists, many of whom were anti-war, ran afoul of the Espionage Act of 1917. Prominent among them was Mrs. Rose Pastor Stokes, a Russian-born Jewess who had worked in America as a cigarmaker and who became a prominent social worker and propagandist for socialism. Referring to American soldiers, she remarked that they were "not fighting for democracy but for the protection and safeguarding of Morgan's millions." In a letter to the Kansas City *Star* she wrote: "No government which is for the profiteers can also be for the people, and I am for the people, while the Government is for the profiteers." She was sentenced to ten years in prison, though a higher court later reversed the decision. President Wilson approved of her original conviction. Professor Zechariah Chafee, Jr., of the Harvard Law School, a prominent liberal, made the following comments on these espionage cases shortly after the war had ended. How does he support his assumption that the suppression of free speech can be self-defeating and dangerous in the long run?

Never in the history of our country, since the Alien and Sedition Laws of 1798, has the meaning of free speech been the subject of such sharp controversy as to-day. Over two hundred prosecutions and other judicial proceedings during the war, involving speeches, newspaper articles, pamphlets, and books, have been followed since the armistice by a widespread legislative consideration of bills punishing the advocacy of extreme radicalism. . . .

The courts have treated opinions as statements of fact, and then condemned them as false because they differed from the President's speech or the resolution of Congress declaring war. They have made it impossible for an opponent of the war to write an article or even a letter in a newspaper of general circulation, because it will be read in some training camp where it might cause insubordination, or interfere with military success. He cannot address a large audience, because it is liable to include a few men in uniform; and some judges have held him punishable if it contains men between eighteen and forty-five; while Judge Van Valkenburgh, in *United States* v. *Rose Pastor Stokes,* would not even require that, because what is said to mothers, sisters, and sweethearts may lessen their enthusiasm for the war, and "our armies in the field and our navies upon the seas can operate and succeed only so far as they are supported and maintained by the folks at home." . . .

Although we have not gone so far as Great Britain in disregarding constitutional guarantees, we have gone much farther than in any other war, even in the Civil War, with the enemy at our gates. Undoubtedly some utterances had to be suppressed. We have passed through a period of danger, and have reasonably supposed the danger to be greater than it actually was, but the prosecutions in Great Britain during a similar period of peril in the French Revolution have not since been regarded with pride.

Action in proportion to the emergency was justified, but we have censored and punished speech which was very far from direct and dangerous interference with the conduct of the war. The chief responsibility for this must rest, not upon Congress, which was content for a long period with the moderate language of the Espionage Act of 1917, but upon the officials of the Department of Justice and the Post Office, who turned that statute into a drag-net for pacifists, and upon the judges who upheld and approved this distortion of law.

It may be questioned, too, how much has actually been gained. Men have been imprisoned, but their words have not ceased to spread. The poetry in *The Masses* was excluded from the mails only to be given a far wider circulation in two issues of the *Federal Reporter.* The mere publication of Mrs. Stokes' statement in the Kansas City *Star,* "I am for the people and the Government is for the profiteers," was considered so dangerous to the morale of the training camps that she was sentenced to ten years in prison, and yet it was repeated by every important newspaper in the country during the trial. There is an unconscious irony in all suppression. . . .

Those who gave their lives for freedom would be the last to thank us for throwing aside so lightly the great traditions of our race. Not satisfied to have justice and almost all the people with our cause, we insisted on an artificial unanimity of opinion behind the war. Keen intellectual grasp of the President's aims by the nation at large was very difficult when the opponents of his idealism ranged unchecked, while the men who urged greater idealism went to prison. In our efforts to silence those who advocated peace without victory, we prevented at the very start that vigorous threshing out of fundamentals which might to-day have saved us from a victory without peace.

D. THE PROPAGANDA FRONT

1. Creel Spreads Fear Propaganda (*c.* 1918)

George Creel—a young, dynamic, but tactless journalist—headed the nation's great propaganda engine, the Committee on Public Information. He not only prepared documentary movies and unleashed tens of thousands of orators, but issued some 75,000,000 copies of pamphlets. He also employed a galaxy of distinguished historians and other scholars to prepare these propaganda booklets, many of them in paper covers of red, white, and blue. One title, *How the War Came to America,* enjoyed a fantastic distribution of 7,000,000 copies. Professor J. S. P. Tatlock, a Chaucer specialist at Stanford University, wrote the following highly imaginative account, inspired in part by Allied propaganda like the Bryce report. Distributed as a part of a pamphlet entitled *Why America Fights Germany,* it boasted a circulation of about 750,000 copies. To what emotions does it most strongly appeal?

Now let us picture what a sudden invasion of the United States by these Germans would mean; sudden, because their settled way is always to attack suddenly.

First, they set themselves to capture New York City. While their fleet blockades the harbor and shells the city and the forts from far at sea, their troops land somewhere near and advance toward the city in order to cut its rail communications, starve it into surrender, and then plunder it.

One body of from 50,000 to 100,000 men lands, let us suppose, at Barnegat Bay, New Jersey, and advances without meeting resistance, for the brave but small American army is scattered elsewhere. They pass through Lakewood, a station on the Central Railroad of New Jersey. They first demand wine for the officers and beer for the men. Angered to find that an American town does not contain large quantities of either, they pillage and burn the post office and most of the hotels and stores. Then they demand $1,000,000 from the residents. One feeble old woman tries to conceal $20 which she has been hoarding in her desk drawer; she is taken out and hanged (to save a cartridge). Some of the teachers in two district schools meet a fate which makes them envy her. The Catholic priest and Methodist minister are thrown into a pig-sty, while the German soldiers look on and laugh. Some of the officers quarter themselves in a handsome house on the edge of the town, insult the ladies of the family, and destroy and defile the contents of the house.

By this time some of the soldiers have managed to get drunk; one of them discharges his gun accidentally, the cry goes up that the residents are firing on the troops, and then hell breaks loose. Robbery, murder, and outrage run riot. Fifty leading citizens are lined up against the First National Bank Building, and shot. Most of the town and the beautiful pinewoods are burned, and then the troops move on to treat New Brunswick in the same way—if they get there.

This is not just a snappy story. It is not fancy. The general plan of campaign against America has been announced repeatedly by German military

1. J. S. P. Tatlock, *Why America Fights Germany,* War Information Series No. 15, Cantonment Edition (1918), pp. 9–10.

men. *And every horrible detail is just what the German troops have done in Belgium and France.*

2. Wilson Unveils His Fourteen Points (1918)
3. Roosevelt Blunts Wilson's Points (1918)

President Wilson's war-aims speeches were lofty and eloquent, but rather vague and long-winded. An American journalist in Russia suggested that he compress his views into crisp, placard-like paragraphs. This he did in his famed Fourteen Points address to Congress on January 8, 1918. By promising independence (self-determination) to minority groups under enemy rule, and by raising up hopes everywhere for a better tomorrow, the Fourteen Points undermined the foe's will to resist. Simultaneously they inspirited the Allies. George Creel's propaganda machine broadcast the Points in leaflet form throughout the world, while Allied rockets and shells showered them over enemy lines. German desertions multiplied. Form some judgment as to whether Wilson's aims were completely clear and consistent. Determine which ones would be most likely to weaken the resistance of Germany and Austria-Hungary. The frustrated Colonel Roosevelt fulminated against the Fourteen Points in the Kansas City *Star*. Given that before 1917 he had been anti-Wilson, pro-tariff, anti-Germany, pro-Ally, and internationalist-minded, what are the most important inconsistencies in his position?

WILSON'S POINTS

I. Open covenants of peace, openly arrived at, after which there shall be no private international understandings of any kind, but diplomacy shall proceed always frankly and in the public view.

[Wilson finally meant *secret* negotiations but *public* commitments. He had earlier laid himself open to criticism by landing the marines in Haiti and Santo Domingo in 1915 and 1916 to restore order.]

II. Absolute freedom of navigation upon the seas, outside territorial waters, alike in peace and in war, except as the seas may be closed in whole or in part by international action [of the League of Nations] for the enforcement of international covenants.

[Big-navy Britain, fearing to blunt her blockade weapon, refused to accept this point.]

III. The removal, so far as possible, of all economic barriers, and the establishment of an equality of trade

ROOSEVELT'S COMPLAINTS

The President has recently waged war on Haiti and San Domingo, and rendered democracy within these two small former republics not merely unsafe, but non-existent. He has kept all that he has done in the matter absolutely secret. If he means what he says, he will at once announce what open covenant of peace he has openly arrived at with these two little republics, which he has deprived of their right of self-determination.

It makes no distinction between freeing the seas from murder, like that continually practiced by Germany, and freeing them from blockade of contraband merchandise, which is the practice of a right universally enjoyed by belligerents, and at this moment practiced by the United States. Either this proposal is meaningless, or it is a mischievous concession to Germany.

The third point promises free trade among all the nations, unless the words are designedly used to conceal

2. *Congressional Record*, 65 Cong., 2 sess., p. 691.
3. Kansas City *Star*, Oct. 30, 1918. By permission of the Kansas City *Star*. The full text may also be found in Ralph Stout, ed., *Roosevelt in the Kansas City "Star"* (1921), pp. 241–42, 243–46.

conditions among all the nations consenting to the peace, and associating themselves [in the League of Nations] for its maintenance.

[This meant, although not too clearly put, that the United States could still maintain tariffs but could not discriminate among fellow members of the League of Nations. Any commercial favors granted to one fellow member would automatically be extended to all.]

IV. Adequate guarantees given and taken that national armaments will be reduced to the lowest point consistent with domestic safety.

[This meant a force no larger than necessary to control domestic disorders and prevent foreign invasion.]

V. A free, open-minded, and absolutely impartial adjustment of all [wartime] colonial claims, based upon a strict observance of the principle that, in determining all such questions of sovereignty, the interests of the populations concerned must have equal weight with the equitable claims of the Government whose title is to be determined.

[German colonies captured by Britain and Japan might be returned, if this course seemed "equitable."]

VI. The evacuation of all Russian territory [inhabited by Russians], and such a settlement of all questions affecting Russia as will secure the best and freest cooperation of the other nations of the world in obtaining for her an unhampered and unembarrassed opportunity for the independent determination of her own political development and national policy, and assure her of a sincere welcome into the society of free nations, under institutions of her own choosing; and, more than a welcome, assistance also of every kind. . . .

[Wilson had in mind having the German invader evacuate Russian territory, and helping the Russian Poles and other non-Russian nationalities to achieve self-determination. He would

President Wilson's true meaning. This would deny to our country the right to make a tariff to protect its citizens, and especially its workingmen, against Germany or China or any other country. Apparently this is desired on the ground that the incidental domestic disaster to this country will prevent other countries from feeling hostile to us. The supposition is foolish. England practiced free trade and yet Germany hated England particularly. . . .

Either this is language deliberately used to deceive, or else it means that we are to scrap our army and navy, and prevent riot by means of a national constabulary, like the state constabulary of New York or Pennsylvania.

Unless the language is deliberately used to deceive, this means that we are to restore to our brutal enemy the colonies taken by our allies while they were defending us from this enemy. The proposition is probably meaningless. If it is not, it is monstrous.

Point VI deals with Russia. It probably means nothing, but if it means anything, it provides that America shall share on equal terms with other nations, including Germany, Austria, and Turkey [the Central Powers], in giving Russia assistance. The whole proposition would not be particularly out of place in a college sophomore's exercise in rhetoric.

also lend a helping hand to the new Bolshevik government.]

VII. Belgium, the whole world will agree, must be evacuated and restored, without any attempt to limit the sovereignty which she enjoys in common with all other free nations. No other single act will serve as this will serve to restore confidence among the nations in the laws which they have themselves set and determined for the government of their relations with one another. Without this healing act the whole structure and validity of international law is forever impaired.

[Germany, disregarding a neutrality treaty of 1839, had struck through Belgium at France in 1914. The war-minded Roosevelt at first approved this act as one of military necessity, but he soon changed his views. The word "restored" in Point VII implied that the Germans would be assessed an indemnity for the damage they had done.]

Point VII deals with Belgium and is entirely proper and commonplace.

VIII. All French territory should be freed and the invaded portions restored, and the wrong done to France by Prussia in 1871 in the matter of Alsace-Lorraine, which has unsettled the peace of the world for nearly fifty years, should be righted, in order that peace may once more be made secure in the interest of all.

[Wilson intended that Alsace-Lorraine, seized by Prussia [Germany] in 1871, should be returned to France.]

Point VIII deals with Alsace-Lorraine and is couched in language which betrays Mr. Wilson's besetting sin—his inability to speak in a straight-forward manner. He may mean that Alsace and Lorraine must be restored to France, in which case he is right. He may mean that a plebiscite must be held, in which case he is playing Germany's evil game.

IX. A readjustment of the frontiers of Italy should be effected along clearly recognizable lines of nationality.

[Wilson would extend "self-determination" to nearby Italian peoples not under the Italian flag.]

Point IX deals with Italy, and is right.

X. The peoples of Austria-Hungary, whose place among the nations we wish to see safeguarded and assured, should be accorded the freest opportunity of autonomous development.

[This point raised difficulties because of the quarreling minorities of

Point X deals with the Austro-Hungarian Empire, and is so foolish that even President Wilson has abandoned it.

[Wilson later stressed independence rather than local autonomy.]

the "succession states" that rose from the ruins of Austria-Hungary.]

XI. Rumania, Serbia, and Montenegro should be evacuated; occupied territories restored; Serbia accorded free and secure access to the sea; and the relations of the several Balkan states to one another determined by friendly counsel along historically established lines of allegiance and nationality; and international guarantees of the political and economic independence and territorial integrity of the several Balkan states should be entered into.

[This point was also invalidated by the "succession states," including Yugoslavia, which embraced Serbia.]

Point XI proposes that we, together with other nations, including apparently Germany, Austria, and Hungary, shall guarantee justice in the Balkan Peninsula. As this would also guarantee our being from time to time engaged in war over matters in which we had no interest whatever, it is worth while inquiring whether President Wilson proposes that we wage these wars with the national constabulary to which he desired to reduce our armed forces.

XII. The Turkish portions of the present Ottoman Empire should be assured a secure sovereignty, but the other nationalities which are now under Turkish rule should be assured an undoubted security of life and an absolutely unmolested opportunity of autonomous development, and the Dardanelles should be permanently opened as a free passage to the ships and commerce of all nations under international guarantees.

[Wilson's ideal was self-determination for the Greeks, Armenians, Arabs, and other non-Turks in the Turkish empire, much of whose land became mandates of France and Britain under the League of Nations.]

Point XII proposes to perpetuate the infamy of Turkish rule in Europe, and as a sop to the conscience of humanity proposes to give the subject races autonomy, a slippery word which in a case like this is useful only for rhetorical purposes.

XIII. An independent Polish state should be erected which should include the territories inhabited by indisputably Polish populations, which should be assured a free and secure access to the sea, and whose political and economic independence and territorial integrity should be guaranteed by international covenant.

[Poland was to be restored from the territory of Germany, Russia, and Austria-Hungary, despite injustices to German and other minorities.]

Point XIII proposes an independent Poland, which is right; and then proposes that we guarantee its integrity in the event of future war, which is preposterous unless we intend to become a military nation more fit for overseas warfare than Germany is at present.

XIV. A general association [League] of nations must be formed under specific covenants for the purpose of

In its essence Mr. Wilson's proposition for a League of Nations seems to be akin to the Holy Alliance of affording mutual guarantees of political independence and territorial integrity to, great and small states alike.

In regard to these essential rectifications of wrong and assertions of right, we feel ourselves to be intimate partners of all the governments and peoples associated together against the Imperialists. We cannot be separated in interest or divided in purpose. We stand together until the end.

the nations of Europe a century ago, which worked such mischief that the Monroe Doctrine was called into being especially to combat it. If it is designed to do away with nationalism, it will work nothing but mischief. If it is devised in sane fashion as an addition to nationalism and as an addition to preparing our own strength for our own defense, it may do a small amount of good. But it will certainly accomplish nothing if more than a moderate amount is attempted, and probably the best first step would be to make the existing league of the Allies a going concern.

E. THE FACE OF WAR

1. General Pershing Defines American Fighting Tactics (1917–1918)

Generals, it has often been said, have a habit of fighting the previous war—a maxim to which jut-jawed General John J. Pershing, commander of the American Expeditionary Force, was no exception. Pershing had studied Civil War tactics at West Point in the late nineteenth century, and saw no reason why they should not be applied in France in the twentieth century. He expressed criticism bordering on contempt for the French and British fascination with fixed, entrenched warfare. Pershing insisted, therefore, that American troops be trained in battle techniques different from those offered to European troops. This approach contributed to appallingly high American casualty rates when the "doughboys" eventually entered combat. How does Pershing here defend his tactical preferences? What factors might have motivated him to adopt them?

The most important question that confronted us in the preparation of our forces of citizen soldiery for efficient service was training. Except for the Spanish-American War, nearly twenty years before, actual combat experience of the Regular Army had been limited to the independent action of minor commands in the Philippines and to two expeditions into Mexico, each with forces smaller than a modern American division. The World War involved the handling of masses where even a division was relatively a small unit. It was one thing to call one or two million men to the colors, and quite another thing to transform them into an organized, instructed army capable of meeting and holding its own in the battle against the best trained force in Europe with three years of actual war experience to its credit.

Few people can realize what a stupendous undertaking it was to teach these vast numbers their various duties when such a large percentage of them were ignorant of practically everything pertaining to the business of the soldier in war. First of all, most of the officer personnel available had little or no military experience, and had to be trained in the manifold duties of commanders. They had to learn the interior economy of their units—

1. John J. Pershing, *My Experiences in the World War* (1931), Vol. I, pp. 150–154; Vol. II, p. 358.

messing, housing, clothing, and, in general, caring for their men—as well as methods of instruction and the art of leading them in battle. This great task was, of course, under the direction of the War Department. . . .

The British methods of teaching trench warfare appealed to me very strongly. They taught their men to be aggressive and undertook to perfect them in hand-to-hand fighting with bayonet, grenade and dagger. A certain amount of this kind of training was necessary to prepare the troops for trench warfare. Moreover it served to stimulate their morale by giving them confidence in their own personal prowess. Through the kindness of Sir Douglas Haig, we were fortunate early in our experience to have assigned to us Lieutenant General R. H. K. Butler and other officers of the British Army in addition to French officers to assist in this individual training. Later, several French and British officers also came to lecture at a number of our schools.

We found difficulty, however, in using these Allied instructors, in that the French and, to a large extent, the British, had practically settled down to the conviction that developments since 1914 had changed the principles of warfare. Both held that new conditions imposed by trench fighting had rendered previous conceptions of training more or less obsolete and that preparation for open warfare was no longer necessary. . . .

If the French doctrine had prevailed our instruction would have been limited to a brief period of training for trench fighting. A new army brought up entirely on such principles would have been seriously handicapped without the protection of the trenches. It would probably have lacked the aggressiveness to break through the enemy's lines and the knowledge of how to carry on thereafter. It was my opinion that the victory could not be won by the costly process of attrition, but it must be won by driving the enemy out into the open and engaging him in a war of movement. Instruction in this kind of warfare was based upon individual and group initiative, resourcefulness and tactical judgment, which were also of great advantage in trench warfare. Therefore, we took decided issue with the Allies and, without neglecting thorough preparation for trench fighting, undertook to train mainly for open combat, with the object from the start of vigorously forcing the offensive. . . .

For the purpose of impressing our own doctrine upon officers, a training program was issued which laid great stress on open warfare methods and offensive action. The following is a pertinent extract from my instructions on this point:

> The above methods to be employed must remain and become distinctly our own. All instruction must contemplate the assumption of a vigorous offensive. This purpose will be emphasized in every phase of training until it becomes a settled habit of thought.

Intimately connected with the question of training for open warfare was the matter of rifle practice. The earliest of my cablegrams on this subject was in August, in which it was urged that thorough instruction in rifle practice should be carried on at home because of the difficulty of giving it in France:

> Study here shows value and desirability of retaining our existing small arms target practice course. In view of great difficulty in securing ranges in France due to density of the population and cultivation recommend as far as practicable the complete course be given in the United States before troops embark. Special emphasis should be placed on rapid fire.

The armies on the Western Front in the recent battles that I had witnessed had all but given up the use of the rifle. Machine guns, grenades, Stokes mortars, and one-pounders had become the main reliance of the average Allied soldier. These were all valuable weapons for specific purposes but they could not replace the combination of an efficient soldier and his rifle. Numerous instances were reported in the Allied armies of men chasing an individual enemy throwing grenades at him instead of using the rifle. Such was the effect of association that continuous effort was necessary to counteract this tendency among our own officers and men and inspire them with confidence in the efficacy of rifle fire. . . .

My view was that the rifle and bayonet still remained the essential weapons of the infantry, and my cables, stressing the fact that the basic principles of warfare had not changed, were sent in an endeavor to influence the courses of training at home. Unfortunately, however, no fixed policy of instruction in the various arms, under a single authority, was ever carried out there. Unresponsive to my advice, the inclination was to accept the views of French specialists and to limit training to the narrow field of trench warfare. Therefore, in large measure, the fundamentals so thoroughly taught at West Point for a century were more or less neglected. The responsibility for the failure at home to take positive action on my recommendations in such matters must fall upon the War Department General Staff.

There were other causes . . . that led to confusion and irregularity in training to such an extent that we were often compelled during the last stages of the war to send men into battle with little knowledge of warfare and sometimes with no rifle practice at all. . . .

[*On September 5, 1918, Pershing issued the following instructions to his Army, then preparing for its first major battle at St. Mihiel.*]

COMBAT INSTRUCTIONS (EXTRACT)

From a tactical point of view, the method of combat in trench warfare presents a marked contrast to that employed in open warfare, and the attempt by assaulting infantry to use trench warfare methods in an open warfare combat will be successful only at great cost. Trench warfare is marked by uniform formations, the regulation of space and time by higher commands down to the smallest details . . . fixed distances and intervals between units and individuals . . . little initiative . . . . Open warfare is marked by . . . irregularity of formations, comparatively little regulation of space and time by higher commanders, the greatest possible use of the infantry's own fire power to enable it to get forward, variable distances and intervals between units and individuals

. . . brief orders and the greatest possible use of individual initiative by all troops engaged in the action. . . . The infantry commander must oppose machine guns by fire from his rifles, his automatics and his rifle grenades and must close with their crews under cover of this fire and of ground beyond their flanks. . . . The success of every unit from the platoon to the division must be exploited to the fullest extent. Where strong resistance is encountered, reënforcements must not be thrown in to make a frontal attack at this point, but must be pushed through gaps created by successful units, to attack these strong points in the flank or rear.

2. A "Doughboy" Describes the Fighting Front (1918)

Some two million young American men served in the American Expeditionary Force, about half of whom saw combat. Many of these troops had been raised on heroic stories about grandfathers and uncles who had fought in the Civil War, and they expected the war in France to provide the same kind of opportunities for glory that their forebears had found at Antietam and Shiloh, Bull Run and Fredericksburg. For the most part, they were bitterly disappointed when they discovered that modern warfare was a decidedly unheroic, dirty, impersonal, and bloody business. The passages below, taken from the battlefield diary of a 31-year-old draftee from upstate New York who was assigned to an engineering company, vividly convey one soldier's reactions to his baptism of fire. What aspects of combat did he find most remarkable? How did his description of warfare fit with General Pershing's expectations about the role of the individual rifleman and the tactics of mobility and "open warfare"?

Thursday, September 12, 1918. Hiked through dark woods. No lights allowed, guided by holding on the pack of the man ahead. Stumbled through underbrush for about half mile into an open field where we waited in soaking rain until about 10:00 P.M. We then started on our hike to the St. Mihiel front, arriving on the crest of a hill at 1:00 A.M. I saw a sight which I shall never forget. It was the zero hour and in one instant the entire front as far as the eye could reach in either direction was a sheet of flame, while the heavy artillery made the earth quake. The barrage was so intense that for a time we could not make out whether the Americans or Germans were putting it over. After timing the interval between flash and report we knew that the heaviest artillery was less than a mile away and consequently it was ours. We waded through pools and mud across open lots into a woods on a hill and had to pitch tents in mud. Blankets all wet and we are soaked to the skin. Have carried full pack from 10:00 P.M. to 2:00 A.M., without a rest. . . . Despite the cannonading I slept until 8:00 A.M. and awoke to find every discharge of 14-inch artillery shaking our tent like a leaf. Remarkable how we could sleep. No breakfast. . . . The doughboys had gone over the top at 5:00 A.M. and the French were shelling the back areas toward Metz. . . . Firing is incessant, so is rain. See an air battle just before turning in.

Friday, September 13, 1918. Called at 3:00 A.M. Struck tents and started to hike at 5:00 A.M. with full packs and a pick. Put on gas mask at alert position and hiked about five miles to St. Jean, where we unslung full packs

2. Courtesy of Eugene Kennedy Collection, Hoover Institution Archives, Stanford University.

and went on about four miles further with short packs and picks. Passed several batteries and saw many dead horses who gave out at start of push. Our doughboys are still shoving and "Jerry" is dropping so many shells on road into no man's land that we stayed back in field and made no effort to repair shell-torn road. Plenty of German prisoners being brought back. . . . Guns booming all the time.

Saturday, September 14, 1918. Hiked up to same road again with rifle, belt, helmet, gas-mask, and pick. . . . First time under shell fire. Major Judge's horse killed. Gibbs has a finger knocked off each hand [by a sniper's bullet] while burying some of our men killed in opening drive. Clothing, bandages, equipment of all sorts, dead horses and every kind of debris strewn all over. . . .

Tuesday, September 17, 1918. Rolled packs and hiked with them up to road. Worked near town that is reduced to heap of stone. Trenches are 20 feet deep and in some places 15 feet across. The wire entanglement is beyond description. Several traps left by Germans. Man in our division had his arm blown off picking up a crucifix.

[*Along with thousands of other doughboys, Kennedy was soon shifted from the St. Mihiel engagement to the major American battleground a few miles to the north, in the Argonne forest between the Meuse and Aire Rivers. He here describes his role in this, the largest American action of the war.*]

Thursday, October 17, 1918. Struck tents at 8:00 A.M. and moved about four miles to Chatel. Pitched tents on a side hill so steep that we had to cut steps to ascend. Worked like hell to shovel out a spot to pitch tent on. Just across the valley in front of us about two hundred yards distant, there had occurred an explosion due to a mine planted by the "Bosche" [Germans] and set with a time fuse. It had blown two men (French), two horses, and the wagon into fragments. . . . Arriving on the scene we found Quinn ransacking the wagon. It was full of grub. We each loaded a burlap bag with cans of condensed milk, peas, lobster, salmon, and bread. I started back . . . when suddenly another mine exploded, the biggest I ever saw. Rocks and dirt flew sky high. Quinn was hit in the knee and had to go to hospital. . . . At 6:00 P.M. each of our four platoons left camp in units to go up front and throw three foot and one artillery bridge across the Aire River. On way to river we were heavily shelled and gassed. . . . We put a bridge across 75-foot span. . . . Third platoon men had to get into water and swim or stand in water to their necks. The toughest job we had so far.

Friday, October 18, 1918. Bright but cool. Men of third platoon who swam river are drying their clothes. . . . Waiting for night to work under cover of darkness. Started up front at 6:00 P.M. . . . Worked one half hour when "Jerry" shelled us so strong that we had to leave job. We could hear snipers' bullets sing past us and had to make our way back carefully along railroad track bank dodging shells every few steps. Gas so thick that masks had to be kept on, adding to the burden of carrying a rifle, pick, shovel, and hand saw. Had to run from one dug-out to another until it let up somewhat, when we made a break for road and hiked to camp about 3 kilometers, gas masks on most of the way, shells bursting both sides of road.

Monday, October 21, 1918. Fragment from shell struck mess-kit on my back. . . . Equipment, both American and German, thrown everywhere, especially Hun helmets and belts of machine gunners. . . . Went scouting . . . for narrow-gauge rails to replace the ones "Jerry" spoiled before evacuating. Negro engineers working on railroad same as at St. Mihiel, that's all they are good for. . . .

Friday, November 1, 1918. Started out at 4:00 A.M. The drive is on. Fritz is coming back at us. Machine guns cracking, flares and Verry lights, artillery from both sides. A real war and we are walking right into the zone, ducking shells all the way. The artillery is nerve racking and we don't know from which angle "Jerry" will fire next. Halted behind shelter of railroad track just outside of Grand Pre after being forced back off main road by shell fire. Trees splintered like toothpicks. Machine gunners on top of railroad bank. . . . "Jerry" drove Ewell and me into a two-by-four shell hole, snipers' bullets close.

Sunday, November 3, 1918. Many dead Germans along the road. One heap on a manure pile. . . . Devastation everywhere. Our barrage has rooted up the entire territory like a ploughed field. Dead horses galore, many of them have a hind quarter cut off—the Huns need food. Dead men here and there. The sight I enjoy better than a dead German is to see heaps of them. Rain again. Couldn't keep rain out of our faces and it was pouring hard. Got up at midnight and drove stakes to secure shelter-half over us, pulled our wet blankets out of mud and made the bed all over again. Slept like a log with all my equipment in the open. One hundred forty-two planes sighted in evening.

Sunday, November 10, 1918. First day off in over two months. . . . Took a bath and we were issued new underwear but the cooties [lice] got there first. . . . The papers show a picture of the Kaiser entitled "William the Lost," and stating that he had abdicated. Had a good dinner. Rumor at night that armistice was signed. Some fellows discharged their arms in the courtyard, but most of us were too well pleased with dry bunk to get up.

THOUGHT PROVOKERS

1. Discuss the shortcomings of volunteering, and explain why it would have been more dangerous in World War I than in preceding wars. In what ways can unpreparedness be more costly, financially and otherwise, than preparedness?

2. Why was there more anti-enemy hysteria in the United States in 1917–1918 than in World War II, when the nation was in graver danger? Why was not America's sense of fair play aroused in behalf of conscientious objectors? How are they dealt with today?

3. In connection with Point I of Wilson's Fourteen Points, why is it impossible to conduct diplomacy with complete openness at all stages of the negotiations? Criticize Roosevelt's criticisms of the Fourteen Points.

4. What was "modern" about the fighting American troops encountered in World War I? Were the "doughboys" well prepared for the war they found in France?

37 · *Making and Unmaking the Peace*

Dare we reject it [the League of Nations] and break the heart of the world?

WOODROW WILSON, JULY 10, 1919

PROLOGUE: Wilson blundered when in October, 1918, he bluntly appealed for a Democratic Congress. Repudiated at the polls the next month, he further antagonized the Republicans by his decision to attend the Paris Peace Conference. The resulting Treaty of Versailles, with the League of Nations riveted in, was disillusioning. Wilson had been forced to compromise away many of his Fourteen Points in order to save his Fourteenth—the League. Returning to America, he bitterly opposed the nationalistic reservations to the Treaty sponsored by his arch-foe, Senator Lodge. With deadlock imminent, Wilson embarked upon a barn-storming appeal to the country, during which he collapsed. When the time came for a vote, the invalid President twice instructed the Democratic Senators to reject the Treaty with the hated Lodge reservations attached. This they dutifully did. Rather than yield to Lodge, Wilson appealed to the country for a "solemn referendum" in the 1920 presidential election. In a highly confused campaign, the Republican Harding won by a tremendous plurality. The idea of American membership in the League was doomed.

A. THE OCTOBER APPEAL

1. Wilson Asks for a Democratic Congress (1918)

President Wilson, now at the peak of his prestige, planned to attend the Paris Peace Conference. The mid-term November elections were nearing, and he feared that a Democratic defeat would weaken his hand. He therefore decided to issue the following appeal on October 25, 1918, more than two weeks before the Armistice with Germany. The Republicans in Congress had supported Wilson's war effort with conspicuous loyalty, and their leaders now reacted angrily to this "challenge" and "insult." Why did Wilson pursue this risky course?

My fellow countrymen: The Congressional elections are at hand. They occur in the most critical period our country has ever faced or is likely to face in our time. If you have approved of my leadership and wish me to continue to be your unembarrassed spokesman in affairs at home and abroad, I earnestly beg that you will express yourselves unmistakably to that effect by returning a Democratic majority to both the Senate and the House of Representatives. I am your servant and will accept your judgment without cavil, but my power to administer the great trust assigned me by the Constitution would be seriously impaired should your judgment be

1. *Congressional Record*, 65 Cong., 2 sess., p. 11494.

adverse, and I must frankly tell you so because so many critical issues depend upon your verdict. . . .

I have no thought of suggesting that any political party is paramount in matters of patriotism. I feel too keenly the sacrifices which have been made in this war by all our citizens, irrespective of party affiliations, to harbor such an idea. I mean only that the difficulties and delicacies of our present task are of a sort that makes it imperatively necessary that the Nation should give its undivided support to the Government under a unified leadership, and that a Republican Congress would divide the leadership.

The leaders of the minority in the present Congress have unquestionably been pro-war, but they have been anti-administration. At almost every turn, since we entered the war, they have sought to take the choice of policy and the conduct of the war out of my hands and put it under the control of instrumentalities of their own choosing. This is no time either for divided counsel or for divided leadership. . . .

The return of a Republican majority to either House of the Congress would, moreover, certainly be interpreted on the other side of the water as a repudiation of my leadership. Spokesmen of the Republican Party are urging you to elect a Republican Congress in order to back up and support the President, but even if they should in this way impose upon some credulous voters on this side of the water, they would impose on no one on the other side. It is well understood there as well as here that the Republican leaders desire not so much to support the President as to control him. . . .

I need not tell you, my fellow countrymen, that I am asking your support not for my own sake or for the sake of a political party, but for the sake of the Nation itself, in order that its inward unity of purpose may be evident to all the world. In ordinary times I would not feel at liberty to make such an appeal to you. In ordinary times divided counsels can be endured without permanent hurt to the country. But these are not ordinary times.

2. Roosevelt Assails Wilson's Appeal (1918)

The aroused Republicans carried both Houses of Congress in November, and Wilson, having needlessly laid his prestige on the line, was a repudiated leader. Ex-President Roosevelt, who remembered that the Republican minority had supported crucial war measures like conscription in the teeth of considerable Democratic opposition, let fly this editorial blast. Did this criticism weaken Wilson as a negotiator in Paris? Was it unpatriotic?

Ten days before election Mr. Wilson issued an appeal to the American people, in which he frankly abandoned the position of President of the whole people; assumed the position, not merely of party leader, but of party dictator; and appealed to the voters as such. . . .

The Americans refused to sustain Mr. Wilson. They elected a heavily

2. Kansas City *Star*, Nov. 26, 1918. By permission of the Kansas City *Star*. The full text may also be found in Ralph Stout, ed., *Roosevelt in the Kansas City "Star"* (1921), pp. 272–77.

Republican House and, to the surprise of everyone, carried a majority in the Senate. On Mr. Wilson's own say-so they repudiated his leadership. In no other free country in the world to-day would Mr. Wilson be in office. He would simply be a private citizen like the rest of us.

Under these circumstances our allies and our enemies, and Mr. Wilson himself, should all understand that Mr. Wilson has no authority whatever to speak for the American people at this time. His leadership has just been emphatically repudiated by them. The newly elected Congress comes far nearer than Mr. Wilson to having a right to speak the purposes of the American people at this moment.

Mr. Wilson and his fourteen points and his four supplementary points and his five complementary points and all his utterances every which way have ceased to have any shadow of right to be accepted as expressive of the will of the American people. He is President of the United States, he is part of the treaty-making power, but he is only part. If he acts in good faith to the American people, he will not claim on the other side of the water any representative capacity in himself to speak for the American people. He will say frankly that his personal leadership has been repudiated and that he now has merely the divided official leadership which he shares with the Senate.

B. THE TREATY OF VERSAILLES

1. General Smuts Lectures Wilson (1919)

Wilson battled valiantly for his Fourteen Points at Paris, but the grasping Allies and harsh realities forced him to compromise. The result was that only about four of his original Fourteen Points and principles were found intact in the final Treaty. He consoled himself with the hope that the new League of Nations, which he had forced into the pact as its very first section, would iron out injustices. But the Germans, who had laid down their arms on the strength of promises that they would be granted a peace based on the Fourteen Points, complained bitterly of betrayal as they criticized the draft Treaty of Versailles. General Jan C. Smuts, who had fought the British in the Boer War but who had recently fought for them against Germany, was a South African delegate to the Paris Peace Conference. As a distinguished liberal leader and friend of the League of Nations, he made this last-minute appeal to Wilson. Why is he so deeply concerned about the ethical aspects of the draft Treaty of Versailles?

Dear President Wilson,

Even at the risk of wearying you I venture to address you once more.

The German answer to our draft Peace Terms seems to me to strike the fundamental note which is most dangerous to us, and which we are bound to consider most carefully. They say in effect that we are under solemn obligation to them to make a Wilson Peace, a peace in accordance with your Fourteen Points and other Principles enunciated in 1918. To my mind there is absolutely no doubt that this is so. Subject to the two reservations made

1. Excerpt from *Woodrow Wilson and World Settlement* by R. S. Baker. Copyright 1922 by Doubleday & Company, Inc. Reprinted by permission of the publisher.

by the Allies before the Armistice,* we are bound to make a peace within the four corners of your Points and Principles, and any provisions of the Peace Treaty which either go contrary to or beyond their general scope and intent would constitute a breach of agreement.

NOT FOURTEEN—ONLY TWO—POINTS LEFT

Although the promised 14 Points were not satisfactorily embodied in the treaty, Germany had no alternative but to sign or be invaded. Cincinnati *Post*, 1919.

This seems to my mind quite clear, and the question of fact remains whether there are any such provisions. If there are, then our position is indeed serious, as I understand it.

This war began with a breach of a solemn international undertaking [regarding Belgium], and it has been one of our most important war aims to vindicate international law and the sanctity of international engagements. If the Allies end the war by following the example of Germany at the beginning, and also confront the world with a "scrap of paper," the discredit on us will be so great that I shudder to think of its ultimate effect on public opinion. We would indeed have done a worse wrong than Germany because of all that has happened since August, 1914, and the fierce light which has been concentrated on this very point.

The question becomes, therefore, most important whether there are important provisions of the Treaty which conflict with or are not covered by, but go beyond, your Points and Principles. I notice a tendency to put the whole responsibility for deciding this question on you, and to say that after all President Wilson agrees to the Treaty and he knows best what the Points and Principles mean. This is most unfair to you, and I think we should all give the gravest consideration to the question whether our Peace Treaty is within the four corners of your Speeches of 1918.

Frankly I do not think this is so, and I think the Germans make out a good case in regard to a number of provisions. All the one-sided provisions, which exclude reciprocity or equality, and all the pinpricks, with which the Treaty teems, seem to me to be both against the letter and the spirit of your Points.

* The British had entered a reservation regarding freedom of the seas; the French, a reservation regarding the collection of reparations.

I cannot find anything in the Points or the Principles which should cover, for instance, the one-sided internationalization of German rivers, and the utterly bad and one-sided administration arranged in respect of them. Reparation by way of coal cannot cover the arrangements made in respect of the Saar Basin and its people. I even doubt whether the Occupation of the Rhine for fifteen years could be squared either with the letter or the spirit of your Points and Principles. And there are many other points to which I shall not refer, but which no doubt your Advisers will consider.

There will be a terrible disillusion if the peoples come to think that we are not concluding a Wilson Peace, that we are not keeping our promises to the world or faith with the public. But if in so doing we appear also to break the formal agreement deliberately entered into (as I think we do), we shall be overwhelmed with the gravest discredit, and this Peace may well become an even greater disaster to the world than the war was.

Forgive me for troubling you with this matter, but I believe it goes to the root of our whole case.

2. Colonel House Appraises the Conference (1919)

Colonel (honorary) E. M. House, a quiet and self-effacing Texan who had retired from cotton planting, became Wilson's intimate adviser in 1912—"the strangest friendship in history." As an influential member of the five-man American delegation at Paris, House acted as the President's deputy during Wilson's absence or incapacity. House's diary analysis of what went wrong is a classic. In the following excerpt, why does he believe that Wilson personally failed, and why does he think that disappointment is inevitable?

June 29, 1919: I am leaving Paris, after eight fateful months, with conflicting emotions. Looking at the Conference in retrospect, there is much to approve and much to regret. It is easy to say what should have been done, but more difficult to have found a way for doing it.

The bitterness engendered by the war, the hopes raised high in many quarters because of victory, the character of the men having the dominant voices in the making of the Treaty, all had their influence for good or for evil, and were to be reckoned with. There seemed to be no full realization of the conditions which had to be met.

An effort was made to enact a peace upon the usual lines. This should never have been attempted. The greater part of civilization had been shattered, and history could guide us but little in the making of this peace.

How splendid it would have been had we blazed a new and better trail! However, it is to be doubted whether this could have been done, even if those in authority had so decreed, for the peoples back of them had to be reckoned with. It may be that Wilson might have had the power and influence if he had remained in Washington and kept clear of the Conference. When he stepped from his lofty pedestal and wrangled with

2. From *The Intimate Papers of Colonel House* by Charles Seymour. Copyright 1928, 1956 by Charles Seymour. Reprinted by permission of Houghton Mifflin Company.

representatives of other states upon equal terms, he became as common clay. . . .

To those who are saying that the Treaty is bad and should never have been made and that it will involve Europe in infinite difficulties in its enforcement, I feel like admitting it. But I would also say in reply that empires cannot be shattered and new states raised upon their ruins without disturbance. To create new boundaries is always to create new troubles. The one follows the other. While I should have preferred a different peace, I doubt whether it could have been made, for the ingredients for such a peace as I would have had were lacking at Paris. And even if those of us like Smuts, Botha, and Cecil* could have had our will, as much trouble might have followed a peace of our making as seems certain to follow this.

The same forces that have been at work in the making of this peace would be at work to hinder the enforcement of a different kind of peace, and no one can say with certitude that anything better than has been done could be done at this time. We have had to deal with a situation pregnant with difficulties and one which could be met only by an unselfish and idealistic spirit, which was almost wholly absent and which was too much to expect of men come together at such a time and for such a purpose.

And yet I wish we had taken the other road, even if it were less smooth, both now and afterward, than the one we took. We would at least have gone in the right direction, and if those who follow us had made it impossible to go the full length of the journey planned, the responsibility would have rested with them and not with us.

3. Editor Villard Reproaches Wilson (1939)

Oswald Garrison Villard, grandson of the abolitionist William Lloyd Garrison, was a fearless crusader in his own right. As editor and owner of the ultra-liberal New York *Nation*, he flailed away at the illiberal Treaty of Versailles. His earlier criticisms of Allied practices and Wilsonian unneutrality had already earned him the label "pro-German." Suspicion was increased by the fact of his birth in Germany while his parents were temporarily residing abroad, and by his ownership of a brown dachshund named Fritz. The following latter-day condemnation of the Conference appeared in his memoirs, published the year Hitler started World War II. How plausible is Villard's argument that America should have browbeaten the Allies instead of betraying the enemy?

As one who at the time approved of Mr. Wilson's going to Paris, I have come to realize the fatal mistake it was. What the occasion needed was a much more determined man. He had the whip hand; in fact, every card in the deck. He had the freshest, best-equipped, and only increasing army in France; he had all the money left in the world and controlled the bulk of the food. Without him the Allies could do nothing. Some of the money

---

* Louis Botha, South African Prime Minister, was a liberal colleague of General Smuts at the Conference; Lord Robert Cecil, a British liberal, was at Paris as one of the chief architects of the League of Nations.
3. O. G. Villard, *Fighting Years* (1939), p. 453. By permission of Henry H. Villard.

they owe us was still being poured out to them. A threat to make the separate treaty with Germany which we afterwards did make, a threat to withdraw our army at once and to loan not a dollar more, would have reduced the Allied leaders to pulp.

Against this, some defenders of Woodrow Wilson protest. It would have been outrageous, they say, thus arrogantly to have dictated the peace. But it would not have been dictation, only a righteous demand that the Allies live up to their pledges made to us and to Germany to make peace on the fourteen peace points. Our failure to insist upon this, whether politely or arrogantly, put us in the position of having broken faith with our enemy, of having tricked them.

Can anyone look at the world today and deny that this policy would have been better than to do what we did: help frame a wicked peace which has revived in worse form the German militarism which we set out to destroy, given rise to Fascism in Italy and elsewhere, and completely disappointed the hopes and the ambitions of millions everywhere for a better world?

C. THE ISSUE OF ARTICLE X

1. The Test of Article X (1919)

Wilson regarded the League of Nations as the backbone of the Treaty of Versailles, and Article X of the League Covenant, which he had partly authored, as the heart of the League. He envisaged the members of the League constituting a kind of police force to prevent aggression. What weaknesses are contained in the wording of this article?

The Members of the League undertake to respect and preserve, as against external aggression, the territorial integrity and existing political independence of all Members of the League. In case of any such aggression, or in case of any threat or danger of such aggression, the Council shall advise upon the means by which this obligation shall be fulfilled.

[*All member nations were represented in the Assembly of the League of Nations; only the Great Powers (originally Britain, France, Italy, and Japan) were represented in the Council. The same general scheme was adopted by the United Nations in 1945.*]

2. Editor Harvey Belittles Article X (1919)

The journalist George Harvey, who had launched a Wilson-for-President boom as early as 1906, ultimately became a venomous Wilson-hater. Founding *Harvey's Weekly* in 1918 as a vehicle for his barbed irony, he consistently jeered at "The Fourteen Commandments." In this excerpt, is he right in his view that Article X is completely toothless?

1. *Senate Executive Documents,* 67 Cong., 4 sess., VIII, No. 348, p. 3339.
2. *Harvey's Weekly,* Aug. 9, 1919, pp. 6–7. This short-lived journal was published between 1918 and 1921.

If Article X of the League Covenant means what Mr. Wilson says it means, then it means nothing. If it means nothing, then its proper destination is the wastebasket. It should be stricken out *in toto* as so much sheer surplusage.

The first sentence of the Article provides that "the members of the League undertake to respect and preserve as against external aggression the territory and existing political independence of all members of the League." The second sentence provides that the League Council shall advise upon the means by which the obligation involved in the first sentence shall be fulfilled.

Mr. Wilson's interpretation of this second sentence, as presented in his message transmitting the Franco-American alliance treaty,* is that after the League Council's advice has been duly given, the League members will do precisely as they please about following it. In the first sentence, the members of the League solemnly agree to respect and protect each other as against external aggression. In the second sentence—according to Mr. Wilson's interpretation—a League member will act upon the League Council's advice in a given aggression case "only if its own judgment justifies such action." In other words, the second sentence of the Article completely cancels the first sentence, leaving zero as the remaining total.

Mr. Hughes [Republican nominee in 1916] said of Article X that it was an "illusory engagement." Mr. Wilson goes Mr. Hughes one better. He says, in substance, that it is no engagement at all, illusory or otherwise. The League Council may advise until it is black in the face, and the League members may go serenely on their respective ways without giving the slightest heed to this advice. And both League members and League Council will equally have done their full duty under Article X.

If Article X be interpreted to mean anything, that meaning necessarily is that we engage to send our armed forces wherever and whenever a super-government of foreigners sitting in Switzerland orders us to send them. If it be interpreted as Mr. Wilson interprets it, the foreign super-government's powers extend only to the giving of advice which we agree to heed or ignore as our judgment dictates. One interpretation is an insult to our self-respect as a nation. The other reduces the whole of Article X to a vacuum.

The way to treat Article X is to strike it out.

3. Wilson Testifies for Article X (1919)

The already ominous mood of the Senate had grown uglier when Wilson conspicuously snubbed that body in framing the peace. The Republican majority was led by the aristocratic Senator Lodge of Massachusetts, who was also chairman of the potent

---

* This alliance, signed by Wilson at Paris, was designed to defend France against future German aggression. The Senate pigeonholed it.
3. *Senate Documents*, No. 76, 66 Cong., 1 sess., XIII, pp. 6, 19.

Committee on Foreign Relations. He was determined to Republicanize and American-ize the pact by adding reservations which would adequately safeguard American in-terests. To avert such a watering-down, Wilson met with the entire Foreign Relations Committee at the White House on August 19, 1919, and underwent about three and a half hours of grilling. Much of the discussion revolved about Article X. How persuasive is Wilson's defense?

Article X is in no respect of doubtful meaning, when read in the light of the Covenant as a whole. The Council of the League can only "advise upon" the means by which the obligations of that great article are to be given effect to. Unless the United States is a party to the policy or action in question, her own affirmative vote in the Council is necessary before any advice can be given, for a unanimous vote of the Council is required. If she is a party, the trouble is hers anyhow. And the unanimous vote of the Council is only advice in any case. Each Government is free to reject it if it pleases.

Nothing could have been made more clear to the [Paris] conference than the right of our Congress under our Constitution to exercise its independent judgment in all matters of peace and war. No attempt was made to question or limit that right.

The United States will, indeed, undertake under Article X to "respect and preserve as against external aggression the territorial integrity and existing political independence of all members of the League," and that engagement constitutes a very grave and solemn moral obligation. But it is a moral, not a legal, obligation, and leaves our Congress absolutely free to put its own interpretation upon it in all cases that call for action. It is bind-ing in conscience only, not in law.

Article X seems to me to constitute the very backbone of the whole Covenant. Without it the League would be hardly more than an influential debating society. . . .

Senator [Warren G.] HARDING. Right there, Mr. President, if there is nothing more than a moral obligation on the part of any member of the League, what avail Articles X and XI?

The PRESIDENT. Why, Senator, it is surprising that that question should be asked. If we undertake an obligation we are bound in the most solemn way to carry it out. . . . There is a national good conscience in such a matter. . . .

When I speak of a legal obligation, I mean one that specifically binds you to do a particular thing under certain sanctions. That is a legal obliga-tion. Now a moral obligation is of course superior to a legal obligation, and, if I may say so, has a greater binding force. . . .

[*Never too respectful of the "bungalow-minded" members of the Senate, Wilson remarked several days later that Senator Harding, destined to be his successor, "had a disturbingly dull mind, and that it seemed impossible to get any explana-tion to lodge in it."*]

4. The Lodge-Hitchcock Reservations (1919)

Wilson finally agreed to accept mildly interpretative Senate reservations which the other powers would not have to approve. But he balked at the more restrictive terms of the fourteen Lodge reservations. These were made a part of the resolution of ratification, and would require the assent of three of the four other major powers (Britain, France, Italy, Japan). To Wilson, such a course was unmanly and humiliating; besides, he detested Senator Lodge. He insisted that the Republican Lodge reservations, notably the one on Article X, devitalized the entire treaty. Below, on the left, appears the Lodge reservation to Article X, which Wilson resentfully rejected. On the right appears the Democratic interpretative reservation, which Senator Hitchcock (the Senate minority leader) had drafted after consulting Wilson. This version Wilson was willing to accept. What are the main differences between the two versions? Are those differences substantial enough to justify Wilson's refusal to accept the Lodge reservation?

LODGE RESERVATION
TO ARTICLE X
(November, 1919)

The United States assumes no obligation to preserve the territorial integrity or political independence of any other country or to interfere in controversies between nations — whether members of the League or not — under the provisions of Article X, or to employ the military or naval forces of the United States under any article of the treaty for any purpose, unless in any particular case the Congress, which, under the Constitution, has the sole power to declare war or authorize the employment of the military or naval forces of the United States, shall by act or joint resolution so provide.

HITCHCOCK RESERVATION
TO ARTICLE X
(November, 1919)

That the advice mentioned in Article X of the covenant of the League which the Council may give to the member nations as to the employment of their naval and military forces is merely advice which each member nation is free to accept or reject according to the conscience and judgment of its then existing Government, and in the United States this advice can only be accepted by action of the Congress at the time in being, Congress alone under the Constitution of the United States having the power to declare war.

D. THE DEFEAT OF THE TREATY

1. Mrs. Wilson as Assistant President (1919)

Rather than knuckle under to Lodge, a weary Wilson spurned the advice of doctors and embarked upon a spectacular speechmaking appeal to the country. He journeyed as far west as the Pacific Coast, and on the return trip collapsed after delivering an emotional speech at Pueblo, Colorado. Shortly thereafter he suffered a stroke, which paralyzed the left side of his body and left him bedridden for many weeks. He did not meet his Cabinet for more than seven months. His devoted wife tells how the government was run. Should Wilson have resigned? Were the interests of Wilson as an individual put above those of the country? To what extent was Mrs. Wilson actually President of the United States?

4. Quoted in T. A. Bailey, *Woodrow Wilson and the Great Betrayal* (1945), pp. 388, 393–94. The Hitchcock reservation follows almost verbatim a reservation that Wilson had himself secretly drafted in September, 1919, and on which Hitchcock had based his. *Ibid.*, p. 393.
1. Edith B. Wilson, *My Memoir* (1939), pp. 288–90. Copyright 1938, 1939 by Edith Bolling Wilson; reprinted by special permission of the publishers. The Bobbs-Merrill Company, Inc.

Once my husband was out of immediate danger, the burning question was how Mr. Wilson might best serve the country, preserve his own life, and, if possible, recover. Many people, among them some I had counted as friends, have written of my overwhelming ambition to act as President; of my exclusion of all advice, and so forth. I am trying here to write as though I had taken the oath to tell the truth, the whole truth, and nothing but the truth—so help me God.

I asked the doctors to be frank with me; that I must know what the outcome would probably be, so as to be honest with the people. They all said that, as the brain was as clear as ever, with the progress made in the past few days there was every reason to think recovery possible. Dr. Dercum told me of the history of Pasteur, who had been stricken exactly in this way, but who recovered and did his most brilliant intellectual work afterwards. He sent me a copy of a remarkable book, *The Life of Pasteur*.

But recovery could not be hoped for, they said, unless the President were released from every disturbing problem during these days of Nature's effort to repair the damage done.

"How can that be," I asked the doctors, "when everything that comes to an Executive is a problem? How can I protect him from problems when the country looks to the President as the leader?"

Dr. Dercum leaned towards me and said: "Madam, it is a grave situation, but I think you can solve it. Have everything come to you: weigh the importance of each matter, and see if it is possible by consultations with the respective heads of the Departments to solve them without the guidance of your husband. In this way you can save him a great deal. But always keep in mind that every time you take him a new anxiety or problem to excite him, you are turning a knife in an open wound. His nerves are crying out for rest, and any excitement is torture to him."

"Then," I said, "had he better not resign, let Mr. [Vice-President] Marshall succeed to the Presidency, and he himself get that complete rest that is so vital to his life?"

"No," the Doctor said, "not if you feel equal to what I suggested. For Mr. Wilson to resign would have a bad effect on the country, and a serious effect on our patient. He has staked his life and made his promise to the world to do all in his power to get the Treaty ratified and make the League of Nations complete. If he resigns, the greatest incentive to recovery is gone; and as his mind is clear as crystal, he can still do more with even a maimed body than anyone else. He has the utmost confidence in you. Dr. Grayson [Wilson's personal physician] tells me he has always discussed public affairs with you; so you will not come to them uninformed."

So began my stewardship. I studied every paper, sent from the different Secretaries or Senators, and tried to digest and present in tabloid form the things that, despite my vigilance, had to go to the President. I, myself, never made a single decision regarding the disposition of public affairs. The only decision that was mine was what was important and what was not, and the *very* important decision of when to present matters to my husband.

He asked thousands of questions, and insisted upon knowing everything, particularly about the Treaty. He would dictate notes to me to send to Senator Hitchcock, who was leading the fight for the Treaty in the Senate. Or he would tell me what Senators to send for, and what suggestions he had to make to them. These directions I made notes of, so, in transmitting his views, I should make no mistake; and I would read them to him before going to the interviews.

This method of handling interviews was another suggestion of the doctors. It is always an excitement for one who is ill to see people. The physicians said that if I could convey the messages of Cabinet members and others to the President, he would escape the nervous drain audiences with these officials would entail. Even the necessary little courteous personal conversations that go with an official interview would consume the President's strength.

These instructions from the medical men were far from easy to carry out. Picture the situation when my husband was stricken: his tour a success; public sentiment which had been worked upon incessantly by the enemies of the League once more responding to Mr. Wilson's logic; the initiative again in the hands of friends of the Treaty; Mr. Hitchcock and the other pro-Treaty Senators eager to push their advantage. And then—the President laid low, ruled out of the fight which he would have continued though he knew it would cost him his life.

Upon all sides I was literally besieged by those who "must" see the President. But I carried out the directions of the doctors—and my heart was in it. Woodrow Wilson was first my beloved husband whose life I was trying to save, fighting with my back to the wall—after that he was the President of the United States.

2. The Aborted Lodge Compromise (1919)

Colonel House, Wilson's onetime intimate adviser, had likewise fallen ill and was confined to his bed in New York. He turned to Stephen Bonsal, a distinguished newspaper correspondent who had been attached to the American peace mission in Paris. Bonsal was instructed to go to Washington, confer with Lodge, and ascertain the Senator's minimum terms for compromise. The meeting took place late in October, 1919, and on November 16 Bonsal recorded the following account of the conference. In what respects does this account qualify the traditional concept of Lodge as a vindictive and uncompromising former student from Harvard who was locking horns with the former professor from Princeton?

The Senator and I went over the [League] Covenant, Article by Article. Here are some of the details. In our final session there was an official copy of the Treaty on the library table, also one of the so-called Lodge Reservations before the Senate but, so far as I can remember, we did not once refer to them. It was on the printed copy of the Covenant that I brought

2. Excerpt from *Unfinished Business* by Stephen Bonsal. Copyright 1944 by Stephen Bonsal. Reprinted by permission of Doubleday and Company, Inc.

with me that the Senator made the changes and inserted the interlineations which, if accepted, he thought would smooth the way to ratification.

The changes ran to about forty words, the "inserts" to about fifty. It seemed to me they were more concerned with verbiage than with the object and the intent of the instrument. In my judgment, they were complementary to, rather than limiting, any substantial purpose of the Covenant. In this they differed sharply from the Reservations Lodge had introduced into the Senate and which are now blocking the path to ratification.

The Senator, frankly and repeatedly, stated that his interest, or, as he put it several times, his anxiety, centered around Article X, which the President often refers to as the "heart of the Covenant," and his suggestion, indeed his demand, was to the effect that none of the obligations or commitments incurred under this provision should be undertaken without the approval of the Senate and the concurrence of the House.

When Lodge had finished what he had to say, I expressed my pleasure at the helpful collaboration of the chairman of the Committee, and with reason, I think. What he asked for now was decidedly milder than the reservations before the Senate, but there was, I ventured to point out, one drawback to any change, even if merely of verbiage, because, in this case, the document would have to be referred back to all the co-signers of the Covenant, and this might open the gates to other changes and would certainly result in delay.

TEACHING HIM WHAT TO SAY

Democratic cartoon stressing Lodge's partisan obstructionism. The Republicans stressed Wilson's uncompromising stubbornness. New York *World,* 1920.

I also ventured to say that the clarification of Article X which he urged was implicit in the Article itself. I argued "it goes without saying," for a variety of obvious reasons, that the sanction of the Senate and the approval of the House, which alone can furnish the money, would have to be forthcoming before aggressive or even defensive action against an aggressor nation could be undertaken.

"If it goes without saying," commented the Senator somewhat tartly, "there is no harm in saying it—and much advantage."

Good-naturedly the Senator now chaffed me about the expression I had used, "it goes without saying," which he thought was a "barbarism." He then went on to express his opinion of the language in which the world charter was drawn, and it was a poor one.

"As an English production it does not rank high." Then, more in chaff than in earnest, he said: "It might get by at Princeton but certainly not at Harvard."

[*With high hopes, Colonel House dispatched the new Lodge concessions to the White House. There was no reply, no acknowledgment. Perhaps Mrs. Wilson thought the memorandum unimportant or too important. Wilson might be upset and suffer a relapse. Or Wilson may have decided merely to treat Lodge's proffered hand with the contempt that he felt for the Senator. Rebuffed and perhaps humiliated, Lodge now fought even more adamantly for his Fourteen Reservations.*]

3. Wilson Defeats Lodge's Reservations (1919)

The debate in the Senate ended in November, 1919, and Lodge was ready for a vote on the Treaty of Versailles with his Fourteen Reservations attached. In general, these reaffirmed American traditional or constitutional safeguards. But Wilson believed that if the odious Lodge reservations were voted down, the Treaty would then be approved without "crippling" reservations. Yet the Democrats, now a minority, could not muster a simple majority, much less the two-thirds vote needed to approve a treaty. The naturally stubborn Wilson, shielded from disagreeable realities by his anxious wife, believed that the great body of public opinion was behind him and would prevail. He evidently had not been told, or would not believe, that public opinion was shifting around in favor of reservations. When the Democratic Senator Hitchcock suggested compromise, Wilson sternly replied, "Let Lodge compromise." Mrs. Wilson again tells the story. How does she describe the President's basic position?

All this time the fight for the reservations to the Covenant of the League was being pressed in the Senate. Deprived of Executive leadership because of the illness of my husband, friends of the Treaty were on the defensive. The ground gained on the Western tour had been gradually lost until things were worse than when he started. Friends, including such a valued and persuasive friend as Mr. Bernard M. Baruch, begged Mr. Wilson to accept a compromise, saying "half a loaf is better than no bread." I cannot be unsympathetic with them, for in a moment of weakness I did the same. In my anxiety for the one I loved best in the world, the long-drawn-out fight was eating into my very soul, and I felt nothing mattered but to get the Treaty ratified, even with those reservations.

On November 19th the Senate was to vote on the reservations. Senator Hitchcock came to tell me that unless the Administration forces accepted them, the Treaty would be beaten—the struggle having narrowed down to a personal fight against the President by Lodge and his supporters. In des-

3. Edith B. Wilson, *My Memoir* (1939), pp. 296–97. Copyright 1938, 1939 by Edith Bolling Wilson; reprinted by special permission of the publishers, The Bobbs-Merrill Company, Inc.

peration I went to my husband. "For my sake," I said, "won't you accept these reservations and get this awful thing settled?"

He turned his head on the pillow and stretching out his hand to take mine answered in a voice I shall never forget: "Little girl, don't you desert me; that I cannot stand. Can't you see that I have no moral right to accept any change in a paper I have signed without giving to every other signatory, even the Germans, the right to do the same thing? It is not I that will not accept; it is the Nation's honor that is at stake."

His eyes looked luminous as he spoke, and I knew that he was right. He went on quietly: "Better a thousand times to go down fighting than to dip your colours to dishonorable compromise."

I felt like one of his betrayers to have ever doubted. Rejoining Senator Hitchcock outside, I told him that for the first time I had seen the thing clearly and I would never ask my husband again to do what would be manifestly dishonorable. When I went back to the President's room, he dictated a letter to Senator Hitchcock, saying: "In my opinion the resolution in that form [embodying the reservations] does not provide for ratification but rather for nullification of the Treaty. . . . I trust that all true friends of the Treaty will refuse to support the Lodge resolution."

That same day the Senate voted. The Administration forces, voting against ratification *with* the Lodge reservations, defeated it. The vote was then on the ratification of the Treaty without reservations—the Treaty as Mr. Wilson had brought it from France. The result was defeat.

When the word came from the Capitol, I felt I could not bear it and that the shock might be serious for my husband. I went to his bedside and told him the fatal news. For a few moments he was silent, and then he said: "All the more reason I must get well and try again to bring this country to a sense of its great opportunity and greater responsibility."

4. Lodge Blames Wilson (1919)

The crucial vote had come in the Senate on November 19, 1919, when the Treaty with the Lodge reservations commanded only 39 yeas to 55 nays. The bulk of the Democrats, heeding Wilson's plea, voted against it. The vote for the Treaty without any reservations was 38 yeas to 53 nays. The bulk of the Republicans voted against it. Lodge wrote in bitterness as follows to his friend, former Secretary of State Root. Is he correct in his assessment of the blame?

If Wilson had not written his letter to the Democratic caucus, calling on them to kill the treaty rather than accept the reservations, the treaty would have been ratified on the 19th of November. There would have been enough Democrats voting with us to have done it. It was killed by Wilson. He has been the marplot from the beginning. All the delays and all the troubles have been made by him. . . . We have worked for more than two months over those reservations, and they represent an amount of labor and modification and concession that it would take me a long time to

4. J. A. Garraty, *Henry Cabot Lodge* (1953), p. 379. By permission of Henry Cabot Lodge, Jr.

explain to you. He can have the treaty ratified at any moment if he will accept the reservations, and if he declines to do so we are not in the least afraid to meet him at the polls on that issue.

[A shocked public forced the Senate to reconsider the Treaty, which now emerged with fifteen revamped Lodge reservations tacked on. Wilson refused to budge an inch from his previous position, and sent another stern letter to the Democrats in the Senate urging them to vote down the odious package. Lodge, no less stubborn, made it clear that the Senate would have to gag down the Treaty with his reservations or there would be no treaty. Faced with naked realities, twenty-one Democrats deserted Wilson and supported ratification. The final vote, March 19, 1920 was 49 yeas to 35 nays, or seven short of the necessary two-thirds. A total of twenty-three loyal Democrats voted "nay." Senator Ashurst of Arizona, a "disloyal" Democrat, declared bitterly, "As a friend of the President, as one who has loyally followed him, I solemnly declare to him this morning: If you want to kill your own child because the Senate straightens out its crooked limbs, you must take the responsibility and accept the verdict of history" (Congressional Record, 66 Cong., 2 sess., p. 4164).]

E. THE PRESIDENTIAL CAMPAIGN OF 1920

1. Wilson Suggests a "Solemn Referendum" (1920)

Wilson had long been addicted to the habit of appealing directly to the people. Unwilling to compromise with Lodge, he was prepared to force the infant League to run in the presidential campaign of 1920. On January 8, 1920, some two months before the second rejection of the Treaty, he sent the following plea to the Democratic National Chairman. He was evidently blind to the fact that even if all of the anti-League Senators up for re-election in 1920 were defeated, and replaced by pro-League Senators, he would still lack a two-thirds vote for the unreserved Treaty. What further evidence does this appeal provide that Wilson was out of touch with reality, especially since three and one-half months had elapsed since his speechmaking tour?

Personally, I do not accept the action of the Senate of the United States as the decision of the Nation.

I have asserted from the first that the overwhelming majority of the people of this country desire the ratification of the treaty, and my impression to that effect has recently been confirmed by the unmistakable evidences of public opinion given during my visit to seventeen of the States.

I have endeavored to make it plain that if the Senate wishes to say what the undoubted meaning of the League is, I shall have no objection. There can be no reasonable objection to interpretations accompanying the act of ratification itself. But when the treaty is acted upon, I must know whether it means that we have ratified or rejected it.

We cannot rewrite this treaty. We must take it without changes which alter its meaning, or leave it, and then, after the rest of the world has signed it, we must face the unthinkable task of making another and separate treaty with Germany.

1. *Congressional Record,* 66 Cong., 2 sess., p. 1249.

But no mere assertions with regard to the wish and opinion of the country are credited. If there is any doubt as to what the people of the country think on this vital matter, the clear and single way out is to submit it for determination at the next election to the voters of the Nation, to give the next election the form of a great and solemn referendum, a referendum as to the part the United States is to play in completing the settlements of the war and in the prevention in the future of such outrages as Germany attempted to perpetrate.

2. Harding Sidetracks the League (1920)

The pro-League Democrats chose as their 1920 presidential standard-bearer James M. Cox, an Ohio newspaperman. The Old Guard Republicans, supremely confident of victory, nominated the handsome Senator Harding, likewise an Ohio newspaperman. His catch-all platform was artfully designed to attract both anti-League and pro-League Republicans. "Wobbly Warren" Harding straddled over various positions on the League, but in his Des Moines speech he put both feet under himself. In the light of his assertions, determine why he opposed clarifying reservations, and whether a pro-League Republican could conscientiously vote for him. Is his proposed substitute for the League of Nations feasible?

The [Democratic] platform, to be sure, approaches its indorsement [of the League] with winding words and sly qualifications . . . but it does, nevertheless, indorse the League as it stands. It does not advocate or favor any reservations or amendments or changes or qualifications. It goes no further than to suggest that reservations will not be opposed which make clearer or more specific the obligations of the United States and the League.

But there is no need of reservations of this character. The obligations are clear enough and specific enough. I

THE SAME PLATFORM

The Republican platform was so ambiguous that the anti-League Senator Johnson could promise defeat of *the* League while the pro-League ex-President Taft could promise *a* League. Dallas *News*, 1920.

2. New York *Times*, Oct. 8, 1920.

oppose the League not because I fail to understand what . . . "we are being let in for," but because I believe I understand precisely what we are being let in for.

I do not want to clarify these obligations; I want to turn my back on them. It is not interpretation but rejection that I am seeking. My position is that the present League strikes a deadly blow at our constitutional integrity and surrenders to a dangerous extent our independence of action. . . .

The issue therefore is clear. I understand the position of the Democratic candidate and he understands mine. . . . In simple words, it is that he favors going into the Paris League and I favor staying out. . . .

As soon as possible after my election I shall advise with the best minds in the United States. . . . I shall do this to the end that we shall have an association of nations for the promotion of international peace, but one which shall so definitely safeguard our sovereignty and recognize our ultimate and unmortgaged freedom of action that it will have back of it not a divided and distracted sentiment, but the united support of the American people.

3. An Editor Dissects the "Referendum" (1920)

Wilson had asked for a referendum on the League. The sovereign voters rose up and swept the anti-League Harding into the White House by the unprecedented plurality of more than 7,000,000 votes. The Republicans exulted that Wilson now had his mandate—in reverse. Disheartened Democrats replied that the results could be no true mandate. The pro-Democratic New York *Times* stated that with pro-League Democrats voting for Cox and pro-League Republicans (reassured by the "Illustrious Thirty-one") voting for Harding, the result could be interpreted, if anything, as a mandate *for* the League. What does the following editorial in the New York *Evening Post* suggest about why any incumbent administration probably would have been repudiated, how "opposites" contributed to the same result, and why Harding could not have received a clear-cut mandate on the League?

We are in the backwash from the mighty spiritual and physical effort to which America girded herself when she won the war for the Allies and saved the world from a fate which America would again challenge if the need arose. The war has not been repudiated, tho the administration that fought it has been overwhelmed. We are now in the chill that comes with the doctor's bills.

As we see it now, any man in the Presidency, and any party in power, would have met the same punishment that was meted out to Woodrow Wilson and the Democratic party. Any Administration that conducted the war would now be the target of the bewildering number of protests that merged into one gigantic protest.

There entered into Harding's majorities the votes of those who were against war with Germany in 1917 and the votes of those who were for war with Germany in 1914; the votes of those who think the peace imposed

3. New York *Evening Post*, quoted in *Literary Digest*, LXVII, 13 (Nov. 13, 1920).

upon Germany too crushing, and the votes of those who think the treatment of Germany not drastic enough; the votes of those who resent the restriction upon the liberties of the American people resulting from the war, and the votes of those who resent the Administration's supposed tenderness for "Bolshevism." Opposites combined to swell Harding's majorities.

But these were by no means the principal factors. The American people as a whole was tired of the Administration. Resentment both against the Treaty and against delay in the Treaty, resentment both against the high prices which were here until the other day and against falling prices to-day, resentment against the "exactions" of labor up to the other day and against the industrial decline and rising unemployment to-day—all these opposites combined in one great weariness, into one mighty desire for a change.

Warren G. Harding and the Republican party have profited thereby. They have come into power upon a mighty wave of protest. It is now for them to decide just what that protest means when it comes to satisfying it in specific concrete terms. The votes of mutually hostile interests count if thrown into the same ballot-box. They can not all be honored by an Administration that hopes to shape anything like a policy and a program.

[*Neither of the two among the "Illustrious Thirty-one" who became members of President Harding's Cabinet staged a revolt to implement their implicit pledge to join an amended League. Secretary of State Hughes recoiled before the threats of the irreconcilable anti-League Senators to tear the administration to pieces. So the United States joined neither a League nor an Association of Nations.*]

THOUGHT PROVOKERS

1. The party in power normally loses seats during the mid-term Congressional elections. What would Wilson's position have been if he had issued no October appeal and had still lost Congress? Such presidential appeals are now commonplace. Why do they not arouse the same resentment as in 1918?

2. In what sense was the Treaty of Versailles a betrayal of Germany? Would Wilson have achieved a better treaty if he had directed the negotiations by wire from Washington? Argue both sides and come to a conclusion.

3. With reference to Article X, is a moral obligation more binding on a person or a nation than a legal one? Is it more binding on a great nation than on a weaker one?

4. It has been said that if Wilson had resigned after his collapse, the United States would have joined the League of Nations. Explain. Would the results have been better if the United States had had a law on the books under which Wilson could have been declared disabled and temporarily out of the Presidency? In the last analysis who was more responsible for keeping America out of the League of Nations, Wilson or Lodge?

5. It has been said that no presidential election can ever be a true mandate on an issue of foreign affairs, or on any single issue. Explain.

38 · *American Life in the Roaring Twenties*

> *You are all a lost generation.*
> Attributed by Ernest Hemingway to Gertude Stein, 1926

PROLOGUE: Disappointed at the results of their intervention in the European War, Americans turned inward in the post-war decade. They repudiated all things allegedly "foreign," including radical political ideas and, especially, immigrants. A witch-hunting, frenzied "Red Scare" rocked the country in the immediate post-war months, capped by the arrest and eventual execution of the Italian anarchists Sacco and Vanzetti. A revived Ku Klux Klan vented its hatred on Catholic and Jewish newcomers, as well as on blacks. Three centuries of virtually unrestricted immigration to America came to a halt with the passage of the restrictive Immigration Act of 1924. The prohibition "experiment" divided "wets" from "drys." In religion, fundamentalists warred against modernists, most famously in the Scopes "Monkey Trial" in Tennessee. "Flappers" flamboyantly displayed the new freedom of young women, one of whose champions was Margaret Sanger, pioneer of the birth-control movement. Meanwhile, a high-mass-consumption economy began fully to flower, typified by the booming automobile industry and by the emergence of advertising and the huge entertainment industries of radio and the movies. A literary renaissance blossomed, led by F. Scott Fitzgerald, William Faulkner, Sherwood Anderson, Eugene O'Neill, Sinclair Lewis, and Ernest Hemingway. Many of these authors sharply criticized the materialist culture of the decade, symbolized by the rampant speculation on the stock market, which crashed in 1929.

A. THE REVIVAL OF ANTI-FOREIGNISM

1. William A. White Condemns Deportations (1922)

Russian Bolshevism inspired a wave of hysteria which swept the United States after World War I and continued into 1920–1921. Strikes, bomb explosions, and other acts of violence were branded the work of alien "Reds," scores of whom were rounded up and deported. In 1919 a total of 249 undesirables were loaded onto a ship known as the "Soviet Ark" and bundled off to the Russian "paradise." Guy Empey, who applauded the "deportation delirium," wrote: "My motto for the Reds is S.O.S.—ship or shoot. I believe we should place them all on a ship of stone, with sails of lead, and that their first stopping place should be hell." By early 1920 newspaper editor William Allen White was calling for sanity. In this excerpt, does he call for absoute freedom of speech? What does he think is the greatest harm done by the indiscriminate persecution of "radicals"?

1. Emporia (Kansas) *Gazette*, Jan. 8, 1920. By permission of the Emporia *Gazette*.

The Attorney General seems to be seeing red. He is rounding up every manner of radical in the country; every man who hopes for a better world is in danger of deportation by the Attorney General. The whole business is un-American. There are certain rules fundamental which should govern in the treason cases.

First, it should be agreed that a man should believe what he chooses.

Second, it should be agreed that when he preaches violence he is disturbing the peace and should be put in jail. Whether he preaches violence in politics, business, or religion, whether he advocates murder and arson and pillage for gain or for political ends, he is violating the common law and should be squelched—jailed until he is willing to quit advocating force in a democracy.

Third, he should be allowed to say what he pleases so long as he advocates legal constitutional methods of procedure. Just because a man does not believe this government is good is no reason why he should be deported.

Abraham Lincoln did not believe this government was all right seventy-five years ago. He advocated changes, but he advocated constitutional means, and he had a war with those who advocated force to maintain the government as it was.

Ten years ago [Theodore] Roosevelt advocated great changes in our American life—in our Constitution, in our social and economic life. Most of the changes he advocated have been made, but they were made in the regular legal way. He preached no force. And if a man desires to preach any doctrine under the shining sun, and to advocate the realization of his vision by lawful, orderly, constitutional means—let him alone. If he is Socialist, anarchist, or Mormon, and merely preaches his creed and does not preach violence, he can do no harm. For the folly of his doctrine will be its answer.

The deportation business is going to make martyrs of a lot of idiots whose cause is not worth it.

2. Vanzetti Condemns Judge Thayer (1927)

The most notorious case associated with the Red Scare involved Nicola Sacco, a shoemaker, and Bartolomeo Vanzetti, a fish peddler. They were convicted of the 1920 murder of a paymaster and his guard at South Braintree, Massachusetts. When arrested, both men were carrying revolvers and both told numerous lies. Moreover, they were both aliens (Italians), atheists, conscientious objectors ("draft dodgers"), and radicals. Their conviction by a jury in the anti-Red atmosphere of the time, despite serious flaws in the evidence, raised grave doubts as to the fairness of the trial and the presiding judge, Webster Thayer. Many critics believed that the accused had been found guilty of radicalism rather than murder; that they were martyrs in the "class struggle." Numerous demonstrations in their favor were staged by radical groups

2. *The Sacco-Vanzetti Case; Transcript of the Record of the Trial . . . and Subsequent Proceedings, 1920–27* (5 vols., New York, 1928–1929), pp. 4898–99, 4904.

in foreign countries. After six years of fruitless appeal, the conviction of Sacco and Vanzetti was upheld, and they were condemned to death in the electric chair. Vanzetti's
defiant words to Judge Thayer upon being sentenced are a classic. Why, in his view,
is he being executed?

You see, it is seven years that we are in jail. What we have suffered
during these seven years no human tongue can say; and yet you see me
before you, not trembling, you see me looking you in your eyes straight,
not blushing, nor changing color, not ashamed or in fear.

Eugene Debs [the Socialist] say that not even a dog—something like
that—not even a dog that kill the chickens would have been found guilty
by American jury with the evidence that the Commonwealth have produced against us. I say that not even a leprous dog would have his appeal
refused two times by the Supreme Court of Massachusetts—not even a
leprous dog. . . .

We have proved that there could not have been another Judge on the
face of the earth more prejudiced and more cruel than you [Thayer] have
been against us. We have proven that. Still they refuse the new trial. We
know, and you know in your heart, that you have been against us from the
very beginning, before you see us. Before you see us you already know
that we were radicals, that we were underdogs, that we were the enemy
of the institution that you can believe in good faith in their goodness—
I don't want to condemn that—and that it was easy on the time of the first
trial to get a verdict of guiltiness.

We know that you have spoke yourself and have spoke your hostility
against us, and your despisement against us with friends of yours on the
train, at the University Club of Boston, on the Golf Club of Worcester,
Massachusetts. I am sure that if the people who know all what you say
against us would have the civil courage to take the stand, maybe your
Honor—I am sorry to say this because you are an old man, and I have an
old father—but maybe you would be beside us in good justice at this
time. . . .

This is what I say: I would not wish to a dog or to a snake, to the most
low and misfortunate creature of the earth—I would not wish to any of
them what I have had to suffer for things that I am not guilty of. But my
conviction is that I have suffered for things that I am guilty of. I am suffering because I am a radical and indeed I am a radical; I have suffered
because I was an Italian, and indeed I am an Italian; I have suffered more
for my family and for my beloved than for myself; but I am so convinced
to be right that if you could execute me two times, and if I could be reborn
two other times, I would live again to do what I have done already.

[*A later investigation, using ballistic tests and other evidence, concluded that
Vanzetti probably was innocent, while Sacco may have been guilty. See Francis
Russell, "Sacco Guilty, Vanzetti Innocent?"* in American Heritage, XIII, 5–9, 107–
11 *(June, 1962); also the same author's* Tragedy in Dedham *(1962)*].

3. Lippmann Pleads for Sacco and Vanzetti (1927)

Four days before the execution, which was scheduled for August 23, 1927, the militant New York *World* ran a full-page editorial, written by its chief editorial writer, pundit Walter Lippmann, pleading for a stay of execution. On what grounds does Lippmann base his appeal?

We recognize perfectly well that no government can with self-respect yield to the clamor of ignorance and sentimentality and partisanship. We realize perfectly well how much more difficult it is for the Governor to commute these sentences in the face of organized threats and of sporadic outrages. It will take greatness of mind and heart for the Governor and his Council to choose the wiser course. . . .

If Governor Fuller commutes these sentences, the Communists and Anarchists will shout that they coerced him. They will make the most of it for a day, a week, a month. The extremists on the other side will call him a weakling, and sneer. They will make the most of it for a day, a week, a month. But in the meantime moderate and disinterested opinion, which is never very talkative, will mobilize behind him and will recognize that he did a wise and a brave thing. . . .

Therefore we plead with the Governor to see this matter in the light, not of to-day and to-morrow, but of years to come. We plead with him to stay the execution because it will defeat the only purpose for which the death penalty can be exacted. We plead with him to remember that, however certain he may be in his own mind that the two men are guilty, no such certainty exists in the minds of his fellow-citizens. . . .

The Sacco-Vanzetti case is clouded and obscure. It is full of doubt. The fairness of the trial raises doubt. The evidence raises doubt. The inadequate review of the evidence raises doubt. The Governor's inquiry has not appeased these doubts. The report of his Advisory Committee has not settled these doubts. Everywhere there is doubt so deep, so pervasive, so unsettling, that it cannot be denied and it cannot be ignored. No man, we submit, should be put to death where so much doubt exists.

The real solution of this case would be a new trial before a new judge under new conditions. Fervently we hope that the Supreme Judicial Court of Massachusetts will decide that under the law such a new trial can be held. But if it does not, then to the Governor, to his Council, and to the friends of justice in Massachusetts we make this plea:

Stay the execution. Wait. The honor of an American Commonwealth is in your hands. Listen, and do not put an irrevocable end upon a case that is so full of doubt. It is human to err, and it is possible in the sight of God that the whole truth is not yet known.

[*As the condemned men were being prepared for execution, mobs stoned American embassies in European and South American capitals, while aroused*

---

3. New York *World*, Aug. 19, 1927. A longer extract appears in R. P. Weeks, ed., *Common wealth vs. Sacco and Vanzetti* (1958), pp. 240–46.

workers went on strike in Italy, France, and the United States. As Sacco was strapped to the electric chair he cried out in Italian, "Long live anarchy!" Some five months earlier a reporter for the New York World *had visited Vanzetti in his cell and recorded the following remarks by the prisoner, which were published in the* World *on May 13, 1927, and which have become famous:*

"If it had not been for these thing, I might have live out my life, talking at street corners to scorning men. I might have die, unmarked, unknown, a failure. Now we are not a failure. This is our career and our triumph. Never in our full life can we hope to do such work for tolerance, for joostice, for man's onderstanding of man, as now we do by an accident.

"Our word—our lives—our pains—nothing! The taking of our lives—lives of a good shoemaker and a poor fish peddler—all! That last moment belong to us— that agony is our triumph!"]

B. THE RECONSTITUTED KU KLUX KLAN

1. Tar-Bucket Terror in Texas (1921)

The hysterical atmosphere of the Red Scare was also partly responsible for the revival of the Ku Klux Klan in the 1920's. The bed sheets, hoods, and lashes were old, but the principles, aside from hatred of blacks, were new. The revamped Klan was anti-foreign, anti-Catholic, anti-Jewish, and anti-Communist. It professed to uphold Christianity, the Bible, prohibition, clean movies, the law, the Constitution, the public schools, the home, the marriage vows. It undertook to persuade unchaste people, especially women, to mend their ways by giving them a dose of the lash and a coat of tar and feathers. The press reported in 1921 that a black bellboy had been branded on the forehead with the letters K.K.K.; that in Florida an Episcopal archdeacon had been whipped, tarred, and feathered; and that there had been forty-three tar-bucket parties in Texas in six months. The Houston *Chronicle* here addresses a protest to the Klan members. Does it register any sympathy for the Klan? What does it see as the Klan's greatest outrages?

Boys, you'd better disband. You'd better take your sheets, your banners, your masks, your regalia, and make one fine bonfire.

Without pausing to argue over the objects you have in mind, it is sufficient to say that your methods are hopelessly wrong. Every tradition of social progress is against them. They are opposed to every principle on which this Government is founded. They are out of keeping with civilized life.

You seem to forget that the chief advantage of democracy is to let in the daylight, to prevent secret punishment, to insure a fair hearing for every person, to make impossible that kind of tyranny which can only flourish in the dark.

The newspapers of last Sunday were disgraced with the account of four illegal, unnecessary, and wholly ineffectual outrages. Without assuming that your organization was directly responsible for any or all of them, it was, in large measure, indirectly responsible. Your organization has made the thought of secretly organized violence fashionable.

---

1. Houston *Chronicle*, quoted in *Literary Digest*, LXX, 12 (Aug. 27, 1921).

It matters not who can get into your organization or who is kept out; any group of men can ape your disguise, your methods, and your practices. If outrages occur for which you are not accountable—and they will—you have no way of clearing yourselves, except by throwing off your disguise and invoking that publicity you have sought to deny. Your rôle of masked violence, of purification by stealth, of reform by terrorism is an impossible one. Your position is such that you must accept responsibility for every offense which smacks of disguised tryanny. . . .

Who was responsible for the Tenaha case, where a woman was stripped naked and then covered with tar and feathers? Has there ever been any crime committed in this state so horrible or one that brought such shame on Texas? Is there any member of the Ku Klux Klan in Texas so pure and holy that he can condemn even the vilest woman to such disgrace and torture?

Masked men did it, and the world was told in press dispatches that they were the hooded Klansmen of Texas.

If that outrage was done by Ku Klux Klansmen, then every decent man who was inveigled into the order should resign immediately. If it was not the work of the real order, its members should disband because of this one act, if for no other reason.

The Ku Klux Klan, as recently rejuvenated, serves no useful purpose. On the other hand, it makes room for innumerable abuses. The community—meaning the whole nation—is against it, and the community will grow more resolutely against it as time goes on. Those who brought it into being, no matter what their intentions, would better bring about its dissolution before the storm breaks.

"PUT IT ON AGAIN!"

The highest type of citizen did not wear bed sheets. Baltimore *Sun*, 1928.

2. A Methodist Editor Clears the Klan (1923)

The brutal excesses of the Ku Klux Klan (or its imitators) brought it into disrepute, and by the mid-1920's it was rapidly disintegrating. But for several years, with its hundreds of thousands of members, it remained a potent political force. The Reverend Bob Shuler (Methodist), editor of *Shuler's Magazine* and the Fundamentalist pastor of a large Los Angeles church, published the following advertisement in the

2. Eugene *Register,* quoted in *Literary Digest,* LXXVI, 18–19 (Jan. 20, 1923). By permission of the Eugene *Register.*

Eugene (Oregon) *Register.* What biases form the basis of his pro-Klan views? Is vigilantism ever justified? How valid is the author's comparison of the Klan with the Knights of Columbus?

This editor has repeatedly affirmed privately and publicly that he is not a member of the Ku Klux or any other secret organization. But when it comes to secret societies, he sees no difference absolutely between the Ku Klux and many others, the Knights of Columbus,° for instance. The Knights of Columbus has an oath, just as binding, or more so, than the Ku Klux oath. Moreover, the Knights of Columbus' oath is not one-half so American as the Ku Klux. If you charge that the Ku Klux has put over mobs, I answer that the Knights of Columbus has put over two mobs to where any other secret organization on earth has ever put over one.

This editor has been favored recently by being permitted to look over documentary evidence as to the tenets, principles, and aims of the Ku Klux Klan. He finds that this organization stands with positive emphasis for Americanism as opposed to foreign idealism; for the principles of the Christian religion as opposed to Roman Catholicism and infidelity; for the American public schools and for the placing of the Holy Bible in the schoolrooms of this nation; for the enforcement of the laws upon the statute books and for a wholesome respect for the Constitution of the United States; for the maintenance of virtue among American women, sobriety and honor among American men, and for the eradication of all agencies and influences that would threaten the character of our children. So the principles of the Klan are not so damnable as pictured, it would seem.

This organization is opposing the most cunning, deceitful, and persistent enemy that Americanism and Protestant Christianity have ever had—the Jesuits. Speaking of "invisible empires," of forces that creep through the night and do their dirty work under cover, influences that are set going in the secret places of darkness, the Jesuits are the finished product. They have burned, killed, defamed, blackmailed, and ruined their enemies by the hundreds. History reeks with it. Though I disagree with the logic of the Klan, the members of that organization declare that they can only fight such a foe by using his own fire.

As to the charge that the Ku Klux Klan has functioned in mob violence in their efforts to correct conditions, I have this to say: I am convinced that most of the mobs reported have not been ordered and directed by the Klan as an organization. I am moreover convinced that many of them have been put over by forces opposed to the Klan and for the purpose of seeking to place the guilt for mob rule upon the Klan. The most of these mobs have been, according to investigation, not Ku Klux mobs at all, but gatherings of indignant citizens, bent on correcting conditions that the officers of the law refused to correct. The way to cause the Ku Klux to retire from the field is for the officers of the law to take that field and occupy it.

° An American Roman Catholic society for men, founded in 1882.

The Ku Klux has the same right to exist so long as it obeys the law that any other organization has. We have not heard of any investigation of the Knights of Columbus, although their un-American oaths are historic and their mob activities have been repeatedly published and heralded from platforms far and near.

C. THE WETS VERSUS THE DRYS

1. A German Observes Bootlegging (1928)

Before the end of World War I most of the states had decreed the prohibition of alcoholic beverages. Nationwide prohibition, authorized by the 18th Amendment in 1919, resulted largely from the spirit of self-sacrifice aroused by the war. A militant majority was thus able to force its will upon a large and vocal minority, especially in the big cities, where the foreign-born population was accustomed to the regular consumption of alcohol. "The Sea Devil" Felix von Luckner, a German naval hero who had destroyed some $25,000,000 worth of Allied commerce with his raider the *Seeadler* (*Sea Eagle*) during World War I, visited America as a lecturer and recorded his curious experiences with alcohol. What does he see as the good and bad features of prohibition? What conditions made enforcement peculiarly difficult?

My first experience with the ways of prohibition came while we were being entertained by friends in New York. It was bitterly cold. My wife and I rode in the rumble seat of the car, while the American and his wife, bundled in furs, sat in front. Having wrapped my companion in pillows and blankets so thoroughly that only her nose showed, I came across another cushion that seemed to hang uselessly on the side. "Well," I thought, "this is a fine pillow; since everyone else is so warm and cozy, I might as well do something for my own comfort. This certainly does no one any good hanging on the wall." Sitting on it, I gradually noticed a dampness in the neighborhood that soon mounted to a veritable flood. The odor of fine brandy told me I had burst my host's peculiar liquor flask.

In time, I learned that not everything in America was what it seemed to be. I discovered, for instance, that a spare tire could be filled with substances other than air, that one must not look too deeply into certain binoculars, and that the Teddy Bears that suddenly acquired tremendous popularity among the ladies very often had hollow metal stomachs.

"But," it might be asked, "where do all these people get the liquor?" Very simple. Prohibition has created a new, a universally respected, a well-beloved, and a very profitable occupation, that of the bootlegger who takes care of the importation of the forbidden liquor. Everyone knows this, even the powers of government. But this profession is beloved because it is essential, and it is respected because its pursuit is clothed with an element of danger and with a sporting risk. . . .

Yet it is undeniable that prohibition has in some respects been signally successful. The filthy saloons, the gin mills which formerly flourished on every corner and in which the laborer once drank off half his wages, have disappeared. Now he can instead buy his own car, and ride off for a week-end or a few days with his wife and children in the country or at the sea. But, on the other hand, a great deal of poison and methyl alcohol has taken the place of the good old pure whiskey. The number of crimes and misdemeanors that originated in drunkenness has declined. But by contrast, a large part of the population has become accustomed to disregard and to violate the law without thinking. The worst is that, precisely as a consequence of the law, the taste for alcohol has spread ever more widely among the youth. The sporting attraction of the forbidden and the dangerous leads to violations. My observations have convinced me that many fewer would drink were it not illegal.

2. La Guardia Pillories Prohibition (1926)

The wholesale violations of the prohibition law became so notorious that in 1926 a Senate judiciary subcommittee held extended hearings. It uncovered shocking conditions. Stubby, turbulent, fiery Fiorello ("The Little Flower") La Guardia, then a Congressman from New York and later to be the controversial reform mayor of New York City, expressed characteristically vigorous views. Which of his statistics seem least susceptible of proof? Which of his arguments would probably carry the most weight with the average taxpayer?

It is impossible to tell whether prohibition is a good thing or a bad thing. It has never been enforced in this country.

There may not be as much liquor in quantity consumed to-day as there was before prohibition, but there is just as much alcohol.

At least 1,000,000 quarts of liquor is consumed each day in the United States. In my opinion such an enormous traffic in liquor could not be carried on without the knowledge, if not the connivance, of the officials entrusted with the enforcement of the law.

I am for temperance; that is why I am for modification.

I believe that the percentage of whisky drinkers in the United States now is greater than in any other country of the world. Prohibition is responsible for that. . . .

At least $1,000,000,000 a year is lost to the National Government and the several states and counties in excise taxes. The liquor traffic is going on just the same. This amount goes into the pockets of bootleggers and into the pockets of the public officials in the shape of graft. . . .

I will concede that the saloon was odious, but now we have delicatessen stores, pool rooms, drug stores, millinery shops, private parlors, and 57 other varieties of speakeasies selling liquor and flourishing.

2. *Hearings before the Subcommittee of the Committee on the Judiciary, United States Senate, Sixty-ninth Congress, First Session, on . . . Bills to Amend the National Prohibition Act,* I, 649–51.

I have heard of $2,000 a year prohibition agents who run their own cars with liveried chauffeurs.

It is common talk in my part of the country that from $7.50 to $12 a case is paid in graft from the time the liquor leaves the 12-mile limit until it reaches the ultimate consumer. There seems to be a varying market price for this service created by the degree of vigilance or the degree of greed of the public officials in charge.

It is my calculation that at least $1,000,-000 a day is paid in graft and corruption to Federal, state, and local officers. Such a condition is not only intolerable, but it is demoralizing and dangerous to organized government. . . .

The Prohibition Enforcement Unit has entirely broken down. It is discredited; it has become a joke. Liquor is sold in every large city. . . .

Only a few days ago I charged on the floor of the House that 350 cases of liquor of a seizure of 1,500 made by Federal officials and

THE NATIONAL GESTURE

Every official seemingly had his hand out for a bribe. *Judge*, c. 1930, in Andrew Sinclair, *Prohibition*, 1962.

stored in the Federal building at Indianapolis, Ind., had been removed. The Department of Justice, under date of April 9, 1926, confirmed my charge. The Attorney General admits that since this liquor was in the possession of the Federal authorities in the Federal building at Indianapolis, 330 cases are missing. If bootleggers can enter Federal buildings to get liquor, the rest can be easily imagined. . . .

I have been in public office for a great many years. I have had the opportunity to observe first the making of the present prohibition laws as a member of Congress, and later as president of the Board of Aldermen of the largest city in this country its attempted enforcement. In order to enforce prohibition in New York City I estimated at the time would require a police force of 250,000 men and a force of 200,000 men to police the police.

3. The W.C.T.U. Upholds Prohibition (1926)

Before the same Senate judiciary subcommittee, and from the same metropolitan area as La Guardia, appeared Mrs. Ella A. Boole, president of the National Woman's Christian Temperance Union. A member of the D.A.R., a Ph.D. from the University of Wooster, and a Presbyterian, she had run unsuccessfully for the United States Senate on the Prohibition ticket in 1920. What values underlie her insistence on enforcing unpopular laws, despite widespread flouting?

You have listened to testimony of shocking conditions due to corruption of officials, and lack of enforcement, some of which suggested no remedy except a surrender to those who violate the law, while the propaganda of all these organizations is encouraging continued violation. Permit me to show another side of the picture, and propose that instead of lowering our standards we urge that the law be strengthened, and in that way notice be served on law violators that America expects her laws to be enforced and to be obeyed. . . .

Enforcement has never had a fair trial. Political patronage, leakage through the permit system, connivance at the violation of law, and spread of the propaganda that it is not obligatory to obey a law unless you believe in it, and to the effect that the responsibility for the enforcement of law rested with the officers alone, when it should be shared by the individual citizen, have materially hindered the work of enforcement—all this with the result that the United States has not derived from prohibition what it would have derived had all the people observed the law and had there been hearty cooperation of the press and the people. . . .

It is not easy to get at the facts about the effect of prohibition on health, morals, and economic [life] because they are interwoven with other causes, and partial statistics may be misleading. But the elimination of a preventable cause of poverty, crime, tuberculosis, the diseases of middle life, unhappy homes, and financial depression brings results insofar as the law is observed and enforced. . . .

The closing of the open saloon with its doors swinging both ways, an ever-present invitation for all to drink—men, women, and boys—is an outstanding fact, and no one wants it to return. It has resulted in better national health, children are born under better conditions, homes are better, and the mother is delivered from the fear of a drunken husband. There is better food. Savings-banks deposits have increased, and many a man has a bank account to-day who had none in the days of the saloon.

The increase in home owning is another evidence that money wasted in drink is now used for the benefit of the family. Improved living conditions are noticeable in our former slum districts. The Bowery and Hell's Kitchen are transformed.

Safety-first campaigns on railroads and in the presence of the increasing number of automobiles are greatly strengthened by prohibition.

3. *Ibid.,* pp. 1068–71.

The prohibition law is not the only law that is violated. Traffic laws, anti-smuggling laws, as well as the Volstead [prohibition] Act, are held in contempt. It is the spirit of the age.

Life-insurance companies have long known that drinkers were poor risks, but they recognize the fact that prohibition has removed a preventable cause of great financial loss to them.

The wonderful advances in mechanics in the application of electricity and in transportation demand brains free from the fumes of alcohol, hence law enforcement and law observance contribute to this progress. . . .

Your attention has been called to the failures. We claim these have been the result of lax enforcement. The machinery of enforcement should be strengthened.

[*The federal enforcement machinery finally broke down, and the 18th Amendment was repealed in 1933. Prohibition had done much good but at a staggering cost. In addition to the evils already noted, gangsterism was flourishing and the courts and jails were clogged. With repeal, the control of liquor went back to state and local governments.*]

D. THE AUTOMOBILE AGE DAWNS

1. Henry Ford Discusses Manufacturing and Marketing (1922)

Henry Ford had little formal schooling, but he became America's most famous industrial genius. Beginning as a machine-shop apprentice and traveling repair man for a farm-machinery company, he built his first motor-car in 1896 and organized the Ford Motor Co. seven years later. Its growth was phenomenal, as was the impact of the automobile on American life. Ford's manufacturing techniques, philosophy of labor relations, and marketing ideas were widely imitated. In the following excerpt from his autobiography, he discusses the early days of his industrial career. Which of his ideas were most innovative? Which seem most attractive today? Which seem most outdated?

In 1909 I announced one morning, without any previous warning, that in the future we were going to build only one model, that the model was going to be "Model T," and that the chassis would be exactly the same for all cars, and I remarked:

"Any customer can have a car painted any colour that he wants so long as it is black."

I cannot say that any one agreed with me. . . . A motor car was still regarded as something in the way of a luxury. The manufacturers did a good deal to spread this idea. Some clever persons invented the name "pleasure car" and the advertising emphasized the pleasure features. The sales people had ground for their objection and particularly when I made the following announcement:

I will build a motor car for the great multitude. It will be large enough for the family but small enough for the individual to run and care for. It will be con-

1. Henry Ford, in collaboration with Samuel Crowther, *My Life and Work* (1922), passim.

structed of the best materials, by the best men to be hired, after the simplest designs that modern engineering can devise. But it will be so low in price that no man making a good salary will be unable to own one—and enjoy with his family the blessing of hours of pleasure in God's great open spaces. . . .

The more economical methods of production did not begin all at once. They began gradually—just as we began gradually to make our own parts. "Model T" was the first motor that we made ourselves. The great economies began in assembling and then extended to other sections so that, while to-day we have skilled mechanics in plenty, they do not produce automobiles—they make it easy for others to produce them. Our skilled men are the tool makers, the experimental workmen, the machinists, and the pattern makers. They are as good as any men in the world—so good, indeed, that they should not be wasted in doing that which the machines they contrive can do better. The rank and file of men come to us unskilled; they learn their jobs within a few hours or a few days. If they do not learn within that time they will never be of any use to us. These men are, many of them, foreigners, and all that is required before they are taken on is that they should be potentially able to do enough work to pay the overhead charges on the floor space they occupy. They do not have to be able-bodied men. We have jobs that require great physical strength—although they are rapidly lessening; we have other jobs that require no strength whatsoever—jobs which, as far as strength is concerned, might be attended to by a child of three. . . .

A Ford car contains about five thousand parts—that is counting screws, nuts, and all. Some of the parts are fairly bulky and others are almost the size of watch parts. In our first assembling we simply started to put a car together at a spot on the floor and workmen brought to it the parts as they were needed in exactly the same way that one builds a house. When we started to make parts it was natural to create a single department of the factory to make that part, but usually one workman performed all of the operations necessary on a small part. The rapid press of production made it necessary to devise plans of production that would avoid having the workers falling over one another. The undirected worker spends more of his time walking about for materials and tools than he does in working; he gets small pay because pedestrianism is not a highly paid line.

The first step forward in assembly came when we began taking the work to the men instead of the men to the work. We now have two general principles in all operations—that a man shall never have to take more than one step, if possibly it can be avoided, and that no man need ever stoop over.

The principles of assembly are these:

1. Place the tools and the men in the sequence of the operation so that each component part shall travel the least possible distance while in the process of finishing.

2. Use work slides or some other form of carrier so that when a workman

completes his operation, he drops the part always in the same place—which place must always be the most convenient place to his hand—and if possible have gravity carry the part to the next workman for his operation.

3. Use sliding assembling lines by which the parts to be assembled are delivered at convenient distances.

The net result of the application of these principles is the reduction of the necessity for thought on the part of the worker and the reduction of his movements to a minimum. He does as nearly as possibly only one thing with only one movement.

The assembling of the chassis is, from the point of view of the nonmechanical mind, our most interesting and perhaps best known operation, and at one time it was an exceedingly important operation. We now [1922] ship out the parts for assembly at the point of distribution.

Along about April 1, 1913, we first tried the experiment of an assembly line. We tried it on assembling the fly-wheel magneto. We try everything in a little way first—we will rip out anything once we discover a better way, but we have to know absolutely that the new way is going to be better than the old before we do anything drastic.

I believe that this was the first moving line ever installed. The idea came in a general way from the overhead trolley that the Chicago packers use in dressing beef. We had previously assembled the fly-wheel magneto in the usual method. With one workman doing a complete job he could turn out from thirty-five to forty pieces in a nine-hour day, or about twenty minutes to an assembly. What he did alone was then spread into twenty-nine operations; that cut down the assembly time to thirteen minutes, ten seconds. Then we raised the height of the line eight inches—this was in 1914—and cut the time to seven minutes. Further experimenting with the speed that the work should move at cut the time down to five minutes. In short, the result is this: by the aid of scientific study one man is now able to do somewhat more than four did only a comparatively few years ago. That line established the efficiency of the method and we now use it everywhere. The assembling of the motor, formerly done by one man, is now divided into eighty-four operations—those men do the work that three times their number formerly did. In a short time we tried out the plan on the chassis.

About the best we had done in stationary chassis assembly was an average of twelve hours and twenty-eight minutes per chassis. We tried the experiment of drawing the chassis with a rope and windlass down a line two hundred fifty feet long. Six assemblers travelled with the chassis and picked up the parts from piles placed along the line. This rough experiment reduced the time to five hours fifty minutes per chassis. In the early part of 1914 we elevated the assembly line. We had adopted the policy of "man-high" work; we had one line twenty-six and three quarter inches and another twenty-four and one half inches from the floor—to suit squads of different heights. The waist-high arrangement and a further subdivision of work so that each man had fewer movements cut down the labour time per chassis to one hour thirty-three minutes. Only the chassis was then assembled in the line. The body was placed on in "John R. Street"—the famous street that runs through our Highland Park factories. Now the line assembles the whole car.

It must not be imagined, however, that all this worked out as quickly as it sounds. The speed of the moving work had to be carefully tried out; in the fly-wheel magneto we first had a speed of sixty inches per minute. That was too fast. Then we tried eighteen inches per minute. That was too slow. Finally we settled on forty-four inches per minute. The idea is that a man must not be hurried in his work—he must have every second necessary but not a single unnecessary second. We have worked out speeds for each assembly, for the success of the chassis assembly caused us gradually to overhaul our entire method of manufacturing and to put all assembling in mechanically driven lines. The chassis assembling line, for instance, goes at a pace of six feet per minute; the front axle assembly line goes at one hundred eighty-nine inches per minute. In the chassis assembling are forty-five separate operations or stations. The first men fasten four mudguard brackets to the chassis frame; the motor arrives on the tenth operation and so on in detail. Some men do only one or two small operations, others do more. The man who places a part does not fasten it—the part may not be fully in place until after several operations later. The man who puts in a bolt does not put on the nut; the man who puts on the nut does not tighten it. On operation number thirty-four the budding motor gets its gasoline; it has previously received lubrication; on operation number forty-four the radiator is filled with water, and on operation number forty-five the car drives out onto John R. Street. . . .

Our policy is to reduce the price, extend the operations, and improve the article. You will notice that the reduction of price comes first. We have never considered any costs as fixed. Therefore we first reduce the price to a point where we believe more sales will result. Then we go ahead and try to make the price. We do not bother about the costs. The new price forces the costs down. . . .

The payment of high wages fortunately contributes to the low costs because the men become steadily more efficient on account of being relieved of outside worries. The payment of five dollars a day for an eight-hour day was one of the finest cost-cutting moves we ever made, and the six-dollar day wage is cheaper than the five. How far this will go, we do not know.

We have always made a profit at the prices we have fixed and, just as we have no idea how high wages will go, we also have no idea how low prices will go, but there is no particular use in bothering on that point. The tractor, for instance, was first sold for $750, then at $850, then at $625, and the other day we cut it 37 per cent to $395. . . .

The standardization that effects large economies for the consumer results in profits of such gross magnitude to the producer that he can scarcely know what to do with his money. But his effort must be sincere, painstaking, and fearless. Cutting out a half-a-dozen models is not standardizing. It may be, and usually is, only the limiting of business, for if one is selling on the ordinary basis of profit—that is, on the basis of taking as much money away from the consumer as he will give up—then surely the consumer ought to have a wide range of choice.

Standardization, then, is the final stage of the process. We start with [the] consumer, work back through the design, and finally arrive at manufacturing. The manufacturing becomes a means to the end of service.

It is important to bear this order in mind. As yet, the order is not thoroughly understood. The price relation is not understood. The notion persists that prices ought to be kept up. On the contrary, good business—large consumption—depends on their going down.

And here is another point. The service must be the best you can give. It is considered good manufacturing practice, and not bad ethics, occasionally to change designs so that old models will become obsolete and new ones will have to be bought either because repair parts for the old cannot be had, or because the new model offers a new sales argument which can be used to persuade a consumer to scrap what he has and buy something new. We have been told that this is good business, that it is clever business, that the object of business ought to be to get people to buy frequently and that it is bad business to try to make anything that will last forever, because when once a man is sold he will not buy again.

Our principle of business is precisely to the contrary. We cannot conceive how to serve the consumer unless we make for him something that, as far as we can provide, will last forever. We want to construct some kind of a machine that will last forever. It does not please us to have a buyer's car wear out or become obsolete. We want the man who buys one of our products never to have to buy another. We never make an improvement that renders any previous model obsolete. The parts of a specific model are not only interchangeable with all other cars of that model, but they are interchangeable with similar parts on all the cars that we have turned out. You can take a car of ten years ago and, buying to-day's parts, make it with very little expense into a car of to-day. Having these objectives the costs always come down under pressure. And since we have the firm policy of steady price reduction, there is always pressure. Sometimes it is just harder! . . .

Now as to saturation. We are continually asked:

"When will you get to the point of overproduction? When will there be more cars than people to use them?"

We believe it is possible some day to reach the point where all goods are produced so cheaply and in such quantities that overproduction will be a reality. But as far as we are concerned, we do not look forward to that condition with fear—we look forward to it with great satisfaction. Nothing could be more splendid than a world in which everybody has all that he wants. Our fear is that this condition will be too long postponed. As to our own products, that condition is very far away. We do not know how many motor cars a family will desire to use of the particular kind that we make. We know that, as the price has come down, the farmer, who at first used one car (and it must be remembered that it is not so very long ago that the farm market for motor cars was absolutely unknown—the limit of sales was at that time fixed by all the wise statistical sharps at somewhere near the number of millionaires in the country) now often uses two, and also he buys a truck. Perhaps, instead of sending workmen out to scattered jobs in a single car, it will be cheaper to send each worker out in a car of his own. That is happening with salesmen. The public finds its own consumptive needs with unerring accuracy, and since we no longer make motor cars or tractors, but merely the parts which when assembled become motor cars and tractors, the facilities as now provided would hardly be sufficient to provide replacements for ten million cars. And it would be quite the same with any business. We do not have to bother about overproduction for some years to come, provided the prices are right. It is the refusal of people to buy on account of price that really stimulates real business. Then if we want to do business we have to get the prices down without hurting the quality. Thus price reduction forces us to learn improved and less wasteful methods of production. One big part of the discovery of what is "normal" in industry depends on managerial genius discovering better ways of doing things. If a man reduces his selling price to a point where he is making no profit or incurring a loss, then he simply is forced to discover how to make as good an article by a better method—making his new method produce the profit, and not producing a profit out of reduced wages or increased prices to the public. . . .

2. Labor Policies at the Ford Motor Company (1916)

By the 1920's the automobile industry, though barely two decades old, was the nation's largest. More than one and one half million cars rolled off Ford's assembly lines in 1923, and in the Detroit area alone Ford, who had employed barely 300 persons just two decades earlier, had some 24,000 people on his payroll. Always a dedicated if eccentric idealist, Ford tried to deal with his employees in innovative ways. His boldest and most controversial stroke came in 1914, when he reduced the work day to eight hours and raised a day's pay to the then unheard-of sum (for manufacturing workers) of five dollars. In the following article by Ford's first personnel manager, what motives are offered for this apparently benevolent, enlightened policy? Was it entirely benevolent? How would workers today greet a comparable policy?

It was along in 1912 that we began to realize something of the relative value of men, mechanism and material in the threefold phase of manufacturing, so to speak, and we confess that up to this time we had believed that mechanism and material were of the larger importance and that some-

2. John R. Lee, "The So-Called Profit Sharing System in the Ford Plant," *Annals of the American Academy of Political and Social Science,* Vol. 65 (May 1916), pp. 299–305, 308.

how or other the human element or our men were taken care of automatically and needed little or no consideration.

During that year there were a number of things that happened that made their impression upon the minds of the executives of the company.

I recall a drop hammer operation that had gone along for a number of years at an even output, when somehow, the standard dropped off. The hammer was in good condition, the man who had operated the machine for years was on the job, but the finished output failed to appear in the old proportions that we were looking for and had the right to expect.

A superficial analysis of things brought no light, but a little talk with the operator revealed a condition of things entirely outside of business, that was responsible for our depleted production. Sickness, indebtedness, and fear and worry over things that related entirely to the home, had crept in and had put a satisfactory human unit entirely out of harmony with the things that were necessary for production.

This is the type of incident that played an important part in the conclusions that we reached.

Our first step was to reduce our working day from ten to nine hours and to give our men an increase of about 15 per cent for nine hours over what they had received for ten.

Following this we instituted a plan for grading employes according to skill, with the idea of eliminating, as far as possible, petty discrimination, misfits, and those unsatisfactory conditions which obtain now and then, possibly through the more aggressive making their worth felt and known than men of more retiring dispositions are wont to do, or to prevent the favoritism of a foreman for an employe, overstepping the bounds of merit or consistency in any case. . . .

Moreover, we laid down a rule whereby a foreman might eliminate a man from his particular department but could not discharge him from the employ of the company. . . .

It may be startling for some of you to know that in the last six months there has been but one man discharged from the Ford organization.

. . . Suffice it to say that the good things and the substantial increases that came to the company through their efforts in the directions indicated gave rise to a further consideration of the human element which has resulted in our so-called profit sharing plan.

Now, I should like to impress upon you the fact that this profit sharing work was in no sense instituted as a spasmodic thing, was not designed or conceived for the sake of business expedient or advertising. We were perfectly satisfied with what each man was giving us, as far as daily return was concerned. We did not seek to advertise the car nor the company through this plan, but rather we felt that we owed it to our men at that time to give them all the help we consistently could to better their financial and their moral status, and to insure, as far as we could, a life worth while, and not merely a bare living.

It was established some time prior to this work that a man who comes out of a home well balanced, who has no fear for the necessities of life for those he is taking care of, who is not in constant dread of losing his position for reasons beyond his control, is the most powerful economic factor that we can use in the shape of a human being.

The profit sharing plan of the Ford Motor Company gives unto every man who can use it within limitations which I shall state, in addition to his wage, a certain amount, according to his worth and what his skill and ability merit for him, to have and to use according to his individual needs for his health and happiness in youth and in old age.

Now, over against each of the eight rates of wage we have set a profit sharing rate, and the lowest total daily income that a worker receives under the profit sharing plan is $5 a day.

This $5 a day, or 62½ cents an hour, is not the lowest minimum wage of the Ford worker; 34 cents is the minimum hourly wage and 28½ cents the minimum share of profits, totaling 62½ cents, which makes a total daily income of $5.

There are three groups under which each employe is considered for profit sharing—these, practically, are all the rules and regulations in connection with the work.

1. All married men living with and taking good care of their families.

2. All single men, over twenty-two, of proven thrifty habits.

3. Men, under twenty-two years of age, and women, who are the sole support of some next of kin or blood relative.

It was clearly foreseen that $5 a day in the hands of some men would work a tremendous handicap along the paths of rectitude and right living and would make of them a menace to society in general and so it was established at start that no man was to receive the money who could not use it advisedly and conservatively; also, that where a man seemed to qualify under the plan and later developed weaknesses, that it was within the province of the company to take away his share of the profits until such time as he could rehabilitate himself; nor was any man urged against his own judgment, likes or dislikes, to change his mode of living and to qualify under that plan if he did not willingly so elect.

The company organized a band of thirty men who were chosen because of their peculiar fitness for the work to act as investigators. The whole work was put into effect and supervised by the employes of the company—no outside talent or assistance was asked. We have worked out the whole scheme with Ford men.

This band of thirty men was commissioned to see each individual employe and to report as to whether, in their judgment, a man was eligible for a share in the profits. These reports were in turn reviewed by a committee and each case passed upon individually.

As a result of this work our employes were grouped as follows:

First Group. Those who were firmly established in the ways of thrift and who would carry out the spirit of the plan themselves were catalogued as one group.

Second Group. Those who had never had a chance but were willing to grasp the opportunity in the way every man should, were catalogued in the second group.

Third Group. Those who had qualified but we were in doubt about as to their strength of character to continue in the direction they had started in, were placed in the third group.

Fourth Group. And the men who did not or could not qualify were put into a fourth group.

The first group of men were never bothered except when we desired information for annual or semi-annual reports or something of that kind.

The second group were looked up as often as in the judgment of the investigation department, so called, we could help them or strengthen their purpose by kindly suggestion.

The third group were dealt with in much the same fashion, although some detailed plans had to be laid for them.

The fourth group were very carefully and thoroughly studied in the hope that we might bring them, with the others, to a realization of what we were trying to accomplish, and to modifications, changes and sometimes complete revamping of their lives and habits, in order that they might receive what the company wanted to give them.

During the first six months 69 per cent of our force qualified. At the end of the first year about 87 per cent were on a profit sharing basis, and at the present time about 90 per cent are receiving the benefits under this plan. . . .

The profits are paid to each employe with his wages in his pay envelope every two weeks. He is not influenced or coerced to spend his money for any one especial thing. The policy of the company is not to sell its men anything or influence them to buy anything—with the exception of Ford cars.

Our legal department has been enlarged so that men may come for counsel and suggestion as to ways and means for employing professional help.

As a part and parcel of the legal department also, we have a committee that makes appraisals of property for employes. A man who has picked out a home and gotten a price upon it, may submit the facts to our legal department, and without charge get from them an idea as to the worth of the property in connection with the price asked, also a general report as to the worth of the house, from the standpoint of construction, finishing and equipment.

We are also doing, in connection with the investigation work, something that is of great benefit both to the men and to the company.

Every morning there is turned over from the time department to our investigation staff a list of the absentees of the day previous, which is carefully looked up. If a man is in trouble he gets help; if a man has been wasting his time and himself, he is reminded of the fact quite forcibly, and is made to feel that to hold his position he must realize the necessity of coöperation.

This little scheme, which is merely eternal vigilance, has cut the number of our daily absentees from 10 per cent to less than one-half of 1 per cent, exclusive of the times when epidemics of grippe, cold, and other human ills prevail, and then it is increased by just the proportion that our men bear to the number afflicted.

It has been no easy task to add to the number of men we originally had, twenty more of the same type and calibre to act as investigators as our forces grew.

Two years ago we were employing some thirteen thousand men; today we have some twenty-four thousand, but we have gained rather than lost in the kind of men and in the spirit and energy shown, as far as this force is concerned.

At the present time we have divided the whole number so that those especially gifted in cases of domestic infelicity might tackle jobs of this type; those who have evidenced unusual skill in handling men with criminal records, are detailed to such cases, and so on.

As you probably know, of necessity rather than choice, a large part of our working force is made up of non-English-speaking men.

It was utterly impossible to reach these men with an explanation of our work through the medium of interpreters, and besides, we found a mercenary unwillingness, if you please, on the part of sophisticated fellow countrymen to aid us in helping this great army of men, which comprised 50 to 60 per cent of the entire number of Ford employes. . . .

We sought out Dr. Roberts—he came to Detroit, and there was organized the plan for giving all non-English-speaking employes a good basic knowledge of the English language through this system.

At the present time we have enrolled in our shop some 1,500, who are taught by volunteer teachers,—foremen, sub-foremen and graduates of the school, who receive in six or eight months, not a lot of grammar or mathematics, or geography, but the ground work of the English language, which enables them to read, write, speak and understand our tongue.

In our motor department there has been a gradual voluntary increase of production (the general layout and operations being practically the same as before with the same number of men), of from 6,125 motors in a 9-hour day to 7,200 in an 8-hour day.

The assembly of radiator cores, for example, has jumped so that a unit of men, previously putting together 750 in nine hours, now assemble 1,300 in eight, and a single group in the fender department heretofore making 38 fenders in nine hours are today producing 50 in eight.

In the making of gasoline tanks, 1,200 for 60 men is the output in eight hours versus 800 by 65 in nine hours.

Many of the methods and schemes used in our factory which have lately helped us so much in cutting out waste motion and lost time, are the direct results of the new spirit in the men and come to us from the rank and file of our employes.

We are finding additional capacity that is willing and always available if justly recognized and amply rewarded.

We used to hire from 40 to 60 per cent of our force each month to maintain it. In the year 1913 between 50,000 and 60,000 people passed through our employment office. In the year 1915 we employed about 7,000, of which number only 2,000 can be used in contrast with the 50,000 mentioned, because the 5,000 were for new jobs and for the enlargement of forces.

As I have previously stated, our daily absentees have decreased from 10 per cent to less than one-half of 1 per cent.

E. NEW GOALS FOR WOMEN

1. Margaret Sanger Campaigns For Birth Control (1920)

Few feminists could rival Margaret Sanger's energy, daring, and genius for organization and publicity. Prosecuted in 1914 for publishing a radical journal, *The Woman Rebel*, she fled to England, where she made the acquaintance of the noted sexual theorist, Havelock Ellis. She returned to America in 1915, and launched herself on a life-long crusade for birth control. Despite being arrested several more times in subsequent years, she persevered in founding the American Birth Control League (later Planned Parenthood) in 1921. For the next decade and more, Sanger tirelessly championed her cause. What arguments does she here emphasize in favor of contraception? What is her view of women? of men? of the relation between the sexes? Critics sometimes accused her of drinking too deeply from the well of racism and nativism that seemed to overflow in the 1920's. Do the remarks that follow offer any evidence in support of such a charge?

The most far-reaching social development of modern times is the revolt of woman against sex servitude. The most important force in the remaking of the world is a free motherhood. Beside this force, the elaborate international programmes of modern statesmen are weak and superficial. . . .

Only in recent years has woman's position as the gentler and weaker half of the human family been emphatically and generally questioned. Men assumed that this was woman's place; woman herself accepted it. It seldom occurred to anyone to ask whether she would go on occupying it forever. . . .

Caught in this "vicious circle," woman has, through her reproductive ability, founded and perpetuated the tyrannies of the Earth. Whether it was the tyranny of a monarchy, an oligarchy or a republic, the one indispensable factor of its existence was, as it is now, hordes of human beings —human beings so plentiful as to be cheap, and so cheap that ignorance was their natural lot. . . .

The creators of over-population are the women, who, while wringing their

1. Margaret Sanger, *Woman and the New Race* (Brentano's, 1920), passim. Reprinted by permission of the estate of Margaret Sanger.

hands over each fresh horror, submit anew to their task of producing the multitudes who will bring about the *next* tragedy of civilization.

While unknowingly laying the foundations of tyrannies and providing the human tinder for racial conflagrations, woman was also unknowingly creating slums, filling asylums with insane, and institutions with other defectives. She was replenishing the ranks of the prostitutes, furnishing grist for the criminal courts and inmates for prisons. Had she planned deliberately to achieve this tragic total of human waste and misery, she could hardly have done it more effectively. . . .

It is true that, obeying the inner urge of their natures, *some* women revolted. They went even to the extreme of infanticide and abortion. Usually their revolts were not general enough. They fought as individuals, not as a mass. . . .

To-day, however, woman is rising in fundamental revolt. Even her efforts at mere reform are, as we shall see later, steps in that direction. Underneath each of them is the feminine urge to complete freedom. Millions of women are asserting their right to voluntary motherhood. They are determined to decide for themselves whether they shall become mothers, under what conditions and when. This is the fundamental revolt referred to. It is for woman the key to the temple of liberty.

Even as birth control is the means by which woman attains basic freedom, so it is the means by which she must and will uproot the evil she has wrought through her submission. . . .

Two chief obstacles hinder the discharge of this tremendous obligation. The first and the lesser is the legal barrier. Dark-Age laws would still deny to her the knowledge of her reproductive nature. Such knowledge is indispensable to intelligent motherhood and she must achieve it, despite absurd statutes and equally absurd moral canons.

The second and more serious barrier is her own ignorance of the extent and effect of her submission. Until she knows the evil her subjection has wrought to herself, to her progeny and to the world at large, she cannot wipe out that evil. . . .

What effect will the practice of birth control have upon woman's moral development? . . . It will break her bonds. It will free her to understand the cravings and soul needs of herself and other women. It will enable her to develop her love nature separate from and independent of her maternal nature.

It goes without saying that the woman whose children are desired and are of such number that she can not only give them adequate care but keep herself mentally and spiritually alive, as well as physically fit, can discharge her duties to her children much better than the overworked, broken and querulous mother of a large, unwanted family. . . .

To achieve this she must have a knowledge of birth control. She must also assert and maintain her right to refuse the marital embrace except when urged by her inner nature. . . .

What can we expect of offspring that are the result of "accidents"—who are brought into being undesired and in fear? What can we hope for from a morality that surrounds each physical union, for the woman, with an atmosphere of submission and shame? What can we say for a morality that leaves the husband at liberty to communicate to his wife a venereal disease?

Subversion of the sex urge to ulterior purposes has dragged it to the level of the gutter. Recognition of its true nature and purpose must lift the race to spiritual freedom. Out of our growing knowledge we are evolving new and saner ideas of life in general. Out of our increasing sex knowledge we shall evolve new ideals of sex. These ideals will spring from the innermost needs of women. They will serve these needs and express them. They will be the foundation of a moral code that will tend to make fruitful the impulse which is the source, the soul and the crowning glory of our sexual natures.

When women have raised the standards of sex ideals and purged the human mind of its unclean conception of sex, the fountain of the race will nave been cleansed. Mothers will bring forth, in purity and in joy, a race that is morally and spiritually free. . . .

Birth control itself, often denounced as a violation of natural law, is nothing more or less than the facilitation of the process of weeding out the unfit, of preventing the birth of defectives or of those who will become defectives. So, in compliance with nature's working plan, we must permit womanhood its full development before we can expect of it efficient motherhood. If we are to make racial progress, this development of womanhood must precede motherhood in every individual woman. Then and then only can the mother cease to be an incubator and be a mother indeed. Then only can she transmit to her sons and daughters the qualities which make strong individuals and, collectively, a strong race. . . .

2. The Lynds Discover Changes in the Middle American Home (1929)

In 1924 the sociologists Robert S. Lynd and Helen Merrell Lynd arrived in Muncie, Indiana, with a team of researchers. They spent the next eighteen months studying the pattern and texture of life in Muncie, and in 1929 they published the results of their research in *Middletown: A Study in Modern American Culture. Middletown* has ever since been recognized as a classic work of American scholarship, perhaps the most detailed, thoughtful portrait ever drawn of life in an American community. The Lynds described the changes in the lives of ordinary, "average" people since the 1890's. (One of the most striking changes they found was that the traditional prohibition on discussing sexual matters, including birth control, was weakening. Among the more prosperous segments of Middletown's population, most women by 1924 not only discussed birth control but practiced it. The practice was much less widespread among the poorer elements of the populace.) Their research revealed that the pace of change was faster among "business class" people than among the "working class." In the following selection about

2. Excerpts from *Middletown*, pp. 167–173, by Robert S. and Helen M. Lynd are reprinted by permission of Harcourt Brace Jovanovich, Inc.; copyright 1929 by Harcourt Brace Jovanovich, Inc., renewed 1957 by Robert S. and Helen M. Lynd.

housework, what are the major differences between the lives of women in the 1890's and the 1920's? How do the lives of women in the two social classes differ? What are the effects on family life of the emergence of a high-mass-consumption economy in the 1920's?

At no point can one approach the home life of Middletown without becoming aware of the shift taking place in the traditional activities of male and female. This is especially marked in the complex of activities known as "housework," which have always been almost exclusively performed by the wife, with more or less help from her daughters. In the growing number of working class families in which the wife helps to earn the family living, the husband is beginning to share directly in housework. Even in families of the business class the manual activities of the wife in making a home are being more and more replaced by goods and services produced or performed by other agencies in return for a money price, thus throwing ever greater emphasis upon the money-getting activities of the husband. . . .

The rhythm of the day's activities varies according to whether a family is of the working or business class, most of the former starting the day at six or earlier and the latter somewhat later. . . .

Dorothy Dix catches the traditional situation in her remark, "Marriage brings a woman a life sentence of hard labor in her home. Her work is the most monotonous in the world and she has no escape from it." Many working class housewives, struggling to commute this sentence for their daughters if not for themselves, voiced in some form the wish of one mother, "I've always wanted my girls to do something other than housework; I don't want *them* to be house drudges like me!" And both groups are being borne along on the wave of material changes toward a somewhat lighter sentence to household servitude. Of the ninety-one working class wives who gave data on the amount of time their mothers spent on housework as compared with themselves, sixty-six (nearly three-fourths) said that their mothers spent more time, ten approximately the same, and fifteen less time. Of the thirty-seven wives of the business group interviewed who gave similar data, seventeen said that their mothers spent more time, eight about the same, and twelve less time.

The fact that the difference between the women of this business group and their mothers is less marked than that between the working class women and their mothers is traceable in part to the decrease in the amount of paid help in the homes of the business class. It is apparently about half as frequent for Middletown housewives to hire full-time servant girls to do their housework today as in 1890. The thirty-nine wives of the business group answering on this point reported almost precisely half as many full-time servants as their mothers in 1890, and this ratio is supported by Federal Census figures; thirteen of the thirty-nine have full-time servants, only two of them more than one. But if the women of the business class have fewer servants than their mothers, they are still markedly more served than the working class. One hundred and twelve out of 118 working class women had no paid help at all during the year preceding the interview, while only four of the thirty-nine women of the business group interviewed had had no help; one of the former group and twenty-five of the latter group had the equivalent of one or more days a week. Both groups of housewives have been affected by the reduction in the number of "old maid" sisters and daughters performing the same duties as domestic servants but without receiving a fixed compensation. Prominent among the factors involved in this diminution of full-time servants are the increased opportunities for women to get a living in other kinds of work; the greater cost of a "hired girl," ten to fifteen dollars a week as against three dollars in 1890; and increased attention to child-rearing, making mothers more careful about the kind of servants they employ. "Every one has the same problem today," said one thoughtful mother. "It is easy to get good girls by the hour but very difficult to get any one good to stay all the time. Then, too, the best type of girl, with whom I feel safe to leave the children, wants to eat with the family." The result is a fortification of the tendency to spend time on the children and transfer other things to service agencies outside the home. A common substitute for a full-time servant today is the woman who "comes in" one or two days a week. A single day's labor of this sort today costs approximately what the housewife's mother paid for a week's work.

Smaller houses, easier to "keep up," labor-saving devices, canned goods, baker's bread, less heavy meals, and ready-made clothing are among the places where the lack of servants is being compensated for and time saved today. Working class housewives repeatedly speak, also, of the use of running water, the shift from wood to coal fires, and the use of linoleum on floors as time-savers. Wives of the business class stress certain non-material changes as well. "I am not as particular as my mother," said many of these housewives, or "I sometimes leave my supper dishes until morning, which my mother would never have thought of doing. She used to do a much more elaborate fall and spring cleaning, which lasted a week or two. I consider time for reading and clubs and my children more important than such careful housework and I just don't do it." These women, on the other hand, mention numerous factors making their work harder than their mothers'. "The constant soot and cinders in this soft-coal city and the hard, alkaline water make up for all you save by new conveniences." A number feel that while the actual physical labor of housework is less and one is less particular about many details, rising standards in other respects use up the saved time. "People are more particular about diet today. They care more about having things nicely served and dressing for dinner. So many things our mothers didn't know about we feel that we ought to do for our children."

Most important among these various factors affecting women's work is the increased use of labor-saving devices. Just as the advent of the Owens machine in one of Middletown's largest plants has unseated a glass-blowing process that had come down largely unchanged from the days of the early

Egyptians, so in the homes of Middletown certain primitive hand skills have been shifted overnight to modern machines. The oil lamp, the gas flare, the broom, the pump, the water bucket, the washboard, the flatiron, the cook stove, all only slightly modified forms of some of man's most primitive tools, dominated Middletown housework in the nineties. In 1924, as noted above, all but 1 per cent. of Middletown's houses were wired for electricity. Between March, 1920, and February, 1924, there was an average increase of 25 per cent. in the K.W.H. [kilowatt hours] of current used by each local family. How this additional current is being used may be inferred from the following record of sales of electrical appliances by five local electrical shops, a prominent drug store, and the local electric power company for the only items it sells, irons and toasters, over the six-month period from May first to October thirty-first, 1923: curlers sold, 1,173; irons, 1,114; vacuum cleaners, 709; toasters, 463; washing machines, 371; heaters, 114; heating pads, 18; electric refrigerators, 11; electric ranges, 3; electric ironers, 1. The manger of the local electric power company estimates that nearly 90 per cent. of Middletown homes have electric irons.

It is in part by compelling advertising couched in terms of certain of women's greatest values that use of these material tools is being so widely diffused:

"Isn't Bobby more important than his clothes?" demands an advertisement of the "Power Laundries" in a Middletown paper.

The advertisment of an electrical company reads:

This is the test of a successful mother—she puts first things first. She does not give to sweeping the time that belongs to her children. . . . Men are judged successful according to their power to delegate work. Similarly the wise woman delegates to electricity all that electricity can do. She cannot delegate the one task most important. Human lives are in her keeping; their future is molded by her hands and heart.

Another laundry advertisement beckons:

Time for sale! Will you buy? Where can you buy back a single yesterday? Nowhere, of course. Yet, right in your city, you can purchase tomorrows. Time for youth and beauty! Time for club work, for church and community activities. Time for books and plays and concerts. Time for home and children. . . .

THOUGHT PROVOKERS

1. Why did anti-foreignism flare up so viciously in the postwar years? Could America have continued indefinitely to allow unlimited immigration? Were Sacco and Vanzetti villains or scapegoats?
2. What was the relation of the revived Ku Klux Klan in the 1920's to the original Klan of Reconstruction days? Why does America periodically spawn violent vigilante-style movements?
3. Was Prohibition a typically American "experiment"? Under what circumstances

does the government have a right to regulate personal behavior, such as drinking alcoholic beverages?

4. In what ways was automobile manufacturing the characteristic industry of early twentieth-century America? How would American life have been different if the internal combustion engine (and hence the automobile) had never been developed?

5. In what ways was the urbanized economic order of the 1920's a "new frontier" for women? How did the spreading practice of birth control reflect changes in the values and styles of family life?

39 · *The Politics of Boom and Bust, 1920 - 1932*

The country is in the midst of an era of prosperity more extensive and of peace more permanent than it has ever before experienced.

PRESIDENT CALVIN COOLIDGE, 1928

PROLOGUE: Warren G. Harding won the presidency by a landslide vote in 1920, campaigning on a promise to return to "normalcy" in the nation's war-strained affairs. As president, Harding soon turned his back on America's recent comrades-in-arms, and made a separate peace with recent enemies. But he responded to pressures from League of Nations advocates and called the Washington Conference on the Limitation of Armament (1921–1922). There the United States secured agreement on limited naval disarmament by making what proved to be costly concessions in the Pacific. Harding was spared the worst embarrassments of his scandal-ridden administration by his death in 1923. Puritanical and tight-lipped Calvin Coolidge succeeded him. Coolidge tried to force the now-unpopular Allies to pay a substantial part of their war debt to the United States, thus aggravating postwar international economic dislocations. Onetime Progressive Herbert Hoover defeated earthy New York Democrat Al Smith for the Presidency in 1928, but his administration was almost immediately engulfed by the steepest and deepest economic downturn in American history.

A. HARDING AND THE WASHINGTON CONFERENCE

1. Harding Hates His Job (*c.* 1922)

The Old Guard Republicans had nominated President Harding largely because he was a second-rater whom they could easily manage. The times, one of them said, did not demand "first-raters." Harding, according to Alice Roosevelt, "was not a bad man. He was just a slob." In beyond his depth, Harding privately moaned that the job was too big for him. William Allen White, the peppery Kansas journalist, visited the White House and talked with the President's secretary, Jud Welliver, an old friend, who (as White remembered it) burst out with the following monologue. What does he identify as Harding's most serious disqualifications for the presidency?

"Lord, Lord, man! You can't know what the President is going through. You see he doesn't understand it; he just doesn't know a thousand things that he ought to know. And he realizes his ignorance, and he is afraid. He has no idea where to turn.

"Not long ago, when the first big tax bill came up, you remember there were two theories of taxation combating for the administration's support. He would listen for an hour to one side, become convinced; and then the other side would get him and overwhelm him with its contentions. Some

1. W. A. White, *Autobiography* (1946), p. 616. By permission of The Macmillan Company.

728

good friend would walk into the White House all cocked and primed with facts and figures to support one side, and another man who he thought perhaps ought to know would reach him with a counter argument which would brush his friend's theory aside.

"I remember he came in here late one afternoon after a long conference, in which both sides appeared, talked at each other, wrangled over him. He was weary and confused and heartsick, for the man really wants to do the right and honest thing. But I tell you, he doesn't know. That afternoon he stood at my desk and looked at me for a moment and began talking out loud:

"'Jud,' he cried, 'you have a college education, haven't you? I don't know what to do or where to turn in this taxation matter. Somewhere there must be a book that tells all about it, where I could go to straighten it out in my mind. But I don't know where the book is, and maybe I couldn't read it if I found it! And there must be a man in the country somewhere who could weigh both sides and know the truth. Probably he is in some college or other. But I don't know where to find him. I don't know who he is, and I don't know how to get him. My God, but this is a hell of a place for a man like me to be!'"

2. Hearst Blasts Disarmament at Washington (1922)

The infant League of Nations was designed in part to bring about disarmament. But with the powerful United States not a cooperating member, a feverish naval race was clattering forward. Rich Uncle Sam, though still slightly behind Britain, could outstrip all others. But the American taxpayers balked, and a popular clamor forced Harding to summon a multi-power conference at Washington for arms limitation. After prolonged wrangling, the conferees agreed that certain capital ships of the major powers—America, Britain, Japan, France, Italy—were to be scrapped and the remainder pegged at a tonnage ratio of 5–5–3–1.7–1.7. The sensitive Japanese were induced to accept an inferior ratio after receiving pledges from America and Britain not to fortify further their Far Eastern bases, including the Philippines and Guam. The surrender of potential (but expensive) naval supremacy by "Uncle Sap" aroused much criticism in America. The influential Hearst newspapers, traditionally anti-Japanese and anti-British, protested vehemently as follows: In what ways does its protest reflect the mood of the age, as revealed in the preceding chapter?

Great Britain and Japan are the ones who gain in this Conference, the ones who are going home satisfied.

England, a naval empire, and Japan, a militaristic empire, have won all the points at the expense of the Republic of France, the Republic of China, the Republic of Russia, and the United States. . . .

We have surrendered Guam and the fortifications of our island possessions, so that the American Navy would have no bases for naval operations in case war should ever be forced upon us.

We have surrendered the naval supremacy that lay within our grasp,

2. *Selections from the Writings and Speeches of William Randolph Hearst* (1948), pp. 193–94. By permission.

and which would always have protected us from any attack by overseas nations. . . .

We have surrendered the adequate development of our merchant marine, and not even the battleships to be put out of commission by the decision of this Conference can be transformed into merchant vessels.

The United States, the one first-class Power of the world, in wealth, in potential strength, in strategic position and condition, has been transformed into distinctly a second-class Power by the subordinate position it has voluntarily taken with regard to England and Japan.

But worst of all is the fact that Japan, by the recognition formally accorded it in this Conference, has been made the dominant nation among the yellow nations of the world, the militaristic leader of a thousand million racial enemies of the white peoples.

Not only the people of the United States but the peoples of Europe, the white race throughout the world, will pay dearly for this act of criminal folly in times to come.

3. Japan Resents the Washington Setback (1922)

If the Japanese won a great diplomatic victory at Washington, they were unaware of it. A Tokyo newspaper (*Yorodzu*) lamented that Uncle Sam, a "hateful and haughty" "international boor," though professing to work for peace, had invited the nations to Washington, where he had "tricked them one and all." Indignant mass meetings were held at various places in Japan. The consensus of the Japanese press was that Britain had gained the most, while Japan had lost the most. Japan was forced to junk the formidable Anglo-Japanese military alliance, which seemed to menace the United States, and accept for the Pacific a weak four-power consultative pact (U.S., Britain, Japan, France). "We have discarded whiskey and accepted water," moaned one Japanese diplomat. What aspect of the conference results rankled the Japanese most deeply?

Our Navy will not have more than 60 percent of the American naval strength hereafter. We must think of some way of improving our relations with America.

Our Government and delegates have brought forth a quadruple agreement [Four Power Pact], replacing the Anglo-Japanese Alliance. It now becomes clear that Japan's claims will not be granted in future without a judgment by the four Powers. Although there are four nations, England is now in a state so that she cannot oppose the will of America. Any decision in a trial of the court of four Powers will be rendered as America sees fit.

Under the circumstances, no Japanese, however optimistic, will have the heart to be optimistic of Japan's future. No one will be able to deny that Japan has [had] her hands and feet cut off in Washington.

We do not advocate pessimistic views by choice. If there be any material by which we can be optimistic, we [should] like to know what it is. If Japan's position has been improved in any way by the Washington Con-

3. Tokyo *Kokumin,* quoted in *Literary Digest,* LXXII, 18 (Jan. 28, 1922).

ference, we [should] like to be informed of it. Reflecting upon Japan, which was thus reduced to a state of blockade on all sides, we cannot but deeply sigh with despair. . . .

American public opinion makes it believed that benefits have been conferred upon Japan. Japan was in a position wherein she was obliged to abandon the Anglo-Japanese Alliance. In place of the Alliance, a quadruple agreement was given to Japan. Thus America has saved Japan's face, American public opinion claims.

By virtue of the quadruple entente, Japan decided not to make an issue out of a race discrimination in America. Our Government and delegates are so magnanimous that they would not raise an issue out of the race discrimination which is insulting to the Japanese race. Nay, our governing classes are never magnanimous. They have never been magnanimous to our countrymen. They are magnanimous to Western peoples. Because they are afraid of Western peoples, they feign to be magnanimous. While being governed by such weak-kneed statesmen, the Japanese race cannot expect to rise above water.

B. DUNNING THE DEBTORS

1. Hoover Opposes Cancellation (1922)

During the war to make the world "safe for democracy," the United States advanced to its associates nearly $10 billion in credits (not gold). The expectation was that these sums would be repaid at 5% interest, although at the time there was some talk of an outright gift. The then deserving Allies were holding back the common enemy while America was belatedly raising an army. When the war ended with the world definitely not "safe for democracy," disillusionment with the "imperialistic" Allies set in. Demands for repayment more than canceled out those for cancellation. Secretary of Commerce Hoover, a hardheaded businessman who shared the current disillusionment, was dead set against cancellation. He was technically right in insisting that the debts were not connected with reparations, but the Allies were counting on reparations from Germany to pay their debts to America. Hoover expressed his views forcefully in this 1922 speech in Toledo. How persuasive is he? What would have been the financial consequences for Americans of cancellation?

Proposals have been repeatedly made over the last three years that the loans from our government to foreign countries during the war should in part or in whole be canceled, either for moral reasons or in the interest of economic stability. Less sweeping proposals have been made that the payments of interest and installments, as required by Congress, should be further postponed or moderated. . . .

These loans are often spoken of as debts to our government. They are, in fact, debts owing to our taxpayers. These loans were made at the urgent request of the borrowers and under their solemn assurance of repayment. The loans were individual to each nation. They have no relation to other

1. *Excerpts from Speeches and Writings of Herbert Hoover* (Hoover-for-President Washington Committee, 1928), pp. 38–39.

UNCLE SAM BECOMES UNCLE SHYLOCK
The Allied debt wrangle changes attitudes. St. Louis
Post-Dispatch, 1926.

nations or other debts [reparations]. The American taxpayer did not participate in reparations and acquired no territory or any other benefits under the treaty, as did our debtors.

There is no question as to the moral or contractual obligation. The repudiation of these loans would undermine the whole fabric of international good faith. I do not believe any public official, either of the United States or any other country, could or should approve their cancellation. Certainly I do not. . . .

America earnestly wishes to be helpful to Europe, but economic matters require a degree of realism that will do justice to the American people, as well as be helpful to peoples abroad.

[*Hoover consistently stressed the theme that if the debts were canceled, the American taxpayer would have to assume the burden (which was all too true), and that the debtors should pay off their obligation with the money they were spending on armaments. The European arms race was largely a product of America's desertion of the Allies; and, as one journal pointed out, no city was going to dismiss its police force to meet payments on its bonded indebtedness.*]

2. Baker Urges Cancellation (1926)

The ex-Allies regarded the debts not as loans but as subsidies to comrades-in-arms. The war-ravaged French argued that they were not asking for their dead soldiers back; America should not ask for her dead dollars back. Washington nevertheless used economic pressure to force the debtors to sign installment-payment agreements spread over sixty-two years. No reduction of the principal sums was granted, but in all cases the interest was lowered from the expected 5%, with a consequent cancellation of a large part of the over-all indebtedness. Americans preened themselves on their generosity, while the Allies complained bitterly about two generations of "USury" to "Uncle $am." Newton D. Baker, who had been Secretary of War under Wilson and was now associated with Cleveland bankers, published the following appeal. Why does he believe that the best interests of both the American bankers and the United States would have been served by an all-around cancellation?

The fact is that not a penny of this money would have been lent by us, or have been borrowed by any of our debtor nations, but for the war. Their need for it arose out of the contributions and sacrifices made by them in the war, and our willingness to supply it arose out of our belief that it was necessary, to our own interest, to sustain their military efficiency until the Armistice, and their economic stability after the Armistice, in order to prevent a collapse which would have cost us vastly more than the money which we supplied.

Nor is it very important to inquire whether, at the time of the making of these so-called loans, there was an expectation that they should be repaid. The question is not what did somebody think in 1917, but what is it wise to think now?

In the modern world, industrial nations are so integrated, by mutual investment and by trade relations, that political isolation is an illusion. . . . The overseas investments of the people of the United States now aggregate perhaps eleven billions of dollars, and we are investing annually overseas at the rate of a billion a year.

Europe to-day is, and long has been, our best customer, consuming of our total exports more than double the amount of any other continent. In a very real sense, therefore, European buying in the world markets is a decisive factor in maintaining the price of our entire home product. It is not conceivable that the rest of the world will continue to trade with us during sixty-two years in which every one of them would have its own industries burdened by crushing taxes.

Every country in the world has had the experience of a vast and hopeless debtor class, and has realized that every so often it is necessary to wipe off the slate and start afresh, as in a Scriptural year of Jubilee. This releases the energies of men, restores hope, cures political disorder, and gives life a fresh start. The analogy applies perfectly to the present international situation. The United States needs, not dollars, but a confident, prosperous, and peaceful world as a field for its industrial and commercial

2. *Trade Winds* (Cleveland), quoted in *Literary Digest*, XC, 10 (Sept. 18, 1926).

operations. That condition cannot be brought about so long as we continue to exact payments up to the capacity of the debtors to pay.

If the foregoing observations are sound, the United States is not justified either in morals, or in a long view of its own best industrial and commercial interests, in adhering to its present policy with regard to the settlement of the inter-allied debts. The time has come when these questions, including the British settlement, ought to be reopened.

Personally, I believe that a mutual cancellation policy will be wise. Such a policy ought to relieve England, France, Italy, Belgium, and the rest of our war allies both as to their debts to us and their debts among themselves, and in turn ought to require the release of some part of the [reparations] burdens imposed upon Germany. This should be done at a round table, where a representative of the United States should be authorized to speak with authority and to demonstrate to the rest of the world that America's interest is not in dollars but in a reconstructed international order.

3. Lippmann Foresees Default (1926)

The debtors, though grumbling, kept up their payments until the early 1930's, when the Great Depression descended with devastating force. Then they all defaulted (save for "brave little Finland") and the debts were dead, except to the American taxpayer and the Treasury bookkeepers. The brilliantly prophetic Walter Lippmann, then on the editorial staff of the New York *World*, predicted what would happen. What are his reasons for believing that the debts would never be paid? Is he correct in distinguishing between war debts and ordinary debts? What additional events of the 1930's and 1940's made for default?

The fundamental reason why these great international war debts cannot be regarded as ordinary debts is that they are dead. They do not represent capital invested in a living enterprise, which produces as it goes along the interest and the principal to repay the money which was loaned. An ordinary debt is productive for the debtor, but these international debts are like bills submitted to pay for the damage done on a wild party by one's grandfather. The payment seems to the debtor like a pure loss, and when it is paid by one nation to another it seems like tribute by the conquered to the conqueror. Money borrowed to build a railroad earns money to pay for itself. But money borrowed to fight a war produces nothing, and if it has to be paid it becomes a dead mortgage superimposed upon all the living credits of a nation.

The United States has engaged itself to collect for the next two generations the sum of $400,000,000 a year on a dead debt. Most of the veterans of the war will be gone. Their children born after the war, knowing no more of its reality than an American college boy knows of the Civil War, will be elderly men, their children in turn will be approaching middle age, and still the huge payments will go on. The last instalments will be paid out of the

3. New York *World*, July 29, 1926.

earnings of the great-grandsons of the men who directed the war. Is it conceivable that for the rest of the century this thing will go on? Does anybody really think he lives in a world where such things are possible?

Let us not deceive ourselves. Mr. Coolidge and Mr. Mellon [Secretary of the Treasury] and Mr. [Senator] Borah and Mr. Baldwin [of Britain] and M. Briand [of France] and the other gentlemen who have made these arrangements will not bind posterity nor mortgage the future in any such fashion as this. To us the war was a great event. But already there is a generation out in the world which has almost no knowledge of it. In a few years those of us who lived through the war will seem like reminiscent old bores to young people who will have many better things to do than hash over the rights and wrongs of 1914–18. Yet here we are deluding ourselves with the preposterous idea that from now until about 1984 people and governments are going to be bothered with carrying out what to them will be perfectly meaningless settlements.

Already Mr. Mellon and Mr. [Winston] Churchill can't quite remember what the money was spent for. The next generation certainly—our own if it is wise—will say in face of the endless bother and animosity that these settlements entail: Let the past be the past, let the dead bury the dead, let us forget, let us forgive, let us have peace.

C. THE DEPRESSION DESCENDS

1. The Plague of Plenty (1932)

In his acceptance speech of 1928, delivered in the Stanford University football stadium, Hoover optimistically envisioned the day when poverty would be banished from America. A popular Republican slogan was "A Chicken in Every Pot, a Car in Every Garage." The next year the stock market collapsed and depression descended. Hoover was a "rugged individualist" who had pulled himself up by his own bootstraps, and he was unwilling to turn Washington into a gigantic soup kitchen for the unemployed. He struggled desperately to halt the Depression, but in general his efforts were too little and too late. To boost morale, he issued a number of cheery statements to the effect that prosperity was just around the corner. The following testimony of a newspaper editor, Oscar Ameringer of Oklahoma City, was given in 1932 before a House committee. What is particularly paradoxical about the situation he describes?

During the last three months I have visited, as I have said, some twenty states of this wonderfully rich and beautiful country. Here are some of the things I heard and saw:

In the state of Washington I was told that the forest fires raging in that region all summer and fall were caused by unemployed timber workers and bankrupt farmers in an endeavor to earn a few honest dollars as fire-fighters. The last thing I saw on the night I left Seattle was numbers of

---

1. *Unemployment in the United States. Hearings before a Subcommittee of the Committee on Labor, House of Representatives, Seventy-second Congress, First Session, on H. R. 206 . . .* (1932), pp. 98–99.

TWO CHICKENS IN EVERY GARAGE

The "Hoover Depression" brought a parody of the Republican slogan
of 1928: "A chicken in every pot and two cars in every garage."
Reprinted courtesy New York *World-Telegram,* copyright 1932.

women searching for scraps of food in the refuse piles of the principal
market of that city. A number of Montana citizens told me of thousands
of bushels of wheat left in the fields uncut on account of its low price
that hardly paid for the harvesting. In Oregon I saw thousands of bushels
of apples rotting in the orchards. Only absolute[ly] flawless apples were
still salable, at from 40 to 50 cents a box containing 200 apples. At the
same time, there are millions of children who, on account of the poverty
of their parents, will not eat one apple this winter.

While I was in Oregon the Portland *Oregonian* bemoaned the fact that
thousands of ewes were killed by the sheep raisers because they did not
bring enough in the market to pay the freight on them. And while Oregon
sheep raisers fed mutton to the buzzards, I saw men picking for meat scraps
in the garbage cans in the cities of New York and Chicago. I talked to one
man in a restaurant in Chicago. He told me of his experience in raising
sheep. He said that he had killed 3,000 sheep this fall and thrown them
down the canyon, because it cost $1.10 to ship a sheep, and then he would

get less than a dollar for it. He said he could not afford to feed the sheep, and he would not let them starve, so he just cut their throats and threw them down the canyon.

The roads of the West and Southwest teem with hungry hitchhikers. The camp fires of the homeless are seen along every railroad track. I saw men, women, and children walking over the hard roads. Most of them were tenant farmers who had lost their all in the late slump in wheat and cotton. Between Clarksville and Russellville, Ark., I picked up a family. The woman was hugging a dead chicken under a ragged coat. When I asked her where she had procured the fowl, first she told me she had found it dead in the road, and then added in grim humor, "They promised me a chicken in the pot, and now I got mine."

In Oklahoma, Texas, Arkansas, and Louisiana I saw untold bales of cotton rotting in the fields because the cotton pickers could not keep body and soul together on 35 cents paid for picking 100 pounds. . . .

As a result of this appalling overproduction on the one side and the staggering underconsumption on the other side, 70 per cent of the farmers of Oklahoma were unable to pay the interests on their mortgages. Last week one of the largest and oldest mortgage companies in that state went into the hands of the receiver. In that and other states we have now the interesting spectacle of farmers losing their farms by foreclosure and mortgage companies losing their recouped holdings by tax sales.

The farmers are being pauperized by the poverty of industrial populations, and the industrial populations are being pauperized by the poverty of the farmers. Neither has the money to buy the product of the other, hence we have overproduction and underconsumption at the same time and in the same country.

I have not come here to stir you in a recital of the necessity for relief for our suffering fellow citizens. However, unless something is done for them and done soon, you will have a revolution on hand. And when that revolution comes it will not come from Moscow, it will not be made by the poor Communists whom our police are heading up regularly and efficiently. When the revolution comes it will bear the label "Laid in the U.S.A." and its chief promoters will be the people of American stock.

2. Distress in the South (1932)

As the Depression deepened, "Hooverville" shack towns sprang up and millions of footsore men sought non-existent jobs. Some sold apples on wind-swept street corners. Hoover, in his *Memoirs*, advances the improbable thesis that these people were exploited by the apple producers and that "Many persons left their jobs for the more profitable one of selling apples." Blacks—"the last hired and the first fired"— were especially hard hit, but the white sharecropper in the South was scarcely better off.

2. *Unemployment Relief. Hearings before a Subcommittee of the Committee on Manufactures, United States Senate, Seventy-second Congress, First Session, on S. 174* . . . (1932), pp. 244–45.

Hoover's policy was that "no one shall starve in this country," but he was criticized for being more willing to use federal funds to supply seed for farmers and feed for animals than food for human beings. Congressman George Huddleston of Alabama thus described conditions in his state before a Senate committee. What kinds of physical and psychic scars were inflicted by the conditions he describes?

We have a great many tenant farmers there [Alabama]. We have a great many Negro farmers, and practically all of them are tenants. Their ability to survive, to eat, to have a shelter, depends upon the ability of the landlord to supply them with the necessaries of life. They have a system under which they make a contract with the landlord to cultivate his land for the next year, and in the meantime he feeds them through the winter; and at the end of the year they gather their crops and pay for their supplies and rent, if they are able to do so. Conditions in agriculture have been such for several years that the landlords have been gradually impoverished, and their farms are mortgaged to the farm-loan system and to the mortgage companies in a multitude of instances.

In a very large percentage [of cases] the landlord is now unable to finance these tenants for another year. He is unable to get the supplies. He has no security and no money with which to feed and clothe his tenants until they can make another crop. . . .

Many of these people, especially the Negro tenants, are now in the middle of a winter, practically without food and without clothes, and without anything else, and how are they going to live? Many of these local counties have no charitable organizations. They are poor people and impoverished. They have no county funds. There is no place to turn, nobody that has any money that they can turn to and ask for help.

Many white people are in the same kind of a situation. They beg around among their neighbors. The neighbors are poor and they have no means of helping them. They stray here and there.

Any thought that there has been no starvation, that no man has starved, and no man will starve, is the rankest nonsense. Men are actually starving by the thousands to-day, not merely in the general sections that I refer to, but throughout this country as a whole, and in my own district. I do not mean to say that they are sitting down and not getting a bite of food until they actually die, but they are living such a scrambling, precarious existence, with suffering from lack of clothing, fuel, and nourishment, until they are subject to be swept away at any time, and many are now being swept away.

The situation has possibilities of epidemics of various kinds. Its consequences will be felt many years. The children are being stunted by lack of food. Old people are having their lives cut short. The physical effects of the privations that they are forced to endure will not pass away within fifty years, and when the social and civic effects will pass away, only God knows. That is something that no man can estimate.

3. Rumbles of Revolution (1932)

Franklin Roosevelt was later acclaimed as the Messiah whose New Deal saved America for capitalism by averting armed revolution. He was quoted as saying that if he failed he would not be the worst but the last President of the United States. Certainly in 1932 the signs were ominous. Hundreds of Middle Western farmers were picketing the highways to keep their underpriced produce from reaching market, overturning milk trucks, overawing armed deputies, releasing prisoners from jail. With increasing millions of desperate men out of work, and with thousands defying the police, the worst might have happened. The testimony of Oscar Ameringer, the Oklahoma newspaperman, is impressive. Does it confirm that the talk of revolution was to be taken seriously?

Some time ago a cowman came into my office in Oklahoma City. He was one of these double-fisted gentlemen, with the gallon hat and all. He said, "You do not know me from Adam's ox."

I said, "No; I do not believe I know you." . . .

He said, "I came to this country without a cent, but, knowing my onions, and by tending strictly to business, I finally accumulated two sections of land and a fine herd of white-faced Hereford cattle. I was independent."

I remarked that anybody could do that if he worked hard and did not gamble and used good management.

He said, "After the war, cattle began to drop, and I was feeding them corn, and by the time I got them to Chicago the price of cattle, considering the price of corn I had fed them, was not enough to even pay my expenses. I could not pay anything."

Continuing, he said, "I mortgaged my two sections of land, and to-day I am cleaned out; by God, I am not going to stand for it."

I asked him what he was going to do about it, and he said, "We have got to have a revolution here like they had in Russia and clean them up."

I finally asked him, "Who is going to make the revolution?"

He said, "I just want to tell you I am going to be one of them, and I am going to do my share in it."

I asked what his share was and he said, "I will capture a certain fort. I know I can get in with twenty of my boys," meaning his cowboys, "because I know the inside and outside of it, and I [will] capture that with my men."

I rejoined, "Then what?"

He said, "We will have 400 machine guns, so many batteries of artillery, tractors, and munitions and rifles, and everything else needed to supply a pretty good army."

Then I asked, "What then?"

He said, "If there are enough fellows with guts in this country to do like us, we will march eastward and we will cut the East off. We will cut the

3. *Unemployment in the United States. Hearings before a Subcommittee of the Committee on Labor, House of Representatives, Seventy-second Congress, First Session, on H. R. 206 . . .* (1932), pp. 100–01.

East off from the West. We have got the granaries; we have the hogs, the cattle, the corn; the East has nothing but mortgages on our places. We will show them what we can do."

That man may be very foolish, and I think he is, but he is in dead earnest; he is a hard-shelled Baptist and a hard-shelled Democrat, not a Socialist or a Communist, but just a plain American cattleman whose ancestors went from Carolina to Tennessee, then to Arkansas, and then to Oklahoma. I have heard much of this talk from serious-minded prosperous men of other days.

As you know, talk is always a mental preparation for action. Nothing is done until people talk and talk and talk. it, and they finally get the notion that they will do it.

I do not say we are going to have a revolution on hand within the next year or two, perhaps never. I hope we may not have such; but the danger is here. That is the feeling of our people—as reflected in the letters I have read. I have met these people virtually every day all over the country. There is a feeling among the masses generally that something is radically wrong. They are despairing of political action. They say the only thing you do in Washington is to take money from the pockets of the poor and put it into the pockets of the rich. They say that this Government is a conspiracy against the common people to enrich the already rich. I hear such remarks every day.

I never pass a hitchhiker without inviting him in and talking to him. Bankers even are talking about that. They are talking in irrational tones. You have more Bolshevism among the bankers to-day than the hod carriers, I think. It is a terrible situation, and I think something should be done and done immediately.

D. HOOVER CLASHES WITH ROOSEVELT

1. On Public versus Private Power

a. Hoover Upholds Free Enterprise (1932)

Hoover, the wealthy conservative, instinctively shied away from anything suggesting socialism. In 1931 he emphatically vetoed the Muscle Shoals Bill, which would have put the federal government in the electric power business on the Tennessee River. (An expanded version later created the Tennessee Valley Authority [TVA] under President Roosevelt.) Hoover ringingly reaffirmed his basic position in a speech during the Hoover–Roosevelt presidential campaign of 1932. Why is he so strongly opposed to federally owned electric power? Why would he find local community ownership more acceptable?

I have stated unceasingly that I am opposed to the Federal Government going into the power business. I have insisted upon rigid regulation. The

1a. New York *Times*, Nov. 1, 1932 (speech at Madison Square Garden, New York, Oct. 31, 1932).

HOOVER'S CONSOLATION

The Republicans argued that a less experienced Democratic "driver" might have fared still worse. Omaha *World-Herald*, 1932.

Democratic candidate has declared that under the same conditions which may make local action of this character desirable, he is prepared to put the Federal Government into the power business. He is being actively supported by a score of Senators in this campaign, many of whose expenses are being paid by the Democratic National Committee, who are pledged to Federal Government development and operation of electrical power.

I find in the instructions to campaign speakers issued by the Democratic National Committee that they are instructed to criticize my action in the veto of the bill which would have put the Government permanently into the operation of power at Muscle Shoals, with a capital from the Federal Treasury of over $100,000,000. In fact thirty-one Democratic Senators, being all except three, voted to override that veto.

In that bill was the flat issue of the Federal Government permanently in competitive business. I vetoed it because of principle and not because it especially applied to power business. In that veto, I stated that I was firmly opposed to the Federal Government entering into any business, the major purpose of which is competition with our citizens. . . .

From their utterances in this campaign and elsewhere it appears to me that we are justified in the conclusion that our opponents propose to put the Federal Government in the power business.

b. Roosevelt Pushes Public Power (1932)

Franklin Roosevelt, who as governor of New York had shown much concern for the Niagara–St. Lawrence River power resources, had already locked horns with the private utility magnates. As President, he later had a large hand in launching the TVA project, which also involved fertilizer, flood control, and improved navigation. He presented his views on public power as follows during the campaign of 1932. Are his arguments more convincing than Hoover's?

I therefore lay down the following principle: That where a community— a city or county or a district—is not satisfied with the service rendered or the rates charged by the private utility, it has the undeniable basic right, as one of its functions of government, one of its functions of home rule, to set up, after a fair referendum to its voters has been had, its own governmentally owned and operated service. . . .

My distinguished opponent is against giving the Federal Government, in any case, the right to operate its own power business. I favor giving the people this right where and when it is essential to protect them against inefficient service or exorbitant charges.

As an important part of this policy, the natural hydro-electric power resources belonging to the people of the United States, or the several States, shall remain forever in their possession.

To the people of this country I have but one answer on this subject. Judge me by the enemies I have made. Judge me by the selfish purposes of these utility leaders who have talked of radicalism while they were selling watered stock to the people, and using our schools to deceive the coming generation.

My friends, my policy is as radical as American liberty. My policy is as radical as the Constitution of the United States.

I promise you this: Never shall the Federal Government part with its sovereignty or with its control over its power resources, while I am President of the United States.

2. On Government in Business

a. Hoover Assails Federal Intervention (1932)

Hoover's conservative nature recoiled from the prospect of government in business, especially on the scale envisaged by the TVA. Annoyed by Democratic charges that he was a complete reactionary, he struck back in a major campaign speech at Madison Square Garden. Laboriously written by himself (he was the last President to scorn ghost writers), it was perhaps the best-conceived of his campaign. "Every time the Federal Government extends its arm," he declared, "531 Senators and Congressmen become actual boards of directors of that business." What truth is there in his charge that government in business invites a species of servitude?

1b. *Roosevelt's Public Papers,* I, 738, 741–42 (speech at Portland, Oregon, Sept. 21, 1932). By permission of Random House.

2a. New York *Times,* Nov. 1, 1932 (speech at Madison Square Garden, New York, Oct. 31, 1932).

There is one thing I can say without any question of doubt—that is, that the spirit of liberalism is to create free men. It is not the regimentation of men. It is not the extension of bureaucracy. I have said in this city [New York] before now that you can not extend the mastery of government over the daily life of a people without somewhere making it master of people's souls and thoughts.

Expansion of government in business means that the Government, in order to protect itself from the political consequences of its errors, is driven irresistibly, without peace, to greater and greater control of the Nation's press and platform. Free speech does not live many hours after free industry and free commerce die.

It is a false liberalism that interprets itself into Government operation of business. Every step in that direction poisons the very roots of liberalism. It poisons political equality, free speech, free press, and equality of opportunity. It is the road not to liberty but to less liberty. True liberalism is found not in striving to spread bureaucracy, but in striving to set bounds to it. . . .

Even if the Government conduct of business could give us the maximum of efficiency instead of least efficiency, it would be purchased at the cost of freedom. It would increase rather than decrease abuse and corruption, stifle initiative and invention, undermine development of leadership, cripple mental and spiritual energies of our people, extinguish equality of opportunity, and dry up the spirit of liberty and progress.

Men who are going about this country announcing that they are liberals because of their promises to extend the Government in business are not liberals; they are reactionaries of the United States.

b. Roosevelt Attacks Business in Government (1932)

The Reconstruction Finance Corporation (R.F.C.), established late in the Hoover administration, was designed primarily to bail out hard-pressed banks and other big businesses—"a bread line for bankers." Charles G. Dawes, former Vice-President of the United States, hastily resigned as the head of the R.F.C. so that his Chicago bank might secure an emergency loan of $80,000,000 to stave off bankruptcy. The Democrats, who argued that loans to ordinary citizens were no less imperative, attacked this presumed favoritism. How well does Roosevelt, in the following campaign speech, refute the Republican philosophy of separating government and business?

Some of my friends tell me that they do not want the Government in business. With this I agree; but I wonder whether they realize the implications of the past. For while it has been American doctrine that the Government must not go into business in competition with private enterprises, still it has been traditional, particularly in Republican administrations, for business urgently to ask the Government to put at private disposal all kinds of Government assistance.

2b. *Roosevelt's Public Papers*, I, 748 (Commonwealth Club speech, San Francisco, Sept. 23, 1932). By permission of Random House.

The same man who tells you that he does not want to see the Government interfere in business—and he means it, and has plenty of good reasons for saying so—is the first to go to Washington and ask the Government for a prohibitory tariff on his product. When things get just bad enough, as they did two years ago, he will go with equal speed to the United States Government and ask for a loan; and the Reconstruction Finance Corporation is the outcome of it.

Each group has sought protection from the Government for its own special interests, without realizing that the function of Government must be to favor no small group at the expense of its duty to protect the rights of personal freedom and of private property of all its citizens.

3. On Balancing the Budget

a. Hoover Stresses Economy (1932)

Hoover, the Iowa orphan, was dedicated to strict economy, a sound dollar, and the balanced budget. He was alarmed by proposals in the Democratic House to unbalance the budget further by voting huge sums to provide jobs for the unemployed. One proposed public works scheme called for the construction of 2300 new post offices. The upkeep and interest charges on these would cost $14,000,000 a year, whereas, as he noted, "the upkeep and rent of buildings at present in use amounts to less than $3,000,000." Hoover unburdened himself as follows at a press conference. In the light of subsequent developments, does he overstress the effects of an unbalanced budget in relation to uneconomical public works? (Since 1932 the federal Treasury has more often than not shown an annual deficit.)

The urgent question today is the prompt balancing of the Budget. When that is accomplished, I propose to support adequate measures for relief of distress and unemployment.

In the meantime, it is essential that there should be an understanding of the character of the draft bill made public yesterday in the House of Representatives for this purpose. That draft bill supports some proposals we have already made in aid to unemployment, through the use of the Reconstruction Finance Corporation, to make loans for projects which have been in abeyance and which proposal makes no drain on the taxpayer. But in addition it proposes to expend about $900,000,000 for Federal public works.

I believe the American people will grasp the economic fact that such action would require appropriations to be made to the Federal Departments, thus creating a deficit in the Budget that could only be met with more taxes and more Federal bond issues. That makes balancing of the Budget hopeless.

The country also understands that an unbalanced budget means the loss of confidence of our own people and of other nations in the credit and stability of the Government, and that the consequences are national

3a. New York *Times*, May 28, 1932 (Washington press conference of May 27, 1932).

demoralization and the loss of ten times as many jobs as would be created by this program, even if it could be physically put into action. . . .

This is not unemployment relief. It is the most gigantic pork barrel ever proposed to the American Congress. It is an unexampled raid on the public Treasury.

b. Roosevelt Stresses Humanity (1932)

The Democratic platform of 1932, which assailed Republican extravagance and deficits, had come out squarely for a balanced budget. A favorite slogan of the Democrats was "Throw the Spenders Out." When Roosevelt died thirteen years later, the national debt (including war costs) had risen from some $19 billion to $258 billion. During the campaign of 1932 Roosevelt expressed his views on a balanced budget as follows. In light of these views, does his later record constitute a breach of faith with the voters?

Let us have the courage to stop borrowing to meet continuing deficits. Stop the deficits! Let us have equal courage to reverse the policy of the Republican leaders and insist on a sound currency. . . .

This dilemma can be met by saving in one place what we would spend in others, or by acquiring the necessary revenue through taxation. Revenues must cover expenditures by one means or another. Any Government, like any family, can for a year spend a little more than it earns. But you and I know that a continuation of that habit means the poorhouse. . . .

The above two categorical statements are aimed at a definite balancing of the budget. At the same time, let me repeat from now to election day so that every man, woman, and child in the United States will know what I mean: If starvation and dire need on the part of any of our citizens make necessary the appropriation of additional funds which would keep the budget out of balance, I shall not hesitate to tell the American people the full truth and ask them to authorize the expenditure of that additional amount.

4. On Restricted Opportunity

a. Roosevelt Urges Welfare Statism (1932)

"Why Change?" cried Republicans in the campaign of 1932. "Things Could Be Worse." A slight business upturn did occur in the summer, but a sag soon followed, owing, claimed Hoover, to fear of a Rooseveltian revolution. Roosevelt himself jeered that the "No Change" argument was like saying, "Do not swap toboggans while you are sliding downhill." He set forth his own concept of change in his memorable Commonwealth Club speech in San Francisco. Is his argument regarding the over-building of America's industrial plant sound in the light of subsequent history?

3b. *Roosevelt's Public Papers*, I, 662, 663, 810. (The first two paragraphs are taken from a radio address from Albany, July 30, 1932; the last paragraph is taken from a speech at Pittsburgh, Oct. 19, 1932.) By permission of Random House.
4a. *Ibid.*, I, 750–53 (speech of Sept. 23, 1932). By permission of Random House.

A glance at the situation today only too clearly indicates that equality of opportunity, as we have known it, no longer exists. Our industrial plant is built; the problem just now is whether under existing conditions it is not overbuilt.

Our last frontier has long since been reached, and there is practically no more free land. More than half of our people do not live on the farms or on lands, and cannot derive a living by cultivating their own property. There is no safety valve in the form of a Western prairie, to which those thrown out of work by the Eastern economic machines can go for a new start.° We are not able to invite the immigration from Europe to share our endless plenty. We are now providing a drab living for our own people. . . .

Recently a careful study was made of the concentration of business in the United States. It showed that our economic life was dominated by some six hundred odd corporations, who controlled two-thirds of American industry. Ten million small business men divided the other third. More striking still, it appeared that if the process of concentration goes on at the same rate, at the end of another century we shall have all American industry controlled by a dozen corporations, and run by perhaps a hundred men. Put plainly, we are steering a steady course toward economic oligarchy, if we are not there already.

Clearly, all this calls for a re-appraisal of values. A mere builder of more industrial plants, a creator of more railroad systems, an organizer of more corporations, is as likely to be a danger as a help. The day of the great promoter or the financial Titan, to whom we granted anything if only he would build, or develop, is over.

Our task now is not discovery or exploitation of natural resources, or necessarily producing more goods. It is the soberer, less dramatic business of administering resources and plants already in hand, of seeking to re-establish foreign markets for our surplus production, of meeting the problem of underconsumption, of adjusting production to consumption, of distributing wealth and products more equitably, of adapting existing economic organizations to the service of the people. The day of enlightened administration has come.

b. Hoover Calls for New Frontiers (1932)

Roosevelt's annoying vagueness prompted Hoover to refer to "a chameleon on plaid." Smarting from the New Dealish overtones of the Commonwealth Club speech, Hoover struck back in his Madison Square Garden speech. Does he interpret America's past and future with greater accuracy than Roosevelt did?

But I do challenge the whole idea that we have ended the advance of America, that this country has reached the zenith of its power, the height of its development. That is the counsel of despair for the future of America.

° For the safety-valve notion, see note, p. 539.
4b. New York *Times*, Nov. 1, 1932 (speech at Madison Square Garden, New York, Oct. 31, 1932).

1932's SOAP BOX

The Republicans shift ground from 1928 to 1932. St. Louis
Post-Dispatch, 1932.

That is not the spirit by which we shall emerge from this depression. That is
not the spirit that made this country. If it is true, every American must abandon the road of countless progress and unlimited opportunity. I deny that
the promise of American life has been fulfilled, for that means we have
begun the decline and fall. No nation can cease to move forward without
degeneration of spirit.

I could quote from gentlemen who have emitted this same note of
pessimism in economic depressions going back for a hundred years. What
Governor Roosevelt has overlooked is the fact that we are yet but on the
frontiers of development of science, and of invention. I have only to remind
you that discoveries in electricity, the internal-combustion engine, the radio
—all of which have sprung into being since our land was settled—have in
themselves represented the greatest advances in America.

This philosophy upon which the Governor of New York proposes to
conduct the Presidency of the United States is the philosophy of stagnation,
of despair. It is the end of hope. The destinies of this country should not
be dominated by that spirit in action. It would be the end of the American
system.

E. AN APPRAISAL OF HOOVER

1. Hoover Defends His Record (1932)

Hoover smarted under charges that he had not fought the "Hoover depression" with every ounce of energy for the benefit of all the people. Such accusations, he asserted, were "deliberate, intolerable falsehoods." At times he put in an eighteen-hour day, remarking that his office was a "compound hell." When he spoke wearily at St. Paul during the last stages of the campaign of 1932, a man was stationed behind him ready to thrust forward an empty chair if he collapsed. In a major speech at Des Moines, Iowa, he thus refuted charges that he was a "see-nothing, do-nothing President." What is the least convincing part of this recital?

We have fought an unending war against the effect of these calamities upon our people. This is no time to recount the battles on a thousand fronts. We have fought the good fight to protect our people in a thousand cities from hunger and cold.

We have carried on an unceasing campaign to protect the Nation from that unhealing class bitterness which arises from strikes and lockouts and industrial conflict. We have accomplished this through the willing agreement of employer and labor, which placed humanity before money through the sacrifice of profits and dividends before wages.

We have defended millions from the tragic result of droughts.

We have mobilized a vast expansion of public construction to make work for the unemployed.

We [have] fought the battle to balance the Budget.

We have defended the country from being forced off the gold standard, with its crushing effect upon all who are in debt.

We have battled to provide a supply of credits to merchants and farmers and industries.

We have fought to retard falling prices.

We have struggled to save homes and farms from foreclosure of mortgages; battled to save millions of depositors and borrowers from the ruin caused by the failure of banks; fought to assure the safety of millions of policyholders from failure of their insurance companies; and fought to save commerce and employment from the failure of railways.

We have fought to secure disarmament and maintain the peace of the world; fought for stability of other countries whose failure would inevitably injure us. And, above all, we have fought to preserve the safety, the principles, and ideals of American life. We have builded the foundations of recovery. . . .

Thousands of our people in their bitter distress and losses today are saying that "things could not be worse." No person who has any remote understanding of the forces which confronted this country during these last eighteen months ever utters that remark. Had it not been for the immediate and unprecedented actions of our government, things would be infinitely worse today.

1. *Ibid.*, Oct. 5, 1932 (speech of Oct. 4, 1932).

2. Roosevelt Indicts Hoover (1932)

Roosevelt did not use kid gloves in his ghostwritten campaign speeches. (That at Topeka represented his own efforts and those of some twenty-five assistants.) Although crediting Hoover with "unremitting efforts," he assailed him for having claimed credit for prosperity while disclaiming discredit for the Depression; for having placed the blame for the Depression on wicked foreigners instead of on shortsighted Republican economic policies; for having marked time and issued airily optimistic statements when he should have grasped the bull by the horns. At Pittsburgh, Roosevelt cried, "I do indict this Administration for wrong action, for delayed action, for lack of frankness and for lack of courage." At Columbus, Ohio, he presented the following bill of particulars. What is the unfairest part of his indictment?

Finally, when facts could no longer be ignored and excuses had to be found, Washington discovered that the depression came from abroad. In October of last year, the official policy came to us as follows: "The depression has been deepened by events from abroad which are beyond the control either of our citizens or our Government"—an excuse, note well, my friends, which the President still maintained in his acceptance speech last week.

Not for partisan purposes, but in order to set forth history aright, that excuse ought to be quietly considered. The records of the civilized Nations of the world prove two facts: first, that the economic structure of other Nations was affected by our own tide of speculation, and the curtailment of our lending helped to bring on their distress; second, that the bubble burst first in the land of its origin—the United States.

The major collapse in other countries followed. It was not simultaneous with ours. Moreover, further curtailment of our loans, plus the continual stagnation in trade caused by the Grundy [Hawley-Smoot] tariff, has continued the depression throughout international affairs.

So I sum up the history of the present Administration in four sentences:

First, it encouraged speculation and overproduction, through its false economic policies.

Second, it attempted to minimize the [1929 stock market] crash and misled the people as to its gravity.

Third, it erroneously charged the cause to other Nations of the world.

And finally, it refused to recognize and correct the evils at home which had brought it forth; it delayed relief; it forgot reform.

THOUGHT PROVOKERS

1. What lessons does the Washington disarmament conference of 1921–1922 hold for arms-control negotiators?
2. Was the United States justified in insisting on repayment of loans made to the Allies during the war? Would it have been wiser for the United States to have foregone its legal "rights" in this case?

2. *Roosevelt's Public Papers*, I, 677 (speech of Aug. 20, 1932). By permission of Random House.

3. What puzzled people most about the impact of the Great Depression? Who was hardest hit? Why was there not more radicalism in Depression-era America?
4. Hoover was a former associate of Woodrow Wilson, as was Franklin Roosevelt. In what ways might they both be considered "Wilsonians"? What were the sharpest differences between them?
5. No man in America had a higher reputation than Hoover in the 1920's, and none rated lower in public esteem in early 1930's. Was this reversal of public opinion justified? Should Hoover be admired for the constancy of his beliefs, even when under severe criticism?

40 · *The Great Depression and the New Deal*

I pledge you, I pledge myself, to a new deal for the American people.
FRANKLIN D. ROOSEVELT, ACCEPTING NOMINATION
OF DEMOCRATIC NATIONAL CONVENTION, 1932

PROLOGUE: Roosevelt boldly set up numerous New Deal agencies to provide relief, recovery, and reform. Ignored were the campaign pledges that he would reduce government expenses, balance the budget, prune the bureaucracy, maintain a sound currency, and eliminate the improper use of money in politics. But Roosevelt honored other promises, directly or indirectly, in the reciprocal tariff program, the Tennessee Valley Authority, the repeal of prohibition, the insurance of bank deposits, and the encouragement of labor unions. Critics of the New Deal cried that Roosevelt promoted class hatred by setting the poor against the rich. New Dealers retorted that they were merely putting need above greed. The voters endorsed Roosevelt so resoundingly at the polls in 1934 and 1936 that he was emboldened to unveil his scheme for "packing" the Supreme Court in 1937. Although soundly rebuffed, he won an unprecedented third-term election in 1940, with a strong assist from the crisis in Europe and a new war-born prosperity.

A. AN ENIGMA IN THE WHITE HOUSE

1. The Agreeable F.D.R. (1949)

The gay, smiling, wisecracking Franklin Roosevelt could occasionally be brutal when he got his "Dutch up," but ordinarily he recoiled from hurting people's feelings. Senator Huey Long complained, "I wonder if he says 'Fine!' to everybody." This trait of ultra-agreeableness led visitors to suspect a lack of candor and truthfulness. In the following account from Mrs. Roosevelt's memoirs, note particularly why the President was often misunderstood.

The few books that have already been written about Franklin show quite plainly that everyone writes from his own point of view, and that a man like my husband, who was particularly susceptible to people, took color from whomever he was with, giving to each one something different of himself. Because he disliked being disagreeable, he made an effort to give each person who came in contact with him the feeling that he understood what his particular interest was. . . .

Often people have told me that they were misled by Franklin. Even

1. Eleanor Roosevelt, *This I Remember* (1949), p. 2. By permission of Harper and Row, Publishers, Inc.

when they have not said it in so many words, I have sometimes felt that he left them, after an interview, with the idea that he was in entire agreement with them. I would know quite well, however, that he was not, and that they would be very much surprised when later his actions were in complete contradiction to what they thought his attitude would be.

This misunderstanding not only arose from his dislike of being disagreeable, but from the interest that he always had in somebody else's point of view and his willingness to listen to it. If he thought it was well expressed and clear, he nodded his head and frequently said, "I see," or something of the sort. This did not mean that he was convinced of the truth of the arguments, or even that he entirely understood them, but only that he appreciated the way in which they were presented.

2. Coffee for the Veterans (1933)

In 1932, during Hoover's last year as President, some 30,000 unemployed veterans had descended upon Washington to obtain advance bonus payments from Congress. They occupied vacant buildings, erected makeshift camps without proper sanitation, and posed a threat to the public health and safety. A fearful Hoover, having doubled the White House guard, finally gave orders that resulted in their eviction by federal troops with bayonets, tear gas, and torches. A second, smaller bonus army came early in the Roosevelt administration, and Secretary of Labor Frances Perkins (the first woman Cabinet member) describes how Roosevelt welcomed them. How do the political instincts of Roosevelt compare with those of Hoover?

Like other kindhearted, liberal people, Roosevelt had been shocked by President Hoover's orders to drive veterans of World War I out of Anacostia Flats in Washington and to burn their encampment when they had marched there in protest in 1931 [1932]. He had been shocked that the President should fear his fellow citizens. His instinct had cried out that veterans in an illegal encampment in Washington, even if difficult and undesirable, must all be faced in a humane and decent way. He had said little, had just shaken his head and shuddered, when the incident took place.

When the veterans came to Washington in March 1933, in a similar, if smaller, march on the capital followed by an encampment, Roosevelt drove out and showed himself, waving his hat at them. He asked Mrs. Roosevelt and Louis Howe to go. "Above all," he said to them, "be sure there is plenty of good coffee. No questions asked. Just let free coffee flow all the time. There is nothing like it to make people feel better and feel welcome."

After the veterans in 1933 had the free coffee and a visit from Mrs. Roosevelt, they were willing to send a committee to talk with Howe. Gradually they began to go home, and relief funds were found to help them start back.

[*This was the last demonstration of its kind during these years.*]

2. Selection from *The Roosevelt I Knew*, pp. 111–12, by Frances Perkins. Copyright © 1946 by Frances Perkins; renewed 1974 by Susanna W. Coggeshall. Reprinted by permission of Viking Penguin Inc.

3. F.D.R. the Administrative "Artist" (1948)

The numerous and overlapping agencies of the New Deal created an atmosphere of indescribable confusion. Roosevelt was generally reputed to be a wretchedly bad administrator. Rather than face a disagreeable scene by dismissing an incompetent subordinate, he would set up a competing agency. Robert E. Sherwood, playwright and winner of three Pulitzer prizes, served with a government agency (Office of War Information) during World War II. He was forced to discharge one of his employees, and he here tells what happened when he reported this unpleasant incident to the President. In what sense was Roosevelt both a poor administrator and a superior one?

Roosevelt now had an expression of open amazement and said, "I can't believe it. I can't believe you had the courage to fire anybody. I thought you were a complete softy—like me."

That scrap of highly unimportant conversation can indicate why those who knew Roosevelt well could never imagine him assuming the role of dictator. He could be and was ruthless and implacable with those whom he considered guilty of disloyalty; but with those in his Administration who were inefficient or even recalcitrant or hopelessly inept, but loyal, he was "a complete softy." He wasted precious hours of time and incalculable quantities of energy and ingenuity trying to find face-saving jobs—or "kicking upstairs" methods—for incompetents who should have been thrown out unceremoniously.

Roosevelt's methods of administration—typified in his handling of the work relief organization—were, to say the least, unorthodox. They filled some practical-minded observers with apprehension and dismay, and some with disgust; they filled others with awe and wonder. I am sure that no final appraisal of them can be made for a long time to come; but there is one thing that can be said about these methods—whether they were good or bad, sensible or insane, they *worked.*

While preparing this book I interviewed Harold Smith, who was Director of the Budget from 1939 to 1946. Smith was a modest, methodical, precise man, temperamentally far removed from Roosevelt and Hopkins. But I know of no one whose judgment and integrity and downright common sense the President trusted more completely. In the course of a long conversation, Smith said to me:

"A few months ago, on the first anniversary of Roosevelt's death, a magazine asked me to write an article on Roosevelt as an administrator. I thought it over and decided I was not ready to make such an appraisal. I've been thinking about it ever since. When I worked with Roosevelt—for six years—I thought, as did many others, that he was a very erratic administrator. But now, when I look back, I can really begin to see the size of his programs. They were by far the largest and most complex programs that any President ever put through. People like me who had the respon-

3. From pp. 72–73 in *Roosevelt and Hopkins* by Robert E. Sherwood. Copyright 1948 by Robert E. Sherwood. By permission of Harper & Row, Publishers, Inc.

sibility of watching the pennies could only see the five or six or seven per cent of the programs that went wrong, through inefficient organization or direction. But now I can see in perspective the ninety-three or -four or -five per cent that went right—including the winning of the biggest war in history—because of unbelievably skillful organization and direction. And if I were to write that article now, I think I'd say that Roosevelt must have been one of the greatest geniuses as an administrator that ever lived. What we couldn't appreciate at the time was the fact that he was a real *artist* in government."

That word "artist" was happily chosen, for it suggests the quality of Roosevelt's extraordinary creative imagination. I think that he would have resented the application of the word as implying that he was an impractical dreamer; he loved to represent himself as a prestidigitator who could amaze and amuse the audience by "pulling another rabbit out of a hat." But he was an artist and no canvas was too big for him.

B. PLOWING THE SURPLUSES UNDER

1. The Planned-Scarcity Scandal (1934)

> The surest way to raise the prices of farm produce to a profit-making level was to reduce the mountainous surpluses. Under the Agricultural Adjustment Act of 1933 ("Triple A"), six million pigs were slaughtered and one-fourth of the cotton acreage (already planted) was plowed under. The proverbially stubborn mules, trained to walk between rows of cotton, balked at trampling on them. Critics of the New Deal sneered that the mules had more sense than the New Dealers. Norman Thomas —ex-Presbyterian clergyman, orator, author, editor, and six times Socialist candidate for the Presidency (1928–1948)—here vents his indignation. What alternatives were there, given the existing economic and social framework?

Poverty and insecurity are, alas, old stories for men. It remained for this generation, and particularly this generation of Americans, to invent a new and most bitter type of poverty. Pearl Buck's moving description of famine in a Chinese village is the kind of thing which, with minor changes, could have been written about agricultural villages over and over again in almost all parts of the world ever since the dim dawn of history. It remained for us to invent "bread lines knee-deep in wheat."

Other generations have been poor because they could not produce enough. We are told that we are poor because we have produced too much.

For thousands of years man had to accept the inevitability of scarcity. Society would have had the poor always with it, no matter how just and kind might have been its institutions, for the simple reason that man had not learned to harness the powers of nature to help him wrest an abundant living from the earth. It was on the basis of inevitable scarcity that the Greek philosophers tried to justify chattel slavery.

1. From *The Choice before Us* by Norman Thomas, pp. 5–7. Originally published by Macmillan Publishing Company, 1934; reprinted by AMS Press, Inc., 1970.

Today, as everybody admits, the machine is our slave. We depend not upon the energy of men but upon the energy of electricity to give us at once abundance and leisure. And still in a nation like our own, blessed by every gift man's skill and nature's abundance can bestow, millions of children go hungry. Their fathers vainly seek work that does not exist. They and their families are crowded together in shacks and slums and hovels while the builders of skyscrapers are idle.

No satirist ever penned such an indictment of a cruel and lunatic order of society as was written by the author of the Agricultural Adjustment Act in America who saw no way to restore a partial prosperity to farmers except to produce an artificial scarcity by paying agricultural producers from the proceeds of a tax on consumers to destroy the abundance of foodstuffs which men had struggled thousands upon thousands of years to be able to create.

And this, be it remembered, in the midst of a cold and hungry world. The more sincerely one believes that such legislation was an emergency necessity, the more terrible is the indictment of the civilization which brought it about.

2. Wallace Puts People above Pigs (1935)

Henry A. Wallace, a Republican convert to the New Deal, served as Roosevelt's first Secretary of Agriculture. An Iowan who had edited a farm journal and made a fortune in the hybrid-seed business, Wallace was destined to have a controversial career as Vice-President under Roosevelt and as presidential candidate on the Communist-backed Progressive ticket of 1948. Capable administrator, prolific author, and dynamic orator, Wallace was also a starry-eyed idealist who later proposed a quart of milk for all people. In this spirited radio defense of his New Deal policies, why does he claim that the producers of pig iron were more blameworthy than the New Dealers? In what way did the policy of planned scarcity actually save food from destruction?

People are still interested in the six million pigs that were killed in September of 1933. In letters I have received following these radio talks, the pigs are mentioned more often than any one thing except potatoes. One letter says:

"It just makes me sick all over when I think how the government has killed millions and millions of little pigs, and how that has raised pork prices until today we poor people cannot even look at a piece of bacon." ...

So six million little pigs were killed in September of 1933. They were turned into one hundred million pounds of pork. That pork was distributed for relief. It went to feed the hungry. Some very small pigs could not be handled as meat by the packers. These were turned into grease and tankage for fertilizer.

If those six million pigs had grown up they would have been marketed in January, February, and March of 1934. They probably would have

2. From *Democracy Reborn*, pp. 103–06, by Henry A. Wallace; copyright 1944, 1972 by Harcourt Brace Jovanovich, Inc. Reprinted by permission of the publisher.

brought around $2.50 a hundredweight. Instead of that the price of hogs at that time averaged [a profitable] $3.60. . . .

Strange to say, I find myself in strong sympathy with the attitude of many folks who held up their hands in horror about the killing of little pigs. I will go further than most of them in condemning scarcity economics. We want an economy of abundance, but it must be balanced abundance of those things we really want.

The pig-iron reduction control of the big steel companies in 1933 was in principle one thousand times as damnable as the pig-reduction campaign of 1933. Pig-iron production in 1932 was about twenty percent of that in 1929. Pig production in 1933 in pounds was ninety-seven percent of that of 1929. In 1934 pig-iron production was about forty-five percent of that of 1929. Pig production in 1934, the drought year, was eighty percent of that of 1929.

In other words, farmers cut pig production three percent when steel companies cut pig-iron production eighty percent. That sort of industrial reduction program plowed millions of workers out into the streets. It is because of that industrial reduction program that we have to spend billions for relief to keep the plowed-out workers from starvation. I hope industry in future reduction programs will not find it desirable to plow millions of workers out of their jobs. People are more important than pigs. . . .

My attention has been called to a statement by a minister out in the Corn Belt before the district conference of his faith. Concerning the actions of the New Deal he says: ". . . some of them are downright sinful as the destruction of foodstuffs in the face of present want."

I have been used to statements of this sort by partisans, demagogues, politicians, and even newspaper columnists. To men of this sort I pay no attention, because I know that their interest in a cause makes it impossible for them to distinguish truth from falsehood. But when a minister of the gospel makes a statement, we expect it to be the truth.

Just what food does he think this administration has destroyed? We would like to know the specific instances. If he is merely referring to acreage control which enabled us to keep out of use in 1935 some thirty million of the fifty million acres which have produced in the past for markets in foreign countries, I would say, "Yes, we are guilty of acreage control and, depending on variations in weather, we shall continue to be until foreign purchasing power is restored by the breaking down of tariff and quota barriers."

We have not destroyed foodstuffs. We do not contemplate destroying them. However, foodstuffs *were* destroyed back in 1932 by farmers who found it profitable to burn their corn for fuel rather than to sell it for ten cents a bushel (which amounted to $3.33 a ton). It was cheaper for many farmers in the northwest Corn Belt to burn food for fuel at those pitiful prices than to burn coal.

People who believe that we ordered the destruction of food are merely the victims of their prejudices and the misinformation that has been fed to them by interested persons. What we actually did was to stop the destruction of foodstuffs by making it worth while for farmers to sell them rather than to destroy them.

Agricultural Adjustment of the past two years has been a million times as warranted as the industrial reduction policy of the past five years. Why does not the minister attack the industrial reduction which was made possible by corporate and tariff laws? It was this reduction by industry that created the *unemployment* and destroyed the farmers' markets.

C. THE TENNESSEE VALLEY AUTHORITY (TVA)

1. Norris Plays Down Electric Power (1933)

George W. Norris, for thirty years United States Senator from Nebraska, shone as one of the foremost liberals and reformers of his generation. He opposed war with Germany in 1917, fought the Treaty of Versailles, and authored the anti-lame duck (20th) Amendment. Best known as "the Father of the TVA," he fought tirelessly for this revolutionary high-dam project. (His fellow Republicans, finally fed up with his New Deal liberalism, read him out of the party in 1936.) The power companies attacked the TVA as primarily an effort to put the government in the electric power business. Norris replied that power was always secondary to navigation and flood control. He declared that the power trust, which favored a large number of obstructing small dams, "had no fundamental objection to making the Tennessee River navigable, but in pursuance of its own interest it preferred an unnavigable river to any interference with its monopolistic control of the generation and sale of electric power." In the final stages of the debate on the TVA bill, Norris spoke as follows. Why could electric power not have been the primary consideration in all instances?

We are confronted here, however, with the Government undertaking in the Tennessee Valley a great project, what we might call "a reclamation project." We are going to try to control the flow of the streams, particularly of the Tennessee River. We are going to try to control the floods. We are going to try to make the great stream navigable. We are going to reforest some of the land. We are going to put to better use some of the so-called "marginal lands." We are going to develop power. The development of power is only one of a large list of things we are going to try to do. They are all interlocked. In many of these improvements every one of these things will enter as a component part.

As to Dam No. 2,* which we own down there now, nobody that I know of has ever said how much of that dam should be allocated to navigation and how much to power. Most people think of it as a power dam only. They do not realize that if that dam had not been built, some similar improvement would have had to be constructed in order to make the

1. *Congressional Record,* 73 Cong., 1 sess., p. 2684 (May 2, 1933).
* Today's Wilson Dam.

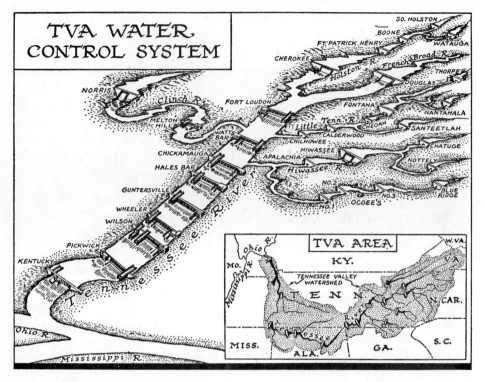

Tennessee River navigable. A great lake has been constructed there over
a portion of the river which at times in the year is just a rippling stream
running over the rocks. . . .

Other dams—smaller dams, without any power—could have been built.
Dam No. 3,* some twelve or fourteen miles above, a well-known dam provided for in the original plan, was never constructed. It strikes me . . . that
no business man would construct Dam No. 3 as a power proposition.
It would not pay; it would not be a good investment; but as a navigation
proposition it is absolutely essential that we shall make the river navigable
during portions of the year at least.

The difficulty arises because all this business is so interlocked and so
interwoven that it is difficult to tell where one begins and the other ends,
but when we put them together as a whole we know what we are going
to get. We are going to get a navigable stream; we are going to get flood
control; we are going to get power as an incident. But while the object of
this bill is to get the maximum amount of flood control, it does not say the
maximum amount of power, as will be noted by anyone who will read
the bill. It provides for securing the maximum amount of flood control, the
maximum amount of navigation—flood control and navigation—and the max-

* Today's Wheeler Dam.

imum amount of power "not inconsistent with navigation and flood control." That, I think, is the language of the bill.

The power is really a secondary proposition. It comes about because it would be sinful to build all these dams and not develop some power. When it shall be developed, what is going to be done with it? The Government has it on its hands, and why should not the people of that great basin have the benefit of it?

2. Willkie Exposes the Rubber Yardstick (1937)

The aroused power companies fought the TVA all the way to the Supreme Court. They contended that expensive high dams would not check erosion, that inexpensive low dams would better serve navigation and flood control, and that the loss to individuals from floods was less than the cost of the grandiose project. Dynamic, tousle-haired, and eloquent Wendell Willkie, later an outspoken liberal and the opponent of Roosevelt in the presidential campaign of 1940, complained as follows in 1937 as president of the competing Commonwealth and Southern power corporation. (In 1939 it sold its Tennessee Electric Power Company to the TVA for some $78,000,000.) How fair or unfair was the so-called yardstick?

Like England's once famous military formation, the British Square, the TVA has had four fronts to present to the public, and it uses the front most suitable to the group which it is addressing. Before the courts it claims that it is not really a power enterprise, but primarily a *conservation* activity: it is a project to prevent floods, promote navigation on the Tennessee River, and check soil erosion in the great Tennessee Valley. Only before a more sympathetic audience is it frankly an instrument for the electrification of America. . . .

The TVA has therefore appeared to be on the side of the angels in the controversy between it and the utilities. But the conservation programme of the TVA is only a masquerade. It has no functional connection with the power programme of the Authority, and the amount spent on it is only an insignificant portion of the Authority's total expenditures. Other departments of government, both state and national, are charged with the duty of caring for soil erosion and are doing such work effectively without the building of dams and power facilities. . . .

The American people, therefore, are paying more than half a billion dollars for eleven dams, chiefly designed to supply power to one area. But this power, as will shortly be demonstrated, is to be supplied to this area at *less than cost*. In other words, the TVA will operate annually at a deficit, and these annual deficits must, of course, be paid for out of the pockets of the taxpayers.

The sponsors of the TVA maintained at the beginning that this vast programme was not designed to create a competitive power system, but to set up a yardstick by which the rates of the private companies could be judged.

2. *Atlantic Monthly*, CLX, 211–14 (Aug., 1937). By permission of the *Atlantic Monthly*.

The yardstick idea was undoubtedly attractive, since, after all, the average consumer did not understand much about electric rates and had no way of personally checking their relative highness or lowness.

Unfortunately, the yardstick is rubber from the first inch to the last.

From the generation of power at the beginning to its distribution to the ultimate consumer at the end, the TVA enjoys privileges and exemptions which are denied to the private utility, which conceal the true cost of TVA power, and the cost of which comes out of the pockets of you and me as taxpayers. These can be best illustrated by a direct comparison between the TVA and the Tennessee Electric Power Company, one of the typical companies in the Commonwealth and Southern System operating in that area.

The first advantage given to the TVA is exemption from practically all taxes. For the fiscal year ended June 30, 1936, the TVA paid only $45,347 in taxes. The Tennessee Electric Power Company (with approximately the same capital investment) paid $2,339,284 in taxes. Here is a difference in this item alone of $2,293,937.

Let us turn to the item of depreciation. This is an expense, a cost of operation, just as much as labor and fuel. This cost to the Tennessee Company, fixed and determined by the Tennessee Railroad and Public Utilities Commission, amounts to $1,260,000 per year. The books of the TVA, however, carry no item for depreciation.

The same is true with respect to interest charges. The Tennessee Company properties were built only in part with borrowed capital. During the twelve months ended June 30, 1936, this company paid interest and preferred dividends amounting to $4,299,022. On the other hand, the property of the TVA is built entirely with borrowed capital. The United States Government is paying interest and will continue to pay interest on such borrowings. The TVA books, however, show no item to cover this interest. It got its property from the Federal Government, which in turn, of course, collected its money from the taxpayer. . . .

Since the TVA is apparently selling its power at less than cost, it should say so. If the people who live in New York City, for example, are to pay part of the electric bill of people who live in Corinth, Mississippi, the people in New York should know about it. Perhaps they will not object. On more than one occasion the American people as a whole have contributed, through taxes, to a development designed to serve only a limited area. Often that is socially desirable. But if we are to pay part of the electric light bills of the Tennessee Valley, the TVA should honestly tell us so.

Also, if the TVA is attempting to force the utilities into public ownership, it should employ means that will neither deceive nor injure the public and will not jeopardize the interests of utility investors. It should announce its intention and proceed, by condemnation proceedings duly instituted in the courts of the land, to take over utility properties with fair compensation to the owners. This is both the honest and the humane method of action.

Also, it gives the people a fair chance to protest if they don't like the change; or if they are still skeptical of political management of a major industry. . . .

3. Displaced Tennesseans (1935)

Architects of the New Deal also designed the TVA to provide employment and to raise the living standards of an impoverished area. Electric lights and appliances were incredibly scarce. Before the valley bottoms were turned into lakes by the high dams, federal agents had to buy out the owners. More than one doughty Tennessean threatened to "shoot them TVA fellers." Form conclusions from this contemporary account as to the need for a TVA. Do the social gains justify the cost?

. . . On Cedar Creek lives Isabel Brantley.

"I was born in this house and so was my pappy before me, and here I've lived and here I'll die, even if I have to bolt the door and let the flood come—but there hain't a-goin' to be no flood!"

This was her greeting to the TVA appraiser, prepared to offer twelve hundred dollars for her log cabin and eroded acres. In the end she was won over by the generosity of TVA's laborers, who offered to move the house in their spare time, without cost to her, to a site below the dam. Persuaded but not softened, she declared, "You got to find me a place with a spring or a well. I don't want none of this newfangled pipe water runnin' into my house."

Such is the sales resistance encountered by Government agents.

When Ezra Hill saw the plans for the home which was to replace his old one in the flood area, he pointed to the place on the print showing the circles and ovals of bathroom fixtures. "What's all this? . . . I won't have it! I guess a privy is still good enough for me."

[*The TVA brought improvement but not paradise; the per capita income of the region remained well below the national average. But the demands of both the government and the people grew so rapidly that by 1962 the TVA had supplementary steam plants capable of producing more than twice the amount of electricity generated by water power.*]

D. LITTLE STEEL VERSUS THE C.I.O.

1. Tom Girdler Girds for Battle (1937)

The New Dealers, with their strong appeal to the low-waged voter, encouraged the unionization of labor, notably through the Wagner Act of 1935. "Big Steel" (including the U.S. Steel Corporation) reluctantly accepted unionization by the C.I.O. (Committee for Industrial Organization). "Little Steel," led by the tough-fisted but mild-appearing Tom Girdler, who became a hero to conservatives, struck back. At his Republic Steel Company's plant in Chicago on Memorial Day, 1937, the police fired upon and killed ten strikers, while wounding many others. Several additional

3. Drew and Leon Pearson, "The Tennessee Valley Experiment," *Harper's Magazine,* CLXX, 707 (May, 1935). Reprinted by permission of the estate of Drew Pearson.
1. "Delivery or Non-Delivery of Mail in Industrial Strife Areas," Senate Committee on Post Offices, *Hearings,* 75 Cong., 1 sess., pp. 207–10.

lives were lost in Ohio cities. Girdler, before a Senate committee, here justifies his opposition. Are the tactics of the C.I.O. defensible (if correctly reported)? Are the accusations regarding Communism convincing?

First of all let me make it clear that the fundamental issue in this strike is not one involving wages, hours, or working conditions in Republic [Steel Company] plants. This is not a strike in the sense that a large body of our employees quit work because of grievances against the company. What has happened is that an invading army descended upon our plants and forced many of our employees from their jobs.

Fully 23,000 of our employees have remained at work throughout the strike despite threats and violence, and many additional thousands have been kept from work against their will.

The basic issue of this strike is the right of American citizens to work, free from molestation, violence, coercion, and intimidation by a labor organization whose apparent policy is either to rule or to ruin American industry. . . .

The difficulties in the present dispute arise from the fact that the company will not enter into a contract, oral or written, with an irresponsible party; and the C.I.O., as presently constituted, is wholly irresponsible. . . .

The irresponsibility of the C.I.O. is well established by the fact that 200 strikes and walk-outs have taken place in the plants of the General Motors Corporation since that corporation signed an agreement with the C.I.O. which called for an end of strikes during the period of the agreement. . . .

Further evidence of the irresponsible character of the C.I.O. is to be seen in the lawless and terroristic conduct of its members since the beginning of the present strike. Republic plants have been surrounded by armed crowds who call themselves pickets and who, by force and violence, have imprisoned in the plants thousands of employees who refused to heed the strike call and remained at work. These men have been prevented from returning to their families when their work is done, and other employees who want to work have been prevented from getting into the plants.

Airplanes delivering food to workers besieged in the plants have been fired upon by armed mobs about the gates. The delivery of the United States mails has been interfered with. Railroad tracks have been dynamited. Families of men who are at work in the plants in certain communities have been threatened, coerced, and stoned. Defiance of law and order has been so flagrant that in some communities law enforcement has completely collapsed.

These illegal practices have not been peculiar to the Republic strike. They have characterized C.I.O. methods since the beginning of its organization drive in many industries. They have more than confirmed the conclusion reached by this company before the present strike ever started that the C.I.O. was and is an irresponsible and dangerous force in America. . . .

We believe that the C.I.O. with its terroristic methods and Communistic

SURE, I'LL WORK FOR BOTH SIDES
Both management and labor resorted to violence. Milwaukee *Journal,* 1935.

technique of picketing constitutes the most dangerous threat to the preservation of democracy in the United States. . . .

Now, let me state a few fundamental conclusions which I have reached about the C.I.O.

First. The C.I.O. has denied to free American citizens who refuse to pay tribute to it the right to work.

Second. The C.I.O. encourages and promotes violence and disregard of law. If this is done under instructions and approval of its leaders, it amounts to a confession on their part that they are deliberately adopting the methods of force and terrorism which have proved so successful for the dictators of Europe. If this is done without their approval and occurs because they cannot control their own men, it is a confession that the C.I.O. is an irresponsible party and that a contract with it would not be worth the paper upon which it is written.

Third. The C.I.O. is associated with Communism. Many of its leaders and organizers are avowed Communists. The *Daily Worker,* the official newspaper of the Communist Party of the United States, gives the C.I.O. its full support. Can any organization which welcomes the support of the International Communist Party still claim that it adheres to the principles of democracy?

2. Lewis Lambasts Girdler (1937)

John L. Lewis—gruff, domineering, shaggy-browed—had risen from the depths of the coal mines to the headship of the potent United Mine Workers of America. Seeking new worlds to conquer, he undertook to unionize mass-production industries through his Committee for Industrial Organization (C.I.O.). The clash between him and Tom Girdler—both strong-minded men—became so noisy that F.D.R. himself burst out, "A plague on both your houses." Four years later, in 1941, Girdler's Little Steel was forced to accept unionization. In this impassioned speech over a radio hookup, Lewis betrays his anger. What is his loudest complaint? Why does he regard people like Girdler as more dangerous than Communists?

Five of the corporations in the steel industry elected to resist collective bargaining and undertook to destroy the steel-workers' union. These companies filled their plants with industrial spies, assembled depots of guns and gas bombs, established barricades, controlled their communities with armed thugs, leased the police power of cities, and mobilized the military power of a state to guard them against the intrusion of collective bargaining within their plants.

During this strike eighteen steel workers were either shot to death or had their brains clubbed out by police, or armed thugs in the pay of the steel companies. . . .

The steel workers have now buried their dead, while the widows weep and watch their orphaned children become objects of public charity. The murder of these unarmed men has never been publicly rebuked by any authoritative officer of the state or federal government. Some of them, in extenuation, plead lack of jurisdiction, but murder as a crime against the moral code can always be rebuked without regard to the niceties of legalistic jurisdiction by those who profess to be the keepers of the public conscience.

[Tom] Girdler, of Republic Steel, in the quiet of his bedchamber, doubtless shrills his psychopathic cackles as he files notches on his corporate gun and views in retrospect the ruthless work of his mercenary killers. . . .

The United States Chamber of Commerce, the National Association of Manufacturers, and similar groups representing industry and financial interests are rendering a disservice to the American people in their attempts to frustrate the organization of labor and in their refusal to accept collective bargaining as one of our economic institutions.

These groups are encouraging a systematic organization of vigilante groups to fight unionization under the sham pretext of local interests. They equip these vigilantes with tin hats, wooden clubs, gas masks, and lethal weapons, and train them in the arts of brutality and oppression. They bring in snoops, finks [strikebreakers], hatchet gangs, and Chowderhead Cohens to infest their plants and disturb the communities.

Fascist organizations have been launched and financed under the shabby pretext that the C.I.O. movement is Communistic. The real breeders of

2. *Vital Speeches*, III, 731 (Sept. 15, 1937; speech of Sept. 3, 1937).

discontent and alien doctrines of government and philosophies subversive of good citizenship are such as these who take the law into their own hands. No tin-hat brigade of goose-stepping vigilantes or bibble-babbling mob of blackguarding and corporation-paid scoundrels will prevent the onward march of labor, or divert its purpose to play its natural and rational part in the development of the economic, political, and social life of our nation. . . .

Do those who have hatched this foolish cry of Communism in the C.I.O. fear the increased influence of labor in our democracy? Do they fear its influence will be cast on the side of shorter hours, a better system of distributed employment, better homes for the underprivileged, social security for the aged, a fairer distribution of the national income?

Certainly the workers that are being organized want a voice in the determination of these objectives of social justice.

E. THE SUPREME COURT FIGHT AND AFTER

1. Ickes Defends His Chief (1937)

The ultra-conservative Supreme Court had repeatedly overthrown crucial New Deal measures for economic and social reform. Roosevelt, intoxicated by his heady majorities of 1932, 1934, and 1936, concluded that in a true democracy the "horse-and-buggy" Court ought to catch up with the will of the people. Two weeks after his second inauguration, he sprang his clever Supreme Court scheme on a surprised Congress and nation. Among other changes, he proposed increasing the membership of the Court from nine to fifteen by appointing additional (New Deal) justices to offset those aged seventy or more who were unwilling to retire. Critics cried that this was "packing" the Court; supporters replied that this was "unpacking" the Court by offsetting reactionaries. "Honest Harold" Ickes, the acid-tongued Secretary of the Interior, here tells how he defended Roosevelt before an audience of Texans. Given that the Court scheme had not received mention in the Democratic platform or in Roosevelt's speeches during the recent campaign of 1936, how persuasive is Ickes' argument regarding a popular mandate?

Then I switched to a discussion of the constitutional situation, with special reference to the recent proposal of the President to change the judiciary system. I could hear a gasp go up as I disclosed my purpose to discuss this issue. A week or ten days ago the Texas State Senate, with only three or four votes opposing, had gone on record as being against the President's proposal. The House decided neither to approve nor disapprove.

I waded right into the constitutional issue with both feet. In my first sentence I asked where had the Supreme Court gotten its supposed power to pass upon the constitutionality of acts of Congress. I read the Tenth Amendment and then I said that this power had been usurped.°

1. *The Secret Diary of Harold L. Ickes*, II, 80. Copyright © 1953 by Simon & Schuster, Inc., renewal © 1981 by Harold M. and Elizabeth Ickes. Reprinted by permission of Simon & Schuster, a Division of Gulf & Western Corporation.
° The 10th Amendment reserved undelegated powers to the states, but the function of judicial review, "usurped" by the Supreme Court, is generally regarded as implicit in the views of the Founding Fathers and in the Constitution.

TO FURNISH THE SUPREME COURT PRACTICAL ASSISTANCE
Roosevelt's proposal to assist the Court by adding a maximum
of six new members was interpreted by critics as an attempt to
"pack" it with his mouthpieces. Washington *Post*, 1937.

I then went on to discuss the supposed checks and balances in our
tripartite Federal system, pointing out that while there were ample checks
and balances with respect to the legislative and executive branches, there
wasn't a single check on the judiciary except that of impeachment, which
was slow and cumbersome and of doubtful efficacy when it came to a
court of nine men. I remarked in passing that one could not be impeached
for being too old, that that was not a crime but merely a misfortune.

I argued that the people had given the President a mandate at the last
election to provide them with such social and economic legislation as is
implicit in the term "New Deal." I said that he would be recreant to his
trust if he didn't do all within his power to give the people what he had
promised them and what they had shown so unmistakably that they wanted.

I expressed the opinion that the people wanted the benefits of the New
Deal now. I pointed out that while those who are opposing the President
pretend to do it on the basis that a constitutional amendment is the proper
procedure, it would take all of twenty years to get such an amendment
through.

With respect to an act or acts of Congress limiting the powers of the
Supreme Court so as to provide, for instance, that no law could be held
to be unconstitutional except on a two-thirds or three-quarters majority,

I ventured to predict that any such law would be declared unconstitutional by the Supreme Court and therefore would be ineffective.

2. Dorothy Thompson Dissents (1937)

As the battle over the Supreme Court mounted, critics accused Roosevelt of perverting the Constitution by destroying the delicate checks and balances, of undermining the integrity and independence of the judiciary, and of grooming himself for dictatorship. Even many New Dealers preferred an unhurried constitutional amendment to a hurried act of Congress. Perhaps most damaging was the suggestion of "slickness," together with Roosevelt's argument, based on false information, that the aged justices were behind in their work. Dorothy Thompson, a noted and respected columnist, sounded the following clarion call. How sound is her view that the people must be protected against fickle majorities, and that haste is not necessary?

If the American people accept this last audacity of the President without letting out a yell to high heaven, they have ceased to be jealous of their liberties and are ripe for ruin.

This is the beginning of pure personal government. Do you want it? Do you like it? Look around about the world—there are plenty of examples [*e.g.,* Hitler]—and make up your mind.

The Executive is already powerful by reason of his overwhelming victory in November, and will be strengthened even more if the reorganization plan for the administration, presented some weeks ago, is adopted. We have, to all intents and purposes, a one-party Congress, dominated by the President. Although nearly 40 percent of the voters repudiated the New Deal at the polls, they have less than 20 percent representation in both houses of Congress. And now the Supreme Court is to have a majority determined by the President and by a Senate which he dominates.

When that happens we will have a one-man Government. It will all be constitutional. So, he claims, is Herr Hitler.

Leave the personality and the intentions of the President out of the picture. They are not the crux of this issue. He may be as wise as Solon, lofty as Plato, and pure as Parsifal. He may have the liberties of the American people deeply at heart. But he will have a successor who may be none of these things. There have been benevolent dictatorships and benevolent tyrannies. They have even, at times in history, worked for the popular welfare. But that is not the welfare which, up to now, the American people have chosen.

And let us not be confused by the words "liberal" and "conservative" or misled into thinking that the expressed will of the majority is the essence of democracy. By that definition Hitler, Stalin, and Mussolini are all great democratic leaders. The essence of democracy is the protection of minorities.

Nor has a majority of this generation the right to mortgage a majority of the next. In the Constitution of the United States are incorporated the rights

2. Washington *Star*, Feb. 10, 1937, quoted in *Congressional Digest*, XVI, 96 (March, 1937).

of the people, rights enjoyed by every American citizen in perpetuity, which cannot be voted away by any majority, ever.

Majorities are temporary things. The Supreme Court is there to protect the fundamental law even against the momentary "will of the people." That is its function. And it is precisely because nine men can walk out and say: "You can't do that!" that our liberties are protected against the mob urge that occasionally overcomes democracies. That is why the Supreme Court has been traditionally divorced from momentary majorities. . . .

The Constitution can be changed. There are ways provided for doing so. To change it will require much deliberation, debate, time. And what is wrong with deliberation and debate and time? What is the hurry? Under what threat are we living at this instant?

This is no proposal to change the Constitution. This is no proposal to limit the powers of the Supreme Court. This is a proposal to capture the Supreme Court. . . .

If, of the six men over 70, four had been "liberals" and two "conservatives," instead of the other way around, do you think that this program would have been proposed? . . .

Don't talk of liberalism! The liberal does not believe that the end justifies the means. Long experience has taught him that the means usually determine the end. No human being can believe in the sincerity of this proposal. It is clever, in a world sick of cleverness and longing for plain talk and simple honesty. Must we begin to examine every message from the President to see whether there is a trick in it somewhere?

[*Roosevelt threw all his weight behind the Supreme Court reform, but suffered his most severe political setback when he lost out on the "packing" feature. He underestimated popular reverence for the Court. But he did win certain other judicial reforms; the Supreme Court did shift to a more liberal position; and within four years he did fill seven vacancies with younger men. He lost a battle but in the end won the war. Yet he lost essential legislative support in Congress.*]

3. Republicans Roast Roosevelt (1940)

The Roosevelt-Willkie presidential campaign of 1940 generated new bitterness. Roosevelt's challenge to the third-term tradition, combined with his unsuccessful attempt to "pack" the Supreme Court and "purge" certain Congressmen hostile to him, accentuated fears of dictatorship. The Democrats argued that Roosevelt had saved capitalism by averting, whatever the monetary cost and confusion, a revolutionary uprising. The Republican platform, invoking the Preamble of the Constitution, found the New Deal wanting on many counts. In the light of subsequent developments, which is the most valid accusation?

Instead of leading us into More Perfect Union, the Administration has deliberately fanned the flames of class hatred.

3. K. H. Porter and D. B. Johnson, eds., *National Party Platforms, 1840–1956* (University of Illinois Press, 1961).

Instead of the Establishment of Justice the Administration has sought the subjection of the Judiciary to Executive discipline and domination.

Instead of insuring Domestic Tranquillity, the Administration has made impossible the normal friendly relation between employers and employees, and has even succeeded in alienating both the great divisions of Organized Labor.

Instead of Providing for the Common Defense, the Administration, notwithstanding the expenditure of billions of our dollars, has left the Nation unprepared to resist foreign attack.

Instead of promoting the General Welfare, the Administration has Domesticated the Deficit, Doubled the Debt, Imposed Taxes where they do the greatest economic harm, and used public money for partisan political advantage.

Instead of the Blessings of Liberty, the Administration has imposed upon us a Regime of Regimentation which has deprived the individual of his freedom and has made of America a shackled giant.

Wholly ignoring these great objectives, as solemnly declared by the people of the United States [in the Constitution], the New Deal Administration has for seven long years whirled in a turmoil of shifting, contradictory, and overlapping administrations and policies. Confusion has reigned supreme. The only steady undeviating characteristic has been the relentless expansion of the power of the Federal government over the everyday life of the farmer, the industrial worker, and the businessman. The emergency demands organization—not confusion. It demands free and intelligent cooperation—not incompetent domination. It demands a change.

The New Deal Administration has failed America.

It has failed by seducing our people to become continuously dependent upon government, thus weakening their morale and quenching the traditional American spirit.

THOUGHT PROVOKERS

1. Compare and contrast the presidential leadership of Hoover and Roosevelt. Temperamentally, could Roosevelt ever have been a true dictator?

2. What probably would have happened if the federal government had refused to provide relief for the 15,000,000 unemployed, as well as for the impoverished farmers? Was planned scarcity immoral?

3. Did the social gains resulting from the TVA more than offset the blow that was directed at legitimate private enterprise? If the TVA was designed as a yardstick, what could it accurately measure? If the TVA has been a success, why has it not been copied more widely elsewhere in the United States?

4. Is the right to work without first joining a union a basic right? Why did the C.I.O. call management Fascist, and why did management call the C.I.O. Communist?

5. Why did Roosevelt's Supreme Court proposal stir up such a hornets' nest? Was Roosevelt justified in breaking his platform promises regarding economy and a balanced budget? Did the New Deal change the basic character of the American people? of the federal government?

41 · *Franklin D. Roosevelt and the Shadow of War*

> *The epidemic of world lawlessness is spreading. . . . There must be positive endeavors to preserve peace.*
>
> FRANKLIN D. ROOSEVELT, 1937

PROLOGUE: The same depression that generated the New Deal at home accelerated the rise of power-hungry dictators abroad: Hitler, Mussolini, and the Japanese war lords. Congress tried to insulate the nation from the imminent world war by arms embargoes and other presumed safeguards. But when Hitler attacked Poland in 1939, the American people found themselves torn between two desires: they wanted to avoid involvement, but they feared for their future security if they did not get involved to the extent of bolstering the democracies. Under Roosevelt's prodding, Congress repealed the arms embargo in 1939, and the administration gradually took a series of steps which removed any pretense of neutrality. Most Americans—but not the die-hard isolationists—were willing to risk hostilities in an effort to help the democracies and halt the aggressors. Roosevelt took the gamble but lost when a shooting war developed with Germany in the Atlantic, and when Japan struck a devastating aerial blow at Pearl Harbor.

A. THE ARMS EMBARGO DEBATE

1. Senator Connally Rejects Rigidity (1935)

By the mid-1930's Hitler was on the rise in Germany and Mussolini was on the loose in Ethiopia. An apprehensive American public was determined to legislate itself out of the next world war by a strait-jacket neutrality law. A special Senate investigation launched in 1934 and headed by the notoriety-seeking Senator Nye had left the impression that the manufacturers of arms had dragged America into World War I. If Congress would only embargo munitions, the nation would (on paper) keep out of World War II. Senator Connally, the long-haired, string-tie Texan orator who headed the Senate Foreign Relations Committee, showed himself unswayed by this logic in the following speech. Does the proposed neutrality legislation provide for true neutrality?

Is it an expression of neutrality to say to two warring nations, one of which has ambitions for territorial conquest, the other unprepared, the other weak, the other trying to pursue its own destiny—is it neutral to say to those nations, "We shall give arms to neither of you," thereby insuring the triumph of the prepared nation, the covetous nation, the ambitious nation, the nation which seeks by force of arms to impose its will on a weaker and defenseless nation?

---

1. *Congressional Record,* 74 Cong., 1 sess., p. 14432 (Aug. 24, 1935).

Mr. President, that is not neutrality; that is a form of unneutrality. That is a form of declaration which announces that the United States will take the side of the strong and powerful against the weak, the unprepared, and the defenseless. Why not leave that determination to the President of the United States when and if, in his conduct of our foreign relations, it becomes a sound American policy for him to take a position in a crisis of that kind? . . .

We cannot now put the United States into an international strait jacket and thereby keep out of war. We cannot by an act of Congress put the United States into a concrete cast internationally which will fit all future occasions and solve all future problems.

2. Roosevelt Pleads for Repeal (1939)

Despite Connally's urging, the arms-embargoing Neutrality Acts of 1935 and 1937 made no distinction between aggressor and victim. When Hitler wantonly launched World War II in September, 1939, the United States could not legally sell munitions to the unprepared democracies, even though American sentiment and self-interest both cried aloud for aid to Britain and France. A worried Roosevelt summoned Congress into special session and made the following dramatic appeal. He was wrong on two counts. First, the arms embargo, as purely domestic legislation, was not a departure from long-established international law. Second, the Jeffersonian embargo and non-intercourse acts did not cause the War of 1812; they came within a few days of averting it. What does this excerpt suggest about Roosevelt's technique as a politician? What does he see as the most dangerous loophole in the existing legislation?

Beginning with the foundation of our constitutional Government in the year 1789, the American policy in respect to belligerent nations, with one notable exception, has been based on international law. . . .

The single exception was the policy adopted by this nation during the Napoleonic Wars, when, seeking to avoid involvement, we acted for some years under the so-called Embargo and Non-Intercourse Acts. That policy turned out to be a disastrous failure—first, because it brought our own nation close to ruin, and, second, because it was the major cause of bringing us into active participation in European wars in our own War of 1812. It is merely reciting history to recall to you that one of the results of the policy of embargo and non-intercourse was the burning in 1814 of part of this Capitol in which we are assembled.

Our next deviation by statute from the sound principles of neutrality, and peace through international law, did not come for 130 years. It was the so-called Neutrality Act of 1935—only 4 years ago—an Act continued in force by the Joint Resolution of May 1, 1937, despite grave doubts expressed as to its wisdom by many Senators and Representatives and by officials charged with the conduct of our foreign relations, including myself.

I regret that the Congress passed that Act. I regret equally that I signed that Act.

On July 14th of this year, I asked the Congress, in the cause of peace

2. *Ibid.*, 76 Cong., 2 sess., pp. 10–11 (Sept. 21, 1939).

and in the interest of real American neutrality and security, to take action to change that Act.

I now ask again that such action be taken in respect to that part of the Act which is wholly inconsistent with ancient precepts of the law of nations —the [arms] embargo provisions. I ask it because they are, in my opinion, most vitally dangerous to American neutrality, American security, and American peace.

These embargo provisions, as they exist today, prevent the sale to a belligerent by an American factory of any completed implements of war, but they allow the sale of many types of uncompleted implements of war, as well as all kinds of general material and supplies. They, furthermore, allow such products of industry [e.g., copper] and agriculture [e.g., cotton] to be taken in American-flag ships to belligerent nations. There in itself— under the present law—lies definite danger to our neutrality and our peace.

3. Senator Vandenberg Fights Repeal (1939)

Senator Arthur H. Vandenberg of Michigan—voluble orator, long-time newspaper-man, and author of books on Alexander Hamilton—was a leader of the Republican isolationists and a serious contender for the presidential nomination in 1940. Later, in 1945, he underwent a spectacular conversion to internationalism, and rose to heights of statesmanship in supporting the Marshall Plan for the rehabilitation of post-war Europe. While fighting against the repeal of the arms embargo in 1939, he wrote in his diary that he deplored Roosevelt's "treacherous" and "cowardly" idea that America could be "half in and half out of this war." Hating Hitlerism, he felt that the honor-able course would be to go in or to stay out—and he much preferred to stay out. In this speech in the Senate against the repeal of the arms embargo, what does he regard as both unneutral and unethical?

Mr. President, I believe this debate symbolically involves the most momentous decision, in the eyes of America and of the world, that the United States Senate has confronted in a generation.

In the midst of foreign war and the alarms of other wars, we are asked to depart basically from the neutrality which the American Congress has twice told the world, since 1935, would be our rule of conduct in such an event. We are particularly asked to depart from it through the repeal of existing neutrality law establishing an embargo on arms, ammunition, and implements of war. We are asked to depart from it in violation of our own officially asserted doctrine, during the [first] World War, that the rules of a neutral cannot be prejudicially altered in the midst of a war.

We are asked to depart from international law itself, as we ourselves have officially declared it to exist. Consciously or otherwise, but mostly consciously, we are asked to depart from it in behalf of one belligerent whom our personal sympathies largely favor, and against another belligerent whom our personal feelings largely condemn. In my opinion, this is the road that may lead us to war, and I will not voluntarily take it. . . .

3. *Ibid.*, p. 95 (Oct. 4, 1939).

The proponents of the change vehemently insist that their steadfast purpose, like ours, is to keep America out of the war, and their sincere assurances are presented to our people. But the motive is obvious, and the inevitable interpretation of the change, inevitably invited by the circumstances, will be that we have officially taken sides.

Somebody will be fooled—either the America which is assured that the change is wholly pacific, or the foreigners who believe it is the casting of our die. Either of these disillusionments would be intolerable. Each is ominous. Yet someone will be fooled—either those at home who expect too much, or those abroad who will get too little.

There is no such hazard, at least to our own America, in preserving neutrality in the existing law precisely as we almost unanimously notified the world was our intention as recently as 1935 and 1937. There is no such jeopardy, at least to our own America, in maintaining the arms embargo as it is. No menace, no jeopardy, to us can thus be persuasively conjured.

Therefore millions of Americans and many members of the Congress can see no reason for the change, but infinite reason to the contrary, if neutral detachment is our sole objective. I am one who deeply holds this view. If I err, I want to err on America's side.

[*Despite such pleas, the arms embargo was repealed early in November, 1939. The vote was 55 to 24 in the Senate; 243 to 172 in the House.*]

B. THE INTERVENTION ISSUE

1. Lindbergh Argues for Isolation (1941)

After France fell to Hitler in 1940, the embattled British stood alone. American interventionists called for a helping hand to Britain; the isolationists called for hands off. The isolationist "America First" group proclaimed, "We have nothing to fear from a Nazi-European victory." Boyish-faced, curly-haired Colonel Charles A. Lindbergh, who had narrowed the Atlantic with his historic solo flight in 1927, stressed the width of the ocean in his new role as a leading isolationist orator. After inspecting Germany's aircraft facilities in 1938, he stoutly maintained that Hitler (who decorated him) could never be conquered in the air. If Lindbergh proved so wrong in an area in which he was a specialist, form some judgment as to the assessment of America's strategic position that he made in this speech before a New York mass meeting in April, 1941. To what extent is interventionism undemocratic, assuming that Lindbergh's figures were correct? Is his analysis of public opinion trustworthy?

We have weakened ourselves for many months, and still worse, we have divided our own people, by this dabbling in Europe's wars. While we should have been concentrating on American defense, we have been forced to argue over foreign quarrels. We must turn our eyes and our faith back to our own country before it is too late. And when we do this, a different vista opens before us.

1. New York *Times*, April 24, 1941, p. 12.

NEW NEUTRALITY LEGISLATION

Dual crises required drastic action. Philadelphia *Inquirer,* 1939.

Practically every difficulty we would face in invading Europe becomes an asset to us in defending America. Our enemy, and not we, would then have the problem of transporting millions of troops across the ocean and landing them on a hostile shore. They, and not we, would have to furnish the convoys to transport guns and trucks and munitions and fuel across three thousand miles of water. Our battleships and our submarines would then be fighting close to their home bases. We would then do the bombing from the air and the torpedoing at sea. And if any part of an enemy convoy should ever pass our navy and our air force, they would still be faced with the guns of our coast artillery, and behind them the divisions of our Army.

The United States is better situated from a military standpoint than any other nation in the world. Even in our present condition of unpreparedness no foreign power is in a position to invade us today. If we concentrate on our own defenses and build the strength that this nation should maintain, no foreign army will ever attempt to land on American shores.

War is not inevitable for this country. Such a claim is defeatism in the true sense. No one can make us fight abroad unless we ourselves are willing to do so. No one will attempt to fight us here if we arm ourselves as a great nation should be armed. Over a hundred million people in this nation are opposed to entering the war. If the principles of democracy mean anything at all, that is reason enough for us to stay out. If we are forced into a war against the wishes of an overwhelming majority of our people, we will have proved democracy such a failure at home that there will be little use fighting for it abroad.

The time has come when those of us who believe in an independent American destiny must band together and organize for strength. We have been led toward war by a minority of our people. This minority has power. It has influence. It has a loud voice. But it does not represent the American people. During the last several years I have traveled over this country from one end to the other. I have talked to many hundreds of men and women, and I have letters from tens of thousands more, who feel the same way as you and I.

[*Public-opinion polls during these months showed contradictory desires. A strong majority of the American people wanted to stay out of war, but a strong majority favored helping Britain even at the risk of war. The Lend-Lease Act of 1941 received about two-to-one support in the public-opinion polls, and more than that in the Congressional voting.*]

2. The New York *Times* Rejects Insulationism (1941)

The New York *Times* challenged Lindbergh's views in a lengthy and well-reasoned editorial that brilliantly set forth the case for intervention. What are its principal points?

Those who tell us now that the sea is still our certain bulwark, and that the tremendous forces sweeping the Old World threaten no danger to the New, give the lie to their own words in the precautions they would have us take.

To a man they favor an enormous strengthening of our defenses. Why? Against what danger would they have us arm if none exists? To what purpose would they have us spend these almost incredible billions upon billions for ships and planes, for tanks and guns, if there is no immediate threat to the security of the United States? Why are we training the youth of the country to bear arms? Under pressure of what fear are we racing against time to double and quadruple our industrial production?

No man in his senses will say that we are arming against Canada or our Latin-American neighbors to the south, against Britain or the captive states of Europe. We are arming solely for one reason. We are arming against Hitler's Germany—a great predatory Power in alliance with Japan.

It has been said, times without number, that if Hitler cannot cross the English Channel he cannot cross three thousand miles of sea. But there is only one reason why he has not crossed the English Channel. That is because forty-five million determined Britons, in a heroic resistance, have converted their island into an armed base, from which proceeds a steady stream of sea and air power. As Secretary Hull has said: "It is not the water that bars the way. It is the resolute determination of British arms. Were the control of the seas by Britain lost, the Atlantic would no longer be an obstacle—rather, it would become a broad highway for a conqueror moving westward."

2. *Ibid.*, April 30, 1941. © 1941 by the New York Times Company. Reprinted by permission.

That conqueror does not need to attempt at once an invasion of continental United States in order to place this country in deadly danger.
We shall be in deadly danger the moment British sea power fails; the
moment the eastern gates of the Atlantic are open to the aggressor; the
moment we are compelled to divide our one-ocean Navy between two
oceans simultaneously.

The combined Axis fleets [German, Italian, Japanese] outmatch our own:
they are superior in numbers to our fleet in every category of vessel, from
warships and aircraft-carriers to destroyers and submarines.* The combined Axis air strength will be much greater than our own if Hitler strikes
in time—and when has he failed to strike in time? The master of Europe
will have at his command shipways that can outbuild us, the resources of
twenty conquered nations to furnish his materials, the oil of the Middle
East to stoke his engines, the slave labor of a continent—bound by no union
rules, and not working on a forty-hour week—to turn out his production.

Grant Hitler the gigantic prestige of a victory over Britain, and who
can doubt that the first result, on our side of the ocean, would be the
prompt appearance of imitation Nazi regimes in a half-dozen Latin-
American nations, forced to be on the winning side, begging favors, clamoring for admission to the Axis? What shall we do then? Make war upon
these neighbors, send armies to fight in the jungles of Central or South
America; run the risk of outraging native sentiment and turning the whole
continent against us? Or shall we sit tight while the area of Nazi influence
draws ever closer to the Panama Canal, and a spreading checkerboard of
Nazi airfields provides ports of call for German planes that may choose
to bomb our cities?

But even if Hitler gave us time, what kind of "time" would we have at
our disposal?

There are moral and spiritual dangers for this country as well as physical
dangers in a Hitler victory. There are dangers to the mind and heart as well
as to the body and the land.

Victorious in Europe, dominating Africa and Asia through his Axis
partners, Hitler could not afford to permit the United States to live an
untroubled and successful life, even if he wished to. We are the arch-
enemy of all he stands for: the very citadel of that "pluto-democracy"
which he hates and scorns. As long as liberty and freedom prevailed in
the United States there would be constant risk for Hitler that our ideas and
our example might infect the conquered countries which he was bending
to his will. In his own interest he would be forced to harry us at every turn.

Who can doubt that our lives would be poisoned every day by challenges and insults from Nazi politicians; that Nazi agents would stir up

---

* Three foreign fleets are not necessarily equal to the sum of all their parts. There are different languages and signals, different-caliber guns and ammunition, different types of maneuvers, etc.

anti-American feeling in every country they controlled; that Nazi spies would overrun us here; that Hitler would produce a continual series of lightning diplomatic strokes—alliances and "non-aggression pacts" to break our will; in short, that a continuous war of nerves, if nothing worse, would be waged against us?

And who can doubt that, in response, we should have to turn our own nation into an armed camp, with all our traditional values of culture, education, social reform, democracy and liberty subordinated to the single, all-embracing aim of self-preservation? In this case we should indeed experience "regimentation." Every item of foreign trade, every transaction in domestic commerce, every present prerogative of labor, every civil liberty we cherish, would necessarily be regulated in the interest of defense.

3. F.D.R. Pledges No Foreign War (1940)

During the hotly contested third-term campaign of 1940, the Republican candidate Wendell Willkie harped on Roosevelt's broken promises. The President's reelection, he charged, would spell war by April 1, 1941. Smarting from this attack, Roosevelt replied as follows in a memorable Boston speech, which later came back to plague him. Inasmuch as Willkie himself later dismissed his own prediction as "a bit of campaign oratory," was Roosevelt bound by this campaign pledge, regardless of subsequent circumstances?

And while I am talking to you fathers and mothers, I give you one more assurance.

I have said this before, but I shall say it again and again and again:

Your boys are not going to be sent into any foreign wars.

They are going into training to form a force so strong that, by its very existence, it will keep the threat of war far away from our shores.

Yes, the purpose of our defense is defense.

[In previous speeches Roosevelt had ordinarily followed the no-war pledge with the words "except in case of attack." To blunt the force of Willkie's accusation, he now left out the qualification. When asked why he was going to do so, he replied somewhat lamely, "It's not necessary. If we're attacked, it's no longer a foreign war."]

C. THE LEND-LEASE CONTROVERSY

1. F.D.R. Drops the Dollar Sign (1940)

A serious student of history, Roosevelt was determined to avoid the blunders of World War I. The post-war quarrel with the Allies over debts lingered in his memory as he groped for some means of bolstering the hard-pressed British without getting involved in a repayment wrangle. Keeping his new brainstorm under his hat until

---

3. *Ibid.*, Oct. 31, 1940 (speech of Oct. 30, 1940).
1. *The Public Papers and Addresses of Franklin D. Roosevelt, 1940 Volume* (1941), pp. 606–08. By permission of The Macmillan Company.

his triumphant re-election over Willkie—he might have lost if he had revealed it before then—he outlined his scheme at one of his breezy, off-the-cuff press conferences. How does he propose to eliminate the root of the debt difficulty?

It is possible—I will put it that way—for the United States to take over British [war] orders, and, because they are essentially the same kind of munitions that we use ourselves, turn them into American orders. We have got enough money to do it. And thereupon, as to such portion of them as the military events of the future determine to be right and proper for us to allow to go to the other side, either lease or sell the materials, subject to mortgage, to the people on the other side. That would be on the general theory that it may still prove true that the best defense of Great Britain is the best defense of the United States, and therefore that these materials would be more useful to the defense of the United States if they were used in Great Britain than if they were kept in storage here.

Now, what I am trying to do is to eliminate the dollar sign. That is something brand new in the thoughts of practically everybody in this room, I think—get rid of the silly, foolish old dollar sign.

Well, let me give you an illustration: Suppose my neighbor's home catches fire, and I have a length of garden hose four or five hundred feet away. If he can take my garden hose and connect it up with his hydrant, I may help him to put out his fire. Now, what do I do? I don't say to him

HANDS ACROSS THE SEA

F.D.R. extends a fist to Hitler and a hand to Britain through lend-lease.
Orr in *Scottish Daily Record* (Glasgow), 1941.

before that operation, "Neighbor, my garden hose cost me $15; you have got to pay me $15 for it." What is the transaction that goes on? I don't want $15—I want my garden hose back after the fire is over. All right. If it goes through the fire all right, intact, without any damage to it, he gives it back to me and thanks me very much for the use of it. But suppose it gets smashed up—holes in it—during the fire; we don't have to have too much formality about it, but I say to him, "I was glad to lend you that hose; I see I can't use it any more, it's all smashed up." He says, "How many feet of it were there?" I tell him, "There were 150 feet of it." He says, "All right, I will replace it." Now, if I get a nice garden hose back, I am in pretty good shape.

In other words, if you lend certain munitions and get the munitions back at the end of the war, if they are intact—haven't been hurt—you are all right. If they have been damaged or have deteriorated or have been lost completely, it seems to me you come out pretty well if you have them replaced by the fellow to whom you have lent them.

[*After the United States entered the war, supplies provided by foreign countries to American forces were credited to their account as reverse lend-lease. The total value of American lend-lease was over $50 billion, less some $7 billion in reverse lend-lease. Some cash was involved in the final settlement of accounts.*]

2. Senator Wheeler Assails Lend-Lease (1941)

Like the interventionists, Roosevelt believed that the salvation of Britain through large-scale military aid was crucial for the defense of the United States. But so strong was isolationist opposition that the proposed lend-lease act could not be entitled "An Act to Intervene in World War II for the Defense of Britain." The official title was "An Act Further to Promote the Defense of the United States." As finally passed, the new law virtually pledged the United States to the full extent of its economic resources to provide military supplies for those who were fighting aggression. Fiery Senator Burton K. Wheeler of Montana, "a born prosecutor" who had run for Vice-President on the left-wing La Follette Progressive ticket of 1924, was one of the most vehement isolationists. In the following radio speech, how prophetic is he?

The lend-lease policy, translated into legislative form, stunned a Congress and a nation wholly sympathetic to the cause of Great Britain. . . . It warranted my worst fears for the future of America, and it definitely stamps the President as war-minded.

The lend-lease-give program is the New Deal's Triple-A foreign policy; it will plow under every fourth American boy.

Never before have the American people been asked or compelled to give so bounteously and so completely of their tax dollars to any foreign nation. Never before has the Congress of the United States been asked by any President to violate international law. Never before has this Nation resorted to duplicity in the conduct of its foreign affairs. Never before has

2. Reprinted in *Congressional Record*, 77 Cong., 1 sess., Appendix, pp. 178–79 (speech of Jan. 12, 1941).

the United States given to one man the power to strip this Nation of its defenses. Never before has a Congress coldly and flatly been asked to abdicate.

If the American people want a dictatorship—if they want a totalitarian form of government and if they want war—this bill should be steam-rollered through Congress, as is the wont of President Roosevelt.

Approval of this legislation means war, open and complete warfare. I, therefore, ask the American people before they supinely accept it, Was the last World War worth while?

If it were, then we should lend and lease war materials. If it were, then we should lend and lease American boys. President Roosevelt has said we would be repaid by England. We will be. We will be repaid, just as England repaid her war debts of the first World War—repaid those dollars wrung from the sweat of labor and the toil of farmers with cries of "Uncle Shylock." Our boys will be returned—returned in caskets, maybe; returned with bodies maimed; returned with minds warped and twisted by sights of horrors and the scream and shriek of high-powered shells.

Considered on its merits and stripped of its emotional appeal to our sympathies, the lend-lease-give bill is both ruinous and ridiculous. . . .

It gives to one man—responsible to no one—the power to denude our shores of every warship. It gives to one individual the dictatorial power to strip the American Army of our every tank, cannon, rifle, or anti-aircraft gun. No one would deny that the lend-lease-give bill contains provisions that would enable one man to render the United States defenseless, but they will tell you, "The President would never do it." To this I say, "Why does he ask the power if he does not intend to use it?" Why not, I say, place some check on American donations to a foreign nation? . . .

I say in the kind of language used by the President—shame on those who ask the powers—and shame on those who would grant them.

[*Talk of "plowing under every fourth American boy" spurred Roosevelt into declaring at his press conference of January 14, 1941, that this was "the most untruthful, as the most dastardly, unpatriotic thing that has ever been said. Quote me on that. That really is the rottenest thing that has been said in public life in my generation." What measure of truth was there in Wheeler's charge?*]

3. Hearst Denounces Aid to Russia (1941)

The fateful lend-lease bill became law in March, 1941. Three months later Hitler treacherously attacked Stalin, his co-conspirator in the non-aggression pact of 1939. Isolationists rejoiced that the two arch-menaces would now bleed each other white, and thus reduce the danger of American involvement. Catholics expressed relief at the weakening of the atheistic menace of Soviet Russia. But Roosevelt, fearful that the Russians could not stem Hitler's mechanized might, promised them lend-lease aid and ultimately delivered supplies worth $11 billion. The Hearst press here expresses distaste for "Bloody Joe" Stalin as a bedfellow. To what extent were its apprehensions justified by events?

3. New York *Journal-American*, Sept. 5, 1941.

If we are fighting against totalitarianism as a foul principle and oppressive policy, why in the name of high heaven should we not desire to see the two totalitarian powers exterminate each other and destroy not only the principle but the practice of despotic government?

If we are citizens—or subjects—of a genuine democracy and if we are devoted to the ideals of democracy, and honestly desirous of preserving and perpetuating those ideals, why should we not desire to see the enemies of democracy destroy each other? . . .

Is our free country piling up deficits, bleeding its citizens white with confiscatory taxation, rushing headlong into national bankruptcy, shoveling out our wealth abroad, and shipping our war materials to alien nations to bolster up Bolshevism in Russia to spread it over all of Europe, including Britain, and to breed it and broadcast it in our own America?

We may not think that this is what we want to do, but this is exactly what we are doing with our Bolshevist alliance, and no smoke screen of fine phrases can obscure that outstanding fact.

No country which fights for Russia can claim to be honestly opposed to tyranny, since Bolshevism is the basest and bloodiest tyranny that has disgraced the supposed civilization of Europe since the time of Ivan the Terrible.

No country can truthfully claim to be crusading for democracy and the four freedoms when it is supporting a tyranny which is the most evil enemy of democracy—a tyranny where all the four freedoms have been brutally suppressed—a tyranny with no liberty, no opportunity, no morality, and no God.

D. WAR IN THE ATLANTIC

1. Framing the Atlantic Charter (1941)

Roosevelt finally met with Prime Minister Churchill in deepest secrecy off the coast of Newfoundland in August, 1941. Major items of discussion were lend-lease shipments, common defense, and the halting of Japanese aggression. Churchill later wrote that for Roosevelt—the head of a technically neutral state—to meet in this way with the prime minister of a belligerent state was "astonishing" and amounted to "warlike action." The most spectacular offspring of the conference was the unofficial Atlantic Charter, which in 1942 became the cornerstone of Allied war aims. An admixture of the old Wilson Fourteen Points (see p. 671) and the new New Deal, it held out seductive hope to the victims of the dictators. What aspects of the Atlantic Charter come closest to "warlike action"?

. . . The President of the United States of America and the Prime Minister, Mr. Churchill, representing His Majesty's Government in the United Kingdom, being met together, deem it right to make known certain common principles in the national policies of their respective countries on which they base their hopes for a better future for the world.

First, their countries seek no aggrandizement, territorial or other;

1. *Department of State Bulletin,* V, 125–26 (Aug. 14, 1941).

Second, they desire to see no territorial changes that do not accord with the freely expressed wishes of the peoples concerned [*i.e.*, self-determination, one of the later 14 Points; in part Points V and XII of the 14];

Third, they respect the right of all peoples to choose the form of government under which they will live; and they wish to see sovereign rights and self-government restored to those who have been forcibly deprived of them [cf. territorial restoration, Points VI, VII, VIII, XI of the 14];

Fourth, they will endeavor, with due respect for their existing obligations, to further the enjoyment by all states, great or small, victor or vanquished, of access, on equal terms, to the trade and to the raw materials of the world which are needed for their economic prosperity [*i.e.*, Point III of 14];

Fifth, they desire to bring about the fullest collaboration between all nations in the economic field with the object of securing, for all, improved labor standards, economic advancement, and social security [a combination of the objectives of the League of Nations and the New Deal];

Sixth, after the final destruction of the Nazi tyranny, they hope to see established a peace which will afford to all nations the means of dwelling in safety within their own boundaries, and which will afford assurance that all the men in all the lands may live out their lives in freedom from fear and want;

Seventh, such a peace should enable all men to traverse the high seas and oceans without hindrance [*i.e.*, freedom of the seas, Point II of 14];

Eighth, they believe that all of the nations of the world, for realistic as well as spiritual reasons, must come to the abandonment of the use of force. Since no future peace can be maintained if land, sea, or air armaments continue to be employed by nations which threaten, or may threaten, aggression outside of their frontiers, they believe, pending the establishment of a wider and permanent system of general security [United Nations, replacing League of Nations], that the disarmament of such nations is essential. They will likewise aid and encourage all other practicable measures which will lighten for peace-loving peoples the crushing burden of armaments [*i.e.*, Point IV of 14].

2. The Chicago *Tribune* Is Outraged (1941)

A highly influential mouthpiece of Middle Western isolationism was the Chicago *Tribune*, self-elected "The World's Greatest Newspaper." Violently anti-Roosevelt and anti-intervention, it resorted to extreme measures, including the publication of Washington's secret war plans three days before Pearl Harbor. To what extent does the *Tribune's* editorial on the Atlantic Conference confirm Churchill's later observation that the deliberations amounted to "warlike action?"

Mr. Roosevelt's dangerous ambition always to do what no other President ever did, and to be the man who shakes the world, led him to meet

2. Chicago *Tribune*, Aug. 15, 1941, as quoted in *A Century of Tribune Editorials* (1947), pp. 129–30. By permission of the Chicago *Tribune*.

Mr. Churchill, as is now disclosed, at sea. There, he, the head of a nation which is not at war, and the head of the British empire, which is at war, signed their names to an eight-point war and peace program, as if both countries not only were fighting side by side but saw their way to victory. . . .

For Mr. Churchill the event would be, he could hope, that last step which would bring him what he has awaited as his salvation—the final delivery on Mr. Roosevelt's commitments, the delivery of the United States with all its man power into the war at all points. Mr. Churchill would appreciate that Mr. Roosevelt in the eyes of the world became his full ally. . . .

Mr. Roosevelt himself had that end in view. As head of a nation at peace he had no right to discuss war aims with the ruler of a country at war. He had no right to take a chair at such a conference. He had no regard for his constitutional duties or his oath of office when he did so. He not only likes to shatter traditions, he likes to shatter the checks and restraints which were put on his office. He is thoroly un-American. His ancestry is constantly emerging. He is the true descendant of that James Roosevelt, his great-grandfather, who was a Tory in New York during the Revolution and took the oath of allegiance to the British king.* . . .

He comes of a stock that has never fought for the country and he now betrays it, altho it has repudiated his program and him with it. . . .

The American people can rest assured that Mr. Churchill was paying little attention to the rehash of the Wilsonian futilities, to the freedom of the seas and the freedom of peoples such as the [British-ruled] people of India, for instance. What he wanted to know of Mr. Roosevelt was: When are you coming across? And it is the answer to that question that concerns the American people, who have voted 4 to 1 that they are not going across at all unless their government drags them in against their will.

One phrase in the statement would have Mr. Churchill's complete approval—"after final destruction of the Nazi tyranny." To that he committed the President of the United States in circumstances as spectacular and theatrical as could be arranged. Mr. Roosevelt pledged himself to the destruction of Hitler and the Nazis. In the circumstances in which this was done Mr. Churchill would insist that it was the pledge of a government, binding upon the country.

The country repudiates it. Mr. Roosevelt had no authority and can find none for making such a pledge. He was more than outside the country. He was outside his office. The spectacle was one of two autocratic rulers, one of them determining the destiny of his country in the matter of war or peace absolutely in his own will, as if his subjects were without voice.

The country rejects that idea of its government.

---

* James Roosevelt, only fifteen years old when the fighting began, was a student at Princeton from 1776 to 1780. His father, a staunch Patriot, was forced to flee New York City. There is no evidence that young James took the alleged oath; the probabilities are strong that he did not. (Information provided by Elizabeth B. Drewry, Director of the Franklin D. Roosevelt Library.)

3. F.D.R. Proclaims Shoot-at-Sight (1941)

Lend-lease carried an implied commitment that the United States would guarantee delivery of arms, even though the law specifically forbade "convoying vessels by naval vessels of the United States." Roosevelt got around this restriction by setting up a system of patrols by American warships working in collaboration with the British. On September 4, 1941, the U.S. destroyer *Greer* in Icelandic waters trailed a German submarine for three and one-half hours, while radioing its position to nearby British aircraft. The U-boat finally fired two torpedoes (which missed), whereupon the *Greer* retaliated with depth bombs (which also missed). Seven days later, after presumably taking time to verify the facts, Roosevelt went on the radio with this sensational shoot-at-sight speech. What liberties does he take with the truth? Did the crisis justify his doing so?

The Navy Department of the United States has reported to me that, on the morning of September fourth, the United States destroyer *Greer*, proceeding in full daylight toward Iceland, had reached a point southeast of Greenland. She was carrying American mail to Iceland. She was flying the American flag. Her identity as an American ship was unmistakable.

She was then and there attacked by a submarine. Germany admits that it was a German submarine. The submarine deliberately fired a torpedo at the *Greer*, followed later by another torpedo attack. In spite of what Hitler's propaganda bureau has invented, and in spite of what any American obstructionist organization may prefer to believe, I tell you the blunt fact that the German submarine fired first upon this American destroyer without warning, and with deliberate design to sink her.

Our destroyer, at the time, was in waters which the Government of the United States has declared to be waters of self-defense—surrounding outposts of American protection in the Atlantic.

In the north, outposts have been established by us in Iceland, Greenland, Labrador, and Newfoundland. Through these waters there pass many ships of many flags. They bear food and other supplies to civilians; and they bear [lend-lease] matériel of war, for which the people of the United States are spending billions of dollars, and which, by Congressional action, they have declared to be essential for the defense of our own land.

The United States destroyer, when attacked, was proceeding on a legitimate mission. . . .

Generation after generation, America has battled for the general policy of the freedom of the seas.* That policy is a very simple one—but a basic, fundamental one. It means that no nation has the right to make the broad oceans of the world, at great distances from the actual theater of land war, unsafe for the commerce of others. . . .

It is no act of war on our part when we decide to protect the seas which

---

3. *Department of State Bulletin*, V, 193, 195, 197 (Sept. 13, 1941).
* The traditional American concept of freedom of the seas did not include the armed convoying of gift lend-lease munitions through German-proclaimed war zones to the enemies of Germany.

are vital to American defense. The aggression is not ours. Ours is solely defense.

But let this warning be clear. From now on, if German or Italian vessels of war enter the waters, the protection of which is necessary for American defense, they do so at their own peril.

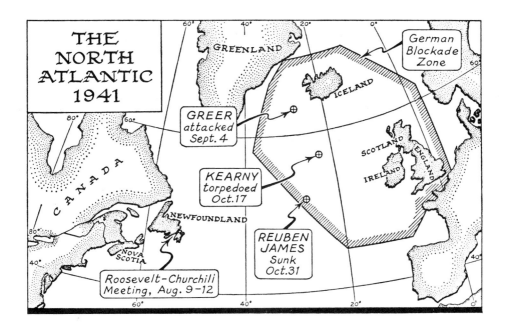

[*Patrolling led to convoying by presidential edict, despite the express terms of the Lend-Lease Act, and convoying led to shooting. In October, 1941, the U.S. destroyer* Kearny *suffered torpedo damage and a loss of eleven lives in a battle with German submarines southwest of Iceland. Later that month the U.S. destroyer* Reuben James *was torpedoed and sunk off Iceland while on convoy duty. An undeclared shooting war with Hitler was now being waged in the Atlantic.*]

E. BLOWUP IN THE PACIFIC

1. Ickes Prepares to "Raise Hell" (1941)

New Japanese aggression in south Indochina, despite warnings from Washington, finally prompted Roosevelt to clamp down a complete embargo on shipments going to Japan when he froze all Japanese assets in the United States on July 25, 1941. Faced with the loss of critical oil supplies, the Tokyo war lords were confronted with agonizing alternatives: yielding some of the fruits of their aggression in the Far East

---

1. *The Secret Diary of Harold L. Ickes,* III, 654–55. Copyright © 1953 by Simon & Schuster, Inc., renewed © 1981 by Harold M. and Elizabeth Ickes. Reprinted by permission of Simon & Schuster, a Division of Gulf & Western Corporation.

or fighting the United States and its allies. America was by no means ready for war in the vast Pacific, and the administration seriously considered a three-month truce— Roosevelt favored six months. But this proposal was never formally presented to Japan. The outspoken Secretary of the Interior Harold Ickes records in his secret diary the story as he heard it. What does this account (November 30) reveal of the inner workings of the Washington government? Why did the truce scheme fail?

Our State Department has been negotiating for several days with Saburo Kurusu, the special envoy sent over from Japan, and with Ambassador Kichisaburo Nomura. I have had a suspicion for a long time that the State Department would resume a policy of appeasement toward Japan, if it could get away with it.

Our State Department, according to a story that I have heard, had actually proposed what it called a "truce" for three months with Japan. We were to resume shipments of cotton and other commodities, but the most important item on the list was gasoline for "civilian" purposes. Now anyone who knows anything about Japan and about the situation there knows that there is very little, if any, civilian use of gasoline. . . . Then a strong protest came in from General Chiang Kai-shek to the effect that to do this would destroy the morale of the Chinese. It was the intention of the State Department to crowd the thing through without even giving Halifax [British ambassador] a chance to refer it to Churchill. However, the British fought for and obtained a sufficient delay to consult Churchill, and he was strongly opposed.

The strong opposition of China and Britain caused the appeasers of the State Department to pause. They went to the White House, and in the end the President refused to go through with the deal.

If it had not been for the strenuous intervention of Churchill and Chiang Kai-shek, the appeasers in the State Department, with the support of the President, would have resumed at least a partial commercial relationship with Japan, as the result of which we would have sent Japan cotton and gasoline and other commodities. . . .

If this negotiation with Japan had been consummated, I would have promptly resigned from the Cabinet with a ringing statement attacking the arrangement and raising hell generally with the State Department and its policy of appeasement. I have no doubt that the country would have reacted violently. As a matter of fact, some of the newspapers indicated that they were uneasy and printed editorials deprecating any attempt at even a partial resumption of relationship with Japan. I believe that the President would have lost the country on this issue and that hell would have been to pay generally.

Now matters are very tense indeed so far as Japan is concerned. The morning papers carry headlines announcing that Japan has solemnly declared her determination "to purge American and British influence from East Asia for the honor and pride of mankind." So it may be, after all, that there will be a clash in the Pacific.

2. Tōgō Blames the United States (1952)

Instead of appeasement, Secretary Hull presented stern terms to the two Japanese envoys in his note of November 26, 1941. Japan would have to withdraw her armed forces from China, after four years of aggression, and from Indochina as well. In return, the United States would unfreeze Japanese assets and make some other secondary concessions. Such loss of face was so abhorrent to the Japanese war lords that Hull had little hope that the terms would be accepted. The next day he told Secretary of War Stimson, "I have washed my hands of it, and it is now in the hands of you and [Secretary of the Navy] Knox—the Army and Navy." The reaction of Japan is described by the then Foreign Minister, Tōgō Shigenori, who later died in prison while serving a twenty-year sentence as a war criminal. Where does he lay the blame for the breakdown of negotiations?

Ambassador Grew, then in Tokyo, later said that when the note of 26 November was sent, the button which set off the war had been pushed.

On the 26th and 27th Secretary Hull held special press conferences at which he gave a full account of the Japanese-American negotiations; the American press responded by reporting almost unanimously that it was Japan's choice whether to accept the Hull Note or go to war. Later—in wartime—an American chronicler wrote that even a Monaco or a Luxemburg would have taken up arms against the United States if it had been handed such a memorandum as that which the State Department presented to the Japanese government. . . .

It is therefore no longer arguable at this time of day that the American authorities, having made all necessary preparations in the expectation that the negotiations would break down and a war ensue, delivered the Hull Note anticipating that Japan would reject it, thus compelling her to elect between total surrender and war. Indeed, remembering that the question of how to insure that Japan should fire the first shot had been in the forefront in the War Cabinet's discussions in Washington, it seems not unwarrantable to construe the note as going beyond the forcing of a choice —it is not too much to say that it was the throwing down of a challenge to Japan, or at the least constituted an ultimatum without time limit.

This we knew in Tokyo—though we could not then know of the words and acts of the high American officials which confirmed our deduction— from the drastic terms of the note and the inclusion among them of conditions never theretofore suggested. Our interpretation was confirmed by the reaction to Hull's disclosures by the American press—which played up, as if at the urging of the governmental authorities, the choice between the terms of the Hull Note and war—and by the plainly visible tightening of the encirclement of Japan.

So far as concerns my own state of mind upon receipt of the Hull Note, I can never forget the despair which overpowered me. I had fought and worked unflaggingly until that moment; but I could feel no enthusiasm for the fight thereafter. I tried as it were to close my eyes and swallow the Hull Note whole, as the alternative to war, but it stuck in the craw. In contrast to my dejection, many of the military men were elated at the uncompromising attitude of the United States, as if to say, "Didn't we tell you so?"—they were by no means easy to be patient with.

"GIVE 'EM BOTH BARRELS"

Uncle Sam aroused by Japanese sneak attack at Pearl Harbor. New Orleans *Times-Picayune*, 1941.

[*The Japanese later argued that they were forced to break out of the economic encircle-ment resulting from Roosevelt's embargo-freezing order of July 25, 1941. This view found surprising sup-port in 1944 from one of America's allies, Cap-tain Oliver Lyttleton, British Minister of Pro-duction. In a London speech he declared, "Japan was provoked into attacking the Amer-icans at Pearl Harbor. It is a travesty on his-tory ever to say that America was forced into the war. . . . It is in-correct to say that America was ever truly neutral. . . . " The sub-sequent uproar in the United States forced Lyttleton hastily to soften his remarks. (New York Times, June 21, 22, 1944.)*]

3. Hull Justifies His Stand (1948)

Isolationist Senator Vandenberg, writing in his diary just after Pearl Harbor, felt that the United States would have had to yield "relatively little" to pacify Japan, and feared that "we may have *driven* her *needlessly* into hostilities through our dog-matic diplomatic attitudes. . . ." "We 'asked for it,' " he added, "and we 'got it.' " Secretary of State Hull, the soft-spoken Tennessean, here outlines three possible alter-natives in his *Memoirs*. Assuming that the ultimate security of the United States required the halting of the Japanese, and knowing that America's navy was not ready for Japan, form conclusions as to the wisdom of Hull's choice among the three possi-bilities. Were other courses open?

There were three methods to meet the danger from Japan. One was by a preventive attack. But democracies do not engage in preventive attacks except with greatest difficulty. Had I suggested to the President that he go to Congress and ask for a declaration of war against Japan at some time after the invasion of southern Indo-China, he could have made a good case concerning the dangers to us inherent in Japan's course of aggression. But, remembering the fact that on August 13, 1941, only three weeks after Japan invaded southern Indo-China, the House of Representatives sustained the Selective Service Act by a majority of just one vote, it seems most unlikely that the President could have obtained a declaration.

Nor would the military and naval authorities have been ready for a preventive attack. The fact that they pleaded for more time solely to prepare our defenses in the Pacific was proof in itself that they were not prepared to take the offensive.

A preventive attack, moreover, would have run counter to our determination to pursue the course of peace to the end, with the hope, however microscopic, that even at the last hour the Japanese might have a change of heart.

The second method to meet the danger was to agree to Japan's demands. This would have given us peace—that is, until Japan, after strengthening herself through the concessions we should have made, was ready to move again. But it would have denied all the principles of right living among nations which we had supported; it would have betrayed the countries [China, Britain] that later became our allies; and it would have given us an infamous place in history.

When we realize that Japan was ruthlessly invading peaceful countries, that the United States had pleaded with her from the beginning to cease her course of military conquest in partnership with Hitler, and that all problems in the Pacific would have practically settled themselves if Japan had adopted a policy of peace, it is evident that Japan had no right to make demands upon us. Japan negotiated as if we, too, were an aggressor, as if both countries had to balance their aggressions. Japan had no more right to make demands upon us than an individual gangster has to make demands upon his intended victim.

The third method was simply to continue discussions with Japan, to convince her that her aggressions cost her more than they were worth, to point out to her that her partnership with Hitler could be as dangerous to her as it was to the rest of the world, to lay before her proposal after proposal which in the long run would have given her in peace the prosperity her military leaders were seeking in conquest.

It was this third that we chose. Of the three, it was the only American method.

[*The Tokyo war lords claimed that they had only two choices—surrender or war. Actually they had a third choice—accommodation. Loss of considerable face would have been better than loss of the war. The argument that Hull's note of November 26 provoked the Japanese into an attack is weakened by two facts. First, the naval force that attacked Pearl Harbor had left its rendezvous in Japan twenty-four hours earlier. Second, early in November the imperial conference had unanimously decided on war, provided that diplomacy had not produced a satisfactory settlement by December 1.]*

THOUGHT PROVOKERS

1. What would have happened if the United States had been truly neutral during World War II? Would the results have been to the nation's best interests?

2. Have the events since 1945 given support to the view that a democratic United States could exist as a kind of fortified island?

3. Lend-lease was designed to defend the United States by helping others fight America's potential enemies with America's weapons. Was there an element of immorality in this policy? Would the United States have kept out of the war if the Lend-Lease Act had not been passed?

4. Assuming that the Atlantic Charter was a warlike step, was it justified? Roosevelt believed that a Hitler victory would be ruinous for the United States, and to combat isolationist pressures he repeatedly misrepresented facts (*Greer* case) or usurped powers (convoying). Was he justified in using such methods to arouse the American people to an awareness of their danger?

5. With regard to the diplomatic breakdown preceding Pearl Harbor, it has been said that both Japan and America were right if one conceded their major premises. Explain fully and form a conclusion.

42 · *America in World War II*

> *No matter how long it may take us to overcome this premeditated invasion [Pearl Harbor], the American people in their righteous might will win through to absolute victory.*
>
> FRANKLIN D. ROOSEVELT, WAR MESSAGE, 1941

PROLOGUE: The nation was plunged into war with the worst naval disaster in its history, and many agonizing months were to pass before the tide in the Pacific began to turn. The American conquest of bomber bases in the Marianas Islands in 1944 ensured that Japan would eventually be blasted into surrender. Meanwhile the Battle of Production at home and the Battle of the Atlantic against German submarines had to be won, as they narrowly were. The hard-pressed and ever-suspicious Soviets, anxious to have the Western allies share equally in the blood-letting, clamored ceaselessly for a second front. Following two widely spaced postponements, the invasion was launched on French soil in 1944, and it teetered so long in the balance as to indicate that earlier invasions would have failed. After Germany was hammered into submission in May, 1945, Japan was atom-bombed into prostration in August, 1945. The Great War ended as the Nuclear Age dawned, ushered in by an ominous mushroom-shaped cloud.

A. THE BLAME FOR PEARL HARBOR

1. War Warnings from Washington (1941)

The military officials in Washington had "cracked" Tokyo's secret code. They therefore knew from intercepted messages, especially after Secretary Hull's final note of November 26, that Japan was about to attack. But they could only guess where. The following war warnings were dispatched to Pacific commanders, including General MacArthur, who was caught with his planes down in the Philippines some eight hours *after* the Pearl Harbor attack on December 7, 1941. The messages from Washington did not mention Hawaii, evidently because of the belief, fortified by reports of massed ship movements, that the Japanese were about to strike in Southeast Asia. The surprised American commanders later complained that they had not been properly warned. Comment critically in the light of these warnings. What grounds existed for the assumption that the attack would not come at Pearl Harbor?

[Navy Department to Pacific Commanders, November 24, 1941]
Chances of favorable outcome of negotiations with Japan very doubtful. This situation, coupled with statements of Japanese Government and movements their naval and military forces, indicates in our opinion that a surprise aggressive movement in any direction, including attack on Philippines or Guam, is a possibility. Chief of Staff has seen this dispatch; concurs

1. *Pearl Harbor Attack; Hearings before the Joint Committee on the Investigation of the Pearl Harbor Attack,* 79 Cong. 1 sess., pt. xiv, pp. 1405, 1406.

791

and requests action [by the respective addressees] to inform senior Army officers their areas. Utmost secrecy necessary in order not to complicate an already tense situation or precipitate Japanese action.

[Navy Department to Asiatic and Pacific Fleets, November 27, 1941]

This despatch is to be considered a war warning. Negotiations with Japan looking toward stabilization of conditions in the Pacific have ceased, and an aggressive move by Japan is expected within the next few days. The number and equipment of Japanese troops, and the organization of naval task forces, indicates an amphibious expedition against either the Philippines, Thai [Siam] or Kra [Malay] peninsula, or possibly Borneo [Dutch East Indies]. . . .

2. Admiral Kimmel Defends Himself (1946)

In 1942, after carrier-based Japanese bombers had crippled the American fleet at Pearl Harbor on that fateful Sunday morning, the special Roberts commission found Admiral H. E. Kimmel and General W. C. Short guilty of "dereliction of duty." But the Army and the Navy conducted their own investigations and concluded that there were no grounds for a court-martial. After the war a full-dress joint Congressional investigation (ten million words) elicited the following testimony from Admiral Kimmel, who must be judged in the light of three points. First, as early as 1932 the Navy had staged a successful mock (Japanese) raid on Pearl Harbor *on a Sunday morning* with carrier-based aircraft. Second, the attacking Japanese carriers had been lost to American naval intelligence for some days. Third, four hours and thirteen minutes before the surprise attack the Navy sighted an enemy submarine off the mouth of Pearl Harbor; an hour and ten minutes before the strike the Navy fired upon and sank a Japanese submarine off the mouth of Pearl Harbor. What were the strengths and weaknesses of Kimmel's defense?

The so-called "war warning" dispatch of November 27 did not warn the Pacific Fleet of an attack in the Hawaiian area. It did not state expressly or by implication that an attack in the Hawaiian area was imminent or probable. It did not repeal or modify the advice previously given me by the Navy Department that no move against Pearl Harbor was imminent or planned by Japan.

The phrase "war warning" cannot be made a catch-all for all the contingencies hindsight may suggest. It is a characterization of the specific information which the dispatch contained. . . .

In brief, on November 27, the Navy Department suggested that I send from the immediate vicinity of Pearl Harbor the carriers of the fleet, which constituted the fleet's main striking defense against an air attack.*

On November 27, the War and Navy Departments suggested that we send from the island of Oahu [site of Pearl Harbor] 50 percent of the Army's resources in pursuit planes.

2. *Ibid.,* pt. VI, pp. 2518, 2520, 2521.
* Fortunately for the United States, the three great carriers were not at Pearl Harbor when the attack came.

These proposals came to us on the very same day of the so-called "war warning."

In these circumstances no reasonable man in my position would consider that the "war warning" was intended to suggest the likelihood of an attack in the Hawaiian area.

From November 27 to the time of the attack, all the information which I had from the Navy Department or from any other source, confirmed, and was consistent with, the Japanese movement in southeast Asia described in the dispatch of November 27. . . .

In short, all indications of the movements of Japanese military and naval forces which came to my attention confirmed the information in the dispatch of 27 November—that the Japanese were on the move against Thailand or the Kra [Malay] Peninsula in southeast Asia.

3. Secretary Stimson Charges Negligence (1946)

General Short, the Army commander in Hawaii, complained that the warnings from Washington were not specific enough regarding a possible Japanese attack. He felt that he should have been advised that Washington was intercepting Japanese coded messages (despite the need for secrecy in using these "magic" intercepts). Yet on November 30—a week early—the Honolulu *Advertiser* had headlined a story "JAPANESE MAY STRIKE OVER WEEKEND." Newly installed Army radar actually picked up the attacking Japanese planes fifty-three minutes in advance, but this evidence stirred no defensive action. Secretary of War Stimson, who had served in three presidential Cabinets, here defends his office before the joint Congressional committee. Is his analogy to a sentinel convincing?

Many of the discussions on this subject indicated a failure to grasp the fundamental difference between the duties of an outpost command and those of the commander in chief of an army or nation and his military advisers.

The outpost commander is like a sentinel on duty in the face of the enemy. His fundamental duties are clear and precise. He must assume that the enemy will attack at his particular post; and that the enemy will attack at the time and in the way in which it will be most difficult to defeat him. It is not the duty of the outpost commander to speculate or rely on the possibilities of the enemy attacking at some other outpost instead of his own. It is his duty to meet him at his post at any time, and to make the best possible fight that can be made against him with the weapons with which he has been supplied.

On the other hand, the Commander in Chief of the Nation (and his advisers) . . . has much more difficult and complex duties to fulfill. Unlike the outpost commander, he must constantly watch, study, and estimate where the principal or most dangerous attack is most likely to come, in order that he may most effectively distribute his insufficient forces and munitions to meet it. He knows that his outposts are not all equally sup-

3. *Ibid.*, pt. XI, pp. 5428–29.

plied or fortified, and that they are not all equally capable of defense. He knows also that from time to time they are of greatly varying importance to the grand strategy of the war. . . .

From the foregoing I believe that it was inevitable and proper that a far greater number of items of information coming through our Intelligence should be collected and considered and appraised by the General Staff at Washington than those which were transmitted to the commander of an outpost.

General Short had been told the two essential facts: (1) A war with Japan is threatening. (2) Hostile action by Japan is possible at any moment. Given those two facts, both of which were stated without equivocation in the message of November 27, the outpost commander should be on the alert to make his fight.

Even without any such message, the outpost commander should have been on the alert. If he did not know that the relations between Japan and the United States were strained and might be broken at any time, he must have been almost the only man in Hawaii who did not know it, for the radio and the newspapers were blazoning out those facts daily, and he had a chief of staff and an intelligence officer to tell him so. And if he did not know that the Japanese were likely to strike without warning, he could not have read his history of Japan or known the lessons taught in Army schools in respect to such matters.*

Under these circumstances, which were of general knowledge and which he must have known, to cluster his airplanes in such groups and positions that in an emergency they could not take to the air for several hours, and to keep his anti-aircraft ammunition so stored that it could not be promptly and immediately available, and to use his best reconnaissance system, the radar, only for a very small fraction of the day and night, in my opinion betrayed a misconception of his real duty which was almost beyond belief.

[*The joint Congressional committee investigating Pearl Harbor was a partisan body which submitted two reports. The majority (six Democrats, joined by two Republicans) generally absolved the Democratic Roosevelt administration of responsibility for the surprise attack, while finding the Hawaii commanders guilty of "errors of judgment and not derelictions of duty." Two Republican Senators filed a minority report highly critical of the Roosevelt administration.*]

4. Roosevelt Awaits the Blow (1941)

On the evening of December 6—the day before Pearl Harbor—American naval intelligence intercepted and decoded the bulk of Tokyo's warlike reply to Secretary Hull's last "tough" note (November 26). Commander Lester Schulz, a naval aide at the White House, promptly delivered these intercepts to the White House. Five years

---

* Attacking without warning had been a feudal practice in Japan. The Japanese attacked the Chinese without warning in 1894 and 1931 and the Russians in 1904. In the Age of Hitler, attacks without warning were commonplace, as indeed they have been throughout history.

4. *Ibid.*, pt. X, pp. 4662–63.

later he testified before the joint Congressional committee as to the President's reaction. Certain critics of Roosevelt claim that he now knew of the Japanese plan to strike Pearl Harbor the next day, and that he deliberately exposed the fleet so as to lure the Japanese into an act of aggression which would unify American opinion. What light does Commander Schulz's testimony shed on this interpretation?

Commander SCHULZ. The President read the papers, which took perhaps ten minutes. Then he handed them to Mr. [Harry] Hopkins. . . . Mr. Hopkins then read the papers and handed them back to the President. The President then turned toward Mr. Hopkins and said in substance . . . "This means war." Mr. Hopkins agreed, and they discussed then, for perhaps five minutes, the situation of the Japanese forces, that is, their deployment and—

MR. RICHARDSON [committee counsel]. Can you recall what either of them said?

Commander SCHULZ. In substance I can. . . . Mr. Hopkins . . . expressed a view that since war was undoubtedly going to come at the convenience of the Japanese, it was too bad that we could not strike the first blow and prevent any sort of surprise. The President nodded and then said in effect, "No, we can't do that. We are a democracy and a peaceful people." Then he raised his voice, and this much I remember definitely. He said, "But we have a good record."

The impression that I got was that we would have to stand on that record; we could not make the first overt move. We would have to wait until it came.

During this discussion there was no mention of Pearl Harbor. The only geographic name I recall was Indochina. The time at which war might begin was not discussed, but from the manner of the discussion there was no indication that tomorrow was necessarily the day.

B. SOVIET-AMERICAN FRICTION

1. Communists Distrust Capitalists (1946)

General John R. Deane, the chief United States military liaison officer in Moscow, found the hard-pressed Russians willing to accept American arms but not American personnel. He concluded that the Communist regime did not want its people tainted by exposure to capitalistic Americans; that it desired the prestige of winning solo victories; and that it regarded World War II as only one campaign in the long war against capitalism. Why permit possible future adversaries like the Americans to spy out the terrain and probe Russia's military weaknesses? In this post-war account, General Deane cites specific cases. Which ones seem to be least credible? What do they foreshadow regarding cooperation with Moscow after the war?

Whatever the reasons, the fact that Russia desired, insofar as possible, to play a lone hand was proved by undeniable evidence. In her darkest

1. Selections from *The Strange Alliance,* pp. 296, 160–61, by J. R. Deane. Copyright 1947 by J. R. Deane; renewed 1974. Reprinted by permission of Viking Penguin Inc.

days she refused to allow a group of Allied bombers to base in the Caucasus
in order to assist her at Stalingrad. Our well-meant voluntary efforts to
support her advance in the Balkans with our Air Force operating from
Italy brought forth protests rather than gratitude. No single American
was allowed to enter the Soviet Union without pressure from the Ambassador or me, and then a visa was granted only after an exhaustive study
of the background of the individual involved. Under these circumstances
it was clear that nothing much could come of a partnership in which one
of the principals was not only reluctant, but proficient in sabotaging its
effectiveness. . . .

When General Eisenhower visted Moscow after the war, he held a press
conference at which he stated that after January 1945 he was kept fully
informed at all times of the essentials of the Red Army's plans, particularly the timing of their offensives, their objectives, and the direction of
their main efforts. This was true, but his possession of such information was
a far cry from the co-operative action that might normally be expected
between allies. All the information Eisenhower had concerning the Red
Army's plans was the result of our initiative in seeking to obtain it, and
then it was only obtained after continuous pressure at the highest levels.

Not once during the war did Stalin or his subordinates seek a meeting
with British or American authorities in order to present proposals for
improving our co-operative effort. It was either the President or the Prime
Minister [Churchill] who proposed [conferences at] Teheran, Yalta, and
Potsdam. No single event of the war irritated me more than seeing the
President of the United States lifted from wheel chair to automobile, to
ship, to shore, and to aircraft, in order to go halfway around the world as
the only possible means of meeting J. V. Stalin.

There were innumerable little ways in which our joint war effort could
have been made more effective. We might have learned something of
immeasurable value in defeating the German submarines had we been
allowed to see Gdynia [naval base] as soon as it was taken; we might have
brought Germany to her knees quicker had we been allowed to establish
radar triangulation stations in Russia as navigational aids to our bomber
formations in eastern Germany. We might have defeated Germany more
quickly had we shared our operational experience by having observers on
each other's fronts. We might have, we might have—on and on. No! In
Soviet Russia each such venture would have meant a closer association
with capitalistic foreigners. Well, perhaps we were among friends, but it
was difficult to believe it.

[Deane further relates (p. 154) that when the British Military Mission in
Moscow was disbanded at war's end, it was discovered that the place was "infested with well-concealed dictaphones." Everything said by these British allies
of the Russians was evidently recorded for the information of the Soviet secret
police.]

2. Stalin Resents Second-Front Delays (1943)

The one kind of help that Stalin consistently demanded was the opening of a second front in France which would draw German divisions off the backs of the reeling Russians. As Stalingrad tottered, Communists and other groups in America demanded a morale-boosting second front in 1942, even though it might end in bloody failure. Conservatives insisted that the two menaces be left alone to cut each other's throats. Drew Pearson, the keyhole columnist, declared in 1943 that this brutal course was the policy of Washington. Secretary Hull thereupon branded such allegations "monstrous and diabolical falsehoods." Stalin was not unaware of such talk when he angrily sent the following secret message to Winston Churchill (June 24, 1943), just after Churchill had again backed down on his promise of a second front in 1943. From the viewpoint of the Allies, what is the most alarming aspect of Stalin's heated response?

. . . When you now write that "it would be no help to Russia if we threw away a hundred thousand men in a disastrous cross-Channel attack," all I can do is remind you of the following:

First, your own Aide-Mémoire of June 1942, in which you declared that preparations were under way for an invasion, not by a hundred thousand, but by an Anglo-American force exceeding one million men at the very start of the operation.

Second, your February [1943] message, which mentioned extensive measures preparatory to the invasion of Western Europe in August or September 1943, which, apparently, envisaged an operation, not by a hundred thousand men, but by an adequate force.

So when you now declare: "I cannot see how a great British defeat and slaughter would aid the Soviet armies," is it not clear that a statement of this kind in re-

NOW!

The *Daily Worker*, a Communist newspaper, began clamoring for an immediate second front less than four months after Pearl Harbor, so as to divert Hitler from his attack on Russia. New York *Daily Worker*, April 9, 1942.

2. Ministry of Foreign Affairs of the U.S.S.R., *Correspondence between the Chairman of the Council of Ministers of the U.S.S.R. and the Presidents of the U.S.A. and the Prime Ministers of Great Britain during the Great Patriotic War of 1941–1945* (1957), II, 75–76.

lation to the Soviet Union is utterly groundless and directly contradicts your previous and responsible decisions, listed above, about extensive and vigorous measures by the British and Americans to organise the invasion this year, measures on which the complete success of the operation should hinge?

I shall not enlarge on the fact that this responsible decision, revoking your previous decisions on the invasion of Western Europe, was reached by you and the President without Soviet participation and without inviting its representatives to the Washington conference, although you cannot but be aware that the Soviet Union's role in the war against Germany and its interest in the problems of the second front are great enough.

There is no need to say that the Soviet Government cannot become reconciled to this disregard of vital Soviet interests in the war against the common enemy.

You say that you "quite understand" my disappointment. I must tell you that the point here is not just the disappointment of the Soviet Government, but the preservation of its confidence in its Allies, a confidence which is being subjected to severe stress. One should not forget that it is a question of saving millions of lives in the occupied areas of Western Europe and Russia, and of reducing the enormous sacrifices of the Soviet armies, compared with which the sacrifices of the Anglo-American armies are insignificant.

3. Roosevelt Manages "Uncle Joe" (1943)

Roosevelt was eager to meet Stalin and soften his suspicions with the famous "Roosevelt charm." "I can handle that old buzzard," he allegedly boasted in private. Late in 1943 the two men met for the first time, together with Prime Minister Churchill, at Teheran, the capital of Persia, which was as far away as Stalin would venture from his direction of the Soviet armies. Roosevelt reported his experiences to his Secretary of Labor, Frances Perkins, who recalls them as follows. How might one account for Stalin's attitude early in the sessions?

"You know [reported Roosevelt], the Russians are interesting people. For the first three days I made absolutely no progress. I couldn't get any personal connection with Stalin, although I had done everything he asked me to do. I had stayed at his Embassy, gone to his dinners, been introduced to his ministers and generals. He was correct, stiff, solemn, not smiling, nothing human to get hold of. I felt pretty discouraged. If it was all going to be official paper work, there was no sense in my having made this long journey which the Russians had wanted. They couldn't come to America or any place in Europe for it. I had come there to accommodate Stalin. I felt pretty discouraged because I thought I was making no personal headway. What we were doing could have been done by the foreign ministers.

3. Selections from *The Roosevelt I Knew*, pp. 83–85, by Frances Perkins. Copyright © 1946 by Frances Perkins; renewed 1974 by Susanna W. Coggeshall. Reprinted by permission of Viking Penguin Inc.

"I thought it over all night and made up my mind I had to do something desperate. I couldn't stay in Teheran forever. I had to cut through this icy surface so that later I could talk by telephone or letter in a personal way. I had scarcely seen Churchill alone during the conference. I had a feeling that the Russians did not feel right about seeing us conferring together in a language which we understood and they didn't.

"On my way to the conference room that morning we caught up with Winston [Churchill] and I had just a moment to say to him, 'Winston, I hope you won't be sore at me for what I am going to do.'

"Winston just shifted his cigar and grunted. I must say he behaved very decently afterward.

"I began almost as soon as we got into the conference room. I talked privately with Stalin. I didn't say anything that I hadn't said before, but it appeared quite chummy and confidential, enough so that the other Russians joined us to listen. Still no smile.

"Then I said, lifting my hand up to cover a whisper (which of course had to be interpreted), 'Winston is cranky this morning, he got up on the wrong side of the bed.'

"A vague smile passed over Stalin's eyes, and I decided I was on the right track. As soon as I sat down at the conference table, I began to tease Churchill about his Britishness, about John Bull, about his cigars, about his [drinking?] habits. It began to register with Stalin. Winston got red and scowled, and the more he did so, the more Stalin smiled. Finally Stalin broke out into a deep, hearty guffaw, and for the first time in three days I saw light. I kept it up until Stalin was laughing with me, and it was then that I called him 'Uncle Joe.' He would have thought me fresh the day before, but that day he laughed and came over and shook my hand.

"From that time on our relations were personal, and Stalin himself indulged in an occasional witticism. The ice was broken and we talked like men and brothers.

"You know . . . he was deeply touched by the presentation of the sword which Churchill brought him from the British people."

[*Relations between Roosevelt and Stalin remained friendly until several weeks before Roosevelt's death in April, 1945. Then Stalin abusively charged bad faith in connection with the surrender of German troops in Italy, while Roosevelt came back with protests against Stalin's violations of his Yalta pledges, notably in connection with Poland.*]

C. THE "UNCONDITIONAL SURRENDER" CONTROVERSY

1. Sherwood Defends F.D.R. (1948)

Late in 1942 the Allies launched a side-issue invasion of French North Africa, but Stalin refused to recognize it as a genuine second front. Shortly thereafter Roosevelt

1. From pp. 695–697 in *Roosevelt and Hopkins* by Robert E. Sherwood. Copyright 1948 by Robert E. Sherwood. By permission of Harper & Row, Publishers, Inc.

flew to Casablanca, in French Morocco, for a conference with Prime Minister Churchill, his eighth cousin once removed. Roosevelt knew that the embittered Stalin was deeply suspicious of a possible "deal" between Hitler and the Allies. The Russians might even make a separate peace with the Germans, as they had done with disastrous effect in 1918. At Roosevelt's instigation, the Casablanca conference proclaimed a policy of "unconditional surrender"—that is, the unconditional surrender of the Axis regimes but not "the destruction of the German populace, nor of the Italian or Japanese populace." Robert E. Sherwood, the ghost-writer associate of Roosevelt, here gives his version. Note how many different objectives the President had in view. Why can one argue that "unconditional surrender" did not prolong German resistance?

There were many propaganda experts, both British and American, who believed that the utterance of these words ["unconditional surrender"] would put the iron of desperate resistance into the Germans, Japanese, and Italians and thereby needlessly prolong the war and increase its cost; there are some who still believe that it did so. These critics were not necessarily opposed to the principle of total defeat—but they considered it a disastrous mistake for the President to announce it publicly. . . .

I wrote Winston Churchill asking him if he had discussed the unconditional surrender statement with Roosevelt before the press conference at Casablanca, and his reply was as follows: "I heard the words 'Unconditional Surrender' for the first time from the President's lips at the Conference. It must be remembered that at that moment no one had a right to proclaim that Victory was assured. Therefore, Defiance was the note. I would not myself have used these words, but I immediately stood by the President and have frequently defended the decision. It is false to suggest that it prolonged the war. Negotiation with Hitler was impossible. He was a maniac with supreme power to play his hand out to the end, which he did; and so did we."

Roosevelt himself absolved Churchill from all responsibility for the statement. Indeed, he suggested that it was an unpremeditated one on his own part. He said, "We had so much trouble getting those two French generals together that I thought to myself that this was as difficult as arranging the meeting of Grant and Lee—and then suddenly the press conference was on, and Winston and I had had no time to prepare for it, and the thought popped into my mind that they had called Grant 'Old Unconditional Surrender' and the next thing I knew, I had said it."

Roosevelt, for some reason, often liked to picture himself as a rather frivolous fellow who did not give sufficient attention to the consequences of chance remarks. In this explanation, indicating a spur-of-the-moment slip of the tongue, he certainly did considerably less than justice to himself. For this announcement of unconditional surrender was very deeply deliberated. Whether it was wise or foolish, whether it prolonged the war or shortened it—or even if it had no effect whatsoever on the duration (which seems possible)—it was a true statement of Roosevelt's considered policy and he refused all suggestions that he retract the statement or soften it and continued refusal to the day of his death. In fact, he restated it a great many times. . . .

What Roosevelt was saying was that there would be no negotiated peace, no compromise with Nazism and Fascism, no "escape clauses" provided by another Fourteen Points which could lead to another Hitler. (The ghost of Woodrow Wilson was again at his shoulder.) Roosevelt wanted this uncompromising purpose to be brought home to the American people and the Russians and the Chinese, and to the people of France and other occupied nations, and he wanted it brought

WILLST DU DER LETZTE TOTE DES KRIEGES SEIN?

("Do you want to be the last dead of the war?") U.S. propaganda leaflet of World War II directed at German soldiers. Hoover Institution, Stanford University.

home to the Germans—that neither by continuance of force nor by contrivance of a new spirit of sweet reasonableness could their present leaders gain for them a soft peace. He wanted to ensure that when the war was won it would stay won.

2. Hull Opposes "Unconditional Surrender" (1948)

"Unconditional surrender" had its warm supporters. In addition to the advantages already indicated, it would hearten German-conquered peoples like the Poles; it would key the Allies up for greater sacrifices; it would postpone disruptive arguments among the Allies as to surrender terms; it would avert a quarrel like that with Germany after 1918 over the Armistice terms. Yet critics like Senator Wheeler of

2. Reprinted with permission of Macmillan Publishing Company from *Memoirs*, Vol. II, by Cordell Hull. Copyright 1948 by Cordell Hull. Copyright renewed.

The principle of unconditional surrender overshadowed our policy toward the Axis and their satellites and our planning for their future.

Originally this principle had not formed part of the State Department's thinking. We were as much surprised as Mr. Churchill when, for the first time, the President, in the Prime Minister's presence, stated it suddenly to a press conference during the Casablanca Conference in January, 1943. I was told that the Prime Minister was dumbfounded.

Basically, I was opposed to the principle for two reasons, as were many of my associates. One was that it might prolong the war by solidifying Axis resistance into one of desperation. The people of the Axis countries, by believing they had nothing to look forward to but unconditional surrender to the will of their conquerors, might go on fighting long after calmer judgment had convinced them that their fight was hopeless.

The President himself had qualified his unconditional surrender phrase by stating at Casablanca that this did not mean the destruction of the people of Germany, Japan, and Italy, but the ending of a philosophy based on conquest and subjugation of other peoples. Nevertheless the phrase itself spread more widely than the qualification, and it became a weapon in the hands of Nazi propagandists.

The second reason was that the principle logically required the victor nations to be ready to take over every phase of the national and local Governments of the conquered countries, and to operate all governmental activities and properties. We and our Allies were in no way prepared to undertake this vast obligation.

I thought that our principle of surrender should be flexible. In some cases the most severe terms should be imposed. I had Germany and Japan in mind in this connection. In other cases we would have preliminary informal conversations that would result in substantial adjustments away from the terms of unconditional surrender. Here I had in mind Italy and the Axis satellite states, Rumania, Hungary, Bulgaria, and Finland.

In our postwar-planning discussions in the State Department, which had begun more than three years prior to the Casablanca Conference, we had not embraced the idea of unconditional surrender. In the United Nations Declaration of January 1, 1942, each Government simply pledged itself not to make a separate armistice or peace with the enemies. Nevertheless, after the President had stated the principle so emphatically at Casablanca, there was nothing we could do except to follow it at least in form. It was to rise on numerous occasions to plague us and to require explanation.

[*Ironically, Japan did not surrender unconditionally in 1945. She held out for the retention of the Emperor.*]

D. DROPPING THE ATOMIC BOMB

1. Japan's Horrified Reaction (1945)

With Germany knocked out of the war, President Truman journeyed to Potsdam, near Berlin, in July, 1945, to concert plans with Stalin and the British leaders. He was there informed that American scientists had experimentally detonated the first atomic bomb in history. The conferees now called upon the Japanese to surrender or be destroyed, although the Potsdam ultimatum made no reference, as perhaps it should have, to the existence of the fantastic new weapon. When Tokyo brushed aside the demand for surrender, Truman ordered the dropping of atomic bombs (the only two the United States then had) on Hiroshima (August 6) and Nagasaki (August 9). The horrified reaction of the *Nippon Times* is herewith given. Determine whether there was force in the Japanese charge of hypocrisy, and whether there is any moral difference between atomic bombing and large-scale incendiary bombing of civilian centers. (The Japanese had already bombed civilian centers, beginning with Shanghai in 1932.) Did the Japanese refusal to respond to the Potsdam ultimatum justify the bombing?

How can a human being with any claim to a sense of moral responsibility deliberately let loose an instrument of destruction which can at one stroke annihilate an appalling segment of mankind? This is not war; this is not even murder; this is pure nihilism. This is a crime against God and humanity which strikes at the very basis of moral existence. What meaning is there in any international law, in any rule of human conduct, in any concept of right and wrong, if the very foundations of morality are to be overthrown as the use of this instrument of total destruction threatens to do?

The crime of the Americans stands out in ghastly repulsiveness all the more for the ironic contradiction it affords to their lying pretensions. For in their noisy statements, they have always claimed to be the champions of fairness and humanitarianism. In the early days of the China Affair [beginning 1937], the United States repeatedly protested against the bombing operations of the Japanese forces, notwithstanding the fact that the Japanese operations were conducted on a limited scale against strictly military objectives. But where its own actions are concerned, the United States seems to see no inconsistency in committing on an unimaginably vast scale the very same crime it had falsely accused others of committing.

This hypocritical character of the Americans had already been amply demonstrated in the previous bombings of Japanese cities. Strewing explosives and fire bombs indiscriminately over an extensive area, hitting large cities and small towns without distinction, wiping out vast districts which could not be mistaken as being anything but strictly residential in character, burning or blasting to death countless thousands of helpless

1. *Nippon Times* (Tokyo), Aug. 10, 1945. The third bomb was not scheduled to be ready until about Aug. 24, two weeks after the dropping of the second one.

women and children, and machine-gunning fleeing refugees, the American raiders had already shown how completely they violate in their actual deeds the principles of humanity which they mouth in conspicuous pretense.

But now beside the latest technique of total destruction which the Americans have adopted, their earlier crimes pale into relative insignificance. What more barbarous atrocity can there be than to wipe out at one stroke the population of a whole city without distinction*—men, women, and children; the aged, the weak, the infirm; those in positions of authority, and those with no power at all; all snuffed out without being given a chance of lifting even a finger in either defense or defiance!

The United States may claim, in a lame attempt to raise a pretext in justification of its latest action, that a policy of utter annihilation is necessitated by Japan's failure to heed the recent demand for unconditional surrender. But the question of surrendering or not surrendering certainly can have not the slightest relevance to the question of whether it is justifiable to use a method which under any circumstance is strictly condemned alike by the principles of international law and of morality. For this American outrage against the fundamental moral sense of mankind, Japan must proclaim to the world its protest against the United States, which has made itself the arch-enemy of humanity.

2. The *Christian Century* Deplores the Bombing (1945)

The use of the atomic bomb was reluctantly but overwhelmingly recommended by Truman's large corps of expert advisers. Some of the scientists at first proposed test demonstrations in an uninhabited place, but the United States had only two bombs, and they might prove to be humiliating duds. They could not wreak much damage in desert areas, and might leave the Japanese unimpressed. If the cities to be bombed were warned in advance, the Japanese might move American prisoners of war to them, and at the same time "ambush" the American bombers. Japan was reeling, but she perhaps had enough suicide resistance left to exact a million casualties, while losing more than a million of her own people. The atomic bomb, indicating that awesome forces were working against the Japanese, might stun them into a quick surrender, as it did. (A dry-run demonstration would have weakened this effect.) The cost was perhaps 150,000 Japanese lives, as against 2,000,000—Japanese, American, and British. The *Christian Century*, a prominent Protestant journal published in Chicago, did not accept the philosophy of a "mercy bombing." Which, if any, of its suggestions would have strengthened the moral position of the United States?

Something like a moral earthquake has followed the dropping of atomic bombs on two Japanese cities. Its continued tremors throughout the world have diverted attention even from the military victory itself. . . . It is our belief that the use made of the atomic bomb has placed our nation in an indefensible moral position.

---

* At Hiroshima about 150,000 people were killed and wounded out of a total population of some 350,000. The fire-bomb raid on Tokyo of March 10, 1945, killed an estimated 83,000 people.

We do not propose to debate the issue of military necessity, though the facts are clearly on one side of this issue. The atomic bomb was used at a time when Japan's navy was sunk, her air force virtually destroyed, her homeland surrounded, her supplies cut off, and our forces poised for the final stroke. Recognition of her imminent defeat could be read between the lines of every Japanese communiqué. Neither do we intend to challenge Mr. Churchill's highly speculative assertion that the use of the bomb saved the lives of more than one million American and 250,000 British soldiers.

IN THE PALM OF HIS HAND

The atomic bomb portends much for civilized man. Jerry Doyle in the Philadelphia *Record*, 1945.

We believe, however, that these lives could have been saved had our government followed a different course, more honorable and more humane. Our leaders seem not to have weighed the moral considerations involved. No sooner was the bomb ready than it was rushed to the front and dropped on two helpless cities, destroying more lives than the United States has lost in the entire war.

Perhaps it was inevitable that the bomb would ultimately be employed to bring Japan to the point of surrender. . . . But there was no military advantage in hurling the bomb upon Japan without warning. The least we might have done was to announce to our foe that we possessed the atomic bomb; that its destructive power was beyond anything known in warfare; and that its terrible effectiveness had been experimentally demonstrated in this country. We could thus have warned Japan of what was in store for her unless she surrendered immediately. If she doubted the good faith of our representations, it would have been a simple matter to select a demonstration target in the enemy's own country at a place where the loss of human life would be at a minimum.

If, despite such warning, Japan had still held out, we would have been in a far less questionable position had we then dropped the bombs on Hiroshima and Nagasaki. At least our record of deliberation and ample warning would have been clear. Instead, with brutal disregard of any principle of humanity, we "demonstrated" the bomb on two great cities, utterly extinguishing them.* This course has placed the United States in a bad light throughout the world. What the use of poison gas did to the reputation of Germany in World War I, the use of the atomic bomb has done for the reputation of the United States in World War II. Our future security is menaced by our own act, and our influence for justice and humanity in international affairs has been sadly crippled.

3. Truman Justifies the Bombing (1945)

German scientists were known to be working on an atomic bomb, and Roosevelt was persuaded to push forward with an ultra-secret competing project that ultimately cost some $2.5 billion. The charge was made—without proof—that Truman had to use the new weapon or face an investigation of squandered money. More probable was his desire to end the Far Eastern war speedily before the bothersome Russians came in. The evidence is strong that they hurried up their six-day participation following the dropping of the first bomb. At all events, President Truman accepted full responsibility for his decision, and later defended it in his *Memoirs,* as excerpted herewith. Did he make the decision by himself? Did he try to use the bomb as a lawful weapon? In the light of conditions at the time, rather than hindsight, was he justified in his action?

My own knowledge of these [atomic] developments had come about only after I became President, when Secretary [of War] Stimson had given me the full story. He had told me at that time that the project was nearing completion, and that a bomb could be expected within another four months. It was at his suggestion, too, that I had then set up a committee of top men and had asked them to study with great care the implications the new weapon might have for us. . . .

It was their recommendation that the bomb be used against the enemy as soon as it could be done. They recommended further that it should be used without specific warning, and against a target that would clearly show its devastating strength. I had realized, of course, that an atomic bomb explosion would inflict damage and casualties beyond imagination. On the other hand, the scientific advisers of the committee reported, "We can propose no technical demonstration likely to bring an end to the war; we see no acceptable alternative to direct military use." It was their conclusion that no technical demonstration they might propose, such as over a deserted island, would be likely to bring the war to an end. It had to be used against an enemy target.

The final decision of where and when to use the atomic bomb was up to

---

* Hiroshima was about three-fourths devastated, Nagasaki, one-third.

3. *Memoirs of Harry S. Truman*: Years of Decisions, Vol. 1, Doubleday & Co., Inc. Copyright © 1955 by Time Inc., renewed 1983 by Margaret Truman Daniel. Reprinted by permission of Time Inc.

me. Let there be no mistake about it. I regarded the bomb as a military weapon, and never had any doubt that it should be used. The top military advisers to the President recommended its use, and when I talked to Churchill, he unhesitatingly told me that he favored the use of the atomic bomb if it might aid to end the war.

In deciding to use this bomb I wanted to make sure that it would be used as a weapon of war in the manner prescribed by the laws of war. That meant that I wanted it dropped on a military target. I had told Stimson that the bomb should be dropped as nearly as possibly upon a war production center of prime military importance. . . .

Four cities were finally recommended as targets: Hiroshima, Kokura, Niigata, and Nagasaki. They were listed in that order as targets for the first attack. The order of selection was in accordance with the military importance of these cities, but allowance would be given for weather conditions at the time of the bombing.

[*The devastating impact of the atomic bomb, together with Russia's sudden entry into the war against Japan, undoubtedly forced the Japanese surrender sooner than otherwise would have been possible. Even so, the fanatical military men in Tokyo almost won out for a last-ditch stand.*

In 1959, during interchanges with the students of Columbia University, ex-President Truman vigorously justified his action. He noted that "When we asked them to surrender at Potsdam, they gave us a very snotty answer. That is what I got. . . . They told me to go to hell, words to that effect." Mr. Truman insisted that the dropping of the bomb was "just a military maneuver, that is all," because "We were destroying the factories that were making more munitions." He then concluded: "All this uproar about what we did and what could have been stopped —should we take these wonderful Monday morning quarterbacks, the experts who are supposed to be right? They don't know what they are talking about. I was there. I did it. I would do it again." (Truman Speaks [1960], pp. 73–74.)]

THOUGHT PROVOKERS

1. Basically why were the defenders at Pearl Harbor caught by surprise, and who deserves the most blame for the surprise?

2. If the situation had been reversed, would Stalin have been more willing than the other Allies to open a second front? Explain.

3. Wilsonian propaganda in 1917–1918 drove a wedge between the German people and their government. Why was this technique less effective in World War II? On balance, and with the benefit of hindsight, was the policy of unconditional surrender "perhaps the biggest political mistake of the war" (Hanson W. Baldwin)?

4. Does the probability that the Germans or the Japanese would have used the atomic bomb against the United States, if they had developed it first, strengthen the moral position of the United States? If Truman had announced at Potsdam that America had the atomic bomb, would the Japanese have been likely to surrender at once? Was the United States shortsighted in establishing a precedent that might one day be used against it? Comment on Secretary Stimson's view that the dropping of the bomb would prove war to be so horrible that there could never be another.

43 · *Harry S Truman and the Cold War*

> *I have been asked whether I have any regrets about any of the major decisions I had to make as President. I have none.*
>
> HARRY S TRUMAN, 1960

PROLOGUE: In February, 1945, while Germany was still fighting desperately and Japan was far from finished, an ailing Roosevelt arrived at Yalta in the Russian Crimea. There, in collaboration with Prime Minister Churchill, he thrashed out final agreements with Stalin. Nine weeks later Roosevelt was dead. The ultimate Communist take-over of the satellite governments of Central Europe, which appeared to contradict Stalin's pledges at Yalta, deepened American fears. President Truman proclaimed the Truman Doctrine in 1947, designed in the short run to shore up Communist-threatened Greece and Turkey, but aiming in the long run to define a global policy of "containment" of Communist expansionism. Truman implemented the Marshall Plan in 1948, designed to rehabilitate war-torn Western Europe. The Marshall Plan proved conspicuously successful in attaining its objectives. But continuing fear of the Soviets forced the United States, despite its ancient anti-alliance tradition, to negotiate in 1949 an epochal military defense alliance in the form of the North Atlantic Treaty Organization. The "containment" policy suffered a severe blow in 1949 when Communists emerged the victors in China's civil war. The "fall" of China touched off bitter political warfare between Republicans and Democrats in the United States, and contributed to the rise of "McCarthyism", or fanatical (and often irresponsible) pursuit of alleged Communist "traitors" in America.

A. THE YALTA AGREEMENTS

1. Roosevelt "Betrays" China and Japan (1945)

One of Roosevelt's primary objectives at the Yalta Conference was to coordinate with Stalin the final blows of the war. The American people were eager to induce Russia to enter the conflict against Japan so as to reduce their anticipated losses in the final stages of the assault. The Soviets had already suffered millions of casualties in fighting Hitler, and Stalin told Roosevelt that he would have to receive concessions if he were to justify another war to his war-weary people. The following, one of the "Top Secret" Yalta agreements hammered out between Roosevelt and Stalin, was not made public until exactly a year later. The basic reason for secrecy was that Russia and Japan were not then at war, and a publication or even leakage of the terms might prompt a Japanese attack before Russia was ready. A need for the utmost secrecy was the excuse given for not then notifying China, an ally of the United States, that her rights were being bartered away in Outer Mongolia and in Manchuria (the Manchurian railroads and the ports of Dairen and Port Arthur). In what ways did the deal "betray" China? Was Roosevelt justified in agreeing to these terms?

---

1. *Foreign Relations of the United States: The Conferences at Malta and Yalta, 1945* (1955), p. 984.

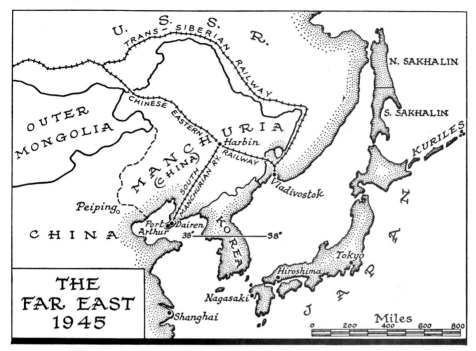

THE FAR EAST 1945

The leaders of the three Great Powers—the Soviet Union, the United States of America, and Great Britain—have agreed that in two or three months* after Germany has surrendered and the war in Europe has terminated, the Soviet Union shall enter into the war against Japan on the side of the Allies on condition that:

1. The *status quo* in Outer Mongolia (the Mongolian People's Republic) shall be preserved; [*This area, twice the size of Texas, had been under China's sway until 1912; it had become a Soviet satellite in 1924.*]

2. The former rights of Russia violated by the treacherous attack of Japan in 1904 shall be restored, *viz.*:

a) The southern part of Sakhalin, as well as all the islands adjacent to it, shall be returned to the Soviet Union, [*Japan and Russia had shared control until 1905, when Japan secured South Sakhalin.*]

b) The commercial port of [China's] Dairen shall be internationalized, the preeminent interests of the Soviet Union in this port being safeguarded, and the lease of [China's] Port Arthur as a naval base of the USSR restored, [*F.D.R. here recognized Russia's age-old need for an ice-free port. Dairen was internationalized, and the Port Arthur naval base was leased to Russia. Both were ultimately restored to Communist China.*]

* Russia entered the Far Eastern war exactly three months after Germany surrendered. Some scholars have argued that America's decision to drop the two atomic bombs on Japan was hastened by the desire to conclude the fighting before Russia could fully enter the war and play a major role. Of course, at the time of Yalta Roosevelt could not know when—or even if—the bombs would be available.

c) The Chinese Eastern Railroad and the South Manchurian Railroad, which provides an outlet to Dairen, shall be jointly operated by the establishment of a joint Soviet-Chinese Company, it being understood that the preeminent interests of the Soviet Union shall be safeguarded and that China shall retain full sovereignty in Manchuria; [*The Yalta agreement insured Russia temporary control of these two key railroads in China's Manchuria.*]

3. The Kurile Islands [of Japan] shall be handed over to the Soviet Union. [*Though colonized by both Russians and Japanese, these islands had become a Japanese possession in 1875. Giving away the territory of enemy Japan raised little protest at the time.*]

It is understood that the agreement concerning Outer Mongolia, and the ports and railroads referred to above, will require concurrence of Generalissimo Chiang Kai-shek. The President will take measures in order to obtain this concurrence on advice from Marshal Stalin.

The Heads of the three Great Powers have agreed that these claims of the Soviet Union shall be unquestionably fulfilled after Japan has been defeated [*that is, whether China consented or not*].

For its part, the Soviet Union expresses its readiness to conclude with the National Government of China a pact of friendship and alliance between the USSR and China in order to render assistance to China with its armed forces for the purpose of liberating China from the Japanese yoke. [*The pact of friendship was concluded after some demur by the Chinese on August 14, 1945, six days after Russia opened war on Japan. Following the dropping of the atomic bomb, the Russians could not wait for China's acquiescence.*]

I. [J.] Stalin
Franklin D. Roosevelt
Winston S. Churchill

2. *The Freeman's* Bill of Indictment (1953)

Roosevelt left Yalta pleased with the victory for Allied unity. He had secured Stalin's consent to a conference at San Francisco to frame the United Nations Charter, and he had won a concession from him limiting the use of the veto. But Roosevelt and Churchill had been forced to agree to Russia's retention of eastern Poland, with compensating western territory to be given to the Poles at the expense of Germany. All this did violence to the rights of millions of Poles and Germans, as well as to the plain terms of the Atlantic Charter of 1941. On the other hand, Stalin had promised free elections for dismembered Poland and for the other satellite nations of Central Europe—a pledge which he later flouted. Critics have charged that

2. *The Freeman* (New York), III, 403 (March 9, 1953). By permission of The Foundation for Economic Education. Admiral Leahy reported in 1950 that at Yalta he had complained to Roosevelt about the vagueness of the agreement regarding a free Poland: " 'Mr. President, this is so elastic that the Russians can stretch it all the way from Yalta to Washington without ever technically breaking it.' The President replied, 'I know, Bill—I know it. But it's the best I can do for Poland at this time.' " W. D. Leahy, *I Was There* (1950), pp. 315–16.

Roosevelt should have known by this time that the Russians did not honor agreements which they found inconvenient, and that he should have stood firm for principle. *The Freeman*, a critical journal, published the following attack eight years later. How balanced is its appraisal?

Yalta was the most cynical and immoral international transaction to which the United States was ever a partner. It was a repudiation of all the ideals for which the war against Nazism was supposedly being fought. America came very close to losing its soul at Yalta. What was even more ominous than the provisions of the agreement was the absence, at the time of its publication, of any loud or audible outcry of protest.* It would seem that the normal American ability to distinguish between right and wrong, freedom and slavery, had been badly blurred.

From the practical standpoint, most of our serious international difficulties at the present time can be traced back to a deal which gave Stalin the keys to Eastern Europe and East Asia in exchange for paper promises which, as anyone with reasonable knowledge of the Soviet record and Soviet psychology could have anticipated, were broken almost as soon as the ink on the Yalta document was dry.

The principle of self-determination for all peoples, spelled out in the first three clauses of the Atlantic Charter [see p. 781], was completely scrapped at Yalta, although there were hypocritical professions of respect for Atlantic Charter principles in the pact. The Soviet annexation of eastern Poland, definitely sanctioned, and the Polish annexation of large slices of ethnic German territory, foreshadowed in the agreement, were obviously against the will of the vast majority of the peoples concerned. There was no pretense of an honest plebiscite. These decisions have created millions of destitute, embittered refugees and have drawn frontier lines which are a very probable cause of future conflict.

Both the freedom and the territorial independence of Poland were offered as sacrifices on the altar of appeasement. The treatment of Poland, carved up territorially and made ripe for a foreign dictatorship, its fate determined by outsiders without even the presence of a Polish spokesman, was similar in many ways to the treatment of Czechoslovakia at Munich. . . .

Two features of the Yalta agreement represent endorsement by the United States of the legitimacy of human slavery—scarcely fit news for the birthday of Abraham Lincoln. There was recognition that German labor could be used as a source of "reparations," which could be invoked as justification for the detention at forced labor of large numbers of German war prisoners in the Soviet Union and also in France and Great Britain. And there was a self-assumed obligation by the United States and Great Britain to repatriate all Soviet citizens in their zones of occupation. So long as this was carried out (it has now, fortunately, long been stopped), there were tragic scenes of actual and attempted suicide on the part of Soviet citizens who

---

* Polish-Americans did protest vigorously at the time; the unpublished secret agreements came out piecemeal later.

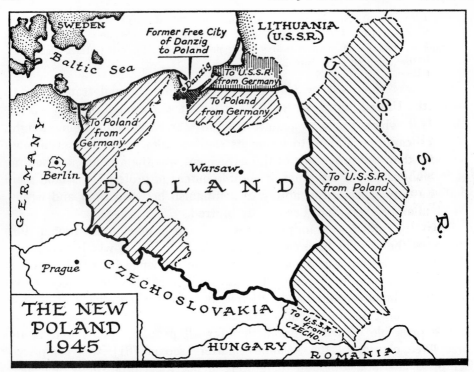

SWEDEN

Former Free City
of Danzig
to Poland

LITHUANIA
(U.S.S.R.)

Baltic Sea

Danzig

To U.S.S.R.
from Germany

To Poland
from Germany

GERMANY

To Poland
from Germany

Berlin

Warsaw

P O L A N D

U.

To U.S.S.R.
from Poland

S.

S.

R.

Prague

C Z E C H O S L O V A K I A

THE NEW
POLAND
1945

To U.S.S.R.
from CZECHO.

HUNGARY

ROMANIA

feared above everything else to return to their homeland of concentration camps.

Finally, the secret clauses of the Yalta agreement, which offered Stalin extensive territorial and economic concessions in the Far East at the expense of China and Japan, were immoral, unnecessary, and unwise. They were immoral because they gave away the rights and interests of an ally, the Nationalist government of China, without consulting or even informing Chiang Kai-shek. They were unnecessary, because Stalin's eagerness to be in at the kill in the Far East was beyond serious doubt or question.

[The Freeman *was more sympathetic toward Germans than were most Americans. Putting Germans under Polish rule and using German slave labor in Russia for reparations did not seem immoral to many Americans in 1945, especially in view of Hitler's diabolical slaughter of some 6,000,000 Jews. As for returning tens of thousands of anti-Communist refugees to Soviet tyranny, many Americans felt that this was not an unreasonable request to grant to their good Russian ally. Eight years later, perspectives had radically changed, as regards both Germany and Russia.*]

3. Secretary Stettinius Defends Yalta (1949)

Handsome Secretary of State Stettinius—he of the prematurely white hair and flashing white teeth—replaced the aged and ailing Secretary Hull late in 1944. With-

3. Excerpt from *Roosevelt and the Russians: The Yalta Conference* by Edward R. Stettinius. Copyright 1949 by The Stettinius Fund, Inc. Reprinted by permission cf Doubleday & Company, Inc.

out political influence or diplomatic experience, he was expected to be a kind of errand boy for President Roosevelt, who took him along to Yalta. Stettinius here presents a spirited defense of the controversial agreements. What conditions existing *at the time* cause the Yalta decisions to appear in a less sinister light than was later cast upon them?

What did the Soviet Union gain in eastern Europe which she did not already have as the result of the smashing victories of the Red Army? Great Britain and the United States secured pledges at Yalta, unfortunately not honored, which did promise free elections and democratic governments.

What, too, with the possible exception of the Kuriles, did the Soviet Union receive at Yalta which she might not have taken without any agreement? If there had been no agreement, the Soviet Union could have swept into North China, and the United States and the Chinese would have been in no real position to prevent it.

It must never be forgotten that, while the Crimea Conference was taking place, President Roosevelt had just been told by his military advisers that the surrender of Japan might not occur until 1947, and some predicted even later. The President was told that without Russia it might cost the United States a million casualties to conquer Japan.

It must be remembered, too, that at the time of the Yalta Conference it was still uncertain whether the atomic bomb could be perfected and that, since the Battle of the Bulge had set us back in Europe, it was uncertain how long it might take for Germany to crack. There had been immense optimism in the autumn of 1944, as Allied troops raced through France, that the war was nearly over. Then came the Battle of the Bulge, which was more than a military reversal. It cast a deep gloom over the confident expectation that the German war would end soon. In Washington, for instance, the procurement agencies of the armed services immediately began placing orders on the basis of a longer war in Europe than had been estimated.

With hindsight, it can be said that the widespread pessimism was unwarranted. The significant fact is not, however, this hindsight but the effect of this thinking on the strategy and agreements made in the Crimea. It was important to bring the Soviet Union into the united sphere of action. Russian co-operation in the Japanese war ran parallel to their co-operation in the world organization and to united action in Europe.

Furthermore, critics of the Far Eastern agreement have tended to overlook the fact that in the agreement the Soviet Union pledged that China was to retain "full sovereignty in Manchuria" and that the Soviet Union would conclude a pact of friendship with the Chinese Nationalist Government.

It is my understanding that the American military leaders felt that the war had to be concluded as soon as possible. There was the fear that heavy casualties in Japan or the possible lack of continuous victories would have an unfortunate effect on the attitude of the American people.

President Roosevelt had great faith in his Army and Navy staffs, and he relied wholeheartedly upon them. Their insistent advice was that the Soviet Union had to be brought into the Far Eastern war soon after Germany's collapse. The President, therefore, in signing the Far Eastern agreement, acted upon the advice of his military advisers. He did not approve the agreement from any desire to appease Stalin and the Soviet Union.

It is apparently the belief of some critics of the Yalta Conference that it would have been better to have made no agreements with the Soviet Union. Yet if we had made no agreements at Yalta, the Russians still would have been in full possession of the territory in Europe that President Roosevelt is alleged to have given them. The failure to agree would have been a serious blow to the morale of the Allied world, already suffering from five years of war; it would have meant the prolongation of the German and Japanese wars; it would have prevented the establishment of the United Nations; and it would probably have led to other consequences incalculable in their tragedy for the world.

[*The legend has taken root that an ailing Roosevelt, advised by the sickly Harry Hopkins and the Communist-employed Alger Hiss (his role has been exaggerated), was sold a gold brick by crafty "Uncle Joe" Stalin. The secret intelligence reports as to Japan's powers of resistance were faulty, but Roosevelt had to rely on such information as was given him. And if he was sick, what of the hale and hearty Churchill, who signed the agreements? Five months after Yalta, President Truman journeyed to Potsdam, where one of his primary purposes was to hold Stalin to his promise to enter the war against Japan. Truman was not sick, and he had further information as to Japanese powers of resistance. When Russia finally entered the war six days before its end, great was the rejoicing in the United States. As for the charge that America "lost" China because of the Yalta agreements, the fact is that China was never America's to lose. The "salvation" of Nationalist China would probably have involved large numbers of United States troops, and public opinion was unwilling to provide them. As for Japan, there was little opposition at the time of Yalta to depriving a savage enemy of the Kurile Islands and handing them over to a resolute ally.*]

B. THE TRUMAN DOCTRINE

1. Kennan Proposes Containment (1946)

As the Grand Alliance crumbled in the post-war months, American policy-makers groped for ways to understand the Soviet Union, and to respond to Russian provocations. On February 22, 1946, the scholarly chargé d'affaires at the American Embassy in Moscow, George F. Kennan, sent his famous "Long Telegram" to the State Department, giving his views of the sources of Soviet conduct. A later version of this message was published anonymously in *Foreign Affairs* (July, 1947). Kennan's ideas proved immensely influential in defining the so-called "containment doctrine" that dominated American strategic thinking for the next two decades or more of the Cold War. Kennan argued that the Soviet Union regarded itself as encircled by hostile capitalist countries.

1. *Foreign Relations of the United States*, 1946, Vol. VI, pp. 696–709.

In Russian eyes, capitalist governments hoped to avert economic conflict among themselves by seeking war against the socialist world. Kennan denied the accuracy of these Russian perceptions, but insisted that they nonetheless motivated Russian behavior. He painted the Soviet leaders as insecure, fearful, and cynical: "In the name of Marxism they sacrificed every single ethical value in their methods and tactics. Today they cannot dispense with it. It is fig leaf of their moral and intellectual respectability. Without it they would stand before history, at best, as only the last of that long succession of cruel and wasteful Russian rulers who have relentlessly forced their country on to ever new heights of military power in order to guarantee the external security of their internally weak regimes. That is why Soviet purposes must always be solemnly clothed in trappings of Marxism, why no one should underrate importance of dogma in Soviet affairs." Kennan then went on to analyze the practical implications of this diagnosis and to recommend American countermeasures. How prophetic was he? In his memoirs many years later, Kennan pleaded that he had never meant to suggest the kind of massive American military build-up that the containment doctrine was later used to justify. Was he in fact misunderstood? If so, why?

PART THREE: PROJECTION OF SOVIET OUTLOOK IN
PRACTICAL POLICY ON OFFICIAL LEVEL

We have now seen nature and background of Soviet program. What may we expect by way of its practical implementation? . . .

On official plane we must look for following:

(A) Internal policy devoted to increasing in every way strength and prestige of Soviet state's intensive military-industrialization; maximum development of armed forces; great displays to impress outsiders; continued secretiveness about internal matters, designed to conceal weaknesses and to keep opponents in dark.

(B) Wherever it is considered timely and promising, efforts will be made to advance official limits of Soviet power. For the moment, these efforts are restricted to certain neighboring points conceived of here as being of immediate strategic necessity, such as Northern Iran, Turkey, possibly Bornholm. However, other points may at any time come into question, if and as concealed Soviet political power is extended to new areas. Thus a "friendly" Persian Government might be asked to grant Russia a port on Persian Gulf. Should Spain fall under communist control, question of Soviet base at Gibraltar Strait might be activated. But such claims will appear on official level only when unofficial preparation is complete.

(C) Russians will participate officially in international organizations where they see opportunity of extending Soviet power or of inhibiting or diluting power of others. Moscow sees in UNO not the mechanism for a permanent and stable world society founded on mutual interest and aims of all nations, but an arena in which aims just mentioned can be favorably pursued. As long as UNO is considered here to serve this purpose, Soviets will remain with it. But if at any time they come to conclusion that it is serving to embarrass or frustrate their aims for power expansion and if they see better prospects for pursuit of these aims along other lines, they will not hesitate to abandon UNO. This would imply, however, that they felt themselves strong enough to split unity of other nations by their withdrawal, to render UNO ineffective as a threat to their aims or security, and to replace it with an international weapon more effective from their viewpoint. Thus Soviet attitude toward UNO will depend largely on loyalty of other nations to it, and on degree of vigor, decisiveness and cohesion with which these nations defend in UNO the peaceful and hopeful concept of international life, which that organization represents to our way of thinking. I reiterate, Moscow has no abstract devotion to UNO ideals. Its attitude to that organization will remain essentially pragmatic and tactical.

(D) Toward colonial areas and backward or dependent peoples, Soviet policy, even on official plane, will be directed toward weakening of power and influence and contacts of advanced western nations, on theory that in so far as this policy is successful, there will be created a vacuum which will favor communist-Soviet penetration. Soviet pressure for participation in trusteeship arrangements thus represents, in my opinion, a desire to be in a position to complicate and inhibit exertion of western influence at such points rather than to provide major channel for exerting of Soviet power. Latter motive is not lacking, but for this Soviets prefer to rely on other channels than official trusteeship arrangements. Thus we may expect to find Soviets asking for admission everywhere to trusteeship or similar arrangements and using levers thus acquired to weaken western influence among such peoples.

(E) Russians will strive energetically to develop Soviet representation in, and official ties with, countries in which they sense strong possibilities of opposition to western centers of power. This applies to such widely separated points as Germany, Argentina, Middle Eastern countries, etc.

(F) In international economic matters, Soviet policy will really be dominated by pursuit of autarchy for Soviet Union and Soviet-dominated adjacent areas taken together. That, however, will be underlying policy. As far as official line is concerned, position is not yet clear. Soviet Government has shown strange reticence since termination hostilities on subject foreign trade. If large scale long term credits should be forthcoming, I believe Soviet Government may eventually again do lip service, as it did in nineteen-thirties to desirability of building up international economic exchange in general. Otherwise I think it possible Soviet foreign trade may be restricted largely to Soviet's own security sphere, including occupied areas in Germany, and that a cold official shoulder may be turned to principle of general economic collaboration among nations.

(G) With respect to cultural collaboration, lip service will likewise be rendered to desirability of deepening cultural contacts between peoples, but this will not in practice be interpreted in any way which could weaken security position of Soviet peoples. Actual manifestations of Soviet policy in this respect will be restricted to arid channels of closely shepherded official visits and functions, with super-abundance of vodka and speeches and dearth of permanent effects.

(H) Beyond this, Soviet official relations will take what might be called "correct" course with individual foreign governments, with great stress being laid on prestige of Soviet Union and its representatives and with punctilious attention to protocol, as distinct from good manners.

PART FOUR: FOLLOWING MAY BE SAID AS TO
WHAT WE MAY EXPECT BY WAY OF IMPLEMENTATION
OF BASIC SOVIET POLICIES ON UNOFFICIAL,
OR SUBTERRANEAN PLANE, I.E. ON PLANE FOR WHICH
SOVIET GOVERNMENT ACCEPTS NO RESPONSIBILITY

•   •   •

(A) To undermine general political and strategic potential of major western powers. Efforts will be made in such countries to disrupt national self-confidence, to hamstring measures of national defense, to increase social and industrial unrest, to stimulate all forms of disunity. All persons with grievances, whether economic or racial, will be urged to seek redress not in mediation and compromise, but in defiant violent struggle for destruction of other elements of society. Here poor will be set against rich, black against white, young against old, newcomers against established residents, etc.

(B) On unofficial plane particularly violent efforts will be made to weaken power and influence of western powers of colonial, backward, or dependent peoples. On this level, no holds will be barred. . . .

(C) Where individual governments stand in path of Soviet purposes pressure will be brought for their removal from office. . . .

(D) In foreign countries Communists will, as a rule, work toward destruction of all forms of personal independence, economic, political or moral. . . .

(E) Everything possible will be done to set major western powers against each other. . . .

(F) In general, all Soviet efforts on unofficial international plane will be negative and destructive in character, designed to tear down sources of strength beyond reach of Soviet control. This is only in line with basic Soviet instinct that there can be no compromise with rival power and that constructive work can start only when communist power is dominant. But behind all this will be applied insistent, unceasing pressure for penetration and command of key positions in administration and especially in police apparatus of foreign countries. The Soviet regime is a police regime par excellence, reared in the dim half world of Tsarist police intrigue, accustomed to think primarily in terms of police power. This should never be lost sight of in gauging Soviet motives.

PART FIVE

In summary, we have here a political force committed fanatically to the belief that with US there can be no permanent modus vivendi, that it is desirable and necessary that the internal harmony of our society be disrupted, our traditional way of life be destroyed, the international authority of our state be broken, if Soviet power is to be secure. This political force has complete power of disposition over energies of one of world's greatest peoples and resources of world's richest national territory, and is borne along by deep and powerful currents of Russian nationalism. In addition, it has an elaborate and far flung apparatus for exertion of its influence in other countries, an apparatus of amazing flexibility and versatility, managed by people whose experience and skill in underground methods are presumably without parallel in history. Finally, it is seemingly inaccessible to considerations of reality in its basic reactions. For it, the vast fund of objective fact about human society is not, as with us, the measure against which outlook is constantly being tested and re-formed, but a grab bag from which individual items are selected arbitrarily and tendentiously to bolster an outlook already preconceived. This is admittedly not a pleasant picture. Problem of how to cope with this force is undoubtedly greatest task our diplomacy has ever faced and probably greatest it will ever have to face. It should be point of departure from which our political general staff work at present juncture should proceed. It should be approached with same thoroughness and care as solution of major strategic problem in war, and if necessary, with no smaller outlay in planning effort. I cannot attempt to suggest all answers here. But I would like to record my conviction that problem is within our power to solve—and that without recourse to any general military conflict. And in support of this conviction there are certain observations of a more encouraging nature I should like to make:

(One) Soviet power, unlike that of Hitlerite Germany, is neither schematic nor adventuristic. It does not work by fixed plans. It does not take unnecessary risks. Impervious to logic of reason, and it is highly sensitive to logic of force. For this reason it can easily withdraw—and usually does—when strong resistance is encountered at any point. Thus, if the adversary has sufficient force and makes clear his readiness to use it, he rarely has to do so. If situations are properly handled there need be no prestige engaging showdowns.

(Two) Gauged against western world as a whole, Soviets are still by far the weaker force. Thus, their success will really depend on degree of cohesion, firmness and vigor which western world can muster. And this is factor which it is within our power to influence.

(Three) Success of Soviet system, as form of internal power, is not yet finally proven. It has yet to be demonstrated that it can survive supreme test of successive transfer of power from one individual or group to another. Lenin's death was first such transfer, and its effects wracked Soviet state for 15 years after. Stalin's death or retirement will be second. But even this will not be final test. Soviet internal system will now be subjected, by virtue of recent territorial expansions, to series of additional strains which once proved severe tax on Tsardom. We here are convinced that never since termination of civil war have mass of Russian people been emotionally farther removed from doctrines of communist party than they are today. In Russia, party has now become a great and—for the moment—highly successful apparatus of dictatorial administration, but it has ceased to be a source of emotional inspiration. Thus, internal soundness and permanence of movement need not yet be regarded as assured.

(Four) All Soviet propaganda beyond Soviet security sphere is basically negative and destructive. It should therefore be relatively easy to combat it by any intelligent and really constructive program.

For these reasons I think we may approach calmly and with good heart problem of how to deal with Russia. As to how this approach should be made, I only wish to advance, by way of conclusion, following comments:

(One) Our first step must be to apprehend, and recognize for what it is, the nature of the movement with which we are dealing. We must study it with same courage, detachment, objectivity, and same determination not to be emotionally provoked or unseated by it, with which doctor studies unruly and unreasonable individual.

(Two) We must see that our public is educated to realities of Russian situation. I cannot over-emphasize importance of this. Press cannot do this alone. It must be done mainly by government, which is necessarily more experienced and better informed on practical problems involved. In this we need not be deterred by [ugliness—Eds.] of picture. I am convinced that there would be far less hysterical anti-Sovietism in our country today if realities of this situation were better understood by our people. There is nothing as dangerous or as terrifying as the unknown. It may also be argued that to reveal more information on our difficulties with Russia would reflect unfavorably on Russian American relations. I feel that if there is any real risk here involved, it is one which we should have courage to face, and sooner the better. But I cannot see what we would be risking. Our stake in this country, even coming on heels of tremendous demonstrations of our friendship for Russian people, is remarkably small. We have here no investments to guard, no actual trade to lose, virtually no citizens to protect, few cultural contacts to preserve. Our only stake lies in what we hope rather than what we have; and I am convinced we have better chance of realizing those hopes if our public is enlightened and if our dealings with Russians are placed entirely on realistic and matter of fact basis.

(Three) Much depends on health and vigor of our own society. World communism is like malignant parasite which feeds only on diseased tissue. This is point at which domestic and foreign policies meet. Every courageous and incisive measure to solve internal problems of our own society, to improve self-confidence, discipline, morale and community spirit of our own people, is a diplomatic victory over Moscow worth a thousand diplomatic notes and joint communiqués. If we cannot abandon fatalism and indifference in face of deficiencies of our own society, Moscow will profit—Moscow cannot help profiting by them in its foreign policies.

(Four) We must formulate and put forward for other nations a much more positive and constructive picture of sort of world we would like to see than we have put forward in past. It is not enough to urge people to develop political processes similar to our own. Many foreign peoples, in Europe at least, are tired and frightened by experiences of past, and are less interested in abstract freedom than in security. They are seeking guidance rather than responsibilities. We should be better able than Russians to give them this. And unless we do, Russians certainly will.

(Five) Finally we must have courage and self-confidence to cling to our own methods and conceptions of human society. After all, the greatest danger that can befall us in coping with this problem of Soviet Communism, is that we shall allow ourselves to become like those with whom we are coping.

2. Truman Appeals to Congress (1947)

A crisis developed early in 1947 when the bankrupt British served notice on Washington that they could no longer afford to support the "rightist" government of Greece against Communist guerrillas. If Greece fell, Turkey and all the eastern Mediterranean countries would presumably collapse like falling dominoes. After hurried consultations in Washington, President Truman boldly went before Congress to ask for $400,000,000 to provide military and economic assistance to both Greece and Turkey. This was a great deal of money, he conceded, but a trifling sum compared with the more than a third of a trillion dollars already expended in the recent war to guarantee freedom. On what grounds does he base his appeal? Are there any dangers in this approach?

I am fully aware of the broad implications involved if the United States extends assistance to Greece and Turkey, and I shall discuss these implications with you at this time.

One of the primary objectives of the foreign policy of the United States is the creation of conditions in which we and other nations will be able to work out a way of life free from coercion. This was a fundamental issue in the war with Germany and Japan. Our victory was won over countries which sought to impose their will, and their way of life, upon other nations.

To insure the peaceful development of nations, free from coercion, the United States has taken a leading part in establishing the United Nations. The United Nations is designed to make possible lasting freedom and independence for all its members. We shall not realize our objectives, however, unless we are willing to help free peoples to maintain their free institutions and their national integrity against aggressive movements that seek to impose upon them totalitarian regimes. [Applause.] This is no more than a frank recognition that totalitarian regimes imposed upon free peoples, by direct or indirect aggression, undermine the foundations of international peace and hence the security of the United States.

The peoples of a number of countries of the world have recently had

2. *Congressional Record,* 80 Cong., 1 sess., p. 1981 (March 12, 1947).

TURKISH DELIGHTS

The *Daily Worker,* a Moscow-inspired newspaper, condemned the Truman Doctrine for assistance to Greece and Turkey as Truman's pipe dream of a dollar-based world empire. New York *Daily Worker,* 1947.

totalitarian regimes forced upon them against their will. The Government of the United States has made frequent protests against coercion and intimidation, in violation of the Yalta Agreement, in Poland, Rumania, and Bulgaria. I must also state that in a number of other countries there have been similar developments. . . .

I believe that it must be the policy of the United States to support free peoples who are resisting attempted subjugation by armed minorities or by outside pressures.

I believe that we must assist free peoples to work out their own destiny in their own way.

I believe that our help should be primarily through economic and financial aid, which is essential to economic stability and orderly political processes.

The world is not static and the status quo is not sacred. But we cannot allow changes in the status quo in violation of the Charter of the United Nations by such methods as coercion, or by such subterfuge as political infiltration. In helping free and independent nations to maintain their freedom, the United States will be giving effect to the principles of the Charter of the United Nations. . . .

This is a serious course upon which we embark. I would not recommend it except that the alternative is much more serious. [Applause.] . . .

The free peoples of the world look to us for support in maintaining their freedoms.

If we falter in our leadership, we may endanger the peace of the world— and we shall surely endanger the welfare of our own Nation.

Great responsibilities have been placed upon us by the swift movement of events.

I am confident that the Congress will face these responsibilities squarely. [Applause, the members rising.]

3. The Chicago *Tribune* Dissents (1947)

The nation was momentarily stunned by Truman's bombshell. Critics complained that the initial appropriation would be but a drop in the bucket (as it was), that the Soviet Union (though not mentioned by name) would be gravely offended, and that the UN was being rudely bypassed. (Speed was of the essence, and the administration concluded that the Soviets would paralyze action in the UN.) The Chicago *Tribune*, a powerful isolationist newspaper, was vehemently anti-British, anti-Communist, and anti-Roosevelt. Which of its arguments against the Truman Doctrine are persuasive?

Mr. Truman made as cold a war speech yesterday against Russia as any President has ever made except on the occasion of going before Congress to ask for a declaration of war. . . .

The outcome will inevitably be war. It probably will not come this year or next year, but the issue is already drawn. The declaration of implacable hostility between this country and Russia is one which cannot be tempered or withdrawn. . . .

Mr. Truman's statement constituted a complete confession of the bankruptcy of American policy as formulated by Mr. Roosevelt and pursued by himself. We have just emerged from a great war which was dedicated to the extinction of the three nations [Germany, Italy, Japan] which were as vocally opposed to Russia as Mr. Truman proclaims himself to be now. If communism was the real danger all along, why did Mr. Roosevelt and Mr. Truman adopt Russia as an ally, and why, at Teheran, Yalta, and Potsdam, did they build up Russia's power by making her one concession after another?

The Truman speech also leaves the United Nations as a meaningless relic of mistaken intentions. The world league to insure a lasting peace is a fraud and a sham, so impotent that Mr. Truman proposes that the United States ignore it and seek peace by force and threat of force—the very means which U. N. was intended to exclude in international dealings.

The one hope that is left is Congress, but even its peremptory refusal to follow Truman into his anti-communist crusade will not wholly undo the damage which the President has already done. His words cannot be unsaid, nor can their effect upon Russia be canceled out. Already, as witness

3. Chicago *Daily Tribune*, March 13, 1947. By permission of the Chicago *Tribune*.

Moscow's recall of the Soviet Ambassador from Washington, the nations are engaging in the usual preliminaries to war.

When the country views the terrible predicament in which it now finds itself, it cannot avoid the conclusion that wisdom at all times counseled the United States to follow Americanism only, to dedicate itself to the pursuit of its own interests, and to let Europe's wars alone. We have fought two of them without avail, and Mr. Truman is calling upon us to fight a third.

We were drawn into these wars primarily at the behest of Britain, and that nation, by dumping the Greek and Turkish problems into Mr. Truman's lap, is summoning us to the struggle again. If the United States can be induced to crush Russia, Britain again will rise to a station of security and comparative eminence, for it will be the only other surviving major nation.

For 10 years the United States has been dominated by alien interests. These interests, primarily financial, have bought up every newspaper, radio station, columnist, and commentator, and every so-called organization of public opinion that could be purchased. It has killed our sons by the hundreds of thousands and brought the nation to bankruptcy. It will use whatever tactics seem best to rush into World War III. It will coerce the timid and fool the stupid.

Congress must cease being a catspaw for this movement and think of America's interest first—even exclusively.

[*The dangers involved in the Truman Doctrine were great. but the dangers of drifting seemed greater. Congress, by better than a two-to-one vote in both Houses, finally approved the initial appropriation early in 1948.*]

C. THE MARSHALL PLAN

1. Secretary Marshall Speaks at Harvard (1947)

By June of 1947 it was painfully evident that the Truman Doctrine was merely a child on an adult's errand. The hunger and economic prostration produced by the war were providing an alarming hotbed for the propagation of Communism in Europe, especially in Italy and France. A Communist take-over of all Western Europe appeared to be a distinct (and depressing) possibility. At this critical juncture the Secretary of State, General George C. Marshall, speaking at the Harvard University commencement exercises, made the following breath-taking proposal. To what extent is it both selfish and unselfish? What is its relation to the Truman Doctrine?

The truth of the matter is that Europe's requirements for the next three or four years of foreign food and other essential products—principally from America—are so much greater than her present ability to pay that she must have substantial additional help or face economic, social, and political deterioration of a very grave character. . . .

Aside from the demoralizing effect on the world at large and the possibilities of disturbances arising as a result of the desperation of the people

1. *Department of State Bulletin*, XVI, 1159–60 (June 15, 1947; speech of June 5, 1947).

concerned, the consequences to the economy of the United States should be apparent to all. It is logical that the United States should do whatever it is able to do to assist in the return of normal economic health in the world, without which there can be no political stability and no assured peace. Our policy is directed not against any country or doctrine but against hunger, poverty, desperation, and chaos. Its purpose should be the revival of a working economy in the world so as to permit the emergence of political and social conditions in which free institutions can exist.

Such assistance, I am convinced, must not be on a piecemeal basis as various crises develop. Any assistance that this Government may render in the future should provide a cure rather than a mere palliative. Any government that is willing to assist in the task of recovery will find full cooperation, I am sure, on the part of the United States Government. Any government which maneuvers to block the recovery of other countries cannot expect help from us. Furthermore, governments, political parties, or groups which seek to perpetuate human misery in order to profit therefrom politically or otherwise will encounter the opposition of the United States.

It is already evident that, before the United States Government can proceed much further in its efforts to alleviate the situation and help start the European world on its way to recovery, there must be some agreement among the countries of Europe as to the requirements of the situation and the part those countries themselves will take in order to give proper effect to whatever action might be undertaken by this Government.

It would be neither fitting nor efficacious for this Government to undertake to draw up unilaterally a program designed to place Europe on its feet economically. This is the business of the Europeans. The initiative, I think, must come from Europe. The role of this country should consist of friendly aid in the drafting of a European program and of later support of such a program so far as it may be practical for us to do so. The program should be a joint one, agreed to by a number, if not all, European nations.

2. Senator Vandenberg Is Favorable (1947, 1948)

Tax-burdened Americans, having spent billions in World War II, were reluctant to pour more treasure down the "European rathole." Eloquent Senator Vandenberg of Michigan (see p. 772), a recent convert from isolationism to internationalism, was one of the foremost champions in Congress of the Marshall Plan. In the following excerpts from letters to his constituents, what are his arguments for the Marshall Plan? In what ways does he sees the Plan as serving the self-interest of the United States?

I have no illusions about this so-called "Marshall Plan." . . . Furthermore, I certainly do not take it for granted that American public opinion is ready for any such burdens as would be involved unless and until it is far more effectively demonstrated to the American people that this (1) is within

2. From *The Private Papers of Senator Vandenberg*, pp. 381–83, by Arthur Vandenberg, Jr. Copyright 1952 by Arthur Vandenberg, Jr. Copyright © renewed 1980. Reprinted by permission of Houghton Mifflin Company.

the latitudes of their own available resources and (2) serves their own intelligent self-interest.

. . . I am entirely willing to admit that America herself cannot prosper in a broken world. But it is equally true that if America ever sags, the world's hopes for peace will sag with her. Meanwhile, however, there are some very realistic problems which we must face—including the basic fact that even our friends in Western Europe will soon be totally devoid of dollar exchange and therefore unable to buy commodities from us which are indispensable to their own self-rehabilitation. I must confess that this poses a tough conundrum in international economics entirely aside from considerations of "charity" or "communism." . . .

So we have no alternative but to do the best we can, in the absence of certified knowledge, and to balance one "calculated risk" against another. . . .

You are entirely right that an "international WPA"* can't save Europe from communism or anything else. Is somebody proposing one? I hadn't heard about it. The so-called "Marshall Plan" is the exact opposite, if it runs true to form—and it's our business to see that it does. It is a program geared to self-help. It requires beneficiary countries to proceed specifically to do the things for themselves which will put them on their own feet (and off ours) by 1951—and our aid is progressively contingent upon concurrent results.

. . . I respectfully submit that we do "know enough" to know what will happen if it, or something like it, doesn't work. We know that independent governments, whatever their character otherwise, will disappear from Western Europe; that aggressive communism will be spurred throughout the world; and that our concept of free men, free government, and a relatively free international economy will come up against accumulated hazards which can put our own, precious "American way of life" in the greatest, kindred hazard since Pearl Harbor. . . .

Let's be equally frank in our "calculations" as to what happens if the iron curtain reaches the Atlantic; if peace and justice are at the mercy of expanding, hostile totalitarian aggression, and if the greatest creditor and capitalist nation on earth should find itself substantially isolated in a communist world where the competition would force us into complete regimentation of ourselves beyond anything we have ever experienced.

This question of "what the Bill will cost" is a very interesting one. Unfortunately, the critics of the Bill have nothing to say about what the failure to pass the Bill will cost. You can get some direct and specific idea on this latter point by reading the testimony before our Senate Foreign Relations Committee by Secretary of Defense Forrestal and Secretary of the Army Royall, who both assert that without legislation of this character they would find it necessary immediately to ask for heavily increased

---

* Works Progress Administration—a New Deal agency designed to provide employment on public works.

appropriations for military defense. Why? Because it is infinitely cheaper to defend ourselves by economic means.

In other words, in the final analysis, peace is cheaper than war. War has no bargains. Peace does. There is no guarantee that this European Recovery Plan will "work." But certainly there is an even chance that it can succeed. In my opinion, we cannot afford not to take that chance.

3. Moscow's Misrepresentations (*c.* 1947)

The Marshall Plan certainly would not have received Congressional approval if the American people had not been convinced that their security depended on preventing Western Europe from falling under the sway of Soviet Communism. Humanitarian instincts, gratitude to former allies, the creation of prosperous customers for surplus goods —all these points were argued, but security was unquestionably paramount. American critics of the Marshall Plan charged that the poor people of the United States needed help, and that Washington should not subsidize socialism (in Britain and elsewhere). The following description of the Marshall Plan was prepared by Soviet propagandists for a children's magazine. How accurate is it?

The American papers immediately raised a great noise about this [Marshall] plan. In different terms, they emphasized "the magnanimity" of America which had decided to help war-stricken Europe.

However, actually, this cunning plan pursued entirely different aims. The American capitalists want to use the help of the Marshall Plan to overwhelm Europe and bring it into subjection to themselves. The government of the Soviet Union at once recognized the real meaning of the Marshall Plan, and definitely refused to take part in setting it up. So also did the governments of the other democratic lands—Poland, Czechoslovakia, Bulgaria, Yugoslavia, Rumania, Hungary, and also Finland.* But sixteen European states adopted the Marshall Plan against the wishes of their peoples.

Let us see now how the U.S.A. is preparing to carry out the Marshall Plan, and what it promises the European countries which have fallen for the American bait.

Representatives of these sixteen European states met together and calculated that they had to receive from the U.S.A. 29 billion dollars to restore their economies. The Americans answered that this sum was too high, and asked for its reduction to 20–22 billion dollars.

The Americans, moreover, attached the following condition: they themselves will dictate to each European country what branch of economy it must develop and what it must curtail. For example, they say to Britain: "You Britishers, build fewer ships for yourselves; you will buy ships from us in America." They propose to the French a reduction in the production of automobiles—American factories can make automobiles for France.

3. Quoted in W. B. Smith, *My Three Years in Moscow* (1949), pp. 198–200. By permission of Harper & Row, Publishers, Inc.
* Soviet pressures on these satellite countries kept them from accepting the Marshall Plan.

It goes without saying that this was very useful for American capitalists. In America everybody is fearfully awaiting "the economic crisis," i.e., the time when many factories and industries suddenly close and millions of people are left without work. At that time it will be difficult for the manufacturers to get rid of their output. A man out of work has nothing with which to buy them. So the American capitalists are greatly concerned how to sell profitably their output in Europe. Further, the European countries inevitably will become dependent on America: once they make a few machines, tools, and automobiles, it means that willy-nilly they must defer to the Americans.

According to the Marshall Plan, the American capitalists want to restore all the great factories of Western Germany. In other countries they are hastening to close many factories, while in Germany, on the contrary, they are opening them up. Their purpose there, too, is quite understandable: clearly, the U.S.A. considers Western Germany as its colony. By controlling the big industries there which can also make armaments, it will be easy for the Americans to frighten the European countries dependent on them.

The American capitalists counted on using the Marshall Plan to stir up trouble between the peoples of the democratic countries and the Soviet Union. The Americans proposed to these countries as follows: "We will give you dollars if only you will abandon your friendship with the Soviet Union. But if you don't, we won't give you anything." But the peoples of these countries did not fall for the American capitalists' trick. They answered the Americans: "We will not exchange our freedom and independence for dollars." . . .

But this isn't all. The American capitalists have still another dastardly aim. After using the Marshall Plan to reduce the European countries, they want to unite them in a military alliance for a future war against the democratic states.

The Marshall Plan is highly profitable to the United States. For the European countries it brings only poverty. Any land which wants to receive "aid" by means of this plan will be entirely dependent on America. Its economy will not be assisted: on the contrary, it will fall into greater ruin because the country will have to close many of its industries and plants, and hundreds of thousands of people will be out of work. That is why both in America itself and in all other lands progressive people are opposing the Marshall Plan with all their strength.

D. THE NORTH ATLANTIC PACT

1. Senator Connally Pleads for Support (1949)

Soviet critics were right on one count: economic union under the Marshall Plan paved the way for a military alliance. The Communist takeover in Czechoslovakia in 1948 ac-

1. *Congressional Record*, 81 Cong., 1 sess., p. 8818 (July 5, 1949).

celerated the machinery. In 1949, the representatives of ten Western European nations, plus the United States and Canada, met in Washington to sign the epochal North Atlantic Pact. It stipulated that an attack on one was an attack on all, and that such an attack would cause each signatory to take "such action as it deems necessary," including "armed force." Senator Connally, the spellbinding chairman of the Senate Committee on Foreign Relations, here pleads for approval of the treaty. In what ways does he depict the alliance as a logical supplement to the Marshall Plan?

It is obvious that the United States gains much by declaring now, in this written pact, the course of action we would follow even if the treaty did not exist. Without a treaty, we were drawn into two world wars to preserve the security of the North Atlantic community. Can anyone doubt that we would become involved in a third world conflict if it should ever come?

After the United States is involved in war, it cooperates with and coordinates its activities with its allies. A joint enterprise to win the war and defend its cause in union with its associates is launched with all of its power and might. If it is wise and desirable to cooperate with our partners after we shall have been involved in a war, why should it be wrong or unwise to cooperate with them prior to the outbreak of war for the purpose of preventing war?

From now on, no one will misread our motives or underestimate our determination to stand in defense of our freedom. By letting the world know exactly where we stand, we erect a fundamental policy that outlasts the daily fluctuations of diplomacy, and the twists and turns of psychological warfare which the Soviet Union has chosen to wage against us. This public preview of our intentions has a steadying effect upon the course of human events both at home, where our people

LIGHTNING ATTRACTOR?

Isolationists argued that the NATO alliance would attract war to the U.S. Akron *Beacon-Journal,* 1949.

want no more Normandy beachheads, and abroad, where men must work and live in the sinister shadow of aggression.

The treaty, in thus encouraging a feeling of confidence and security, will provide an atmosphere in which the European recovery program can move forward with new vitality. We know that encouraging progress has already been made. We know, too, that momentum of confidence has been building up in Europe as a direct result of our assistance.

But that is not enough. The greatest obstacle that stands in the way of complete recovery is the pervading and paralyzing sense of insecurity. The treaty is a powerful antidote to this poison. It will go far in dispelling the fear that has plagued Europe since the war.

With this protection afforded by the Atlantic Pact, western Europe can breathe easier again. It can plan its future with renewed hope. New business enterprises, increased trade, and planning for long-range recovery should be the direct results.

The treaty is thus a logical and necessary complement to the recovery program. Through it we shall protect our past and future investments in that famous calculated risk which already has paid remarkable dividends. We might even look forward to the time when we can anticipate rather substantial savings in our ECA° expenditures, once the full impact of the treaty has been felt in Europe.

2. Senator Taft Spurns Entanglements (1949)

Balding and bespectacled Senator Robert A. Taft of Ohio, a dyed-in-the-wool isolationist who was dubbed "Mr. Republican," vigorously opposed the pact. A critic quipped that he had the most brilliant mind in Washington until he made it up. What are the strengths and weaknesses of his argument that the United States was embarking upon a war policy rather than a peace policy?

So, Mr. President, I am opposing the treaty. . . . This whole program in my opinion is not a peace program; it is a war program. Mr. President, I do not wish to make so didactic a statement as that, so I shall say that with the arms factor the whole tendency of this program is toward a third world war, instead of away from a third world war; because we are in the first place committing ourselves to a vast program of foreign aid.

In the second place, we are committing ourselves to a policy of war, not a policy of peace. We are building up armaments. We are undertaking to arm half the world against the other half. We are inevitably starting an armament race. The more the pact signatories arm, the more the Russians are going to arm. It is said they are armed too much already. Perhaps that is true. But that makes no difference. The more we arm, the more they will arm, the more they will devote their whole attention to the building up of arms. The general history of armament races in the world is that they have led to war, not to peace.

° Economic Cooperation Administration, which administered Marshall Plan aid.
2. *Ibid.*, pp. 9887–88 (July 21, 1949).

In the third place, we are going back to the old balance-of-power theory. Every American has denounced that theory. Every man who has thoroughly thought out the question of international organization has said the only ultimate hope of peace depends upon the establishment of law and justice among nations, with international action by joint force against an aggressor. We abandon that theory under the treaty and arms program; and we go back to the old balance-of-power theory, which England followed for years. . . . It always led to a series of wars in Europe, and it will lead to a series of wars in the world, if that is all we develop.

[*The New York* Daily Worker, *a Communist sheet that slavishly echoed the Moscow "line," blasted the Atlantic Pact as "terrible hypocrisy," a "criminal scheme," and "Murder, Inc." It fumed that "even a reactionary like Taft" saw through the "evil conspiracy," which involved "Marshall Plan stooges" groomed for "war on the Soviet Union." The Senate nevertheless approved the twenty-year pact, on July 21, 1949, by a vote of 82 to 13.*]

E. THE CHINA TANGLE

1. Secretary Acheson Drops Chiang (1949)

Chiang Kai-shek's Nationalist China was creaking at the joints when its eight-year war with Japan ended in 1945. Washington continued to provide Chiang with arms to fight the Chinese Communists, but many of these supplies were corruptly sold or abjectly surrendered. President Truman finally dispatched the highly respected General Marshall in a fruitless attempt to persuade the Nationalists to form a coalition government with the Communists. After Washington had cut back the flow of arms to Nationalist China, the corruption-riddled regime collapsed; Chiang fled with the remnants of his army to the offshore island of Formosa (Taiwan). The suavely mustached Secretary of State Acheson, whose keen intellect and toplofty manner irritated Congressmen, defended the administration in the following official letter. What part seems least candid? What is Acheson's ability as a prophet? Should the historic policy have been reversed? Would American public opinion have tolerated such a reversal?

A realistic appraisal of conditions in China, past and present, leads to the conclusion that the only alternative open to the United States was full-scale intervention in behalf of a Government which had lost the confidence of its own troops and its own people. Such intervention would have required the expenditure of even greater sums than have been fruitlessly spent thus far, the command of Nationalist armies by American officers, and the probable participation of American armed forces—land, sea, and air—in the resulting war.

Intervention of such a scope and magnitude would have been resented by the mass of the Chinese people, would have diametrically reversed our historic policy, and would have been condemned by the American people. . . .

The unfortunate but inescapable fact is that the ominous result of the civil war in China was beyond the control of the government of the United

1. *United States Relations with China, with Special Reference to the Period 1944–1949* (1949), pp. xv–xvi.

States. Nothing that this country did or could have done within the reasonable limits of its capabilities could have changed that result; nothing that was left undone by this country has contributed to it. It was the product of internal Chinese forces, forces which this country tried to influence but could not. A decision was arrived at within China, if only a decision by default.

And now it is abundantly clear that we must face the situation as it exists in fact. We will not help the Chinese or ourselves by basing our policy on wishful thinking. We continue to believe that, however tragic may be the immediate future of China, and however ruthlessly a major portion of this great people may be exploited by a [Communist] party in the interest of foreign imperialism, ultimately the profound civilization and the democratic individualism of China will reassert themselves, and she will throw off the foreign yoke. I consider that we should encourage all developments in China which now and in the future work toward this end.

2. Senator McCarthy Blasts "Traitors" (1952)

The loss of a half-billion or so Chinese to the Communists was a staggering blow to American policy. Scapegoats had to be found. The violently anti-Communist Republican Senator Joseph R. McCarthy leaped into the fray, flinging accusations wildly and indiscriminately. In his view Secretary Acheson and General Marshall, themselves allegedly "soft" on Communism and advised by Communist "traitors" in the State Department, had deliberately and treasonably allowed China to go down the drain. Senator McCarthy asks himself the following questions—and answers them—in a book published in 1952. Which of his charges seem the most convincing? the most overdrawn? Does he prove that more arms for China would have averted the Communist take-over?

Do you think Acheson realized he was following the Communist Party line in Asia?

Either he knew what he was doing or he was incompetent beyond words. As late as November, 1945, William Z. Foster, head of the Communist Party of the United States, notified the world that China was the prime target of the Soviet Union. He said: "On the international scale, the key task . . . is to stop American intervention in China. . . . The war in China is the key of all problems on the international front."

Less than a month after this Communist proclamation, Marshall embarked upon the "Marshall Mission to China." The testimony before the Russell Committee was that this mission was an Acheson-Marshall-Vincent* project. Before Marshall went to China the Communists occupied a very small portion of China. Their Army numbered less than 300,000 badly equipped troops. When Marshall returned from China to be rewarded by Truman with an appointment as Secretary of State, the Communist-controlled area had greatly increased and the Communist Army had grown from 300,000

2. Quoted from Senator Joseph McCarthy, *McCarthyism: The Fight for America* (1952), pp. 37–40. Published in 1952 by the Devin-Adair Company, New York.
* John C. Vincent was a foreign service officer allegedly "soft" on Communism.

badly equipped troops to an Army of over 2,000,000 relatively well-equipped soldiers.

What about the State Department's excuse that we withdrew aid from Chiang Kai-shek because his government was corrupt?

Chiang Kai-shek had been engaged in conflict and warfare since 1927—first with the Communists, then with Japan, then simultaneously with the Communists and Japan, and after Japan's defeat, again with the Communists. During that time, all the disruption of war beset Chiang's Government. Under the circumstances it would be a miracle if there were no corruption or incompetence in his government.

But if corruption and incompetence are grounds for turning an administration over to the Communists, then Earl Browder should be President of the United States, Harry Bridges should be Secretary of Labor, and Alger Hiss† should be Secretary of Defense.

What about Acheson's claim that we gave Chiang Kai-shek every help which he could utilize, including $2 billion worth of aid since the end of World War II?

That is untrue. Acheson made this claim in a letter to Senator Pat Mc-Carran on March 14, 1949, in arguing against any further aid to anti-Communist China, which according to Acheson "would almost surely be catastrophic."

Of the phony $2 billion figure, $335,800,000 was for repatriating Japanese soldiers in China and transporting Chinese Nationalist armed forces to accept the surrender of the Japanese. Even President Truman declared that those expenditures should properly have been charged to World War II. . . .

Is it true that Marshall, under State Department instructions, signed an order cutting off not only arms to our friends in China, but also all ammunition so that the arms they had would be useless?

Yes. The embargo on all arms and ammunition to China began in 1946 and continued into 1947.

Those were crucial years, and China's plight was so bad that even the New York *Times* reported on June 22, 1947, that the guns of the anti-Communists were so worn and burned out that "bullets fell through them to the ground."

The Communists, on the other hand, were kept well supplied by the Russians. Admiral Cooke has so testified before the McCarran Committee. . . .

Do you claim that General Marshall, who has long worked with Acheson, was knowingly working for the Communist cause in China?

As I stated in my book, *The Story of General George Marshall—America's Retreat from Victory*, I cannot delve into the mind of Marshall. I can only

---

† Alger Hiss was a former State Department official convicted in 1950 of perjury in connection with passing secrets on to the Soviets. Harry Bridges was a Pacific Coast labor leader accused of Communist affiliation. Earl Browder was twice a candidate for the Presidency on the Communist ticket.

present the facts to the American people. Whether Marshall knowingly betrayed China or whether he honestly thought that he was helping China, the results are equally disastrous for America. . . .

Since the fall of China has Acheson ever admitted that his China policy was a failure?

No. There is no indication that Acheson considers the loss of China to Communism a "failure." Instead, he hailed it as "a new day which has dawned in Asia."

[*The Americans supplied Chiang's Nationalists with vastly more arms than the Russians sent to the Chinese Communists, although departing Soviet troops did abandon large quantities of Japanese munitions to the Communists. The Americans also abandoned comparable supplies of their own to the Nationalists. The tale about bullets falling out of worn-out guns came from an unnamed Chinese correspondent's report (New York Times, June 22, 1947, p. 38) that "some machine gun barrels were so burned that bullets fell through them to the ground." Machine guns can be so badly worn as to fire inaccurately, but the bullets are firmly lodged in the cartridges, and the cartridges are either clipped or belted together.*

General Barr, an American military observer, reported to the Department of the Army on November 16, 1948:

"*I am convinced that the military situation has deteriorated to the point where only the active participation of United States troops could effect a remedy. . . . Military matériel and economic aid in my opinion is less important to the salvation of China than other factors. No battle has been lost since my arrival due to lack of ammunition or equipment. Their military debacles in my opinion can all be attributed to the world's worst leadership and many other morale-destroying factors that lead to a complete loss of will to fight. The complete ineptness of high military leaders and the widespread corruption and dishonesty throughout the Armed Forces could, in some measure, have been controlled and directed had the above authority and facilities been available. Chinese leaders completely lack the moral courage to issue and enforce an unpopular decision. . . .*" (United States Relations with China, with Special Reference to the Period 1944–1949 [1949], p. 358.)]

THOUGHT PROVOKERS

1. What choices did Roosevelt have at Yalta? Was he justified in making the concessions that he did to the Soviet Union?
2. Why did George Kennan's views of Soviet behavior prove so influential? What is the role of ideas in the formulation of foreign policy? Was the Truman Doctrine a balanced, proportionate response to the crisis that President Truman faced in the 1940's?
3. To what extent was the Marshall Plan an act of altruism? Of self-interest?
4. Was America justified in departing from tradition to join the NATO alliance? Why was a military alliance considered the right policy at the time? Is NATO's role today the same as it was in the 1940's?
5. Is it proper to speak of the Communist take-over in China as the "fall" of China? Why did Senator McCarthy use the China issue so viciously against the Democrats? Would a different American policy have produced a different outcome in China?

44 · *Korea and the Eisenhower Era*

> *We must guard against the acquisition of unwarranted influence, whether sought or unsought, by the military-industrial complex.*
>
> DWIGHT D. EISENHOWER, 1961

PROLOGUE: A frontal challenge to world peace came in 1950 when the North Koreans, joined later by the Chinese, lunged into South Korea. Hoping to preserve collective security and avert global war, Truman intervened. The United States and the South Koreans, with help from fifteen allies under the auspices of the United Nations, fought the Communists to a bloody standstill. Truman's unwillingness to risk a general war with China and Russia resulted in the dismissal of General MacArthur. The stalemated war helped to invigorate Senator McCarthy's ill-conceived crusade against alleged Communists in government. The resulting witch hunt cruelly wounded many individuals, and left scars on the body politic that took decades to heal. The Supreme Court in 1954 ordered the desegregation of schools, notably in the South. The white South at first resisted massively, but the Court's decision gave momentum to the rising wave of the civil rights movement, which was to crest in the 1960's. The first Republican administration in twenty years, inaugurated under war-hero Dwight Eisenhower's leadership in 1953, proved unable to thaw the Cold War with Russia, though "Ike" did bring an uneasy armistice to Korea. Stalin died in 1953, and the more subtle Khrushchev emerged as the undisputed Soviet leader. The Russians matched the American hydrogen bomb in 1953, and then startled the world by shooting two Sputniks into orbit in 1957. The balance of power, heavily weighted in favor of an atomically armed America after 1945, was clearly shifting to an uneasy balance of terror. Tensions tightened when the Soviets crushed the Hungarian freedom fighters in 1956, backed President Nasser of Egypt during the Suez explosion of 1956, and wooed Cuba's bearded Communist Castro. New leadership and the New Frontier came with the election of Senator Kennedy to the Presidency in the close and colorful campaign of 1960.

A. THE KOREAN CRISIS

1. Senator Connally Writes Off Korea (1950)

Secretary Acheson compounded his China felony, in McCarthyite eyes, by making a memorable speech to the National Press Club of Washington early in 1950. He outlined America's "defensive perimeter" in the Far East, but conspicuously omitted from it the Republic of South Korea and Chiang's last-hope Formosa. He stated that the areas thus excluded would have to depend on themselves for defense and on "the commitments of the entire civilized world under the Charter of the United

---

1. From a copyrighted interview in *U.S. News and World Report*, XXVIII, 30 (May 5, 1950).

Nations. . . ." Some three months later Senator Connally, chairman of the powerful Senate Foreign Relations Committee, gave the following interview. Critics of the Truman administration later charged that the Acheson and Connally statements were open invitations to the Russian-backed North Korean Communists to invade South Korea, as they did in June, 1950. Was this inference fair?

Question. Do you think the suggestion that we abandon South Korea is going to be seriously considered?

Answer. I am afraid it is going to be seriously considered because I'm afraid it's going to happen, whether we want it to or not. I'm for Korea. We're trying to help her—we're appropriating money now to help her. But South Korea is cut right across by this line—north of it are the Communists, with access to the mainland—and Russia is over there on the mainland. So that whenever she takes a notion, she can just overrun Korea, just like she probably will overrun Formosa when she gets ready to do it. I hope not, of course.

Question. But isn't Korea an essential part of the defense strategy?

Answer. No. Of course, any position like that is of some strategic importance. But I don't think it is very greatly important. It has been testified before us that Japan, Okinawa, and the Philippines make the chain of defense which is absolutely necessary. And, of course, any additional territory along in that area would be that much more, but it's not absolutely essential.

2. Truman Accepts the Korean Challenge (1950)

President Truman was forced to make a series of agonizing decisions: the Truman doctrine (1947), the Marshall Plan (1947), the Berlin Airlift (1948), the North Atlantic Pact (1949), the Korean intervention (1950). Speaking later (1959) at Columbia University, he was asked, "Mr. President, what was the most complicated, the one single, most difficult decision you had to make?" Unhesitatingly he replied: "Korea. The reason for that was the fact that the policies of our allies and the members of the United Nations were at stake at the same time as ours." Here in his *Memoirs* he explains more fully the reasons for intervening with armed forces to support the South Korean republic, a special ward of the United Nations. Remembering that the League of Nations had collapsed in the 1930's because it failed to act resolutely, assess the validity of Truman's view that his intervention in Korea averted World War III.

On Saturday, June 24, 1950, I was in Independence, Missouri, to spend the weekend with my family and to attend to some personal family business.

It was a little after ten in the evening, and we were sitting in the library of our home on North Delaware Street when the telephone rang. It was the Secretary of State calling from his home in Maryland.

"Mr. President," said Dean Acheson, "I have very serious news. The North Koreans have invaded South Korea."

My first reaction was that I must get back to the capital, and I told Acheson so. . . .

2. *Memoirs by Harry S. Truman: Years of Trial and Hope* (1956), II, 331–33. Published by Doubleday and Company. Copyright 1956 by Time, Inc. Reprinted by permission of Time, Inc.

The plane left the Kansas City Municipal Airport at two o'clock, and it took just a little over three hours to make the trip to Washington. I had time to think aboard the plane. In my generation, this was not the first occasion when the strong had attacked the weak. I recalled some earlier instances: [Japan in] Manchuria, [Italy in] Ethiopia, [Germany in] Austria. I remembered how each time that the democracies failed to act it had encouraged the aggressors to keep going ahead.

Communism was acting in Korea just as Hitler, Mussolini, and the Japanese had acted ten, fifteen, and twenty years earlier. I felt certain

U.S. DEFENSE PERIMETER JAN. 1950

that if South Korea was allowed to fall, Communist leaders would be emboldened to override nations closer to our own shores. If the Communists were permitted to force their way into the Republic of Korea without opposition from the free world, no small nation would have the courage to resist threats and aggression by stronger Communist neighbors. If this was allowed to go unchallenged it would mean a third world war, just as similar incidents had brought on the second world war. It was also clear to me that the foundations and the principles of the United Nations were at stake unless this unprovoked attack on Korea could be stopped.

B. THE SACKING OF GENERAL MacARTHUR

1. Truman Asserts Civil Supremacy (1951)

General Douglas MacArthur—handsome, proud, dramatic—served brilliantly as United Nations commander in Korea, until rocked back on his heels by the unexpected descent of hordes of Chinese "volunteers." He urged on Washington a blockade of the Chinese coast, a bombing of supply bases in China, and the use of Chiang's Formosan troops in Korea. Russia had a treaty of alliance (1950) with China, and both the Truman administration and its UN allies were anxious to avoid

1. *Memoirs by Harry S. Truman: Years of Trial and Hope* (1956), II, 444–45. Published by Doubleday and Company. Copyright 1956 by Time, Inc. Reprinted by permission of Time, Inc.

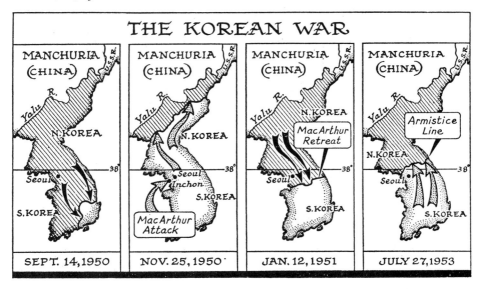

THE KOREAN WAR

MANCHURIA (CHINA)	MANCHURIA (CHINA)	MANCHURIA (CHINA)	MANCHURIA (CHINA)
N.KOREA / Seoul / S.KOREA	N.KOREA / Seoul / Inchon / S.KOREA / MacArthur Attack	N.KOREA / MacArthur Retreat / Seoul / S.KOREA	Armistice Line / N.KOREA / Seoul / S.KOREA
SEPT. 14, 1950	NOV. 25, 1950	JAN. 12, 1951	JULY 27, 1953

a general war in the Far East while the Soviet menace loomed large in Europe. MacArthur, who sharply disagreed with the policy of Washington, ruined Truman's proposed peace negotiations by delivering an ultimatum to the enemy (March 24, 1951). Peppery Harry Truman, who had been an army captain in World War I, would brook no such insubordination. He here expresses his views in his *Memoirs*. How does he defend the view that the military must be subordinate to civil authority?

If there is one basic element in our Constitution, it is civilian control of the military. Policies are to be made by the elected political officials, not by generals or admirals. Yet time and again General MacArthur had shown that he was unwilling to accept the policies of the administration. By his repeated public statements he was not only confusing our allies as to the true course of our policies but, in fact, was also setting his policy against the President's.

I have always had, and I have to this day, the greatest respect for General MacArthur, the soldier. Nothing I could do, I knew, could change his stature as one of the outstanding military figures of our time—and I had no desire to diminish his stature. I had hoped, and I had tried to convince him, that the policy he was asked to follow was right. He had disagreed. He had been openly critical. Now, at last, his actions [in issuing an ultimatum] had frustrated a political course decided upon, in conjunction with its allies, by the government he was sworn to serve. If I allowed him to defy the civil authorities in this manner, I myself would be violating my oath to uphold and defend the Constitution.

I have always believed that civilian control of the military is one of the strongest foundations of our system of free government. Many of our people are descended from men and women who fled their native countries to escape the oppression of militarism. We in America have sometimes failed to give the soldier and the sailor their due, and it has hurt us. But we have always jealously guarded the constitutional provision that prevents the military from taking over the government from the authorities, elected by the people, in whom the power resides.

It has often been pointed out that the American people have a tendency to choose military heroes for the highest office in the land, but I think the statement is misleading. . . . We have chosen men who, in time of war, had made their mark, but until 1952 we had never elevated to the White House any man whose entire life had been dedicated to the military.*

One reason that we have been so careful to keep the military within its own preserve is that the very nature of the service hierarchy gives military commanders little, if any, opportunity to learn the humility that is needed for good public service. The elected official will never forget—unless he is a fool—that others as well or better qualified might have been chosen, and that millions remained unconvinced that the last choice made was the best one possible. . . .

These are things a military officer is not likely to learn in the course of his profession. The words that dominate his thinking are "command" and "obedience," and the military definitions of these words are not definitions for use in a republic.

That is why our Constitution embodies the principle of civilian control of the military. This was the principle that General MacArthur threatened. I do not believe that he purposefully decided to challenge civilian control of the military, but the result of his behavior was that this fundamental principle of free government was in danger.

It was my duty to act.

2. MacArthur Calls for Victory (1951)

Joseph W. Martin, Republican House minority leader, had written to General MacArthur in March, 1951, complaining about the folly of not using Chiang's several hundred thousand orphaned Chinese troops in Korea. (They were needed for the defense of Formosa; they might have defected; they would have been resented by the South Koreans.) Martin solicited MacArthur's views. The outspoken general, without labeling his reply as confidential, wrote as follows. On April 5, 1951, Martin read the letter to the House. Truman had already made up his mind to remove MacArthur, and this indiscreet statement strengthened his determination. What part of the letter reveals most clearly the military man rather than the statesman?

I am most grateful for your note of the eighth forwarding me a copy of your address of February 12. The latter I have read with much interest, and find that with the passage of years you have certainly lost none of your old-time punch.

---

* Truman neglected to say that General Eisenhower had been president of Columbia University for four years.
2. *Congressional Record*, 82 Cong., 1 sess., p. 3380.

My views and recommendations with respect to the situation created by Red China's entry into war against us in Korea have been submitted to Washington in most complete detail. Generally these views are well known and clearly understood, as they follow the conventional pattern of meeting force with maximum counter-force, as we have never failed to do in the past. Your view with respect to the utilization of the Chinese forces on Formosa is in conflict with neither logic nor this tradition.

It seems strangely difficult for some to realize that here in Asia is where the Communist conspirators have elected to make their play for global conquest, and that we have joined the issue thus raised on the battlefield; that here we fight Europe's war with arms while the diplomats there still fight it with words; that if we lose the war to Communism in Asia the fall of Europe is inevitable; win it, and Europe most probably would avoid war and yet preserve freedom.

As you point out, we must win. There is no substitute for victory.

3. Truman Looks beyond Victory (1951)

An angered Truman abruptly dismissed MacArthur from his Far Eastern commands (April 11, 1951), but circumstances conspired to make the General's removal unduly brutal. The five-star general, "fired by a two-bit President," returned home to receive a hero's welcome. He delivered a dramatic speech before Congress in which he repeated the no-substitute-for-victory formula, and then with tear-inducing pathos recited the lines of the old barracks ballad: "Old soldiers never die; they just fade away." The excitement faded away, even though the General did not, and a stalemate truce came to Korea in 1953. A cocksure Truman delivered this rebuttal in his *Memoirs*, taking as his text the indiscreet MacArthur letter to Representative Martin. Why, in Truman's view, was the kind of victory that the General proposed the wrong kind of victory?

Of course the third paragraph of MacArthur's letter was the real "clincher." I do not know through what channels of information the general learned that the Communists had chosen to concentrate their efforts on Asia —and more specifically on his command. . . . Actually, of course, my letter of January 13 [to MacArthur] had made it clear that Communism was capable of attacking not only in Asia but also in Europe, and that this was one reason why we could not afford to extend the conflict in Korea. But then MacArthur added a belittling comment about our diplomatic efforts, and reached his climax with the pronouncement that "there is no substitute for victory."

But there is a right kind and a wrong kind of victory, just as there are wars for the right thing and wars that are wrong from every standpoint.

As General Bradley later said: "To have extended the fighting to the mainland of Asia would have been the wrong war, at the wrong time and in the wrong place."

3. *Memoirs by Harry S. Truman: Years of Trial and Hope* (1956), II, 446–47. Published by Doubleday and Company. Copyright 1956 by Time, Inc. Reprinted by permission of Time, Inc.

"WE'VE BEEN USING MORE OF A ROUNDISH ONE."

General Marshall advises General MacArthur that an expanded war in the Far East might not remain there but
spread to the rest of the globe. Washington *Post*, March,
1951. From *The Herblock Book* (Beacon Press, 1952).

The kind of victory MacArthur had in mind—victory by the bombing of
Chinese cities, victory by expanding the conflict to all of China—would have
been the wrong kind of victory.

To some professional military men, victory—success on the battlefield
alone—becomes something of an end in itself. Napoleon, during his ill-fated
Moscow campaign, said, "I beat them in every battle, but it does not get
me anywhere."

The time had come to draw the line. MacArthur's letter to Congressman
Martin showed that the general was not only in disagreement with the
policy of the government but was challenging this policy in open insubordination to his Commander in Chief.

C. THE McCARTHY HYSTERIA

1. McCarthy Upholds Guilt by Association (1952)

Senator Joseph R. McCarthy of Wisconsin, hitherto unknown to fame, rocketed into the headlines in 1950 when he declared in a political speech that there were scores of known Communists in the State Department. The collapse of Chiang's China and the bloodily indecisive Korean War gave point to his charges, while accelerating the hunt for scapegoats. A few homosexuals, "pinks," and Communist sympathizers were exposed and driven out of government. But persons with liberal or non-conformist ideas were indiscriminately branded as Communists, with a subsequent loss of reputation and jobs. In McCarthy's view, birds that waddled like ducks, quacked like ducks, and associated with ducks were presumed to be ducks. Anti-McCarthyites cited the axiom that it was better to let ten guilty men escape than to condemn one innocent man. McCarthy here defends his tactics. How convincing is he?

One of the safest and most popular sports engaged in today by every politician and office seeker is to "agree with McCarthy's aim of getting rid of Communists in government," but at the same time to "condemn his irresponsible charges and shot-gun technique." It is a completely safe position to take. The Communist Party and their camp followers in press and radio do not strike back as long as you merely condemn Communism in general terms. It is only when one adopts an effective method of digging out and exposing the under-cover, dangerous, "sacred cow" Communists that all of the venom and smear of the Party is loosed upon him.

I suggest to you, therefore, that when a politician mounts the speaker's rostrum and makes the statement that he "agrees with McCarthy's aims but not his methods," that you ask him what methods he himself has used against Communists. I suggest you ask him to name a single Communist or camp follower that he has forced out of the government by his methods. . . .

Is not a person presumed innocent until proven guilty?
Yes.

Why do you condemn people like Acheson, Jessup, Lattimore, Service, Vincent, * *and others who have never been convicted of any crime?*
The fact that these people have not been convicted of treason or of violating some of our espionage laws is no more a valid argument that they are fit to represent this country in its fight against Communism than the argument that a person who has a reputation of consorting with criminals, hoodlums, gamblers, and kidnappers is fit to act as your baby sitter because he has never been convicted of a crime.

1. Quoted from Senator Joseph McCarthy, *McCarthyism: The Fight for America* (1952), pp. 7, 79–80. Published in 1952 by the Devin-Adair Company, New York. *Webster's Third International Dictionary* (1961) defines McCarthyism as "a political attitude of the mid-twentieth century closely allied to know-nothingism, and characterized chiefly by opposition to elements held to be subversive, and by the use of tactics involving personal attacks on individuals by means of widely publicized indiscriminate allegations, especially on the basis of unsubstantiated charges."

* Professors Philip C. Jessup and Owen Lattimore were prominent officials or advisers who were allegedly "soft" on Communism; John S. Service and John C. Vincent were foreign service officers similarly branded by McCarthy.

A government job is a privilege, not a right. There is no reason why men who chum with Communists, who refuse to turn their backs upon traitors† and who are consistently found at the time and place where disaster strikes America and success comes to international Communism, should be given positions of power in government. . . .

I have not urged that those whom I have named be put in jail. Once they are exposed so the American people know what they are, they can do but little damage. . . .

Strangely enough, those who scream the loudest about what they call guilt by association are the first to endorse innocence by association.

For example, those who object most strongly to my showing Jessup's affinity for Communist causes, the Communist money used to support the publication over which he had control, and his close friendship and defense of a Communist spy [Hiss], also argue Hiss' innocence by association. The argument is that Hiss was innocent because Justices Frankfurter and Reed testified they were friends of his, because Acheson chummed and walked with him each morning, because Hiss was the top planner at the United Nations conference and helped to draft the Yalta agreement.

We are not concerned with GUILT by association because here we are not concerned with convicting any individual of any crime. We are concerned with the question of whether the individual who associates with those who are trying to destroy this nation, should be admitted to the high councils of those planning the policies of this nation: whether they should be given access to top secret material to which even Senators and Congressmen are not given access.

2. A Senator Speaks Up (1950)

The infiltration of a few Communists into government was perhaps inevitable, but the embarrassed Truman administration played into the hands of the McCarthyites by its cover-up tactics. In the interests of free debate, the Constitution exempts from libel suits anything that may be said on the floor of Congress. Senator McCarthy clearly abused this privilege. At a time when he was riding high and many Republicans regarded him as a political asset, the tall and gray-haired Republican Margaret Chase Smith of Maine, the only woman United States Senator, courageously spoke out against his excesses. (Later McCarthy vindictively invaded Maine in an unsuccessful effort to defeat her for re-election.) Why does she believe that McCarthy's tactics, whatever his aims, are contrary to the Constitution and basically unAmerican?

I think that it is high time for the United States Senate and its Members to do some real soul searching, and to weigh our consciences as to the manner in which we are performing our duty to the people of America, and the manner in which we are using or abusing our individual powers and privileges.

† After State Department official Alger Hiss was convicted of perjury in connection with Soviet espionage, his friend Secretary of State Acheson loyally but indiscreetly declared, "I do not intend to turn my back [on him]."

2. *Congressional Record*, 81 Cong., 2 sess., pp. 7894–95 (June 1, 1950). Senator Smith simultaneously presented "a Declaration of Conscience" signed by six fellow Senators.

I think it is high time that we remembered that we have sworn to uphold and defend the Constitution. I think it is high time that we remembered that the Constitution, as amended, speaks not only of the freedom of speech but also of trial by jury instead of trial by accusation.

Whether it be a criminal prosecution in court or a character prosecution in the Senate, there is little practical distinction when the life of a person has been ruined.

Those of us who shout the loudest about Americanism in making character assassinations are all too frequently those who, by our own words and acts, ignore some of the basic principles of Americanism—

"FIRE!"

Incipient McCarthyites regard flame in torch of Statue of Liberty as a fire. Washington *Post,* 1951. From *The Herblock Book* (Beacon Press, 1952).

The right to criticize.

The right to hold unpopular beliefs.

The right to protest.

The right of independent thought.

The exercise of these rights should not cost one single American citizen his reputation or his right to a livelihood, nor should he be in danger of losing his reputation or livelihood merely because he happens to know someone who holds unpopular beliefs. Who of us does not? Otherwise none of us could call our souls our own. Otherwise thought control would have set in.

The American people are sick and tired of being afraid to speak their minds lest they be politically smeared as Communists or Fascists by their opponents. Freedom of speech is not what it used to be in America. It has been so abused by some that it is not exercised by others.

The American people are sick and tired of seeing innocent people smeared and guilty people whitewashed. But there have been enough proved cases, such as the *Amerasia* case, the Hiss case, the Coplon case, the Gold case,* to cause nation-wide distrust and strong suspicion that there may be something to the unproved, sensational accusations. . . .

Today our country is being psychologically divided by the confusion and the suspicions that are bred in the United States Senate to spread like cancerous tentacles of "know nothing, suspect everything" attitudes. . . .

As a United States Senator, I am not proud of the way in which the Senate has been made a publicity platform for irresponsible sensationalism. I am not proud of the reckless abandon in which unproved charges have been hurled from this [Republican] side of the aisle. I am not proud of the obviously staged, undignified countercharges which have been attempted in retaliation from the other [Democratic] side of the aisle.

I do not like the way the Senate has been made a rendezvous for vilification, for selfish political gain at the sacrifice of individual reputations and national unity. I am not proud of the way we smear outsiders from the floor of the Senate and hide behind the cloak of congressional immunity, and still place ourselves beyond criticism on the floor of the Senate.

As an American, I am shocked at the way Republicans and Democrats alike are playing directly into the Communist design of "confuse, divide, and conquer." As an American, I do not want a Democratic administration whitewash or cover-up any more than I want a Republican smear or witch hunt.

As an American, I condemn a Republican Fascist just as much as I condemn a Democratic Communist. I condemn a Democratic Fascist just as much as I condemn a Republican Communist. They are equally dangerous to you and me and to our country. As an American, I want to see our Nation recapture the strength and unity it once had when we fought the enemy instead of ourselves.

3. McCarthy Inspires Fear at Harvard (1954)

Senator McCarthy overplayed his hand, notably in the televised investigation of the Army. To millions of viewers he exposed his vindictiveness, arrogance, and intellectual dishonesty. Apologists claimed that his anti-Communist zeal, whether sincere or not, destroyed all sense of fair play. His bubble burst when the Senate "condemned" him in 1954 by a formal vote, not, curiously enough, for his abuses of American citizens but for his contemptuous attitude toward the Senate itself. A petition urging the censure of McCarthy was circulated at Harvard University, and two undergraduates who refused to sign it gave their reasons in the first of the following letters to the Harvard *Crimson.* An English-born student named J. C. P.

---

* *Amerasia* was a Communist-tainted magazine which acquired confidential government documents. Judith Coplon, a Justice Department employee, and Harry Gold, a Philadelphia biochemist, were both convicted in 1950 of spying for Russia.
3. Cited in *Congressional Record,* 83 Cong., 2 sess., p. A6909. Reprinted by permission of the Harvard *Crimson.* The letters appeared in the issues of November 24 and 30, 1954. The Richardson letter ended in the *Crimson* with four dots after "crowd"; the missing five lines are published in the *Congressional Record.*

Richardson, who was backing the petition, took sharp issue with them in the second letter. Who has the sounder position?

To the Editors of the *Crimson:*

This afternoon my roommate and I were asked to sign a petition advocating the censure of Senator Joseph R. McCarthy. We both refused. And yet, we both hope that the censure motion is adopted.

Discussing our actions, we came to the conclusion that we did not sign because we were afraid that sometime in the future McCarthy will point to us as having signed the petition, and, as he has done to others, question our loyalty.

We are afraid that of the thousands of petition signers, one will be proved a Communist, and as a result, McCarthy, or someone like him, will say, because we were both co-signers and classmates of the Communist, that we, too, are Reds.

The fact that two college students and others like us will not sign a petition for fear of reprisal indicates only too clearly that our democracy is in danger. It is clear that McCarthy is suppressing free speech and free actions by thrusting fear into the hearts of innocent citizens.

Let us hope that the Senators of the United States are not victims of the same fear that has infected us.

K. W. L. '58
M. F. G. '58

To the Editors of the *Crimson*:

The letter sent to you by two Harvard students and published yesterday can safely be said to represent the viewpoint of about one half of those who did not sign the anti-McCarthy petition.

The position taken by the authors is common and understandable, but it is by no means justifiable. In a free society, when opinions become unpopular and dangerous, it is most important that they be expressed. To yield to the climate of fear, to become a scared liberal, is to strengthen the very forces which one opposes. Courage must complement conviction, for otherwise each man will become a rubber-stamp, content to spend the rest of his life echoing popular beliefs, never daring to dissent, never having enough courage to say what he thinks, and never living as an individual, but only as part of the crowd.

Yes, our democracy is in danger, but as long as men are not afraid to express their view in spite of the consequences, it shall flourish. Only when fear is allowed to limit dissension does democracy falter.

The blame for America's present intellectual intolerance rests as heavily on those who have bowed to it as it does on those who encourage it.

Sincerely,
J. C. Peter Richardson '56

D. THE SUPREME COURT AND THE BLACK REVOLUTION

1. The Court Rejects Segregation (1954)

The 14th Amendment (1868) had made blacks citizens and assured them "the equal protection of the laws." The Southern states established "separate but equal" facilities in the schools, in public toilets, and in transportation. But in many instances the facilities for blacks, though "separate," were not "equal" to those for whites. In 1892 a Louisianan by the name of Plessy, of one-eighth African blood, was jailed for insisting on sitting in a railroad car reserved for whites. The case was appealed to the Supreme Court, where Plessy lost by a 7 to 1 vote. The Court held that separate but equal public conveyances did not violate the 14th Amendment. This principle was applied to educational facilities until May 17, 1954, when the Supreme Court, by a 9 to 0 vote, reversed its basic policy and decreed that separate educational facilities were not equal within the meaning of the 14th Amendment. In the heart of the decision given here, what ground is there for the white Southern complaint that this was a sociological rather than a legal decision? Are separateness and inequality inseparable?

In approaching this problem, we cannot turn the clock back to 1868 when the [14th] Amendment was adopted, or even to 1896 when *Plessy v. Ferguson* was written. We must consider public education in the light of its full development and its present place in American life throughout the Nation. Only in this way can it be determined if segregation in public schools deprives these plaintiffs of the equal protection of the laws.

Today, education is perhaps the most important function of state and local governments. Compulsory school attendance laws and the great expenditures for education both demonstrate our recognition of the importance of education to our democratic society. It is required in the performance of our most basic public responsibilities, even service in the armed forces. It is the very foundation of good citizenship. Today it is a principal instrument in awakening the child to cultural values, in preparing him for later professional training, and in helping him to adjust normally to his environment. In these days, it is doubtful that any child may reasonably be expected to succeed in life if he is denied the opportunity of an education. Such an opportunity, where the state has undertaken to provide it, is a right which must be made available to all on equal terms.

We come then to the question presented: Does segregation of children in public schools solely on the basis of race, even though the physical facilities and other "tangible" factors may be equal, deprive the children of the minority group of equal educational opportunities? We believe that it does. . . .

Such considerations apply with added force to children in grade and high schools. To separate them from others of similar age and qualifications, solely because of their race, generates a feeling of inferiority as to their status in the community that may affect their hearts and minds in a way unlikely ever to be undone. The effect of this separation on their educational opportunities was well stated by a finding in the Kansas case by a court which nevertheless felt compelled to rule against the Negro plaintiffs:

1. 347 U.S. 492–95. Brown *vs.* Board of Education of Topeka.

"Segregation of white and colored children in public schools has a detrimental effect upon the colored children. The impact is greater when it has the sanction of the law; for the policy of separating the races is usually interpreted as denoting the inferiority of the Negro group. A sense of inferiority affects the motivation of a child to learn. Segregation with the sanction of law, therefore, has a tendency to [retard] the educational and mental development of Negro children, and to deprive them of some of the benefits they would receive in a racial[ly] integrated school system."

Whatever may have been the extent of psychological knowledge at the time of *Plessy v. Ferguson*, this finding is amply supported by modern authority. Any language in *Plessy v. Ferguson* contrary to this finding is rejected.

We conclude that in the field of public education the doctrine of "separate but equal" has no place. Separate educational facilities are inherently unequal. Therefore, we hold that the plaintiffs and others similarly situated for whom the actions have been brought are, by reason of the segregation complained of, deprived of the equal protection of the laws guaranteed by the Fourteenth Amendment.

2. One Hundred Congressmen Dissent (1956)

Chief Justice Earl Warren, a gray-haired, open-faced California governor turned judge, had already come under some fire for his liberal views. Bitter was the outcry of white Southerners against the "Earl Warren Communist Court." Even though the desegregation decision called for gradual implementation, the social upheaval that it foreshadowed was enormous. One hundred Southern members of Congress issued the following manifesto in 1956. The first part of it declared that since the Constitution does not mention education, the schools are solely the concern of the states under reserved powers (10th Amendment). How persuasive is the manifesto's contention that the Court's decision would worsen, rather than improve, race relations?

In the case of *Plessy v. Ferguson*, in 1896, the Supreme Court expressly declared that under the Fourteenth Amendment no person was denied any of his rights if the states provided separate but equal public facilities. This decision has been followed in many other cases. It is notable that the Supreme Court, speaking through Chief Justice Taft, a former President of the United States, unanimously declared in 1927 in *Lum v. Rice* that the "separate but equal" principle is ". . . within the discretion of the state in regulating its public schools and does not conflict with the Fourteenth Amendment."

This interpretation, restated time and again, became a part of the life of the people of many of the states and confirmed their habits, customs, traditions, and way of life. It is founded on elemental humanity and common sense, for parents should not be deprived by Government of the right to direct the lives and education of their own children.

2. *Congressional Record*, 84 Cong., 2 sess., pp. 4515–16 (March 12, 1956). The signers numbered 19 Senators and 81 Representatives.

Though there has been no constitutional amendment or act of Congress changing this established legal principle almost a century old, the Supreme Court of the United States, with no legal basis for such action, undertook to exercise their naked judicial power and substituted their personal political and social ideas for the established law of the land.

This unwarranted exercise of power by the court, contrary to the Constitution, is creating chaos and confusion in the states principally affected. It is destroying the amicable relations between the white and Negro races that have been created through ninety years of patient effort by the good people of both races. It has planted hatred and suspicion where there has been heretofore friendship and understanding.

Without regard to the consent of the governed, outside agitators are threatening immediate and revolutionary changes in our public school systems. If done, this is certain to destroy the system of public education in some of the states.

With the gravest concern for the explosive and dangerous conditions created by this decision and inflamed by outside meddlers:

We reaffirm our reliance on the Constitution as the fundamental law of the land.

We decry the Supreme Court's encroachments on rights reserved to the states and to the people, contrary to established law and to the Constitution.

We commend the motives of those states which have declared the intention to resist forced integration by any lawful means.

We appeal to the states and people who are not directly affected by these decisions to consider the constitutional principles involved against the time when they too, on issues vital to them, may be the victims of judicial encroachment.

Even though we constitute a minority in the present Congress, we have full faith that a majority of the American people believe in the dual system of government which has enabled us to achieve our greatness and will in time demand that the reserved rights of the states and of the people be made secure against judicial usurpation.

We pledge ourselves to use all lawful means to bring about a reversal of this decision, which is contrary to the Constitution, and to prevent the use of force in its implementation.

In this trying period, as we all seek to right this wrong, we appeal to our people not to be provoked by the agitators and troublemakers invading our states and to scrupulously refrain from disorder and lawless acts.

3. Eisenhower Sends Federal Troops (1957)

Following the school-desegregation decision of the "Earl Warren Court," Southern white resistance mounted. A showdown occurred in the autumn of 1957, when angry mobs in Little Rock, Arkansas, prevented nine black pupils from attending the all-

3. *Vital Speeches,* XXIV, 11–12 (Oct. 15, 1957; address of Sept. 24, 1957).

white Central High School. When the governor of the state refused to provide proper protection, President Eisenhower backed up the federal court by sending in federal troops. Under their protective bayonets the black pupils attended the school, despite disagreeable incidents. This ugly episode became a hot issue in the Cold War. Little Rock rapidly became the best-known American city as Communist propagandists had a field day, ignoring the fact that the federal government was trying to help the blacks. President Eisenhower addressed the American people on a nationwide radio and television hookup, explaining why he had regretfully resorted to drastic action. Is he on sound legal ground? Why is he concerned about the foreign implications of the affair?

For a few minutes this evening I want to talk to you about the serious situation that has arisen in Little Rock. To make this talk I have come to the President's office in the White House. I could have spoken from Rhode Island, where I have been staying recently, but I felt that, in speaking from the house of Lincoln, of Jackson, and of Wilson, my words would better convey both the sadness I feel in the action I was compelled today to take and the firmness with which I intend to pursue this course until the orders of the Federal Court at Little Rock can be executed without unlawful interference.

In that city, under the leadership of demagogic extremists, disorderly mobs have deliberately prevented the carrying out of proper orders from a Federal Court. Local authorities have not eliminated that violent opposition and, under the law, I yesterday issued a Proclamation calling upon the mob to disperse.

This morning the mob again gathered in front of the Central High School of Little Rock, obviously for the purpose of again preventing the carrying out of the Court's order relating to the admission of Negro children to that school.

Whenever normal agencies prove inadequate to the task and it becomes necessary for the Executive Branch of the Federal Government to use its powers and authority to uphold Federal Courts, the President's responsibility is inescapable.

In accordance with that responsibility, I have today issued an Executive Order directing the use of troops under Federal authority to aid in the execution of Federal law at Little Rock, Arkansas. This became necessary when my Proclamation of yesterday was not observed, and the obstruction of justice still continues. . . .

Our personal opinions about the decision have no bearing on the matter of enforcement; the responsibility and authority of the Supreme Court to interpret the Constitution are very clear. . . .

Mob rule cannot be allowed to override the decisions of our courts.

Now, let me make it very clear that Federal troops are not being used to relieve local and state authorities of their primary duty to preserve the peace and order of the community. Nor are the troops there for the purpose of taking over the responsibility of the School Board and the other responsible local officials in running Central High School. The running of our

"FIRST WE CLOSED OUR SCHOOLS, THEN ONE THING LED TO ANOTHER!"

The Atlanta *Constitution*, though in the center of the "massive resistance" area, regarded closing of the schools as a poor way to fight integration. Atlanta *Constitution*, 1959.

school system and the maintenance of peace and order in each of our states are strictly local affairs, and the Federal Government does not interfere, except in very special cases and when requested by one of the several states. In the present case the troops are there, pursuant to law, solely for the purpose of preventing interference with the orders of the Court. . . .

In the South, as elsewhere, citizens are keenly aware of the tremendous disservice that has been done to the people of Arkansas in the eyes of the nation, and that has been done to the nation in the eyes of the world.

At a time when we face grave situations abroad because of the hatred that Communism bears toward a system of government based on human rights, it would be difficult to exaggerate the harm that is being done to the prestige and influence and, indeed, to the safety of our nation and the world.

Our enemies are gloating over this incident and using it everywhere to misrepresent our whole nation. We are portrayed as a violator of those standards of conduct which the peoples of the world united to proclaim in

the Charter of the United Nations. There they affirmed "faith in fundamental human rights" and "in the dignity and worth of the human person,"
and they did so "without distinction as to race, sex, language, or religion."

And so, with deep confidence, I call upon citizens of the State of Arkansas
to assist in bringing to an immediate end all interference with the law and
its processes. If resistance to the Federal Court order ceases at once, the
further presence of Federal troops will be unnecessary and the city of
Little Rock will return to its normal habits of peace and order—and a blot
upon the fair name and high honor of our nation will be removed.

Thus will be restored the image of America and of all its parts as one
nation, indivisible, with liberty and justice for all.

4. The *Arkansas Democrat* Protests (1958)

Occupying federal troops—the first in the South since 1877—remained eight months,
until the nine black pupils could attend the high school without serious molestation.
Many white Southerners who were resigned to gradual integration of the schools bitterly
resented President Eisenhower's armed intervention. In the light of the following article
in a Little Rock newspaper, explain why. Where is the editor on the weakest ground?
the strongest ground?

Little Rock's Central High School is still under military occupation. The
troops are still there—on the campus, in the building.

The troops are still there, despite the fact that their presence is resented
by the big majority of the students, the parents, and the people in general
throughout the South.

The troops continue to stand guard during school hours, on the grounds
and within the corridors and classrooms, despite the fact that there is no
law or precedent—Federal or State—that permits them to do so.

There is not even an order, or so much as a sanction, from the U.S.
Supreme Court that makes its own "laws" on mixing of races in the public
schools.

Federal troops continue to occupy Central High—in defiance of the
Constitution, law, and precedent—while the Congress of the United States
sits out the sessions and does nothing.

Never before in the history of America has any area of our so-called Free
Republic been so shamefully treated.

When two sections of this country were at war with each other, no troops
ever patrolled the public school buildings and grounds from day to day.
After the South had been beaten down, Federal forces kept the vanquished
under the iron heel for the duration of the "Reconstruction" period. But not
once did they molest the public schools with troop occupation.

Education, or attempted education, under the scrutiny of armed troops
is un-American, un-Godly.

It is not even Communistic. Russia, in all her cruelty, has never bothered

4. *Arkansas Democrat* (Little Rock), March 10, 1958. By Karr Shannon. Reprinted by permission.

school children in occupied territory by stationing armed soldiers on the grounds and in the buildings. Germany never did it.

No other nation, however barbaric and cruel and relentless, ever—in the history of the human race—resorted to such tactics—only the United States, which sets itself up as a world example of peace, freedom, and democracy, forces the military upon a free school.

How much longer will Congress sit idly by and let such brazen violation of American principle and law continue on and on and on?

5. A Black Newspaper Praises Courage (1958)

The conduct of the nine black pupils at Central High School, in the face of the sneers, jeers, jostling, spitting, and other insults, evoked praise in varied places. A black newspaper in Chicago paid them the following tribute. What parts of their ordeal must have taken the most courage?

Few incidents in recent American history can match the courage shown by the nine teen-age Negroes of Little Rock. They risked their lives for the sake of establishing a principle: the right to attend an integrated high school. They did it in the face of ugly and determined opposition; they did it under circumstances that would have caused many stout-hearted grown-ups to withdraw behind the protective shield of their own homes.

This was the most severe test of the law. The Federal courts paved the way; Federal troops held the angry mob at bay. But the nine Negro pupils did not have to march through the guardsmen to enter Little Rock's Central High School. They could have waited until public indignation had subsided; or they could have decided to attend a nearby Negro school rather than avail themselves of their legal rights. They didn't. Instead they went ahead, despite jeers and bitter invectives.

How many of us would have had the fortitude to do what these youngsters have done? How often have we failed to take advantage of victories won for us? It is therefore the more remarkable that these young Negroes, living in the Deep South, fearlessly implemented the Court's action by their daily presence at Central High School.

Though their lot was not a happy one even inside the high school building, though they were pushed around, insulted, and beaten by some of the white students, the Negro pupils held their ground. The Supreme Court's integration ruling would have been meaningless had these Negro boys and girls failed to follow the course mapped out for them by the law. They should be applauded by all of us.

E. EISENHOWER SAYS FAREWELL (1961)

Dwight Eisenhower, the war hero, presided over nearly eight years of peaceful American relations with the rest of the world. Yet Eisenhower also presided over the largest

5. Chicago *Daily Defender*, May 28, 1958. Reprinted by permission.
From: *Public Papers of the President: Dwight D. Eisenhower, 1960–1961* (1961), pp. 1036–1039.

peace-time build-up of armaments in American history up to that time. In his final message to the American people as President, the popular ex-soldier sounded a surprising warning about the economic, political, and social consequences of the garrison state that America was apparently becoming. His speech is justly remembered as one of the most telling criticisms of the domestic consequences of the Cold War. What are the most worrisome aspects of the "military-industrial complex" that Eisenhower described? Why did he wait until he was on his way out of office to express his alarm?

Good evening, my fellow Americans:

First, let me express my gratitude to the radio and television networks for the opportunity to express myself to you during these past eight years and tonight.

Three days from now, after half a century in the service of our country, I shall lay down the responsibilities of office as, in traditional solemn ceremony, the authority of the President is vested in my successor.

This evening I come to you with a message of leave-taking and farewell, and to share a few final thoughts with you, my countrymen. . . .

We now stand ten years past the midpoint of a century that has witnessed four major wars among great nations. Three of these involved our own country. Despite these holocausts America is today the strongest, the most influential, and most productive nation in the world. Understandably proud of this pre-eminence, we yet realize that America's leadership and prestige depend, not merely upon our unmatched material progress, riches, and material strength, but on how we use our power in the interests of world peace and human betterment.

Throughout America's adventure in free government, our basic purposes have been to keep the peace; to foster progress in human achievement; and to enhance liberty, dignity, and integrity among people and among nations. To strive for less would be unworthy of a free and religious people. Any failure traceable to arrogance, or our lack of comprehension or readiness to sacrifice would inflict upon us grievous hurt both at home and abroad.

Progress toward these noble goals is persistently threatened by the conflict now engulfing the world. It commands our whole attention, absorbs our very beings. We face a hostile ideology—global in scope, atheistic in character, ruthless in purpose, and insidious in method. Unhappily the danger it poses promises to be of indefinite duration. To meet it successfully, there is called for, not so much the emotional and transitory sacrifices of crisis, but rather those which enable us to carry forward steadily, surely, and without complaint the burdens of a prolonged and complex struggle—with liberty the stake. Only thus shall we remain, despite every provocation, on our chartered course toward permanent peace and human betterment.

Crises there will continue to be. In meeting them, whether foreign or domestic, great or small, there is a recurring temptation to feel that some spectacular and costly action could become the miraculous solution to all current difficulties. A huge increase in newer elements of our defense; development of unrealistic programs to cure every ill in agriculture; a dramatic expansion in basic and applied research—these and many other possibilities, each possibly promising in itself, may be suggested as the only way to the road we wish to travel.

But each proposal must be weighed in the light of a broader consideration: the need to maintain balance in and among national problems—balance between the private and the public economy, balance between cost and hoped for advantage—balance between the clearly necessary and the comfortably desirable; balance between our essential requirements as a nation and the duties imposed by the nation upon the individual; balance between actions of the moment and the national welfare of the future. Good judgment seeks balance and progress; lack of it eventually finds imbalance and frustration.

The record of many decades stands as proof that our people and their government have, in the main, understood these truths and have responded to them well, in the face of stress and threat. But threats, new in kind or degree, constantly arise. I mention two only.

A vital element in keeping the peace is our military establishment. Our arms must be mighty, ready for instant action, so that no potential aggressor may be tempted to risk his own destruction.

Our military organization today bears little relation to that known by any of my predecessors in peacetime, or indeed by the fighting men in World War II or Korea.

Until the latest of our world conflicts, the United States had no armaments industry. American makers of plowshares could, with time and as required, make swords as well. But now we can no longer risk emergency improvision of national defense; we have been compelled to create a permanent armaments industry of vast proportions. Added to this, three and a half million men and women are directly engaged in the defense establishment. We annually spend on military security more than the net income of all United States corporations.

This conjunction of an immense military establishment and a large arms industry is new in American experience. The total influence—economic, political, even spiritual—is felt in every city, every state house, every office of the federal government. We recognize the imperative need for this development. Yet we must not fail to comprehend its grave implications. Our toil, resources and livelihood are all involved; so is the very structure of our society.

In the councils of government, we must guard against the acquisition of unwarranted influence, whether sought or unsought, by the military-industrial complex. The potential for the disastrous rise of misplaced power exists and will persist.

We must never let the weight of this combination endanger our liberties or democratic processes. We should take nothing for granted. Only an alert and knowledgeable citizenry can compel the proper meshing of the huge industrial and military machinery of defense with our peaceful methods and goals, so that security and liberty may prosper together.

Akin to, and largely responsible for the sweeping changes in our industrial-military posture, has been the technological revolution during recent decades.

In this revolution, research has become central; it also becomes more formalized, complex, and costly. A steadily increasing share is conducted for, by, or at the direction of, the federal government.

Today, the solitary inventor, tinkering in his shop, has been overshadowed by task forces of scientists in laboratories and testing fields. In the same fashion, the free university, historically the fountainhead of free ideas and scientific discovery, has experienced a revolution in the conduct of research. Partly because of the huge costs involved, a government contract becomes virtually a substitute for intellectual curiosity. For every old blackboard there are now hundreds of new electronic computers.

The prospect of domination of the nation's scholars by federal employment, project allocations, and the power of money is ever present and is gravely to be regarded.

Yet, in holding scientific research and discovery in respect, as we should, we must also be alert to the equal and opposite danger that public policy could itself become the captive of a scientific-technological elite.

It is the task of statesmanship to mold, to balance, and to integrate these and other forces, new and old, within the principles of our democratic system—ever aiming toward the supreme goals of our free society.

Another factor in maintaining balance involves the element of time. As we peer into society's future, we—you and I, and our government—must avoid the impulse to live only for today, plundering, for our own ease and convenience, the precious resources of tomorrow. We cannot mortgage the material assets of our grandchildren without risking the loss also of their political and spiritual heritage. We want democracy to survive for all generations to come, not to become the insolvent phantom of tomorrow.

Down the long lane of the history yet to be written America knows that this world of ours, ever growing smaller, must avoid becoming a community of dreadful fear and hate, and be, instead, a proud confederation of mutual trust and respect.

Such a confederation must be one of equals. The weakest must come to the conference table with the same confidence as we do, protected as we are by our moral, economic, and military strength. That table, though scarred by many past frustrations, cannot be abandoned for the certain agony of the battlefield.

Disarmament, with mutual honor and confidence, is a continuing imperative. Together we must learn how to compose differences, not with arms, but with intellect and decent purpose. Because this need is so sharp and apparent I confess that I lay down my official responsibilities in this field with a definite sense of disappointment. As one who has witnessed the horror and the lingering sadness of war—as one who knows that another war could utterly destroy this civilization which has been so slowly and painfully built over thousands of years—I wish I could say tonight that a lasting peace is in sight.

Happily, I can say that war has been avoided. Steady progress toward our ultimate goal has been made. But, so much remains to be done. As a private citizen, I shall never cease to do what little I can to help the world advance along that road.

So—in this my last good night to you as your President—I thank you for the many opportunities you have given me for public service in war and peace. I trust that in that service you find some things worthy; as for the rest of it, I know you will find ways to improve performance in the future.

You and I—my fellow citizens—need to be strong in our faith that all nations, under God, will reach the goal of peace with justice. May we be ever unswerving in devotion to principle, confident but humble with power, diligent in pursuit of the nation's great goals.

To all the peoples of the world, I once more give expression to America's prayerful and continuing aspiration:

We pray that peoples of all faiths, all races, all nations may have their great human needs satisfied; that those now denied opportunity shall come to enjoy it to the full; that all who yearn for freedom may experience its spiritual blessings; that those who have freedom will understand, also, its heavy responsibilities; that all who are insensitive to the needs of others will learn charity; that the scourges of poverty, disease, and ignorance will be made to disappear from the earth, and that, in the goodness of time, all peoples will come to live together in a peace guaranteed by the binding force of mutual respect and love.

Now on Friday noon I am to become a private citizen. I am proud to do so. I look forward to it.

THOUGHT PROVOKERS

1. Was Korea a necessary war for the United States? What would have happened if the Americans had stayed out?
2. Was Truman wise to fire General MacArthur? When is a military officer justified in disobeying orders? MacArthur believed that there was "no substitute for victory." Would his policies have brought victory or simply more bloodshed in Korea?
3. Did Senator McCarthy help or hinder the cause of anticommunism? Is American society peculiarly vulnerable to his kind of demagoguery? What finally stopped McCarthy? Did McCarthyism perish with Joseph McCarthy?
4. Progressives and liberals have historically argued that the courts should take a hands-off policy toward legislation in the economic realm, yet they applauded the Supreme Court's activist role in civil rights matters. Were they being inconsistent? What were the greatest obstacles to the success of the civil rights movement? What were its greatest assets?
5. How prophetic was Eisenhower's warning about the "military-industrial complex"? Is that complex more or less powerful now than in Eisenhower's day? To what extent was it an inevitable product of the Cold War?

45 · *The Stormy Sixties*

And so, my fellow Americans: ask not what your country can do for you—ask what you can do for your country.

PRESIDENT JOHN F. KENNEDY, 1961

PROLOGUE: Youthful President John F. Kennedy launched his administration with high hopes and great vigor. Young people seemed particularly attracted to the tough-minded yet idealistic style of Kennedy's presidency. Yet Kennedy's record in office, before his tragic assassination in 1963, was spotty. He presided over a botched invasion of Cuba in 1961, and in the same year took the first fateful steps into the Vietnam quagmire. In 1962 he emerged victorious from a tense stand-off with the Russians over the emplacement of Soviet missiles in Cuba. Sobered by this brush with the prospect of nuclear holocaust, Kennedy initiated a new policy of realistic accommodation with the Soviets—while the Soviets, determined never again to be so humiliated, began a massive military build-up. At home, the black revolution, led most conspicuously by Martin Luther King, exploded with a vengeance. Lyndon Johnson, ascending to the presidency after Kennedy's death, won election in his own right in 1964, and promptly threw his support behind the cause of civil rights. In a remarkable burst of political leadership, Johnson persuaded the Congress to pass a vast array of social welfare legislation, known collectively as the Great Society programs. But Johnson's dreams for a happier America were blasted by the mounting unpopularity of the war in Vietnam, which had drawn half a million American troops by the mid-1960's. Bedeviled by the Vietnam problem, Johnson withdrew from the 1968 presidential race, paving the way for the election of Richard Nixon.

A. THE CUBAN MISSILE CRISIS

1. Kennedy Proclaims a "Quarantine" (1962)

After the abortive Bay of Pigs invasion in 1961, the United States watched Castro's Cuba for further trouble. Officials in Washington knew that the Soviets were sending Castro immense quantities of weapons, which Moscow repeatedly claimed were defensive.* In mid-October, 1962, high-flying American spy planes returned with startling photographic evidence that Russian technicians were installing about forty nuclear missiles with a striking range of about 2200 miles. Rather than forewarn Premier Khrushchev in Moscow, Kennedy quietly consulted with members of Congress, and then went on radio and television with a bombshell address which caught the Soviets

---

1. *Public Papers of the Presidents of the United States, John F. Kennedy: 1962* (1963), pp. 807–08 (October 22, 1962).
* The Soviets were correct in the sense that so-called offensive weapons aimed at the United States were defensive in that they would deter an invasion of Cuba.

off guard. In this excerpt, what options does he leave for himself if the initial "quarantine" should fail? What are the risks in Kennedy's strategy? Are they worth it?

Acting, therefore, in the defense of our own security and of the entire Western Hemisphere, . . . I have directed that the following *initial* steps be taken immediately:

First: To halt this offensive buildup, a strict quarantine on all offensive military equipment under shipment to Cuba is being initiated. All ships of any kind bound for Cuba from whatever nation or port will, if found to contain cargoes of offensive weapons, be turned back. This quarantine will be extended, if needed, to other types of cargo and carriers. We are not at this time, however, denying the necessities of life, as the Soviets attempted to do in their Berlin blockade of 1948.

Second: I have directed the continued and increased close [aerial] surveillance of Cuba and its military buildup. . . .

Third: It shall be the policy of this Nation to regard any nuclear missile launched from Cuba against any nation in the Western Hemisphere as an attack by the Soviet Union on the United States, requiring a full retaliatory response upon the Soviet Union.

Fourth: As a necessary military precaution, I have reinforced our base at Guantanamo [Cuba], evacuated today the dependents of our personnel there, and ordered additional military units to be on a standby alert basis.

Fifth: We are calling tonight for an immediate meeting of the Organ of Consultation under the Organization of American States, to consider this threat to hemispheric security and to invoke Articles 6 and 8 of the Rio Treaty in support of all necessary action. . . . Our other allies around the world have also been alerted.

Sixth: Under the Charter of the United Nations, we are asking tonight that an emergency meeting of the Security Council be convoked without delay to take action against this latest Soviet threat to world peace. Our resolution will call for the prompt dismantling and withdrawal of all offensive weapons in Cuba, under the supervision of U.N. observers, before the quarantine can be lifted.

Seventh and finally: I call upon Chairman Khrushchev to halt and eliminate this clandestine, reckless, and provocative threat to world peace and to stable relations between our two nations. I call upon him further to abandon this course of world domination, and to join in an historic effort to end the perilous arms race and to transform the history of man.

2. Khrushchev Proposes a Swap (1962)

During the tense six days after Kennedy's proclamation of a "quarantine," Soviet technicians in Cuba worked feverishly to emplace the missiles. A number of approaching Russian merchant ships, presumably loaded with "offensive" weapons, turned back.

. 2. *Department of State Bulletin,* XLVII, p. 742 (November 12, 1962).

Several, not carrying such cargoes, were allowed to reach Cuba. Premier Khrushchev, at first disposed to give some ground in a letter of October 26 to Kennedy, took a tougher stand in the following message of October 27 and proposed a swap. The American missiles in Turkey were so obsolete that two months earlier President Kennedy had given orders for their withdrawal, but they were still there. He and his advisers felt that to remove them, as Khrushchev asked, on an exchange basis would weaken the morale of Turkey, the eastern anchor of the North Atlantic Treaty Organization. **Was Kennedy right in risking nuclear incineration for the sake of Turkey? How much plausibility is there in Khrushchev's proposal?**

Our purpose has been and is to help Cuba, and no one can challenge the humanity of our motives aimed at allowing Cuba to live peacefully and develop as its people desire. You want to relieve your country from danger and this is understandable. However, Cuba also wants this. All countries want to relieve themselves from danger.

But how can we, the Soviet Union and our government, assess your actions which, in effect, mean that you have surrounded the Soviet Union with military bases, surrounded our allies with military bases, set up military bases literally around our country, and stationed your rocket weapons at them? This is no secret. High-placed American officials demonstratively declare this. Your rockets are stationed in Britain and in Italy and pointed at us. Your rockets are stationed in Turkey.

You are worried over Cuba. You say that it worries you because it lies at a distance of 90 miles across the sea from the shores of the United States. However, Turkey lies next to us. Our sentinels are pacing up and down and watching each other. Do you believe that you have the right to demand security for your country and the removal of such weapons that you qualify as offensive, while not recognizing this right for us? . . .

This is why I make this proposal: We agree to remove those weapons from Cuba which you regard as offensive weapons. We agree to do this and to state this commitment in the United Nations. Your representatives will make a statement to the effect that the United States, on its part, bearing in mind the anxiety and concern of the Soviet state, will evacuate its analogous weapons from Turkey. Let us reach an understanding on what time you and we need to put this into effect.

After this, representatives of the U.N. Security Council could control on-the-spot the fulfillment of these commitments.

3. Kennedy Advances a Solution (1962)

President Kennedy skillfully avoided an argument over a missile swap by ignoring his opponent's suggestion. Referring to Khrushchev's more promising letter of the previous day, he advanced the following proposals on October 27. The tension was building up, and an airstrike against Cuba was scheduled for three days later, before the nuclear missiles could become fully operative. **In this letter, what restrictions is Kennedy prepared to place on the United States?**

3. *Ibid.*, p. 743.

Dear Mr. Chairman:

I have read your letter of October 26th with great care and welcomed the statement of your desire to seek a prompt solution to the problem. The first thing that needs to be done, however, is for work to cease on offensive missile bases in Cuba and for all weapons systems in Cuba capable of offensive use to be rendered inoperable, under effective United Nations arrangements.

Assuming this is done promptly, I have given my representatives in New York instructions that will permit them to work out this weekend—in cooperation with the Acting Secretary General and your representative—an arrangement for a permanent solution to the Cuban problem along the lines suggested in your letter of October 26th. As I read your letter, the key elements of your proposals—which seem generally acceptable as I understand them—are as follows:

1) You would agree to remove these weapons systems from Cuba under appropriate United Nations observation and supervision; and undertake, with suitable safeguards, to halt the further introduction of such weapons systems into Cuba.

2) We, on our part, would agree—upon the establishment of adequate arrangements through the United Nations to ensure the carrying out and continuation of these commitments—(a) to remove promptly the quarantine measures now in effect and (b) to give assurances against an invasion of Cuba. I am confident that other nations of the Western Hemisphere would be prepared to do likewise.

If you will give your representative similar instructions, there is no reason why we should not be able to complete these arrangements and announce them to the world within a couple of days.

[*The next day, October 28, 1962, Khrushchev consented to Kennedy's terms, and a great sense of relief swept over the world. Kennedy himself had privately reckoned that the odds in favor of a nuclear blowup ran as high as fifty-fifty.*]

4. The Russians Save Face (1962)

The Soviets, claiming that they had achieved their objective of preventing an invasion of Cuba, gathered up and (ostensibly) shipped home their forty-two nuclear missiles. The United States in truth won only a partial diplomatic victory. Thousands of Russian workmen stayed behind, and Castro remained defiant with Russian weapons and backing. The official Soviet newspaper *Izvestia* put the best possible face it could on the diplomatic setback. What gains for Soviet diplomacy does it claim were achieved?

The threat to peace was created by hostile, adventurist schemes aimed at the very existence of the Cuban Republic. The Soviet Union could not disregard Cuba's predicament in the face of the imperialistic provocations. Our

4. Translation copyright 1962 by *The Current Digest of the Soviet Press,* published weekly at The Ohio State University; reprinted by permission.

country, fulfilling its international duty, came to the fraternal assistance of the Cuban people, and in these troubled days of the provocational aggravation . . . it has stood, stands, and will continue to stand firmly with Cuba.

The contemplated scheme of aggression against Cuba was built upon a very shaky foundation, but the danger with which Cuba was threatened was not thereby diminished. The pretext that was advanced in the U.S.A. for action against Cuba was the presence of Soviet weapons in Cuba that the United States termed "offensive." These weapons were depicted as representing a "threat" to America and the whole Western Hemisphere, although neither Cuba nor the Soviet Union was threatening the United States with its actions, while at the same time extremist, militant circles in the U.S. revealed . . . a desire to end the independence of the Cuban Republic.

In that tense moment the Soviet government, which had displayed the utmost self-control, calm and firmness, took speedy and efficient action to prevent the outbreak of the imminent conflict and thereby preserve universal peace.

The progression of events showed that the far-seeing, wise course of the Soviet government was the only correct one in the situation that had developed and led in a short time to the start of the normalization of the situation and the creation of conditions in which the interests of universal peace and of the . . . integrity of the Cuban Republic will be assured.

The decisive step of the Soviet Union—which foiled the aggressive plans of an attack on Cuba and deprived the authors of these plans of a reason and pretext for military action—was the indication that appropriate measures were being taken to stop the build-up in Cuba of objectives depicted by the United States as threatening American security, to dismantle these objectives and return them to the Soviet Union.

This step by the Soviet government was made possible as a result of the statement made by U.S. President Kennedy in his message of Oct. 27 to N. S. Khrushchev. The message states that there will be no attacks on Cuba, no invasion, not only on the part of the United States but on the part of the other countries of the Western Hemisphere as well, if the weapons termed "offensive" by the U.S.A. are shipped out of Cuba.

Thus reason and wisdom prevailed. At present, all conditions exist for the total elimination of the conflict and for further efforts toward the strengthening of peace and security. All honest people, anxious over the fate of peace, render their due to our Communist Party, to the Soviet government and to Nikita Sergeyevich Khrushchev for the fact that the forces of aggression and war have been restrained and reason in international relations has prevailed over folly.

These days telegrams are being received in Moscow, in the Kremlin, from all corners of the globe. They express the impassioned voices of people of good will, conveying their support of the peace-loving position of the Soviet Union. . . .

B. THE "GREAT SOCIETY"

1. President Johnson Declares War on Poverty (1964)

America in the 1960s continued to present appalling contrasts in wealth. An official government report in 1964 declared that one-fifth of the families in the country—9.3 million in all—"enjoyed" annual incomes of less than $3,000. Under President Kennedy, Congress made a modest beginning by passing several laws providing for self-help and job retraining. President Johnson threw his full weight behind the Economic Opportunity Act of 1964, which a Democratic Congress approved and implemented with an initial appropriation of $947.5 million. This legislation included provisions for a Job Corps that would provide training for unskilled young men and women, aid for education, and a domestic Peace Corps to work with Indians and other disadvantaged groups. In a part of his message to Congress the President made the following plea. Is he convincing in his argument that these heavy outlays would in the long run help the taxpayer?

I have called for a national war on poverty. Our objective: total victory.

There are millions of Americans—one fifth of our people—who have not shared in the abundance which has been granted to most of us, and on whom the gates of opportunity have been closed.

What does this poverty mean to those who endure it?

It means a daily struggle to secure the necessities for even a meager existence. It means that the abundance, the comforts, the opportunities they see all around them are beyond their grasp.

Worst of all, it means hopelessness for the young.

The young man or woman who grows up without a decent education, in a broken home, in a hostile and squalid environment, in ill health or in the face of racial injustice—that young man or woman is often trapped in a life of poverty.

He does not have the skills demanded by a complex society. He does not know how to acquire those skills. He faces a mounting sense of despair which drains initiative and ambition and energy. . . .

The war on poverty is not a struggle simply to support people, to make them dependent on the generosity of others.

It is a struggle to give people a chance.

It is an effort to allow them to develop and use their capacities, as we have been allowed to develop and use ours, so that they can share, as others share, in the promise of this nation.

We do this, first of all, because it is right that we should.

From the establishment of public education and land grant colleges through agricultural extension and encouragement to industry, we have pursued the goal of a nation with full and increasing opportunities for all its citizens.

The war on poverty is a further step in that pursuit.

We do it also because helping some will increase the prosperity of all.

Our fight against poverty will be an investment in the most valuable of our resources—the skills and strength of our people.

1. *Public Papers of the Presidents of the United States: Lyndon B. Johnson, 1963–1964* (1965), I, pp. 376–77 (March 16, 1964).

And in the future, as in the past, this investment will return its cost many fold to our entire economy.

If we can raise the annual earnings of 10 million among the poor by only $1,000 we will have added 14 billion dollars a year to our national output. In addition we can make important reductions in public assistance payments which now cost us 4 billion dollars a year, and in the large costs of fighting crime and delinquency, disease and hunger.

This is only part of the story.

Our history has proved that each time we broaden the base of abundance, giving more people the chance to produce and consume, we create new industry, higher production, increased earnings and better income for all.

Giving new opportunity to those who have little will enrich the lives of all the rest.

Because it is right, because it is wise, and because, for the first time in our history, it is possible to conquer poverty, I submit, for the consideration of the Congress and the country, the Economic Opportunity Act of 1964.

The Act does not merely expand old programs or improve what is already being done.

It charts a new course.

It strikes at the causes, not just the consequences of poverty.

It can be a milestone in our one-hundred-eighty year search for a better life for our people.

2. War on the Anti-Poverty War

President Johnson's anti-poverty scheme aroused the dogs of criticism, especially among conservatives. They declared that it was contrived to catch votes; that it would undermine individual initiative; that it would inject big government into private affairs; that it was socialistic; that it was a revival of Franklin Roosevelt's Conservation Corps; and that it would burden the taxpayers. In truth, the cost of keeping a high-school dropout in one of the fresh-air training camps was estimated to be about three times that of keeping a student in Harvard University. The executive editor of the Cleveland *Plain Dealer* here speaks out plainly against some of the weaknesses of the scheme. What are his most telling points?

The political astuteness of President Johnson is nowhere better illustrated than by his proposal described as the "antipoverty program" or the "war on poverty." It has more than a faint odor of hokum about it, but its implications are that anyone bold enough to question or peer deeply into it must be in favor of poverty—and that's politically and socially disastrous.

The present level of extravagance in the American uppercrust, affluence in the middle class, and considerable comfort even in the lower pay brackets is so widely taken for granted these days that a campaigner against poverty has to hunt around for groups and areas to help. . . .

But there are increasingly large numbers of Negro dropouts from high school and teenage unemployment. And small farmers who can't seem to get

2. Philip W. Porter, Cleveland *Plain Dealer*, March 28, 1964. By permission of the Cleveland *Plain Dealer*.

ahead. And inhabitants of "Appalachia," the mountains where coal mining has gone to pot. These are areas with average incomes of $3,000 a year or under. They've got to be saved from themselves by the Federal Government. Hence, the "war on poverty," a colorful phrase much favored by newspapers, TV, and radio.

There's really no war on anything. The Johnson proposal is an attempt to sop up some unemployed teens by giving them jobs in conservation camps, to lend some money to the hardscrabble farmers, to produce some loan help for college students—and, just as important, add some new bureaucrats to the payroll.

The objective is good, particularly the movement of dropouts from the street corner to the forest. But the only way to solve the Appalachia problem is to transplant whole families and villages to places where there are jobs— but they won't leave. And lending money to marginal farmers is fruitless; the quicker they give up small uneconomical "family" units, and try to earn money elsewhere, the better off they'll be.

Some individuals will be helped, no doubt. The politicians have something new to promise. But eradicating all poverty is about as unlikely an attainment as entering the Kingdom of Heaven, which our grandmothers talked so much about.

The objective, though vague and built of goober feathers, is good. But will it work on those of low mentality who are not educable, or those who lack desire to improve themselves? And in reverse, is it really needed by the determined individual, the man already moonlighting to go to law school, or waiting table to pay for college?

Has the Horatio Alger, Jr., concept, the bootblack who became a tycoon, vanished completely? Andrew Carnegie built a fortune from little. So did Henry Ford. Lyndon Johnson himself started from scratch. . . .

But today the Federal Government has got to get into the act. And anyone who asks questions or objects is automatically a stinker.

[*The war against poverty, though it improved the quality of life for many underprivileged Americans, fell far short of the roseate forecasts of its sponsors. The war in Vietnam began to siphon away billions of dollars, and the national budget could not fully support both wars. Bureaucratic bungling, political favoritism, and outright graft combined to bring the program into considerable disrepute and to undermine its nobler purposes.*]

C. THE BLACK REVOLUTION ERUPTS

1. Martin Luther King Writes from a Birmingham Jail (1963)

The year 1963 marked the one hundredth anniversary of the Emancipation Proclamation, yet millions of American blacks remained enchained by racism. Though racial

JUNE 1963
THE MOMENT SEEMS TO BE NOW
© The London *Daily Mail.* Illingworth.

prejudice was a national curse, it worked most viciously in the South, the ancient home-land of slavery. Nearly a decade after the Supreme Court's desegregation order, fewer than 10 percent of black children in the South attended classes with white children. The problem was especially acute in Birmingham, Alabama, the most segregated big city in America. Segregation was the rule in schools, restaurants, rest rooms, ball parks, libraries, and taxicabs. Though blacks were nearly half the city's residents, they constituted less than 15 percent of the city's voters. More than fifty cross-burnings and eighteen racial bombings between 1957 and 1963 had earned the city the nickname of "Bombingham" among blacks. Thus Birmingham was a logical choice—and a courageous one—as the site of a mass protest by the Reverend Martin Luther King, Jr., and his Southern Chris-tian Leadership Conference. Arrested during a protest demonstration on Good Friday, 1963, King penned the following letter from jail, writing on scraps of paper smuggled to him by a prison trusty. He was responding to criticism from eight white Alabama clergymen who had deplored his tactics as "unwise and untimely"—though King through-out his life preached the wisdom of nonviolence. Why does King believe that black Americans could wait no longer for their civil rights? How does he view himself in rela-tion to white "moderates" and black extremists?

My Dear Fellow Clergymen:

•   •   •

You deplore the demonstrations taking place in Birmingham. But your statement, I am sorry to say, fails to express a similar concern for the con-ditions that brought about the demonstrations. I am sure that none of you would want to rest content with the superficial kind of social analysis that deals merely with effects and does not grapple with underlying causes. It is unfortunate that demonstrations are taking place in Birmingham, but it is even more unfortunate that the city's white power structure left the Negro community with no alternative. . . .

We know through painful experience that freedom is never voluntarily given by the oppressor; it must be demanded by the oppressed. Frankly, I have yet to engage in a direct-action campaign that was "well timed" in the view of those who have not suffered unduly from the disease of segregation. For years now I have heard the word "Wait!" It rings in the ear of every Negro with piercing familiarity. This "Wait" has almost always meant "Never." We must come to see, with one of our distinguished jurists, that "justice too long delayed is justice denied."

We have waited for more than 340 years for our constitutional and God-given rights. The nations of Asia and Africa are moving with jetlike speed toward gaining political independence, but we still creep at horse-and-buggy pace toward gaining a cup of coffee at a lunch counter. Perhaps it is easy for those who have never felt the stinging darts of segregation to say, "Wait." But when you have seen vicious mobs lynch your mothers and fathers at will and drown your sisters and brothers at whim; when you have seen hate-filled policemen curse, kick, and even kill your black brothers and sisters; when you see the vast majority of your twenty million Negro brothers smothering in an airtight cage of poverty in the midst of an affluent society; when you suddenly find your tongue twisted and your speech stammering as you seek to explain to your six-year-old daughter why she can't go to the public amusement park that has just been advertised on television, and see tears welling up in her eyes when she is told that Funtown is closed to colored children, and see ominous clouds of inferiority beginning to form in her little mental sky, and see her beginning to distort her personality by developing an unconscious bitterness toward white people; when you have to concoct an answer for a five-year-old son who is asking: "Daddy, why do white people treat colored people so mean?"; when you take a cross-country drive and find it necessary to sleep night after night in the uncomfortable corners of your automobile because no motel will accept you; when you are humiliated day in and day out by nagging signs reading "white" and "colored"; when your first name becomes "nigger," your middle name becomes "boy" (however old you are) and your last name becomes "John," and your wife and mother are never given the respected title "Mrs."; when you are harried by day and haunted by night by the fact that you are a Negro, living constantly at tiptoe stance, never quite knowing what to expect next, and are plagued with inner fears and outer resentments; when you are forever fighting a degenerating sense of "nobodiness"—then you will understand why we find it difficult to wait. There comes a time when the cup of endurance runs over, and men are no longer willing to be plunged into the abyss of despair. I hope, sirs, you can understand our legitimate and unavoidable impatience. . . .

You speak of our activity in Birmingham as extreme. At first I was rather disappointed that fellow clergymen would see my nonviolent efforts as those of an extremist. I began thinking about the fact that I stand in the middle of two opposing forces in the Negro community. One is a force of complacency, made up in part of Negroes who, as a result of long years of oppression, are so drained of self-respect and a sense of "somebodiness" that they have adjusted to segregation; and in part of a few middle-class Negroes who, because of a degree of academic and economic security and because in some ways they profit by segregation, have become insensitive to the problems of the masses. The other force is one of bitterness and hatred, and it comes perilously close to advocating violence. It is expressed in the various black nationalist groups that are springing up across the nation, the largest and best-known being Elijah Muhammad's Muslim movement. Nourished by the Negro's frustration over the continued existence of racial discrimination, this movement is made up of people who have lost faith in America, who have absolutely repudiated Christianity, and who have concluded that the white man is an incorrigible "devil."

I have tried to stand between these two forces, saying that we need emulate neither the "do-nothingism" of the complacent nor the hatred and despair of the black nationalist. For there is the more excellent way of love and nonviolent protest. I am grateful to God that, through the influence of the Negro church, the way of nonviolence became an integral part of our struggle.

If this philosophy had not emerged, by now many streets of the South would, I am convinced, be flowing with blood. And I am further convinced that if our white brothers dismiss as "rabble-rousers" and "outside agitators" those of us who employ nonviolent direct action, and if they refuse to support our nonviolent efforts, millions of Negroes will, out of frustration and despair, seek solace and security in black-nationalist ideologies—a development that would inevitably lead to a frightening racial nightmare.

Oppressed people cannot remain oppressed forever. The yearning for freedom eventually manifests itself, and that is what has happened to the American Negro. Something within has reminded him of his birthright of freedom, and something without has reminded him that it can be gained. . . .

When I was suddenly catapulted into the leadership of the bus protest in Montgomery, Alabama, a few years ago, I felt we would be supported by the white church. I felt that the white ministers, priests and rabbis of the South would be among our strongest allies. Instead, some have been outright opponents, refusing to understand the freedom movement and misrepresenting its leaders; all too many others have been more cautious than courageous and have remained silent behind the anesthetizing security of stained-glass windows. . . .

Before closing I feel impelled to mention one other point in your statement that has troubled me profoundly. You warmly commended the Birmingham police force for keeping "order" and "preventing violence." I doubt that you would have so warmly commended the police force if you had seen its dogs sinking their teeth into unarmed, nonviolent Negroes. I doubt that you would so quickly commend the policemen if you were to observe their ugly and inhumane treatment of Negroes here in the city jail; if you were to watch them push and curse old Negro women and young Negro girls; if you were to see them slap and kick old Negro men and young boys; if you were to observe them, as they did on two occasions, refuse to give us food because we wanted to sing our grace together. I cannot join you in your praise of the Birmingham police department. . . .

I wish you had commended the Negro sit-inners and demonstrators of Birmingham for their sublime courage, their willingness to suffer and their amazing discipline in the midst of great provocation. One day the South will recognize its real heroes. They will be the James Merediths, with the noble sense of purpose that enables them to face jeering and hostile mobs, and with the agonizing loneliness that characterizes the life of the pioneer. They will be old, oppressed, battered Negro women, symbolized in a seventy-two-year-old woman in Montgomery, Alabama, who rose up with a sense of dignity and with her people decided not to ride segregated buses, and who responded with ungrammatical profundity to one who inquired about her weariness: "My feets is tired, but my soul is at rest." They will be the young high school and college students, the young ministers of the gospel and a host of their elders, courageously and nonviolently sitting in at lunch counters and willingly going to jail for conscience' sake. One day the South will know that when these disinherited children of God sat down at lunch counters, they were in reality standing up for what is best in the American dream and for the most sacred values in our Judaeo-Christian heritage, thereby bringing our nation back to those great wells of democracy which were dug deep by the founding fathers in their formulation of the Constitution and the Declaration of Independence. . . .

Yours for the cause of Peace and Brotherhood,
Martin Luther King, Jr.

2. President Johnson Supports Civil Rights (1965)

Prompted largely by the mass outpouring of sentiment inspired by Martin Luther King, Congress passed a major Civil Rights Act in 1964. It prohibited discrimination in most public places, forbade employers or unions to discriminate on the basis of race, and created an Equal Employment Opportunity Commission to provide enforcement. Yet King and other black leaders were determined not to rest until they had secured federal legislation protecting the right of black people to vote. Once again, King chose Alabama as the stage for demonstrations designed to force the Johnson Administration's hand. On March 7, 1965, demonstraters marching from Selma, Alabama, to the state capital at Montgomery were brutally beaten and dispersed by state troopers and hastily

2. *Public Papers of the Presidents of the United States: Lyndon B. Johnson, 1965*, Book 1 (1966), pp. 281–287.

deputized "possemen." Millions of Americans witnessed the violent assault on television, and within days hundreds of clergymen and clergywomen of all faiths had poured into Selma to aid Reverend King. One of them, a Boston Unitarian minister, died after having been clubbed by a gang of white hooligans. The pressure on Washington to act mounted to irresistible proportions, and on March 15 President Johnson addressed Congress and the nation, as follows, to plead for a voting rights bill. Though Johnson had in fact tried to discourage King from marching in Alabama, he now threw the full moral and legal weight of his office behind the cause of black voting rights. In what broader context does he try to set the black civil rights movement? How do his personal feelings and experiences influence his political action?

Mr. Speaker, Mr. President, Members of the Congress:

I speak tonight for the dignity of man and the destiny of democracy.

I urge every member of both parties, Americans of all religions and of all colors, from every section of this country, to join me in that cause.

At times history and fate meet at a single time in a single place to shape a turning point in man's unending search for freedom. So it was at Lexington and Concord. So it was a century ago at Appomattox. So it was last week in Selma, Alabama.

There, long-suffering men and women peacefully protested the denial of their rights as Americans. Many were brutally assaulted. One good man, a man of God, was killed.

There is no cause for pride in what has happened in Selma. There is no cause for self-satisfaction in the long denial of equal rights of millions of Americans. But there is cause for hope and for faith in our democracy in what is happening here tonight.

For the cries of pain and the hymns and protests of oppressed people have summoned into convocation all the majesty of this great Government —the Government of the greatest Nation on earth.

Our mission is at once the oldest and the most basic of this country: to right wrong, to do justice, to serve man.

In our time we have come to live with moments of great crisis. Our lives have been marked with debate about great issues; issues of war and peace, issues of prosperity and depression. But rarely in any time does an issue lay bare the secret heart of America itself. Rarely are we met with a challenge, not to our growth or abundance, our welfare or our security, but rather to the values and the purposes and the meaning of our beloved Nation.

The issue of equal rights for American Negroes is such an issue. And should we defeat every enemy, should we double our wealth and conquer the stars, and still be unequal to this issue, then we will have failed as a people and as a nation.

For with a country as with a person, "What is a man profited, if he shall gain the whole world, and lose his own soul?"

There is no Negro problem. There is no Southern problem. There is no Northern problem. There is only an American problem. And we are met here tonight as Americans—not as Democrats or Republicans—we are met here as Americans to solve that problem.

This was the first nation in the history of the world to be founded with a purpose. The great phrases of that purpose still sound in every American heart, North and South: "All men are created equal"—"government by consent of the governed"—"give me liberty or give me death." Well, those are not just clever words, or those are not just empty theories. In their name Americans have fought and died for two centuries, and tonight around the world they stand there as guardians of our liberty, risking their lives.

Those words are a promise to every citizen that he shall share in the dignity of man. This dignity cannot be found in a man's possessions; it cannot be found in his power, or in his position. It really rests on his right to be treated as a man equal in opportunity to all others. It says that he shall share in freedom, he shall choose his leaders, educate his children, and provide for his family according to his ability and his merits as a human being.

To apply any other test—to deny a man his hopes because of his color or race, his religion or the place of his birth—is not only to do injustice, it is to deny America and to dishonor the dead who gave their lives for American freedom.

THE RIGHT TO VOTE

Our fathers believed that if this noble view of the rights of man was to flourish, it must be rooted in democracy. The most basic right of all was the right to choose your own leaders. The history of this country, in large measure, is the history of the expansion of that right to all of our people.

Many of the issues of civil rights are very complex and most difficult. But about this there can and should be no argument. Every American citizen must have an equal right to vote. There is no reason which can excuse the denial of that right. There is no duty which weighs more heavily on us than the duty we have to ensure that right.

Yet the harsh fact is that in many places in this country men and women are kept from voting simply because they are Negroes.

Every device of which human ingenuity is capable has been used to deny this right. The Negro citizen may go to register only to be told that the day is wrong, or the hour is late, or the official in charge is absent. And if he persists, and if he manages to present himself to the registrar, he may be disqualified because he did not spell out his middle name or because he abbreviated a word on the application.

And if he manages to fill out an application he is given a test. The registrar is the sole judge of whether he passes this test. He may be asked to recite the entire Constitution, or explain the most complex provisions of State law. And even a college degree cannot be used to prove that he can read and write.

For the fact is that the only way to pass these barriers is to show a white skin.

Experience has clearly shown that the existing process of law cannot overcome systematic and ingenious discrimination. No law that we now have on the books—and I have helped to put three of them there—can ensure the right to vote when local officials are determined to deny it.

In such a case our duty must be clear to all of us. The Constitution says that no person shall be kept from voting because of his race or his color. We have all sworn an oath before God to support and to defend that Constitution. We must now act in obedience to that oath.

GUARANTEEING THE RIGHT TO VOTE

Wednesday I will send to Congress a law designed to eliminate illegal barriers to the right to vote.

The broad principles of that bill will be in the hands of the Democratic and Republican leaders tomorrow. After they have reviewed it, it will come here formally as a bill. I am grateful for this opportunity to come here tonight at the invitation of the leadership to reason with my friends, to give them my views, and to visit with my former colleagues.

I have had prepared a more comprehensive analysis of the legislation which I had intended to transmit to the clerk tomorrow but which I will submit to the clerks tonight. But I want to really discuss with you now briefly the main proposals of this legislation.

This bill will strike down restrictions to voting in all elections—Federal, State, and local—which have been used to deny Negroes the right to vote.

This bill will establish a simple, uniform standard which cannot be used, however ingenious the effort, to flout our Constitution.

It will provide for citizens to be registered by officials of the United States Government if the State officials refuse to register them.

It will eliminate tedious, unnecessary lawsuits which delay the right to vote.

Finally, this legislation will ensure that properly registered individuals are not prohibited from voting.

I will welcome the suggestions from all of the Members of Congress—I have no doubt that I will get some—on ways and means to strengthen this law and to make it effective. But experience has plainly shown that this is the only path to carry out the command of the Constitution.

To those who seek to avoid action by their National Government in their own communities; who want to and who seek to maintain purely local control over elections, the answer is simple:

Open your polling places to all your people.

Allow men and women to register and vote whatever the color of their skin.

Extend the rights of citizenship to every citizen of this land.

THE NEED FOR ACTION

There is no constitutional issue here. The command of the Constitution is plain.

There is no moral issue. It is wrong—deadly wrong—to deny any of your fellow Americans the right to vote in this country.

There is no issue of States rights or national rights. There is only the struggle for human rights.

I have not the slightest doubt what will be your answer. . . .

This time, on this issue, there must be no delay, no hesitation and no compromise with our purpose.

We cannot, we must not, refuse to protect the right of every American to vote in every election that he may desire to participate in. And we ought not and we cannot and we must not wait another 8 months before we get a bill. We have already waited a hundred years and more, and the time for waiting is gone. . . .

WE SHALL OVERCOME

But even if we pass this bill, the battle will not be over. What happened in Selma is part of a far larger movement which reaches into every section and State of America. It is the effort of American Negroes to secure for themselves the full blessings of American life.

Their cause must be our cause too. Because it is not just Negroes, but really it is all of us, who must overcome the crippling legacy of bigotry and injustice.

And we shall overcome.

As a man whose roots go deeply into Southern soil I know how agonizing racial feelings are. I know how difficult it is to reshape the attitudes and the stucture of our society.

But a century has passed, more than a hundred years, since the Negro was freed. And he is not fully free tonight.

It was more than a hundred years ago that Abraham Lincoln, a great President of another party, signed the Emancipation Proclamation, but emancipation is a proclamation and not a fact.

A century has passed, more than a hundred years, since equality was promised. And yet the Negro is not equal.

A century has passed since the day of promise. And the promise is unkept.

The time of justice has now come. I tell you that I believe sincerely that no force can hold it back. It is right in the eyes of man and God that it should come. And when it does, I think that day will brighten the lives of every American.

For Negroes are not the only victims. How many white children have gone uneducated, how many white families have lived in stark poverty, how many white lives have been scarred by fear, because we have wasted our energy and our substance to maintain the barriers of hatred and terror?

So I say to all of you here, and to all in the Nation tonight, that those who appeal to you to hold on to the past do so at the cost of denying you your future.

This great, rich, restless country can offer opportunity and education and hope to all: black and white, North and South, sharecropper and city dweller. These are the enemies: poverty, ignorance, disease. They are the enemies and not our fellow man, not our neighbor. And these enemies too, poverty, disease and ignorance, we shall overcome. . . .

THE PURPOSE OF THIS GOVERNMENT

My first job after college was as a teacher in Cotulla, Tex., in a small Mexican-American school. Few of them could speak English, and I couldn't speak much Spanish. My students were poor and they often came to class without breakfast, hungry. They knew even in their youth the pain of prejudice. They never seemed to know why people disliked them. But they knew it was so, because I saw it in their eyes. I often walked home late in the afternoon, after the classes were finished, wishing there was more that I could do. But all I knew was to teach them the little that I knew, hoping that it might help them against the hardships that lay ahead.

Somehow you never forget what poverty and hatred can do when you see its scars on the hopeful face of a young child.

I never thought then, in 1928, that I would be standing here in 1965. It never even occurred to me in my fondest dreams that I might have the chance to help the sons and daughters of those students and to help people like them all over this country.

But now I do have that chance—and I'll let you in on a secret—I mean to use it. And I hope that you will use it with me.

This is the richest and most powerful country which ever occupied the globe. The might of past empires is little compared to ours. But I do not want to be the President who built empires, or sought grandeur, or extended dominion.

I want to be the President who educated young children to the wonders of their world. I want to be the President who helped to feed the hungry and to prepare them to be taxpayers instead of taxeaters.

I want to be the President who helped the poor to find their own way and who protected the right of every citizen to vote in every election.

I want to be the President who helped to end hatred among his fellow men and who promoted love among the people of all races and all regions and all parties.

I want to be the President who helped to end war among the brothers of this earth. . . .

Beyond this great chamber, out yonder in 50 States, are the people that we serve. Who can tell what deep and unspoken hopes are in their hearts tonight as they sit there and listen. We all can guess, from our own lives, how difficult they often find their own pursuit of happiness, how many problems each little family has. They look most of all to themselves for their futures. But I think that they also look to each of us.

Above the pyramid on the great seal of the United States it says—in Latin
—"God has favored our undertaking."

God will not favor everything that we do. It is rather our duty to divine
His will. But I cannot help believing that He truly understands and that He
really favors the undertaking that we begin here tonight.

3. A Conservative Denounces Black Rioters (1965)

With the passage of the Voting Rights Act in the summer of 1965, the civil rights
movement seemed to stand triumphant, and the Johnson Administration seemed at last
to have fulfilled the promises of emancipation made a century earlier. But the moment
of satisfaction was brief. Just five days after President Johnson signed the Voting Rights
Act, a rampaging riot swept through the black Los Angeles ghetto of Watts, leaving
some 34 persons dead. Moderates were shocked and disillusioned; conservatives were
angry. They turned their rage on black leaders like Martin Luther King. In the following
selection Dr. Will Herberg, a noted conservative intellectual of the day, denounces the
Watts rioters and blames King for their actions. Is his assessment of King's role fair?

The country is still reeling from the shock of what happened in Los Angeles. Six days of "racial" rioting, of violence uncontrolled and uncontrollable. Thousands of Negroes running wild, burning, destroying, looting,
spreading from the Negro section outward, on a scale that made a senior
officer of the National Guard, which finally quelled the rioting, describe it
as veritable insurrection.

The fury of hate and violence revealed in these six dreadful days has
engendered a profound uneasiness through every part of the country. How
could it have happened? After all, Los Angeles is not the Congo—or is it?

Of course, the politicians and the professional bleeding hearts immediately began to mumble the tired old phrases about "poverty" and "frustration," as though nobody was, or ever had been, poor or frustrated except
the Los Angeles Negroes. (The living standards and conditions of life of the
Negroes in Los Angeles, bad as they are, would have seemed something
near to heaven to most of the immigrants who came to this country in earlier
years.). . .

Internal order is the first necessity of every society. Even justice is secondary to order, because without order there can be no society and no
justice, however partial and fragmentary. . . .

But the internal order of a community, which is so primary and precious
to it, is always precarious. . . .

It is preserved by force—by the naked force of police . . . but more immediately by the force of custom and respect for constituted authority. It
is these two—custom and respect for constituted authority—that do the everyday work of maintaining order and security. When these are weakened or
destroyed, hell breaks loose—whether it is in the Congo or in Los Angeles,
whether it is Negroes or whites who do the devil's work. . . .

3. *National Review*, XVII, 769–70 (Sept. 7, 1965), 150 E. 35th St., New York, N.Y., 10016.
By permission.

This internal order is now in jeopardy; and it is in jeopardy because of the doings of such highminded, self-righteous "children of light" as the Rev. Dr. Martin Luther King and his associates in the leadership of the "civil rights" movement. If you are looking for those ultimately responsible for the murder, arson, and looting in Los Angeles, look to them: they are the guilty ones, these apostles of "non-violence."

For years now, the Rev. Dr. Martin Luther King and his associates have been deliberately undermining the foundations of internal order in this country. With their rabble-rousing demagoguery, they have been cracking the "cake of custom" that holds us together. With their doctrine of "civil disobedience," they have been teaching hundreds of thousands of Negroes—particularly the adolescents and the children—that it is perfectly all right to break the law and defy constituted authority if you are a Negro-with-a-grievance; in protest against injustice. And they have done more than talk. They have on occasion after occasion, in almost every part of the country, called out their mobs on the streets, promoted "school strikes," sit-ins, lie-ins, in explicit violation of the law and in explicit defiance of the public authority. They have taught anarchy and chaos by word and deed—and, no doubt, with the best of intentions—and they have found apt pupils everywhere, with intentions *not* of the best. Sow the wind, and reap the whirlwind. But it is not they alone who reap it, but we as well; the entire nation.

It is worth noting that the worst victims of these high-minded rabble-rousers are not so much the hated whites, but the great mass of the Negro people themselves. The great mass of the Negro people cannot be blamed for the lawlessness and violence in Harlem, Chicago, Los Angeles, or elsewhere. All they want to do is what decent people everywhere want to do: make a living, raise a family, bring up their children as good citizens, with better advantages than they themselves ever had. The "civil rights" movement and the consequent lawlessness has well nigh shattered these hopes; not only because of the physical violence and insecurity, but above all because of the corruption and demoralization of the children, who have been lured away from the steady path of decency and self-government to the more exhilarating road of "demonstrating"—and rioting. An old friend of mine from Harlem put it to me after the riots last year: "For more than fifteen years we've worked our heads off to make something out of these boys. Now look at them—they're turning into punks and hoodlums roaming the streets."

Shall we wreak our wrath upon such "punks" and "hoodlums," the actual rioters, and allow those ultimately responsible, the Martin Luther Kings, the inciters to law-defiance in the name of "conscience," to go immune in their self-righteousness? They stand horrified at the rioting and violence. But isn't it all the handiwork of the demons they themselves raised? They are the guilty ones—despite the best intentions. If they have any conscience left besides that which they use as justification for the violation of law, let them search it now.

4. A Christian Journal Takes the Long View (1965)

A long-established weekly religious magazine, the non-denominational *Christian Century*, judged the Watts riots with more compassion than many. In the light of its **views, why is the answer to the black disorders not simply bigger and better police forces?**

Respectable, law-abiding white and Negro America condemns the arson, pillage and vandalism which erupted in Los Angeles and to a lesser degree in other cities in mid-August. In that condemnation there is more fear and contempt than there is compassion, more haughty bigotry than understanding, more irritation with the rampaging Negro mobs than concern about them. Does comfortable, secure white and Negro America also deplore the circumstances which make explosions in the black ghettos of the nation's megalopolises inevitable? Does it lament the ghettos' filth and stench, the vermin-infested tenements, the broken families, the legacy of cultural blight, the unemployment, the dropouts? Does it understand, does it want to understand people whose despair runs so deep that they sense no identity with any of the social structures and view all of them as enemies? Whence this wild hatred which roves the streets crying "Let's kill whitey"? Are we willing to ask that question? Are we able to face the answer?

Responsible whites and Negroes know that when such riots break out, adequate restraints must be employed to replace anarchy with order. But if we do nothing more than this, if policemen and soldiers are our only reply to the rebellion bred in the slums, then we merely intensify the pressures which produce riots. Peaceful citizens want themselves and their property protected by the law and by law enforcement agencies—a reasonable desire. But out of the steaming slums comes a hysteria to which such reasonableness is wholly alien. What appeal do the standards of an orderly society have for a poor, ignorant man who believes himself cut off from all the benefits of a good society? . . . Do we not have the right to demand that riots cease, to insist and to enforce our insistence that there be law and order in the streets? We do. But we might as well accept the realities of the situation, one of which is that the systems we trust and defend have impregnated some Negroes with a deep, implacable contempt for those systems. . . .

The riots are painful warnings that the nation faces major catastrophes in its industrial and commercial centers. The slums of these centers are tightly packed with Negroes and other minorities who are condemned to unemployment or underemployment, to bad housing at high cost, to poor schools, to the enticements and intimidations of criminals, to the incitements of rabble rousers and to all the miseries which attend human congestion.

In these settings—as in Los Angeles—minor incidents inexplicably explode long-accumulated charges of frustration, bitterness and hatred. The slums of the great cities are a multifaceted problem for which there is no cure-all, no quick and easy remedy. The problems are too big for the cities to handle alone, particularly since the cities are usually surrounded by white suburbs which view with horror what occurs at the metropolitan core but which resist all efforts to change the circumstances producing race riots.

It is a state problem and a national one. Nothing done yet at these levels acknowledges the gravity of the situation. The nation must now with its full strength relieve the plight of the Negroes in urban slums or turn its metropolises into garrisoned cities. The best way for the Negro and for the general society is long and hard; but we must take it.

D. VIETNAM TROUBLES

1. The Joint Chiefs of Staff Propose a Wider War (1964)

United States involvement in Vietnam went back at least as far as 1950, when President Truman began aiding the French in their effort to suppress a nationalist insurgency in their Indochinese colony. Despite American help, the French forces collapsed in 1954. An international conference in Geneva, Switzerland, in 1954 divided Vietnam at the 17th parallel, and called for elections in *all* of Vietnam in 1956. The elections were never held, primarily because the government in South Vietnam, encouraged by the United States, feared that the Communists in the North, led by Ho Chi Minh, would score a massive victory. President Eisenhower pledged in 1954 to provide military assistance to the government of South Vietnam, and by the end of Eisenhower's term in office about 700 American "advisers" were helping to bolster the Vietnamese military. President Kennedy thus inherited a risky but limited commitment to South Vietnam. Meanwhile, Communist-led nationalist forces, abetted by the Communist regime in North Vietnam, were stepping up the pressure on the shaky South Vietnamese government in Saigon. A bloody military coup in late 1963 brought a new, apparently tougher, government to Saigon, setting the stage for increasing American involvement. A few months later, General Maxwell D. Taylor, the chairman of the Joint Chiefs of Staff, sent the following memorandum to Secretary of Defense Robert S. McNamara, proposing intensified American military actions in Vietnam. What reasons does he offer for such actions? How persuasive are his reasons?

1. National Security Action Memorandum No. 273 makes clear the resolve of the President to ensure victory over the externally directed and supported communist insurgency in South Vietnam. In order to achieve that victory, the Joint Chiefs of Staff are of the opinion that the United States must be prepared to put aside many of the self-imposed restrictions which now limit our efforts, and to undertake bolder actions which may embody greater risks.

2. The Joint Chiefs of Staff are increasingly mindful that our fortunes in South Vietnam are an accurate barometer of our fortunes in all of Southeast Asia. It is our view that if the U.S. program succeeds in South Vietnam it will go far toward stabilizing the total Southeast Asia situation. Conversely, a loss of South Vietnam to the communists will presage an early erosion of the remainder of our position in that subcontinent.

1. *The Pentagon Papers, New York Times* edition (1971), pp. 274–277.

3. Laos, existing on a most fragile foundation now, would not be able to endure the establishment of a communist—or pseudo neutralist—state on its eastern flank. Thailand, less strong today than a month ago by virtue of the loss of Prime Minister Sarit would probably be unable to withstand the pressures of infiltration from the north should Laos collapse to the communists in its turn. Cambodia apparently has estimated that our prospects in South Vietnam are not promising and, encouraged by the actions of the French, appears already to be seeking an accommodation with the communists. Should we actually suffer defeat in South Vietnam, there is little reason to believe that Cambodia would maintain even a pretense of neutrality.

4. In a broader sense, the failure of our programs in South Vietnam would have heavy influence on the judgments of Burma, India, Indonesia, Malaysia, Japan, Taiwan, the Republic of Korea, and the Republic of the Philippines with respect to U.S. durability, resolution, and trustworthiness. Finally, this being the first real test of our determination to defeat the communist wars of national liberation formula, it is not unreasonable to conclude that there would be a corresponding unfavorable effect upon our image in Africa and in Latin America.

5. All of this underscores the pivotal position now occupied by South Vietnam in our world-wide confrontation with the communists and the essentiality that the conflict there would be brought to a favorable end as soon as possible. However, it would be unrealistic to believe that a complete suppression of the insurgency can take place in one or even two years. The British effort in Malaya is a recent example of a counterinsurgency effort which required approximately ten years before the bulk of the rural population was brought completely under control of the government, the police were able to maintain order, and the armed forces were able to eliminate the guerrilla strongholds.

6. The Joint Chiefs of Staff are convinced that, in keeping with the guidance in NSAM 273, the United States must make plain to the enemy our determination to see the Vietnam campaign through to a favorable conclusion. To do this, we must prepare for whatever level of activity may be required and, being prepared, must then proceed to take actions as necessary to achieve our purposes surely and promptly.

7. Our considerations, furthermore, cannot be confined entirely to South Vietnam. Our experience in the war thus far leads us to conclude that, in this respect, we are not now giving sufficient attention to the broader area problems of Southeast Asia. The Joint Chiefs of Staff believe that our position in Cambodia, our attitude toward Laos, our actions in Thailand, and our great effort in South Vietnam do not comprise a compatible and integrated U.S. policy for Southeast Asia. U.S. objectives in Southeast Asia cannot be achieved by either economic, political, or military measures alone. All three fields must be integrated into a single, broad U.S. program for Southeast Asia. The measures recommended in this memorandum are a partial contribution to such a program.

8. Currently we and the South Vietnamese are fighting the war on the enemy's terms. He has determined the locale, the timing, and the tactics of the battle while our actions are essentially reactive. One reason for this is the fact that we have obliged ourselves to labor under self-imposed restrictions with respect to impeding external aid to the Viet Cong. These restrictions include keeping the war within the boundaries of South Vietnam, avoiding the direct use of U.S. combat forces, and limiting U.S. direction of the campaign to rendering advice to the Government of Vietnam. These restrictions, while they may make our international position more readily defensible, all tend to make the task in Vietnam more complex, time-consuming, and in the end, more costly. In addition to complicating our own problem, these self-imposed restrictions may well now be conveying signals of irresolution to our enemies--encouraging them to higher levels of vigor and greater risks. A reversal of attitude and the adoption of a more aggressive program would enhance greatly our ability to control the degree to which escalation will occur. It appears probable that the economic and agricultural disappointments suffered by Communist China, plus the current rift with the Soviets, could cause the communists to think twice about undertaking a large-scale military adventure in Southeast Asia.

9. In adverting to actions outside of South Vietnam, the Joint Chiefs of Staff are aware that the focus of the counterinsurgency battle lies in South Vietnam itself, and that the war must certainly be fought and won primarily in the minds of the Vietnamese people. At the same time, the aid now coming to the Viet Cong from outside the country in men, resources, advice, and direction is sufficiently great in the aggregate to be significant—both as help and as encouragement to the Viet Cong. It is our conviction that if support of the insurgency from outside South Vietnam in terms of operational direction, personnel, and material were stopped completely, the character of the war in South Vietnam would be substantially and favorably altered. Because of this conviction, we are wholly in favor of executing the covert actions against North Vietnam which you have recently proposed to the President. We believe, however, that it would be idle to conclude that these efforts will have a decisive effect on the communist determination to support the insurgency; and it is our view that we must therefore be prepared fully to undertake a much higher level of activity, not only for its beneficial tactical effect, but to make plain our resolution, both to our friends and to our enemies.

10. Accordingly, the Joint Chiefs of Staff consider that the United States must make ready to conduct increasingly bolder actions in Southeast Asia; specifically as to Vietnam to:

a. Assign to the U.S. military commander responsibilities for the total U.S. program in Vietnam.

b. Induce the Government of Vietnam to turn over to the United States military commander, temporarily, the actual tactical direction of the war.

c. Charge the United States military commander with complete responsibility for conduct of the program against North Vietnam.

d. Overfly Laos and Cambodia to whatever extent is necessary for acquisition of operational intelligence.

e. Induce the Government of Vietnam to conduct overt ground operations in Laos of sufficient scope to impede the flow of personnel and material southward.

f. Arm, equip, advise, and support the Government of Vietnam in its conduct of aerial bombing of critical targets in North Vietnam and in mining the sea approaches to that country.

g. Advise and support the Government of Vietnam in its conduct of large-scale commando raids against critical targets in North Vietnam.

h. Conduct aerial bombing of key North Vietnam targets, using U.S. resources under Vietnamese cover, and with the Vietnamese openly assuming responsibility for the actions.

i. Commit additional U.S. forces, as necessary, in support of the combat action within South Vietnam.

j. Commit U.S. forces as necessary in direct actions against North Vietnam.

11. It is our conviction that any or all of the foregoing actions may be required to enhance our position in Southeast Asia. The past few months have disclosed that considerably higher levels of effort are demanded of us if U.S. objectives are to be attained.

12. The governmental reorganization which followed the coup d'etat in Saigon should be completed very soon, giving basis for concluding just how strong the Vietnamese Government is going to be and how much of the load they will be able to bear themselves. Additionally, the five-month dry season, which is just now beginning, will afford the Vietnamese an opportunity to exhibit their ability to reverse the unfavorable situation in the critical Mekong Delta. The Joint Chiefs of Staff will follow these important developments closely and will recommend to you progressively the execution of such of the above actions as are considered militarily required, providing, in each case, their detailed assessment of the risks involved.

13. The Joint Chiefs of Staff consider that the strategic importance of Vietnam and of Southeast Asia warrants preparations for the actions above and recommend that the substance of this memorandum be discussed with the Secretary of State.

2. President Johnson Asserts His War Aims (1965)

On August 2–4, 1964, two American destroyers in the Gulf of Tonkin were reportedly fired upon by North Vietnamese torpedo boats. President Johnson, concealing the fact that the destroyers had been engaging in provocative raids on North Vietnam, used the incident to secure from Congress a sweeping mandate for American military intervention (The "Gulf of Tonkin Resolution"). Then in February, 1965, Viet Cong guerillas attacked an American base at Pleiku, South Vietnam, and Johnson seized the occasion to begin an enormous escalation of the American military presence in Southeast Asia. He

2. *Public Papers of the Presidents of the United States: Lyndon B. Johnson* (1966), p. 395.

ordered virtually continuous bombing of North Vietnam, and sharply increased the number of American troops in South Vietnam (to nearly 200,000 by the end of 1965). On April 7, 1965, in a major address at Johns Hopkins University, Johnson set forth his reasons for the increasing American commitment. Just two weeks earlier, the Assistant Secretary of Defense for International Security Affairs had noted in a private memorandum that American war aims were "70%—to avoid a humiliating U.S. defeat (to our reputation as a guarantor). 20%—to keep South Vietnam (and the adjacent) territory from Chinese hands, 10%—to permit the people of South Vietnam to enjoy a better, freer way of life. Also—to emerge from crisis without unacceptable taint from methods used. Not—to 'help a friend.' " Was Johnson's speech consistent with that thinking?

. . . Why are we in South Viet-Nam?

We are there because we have a promise to keep. Since 1954 every American President has offered support to the people of South Viet-Nam. We have helped to build, and we have helped to defend. Thus, over many years, we have made a national pledge to help South Viet-Nam defend its independence.

And I intend to keep that promise.

To dishonor that pledge, to abandon this small and brave nation to its enemies, and to the terror that must follow, would be an unforgivable wrong.

We are also there to strengthen world order. Around the globe from Berlin to Thailand are people whose well being rests in part on the belief that they can count on us [to honor some forty defensive alliances] if they are attacked. To leave Viet-Nam to its fate would shake the confidence of all these people in the value of an American commitment and in the value of America's word. The result would be increased unrest and instability, and even wider war.

We are also there because there are great stakes in the balance. Let no one think for a moment that retreat from Viet-Nam would bring an end to conflict. The battle would be renewed in one country and then another. The central lesson of our time is that the appetite of aggression is never satisfied. . . .

Our objective is the independence of South Viet-Nam and its freedom from attack. We want nothing for ourselves—only that the people of South Viet-Nam be allowed to guide their own country in their own way.

We will do everything necessary to reach that objective and we will do only what is absolutely necessary.

3. British Prime Minister Criticizes American Bombing (1965)

"Operation Rolling Thunder"—large-scale bombing raids on North Vietnam—evoked world-wide criticism in 1965. Even America's allies grew restive. On June 3, 1965, British Prime Minister Harold Wilson sent the following cable to President Johnson, gently but firmly taking issue with American policy in Vietnam. What does Wilson find most objectionable?

3. *Pentagon Papers, New York Times* edition (1971), pp. 448–449.

I was most grateful to you for asking Bob McNamara to arrange the very full briefing about the two oil targets near Hanoi and Haiphong that Col. Rogers gave me yesterday. . . .

I know you will not feel that I am either unsympathetic or uncomprehending of the dilemma that this problem presents for you. In particular, I wholly understand the deep concern you must feel at the need to do anything possible to reduce the losses of young Americans in and over Vietnam; and Col. Rogers made it clear to us what care has been taken to plan this operation so as to keep civilian casualties to the minimum.

However, . . . I am bound to say that, as seen from here, the possible military benefits that may result from this bombing do not appear to outweigh the political disadvantages that would seem the inevitable consequence. If you and the South Vietnamese Government were conducting a declared war on the conventional pattern . . . this operation would clearly be necessary and right. But since you have made it abundantly clear—and you know how much we have welcomed and supported this—that your purpose is to achieve a negotiated settlement, and that you are not striving for total military victory in the field, I remain convinced that the bombing of these targets, without producing decisive military advantage, may only increase the difficulty of reaching an eventual settlement. . . .

The last thing I wish is to add to your difficulties, but, as I warned you in my previous message, if this action is taken we shall have to dissociate ourselves from it, and in doing so I should have to say that you had given me advance warning and that I had made my position clear to you. . . .

Nevertheless I want to repeat . . . that our reservations about this operation will not affect our continuing support for your policy over Vietnam, as you and your people have made it clear from your Baltimore speech onwards. But, while this will remain the Government's position, I know that the effect on public opinion in this country—and I believe throughout Western Europe—is likely to be such as to reinforce the existing disquiet and criticism that we have to deal with.

4. Defense Secretary McNamara Foresees a Stalemate (1965)

Despite intense air attacks on North Vietnam, and swelling contingents of American troops, the United States and its South Vietnamese allies made little headway in Vietnam. At home, conservative critics demanded that the military be given a free hand to deliver a knockout blow to the Communist forces. But the government's policy was to increase its application of force only in carefully measured increments. In an assessment of the war effort in December, 1965, Secretary of Defense Robert S. McNamara suggested one reason for this policy of cautious "escalation." What does he see as the greatest restraint on America's ability to raise the stakes in Vietnam?

. . . We believe that, whether or not major new diplomatic initiatives are made, the U.S. must send a substantial number of additional forces to VN [Vietnam] if we are to avoid being defeated there. (30 Nov program; concurred in by JCS [Joint Chiefs of Staff])

4. *Pentagon Papers,* New York Times edition (1971), pp. 489–490.

IV. Prognosis assuming the recommended deployments

Deployments of the kind we have recommended will not guarantee success. Our intelligence estimate is that the present Communist policy is to continue to prosecute the war vigorously in the South. They continue to believe that the war will be a long one, that time is their ally, and that their own staying power is superior to ours. They recognize that the U.S. reinforcements of 1965 signify a determination to avoid defeat, and that more U.S. troops can be expected. Even though the Communists will continue to suffer heavily from GVN [Government of Vietnam] and U.S. ground and air action, we expect them, upon learning of any U.S. intentions to augment its forces, to boost their own commitment and to test U.S. capabilities and will to persevere at higher level of conflict and casualties (U.S. KIA [Killed In Action] with the recommended deployments can be expected to reach 1000 a month).

If the U.S. were willing to commit enough forces—perhaps 600,000 men or more—we could ultimately prevent the DRV/VC [Democratic Republic of Vietnam/Viet Cong] from sustaining the conflict at a significant level. When this point was reached, however, the question of Chinese intervention would become critical. (*We are generally agreed that the Chinese Communists will intervene with combat forces to prevent destruction of the Communist regime in the DRV. It is less clear whether they would intervene to prevent a DRV/VC defeat in the South.) The intelligence estimate is that the chances are a little better than even that, at this stage, Hanoi and Peiping would choose to reduce the effort in the South and try to salvage their resources for another day; but there is an almost equal chance that they would enlarge the war and bring in large numbers of Chinese forces (they have made certain preparations which could point in this direction).

It follows, therefore, that the odds are about even that, even with the recommended deployments, we will be faced in early 1967 with a military standoff at a much higher level, with pacification still stalled, and with any prospect of military success marred by the chances of an active Chinese intervention. . . .

5. Secretary McNamara Opposes Further Escalation (1966)

By the end of 1966 Vietnam was beginning to look like a bottomless pit into which America was dumping precious money and more precious men. Secretary of Defense McNamara, one of the original architects of American involvement, was among the first high-level officials to grow disenchanted with the course of the war. In his report to the President, given below, he gives his increasingly pessimistic assessment of American prospects in Southeast Asia. Such views did not endear him to Johnson, who clung to the hope that the United States could salvage some kind of victory from the Vietnam quagmire, and McNamara soon left the Cabinet. But when military men in the spring of 1968 requested an additional 200,000 troops for Vietnam, Johnson at last drew the line. He put a ceiling on American troop commitments, and withdrew from the 1968 presidential race so as to pursue peace more effectively. For Johnson, it was too little too late. There was no peace in 1968 (the war dragged on five more years), and his

5. *Pentagon Papers, New York Times* edition (1971), pp. 542–551.

party lost the White House in that year to the Republican Richard M. Nixon. Nixon soon announced a policy of "Vietnamization"—increasing the role of the Vietnamese in their own war, while simultaneously decreasing the American role. In what ways does McNamara's 1966 report foreshadow Nixon's approach? Why is McNamara pessimistic? What is his view of the bombing operation over North Vietnam?

1. Evaluation of the situation. In the report of my last trip to Vietnam almost a year ago, I stated that the odds were about even that, even with the then-recommended deployments, we would be faced in early 1967 with a military stand-off at a much higher level of conflict and with "pacification" still stalled. I am a little less pessimistic now in one respect. We have done somewhat better militarily than I anticipated. We have by and large blunted the communist military initiative—any military victory in South Vietnam the Viet Cong may have had in mind 18 months ago has been thwarted by our emergency deployments and actions. And our program of bombing the North has exacted a price.

My concern continues, however, in other respects. This is because I see no reasonable way to bring the war to an end soon. Enemy morale has not broken—he apparently has adjusted to our stopping his drive for military victory and has adopted a strategy of keeping us busy and waiting us out (a strategy of attriting our national will). He knows that we have not been, and he believes we probably will not be, able to translate our military successes into the "end products"—broken enemy morale and political achievements by the GVN [Government of Vietnam].

The one thing demonstrably going for us in Vietnam over the past year has been the large number of enemy killed-in-action resulting from the big military operations. Allowing for possible exaggeration in reports, the enemy must be taking losses—deaths in and after battle—at the rate of more than 60,000 a year. The infiltration routes would seem to be one-way trails to death for the North Vietnamese. Yet there is no sign of an impending break in enemy morale and it appears that he can more than replace his losses by infiltration from North Vietnam and recruitment in South Vietnam.

Pacification is a bad disappointment. We have good grounds to be pleased by the recent elections, by Ky's 16 months in power, and by the faint signs of development of national political institutions and of a legitimate civil government. But none of this has translated itself into political achievements at Province level or below. Pacification has if anything gone backward. As compared with two, or four, years ago, enemy full-time regional forces and part-time guerrilla forces are larger; attacks, terrorism and sabotage have increased in scope and intensity; more railroads are closed and highways cut; the rice crop expected to come to market is smaller; we control little, if any, more of the population; the VC political infrastructure thrives in most of the country, continuing to give the enemy his enormous intelligence advantage; full security exists nowhere (not even behind the U.S. Marines' lines and in Saigon); in the countryside, the enemy almost completely controls the night.

"WE ARE WINNING THE WAR"

The wasteland refrain of Presidents Johnson and Ho in 1967
Courtesy, the Boston *Globe*. Cartoonist Paul Szep.

Nor has the Rolling Thunder program of bombing the North either significantly affected infiltration or cracked the morale of Hanoi. There is agreement in the intelligence community on these facts. . . .

In essence, we find ourselves—from the point of view of the important war (for the complicity of the people)—no better, and if anything worse off. This important war must be fought and won by the Vietnamese themselves. We have known this from the beginning. But the discouraging truth is that, as was the case in 1961 and 1963 and 1965, we have not found the formula, the catalyst, for training and inspiring them into effective action.

2. Recommended actions. In such an unpromising state of affairs, what should we do? We must continue to press the enemy militarily; we must make demonstrable progress in pacification; at the same time, we must add a new ingredient forced on us by the facts. Specifically, we must improve our position by getting ourselves into a military posture that we credibly would maintain indefinitely—a posture that makes trying to "wait us out" less attractive. I recommend a five-pronged course of action to achieve those ends.

a. Stabilize U.S. force-levels in Vietnam. It is my judgment that, barring a dramatic change in the war, we should limit the increase in U.S. forces in

THE VIETNAM NIGHTMARE

Cartoon by Paul Szep. Courtesy The Swann Collection of Caricatures and Cartoons, Library of Congress.

SVN in 1967 to 70,000 men and we should level off at the total of 470,000 which such an increase would provide.° It is my view that this is enough to punish the enemy at the large-unit operations level and to keep the enemy's main forces from interrupting pacification. I believe also that even many more than 470,000 would not kill the enemy off in such numbers as to break their morale so long as they think they can wait us out. It is possible that such a 40 percent increase over our present level of 325,000 will break the enemy's morale in the short term; but if it does not, we must, I believe, be prepared for and have underway a long-term program premised on more than breaking the morale of main force units. A stabilized U.S. force level would be part of such a long-term program. It would put us in a position where negotiations would be more likely to be productive, but if they were not we could pursue the all-important pacification task with proper attention and resources and without the spectre of apparently endless escalation of U.S. deployments.

b. Install a barrier. A portion of the 470,000 troops—perhaps 10,000 to 20,000—should be devoted to the construction and maintenance of an infiltration barrier. Such a barrier would lie near the 17th parallel—would run from the sea, across the neck of South Vietnam (choking off the new infiltration routes through the DMZ [Demilitarized Zone] and across the trails

° Admiral Sharp has recommended a 12/31/67 strength of 570,000. However, I believe both he and General Westmoreland recognize that the danger of inflation will probably force an end 1967 deployment limit of about 470,000.

in Laos. This interdiction system (at an approximate cost of $1 billion) would comprise to the east a ground barrier of fences, wire, sensors, artillery, aircraft and mobile troops; and to the west—mainly in Laos—an interdiction zone covered by air-laid mines and bombing attacks pinpointed by air-laid acoustic sensors.

The barrier may not be fully effective at first, but I believe that it can be effective in time and that even the threat of its becoming effective can substantially change to our advantage the character of the war. It would hinder enemy efforts, would permit more efficient use of the limited number of friendly troops, and would be persuasive evidence both that our sole aim is to protect the South from the North and that we intend to see the job through.

c. Stabilize the Rolling Thunder program against the North. Attack sorties in North Vietnam have risen from about 4,000 per month at the end of last year to 6,000 per month in the first quarter of this year and 12,000 per month at present. Most of our 50 percent increase of deployed attack-capable aircraft has been absorbed in the attacks on North Vietnam. In North Vietnam, almost 84,000 attack sorties have been flown (about 25 percent against fixed targets), 45 percent during the past seven months.

Despite these efforts, it now appears that the North Vietnamese-Laotian road network will remain adequate to meet the requirements of the Communist forces in South Vietnam—this is so even if its capacity could be reduced by one-third and if combat activities were to be doubled. North Vietnam's serious need for trucks, spare parts and petroleum probably can, despite air attacks, be met by imports. The petroleum requirement for trucks involved in the infiltration movement, for example, has not been enough to present significant supply problems, and the effects of the attacks on the petroleum distribution system, while they have not yet been fully assessed, are not expected to cripple the flow of essential supplies. Furthermore, it is clear that, to bomb the North sufficiently to make a radical impact upon Hanoi's political, economic and social structure, would require an effort which we could make but which would not be stomached either by our own people or by world opinion; and it would involve a serious risk of drawing us into open war with China.

The North Vietnamese are paying a price. They have been forced to assign some 300,000 personnel to the lines of communication in order to maintain the critical flow of personnel and material to the South. Now that the lines of communication have been manned, however, it is doubtful that either a large increase or decrease in our interdiction sorties would substantially change the cost to the enemy of maintaining the roads, railroads, and waterways or affect whether they are operational. It follows that the marginal sorties—probably the marginal 1,000 or even 5,000 sorties—per month against the lines of communication no longer have a significant impact on the war. . . .

When this marginal inutility of added sorties against North Vietnam and

Laos is compared with the crew and aircraft losses implicit in the activity (four men and aircraft and $20 million per 1,000 sorties), I recommend, as a minimum, against increasing the level of bombing of North Vietnam and against increasing the intensity of operations by changing the areas or kinds of targets struck.

Under these conditions, the bombing program would continue the pressure and would remain available as a bargaining counter to get talks started (or to trade off in talks). But, as in the case of a stabilized level of U.S. ground forces, the stabilization of Rolling Thunder would remove the prospect of ever escalating bombing as a factor complicating our political posture and distracting from the main job of pacification in South Vietnam.

At the proper time, as discussed on pages 6–7 below, I believe we should consider terminating bombing in all of North Vietnam, or at least in the Northeast zones, for an indefinite period in connection with covert moves toward peace.

d. Pursue a vigorous pacification program. As mentioned above, the pacification (Revolutionary Development) program has been and is thoroughly stalled. The large-unit operations war, which we know best how to fight and where we have had our successes, is largely irrelevant to pacification as long as we do not lose it. By and large, the people in rural areas believe that the GVN when it comes will not stay but that the VC [Viet Cong] will; that cooperations with the GVN will be punished by the VC; that the GVN is really indifferent to the people's welfare; that the low-level GVN are tools of the local rich; and that the GVN is ridden with corruption.

Success in pacification depends on the interrelated functions of providing physical security, destroying the VC apparatus, motivating the people to cooperate and establishing responsive local government. An obviously necessary but not sufficient requirement for success of the Revolutionary Development cadre and police is vigorously conducted and adequately prolonged clearing operations by military troops, who will "stay" in the area, who behave themselves decently and who show some respect for the people.

This elemental requirement of pacification has been missing.

In almost no contested area designated for pacification in recent years have ARVN [Army of the Republic of Viet Nam] forces actually "cleared and stayed" to a point where cadre teams, if available, could have stayed overnight in hamlets and survived, let alone accomplish their mission. VC units of company and even battalion size remain in operation, and they are more than large enough to overrun anything the local security forces can put up.

Now that the threat of a Communist main-force military victory has been thwarted by our emergency efforts, we must allocate far more attention and a portion of the regular military forces (at least half of the ARVN and perhaps a portion of the U.S. forces) to the task of providing an active and permanent security screen behind which the Revolutionary Development teams and police can operate and behind which the political struggle with the VC infrastructure can take place.

The U.S. cannot do this pacification security job for the Vietnamese. All we can do is "Massage the heart." For one reason, it is known that we do not intend to stay; if our efforts worked at all, it would merely postpone the eventual confrontation of the VC and GVN infrastructures. The GVN must do the job; and I am convinced that drastic reform is needed if the GVN is going to be able to do it. . . .

3. The prognosis. The prognosis is bad that the war can be brought to a satisfactory conclusion within the next two years. The large-unit operations probably will not do it; negotiations probably will not do it. *While we should continue to pursue both of these routes in trying for a solution in the short run, we should recognize that success from them is a mere possibility, not a probability.*

The solution lies in girding, openly, for a longer war and in taking actions immediately which will in 12 to 18 months give clear evidence that the continuing costs and risks to the American people are acceptably limited, that the formula for success has been found, and that the end of the war is merely a matter of time. All of my recommendations will contribute to this strategy, but the one most difficult to implement is perhaps the most important one—enlivening the pacification program. The odds are less than even for this task, if only because we have failed consistently since 1961 to make a dent in the problem. But, because the 1967 trend of pacification will, I believe, be the main talisman of ultimate U.S. success or failure in Vietnam, extraordinary imagination and effort should go into changing the stripes of that problem.

President Thieu and Prime Minister Ky are thinking along similar lines. They told me that they do not expect the Enemy to negotiate or to modify his program in less than two years. Rather, they expect that enemy to continue to expand and to increase his activity. They expressed agreement with us that the key to success is pacification and that so far pacification has failed. They agree that we need clarification of GVN and U.S. roles and that the bulk of the ARVN should be shifted to pacification. Ky will, between January and July 1967, shift all ARVN infantry divisions to that role. And he is giving Thang, a good Revolutionary Development director, added powers. Thieu and Ky see this as part of a two-year (1967–68) schedule, in which offensive operations against enemy main force units are continued, carried on primarily by the U.S. and other Free-World forces. At the end of the two-year period, they believe the enemy may be willing to negotiate or to retreat from his current course of action. . . .

6. The Soldier's War (1966)

Hundreds of thousands of young Americans served in Vietnam; more than 50,000 lost their lives there during the decade-long conflict (it was America's longest war). Much of the fighting was not conventional warfare, with front lines and well-identified foes facing one another. Instead, the Americans faced guerilla adversaries and their

6. Glenn Munson, ed., *Letters from Viet Nam* (1966), pp. 104, 118.

civilian supporters who were indistinguishable from the "friendly" South Vietnamese. In the absence of a defined front, there was no "rear," and American troops often felt themselves to be adrift in a hostile sea of treacherous enemies. Brutality was inevitable in this kind of environment. Two wartime letters from American servicemen follow. What opinion do the writers have of the war? of their own role in it? of antiwar protesters at home?

Dear Mom, . . .

Yesterday I witnessed something that would make any American realize why we are in this war. At least it did me. I was on daylight patrol. We were on a hill overlooking a bridge that was out of our sector. I saw a platoon of Vietcong stopping traffic from going over the bridge. They were beating women and children over the head with rifles, clubs, and fists. They even shot one woman and her child. They were taking rice, coconuts, fish, and other assorted foods from these people. The ones that didn't give they either beat or shot. I think you know what I tried to do. I wanted to go down and kill all of those slant-eyed bastards. I started to and it took two men to stop me. These slobs have to be stopped, even if it takes every last believer in a democracy and a free way of life to do it. I know after seeing their brave tactics I'm going to try my best. So please don't knock [President] Johnson's policy in Vietnam. There is a good reason for it. I'm not too sure what it is myself, but I'm beginning to realize, especially after yesterday. . . .

Love, Bill

How are the people taking to the war in Portland? I've read too much . . . about the way some of those cowardly students are acting on campuses. They sure don't show me much as far as being American citizens. They have the idea that they are our future leaders. Well, I won't follow nobody if he isn't going to help fight for my freedom.

A few weeks ago, I had the chance to talk with some Marines who had come to Okinawa for four (lousy) days of leave. They were more than happy because they had been fighting for six months with no let-up. We sat in a restaurant all the time, and I wish I could have taped it on my recorder. What they had to say would have had an impact on the people back home. One showed me where he had been shot. I asked if it hurt, and he didn't feel it. Not until after he got the — — that shot him. He was more angry than hurt. They told me of some of their patrols and how they would be talking to a buddy one minute and watch him die the next. Or wake up in the morning and see a friend hung from a tree by hooks in his armpits with parts of his body cut and shoved into his mouth. From what they said, the Vietcong aren't the only ruthless ones. *We* have to be, too. *Have* to. You'd be surprised to know that a guy you went to school with is right now shooting a nine-year-old girl and her mother. He did it because if they got the chance they would kill him. Or throwing a Vietcong out of a helicopter because he wouldn't talk.

One guy (who had broke down and cried) said that his one desire is to

Vietnam and Southeast Asia map showing Burma, China, North Viet-Nam, Laos, Thailand, Cambodia, South Viet-Nam, with labels including "1954 French Surrender," "U.S. Destroyers Attacked, 1964," "1st attack Aug. 2," "2nd attack Aug. 4," "Demarcation Line July 22, 1954," "Da Nang (U.S. Base)," "Gulf of Tonkin," "Hainan," "South China Sea," "Gulf of Siam," and cities Hanoi, Haiphong, Dien Bien Phu, Luang Prabang, Vientiane, Hué, Bangkok, Phnom Penh, Saigon, Nanning.

get enough leave to go home and kick three of those demonstrators in a well-suited place and bring him back. I tell you, it's horrible to read a paper and see your own people aren't backing you up.

E. THE POLITICS OF PROTEST IN THE 1960's

1. Students for a Democratic Society Issues a Manifesto (1962)

The civil rights struggle and the continuing Cold War inspired many young people who came of age in the 1960's to take a radically critical look at American society—

1. From The Port Huron Statement. Reprinted by permission of Tom Hayden, a founding member of Students for a Democratic Society and principal author of The Port Huron Statement. He was elected to the California legislature in 1982.

even before the worsening Vietnam imbroglio made radical disenchantment almost fashionable among the young. One of the earliest and most thoughtful expressions of this incipient youthful radicalism was the Port Huron Statement, drafted by Tom Hayden and adopted by the fledgling Students for a Democratic Society (then in a relatively moderate phase of development) at its national convention at Port Huron, Michigan, in 1962. This statement later proved enormously influential in shaping the political views of many young activists. What aspects of the American situation does it find most deplorable? How truly "radical" are the sentiments it expresses?

We are people of this generation, bred in at least modest comfort, housed now in universities, looking uncomfortably to the world we inherit.

When we were kids the United States was the wealthiest and strongest country in the world; the only one with the atom bomb, the least scarred by modern war, an initiator of the United Nations that we thought would distribute Western influence throughout the world. Freedom and equality for each individual, government of, by, and for the people—these American values we found good, principles by which we could live as men. Many of us began maturing in complacency.

As we grew, however, our comfort was penetrated by events too troubling to dismiss. First, the permeating and victimizing fact of human degradation, symbolized by the Southern struggle against racial bigotry, compelled most of us from silence to activism. Second, the enclosing fact of the Cold War, symbolized by the presence of the Bomb, brought awareness that we ourselves, and our friends, and millions of abstract "others'" we knew more directly because of our common peril, might die at any time. We might deliberately ignore, or avoid, or fail to feel all other human problems, but not these two, for these were too immediate and crushing in their impact, too challenging in the demand that we as individuals take the responsibility for encounter and resolution.

While these and other problems either directly oppressed us or rankled our consciences and became our own subjective concern, we began to see complicated and disturbing paradoxes in our surrounding America. The declaration "all men are created equal . . ." rang hollow before the facts of Negro life in the South and the big cities of the North. The proclaimed peaceful intentions of the United States contradicted its economic and military investments in the Cold War status quo.

We witnessed, and continue to witness, other paradoxes. With nuclear energy whole cities can easily be powered, yet the dominant nation-states seem more likely to unleash destruction greater than that incurred in all wars of human history. Although our own technology is destroying old and creating new forms of social organization, men still tolerate meaningless work and idleness. While two-thirds of mankind suffers undernourishment, our own upper classes revel amidst superfluous abundance. Although world population is expected to double in forty years, the nations still tolerate anarchy as a major principle of international conduct and uncontrolled exploitation governs the sapping of the earth's physical resources. Although mankind desperately needs revolutionary leadership, America rests in national stalemate, its goals ambiguous and tradition-bound instead of informed and clear, its democratic system apathetic and manipulated rather than "of, by, and for the people."

Not only did tarnish appear on our image of American virtue, not only did disillusion occur when the hypocrisy of American ideals was discovered, but we began to sense that what we had originally seen as the American Golden Age was actually the decline of an era. The worldwide outbreak of revolution against colonialism and imperialism, the entrenchment of totalitarian states, the menace of war, overpopulation, international disorder, supertechnology—these trends were testing the tenacity of our own commitment to democracy and freedom and our abilities to visualize their application to a world in upheaval.

Our work is guided by the sense that we may be the last generation in the experiment with living. But we are a minority—the vast majority of our people regard the temporary equilibriums of our society and world as eternally functional parts. In this is perhaps the outstanding paradox: we ourselves are imbued with urgency, yet the message of our society is that there is no viable alternative to the present. Beneath the reassuring tones of the politicians, beneath the common opinion that America will "muddle through," beneath the stagnation of those who have closed their minds to the future, is the pervading feeling that there simply are no alternatives, that our times have witnessed the exhaustion not only of Utopias, but of any new departures as well. Feeling the press of complexity upon the emptiness of life, people are fearful of the thought that at any moment things might be thrust out of control. They fear change itself, since change might smash whatever invisible framework seems to hold back chaos for them now. For most Americans, all crusades are suspect, threatening. The fact that each individual sees apathy in his fellows perpetuates the common reluctance to organize for change. The dominant institutions are complex enough to blunt the minds of their potential critics, and entrenched enough to swiftly dissipate or entirely repel the energies of protest and reform, thus limiting human expectancies. Then, too, we are a materially improved society, and by our own improvements we seem to have weakened the case for further change.

Some would have us believe that Americans feel contentment amidst prosperity—but might it not better be called a glaze above deeply felt anxieties about their role in the new world? And if these anxieties produce a developed indifference to human affairs, do they not as well produce a yearning to believe there *is* an alternative to the present, that something *can* be done to change circumstances in the school, the workplaces, the bureaucracies, the government? It is to this latter yearning, at once the spark and engine of change, that we direct our present appeal. The search for truly democratic alternatives to the present, and a commitment to social experimentation with them, is a worthy and fulfilling human enterprise, one which moves us and, we hope, others today. On such a basis do we offer this document of our convictions and analysis: as an effort in understanding and changing the conditions of humanity in the late twentieth century, an effort rooted in the ancient, still unfulfilled conception of man attaining determining influence over his circumstances of life.

2. A War Protestor Decides to Resist the Draft (1966)

No issue did more to breed disenchantment among young people in the 1960's than the war in Vietnam. As revelations spread about the deepening American involvement there, and as the government in Washington proved increasingly unable to justify the conflict to the American public, countless people, especially college youths, expressed their disaffection. For many young men of draft age, their relationship with the Selective Service System became both a political and a moral issue. One young man who decided to resist the draft was David Harris, a former Boy-of-the-Year from Fresno, California, and, in 1966, president of the student body at Stanford University. With his friend Dennis Sweeney—who a decade and a half later would be convicted of murdering former Congressman Allard K. Lowenstein, another anti-war activist—Harris helped to organize a draft resistance "movement" among college students. In the following passage, Harris describes his own decision to become a draft resister. (He would later spend nearly two years in a federal penitentiary as a consequence.) What are his motives? Is he justified in reaching his decision?

The more we learned about the war, the worse it seemed. Late in July, Cooley Street attended a lecture by a Canadian journalist who had just returned from North Vietnam. Dennis and the Channing Street group were at the lecture as well.

With what amounted to only a fledgling air defense system, explained the journalist, North Vietnam had no hope of turning the American Air Force back. Theoretically, strategic air power destroys the enemy's industrial, logistic, and transportation systems, but North Vietnam possessed little centralized industry and only a rudimentary transportation system. Consequently, the target increasingly became the population itself. The American strategy's starting point was a calculation by Defense Department planners that it took only two Vietnamese to deal with one of their dead countrymen, but one wounded required five. Mass woundings, it was assumed, would tie the enemy's hands, and the American arsenal had developed wounding devices in great variety.

The CBU 46 was a small explosive package stuffed with hundreds of one-inch steel darts, each shaped with fins, designed to "peel off" the outer flesh, make "enlarged wounds," and "shred body organs" before "lodging in the blood vessels." They were dropped a thousand at a time from 30,000 feet. The BLU 52 was 270 pounds of "riot control" chemical that induced vomiting, nausea, and muscle spasms, occasionally fatal to old people and children. The M-36 was an 800-pound casing containing 182 separate "incendiary bomblets," the most horrendous of which were manufactured from phosphorus, commonly lodging in the flesh and continuing to burn for as

2. *Dreams Die Hard: Three Men's Journey Through the Sixties* by David Harris. Copyright © 1982 by David Harris. Reprinted by permission of St. Martin's/Marek, New York.

long as fifteen days, causing its victims' wounds to glow with an eerie green light.

The two antipersonnel weapons then in most common use were versions of the BLU $2\frac{4}{26}$. The "pineapple bomb" was the earliest model. A yellow cylinder, it contained 250 steel ball-bearing pellets packed around an explosive charge. On impact, its pellets fired out horizontally. A batch of a thousand pineapples would cover an area the size of four football fields, leaving anything above ground level a casualty. The "guava bomb" was the pineapple's successor. Gray and round, it doubled the number of pellets and had a fuse that let it either explode at a set altitude or on impact. Since it fired its pellets diagonally instead of on the horizontal, the Guava also fired into the holes where people might be hiding.

After the program was over, we all decided to proceed to a place we called End of the World Beach. It was the edge of a causeway supporting the eastern approach to the Dunbarton Bridge, where beer bottles, old tires, two-by-fours, tennis shoes, condoms, dead fish, and seaweed were strung out for half a mile. It captured the devastation still haunting everyone's thinking. At one point, Dennis and I stood next to each other, staring across the refuse at the blinking lights of civilization on the other side of the bay.

Without looking at Dennis, I spoke up.

"You know," I said, "those bastards have got to be stopped."

When I turned to Sweeney, he was nodding his head like he knew exactly what I meant.

Three weeks later I sat at my typewriter and wrote local Draft Board 71 in Fresno, California, a letter "To whom it may concern." I enclosed a Selective Service classification card indicating that the bearer, David Victor Harris, possessed a student deferment. The letter informed my draft board that I could no longer in good conscience carry the enclosed document or accept the deferment it signified. It was a privilege I found unwarranted for any student. It also signified tacit assent on my part for both the task the Selective Service System was performing and the power it had assumed over my life. Being even implicitly a party to the destruction of Indochina was not part of my plans. If they ordered me for induction, I warned them, I would refuse to comply.

I feel as though I have explained that act of defiance a million times in the intervening years without ever quite capturing it. The repetition eventually burdened my explanation with a shell of distance and matter-of-factness that distorts what I did. It was an act of wonderment and impulse, taken in the calmest and most practical frame of mind. I was prepared to abandon what seemed a promising future and pit myself against the war one on one, believing I would redeem my country and realize myself in the process. It seemed that to do anything else would have dishonored both. There was nothing matter-of-fact or distant about it that August. I took my life in my hands and it was the bravest I have ever been. It was also, I think, the most right. That I have never doubted. Times change and I am no longer the same person, but my past and I are still directly related.

I remember mailing that letter at the mailbox next to the neighborhood store, scuffing along in the dust at the road edge, wearing Levis, moccasins, and a brown khaki work shirt. My moustache had become a full beard and my hair covered the top of my ears. I was both frightened and exhilarated. The last barrier was down. Henceforth, I was my own soldier advancing in my own kind of war.

My adrenaline didn't diminish until long after midnight. Lying in my bed, I pictured the penitentiary as a very cold and lonely place that I planned to endure for the sake of us all.

3. George Kennan Chastises The Student Left (1968)

George F. Kennan, the noted scholar, Soviet specialist, and diplomat (see p. 814), gave a controversial speech at the ceremonies dedicating a new library at Swarthmore College on December 11, 1967. Later published as "Rebels Without a Program," Kennan's remarks drew angry responses from many student activists and their (mostly junior) faculty allies. Kennan later replied to his critics in the book from which the selections below are taken. Written in the tumultuous year of 1968, which saw the assassinations of Robert Kennedy and Martin Luther King, Jr., riots in the black ghettos of several cities, and increasingly disruptive anti-war protests on many college campuses, Kennan's opinions are perhaps most remarkable for their comparatively calm, reasoned tone. Many other members of his generation were far less restrained in their hostility to the radical student left. (At Kent State University, in Ohio, National Guardsmen in the spring of 1970 fired at a group of anti-war demonstrators, killing four students; President Nixon shortly thereafter referred to student protesters as "bums".) Yet Kennan makes clear his abundant disagreement with the motives, methods, and goals of the student left. What does he find most objectionable? How fair is his criticism? On what matters does he agree with the student radicals?

The world seems to be full, today, of embattled students. The public prints are seldom devoid of the record of their activities. Photographs of them may be seen daily: screaming, throwing stones, breaking windows, overturning cars, being beaten or dragged about by police and, in the case of those on other continents, burning libraries. That these people are embattled is unquestionable. That they are really students, I must be permitted to doubt. I have heard it freely confessed by members of the revolutionary student generation of Tsarist Russia that, proud as they were of the revolutionary exploits of their youth, they never really learned anything in their university years; they were too busy with politics. The fact of the matter is that the state of being *enragé* is simply incompatible with fruitful study. It implies a degree of existing emotional and intellectual commitment which leaves little room for open-minded curiosity.

I am not saying that students should not be concerned, should not have views, should not question what goes on in the field of national policy and

3. George F. Kennan, *Democracy and the Student Left* (1968), pp. 7–9, 17–18, 224–227. Reprinted by permission of Harriet Wasserman Literary Agency, as agent for the author. Copyright © 1968 by George F. Kennan.

should not voice their questions about it. Some of us, who are older, share many of their misgivings, many of their impulses. Some of us have no less lively a sense of the dangers of the time, and are no happier than they are about a great many things that are now going on. But it lies within the power as well as the duty of all of us to recognize not only the possibility that we might be wrong but the virtual certainty that on some occasions we are bound to be. The fact that this is so does not absolve us from the duty of having views and putting them forward. But it does make it incumbent upon us to recognize the element of doubt that still surrounds the correctness of these views. And if we do that, we will not be able to lose ourselves in transports of moral indignation against those who are of opposite opinion and follow a different line; we will put our views forward only with a prayer for forgiveness for the event that we prove to be mistaken.

I am aware that inhibitions and restraints of this sort on the part of us older people would be attributed by many members of the student left to a sweeping corruption of our moral integrity. Life, they would hold, has impelled us to the making of compromises; and these compromises have destroyed the usefulness of our contribution. Crippled by our own cowardice, prisoners of the seamy adjustments we have made in order to be successfully a part of the American establishment, we are regarded as no longer capable of looking steadily into the strong clear light of truth.

In this, as in most of the reproaches with which our children shower us, there is of course an element of justification. There is a point somewhere along the way in most of our adult lives, admittedly, when enthusiasms flag, when idealism becomes tempered, when responsibility to others, and even affection for others, compels greater attention to the mundane demands of private life. There is a point when we are even impelled to place the needs of children ahead of the dictates of a defiant idealism, and to devote ourselves, pusillanimously, if you will, to the support and rearing of these same children—precisely in order that at some future date they may have the privilege of turning upon us and despising us for the materialistic faintheartedness that made their maturity possible. This, no doubt, is the nature of the compromise that millions of us make with the imperfections of government and society in our time. Many of us could wish that it might have been otherwise—that the idealistic pursuit of public causes might have remained our exclusive dedication down into later life. . . .

. . . Some people, who accept our political system, believe that they have a right to disregard it and to violate the laws that have flowed from it so long as they are prepared, as a matter of conscience, to accept the penalties established for such behavior.

I am sorry; I cannot agree. The violation of law is not, in the moral and philosophic sense, a privilege that lies offered for sale with a given price tag, like an object in a supermarket, available to anyone who has the price and is willing to pay for it. It is not like the privilege of breaking crockery in a tent at the county fair for a quarter a shot. Respect for the law is not an obligation which is exhausted or obliterated by willingness to accept the penalty for breaking it.

To hold otherwise would be to place the privilege of lawbreaking preferentially in the hands of the affluent, to make respect for law a commercial proposition rather than a civic duty and to deny any authority of law independent of the sanctions established against its violation. It would then be all right for a man to create false fire alarms or frivolously to pull the emergency cord on the train, or to do any number of other things that endangered or inconvenienced other people, provided only he was prepared to accept the penalties of so doing. Surely, lawlessness and civil disobedience cannot be condoned or tolerated on this ground; and those of us who care for the good order of society have no choice but to resist attempts at its violation, when this is their only justification. . . .

I said at the outset of this treatise that it would not be addressed to the students themselves. But perhaps I may attempt now, in conclusion, to sum up what I might say to a composite student activist if I had him before me and if he would listen that long. It would be something like this:

> I am not as critical of you, when all is said and done, as you think. There is much to be said on your side. Our society *is* endangered. So is world peace. So, indeed, is the very survival of Western civilization—in both the spiritual and physical sense. For all of this your government, and the generation which has supported that government, bear a heavy measure of responsibility. You may well have a sense of grievance over the fact that you have been propelled into such a world.
>
> Your understanding, on the other hand, both of what it is that is wrong and of the elements of responsibility involved, is shallow and inadequate—lacking in historical depth, lacking in understanding for what the human predicament really is, lacking in appreciation for the element of tragedy in human affairs, lacking in feeling for the importance of such things as continuity, custom and familiarity as components in any process of mass adjustment to new conditions. This is why I made the suggestion that so many of you resented: that you take advantage of the opportunity you have now, at college, and will never have again, to do some studying and to deepen understanding in all these respects, so that when you do come to a responsible involvement in public affairs you will be better prepared for it. So long as your analysis of the problem is shallow, the remedies that commend themselves to you are almost bound to suffer from the same distortion, and they are not likely to be effective.
>
> I recognize that the draft, more than any other single factor, causes you to feel that it is not you who have involved yourselves in the affairs of the government, but the government that has involved you. I concede your point, here, and give you my sympathy. I would ask you, however, not to exaggerate and overdramatize your plight. It will not be made easier by your doing so. And I think you should not make such heavy sledding of it from the standpoint of conscience. It was not you who started this war; it is not really you who can stop it. The decision is not yours, nor is the responsibility.
>
> If you are drafted and unhappy about it, I do not think you should go to prison or flee the country. I think it would be in order for you to tell your draft

board, without disrespect, that you consider this a foolish and unjust war, and that you go under protest, without enthusiasm, only as a mark of respect for what your country once was and could someday again be. But I don't think you should defy completely the decision of your government, however foolish and shortsighted, that brings you before that board. To be so lacking in patience is not fair to the country, as a political entity of nearly two hundred years' standing; it is not fair to all the people who are struggling in other, and perhaps more effective, ways for things you care about; just as Thoreau's futile gesture of spending a night by his own insistence in the little Concord jail was scarcely fair to his friends in the New England abolitionist movement who were moving in other ways, and more effective ones, to achieve the same ends, and to whom his gesture came as an unnecessary reproach and claim to moral superiority.

It is perhaps not fair to ask of you that you try to recognize in yourselves the children of a generation of people disoriented by a process of technological change far too sudden and precipitous for human power of adaptation. Such a burden of self-recognition is one not usually placed upon people of your age. But you will be well advised to attempt the feat. And if you attempt it, you will draw the consequence: which will be a feeling of less anger and more sadness; of less self-righteousness and greater understanding and pity for others; of a greater patience, relaxation, resignation and good humor in the face of the ordeals and choices with which our society now confronts you.

THOUGHT PROVOKERS

1. Was the Cuban Missile Crisis a turning point in the Cold War? Who actually "won" the confrontation over the missiles? Was President Kennedy's diplomacy in the crisis courageous or foolhardy?
2. In what ways was Lyndon Johnson an innovative political leader? What did the Great Society program owe to the New Deal? Can America afford the kinds of programs that Johnson dreamed of?
3. Was Martin Luther King, Jr., a "radical"? King took part of his inspiration from the non-violent tactics of Mohandas Gandhi's campaign for independence in India. What conditions are necessary for non-violence to succeed as a political technique? Who deserves more credit for the civil rights advances of the 1960's, Martin Luther King or Lyndon Baines Johnson?
4. Why did the United States become involved in Vietnam? Why did it fight the war in the gradually "escalating" way that it did? Why did the war last so long? In what ways did the Vietnam imbroglio alter America's role in the world?
5. Why did a radical movement well up in the 1960's? Just how truly radical was it? What legacy has the 1960's movement left behind? Are the issues on which it focussed dead?

46 · The Rise and Fall of Richard Nixon

I pledge to you the new leadership will end the war and win the peace in the Pacific.

PRESIDENTIAL CANDIDATE RICHARD NIXON, 1968

PROLOGUE: President Nixon, elected by a minority of the voters in the bitterly contested election of 1968, gave his highest priority to foreign affairs, especially to ending the war in Vietnam. He sought "peace with honor"—a combination that took nearly five years to achieve. When Nixon sent American troops into Cambodia in the spring of 1970, the nation's already seething college campuses erupted. Nixon withstood the storm of unpopularity and finally succeeded in extricating the United States from Vietnam. In the process he re-established American contacts with Communist China, and initiated a period of "détente," or relaxed relations, with the Soviet Union. Nixon also had the opportunty to appoint several Supreme Court justices. He expected them to share his conservative judicial philosophy, which stressed "law and order" and frowned on the kind of judicial activism in behalf of minorities that had characterized the court in the 1950's and 1960's under Chief Justice Earl Warren. Nixon handily won re-election in 1972, but he was soon ensnared in a controversy concerning his role in a politically inspired break-in at the Democratic party offices in Washington's Watergate apartment complex. Threatened with formal impeachment and trial, Nixon resigned the presidency. Gerald Ford, who had been appointed vice-president after Nixon's original running mate had resigned amidst scandalous accusations, became the first person ever elevated to the presidency solely by act of Congress. He speedily lost whatever confidence the public had in him when he extended an unconditional pardon to the fallen Nixon.

A. THE SUPREME COURT "CODDLES" CRIMINALS

1. The Outlawing of Third-degree Confessions (1966)

In the 1960's and even earlier, the Supreme Court was a target for abuse by conservative groups. The more vocal extremists raised the insulting cry, "Impeach Earl Warren," against the liberal Chief Justice. Conservatives were first outraged by a series of rulings which extended Constitutional guarantees to Communists and which ordered desegregation in the schools. Then, in 1962 and 1963, came two decisions

1. *Official Reports of the Supreme Court,* vol. 384 U.S. Pt. 3 (Preliminary Print), pp. 444–481, *passim.* The Court also decreed reapportionment in the state legislatures (1962) and in the Congressional districts (1964) on the basis of "one man, one vote," rather than on the lopsided basis which often gave agricultural areas greater voting power than more populous urban areas.

which banned the recitation of prayers in the public schools. Such a practice was declared to be in violation of the First Amendment, which required a separation of church and state.

In 1963 an epochal decision held that accused criminals must be provided with lawyers in non-capital offenses. In 1964 and 1966 other decisions decreed that confessions obtained by the police in private (and hence under suspicion of physical force) could not be used to convict. The Fifth Amendment had long barred self-incrimination. Finally, on June 13, 1966, the Supreme Court, in a 5 to 4 decision, reversed the conviction of a confessed kidnapper-rapist, Ernesto Miranda, together with three men accused of other felonies. Chief Justice Warren, speaking for the majority, ruled in part as follows. In view of the fact that the crime rate was rising alarmingly and that this decision would make convictions harder to obtain, was the Court to be commended for emphasizing the rights of the individual at the expense of social order?

Prior to any questioning, the person must be warned that he has a right to remain silent, that any statement he does make may be used as evidence against him, and that he has a right to the presence of an attorney, either retained or appointed.

The defendant may waive effectuation of these rights, provided the waiver is made voluntarily, knowingly and intelligently.

If, however, he indicates in any manner and at any stage of the process that he wishes to consult with an attorney before speaking, there can be no questioning.

Likewise, if the individual is alone and indicates in any manner that he does not wish to be interrogated, the police may not question him. The mere fact that he may have answered some questions or volunteered some statements on his own does not deprive him of the right to refrain from answering any further inquiries until he has consulted with an attorney and thereafter consents to be questioned.

The constitutional issue we decide in each of these [four] cases is the admissibility of statements obtained from a defendant questioned while in custody and deprived of his freedom of option. In each, the defendant was questioned by police officers, detectives, or a prosecuting attorney in a room in which he was cut off from the outside world. In none of these cases was the defendant given a full and effective warning of his rights at the outset of the interrogation process. In all the cases, the questioning elicited oral admissions, and in three of them, signed statements as well which were admitted at their trials.

They all thus share salient features—incommunicado * interrogation of individuals in a police-dominated atmosphere, resulting in self-incriminating statements without full warnings of constitutional rights. . . .

From extensive factual studies undertaken in the early [19]30s . . . it is clear that police violence and the "third degree" flourished at that time. In a series of cases decided by this Court long after these studies, the police

---

* That is, without outside communication.

resorted to physical brutality—beatings, hanging, whipping—and to sustained and protracted questioning incommunicado in order to extort confessions. The 1961 Commission on Civil Rights found much evidence to indicate that "some policemen still resort to physical force to obtain confessions."

The use of physical brutality and violence is not, unfortunately, relegated to the past or to any part of the country. Only recently in Kings County, N. Y., the police brutally beat, kicked and placed lighted cigarette butts on the back of a potential witness under interrogation for the purpose of securing a statement incriminating a third party. . . .

The examples given above are undoubtedly the exception now, but they are sufficiently widespread to be the object of concern. . . .

Even without employing brutality, the "third degree" or the specific stratagems described above, the very fact of custodial interrogation exacts a heavy toll on individual liberty and trades on the weakness of individuals. . . .

If an individual indicates that he wishes the assistance of counsel before any interrogation occurs, the authorities cannot rationally ignore or deny his request on the basis that the individual does not have or cannot afford a retained attorney.

The financial ability of the individual has no relationship to the scope of the rights involved here. The privilege against self-incrimination secured by the Constitution applies to all individuals. The need for counsel in order to protect the privilege exists for the indigent as well as the affluent. . . .

This does not mean, as some have suggested, that each police station must have a "station-house lawyer" present at all times to advise prisoners. It does mean, however, that if police propose to interrogate a person they must make known to him that he is entitled to a lawyer and that, if he cannot afford one, a lawyer will be provided for him prior to any interrogation. . . .

Our decision is not intended to hamper the traditiona! function of police officers in investigating crime. . . . When an individual is in custody on probable cause, the police may, of course, seek out evidence in the field to be used at trial against him. Such investigation may include inquiry of persons not under restraint.

General on-the-scene questioning as to facts surrounding a crime or other general questioning of citizens in the fact-finding process is not affected by our holding. It is an act of responsible citizenship for individuals to give whatever information they may have to aid in law enforcement. In such situations the compelling atmosphere inherent in the process of in-custody interrogation is not necessarily present.

In dealing with statements obtained through interrogation, we do not purport to find all confessions inadmissible. Confessions remain a proper element in law enforcement. Any statement given freely and voluntarily without any compelling influence is, of course, admissible in evidence. . . .

In announcing these principles, we are not unmindful of the burdens which law-enforcement officials must bear, often under trying circumstances. We also fully recognize the obligation of all citizens to aid in enforcing the criminal laws.

2. The Minority Supports the Police (1966)

An angered, fist-pounding Mr. Justice Harlan, speaking for three of the four dissenters, put his finger on some of the weaknesses of the majority opinion. In these excerpts from his dissent, is he more realistic than the majority in his approach to the problem, and if so, in what respects?

I believe the decision of the Court represents poor constitutional law and entails harmful consequences for the country at large. How serious these consequences may prove to be only time can tell. But the basic flaws in the Court's justification seem to me readily apparent, now once all sides of the problem are considered. . . .

The new rules are not designed to guard against police brutality or other unmistakably banned forms of coercion. Those who use "third degree" tactics and deny them in court are equally able and destined to lie as skillfully about warnings and waivers.

Rather, the thrust of the new rules is to negate all pressures, to reinforce the nervous or ignorant suspect, and ultimately to discourage any confession at all. The aim, in short, is toward "voluntariness" in a utopian sense, or, to view it from a different angle, voluntariness with a vengeance.

To incorporate this notion into the Constitution requires a strained reading of history and precedent and a disregard of the very pragmatic concerns that alone may on occasion justify such strains. . . .

What the Court largely ignores is that its rules impair, if they will not eventually serve wholly to frustrate, an instrument of law enforcement that has long and quite reasonably been thought worth the price paid for it.

There can be little doubt that the Court's new code would markedly decrease the number of confessions. To warn the suspect that he may remain silent and remind him that his confession may be used in court are minor obstructions. To require also an express waiver by the suspect and an end to questioning whenever he demurs must heavily handicap questioning. And to suggest or provide counsel for the suspect simply invites the end of the interrogation.

How much harm this decision will inflict on law enforcement cannot fairly be predicted with accuracy. Evidence on the role of confessions is notoriously incomplete. . . .

We do know that some crimes cannot be solved without confessions, that ample expert testimony attests to their importance in crime control, and that the Court is taking a real risk with society's welfare in imposing its new regime on the country. The social costs of crime are too great to call the new rules anything but a hazardous experimentation.

2. *Ibid.*, pp. 504–17, *passim.*

3. A Green Light for Criminals (1966)

The increase of crimes of violence in the large cities had become frightening, particularly stabbings, "muggings" (assaults to commit robbery), rapes, and murders. In Washington, D. C., where citizens were frequently attacked within sight of the Capitol dome, one newspaper responded to the *Miranda* decision under the heading "Green Light for Criminals." In what additional respects does this commentary strengthen the view of the Court's minority as to the visionary character of the majority decision?

The Supreme Court's 5 to 4 ruling on police questioning of criminal suspects will be received with rejoicing by every thug in the land. For without a doubt it is a ruling which will grievously handicap the police and make it much easier for a criminal to beat the rap.

The murky torrent of words embodied in Chief Justice Warren's opinion tends to obscure some aspects of the ruling. But the salient points come through clearly enough.

Henceforth, once the police have taken a suspect into custody, they cannot lawfully ask him any questions unless four warnings have been given. (1) The suspect must be plainly advised that he need not make any statement. (2) He must be informed that anything he says may be used against him in a trial. (3) He must be told that he has a right to have an attorney *present* throughout the questioning. (4) If the suspect is an indigent, he must be assured that he will be furnished a lawyer free of charge. Unless all of these conditions are met no confession or other evidence obtained during an interrogation can be used against the suspect.

The Chief Justice makes the remarkable observation that "our decision is not intended to hamper the traditional function of police officers in investigating crime." Intent aside, he must know that this is in fact a decision which will not only hamper but will largely destroy the traditional police function, at least as far as interrogation is concerned.

Why? Because any lawyer called in to sit beside a guilty prisoner is going to tell him to say nothing to the police. He would be derelict in his duty were he to do otherwise. In the face of this, the Chief Justice blandly suggests that there is nothing in the decision which requires "that police stop a person who enters a police station and states that he wishes to confess to a crime." How true! And how often in the proverbial blue moon will this happen?

The deplorable fact is that this ruling, as far as the public is concerned, will most directly affect the vicious types of crime—the murders, the yokings, the robberies and the rapes where it often is impossible to assemble enough evidence, without a confession, to obtain convictions. All the criminal need do is to demand a lawyer—and then the police, under the practical effect of this decision, will be unable to ask him question No. 1. What was it the

"MUM'S THE WORD, BUB"
Courtesy of The News, New York's Picture
Newspaper. Cartoonist Warren King.

President said about ridding our cities of crime so law-abiding citizens will
be safe in their homes, on the streets and in their places of business?

The dissents by Justices Harlan, Clark, Stewart and White were sharply-
worded. It is necessary to read them to understand the frailty of the grounds
upon which the majority rests this unprecedented ruling.

[*An extreme case of the application of the* Miranda *ruling came in February, 1967. In Brooklyn a factory worker had confessed to stabbing to death
his common-law wife and her five children. But he had not been advised of
his "right to silence," and, in the absence of concrete evidence, he was turned
loose. The presiding judge remarked, "Even an animal such as this one . . .
must be protected with all legal safeguards. It is repulsive to let a thing like
this out on the streets."* Time, March 3, 1967, p. 49]

4. President Nixon Outlines His Judicial Philosophy (1971)

Before his election, Nixon made clear his determination to change the complexion of the liberal "Warren Court." He clearly wished to reverse some recent landmark decisions. Two of his early appointees, Justices Burger and Blackmun, were distinguished conservatives. Two nominees, both rejected by the Senate, were of a similar stripe, though conspicuously less able and obviously chosen to discharge a political debt to the South. The next were Lewis F. Powell, Jr., and William H. Rehnquist, both rock-ribbed conservative lawyers with noteworthy intellectual qualifications. In presenting these two nominees, the President set forth at length his judicial philosophy. How does it differ from the values that animated the Warren Court?

These are the criteria I believe should be applied in naming people to the Supreme Court.

First, the Supreme Court is the highest judicial body in this country. Its members, therefore, should, above all, be among the very best lawyers in the Nation. Putting it another way: In the legal profession, the Supreme Court is the fastest track in the Nation, and it is essential that the Justices on that Court be able to keep up with the very able lawyers who will appear before that Court arguing cases. The two individuals I am nominating to the Court meet that standard of excellence to an exceptional degree.

The second consideration is the judicial philosophy of those who are to serve on the Court. Now, I emphasize the word "judicial" because whether an individual is a Democrat or a Republican cannot and should not be a decisive factor in determining whether he should be on the Court.

By "judicial philosophy" I do not mean agreeing with the President on every issue. It would be a total repudiation of our constitutional system if judges on the Supreme Court, or any other Federal court, for that matter, were like puppets on a string pulled by the President who appointed them.

When I appointed Chief Justice Burger, I told him that from the day he was confirmed by the Senate, he could expect that I would never talk to him about a case that was before the Court.

In the case of both Chief Justice Burger and Mr. Justice Blackmun and in the case of the two nominees that I shall be sending to the Senate tomorrow, their sole obligation is to the Constitution and to the American people and not to the President who appointed them to their positions.

As far as judicial philosophy is concerned, it is my belief that it is the duty of a judge to interpret the Constitution and not to place himself above the Constitution or outside the Constitution.

He should not twist or bend the Constitution in order to perpetuate his personal political and social views.

Now, this does not mean that judges who adhere to this philosophy that I have just described will find that they always agree on their interpretation of the Constitution. You seldom find two lawyers who will agree on any close question.

We have an excellent example of this in the record of the two judges whose vacancies I now have the duty to fill, Mr. Justice Black, Mr. Justice Harlan. When they retired from the Court a month ago, most observers labeled Mr. Justice Black as a liberal and Mr. Justice Harlan as a conservative. There was a measure of truth in this, but I would say that both were constitutionalists.

It is true, they disagreed sharply in many cases, but as I learned, not only from reading their opinions over the years, but from appearing twice before them and arguing a case before the Supreme Court, both were great judges with the brilliant ability to ask questions that went to the heart of a matter and then to make a decision based on their honest interpretation of the Constitution.

In the debate over the confirmation of the two individuals I have selected, I would imagine that it may be charged that they are conservatives. This is true, but only in a judicial, not in a political sense.

You will recall, I am sure, that during my campaign for the Presidency, I pledged to nominate to the Supreme Court individuals who shared my judicial philosophy, which is basically a conservative philosophy.

Now, let me give you an example of what that philosophy means.

Twenty-one months ago, Mr. Walter Lippmann wrote, ". . . the balance of power within our society has turned dangerously against the peace forces— against governors and mayors and legislatures, against the police and the courts." I share this view.

Over the past few years, many cases have come before the court involving that delicate balance between the rights of society and the rights of defendants accused of crimes against society. And honest and dedicated constitutional lawyers have disagreed as to where and how to maintain that balance.

As a judicial conservative, I believe some court decisions have gone too far in the past in weakening the peace forces as against the criminal forces in our society. In maintaining, as it must be maintained, the delicate balance between the rights of society and defendants accused of crimes, I believe the peace forces must not be denied the legal tools they need to protect the innocent from criminal elements. And I believe we can strengthen the hand of the peace forces without compromising our precious principle that the rights of individuals accused of crimes must always be protected.

It is with these criteria in mind that I have selected the two men whose names I will send to the Senate tomorrow.

B. NIXON'S CAMBODIAN COUP

1. The President Defends His Incursion (1970)

Nixon's scheme for ending the Vietnam war and winning the peace came to be known as Vietnamization. Pursuant to his "Guam Doctrine" or "Nixon Doctrine" of turning

1. *Weekly Compilation of Presidential Documents*, VI (1970), pp. 597ff.

over Asia's wars to Asians, he announced on November 3, 1969, that he would gradually withdraw American troops from Vietnam in the expectation that an ever-stronger South Vietnam would take up the slack and hold its own. On April 30, 1970, Nixon dramatically appeared on nation-wide television. Pointing out that areas along the border of supposedly neutral Cambodia were being used as hideouts from which enemy troops had long been attacking American and South Vietnamese forces, he announced that he was taking steps to wipe out these sanctuaries. Which of the reasons that he gives for doing so seem most valid and which the least valid? How could an extension of the fighting save American lives?

Cambodia . . . has sent out a call to the United States, to a number of other nations, for assistance. Because if this enemy effort succeeds, Cambodia would become a vast enemy staging area and a springboard for attacks on South Vietnam along 600 miles of frontier—a refuge where enemy troops could return from combat without fear of retaliation.

North Vietnamese men and supplies could then be poured into that country, jeopardizing not only the lives of our own men but the people of South Vietnam as well.

Now confronted with this situation, we have three options.

First, we can do nothing. Well, the ultimate result of that course of action is clear. Unless we indulge in wishful thinking, the lives of Americans remaining in Vietnam after our next withdrawal of 10,000 would be gravely threatened. . . .

Our second choice is to provide massive military assistance to Cambodia itself. Now unfortunately, while we deeply sympathize with the plight of 7 million Cambodians whose country is being invaded, massive amounts of military assistance could not be rapidly and effectively utilized by the small Cambodian Army against the immediate threat. . . .

Our third choice is to go to the heart of the trouble. That means cleaning out major North Vietnamese and Vietcong occupied territories, these sanctuaries which serve as bases for attacks on both Cambodia and American and South Vietnamese forces in South Vietnam. Some of these, incidentally, are as close to Saigon as Baltimore is to Washington. . . .

In cooperation with the armed forces of South Vietnam, attacks are being launched this week to clean out major enemy sanctuaries on the Cambodian-Vietnam border. . . .

This is not an invasion of Cambodia. The areas in which these attacks will be launched are completely occupied and controlled by North Vietnamese forces. Our purpose is not to occupy the areas. Once enemy forces are driven out of these sanctuaries and once their military supplies are destroyed, we will withdraw. . . .

Now let me give you the reasons for my decision.

A majority of the American people, a majority of you listening to me, are for the withdrawal of our forces from Vietnam. The action I have taken tonight is indispensable for the continuing success of that withdrawal program.

A majority of the American people want to end this war rather than to have it drag on interminably. The action I have taken tonight will serve that purpose.

A majority of the American people want to keep the casualties of our brave men in Vietnam at an absolute minimum. The action I take tonight is essential if we are to accomplish that goal.

We take this action not for the purpose of expanding the war into Cambodia but for the purpose of ending the war in Vietnam and winning the just peace we all desire. We have made and we will continue to make every possible effort to end this war through negotiation at the conference table rather than through more fighting on the battlefield. . . .

Tonight, I again warn the North Vietnamese that if they continue to escalate the fighting when the United States is withdrawing its forces, I shall meet my responsibility as Commander in Chief of our Armed Forces to take the action I consider necessary to defend the security of our American men.

The action that I have announced tonight puts the leaders of North Vietnam on notice that we will be patient in working for peace, we will be conciliatory at the conference table, but we will not be humiliated. We will not be defeated. We will not allow American men by the thousands to be killed by an enemy from privileged sanctuaries. . . .

If, when the chips are down, the world's most powerful nation, the United States of America, acts like a pitiful, helpless giant, the forces of totalitarianism and anarchy will threaten free nations and free institutions throughout the world.

Courtesy *Buffalo Evening News,* Cartoonist *Bruce Shanks*

It is not our power but our will and character that is being tested tonight. The question all Americans must ask and answer tonight is this: Does the richest and strongest nation in the history of the world have the character to meet a direct challenge by a group which rejects every effort to win a just peace, ignores our warning, tramples on solemn agreements, violates the neutrality of an unarmed people, and uses our prisoners as hostages?

If we fail to meet this challenge, all other nations will be on notice that despite its overwhelming power the United States, when a real crisis comes, will be found wanting.

During my campaign for the Presidency, I pledged to bring Americans home from Vietnam. They are coming home.

I promised to end this war. I shall keep that promise.

I promised to win a just peace. I shall keep that promise.

We shall avoid a wider war. But we are also determined to put an end to this war.

2. The St. Louis *Post-Dispatch* Dissents (1970)

The sudden invasion of "neutral" Cambodia by U.S. troops, at a time when Nixon was presumably "winding down" the war rather than widening it, provoked an angry uproar in America. No doubt taken aback by the furor, Nixon gave assurances that American forces would withdraw within two months (as they did) and penetrate no farther than about 20 miles (which they did). Some stores of rice, arms, and trucks were captured. The assumption was that the enemy forces would return, as they did, when the Americans left. Nixon was widely upbraided for having turned the Vietnam War into an Indochina War (which to a degree it already was), and this charge was redoubled when, in February 1971, an American-supported South Vietnamese force invaded Laos and was quickly driven back. The St. Louis *Post-Dispatch*, a prominent Democratic newspaper, found the Cambodian incursion illogical and deceptive. Which of its various criticisms seems most trenchant in the light of subsequent events?

President Nixon now has his own Indochina war and his own credibility gap. Neither one is inherited any longer. In asking the American people to support the expansion of the Vietnam war to Cambodia, as he has already expanded it to Laos, he asks them to believe the same false promises which have repeatedly betrayed them against their will into ever deeper involvement on the mainland of Asia.

They are asked to seek peace by making war; to seek withdrawal of our troops by enlarging the arena of combat; to diminish American casualties by sending more young men to their death; to save the lives of 450,000 American troops by one more round of escalation. And all this Mr. Nixon asks in the name of preserving the credibility of America as a great power!

Such an exercise in double-think and double-talk would be unbelievable if the whole nation had not seen an uneasy President floundering in illogic and misrepresentation before its very eyes. It is still hard to understand how

2. St. Louis *Post-Dispatch*, May 3, 1970. By permission of the publisher.

a President who saw his predecessor destroyed by manipulating the people into an unwanted war would now attempt to manipulate them into enlarging the war he promised to end.

When all of Mr. Nixon's patchwork rationalizations are stripped away, it is quite clear what has happened. His policy of Vietnamization is a failure. It always was a fatuous assumption that as American troops withdrew the South Vietnamese would become stronger and Hanoi would be intimidated into accepting defeat. Now that the assumption has been exposed as false—now that the Communists refuse to give up fighting on Mr. Nixon's command —the Pentagon has sold him the bill of goods that escalation will rescue a bankrupt policy.

It is the same bill of goods, slightly worn, that the generals sold Lyndon Johnson. First they promised that a merciless air war would bring Hanoi to its knees; and it didn't. Then, 500,000 ground troops would cow the Viet Cong; and they didn't. Now, "cleaning out" the bases on the Cambodian border, which our forces have lived with for five years, will suddenly win the war—and who can believe, honestly, that it will?

Nor can rational men honestly believe that sending American troops into Cambodia is necessary to save the lives of our garrison in Vietnam. The 450,000 men there, equipped and armed to the hilt, are perfectly able to protect themselves and Mr. Nixon knows it. So he fuzzes up the argument by saying that the object is to protect the lives of those Americans who will be left in Vietnam after mid-1971, when the current withdrawal schedule has been fulfilled.

This adds up to an interesting confession that Mr. Nixon intends to leave some 300,000 troops in Vietnam after his third year in office, but it is no more persuasive than the other. The plain truth is that Vietnamization has failed, the withdrawal schedule is threatened, Mr. Nixon because of his marriage to the Thieu-Ky regime [in South Vietnam] refuses to negotiate a compromise political settlement, and so he buys the old, battered nostrum of escalation. . . .

It is no wonder that moderate and thoughtful men like Republican Senator Mark Hatfield of Oregon are coming to the conclusion that the only way left to carry out the public will is to exercise the constitutional powers of Congress in a way that guarantees an end to the war. . . . Senator Hatfield is proposing that Congress stipulate a cut-off date after which no more funds will be appropriated for military operations in Indochina.

We favor such a measure. The cut-off date could be set far enough ahead to avoid any perils of precipitate withdrawal. It would not interfere with, but would reinforce, an orderly and secure disengagement. It would do no more than to write into law what Mr. Nixon claims to be his policy of ending the war. Its most immediate effect, we imagine, would be to compel Mr. Nixon to negotiate a reasonable political settlement based on a coalition government, to be followed by elections in which the Vietnamese people determine their own future. And what is wrong with that?

3. Kissinger Dissects the Dissenters

Henry Kissinger, a brilliant, German-born former Harvard professor, was serving in 1970 as President Nixon's National Security Assistant—a highly powerful position from which he exerted great influence on foreign policy. (He would later exercise still more power as Secretary of State in the second Nixon administration, and in the short-lived Ford administration.) In the passage from his memoirs given below, he offers his view of the anti-war protesters who convulsed the country in the wake of the Cambodian incursion. How does he judge the behavior of the Nixon administration toward the protesters? What is his assessment of their motives? Of their effect on policy? What did the crisis do to his relations with his one-time academic colleagues?

. . . I had entered government with the hope that I could help heal the schisms in my adopted country by working to end the war. I sympathized with the anguish of the students eager to live the American dream of a world where ideas prevailed by their purity without the ambiguities of recourse to power. The war in Vietnam was the first conflict shown on television and reported by a largely hostile press. The squalor and suffering and confusion inseparable from any war became part of the living experience of Americans; too many ascribed its agony to the defects of their own leaders.

Repellent as I found the self-righteousness and brutality of some protesters, I had a special feeling for the students. They had been brought up by skeptics, relativists, and psychiatrists; now they were rudderless in a world from which they demanded certainty without sacrifice. My generation had failed them by encouraging self-indulgence and neglecting to provide roots. I spent a disproportionate amount of time in the next months with student groups—ten in May alone. I met with protesters at private homes. I listened, explained, argued. But my sympathy for their anguish could not obscure my obligation to my country as I saw it. They were, in my view, as wrong as they were passionate. Their pressures delayed the end of the war, not accelerated it; their simplifications did not bring closer the peace, of the yearning for which they had no monopoly. Emotion was not a policy. We had to end the war, but in conditions that did not undermine America's power to help build the new international order upon which the future of even the most enraged depended. . . .

. . . The President's statements, oscillating between the maudlin and the strident, did not help in a volatile situation where everything was capable of misinterpretation. His May 1 off-the-cuff reference to "bums . . . blowing up campuses," a gibe overheard by reporters during a visit to the Pentagon, was a needless challenge, although it was intended to refer only to a tiny group of students who had firebombed a building and burned the life's research of a Stanford professor. When on May 4, four students at Kent State University were killed by rifle fire from National Guardsmen dispatched

by Ohio Governor James Rhodes to keep order during several days of violence, there was a shock wave that brought the nation and its leadership
close to psychological exhaustion.

The Administration responded with a statement of extraordinary insensi-
tivity. Ron Ziegler was told to say that the killings "should remind us all
once again that when dissent turns to violence it invites tragedy."

The momentum of student strikes and protests accelerated immediately.
Campus unrest and violence overtook the Cambodian operation itself as
the major issue before the public. Washington took on the character of a
besieged city. A pinnacle of mass public protest was reached by May 9
when a crowd estimated at between 75,000 and 100,000 demonstrated on a
hot Saturday afternoon on the Ellipse, the park to the south of the White
House. Police surrounded the White House; a ring of sixty buses was used
to shield the grounds of the President's home. . . .

All this accelerated the processes of disenchantment. Conservatives were
demoralized by a war that had turned into a retreat and liberals were paralyzed by what they themselves had wrought—for they could not completely
repress the knowledge that it was a liberal Administration that had sent
half a million Americans to Indochina. They were equally reluctant to face
the implications of their past actions or to exert any serious effort to maintain calm. There was a headlong retreat from responsibility. Extraordinarily
enough, all groups, dissenters and others, passed the buck to the Presidency.
It was a great joke for undergraduates when one senior professor proclaimed
"the way to get out of Vietnam is by ship." The practical consequence was
that in the absence of any serious alternative the government was left with
only its own policy or capitulation.

The very fabric of government was falling apart. The Executive Branch
was shell-shocked. After all, their children and their friends' children took
part in the demonstrations. Some two hundred and fifty State Department
employees, including fifty Foreign Service Officers, signed a statement objecting to Administration policy. The ill-concealed disagreement of Cabinet
members showed that the Executive Branch was nearly as divided as the
country. Interior Secretary Walter Hickel protested in public. The *New
York Times* on May 9 reported that the Secretary of State had prohibited
any speculation on his own attitude—hardly a ringing endorsement of the
President. A group of employees seized the Peace Corps building and flew
a Viet Cong flag from it. Robert Finch, Secretary of Health, Education, and
Welfare, refused to disagree publicly with his President and old friend—as
indeed he did privately—and a large number of his officials occupied the
department's auditorium in protest. The President saw himself as the firm
rock in this rushing stream, but the turmoil had its effect on him as well.
Pretending indifference, he was deeply wounded by the hatred of the protesters. He would have given a great deal to gain a measure of the affection
in which the students held the envied and admired Kennedys. In his am-
bivalence Nixon reached a point of exhaustion that caused his advisers deep

concern. His awkward visit to the Lincoln Memorial to meet students at 5:00 A.M. on May 9 was only the tip of the psychological iceberg.

Exhaustion was the hallmark of us all. I had to move from my apartment ringed by protesters into the basement of the White House to get some sleep. Despite the need to coordinate the management of the crisis, much of my own time was spent with unhappy, nearly panicky, colleagues; even more with student and colleague demonstrators. I talked at some length to Brian McDonnell and Thomas Mahoney, two young pacifists who announced they would fast in Lafayette Park until all American troops had been withdrawn. I talked in the Situation Room with groups of students from various colleges and graduate schools about the root causes, as I saw them, of their despair, which I thought deeper than anxiety about the war.

I found these discussions with students rather more rewarding than those with their protesting teachers. When I had lunch in the Situation Room with a group of Harvard professors, most of whom had held high governmental posts, at their request, I offered to engage in a candid discussion of the reasoning behind the decision, but on an off-the-record basis. Most had been my close colleagues and friends. They would not accept this offer. They were there not as eminent academicians but as political figures representing a constituency at home, a campus inflamed by the Kent State tragedy as much as by the war. They had proclaimed to the newspapers beforehand —but not to me—that they were there to confront me; they announced that they would henceforth refuse any research or advisory relationship with the government.

Their objections to the Cambodian decision illustrated that hyperbole was not confined to the Administration. One distinguished professor gave it as his considered analysis that "somebody had forgotten to tell the President that Cambodia was a country; he acted as if he didn't know this. Had we undertaken a large commitment to Cambodia? If we had, this was rotten foreign policy. If we hadn't, this was rotten foreign policy." He was convinced that this action "clearly jeopardized American withdrawals"— though in fact it did the opposite. This professor was prepared to believe, on the basis of no evidence whatsoever, that Secretary of Defense Laird had been unaware of the military operations before the President announced them. He held the amazing view that "it was a gamble that shouldn't have been taken even if it succeeds on its own terms." Others said the decision was "incomprehensible," "more horrible than anything done by LBJ," "dreadful." One professor advanced the extraordinary hypothesis that an operation lasting eight weeks to a distance of twenty-one miles might lead our military commanders to believe that the use of nuclear weapons was now conceivable. Another declared that we had provoked all the actions of the other side.

The meeting completed my transition from the academic world to the world of affairs. These were the leaders of their fields; men who had been my friends, academicians whose lifetime of study should have encouraged a sense of perspective. That they disagreed with our decision was understandable; I had myself gone through a long process of hesitation before I became convinced that there was no alternative. But the lack of compassion, the overweening righteousness, the refusal to offer an alternative, reinforced two convictions: that for the internal peace of our country the war had to be ended, but also that in doing so on terms compatible with any international responsibility we would get no help from those with whom I had spent my professional life. The wounds would have to be healed after the war was over; in the event, these were not.

Cambodia was *not* a moral issue; neither Nixon nor his opponents should ever have presented it in those terms. What we faced was an essentially tactical choice: whether the use of American troops to neutralize the sanctuaries for a period of eight weeks was the best way to maintain the established pace and security of our exit from Vietnam and prevent Hanoi from overrunning Indochina. Reasonable men might differ; instead, rational discussion ended. The President's presentation that elevated his decision to the same level of crisis as some of the crucial choices of World War II was countered by the critics with the image of an out-of-control President acting totally irrationally, who had provoked the enemy and whose actions were immoral even if they *succeeded.*

But it was not the incursion into Cambodia that was the real subject of debate. It was the same issue that had torn the country during the Moratorium the previous year: whether there were any terms that the United States should insist on for its honor, its world position, and the sacrifices already made, or whether it should collapse its effort immediately and unconditionally. A political settlement as urged by Senator Fulbright—other than the quick imposition of a Communist government in Saigon—was precisely what Hanoi had always rejected, as Le Duc Tho had confirmed to me in the most unqualified terms not three weeks earlier. What none of the moderate critics was willing to admit was that if we followed their recommendations of refusing aid to Cambodia, we would soon have no choice but to accept Hanoi's terms, which none of them supported. Our opponents kept proclaiming an assumption for which there did not exist the slightest evidence—that there was some unspecified political alternative, some magic formula of neutrality, which was being willfully spurned. The panicky decision to set a June 30 deadline for the removal of our forces from Cambodia was one concrete result of public pressures. . . .

Unfortunately, the arguments for a withdrawal deadline had not improved with age. Either the deadline was compatible with Vietnamization, in which case it coincided with our own policy but would deprive us of negotiating leverage. Or it was arbitrary, in which case it was a euphemism for a collapse; and it would have been nearly impossible to justify risking lives in the interval before the deadline expired. So we ended the Cambodia operation still on the long route out of Vietnam, confronting an implacable enemy and an equally implacable domestic opposition.

C. WINDING DOWN THE VIETNAM WAR

1. Nixon's Grand Plan in Foreign Policy (1968–69)

Richard Nixon built his pre-presidential career on a strong reputation as a hawkish cold warrior—and thus, ironically, he was in a particularly favorable position to bring some thaw to the chilly cold war. As a certified conservative, he had a freedom of maneuver that would not have been available to a liberal Democrat, who would have been vulnerable to criticism from the very right wing that Nixon could easily control. Nixon shrewdly saw the implications of the split between China and the Soviet Union that had developed in the 1960's, and he was determined to turn that split to American advantage. In the following passage from his memoirs, Nixon describes his thinking about global affairs as he embarked upon his presidency. What does he mean when he says that "the key to a Vietnam settlement lay in Moscow and Peking rather than in Hanoi"?

In the late 1940s and during the 1950s I had seen communism spread to China and other parts of Asia, and to Africa and South America, under the camouflage of parties of socialist revolution, or under the guise of wars of national liberation. And, finally, during the 1960s I had watched as Peking and Moscow became rivals for the role of leadership in the Communist world.

Never once in my career have I doubted that the Communists mean it when they say that their goal is to bring the world under Communist control. Nor have I ever forgotten Whittaker Chambers's chilling comment that when he left communism, he had the feeling he was leaving the winning side. But unlike some anticommunists who think we should refuse to recognize or deal with the Communists lest in doing so we imply or extend an ideological respectability to their philosophy and their system, I have always believed that we can and must communicate and, when possible, negotiate with Communist nations. They are too powerful to ignore. We must always remember that they will never act out of altruism, but only out of self-interest. Once this is understood, it is more sensible—and also safer—to communicate with the Communists than it is to live in icy cold-war isolation or confrontation. In fact, in January 1969 I felt the relationship between the United States and the Soviet Union would probably be the single most important factor in determining whether the world would live at peace during and after my administration.

I felt that we had allowed ourselves to get in a disadvantageous position vis-à-vis the Soviets. They had a major presence in the Arab states of the Middle East, while we had none; they had Castro in Cuba; since the mid-1960s they had supplanted the Chinese as the principal military suppliers of North Vietnam; and except for Tito's Yugoslavia they still totally controlled Eastern Europe and threatened the stability and security of Western Europe.

There were, however, a few things in our favor. The most important and

---

1. Reprinted by permission of Grosset and Dunlap, Inc. from *RN: The Memoirs of Richard Nixon,* copyright © 1978 by Richard Nixon.

interesting was the Soviet split with China. There was also some evidence of growing, albeit limited, independence in some of the satellite nations. There were indications that the Soviet leaders were becoming interested in reaching an agreement on strategic arms limitation. They also appeared to be ready to hold serious talks on the anomalous situation in Berlin, which, almost a quarter century after the war had ended, was still a divided city and a constant source of tension, not just between the Soviets and the United States, but also between the Soviets and Western Europe. We sensed that they were looking for a face-saving formula that would lessen the risk of confrontation in the Mideast. And we had some solid evidence that they were anxious for an expansion of trade.

It was often said that the key to a Vietnam settlement lay in Moscow and Peking rather than in Hanoi. Without continuous and massive aid from either or both of the Communist giants, the leaders of North Vietnam would not have been able to carry on the war for more than a few months. Thanks to the Sino-Soviet split, however, the North Vietnamese had been extremely successful in playing off the Soviets and the Chinese against each other by turning support for their war effort into a touchstone of Communist orthodoxy and a requisite for keeping North Vietnam from settling into the opposing camp in the struggle for domination within the Communist world. This situation became a strain, particularly for the Soviets. Aside from wanting to keep Hanoi from going over to Peking, Moscow had little stake in the outcome of the North Vietnamese cause, especially as it increasingly worked against Moscow's own major interests vis-à-vis the United States. While I understood that the Soviets were not entirely free agents where their support for North Vietnam was concerned, I nonetheless planned to bring maximum pressure to bear on them in this area.

I was sure that Brezhnev and Kosygin had been no more anxious for me to win in 1968 than Khrushchev had been in 1960. The prospect of having to deal with a Republican administration—and a Nixon administration at that—undoubtedly caused anxiety in Moscow. In fact, I suspected that the Soviets might have counseled the North Vienamese to offer to begin the Paris talks in the hope that the bombing halt would tip the balance to Humphrey in the election—and if that was their strategy, it had almost worked.

After the election Johnson proposed that as President and President-elect he and I attend a summit meeting with the Soviets in the period before my inauguration. I understood his desire to make one last dramatic demonstration of his dedication to peace, but I saw no solid basis for concluding that the Soviet leaders were prepared to negotiate seriously on any critical issue. Nor did I want to be boxed in by any decisions that were made before I took office.

The most that might come from such a last-minute summit would be a "spirit," like the "Spirit of Glassboro" that followed Johnson's meeting with Kosygin in New Jersey in 1967 or the "Spirit of Camp David" that followed

Eisenhower's meeting with Khrushchev in 1959. It was my feeling that such "spirits" were almost entirely spurious and that they actually worked heavily to the Soviets' advantage. Since public opinion played no role whatever in the Communist system, such summit "spirit" was a one-way street in their direction, because the optimistic attitudes that characterized American public opinion after a summit made it harder for us to assume a tough line in our postsummit dealings with the Soviets.

During the transition period Kissinger and I developed a new policy for dealing with the Soviets. Since U.S.–Soviet interests as the world's two competing nuclear superpowers were so widespread and overlapping, it was unrealistic to separate or compartmentalize areas of concern. Therefore we decided to link progress in such areas of Soviet concern as strategic arms limitation and increased trade with progress in areas that were important to us—Vietnam, the Mideast, and Berlin. This concept became known as linkage.

Lest there be any doubt of my seriousness in pursuing this policy, I purposely announced it at my first press conference when asked a question about starting SALT talks. I said, "What I want to do is to see to it that we have strategic arms talks in a way and at a time that will promote, if possible, progress on outstanding political problems at the same time—for example, on the problem of the Mideast and on other outstanding problems in which the United States and the Soviet Union acting together can serve the cause of peace."

Linkage was something uncomfortably new and different for the Soviets, and I was not surprised when they bridled at the restraints it imposed on our relationship. It would take almost two years of patient and hard-nosed determination on our part before they would accept that linkage with what we wanted from them was the price they would have to pay for getting any of the things they wanted from us.

We made our first contacts with the Soviets during the transition period. In mid-December Kissinger met with a Soviet UN diplomat who was, as we knew, actually an intelligence officer. I wanted it made clear that I was not taken in by any of the optimistic rhetoric that had characterized so much of recent Soviet–American relations. Kissinger therefore stated that while the tendency during the last few years had been to emphasize how much our two nations supposedly had in common, the Nixon administration felt that there were real and substantial differences between us and that an effort to lessen the tension created by these differences should be the central focus of our relationship. Kissinger also said that I did not want a pre-inauguration summit meeting and that if they held one with Johnson I would have to state publicly that I would not be bound by it. Nothing was heard about this summit project.

We received a prompt reply from Moscow. Our UN contact reported that the Soviet leadership was "not pessimistic" because of the election of a Republican President. He said that the Soviet leadership had expressed an interest in knowing if I desired to "open channels of communication." It was with this in mind that I said in my inaugural address, "After a period of confrontation, we are entering an era of negotiation. Let all nations know that during this administration our lines of communication will be open."

2. Nixon's Address to the Nation (1973)

President Nixon had inherited the unwanted war in Vietnam but he kept the bloodshed going for more than four years—longer than America's participation in either World War I or World War II. When the North Vietnamese balked at the peace table in Paris in 1972, he launched his awesome "Christmas blitz" against the North Vietnamese capital, thus prompting the so-called cease-fire that Nixon hailed as "peace with honor." By its terms the United States retrieved some 560 prisoners of war and withdrew its remaining 27,000 troops. The South Vietnamese government of dictatorial President Thieu was permitted to receive replacements of weapons from the United States, as well as other kinds of non-troop support. Yet the North Vietnamese forces still occupied about thirty percent of South Vietnam, and they were allowed to retain there about 145,000 troops that were in a position to renew hostilities. Such was the "honorable" peace that North Vietnam immediately flouted and that vanished in about two years. To what extent does Nixon gloss over the truth in this section of his televised report to the nation on January 23, 1973?

Good evening. I have asked for this radio and television time tonight for the purpose of announcing that we today have concluded an agreement to end the war and bring peace with honor in Vietnam and in Southeast Asia. . . .

We must recognize that ending the war is only the first step toward building the peace. All parties must now see to it that this is a peace that lasts, and also a peace that heals, and a peace that not only ends the war in Southeast Asia, but contributes to the prospects of peace in the whole world.

This will mean that the terms of the agreement must be scrupulously adhered to. We shall do everything the agreement requires of us and we shall expect the other parties to do everything it requires of them. We shall also expect other interested nations to help insure that the agreement is carried out and peace is maintained.

As this long and very difficult war ends, I would like to address a few special words to each of those who have been parties in the conflict.

First, to the people and Government of South Vietnam: By your courage, by your sacrifice, you have won the precious right to determine your own future and you have developed the strength to defend that right. We look forward to working with you in the future, friends in peace as we have been allies in war.

To the leaders of North Vietnam: As we have ended the war through negotiations, let us now build a peace of reconciliation. For our part, we are prepared to make a major effort to help achieve that goal. But just as reciprocity was needed to end the war, so, too, will it be needed to build and strengthen the peace.

2. *Weekly Compilation of Presidential Documents*, IX (1973), pp. 43–44.

THE CEASE-FIRE THAT WAS NEVER KEPT
Reprinted with permission of the Toronto *Star*. Cartoonist Doug Sneyd.

To the other major powers [China, Russia] that have been involved even indirectly: Now is the time for mutual restraint so that the peace we have achieved can last.

And finally, to all of you who are listening, the American people: Your steadfastness in supporting our insistence on peace with honor has made peace with honor possible. I know that you would not have wanted that peace jeopardized. With our secret negotiations at the sensitive stage they were in during this recent period, for me to have discussed publicly our efforts to secure peace would not only have violated our understanding with North Vietnam, it would have seriously harmed and possibly destroyed the chances for peace. Therefore, I know that you now can understand why, during these past several weeks, I have not made any public statements about those efforts.

The important thing was not to talk about peace, but to get peace and to get the right kind of peace. This we have done.

Now that we have achieved an honorable agreement, let us be proud that America did not settle for a peace that would have betrayed our allies, that would have abandoned our prisoners of war, or that would have ended the war for us but would have continued the war for the 50 million people of Indochina. Let us be proud of the 2½ million young Americans who served in Vietnam, who served with honor and distinction in one of the most selfless enterprises in the history of nations. And let us be proud of those who sacrificed, who gave their lives so that the people of South Vietnam might live in freedom and so that the world might live in peace.

3. Canadians See Neither Peace Nor Honor (1973)

Much of the free world, in addition to the Communist countries, had deplored the American intervention in Vietnam. Canada, to which many draft-dodgers had fled, was conspicuous among the critics. The "peace with honor" that Nixon announced was actually violated in a wholesale fashion by both sides from the day of signing in January 1973 until the disgraceful rout in April 1975. During the first year of "peace" alone an estimated 50,000 Vietnamese were killed. To what extent does the following editorial from the Toronto Star *seem justified in light of the facts?*

It's evidently impossible for a president of the United States to come clean about Viet Nam; there is too much shame and failure in the American record there to be even hinted at. Thus President Nixon kept proclaiming the achievement of "peace with honor" last night, when all he can really promise is that the Americans are going to pull out of that wretched war in fairly good order, with their prisoners returned, instead of fleeing in abject humiliation.

"Exit with face saved" would have been a more accurate phrase than peace with honor; for, whatever the terms of the Paris agreement may say, it's obvious that there is no guarantee of peace between North and South Viet Nam. Hanoi maintains its goal of unifying all Viet Nam under Communist rule, while the government of South Viet Nam and a considerable number of its people mean to resist that dubious blessing.

The president felt obliged to insist that the principal war aim of the United States had been achieved; he told the South Vietnamese that their right to determine their own future has been won. That's uncertain, to put it mildly, since they have so far been incapable of defeating the Communists with the full participation of the United States on their side.

It would have been enough good news for Nixon to say what he can say credibly, that the United States is getting out. Not that the basic purpose of the American intervention—to keep South Viet Nam from being taken over by the Communists—was dishonorable. But the way the Americans fought the war has been calamitous for both Viet Nam and the United States.

The United States waged war with incredible stupidity and callousness. Counting social as well as material and human destruction, it probably harmed its ally South Viet Nam more than its enemy North Viet Nam. The land was transformed from one of hamlets and villages to one of shantytown cities living off the American war machine. Bombing and clearance orders—in South Viet Nam—created millions of refugees and caused hundreds of thousands of civilian casualties. In terms of military efficiency, the profligate

3. The Toronto *Star*, Jan. 24, 1973. Reprinted with permission of the Toronto *Star*.

American operation was comparable to shooting mosquitoes with a machine-gun. The Viet Cong and the North Vietnamese troops were equally callous, but couldn't match the American power to destroy and disrupt.

Let us hope that peace is indeed near for the tortured people of Viet Nam. But the prospects are highly doubtful, and depend heavily on the willingness of the Soviet Union and China on one side, and the United States on the other, to restrain their respective allies. For now, it is sufficient to know that the most blunderingly destructive element of all—the American presence —is to be removed.

4. The Expulsion from Vietnam (1975)

Early in 1975 the North Vietnamese launched a furious assault, and the South Vietnamese defenses crumpled like cardboard. As Saigon was caving in, helicopters airlifted out American personnel and also rescued an estimated 140,000 Vietnamese who were supposedly marked for extermination by the victors. The escape from Vietnam was a defeat not so much for the United States as it was for the American policy of supporting Communist-threatened regimes in distant parts of the globe. The American forces had fought the enemy to a standstill and had withdrawn "with honor" after fighting to at least a stalemate in 1973. The South Vietnamese, with continued American military supplies, lost the war and the United States consequently lost face. In the light of these circumstances, was the Des Moines *Register* unduly critical in its assessment?

The war in Vietnam, like the war in Cambodia, has ended with a victory for the Communist-led revolutionary forces and a defeat for the upholders of the old ruling classes. That includes the United States, which for 25 years —since the first aid to France in support of that country's effort to maintain its Indochina colony—has been upholding the old regimes.

The incredible thing, still, is the stubborn failure of United States leaders to see what was going on, to see the hopelessness of their cause and to get out. A quarter of a century!

The American public and press must share the blame for this disaster of American foreign policy. With rare and honorable exceptions, Americans went along, bemused by the concept of American leadership of a "free world" struggle against Communism.

A succession of American presidents, secretaries of state, defense secretaries and generals told the people over and over that America was winning. They distorted the evidence; they told outright lies. The facts were that the side America was supporting was losing.

Each American president since Eisenhower has had the opportunity to move toward a political compromise in Vietnam. Each one lacked the courage to take a step which he feared might look like an American "defeat" or, as President Ford and Secretary Kissinger have been putting it, like a failure to make good on a commitment.

In the end, this policy led to a much worse defeat and a much worse dis-

4. Des Moines *Register*, April 30, 1975. Reprinted with permission of the Des Moines *Register*.

Lou Grant, Copyright © 1975, The Oakland *Tribune*.
Reprinted with permission Los Angeles *Times* Syndicate.

crediting of America's international behavior than early withdrawal would have meant.

The fear of Communist takeovers, of a phony "domino" theory of collapsing "democracies", has been dominant in U.S. policy—even after the moves toward détente with the big Communist countries.

The misguided quarter century is now behind America, as President Ford said recently, although not in those words. Instead of losing face or encouraging Communism or losing confidence of the rest of the world, the United States probably will gain in these respects from finally ending its military role in Asia.

The nation would have gained respect sooner if the government had acted on its own—10, 15 or more years ago. Instead, action to end the Indochina connection came only after the arousal of public opinion which drove one president out of public life, and led to the near-impeachment of another on charges of abuse of constitutional power. Even the ending was a foot-dragging business with Ford, Kissinger and Ambassador Graham Martin holding the line in Saigon.

But public opinion finally did prevail; the machinery of democracy did work, though slowly. The country will be stronger, wiser and more effective in world affairs, we believe, as a result of ending this misadventure. The illusions of imperialism, of world leadership in terms of military power, of executive primacy in foreign affairs—those illusions, we hope and believe, are vanishing.

D. THE MOVE TO IMPEACH NIXON

1. The First Article of Impeachment (1974)

During the Nixon-McGovern campaign of 1972, a bungled burglary had occurred in the Democratic Watergate headquarters in Washington. After Nixon's re-election, evidence turned up that the culprits, with close White House connections, had been working for the Republican Committee for the Re-election of the President (CREEP). A Senate investigating committee uncovered proof that the President had secretly recorded relevant White House conversations on tapes. After much foot-dragging and legal obstruction by Nixon, enough of the damning tapes were surrendered to prove beyond doubt that he had known of the attempted cover-up from an early date and had actively participated in it. After extensive hearings, the House Judiciary Committee voted three articles of impeachment, of which the following, relating to the crime of obstructing justice, was the first. This article was approved on July 27, 1974, by a committee vote of 27 to 11, with all of the Democrats being joined by six Republicans. Assuming that these charges were true, do they add up to "high crimes and misdemeanors" as specified by the Constitution?

1. *House of Representatives Report No. 93–1305* (House Calendar No. 426), 93 Cong., 2 sess., pp. 1–2.

Article I

In his conduct of the office of President of the United States, Richard M. Nixon, in violation of his constitutional oath faithfully to execute the office of President of the United States and, to the best of his ability, preserve, protect, and defend the Constitution of the United States, and in violation of his constitutional duty to take care that the laws be faithfully executed, has prevented, obstructed, and impeded the administration of justice, in that:

On June 17, 1972, and prior thereto, agents of the Committee for the Re-election of the President committed unlawful entry of the headquarters of the Democratic National Committee in Washington, District of Columbia, for the purpose of securing political intelligence. Subsequent thereto, Richard M. Nixon, using the powers of his high office, engaged personally and through his subordinates and agents, in a course of conduct or plan designed to delay, impede, and obstruct the investigation of such unlawful entry; to cover up, conceal and protect those responsible; and to conceal the existence and scope of other unlawful covert activities.

The means used to implement this course of conduct or plan included one or more of the following:

(1) making or causing to be made false or misleading statements to lawfully authorized investigative officers and employees of the United States;

(2) withholding relevant and material evidence or information from lawfully authorized investigative officers and employees of the United States;

(3) approving, condoning, acquiescing in, and counseling witnesses with respect to the giving of false or misleading statements to lawfully authorized investigative officers and employees of the United States and false or misleading testimony in duly instituted judicial and congressional proceedings;

(4) interfering or endeavoring to interfere with the conduct of investigations by the Department of Justice of the United States, the Federal Bureau of Investigation, the Office of Watergate Special Prosecution Force, and Congressional Committees;

(5) approving, condoning, and acquiescing in, the surreptitious payment of substantial sums of money for the purpose of obtaining the silence or influencing the testimony of witnesses, potential witnesses or individuals who participated in such unlawful entry and other illegal activities;

(6) endeavoring to misuse the Central Intelligence Agency, an agency of the United States;

(7) disseminating information received from officers of the Department of Justice of the United States to subjects of investigations conducted by lawfully authorized investigative officers and employees of the United States, for the purpose of aiding and assisting such subjects in their attempts to avoid criminal liability;

(8) making false or misleading public statements for the purpose of deceiving the people of the United States into believing that a thorough and complete investigation had been conducted with respect to allegations of misconduct on the part of personnel of the executive branch of the United States and personnel of the Committee for the Re-election of the President, and that there was no involvement of such personnel in such misconduct; or

(9) endeavoring to cause prospective defendants, and individuals duly tried and convicted, to expect favored treatment and consideration in return for their silence or false testimony, or rewarding individuals for their silence or false testimony.

In all of this, Richard M. Nixon has acted in a manner contrary to his trust as President and subversive of constitutional government, to the great prejudice of the cause of law and justice and to the manifest injury of the people of the United States.

Wherefore Richard M. Nixon, by such conduct, warrants impeachment and trial, and removal from office.

2. Impeachment as a Partisan Issue (1974)

The second and third articles of impeachment approved by the House Judiciary Committee related to (a) repeated abuses of Presidential power and to (b) prolonged contempt of Congress. The second article passed the Committee by a tally of 28 to 10; all Democrats, as well as seven Republicans, voted yea. The third article charged Nixon with contempt of Congress for refusing to comply with eight subpoenas for the White House tapes. It was regarded as the least damaging of the three, for it failed to gain broad partisan backing when it squeezed through by a narrow vote of 21 to 17. Even after his complete disgrace, Nixon had millions of supporters who believed that his removal was unjustified. The following is a part of the minority report of the House Committee, signed by 10 of its 17 Republican members, and dated August 20, 1974, eleven days after Nixon's formal resignation. What light does it throw on the alleged partisanship of the impeachment move?

Richard Nixon served his country in elective office for the better part of three decades and, in the main, he served it well. Each of the undersigned voted for him, worked for and with him in election campaigns, and supported the major portion of his legislative program during his tenure as President. Even at the risk of seeming paradoxical, since we were prepared to vote for his impeachment on proposed Article I had he not resigned his office, we hope that in the fullness of time it is his accomplishments—and they were many and significant—rather than the conduct to which this Report is addressed for which Richard Nixon is primarily remembered in history.

We know that it has been said, and perhaps some will continue to say, that Richard Nixon was "hounded from office" by his political opponents and media critics. We feel constrained to point out, however, that it was

2. *Ibid.*, p. 361.

Richard Nixon who impeded the FBI's investigation of the Watergate affair by wrongfully attempting to implicate the Central Intelligence Agency; it was Richard Nixon, who created and preserved the evidence of that transgression and who, *knowing that it had been subpoenaed by this Committee and the Special Prosecutor,* concealed its terrible import, even from his own counsel, until he could do so no longer. And it was a unanimous Supreme Court of the United States which, in an opinion authored by the Chief Justice whom he appointed, ordered Richard Nixon to surrender that evidence to the Special Prosecutor, to further the ends of justice.

The tragedy that finally engulfed Richard Nixon had many facets. One was the very self-inflicted nature of the harm. It is striking that such an able, experienced and perceptive man, whose ability to grasp the global implications of events little noticed by others may well have been unsurpassed by any of his predecessors, should fail to comprehend the damage that accrued daily to himself, his Administration, and to the Nation, as day after day, month after month, he imprisoned the truth about his role in the Watergate cover-up so long and so tightly within the solitude of his Oval Office that it could not be unleashed without destroying his Presidency.

3. Nixon Incriminates Himself (1972)

By August 5, 1974, much evidence of Presidential misconduct and wrongdoing had been uncovered, but where was the high crime? Where was the "smoking pistol"? It finally surfaced on that day when Nixon, forced by a unanimous decision of the Supreme Court to yield crucial tape recordings, revealed a White House conversation of June 23, 1972. In it the President was heard instructing his chief aide to use the Central Intelligence Agency to quash an investigation by the Federal Bureau of Investigation. Obstruction of justice of this type was a clear-cut crime. Support for Nixon in Congress collapsed, and he was faced with the dilemma of resigning or of being thrown out of office without retirement benefits amounting to more than $150,000 a year. He wisely chose to announce his resignation on August 8. How damning is the evidence in the following transcript of the conversation of June 23, 1972?

TRANSCRIPT OF A RECORDING OF A MEETING
BETWEEN THE PRESIDENT AND H. R. HALDEMAN,
THE OVAL OFFICE, JUNE 23, 1972, FROM 10:04 TO
1:39 A.M.

HALDEMAN. Okay—that's fine. Now, on the investigation, you know, the Democratic break-in thing, we're back to the—in the, the problem area because the FBI is not under control, because Gray doesn't exactly know how to control them, and they have, their investigation is now leading into some productive areas, because they've been able to trace the money, not through the money itself, but through the bank, you know, sources—the banker himself. And, and it goes in some directions we don't want it to

3. *Statement of Information* Appendix 3, *Hearings before the Committee on the Judiciary,* House of Representatives, 93rd Cong., 2d sess., pursuant to HR 803, p. 39.

go. Ah, also there have been some things, like an informant came in off the street to the FBI in Miami, who was a photographer or has a friend who is a photographer who developed some films through this guy, Barker, and the films had pictures of Democratic National Committee letter head documents and things. So I guess, so it's things like that are gonna, that are filtering in. Mitchell came up with yesterday, and John Dean analyzed very carefully last night and concludes, concurs now with Mitchell's recommendation that the only way to solve this, and we're set up beautifully to do it, ah, in that and that . . . the only network that paid any attention to it last night was NBC . . . they did a massive story on the Cuban . . .

PRESIDENT. That's right.

HALDEMAN. . . . thing.

PRESIDENT. Right.

HALDEMAN. That the way to handle this is for us to have Walters call Pat Gray and just say, "Stay the hell out of this . . . this is ah, business here we don't want you to go any further on it." That's not an unusual development, . . .

PRESIDENT. Um huh.

HALDEMAN. . . . and, uh, that would take care of it.

PRESIDENT. What about Pat Gray, ah, you mean he doesn't want to?

HALDEMAN. Pat does want to. He doesn't know how to, and he doesn't have, he doesn't have any basis for doing it. Given this, he will then have the basis. He'll call Mark Felt in, and the two of them . . . and Mark Felt wants to cooperate because . . .

PRESIDENT. Yeah.

HALDEMAN. . . . he's ambitious . . .

PRESIDENT. Yeah.

HALDEMAN. Ah, he'll call him in and say, "We've got the signal from across the river to, to put the hold on this." And that will fit rather well because the FBI agents who are working the case, at this point, feel that's what it it. This is CIA.

PRESIDENT. But they've traced the money to 'em.

HALDEMAN. Well they have, they've traced to a name, but they haven't gotten to the guy yet.

PRESIDENT. Would it be somebody here?

HALDEMAN. Ken Dahlberg.

PRESIDENT. Who the hell is Ken Dahlberg?

HALDEMAN. He's ah, he gave $25,000 in Minnesota and ah, the check went directly in to this, to this guy Barker.

PRESIDENT. Maybe he's a . . . bum.

•　　　•　　　•

PRESIDENT. He didn't get this from the committee though, from Stans.

HALDEMAN. Yeah. It is. It is. It's directly traceable and there's some more through some Texas people in—that went to the Mexican bank which they can also trace to the Mexican bank . . . they'll get their names today. And [*pause*].

PRESIDENT. Well, I mean, ah, there's no way . . . I'm just thinking if they don't cooperate, what do they say? They they, they were approached by the Cubans. That's what Dahlberg has to say, the Texans too. Is that the idea?

HALDEMAN. Well, if they will. But then we're relying on more and more people all the time. That's the problem. And ah, they'll stop if we could, if we take this other step.

PRESIDENT. All right. Fine.

HALDEMAN. And, and they seem to feel the thing to do is get them to stop?

PRESIDENT. Right, fine.

HALDEMAN. They say the only way to do that is from White House instructions. And it's got to be to Helms and, ah, what's his name . . . ? Walters.

PRESIDENT. Walters.

HALDEMAN. And the proposal would be that Ehrlichman [*coughs*] and I call them in . . .

PRESIDENT. All right, fine.

HALDEMAN. . . . and say, ah . . .

PRESIDENT. How do you call him in, I mean you just, well, we protected Helms from one hell of a lot of things.

HALDEMAN. That's what Ehrlichman says.

PRESIDENT. Of course, this is a, this is a Hunt, you will—that will uncover a lot of things. You open that scab there's a hell of a lot of things and that we just feel that it would be very detrimental to have this thing go any further. This involves these Cubans, Hunt, and a lot of hanky-panky that we have nothing to do with ourselves. Well what the hell, did Mitchell know about this thing to any much of a degree?

HALDEMAN. I think so. I don't think he knew the details, but I think he knew.

PRESIDENT. He didn't know how it was going to be handled though, with Dahlberg and the Texans and so forth? Well who was the asshole that did? [*Unintelligible*] Is it Liddy? Is that the fellow? He must be a little nuts.

HALDEMAN. He is.

PRESIDENT. I mean he just isn't well screwed on is he? Isn't that the problem?

HALDEMAN. No, but he was under pressure, apparently, to get more information, and as he got more pressure, he pushed the people harder to move harder on . . .

PRESIDENT. Pressure from Mitchell?

HALDEMAN. Apparently.

PRESIDENT. Oh, Mitchell, Mitchell was at the point that you made on this, that exactly what I need from you is on the—

HALDEMAN. Gemstone, yeah.

PRESIDENT. All right, fine, I understand it all. We won't second-guess Mitchell and the rest. Thank God it wasn't Colson.

HALDEMAN. The FBI interviewed Colson yesterday. They determined that would be a good thing to do.

PRESIDENT. Um hum.

HALDEMAN. Ah, to have him take a . . .

PRESIDENT. Uh hum.

HALDEMAN. An interrogation, which he did, and that, the FBI guys working the case had concluded that there were one or two possibilities, one, that this was a White House, they don't think that there is anything at the Election Committee, they think it was either a White House operation and they had some obscure reasons for it, nonpolitical. . . .

PRESIDENT. Uh huh.

HALDEMAN. . . . or it was a . . .

PRESIDENT. Cuban thing—

HALDEMAN. Cubans and the CIA. And after their interrogation of, of . . .

PRESIDENT. . . . Colson.

HALDEMAN. Colson, yesterday, they concluded it was not the White House, but are now convinced it is a CIA thing, so the CIA turnoff would . . .

PRESIDENT. Well, not sure of their analysis, I'm not going to get that involved. I'm [*unintelligible*].

HALDEMAN. No, sir. We don't want you to.

PRESIDENT. You call them in.

•   •   •

PRESIDENT. Good. Good deal. Play it tough. That's the way they play it and that's the way we are going to play it.

HALDEMAN. O.K. We'll do it.

PRESIDENT. Yeah, when I saw that news summary item, I of course knew it was a bunch of crap, but I thought, ah, well it's good to have them off on this wild hair thing because when they start bugging us, which they have, we'll know our little boys will not know how to handle it. I hope they will though. You never know. Maybe, you think about it. Good!

•   •   •

PRESIDENT. When you get in these people . . . when you get these people in, say: "Look, the problem is that this will open the whole, the whole Bay of Pigs thing, and the President just feels that" ah, without going into the details . . . don't, don't lie to them to the extent to say there is no involvement, but just say this is sort of a comedy of errors, bizarre, without getting into it, "the President believes that it is going to open the whole Bay of Pigs thing up again. And, ah because these people are plugging for, for keeps and that they should call the FBI in and say that we wish for the country, don't go any further into this case," period!

HALDEMAN. OK.

PRESIDENT. That's the way to put it, do it straight. [*Unintelligible*]

HALDEMAN. Get more done for our cause by the opposition than by us at this point.

PRESIDENT. You think so?

HALDEMAN. I think so, yeah.

TRANSCRIPT OF A RECORDING OF A MEETING
BETWEEN THE PRESIDENT AND H. R. HALDEMAN,
THE OVAL OFFICE, JUNE 23, 1972, FROM 1:04 TO
1:13 P.M.

[*Background noise, sound of writing and some unintelligible conversation*]

HALDEMAN. [*On the phone*] [*Unintelligible*] Where are they? Okay. I'll be up in just a minute.

[*40-second pause, with sounds of writing*]

HALDEMAN. I see a time way back [*unintelligible*] might find out about that report before we do anything.

PRESIDENT. [*Unintelligible*]

[*35-second pause*]

PRESIDENT. Okay [*unintelligible*] and, ah, just, just postpone the [*unintelligible, with noises*] hearings [*15-second unintelligible, with noises*] and all that garbage. Just say that I have to take a look at the primaries [*unintelligible*] recover [*unintelligible*] I just don't [*unintelligible*] very bad, to have this fellow Hunt, ah, you know, ah, it's, he, he knows too damn much and he was involved, we happen to know that. And that it gets out that the whole, this is all involved in the Cuban thing, that it's a fiasco, and it's going to make the FB, ah CIA look bad, it's going to make Hunt look bad, and it's likely to blow the whole, uh, Bay of Pigs thing which we think would be very unfortunate for CIA and for the country at this time, and for American foreign policy, and he just better tough it and lay it on them. Isn't that what you . . .

HALDEMAN. Yeah, that's, that's the basis we'll do it on and just leave it at that.

PRESIDENT. I don't want them to get any ideas we're doing it because our concern is political.

HALDEMAN. Right.

PRESIDENT. And at the same time, I wouldn't tell them it is not political . . .

HALDEMAN. Right.

PRESIDENT. I would just say "Look, it's because of the Hunt involvement," just say [*unintelligible, with noise*] sort of thing, the whole cover is, uh, basically this [*unintelligible*].

HALDEMAN. [*Unintelligible*] Well they've got some pretty good ideas on this need thing.

PRESIDENT. George Schultz did a good paper on that, I read it . . .

[*Unintelligible voices heard leaving the room*]

4. A Critical Canadian Viewpoint (1974)

From the objective vantage point of Canada, the Toronto *Star* newspaper pronounced this judgment on Nixon's resignation. Is it unduly harsh?

Richard Nixon leaves the presidency the way he operated it—dishonestly.

The man who approved the Watergate cover-up six days after the break-in continued to hide his guilt right to the end. In his resignation speech last night, there was no admission of wrong-doing, no acceptance of personal responsibility for the scandal that ripped apart U.S. society, paralyzed its government and, for a time, threatened to destroy public confidence in the democratic system.

It is happily true that ultimately the process that forced Nixon from office was a triumph of the system he tried to subvert. A free press in its role as watchdog uncovered the scandal and an independent judiciary affirmed the principle that under the rule of law, no men are above the law. The checks and balances needed to make democracy work came through when it counted.

All this is the positive side of Watergate, and its significance is great. An open society has openly met its problems and emerged healthier and stronger. The American system has shown that it could meet stern tests. The confidence of ordinary people in the institutions that govern them has been restored, and they can make a fresh start with a fresh president. The western world, which depends on U.S. leadership, is grateful.

But it wasn't the rule of law and his own personal culpability that Nixon cited as his reason for leaving office. No one would know from his speech last night that he had done anything wrong. Oh, some errors in judgment, sure. But nothing serious. The reason he gave for leaving rested on the narrow base that he had lost the political support in Congress that he needed both to stay in office and to fight the attempts to oust him.

If 20 or so senators hadn't changed their minds, he'd still be in there fighting.

That in effect is what he was saying.

This manner of leaving does not satisfy the rule of law, for if it is true that no man is above the law, it must also be true that all men are equal before it.

So what is Richard Nixon's punishment for breaking the law? The $60,000 pension that he gets because he resigned and which he would have lost if he had been ousted by impeachment? Where is the equality in a jail sentence for John Dean, the former presidential counsel whose Watergate testimony first accused Nixon, while the man who gave him his orders goes free? Where is equality in proceeding with cover-up charges against former presidential chief-of-staff H. R. Haldeman with the prime evidence a tape on which Nixon is approving the cover-up?

If Nixon had openly admitted his guilt and responsibility, then it would at least be clear that his resignation was his punishment. This was the

4. The Toronto *Star*, Aug. 9, 1974. Reprinted with permission of the Toronto *Star*.

formula followed by Spiro Agnew when he resigned as vice-president. He pleaded guilty but avoided jail. One might then argue whether the punishment fitted the crime, but at least the record would be clear about guilt.

At present there is no such clear-cut record. Nixon is out, but he has admitted nothing. Congress, by halting the impeachment process, has not declared its judgment of his actions.

This judgment may yet come. Leon Jaworski, the special Watergate prosecutor, has made it clear he is prevented by no agreement or understanding from bringing charges against Nixon. State courts or even private citizens could bring suits against him. More taped conversations are to be made public and some of the material may have an impact on the public's judgment about whether a former president should be pursued like a common criminal.

But don't count on it. The Americans have been sweating through Watergate for a long time and many are tired of it. There is a strong feeling that a man shouldn't be kicked when he is down. Many undoubtedly will argue that every effort should go towards a fresh start rather than try further to cleanse the past

If this is the course then America will be whole again, but the stain will remain. Nixon's manipulations will have succeeded. The phony transcripts. The lies. The obstruction. They did not save his office but they saved him from the law.

He left politics as he arrived. Tricky Dick.

[*Despite the three long categories of accusations voted by the House Judiciary Committee, Nixon was not impeached by the full House, tried by the Senate, or even convicted in the courts of any crime. The closest he came to conviction was his uncontested disbarment as a lawyer by the Appellate Division of the state Supreme Court of New York. The decision (July 8, 1976), by a 4 to 1 vote, was the most severe punishment that this body could impose. As for obstruction of justice, the Court found Nixon guilty on five specifications, including improper interference with an FBI investigation of the Watergate break-in; the improper authorization of bribes to silence conspirators; and the improper encouragement of others to commit perjury by concealing evidence of wrongdoing.*]

5. Nixon Accepts a Presidential Pardon (1974)

To complicate the Watergate uproar, Vice-President Agnew, facing unrelated criminal charges, avoided jail by resigning in October 1973. Nixon, pursuant to Amendment XXV of the Constitution, chose as his successor Gerald R. Ford, House minority leader. For about a month the non-elected President enjoyed a "honeymoon," which he abruptly ended by granting Nixon "a full, free, and absolute pardon" for "all offenses against the United States which he, Richard Nixon, has committed or may have committed or taken part in" during his presidency. Nixon promptly accepted the pardon but he was careful not to confess that he had committed any crimes. Mistakes, indecision, poor judgment, yes, but crimes, no. Yet, as President Ford agreed, testifying before a House Judiciary Committee, acceptance of the pardon is "tantamount to an

5. *San Francisco Chronicle,* September 9, 1974.

admission of guilt. . . ." Moreover, many of Nixon's admirers felt that he had humbled himself enough by admitting remorse for acts that he had committed in the line of duty for what he regarded to be the good of the country. Is Nixon's self-justification convincing?

I have been informed that President Ford has granted me a full and absolute pardon for any charges which might be brought against me for actions taken during the time I was President of the United States.

In accepting this pardon, I hope that his compassionate act will contribute to lifting the burden of Watergate from our country.

Here in California, my perspective on Watergate is quite different than it was while I was embattled in the midst of the controversy, and while I was still subject to the unrelenting daily demands of the presidency itself.

Looking back on what is still in my mind a complex and confusing maze of events, decisions, pressures and personalities, one thing I can see clearly now is that I was wrong in not acting more decisively and more forthrightly in dealing with Watergate, particularly when it reached the stage of judicial proceedings and grew from a political scandal into a national tragedy.

No words can describe the depths of my regret and pain at the anguish my mistakes over Watergate have caused the nation and the presidency—a nation I so deeply love and an institution I so greatly respect.

I know many fair-minded people believe that my motivations and action in the Watergate affair were intentionally self-serving and illegal. I now understand how my own mistakes and misjudgments have contributed to that belief and seemed to support it. This burden is the heaviest one of all to bear.

That the way I tried to deal with Watergate was the wrong way is a burden I shall bear for every day of the life that is left to me.

THOUGHT PROVOKERS

1. What is the role of the Supreme Court in the American governmental system? Is its independence compromised because the President has the exclusive power to nominate justices? Would some other system—for example, national election of justices—be better? What, precisely, were the differences between the "Warren Court" of the 1950's and 1960's and the "Burger Court" of the 1970's and 1980's?
2. Was Nixon's Cambodian incursion courageous or foolhardy? Did it shorten or lengthen the war? What effect did the public outcry against the incursion have on the administration's conduct of foreign policy?
3. What was the connection between "détente" and the end of the war in Vietnam? Did Nixon's policies toward the Soviet Union and China mark a fundamental re-orientation in American foreign policy, or simply a convenient maneuver to extricate the United States from the Indochina War?
4. Why was the resolution to impeach President Nixon passed? What exactly did it name as the grounds for impeachment? Nixon later said that he gave his enemies a sword and they cut him down with it. Is that an accurate description of what happened? Should a president be forgiven for lying to the public under some circumstances?

47. *The Carter Interlude and the Reagan Revolution*

> *I went over the complete inventory of U.S. nuclear war-heads, which is really a sobering experience.*
>
> PRESIDENT JIMMY CARTER, diary entry, December 28, 1977.

PROLOGUE: Little-known Jimmy Carter, promising that he "would never lie," capitalized on the Watergate-bred disillusion with Nixon and Ford to win the presidency in 1976. But Carter, though full of good intentions, seemed unable to master the art of exercising power from the White House. He negotiated a new arms-control agreement with the Soviets, but failed to secure its approval by the Senate. He did score notable diplomatic gains in Central America, by signing a treaty giving control of the Panama Canal to the Panamanians. He also won laurels in the Middle East, by presiding over a grueling but ultimately successful reconciliation between the leaders of Egypt and Israel. These successes were soon overshadowed, however, by spiralling inflation, sky-rocketing interest rates, a near-doubling of oil prices in 1979, the Soviet invasion of Afghanistan, and, most of all, by the capture, in November, 1979, of some fifty American hostages by Iranian revolutionaries. Crippled by these blows, Carter was no match for Ronald Reagan, the powerful Republican candidate who emerged victorious in the presidential campaign of 1980. President Reagan set out immediately to implement a virtual revolution in American politics. He attacked head-on the big-government legacy of the New Deal and the Great Society. He slashed the federal budget for social programs, induced Congress to pass a sweeping tax-cut—and called for a massive expansion of military expenditures. "Reaganomics" soon produced deficits in the federal budget in the hundreds-of-billions-of-dollars range, and pushed unemployment to the highest levels since the Great Depression. But Reagan stood by his guns in the hope that his policies would kill the ogre of inflation that had stalked the economy for more than a decade, and lay the foundation for a sustained economic recovery. Meanwhile, Reagan strained relations with the European allies with his revival of Cold War rhetoric and repudiation of "détente."

A. RELINQUISHING CONTROL OF THE PANAMA CANAL

1. Secretary of State Vance Favors Letting Go of the Canal (1977)

Four presidents, beginning with Lyndon Johnson, had tried to negotiate with the government of Panama agreements giving control of the Panama Canal to the Panamanians. To many Latin Americans, the American-administered Canal Zone was an offensive imperialist intrusion by the giant of the North—an unwelcome reminder of Theodore

---

1. *Hearings before the Committee on Foreign Relations, United States Senate,* 95 Cong., 1 sess., pp. 10–15 (September 26, 1977).

Roosevelt's "big-stick" diplomacy at the turn of the century. It fell to the Carter administration to bring these long negotiations to a successful conclusion. Yet many voices were raised in the United States against the alleged "giveaway," and the administration had a difficult task convincing Congress and the public that giving up control of the canal served the nation's best interests. In Secretary of State Cyrus Vance's testimony to the Senate Foreign Relations Committee, excerpted here, how does he defend the new Panama Canal treaties? What benefits does he see flowing from America's withdrawal from the Panamanian isthmus?

Secretary VANCE. Thank you very much, Mr. Chairman and members of the committee. I and my colleagues appreciate very much the opportunity to meet with you today to discuss these vitally important treaties. Today I seek your support for new treaties governing the Panama Canal.

WHAT TREATIES DO AND ARE

First, these treaties protect and advance the national interests of both the United States and Panama.

Second, they provide for an open, neutral, secure, and efficiently operated canal for this hemisphere, and for other nations throughout the world.

Third, they will promote constructive and positive relationships between the United States and other nations in this hemisphere.

These treaties, in my judgment, will gain us respect among other nations of the world, both large and small, because of the responsible way they resolve complex and emotional issues which have been with us for most of this century.

The treaties are the culmination of 13 years' work by four American Presidents of both major political parties, and their Secretaries of State. They are the outcome of patient and skillful negotiation since 1964 by a number of dedicated political leaders, diplomats, and military men. They have been achieved because of valuable counsel and support offered by members of this committee and by representatives of American business and labor who have seen these new treaties as being in their own interest and in the larger national interest.

They are, above all, a triumph for the principle of the peaceful and constructive settlement of disputes between nations. That is a principle we seek to apply in all aspects of American foreign policy.

BASIC QUESTIONS BEING ASKED ABOUT TREATIES

Do these treaties safeguard our national security interest in the Panama Canal? Do they establish a long-term basis for open and effective operation of the canal? Do they enhance our relationships with nations of this hemisphere? Do they place any new burden on the American taxpayer? Do American workers in the Canal Zone get a fair shake? And, without the treaties, what might happen?

I am satisfied in my own mind that these questions have been properly answered, thanks to the skilled and hard bargaining by our negotiators. I will discuss these questions briefly this morning.

LONG-TERM OPERATION OF CANAL

First, as to the long-term operation of the Panama Canal, the United States will control canal operations through a new U.S. Government agency, the Panama Canal Commission, to be supervised by a board composed of five Americans and four Panamanians. The Commission will operate the canal until the end of this century. The present Panama Canal Company will be discontinued.

The United States will maintain responsibility for managing the canal, setting tolls, and enforcing rules of passage until the year 2000. Until the year 2000 the United States will also maintain primary responsibility for the defense of the canal. After that, the United States will have responsibility to maintain the permanent neutrality of the canal to assure that it will remain open to our ships, and those of all other nations on a nondiscriminatory basis.

The treaties further allow for the modernization of the canal through construction of a third lane of locks and foresee the possibility of construction in Panama of a new, sea-level canal. This would provide access for many modern supertankers and warships which are too large to pass through the present canal.

HEMISPHERIC RELATIONS

As to hemispheric relations, I believe the ratification and implementation of these treaties will be the single most positive action to be undertaken in recent years in our relations with Latin America.

Only last month, in Bogota, the democratic Governments of Venezuela, Costa Rica, Colombia, Mexico, and Jamaica issued a joint communique urging the United States and Panama to conclude the new treaties rapidly. For years, Latin American peoples and governments have viewed our negotiations with Panama over the canal as a litmus test of our intentions toward their countries.

These treaties, as negotiated, represent a fair and balanced reconciliation of the interests of the United States and Panama. They create, as has been said already this morning, a partnership under which our two countries can join in the peaceful and efficient operation of the canal. They symbolize our intentions toward the hemisphere, and they prove once and for all the falsity of the tired charges that we are imperialistic exploiters bent only on extracting Latin American raw materials and using the continent for our own economic interests.

NATIONAL SECURITY ASPECTS

As to national security aspects, representatives of the Joint Chiefs of Staff worked closely with the treaty negotiators on the security provisions, and played a major role in drafting the neutrality treaty. The United States will retain all military bases and facilities, all the lands and waters, that we require for the Panama Canal's defense until the year 2000. We may keep the same force levels which we now maintain in the zone, about 9,300, and can increase them if that is necessary.

After the year 2000, as I indicated earlier, the United States will have a permanent right to maintain the Panama Canal's neutrality, including the right to defend the canal if necessary. Our warships are given the right to use the canal expeditiously. . . .

WHAT IF TREATIES ARE REJECTED?

Now, what if the treaties are rejected? It would be all too easy for me to emphasize today that if 13 years of effort were lost, and these treaties were rejected, our relations with Panama would be shattered, our standing in Latin America damaged immeasurably, and the security of the canal itself placed in jeopardy.

Indeed, all of these things could and might happen if these treaties were not ratified. But that is not the major reason for supporting them.

WHY TREATIES DESERVE SUPPORT

They deserve support because they are in our interest as well as the interest of Panama.

For the people and Government of Panama, there is the knowledge that they eventually will assume full jurisdiction over their own territory. There are also the economic benefits to be gained from canal revenues, and from the guarantees, loans and credits, not grants, we have pledged to consider on their behalf. Panama, as a result, will be a more stable and prosperous country.

For us, there is the knowledge that the Panama Canal will be open, neutral, secure, and efficiently operated, for our benefit and for other nations in the world. We are not appropriating American taxpayers' money to accomplish this. And we will have gained respect throughout Latin America and the world for addressing this issue peacefully and constructively.

It is our interests, not foreign pressures, that led us to these treaties. . . .

U.S. USE OF ITS POWER

Both we and others are under considerable pressure in our domestic economies. There is a tendency toward economic protectionism. And there is a question about the most appropriate ways to use our power in a world grown so complex.

Panama is a small country. It would be all too easy for us to lash out, in impatience and frustration, to tell Panama and Latin America, and other countries around the world, that we intended both to speak loudly and carry a big stick and to turn away from the treaties four Presidents have sought over so long a time.

But that, in my judgment, would not be conduct appropriate to a responsible world power or consonant with the character and ideals of the American people.

Any nation's foreign policy is based, in the end, not just upon its interests, and in Panama our interests are clear and apparent. It is also based upon the nature and will of its people. I believe the American people want to live in peace with their neighbors, want to be strong, but to use their strength with restraint, want all peoples everywhere to have their own chance to better themselves and to live in self-respect. That is all a part of our American tradition.

That is why I am convinced that after the national debate they deserve, these treaties will be approved without reservation by the Senate with the strong support of the American people.

Thank you, Mr. Chairman.

The CHAIRMAN. Thank you very much, Mr. Secretary.

Hon. Ellsworth Bunker, Ambassador-at-Large and conegotiator of the Panama Canal Treaties, Department of State. Ambassador, I understand you do have a prepared statement. I have it before me. You may present it as you see fit.

2. Ronald Reagan Denounces the Panama "Giveaway" (1977)

Among the most outspoken critics of the Panama Canal treaties was former California Governor Ronald Reagan, in 1977 still an "undeclared" candidate for the presidency in 1980. What does he find most objectionable about the proposed treaties? Are his concerns purely nationalistic?

For more than 60 years we have operated the Panama Canal efficiently impartially and on a not-for-profit basis. The nations of the Western Hemisphere have to come to rely on our stable presence there to make sure that their commerce would get through unhindered.

We cannot be certain, if these new treaties go into operation, that key personnel now operating the canal will not leave a great deal sooner than expected, thus bringing into question the smooth operation of the canal. We cannot be certain that, as the American presence withdraws from the Canal Zone, new demands for accelerated withdrawal will not be made under threat of violence. We cannot be certain that outside influences hostile to hemispheric security will not make their presence felt much greater than before in Panama. We cannot be certain that Americans operating the canal will not be harrassed by an unstable and power-hungry dictator.

Fidel Castro, whose interest in exporting revolution is well known, has made quite a show of his friendship for the current military regime in Panama. And just this summer, a delegation from the Soviet Union visited Panama to look into trade, investigate possible plant locations and even the possibility of opening a bank in Panama. It should never surprise us that whenever the United States withdraws its presence or its strong interest

2. *Hearings before the Committee on Foreign Relations, United States Senate,* 95 Cong., 1 sess., pt. 2, pp. 96–103 (October 4–5, 1977).

from any area, the Soviets are ready, willing and often able to exploit the situation. Can we believe that the Panama Canal is any exception?

Although the proposed second treaty would continue indefinitely beyond the expiration of the first one in the year 2000, the question must be asked, does it really provide what it says it will, which is the unilateral ability of the United States to step in to defend the canal if its neutrality is threatened?

I believe we will make a very grave mistake if we let ourselves be inveighed into debating what the treaties do or do not say. Yes, on paper, we are told we have the right to step in—even after we have turned over control and removed our forces. But will we?

We are told by the treaty advocates, there will be unpleasantness and trouble if we don't accept these treaties. The same people then assure us we can march back in if there is trouble. But once we have said, in effect, "We don't want trouble; we'll give up the canal," have we not also said, "If the Government of Panama, encouraged by leftist allies, plays fast and loose with the treaty," we'll decide—since we are giving it up anyway—"why bother?"

I don't believe such a concern is unjustified, given the recent history of our Nation. We have shown a reluctance to meet the responsibility of free world leadership, even on occasion to abandon allies.

We have been told the canal is declining in terms of military importance and yet all but a handful of our navy ships can transit the canal. The great bulk of material bound for our forces in Vietnam went by way of the canal. And who can say what shape our navy will take 20 or 30 years from now? It may very well consist in this missile age of small, fast ships relying on quick accessibility from one ocean to another.

President Carter cites a statement by the Joint Chiefs of Staff that the treaty is satisfactory in terms of our defense needs. I mean no disrespect to these fine men. Yet, in a recent letter to the President, four former Chiefs of Naval Operations—now retired and, therefore, free to speak out on this issue—underscored the importance of our keeping active control of the canal. Admirals Arleigh Burke, Thomas Moorer, Robert Carney, and George Anderson said, in part, "As long as most of the world's combatant and commercial tonnage can transit through the canal, it offers inestimable strategic advantages to the U.S., giving us maximum strength at minimum cost.

"By contrast, the Panama Canal, under control of a potential adversary, would become an immediate crucial problem and prove a serious weakness in the overall U.S. defense capability with enormous consequences for evil."

Our continued presence at the canal inhibits potential adventurers from trying to make international trouble there far better than would a piece of paper granting us the right to return after we had once departed.

It is no secret that the Soviet Union believes control over some vital sea lane "choke points" means dominance of the world's oceans. Our presence at one of the busiest and most important of those "choke points" is a definite deterrent.

There is another factor at work which could be harmful to the security of the hemisphere because it could further question our willingness to maintain a leadership role. Let us remember that, for much of the time, while these treaties were being negotiated, we were doing so (especially in the last 2 years) under repeated threats of violence. True, the threats slackened off this year, possibly because General Torrijos saw victory ahead. Some may believe the threats were a bluff, but the fact remains that we did continue to negotiate and, apparently, made concessions in the face of threats. The President seemed anxious to speed up and bring the matter to a conclusion in spite of his previous declarations that he would never relinquish effective control of the canal.

If we accede to a treaty under such circumstances, will this mark the end of further demands? If there are, indeed, radical guerrillas in Panama (as we are told) ready to blow up the canal if we don't sign a treaty, what assurance do we have that they will be satisfied with the terms of these treaties? Already, the government-sponsored student federation in Panama has issued a manifesto supporting the treaties, but also indicating that "the struggle will continue" so long as there is any American presence at the canal. If they should press Torrijos to ignore these treaties, would we not hear the same arguments from the same people for giving in to those new demands that we are hearing today?

Whether or not these treaties ever go into effect, we can expect trouble from leftist elements in Panama and elsewhere. Yes, failure to ratify the treaty will offer an excuse for demonstrations and riots in Panama and very possibly in the U.S. And, behind the scenes, the Russian Bear will do all it can to destabilize the security of the hemisphere and cause a global whirlwind of unfavorable press aimed at us—not because we didn't ratify the treaty but because that's their normal procedure where we are concerned.

LATIN AMERICA

The treaty advocates say failure to ratify and implement these treaties will harm our relations with all of Latin America. Is it possible they believe they are betting on a sure thing? Historically, our Latin American neighbors have felt the need to be somewhat on guard against a United States which to them is the "Colossus of the North." A natural reaction has been to vote as a group on inter-American matters in international forums. This does not mean, however, that all Latin American nations have identical interests or think alike. As a matter of fact, a surprising number have privately expressed concern about our possible withdrawal from the canal.

Frankly, I believe we can question not only the warnings about possible deterioration in our relations with Latin America if we don't ratify the treaty but also the glowing promises of a new era if we do.

The fact is we do not now have a coherent policy toward our Western Hemisphere neighbors. And we should because, over the next few decades, our continued prosperity, possibly even our survival will be closely linked to that of our neighbors within this hemisphere. I do not believe these treaties are a substitute for such a policy. I do believe that the U.S. negotiating from strength and not meekly yielding legitimate rights and responsibilities out of a desire to avoid unpleasantness, can be truly helpful to the people of Panama and to all the hemisphere.

Some of our neighbors need aid we are in a position to give. With others, the need is for increased technology and trade; and with some, unhindered access to capital for needed development. Once our Government recognizes that we must all sink or swim together maybe we'll stop some of our self-defeating practices. It is self-defeating to throttle a nation's ability to obtain capital because it doesn't run its internal politics precisely as we would like. It is self-defeating to keep a neighbor from buying weapons for its police force because someone in Washington sees terrorists as mere political dissidents. Thus, we encourage more terrorism and hurt a nation's chances for economic recovery.

Our neighbors in Latin America ask that we learn enough about them to have some understanding. Sometimes, their problems are similar, sometimes different but each nation is deserving of understanding.

What especially do the Panamanians want? That isn't an easy question to answer since there is no elected government, nor can we be sure a plebiscite of the people on the treaties would give an accurate answer in view of the nature of the government.

We are left with some educated guesses about the wants of the Panamanian people. Thanks in large part to the canal, the Panamanians have the highest per-capita income in Central America and the third and fourth highest in all of Latin America. But their economy is near bankruptcy. They are plagued by inflation and unemployment while natural resources lie undeveloped.

Contrary to what has been implied about my own position, I do not believe that in rejecting these treaties we should simply demand the status quo and not seek answers to problems regarding our relations with the people of Panama.

Early in this century, we realized our dream of a waterway connecting two great oceans. Panama, then a neglected province of Colombia, also realized a dream—to be free and independent. The two dreams were interrelated. Many in our country thought the canal should be in Nicaragua. The Panamanians knew their only chance to have independence and prosperity lay in the canal being built in Panama. And so it was that Panama ratified the Hay-Bunau-Varilla Treaty months before it was ratified by our own Government.

We have nothing to be ashamed of and much to be proud of. We created one of the great wonders of the world and it is doubtful any other nation could have done so. More than that, however, we have managed the canal fairly for all nations at no profit to ourselves and with great economic benefit to Panama. Not only did we deal fairly with the governments of Panama and Colombia, we also bought every piece of privately owned land in the Canal Zone in fee simple from the individual owners. And may I point out the Canal Zone is not flanked by "Berlin Walls." The people of Panama can go in and out of the Zone freely at all times.

But times change and the Panamanians have a growing feeling of nationalism. We, on the other hand, cannot weaken our ability to provide security for our nation and the entire Western Hemisphere. Can ways be found to satisfy some of their national aspirations without compromising our ability to meet security requirements?

RUMORS TO BE DISPELLED

Senator HOLLINGS. They are beginning to give. They see the unfairness and the un-American posture that they are now posing. They see it and they are beginning to feel it. They know now that it is not the title there.

Now we can jump to another very important point, Mr. Chairman, and I only heard this at lunch yesterday. It was said at the back table where several Senators eat, that President Carter was answering questions earlier this year in Mississippi, back in July. The connotation of it all was that without thinking he said he might go somewhere else for a sea-level canal.

Now, after President Carter said that down in Mississippi, Panama actually called him on it, and the United States was pressured into signing a prohibition against negotiating a new canal anywhere else. That is what is said. That is absolutely ridiculous.

I would ask this committee to please get up work sheets on the economy, the military, the defense, the history, the new canal and all of the other issues so that Senators will disabuse themselves from that kind of nonsense. Just what are the facts, really?

Senator CASE. Did the President say that or is it alleged?

Senator HOLLINGS. That is what was said. He did say something in Mississippi about building a new sea-level canal elsewhere and that is when we were being pressured to make a multibillion dollar payment. It is good to bring that into perspective. In June, when they said that the President had already signed the treaty, or whatever, it was, and in July when he was talking in Mississippi, they were still asking for the billions.

But I talked to Mr. Moss, who negotiated this particular session—incidentally, opponents know better. My distinguished senior colleague put into the record on July 17, 1967, the treaty of 1967, which called for a sea-level canal. Now he says that the American people wouldn't think of it. Why they agreed to it in principle 10 years ago. He got the treaty. He put it into the record.

Yesterday afternoon I had that, but I thought there might be something else. So I asked the CIA—since our distinguished Chairman here now headed up the intelligence investigation—the CIA came over in top secret form at 5 o'clock yesterday afternoon, almost with a guard, and said here, classified as "secret," is the 1967 treaty. Strom Thurmond made that public on July 17, 1967–10 years ago, and they are still running around with the "secret" treaty of 1967. [General laughter.]

B. COPING WITH THE ENERGY CRISIS

1. Carter Calls For "The Moral Equivalent of War" (1977)

Newly elected President Jimmy Carter made the "energy crisis" his number one priority upon entering the White House. For many years, oil production in the United States had failed to keep pace with the seemingly insatiable appetite of Americans for more energy. Once a major energy exporter, the United States had become a net importer of oil. Then in 1973–1974 the Organization of Petroleum Exporting Countries (OPEC), a powerful cartel of oil-producers, flexed its muscles, and began pushing the price of oil skyward. America's costly and dangerous dependence on foreign oil was painfully revealed. Determined to make Americans understand the full gravity of their situation, Carter delivered the following televised address on April 18, 1977. What does he see as the greatest menace in America's energy dependence? How sound are his solutions to the problem?

Good evening.

Tonight I want to have an unpleasant talk with you about a problem that is unprecedented in our history. With the exception of preventing war, this is the greatest challenge that our country will face during our lifetime.

The energy crisis has not yet overwhelmed us, but it will if we do not act quickly. It's a problem that we will not be able to solve in the next few years, and it's likely to get progressively worse through the rest of this century.

We must not be selfish or timid if we hope to have a decent world for our children and our grandchildren. We simply must balance our demand for energy with our rapidly shrinking resources. By acting now we can control our future instead of letting the future control us.

Two days from now, I will present to the Congress my energy proposals. Its Members will be my partners, and they have already given me a great deal of valuable advice.

Many of these proposals will be unpopular. Some will cause you to put up with inconveniences and to make sacrifices. The most important thing about these proposals is that the alternative may be a national catastrophe. Further delay can affect our strength and our power as a nation.

Our decision about energy will test the character of the American people and the ability of the President and the Congress to govern this Nation. This difficult effort will be the "moral equivalent of war," except that we will be uniting our efforts to build and not to destroy.

Now, I know that some of you may doubt that we face real energy shortages. The 1973 gas lines are gone, and with this springtime weather, our homes are warm again. But our energy problem is worse tonight than it was

1. *Public Papers of the Presidents of the United States: Jimmy Carter, 1977*, Vol. 1, pp. 656–662.

in 1973 or a few weeks ago in the dead of winter. It's worse because more waste has occurred and more time has passed by without our planning for the future. And it will get worse every day until we act.

The oil and natural gas that we rely on for 75 percent of our energy are simply running out. In spite of increased effort, domestic production has been dropping steadily at about 6 percent a year. Imports have doubled in the last 5 years. Our Nation's economic and political independence is becoming increasingly vulnerable. Unless profound changes are made to lower oil consumption, we now believe that early in the 1980's the world will be demanding more oil than it can produce.

The world now uses about 60 million barrels of oil a day, and demand increases each year about 5 percent. This means that just to stay even we need the production of a new Texas every year, an Alaskan North Slope every 9 months, or a new Saudi Arabia every 3 years. Obviously, this cannot continue.

We must look back into history to understand our energy problem. Twice in the last several hundred years, there has been a transition in the way people use energy.

The first was about 200 years ago, when we changed away from wood—which had provided about 90 percent of all fuel—to coal, which was much more efficient. This change became the basis for the Industrial Revolution.

The second change took place in this century, with the growing use of oil and natural gas. They were more convenient and cheaper than coal, and the supply seemed to be almost without limit. They made possible the age of automobile and airplane travel. Nearly everyone who is alive today grew up during this period, and we have never known anything different.

Because we are now running out of gas and oil, we must prepare quickly for a third change—to strict conservation and to the renewed use of coal and to permanent renewable energy sources like solar power.

The world has not prepared for the future. During the 1950's, people used twice as much oil as during the 1940's. During the 1960's, we used twice as much as during the 1950's. And in each of those decades, more oil was consumed than in all of man's previous history combined.

World consumption of oil is still going up. If it were possible to keep it rising during the 1970's and 1980's by 5 percent a year, as it has in the past, we could use up all the proven reserves of oil in the entire world by the end of the next decade.

I know that many of you have suspected that some supplies of oil and gas are being withheld from the market. You may be right, but suspicions about the oil companies cannot change the fact that we are running out of petroleum.

All of us have heard about the large oil fields on Alaska's North Slope. In a few years, when the North Slope is producing fully, its total output will be just about equal to 2 years' increase in our own Nation's energy demand.

Each new inventory of world oil reserves has been more disturbing than the last. World oil production can probably keep going up for another 6 or 8 years. But sometime in the 1980's, it can't go up any more. Demand will overtake production. We have no choice about that.

But we do have a choice about how we will spend the next few years. Each American uses the energy equivalent of 60 barrels of oil per person each year. Ours is the most wasteful nation on Earth. We waste more energy than we import. With about the same standard of living, we use twice as much energy per person as do other countries like Germany, Japan, and Sweden.

One choice, of course, is to continue doing what we've been doing before. We can drift along for a few more years.

Our consumption of oil would keep going up every year. Our cars would continue to be too large and inefficient. Three-quarters of them would carry only one person—the driver—while our public transportation system continues to decline. We can delay insulating our homes, and they will continue to lose about 50 percent of their heat in waste. We can continue using scarce oil and natural gas to generate electricity and continue wasting two-thirds of their fuel value in the process.

If we do not act, then by 1985 we will be using 33 percent more energy than we used today.

We can't substantially increase our domestic production, so we would need to import twice as much oil as we do now. Supplies will be uncertain. The cost will keep going up. Six years ago, we paid $3.7 billion for imported oil. Last year we spent $36 billion for imported oil—nearly 10 times as much. And this year we may spend $45 billion.

Unless we act, we will spend more than $550 billion for imported oil by 1985—more than $2,500 for every man, woman, and child in America. Along with that money that we transport overseas, we will continue losing American jobs and become increasingly vulnerable to supply interruptions.

Now we have a choice. But if we wait, we will constantly live in fear of embargoes. We could endanger our freedom as a sovereign nation to act in foreign affairs. Within 10 years, we would not be able to import enough oil from any country, at any acceptable price.

If we wait and do not act, then our factories will not be able to keep our people on the job with reduced supplies of fuel.

Too few of our utility companies will have switched to coal, which is our most abundant energy source. We will not be ready to keep our transportation system running with smaller and more efficient cars and a better network of buses, trains, and public transportation.

We will feel mounting pressure to plunder the environment. We will have to have a crash program to build more nuclear plants, strip mine and burn more coal, and drill more offshore wells than if we begin to conserve right now.

Inflation will soar; production will go down; people will lose their jobs.

Intense competition for oil will build up among nations and also among the different regions within our own country. This has already started.

If we fail to act soon, we will face an economic, social, and political crisis that will threaten our free institutions. But we still have another choice. We can begin to prepare right now. We can decide to act while there is still time. That is the concept of the energy policy that we will present on Wednesday.

Our national energy plan is based on 10 fundamental principles. The first principle is that we can have an effective and comprehensive energy policy only if the Government takes responsibility for it and if the people understand the seriousness of the challenge and are willing to make sacrifices.

The second principle is that healthy economic growth must continue. Only by saving energy can we maintain our standard of living and keep our people at work. An effective conservation program will create hundreds of thousands of new jobs.

The third principle is that we must protect the environment. Our energy problems have the same cause as our environmental problems—wasteful use of resources. Conservation helps us solve both problems at once.

The fourth principle is that we must reduce our vulnerability to potentially devastating embargoes. We can protect ourselves from uncertain supplies by reducing our demand for oil, by making the most of our abundant resources such as coal, and by developing a strategic petroleum reserve.

The fifth principle is that we must be fair. Our solutions must ask equal sacrifices from every region, every class of people, and every interest group. Industry will have to do its part to conserve just as consumers will. The energy producers deserve fair treatment, but we will not let the oil companies profiteer.

The sixth principle, and the cornerstone of our policy, is to reduce demand through conservation. Our emphasis on conservation is a clear difference between this plan and others which merely encouraged crash production efforts. Conservation is the quickest, cheapest, most practical source of energy. Conservation is the only way that we can buy a barrel of oil for about $2. It cost about $13 to waste it.

The seventh principle is that prices should generally reflect the true replacement cost of energy. We are only cheating ourselves if we make energy artificially cheap and use more than we can really afford.

The eighth principle is that Government policies must be predictable and certain. Both consumers and producers need policies they can count on so they can plan ahead. This is one reason that I'm working with the Congress to create a new Department of Energy to replace more than 50 different agencies that now have some control over energy.

The ninth principle is that we must conserve the fuels that are scarcest and make the most of those that are plentiful. We can't continue to use oil and gas for 75 percent of our consumption, as we do now, when they only make up 7 percent of our domestic reserves. We need to shift to plentiful coal, while taking care to protect the environment, and to apply stricter safety standards to nuclear energy.

The tenth and last principle is that we must start now to develop the new, unconventional sources of energy that we will rely on in the next century.

Now, these 10 principles have guided the development of the policy that I will describe to you and the Congress on Wednesday night.

Our energy plan will also include a number of specific goals to measure our progress toward a stable energy system. These are the goals that we set for 1985:

—to reduce the annual growth rate in our energy demand to less than 2 percent;

—to reduce gasoline consumption by 10 percent below its current level;

—to cut in half the portion of U.S. oil which is imported—from a potential level of 16 million barrels to 6 million barrels a day;

—to establish a strategic petroleum reserve of one billion barrels, more than a 6-month supply;

—to increase our coal production by about two-thirds to more than one billion tons a year;

—to insulate 90 percent of American homes and all new buildings;

—to use solar energy in more than 2½ million houses.

We will monitor our progress toward these goals year by year. Our plan will call for strict conservation measures if we fall behind. I can't tell you that these measures will be easy, nor will they be popular. But I think most of you realize that a policy which does not ask for changes or sacrifices would not be an effective policy at this late date.

This plan is essential to protect our jobs, our environment, our standard of living, and our future. Whether this plan truly makes a difference will not be decided now here in Washington but in every town and every factory, in every home and on every highway and every farm.

I believe that this can be a positive challenge. There is something especially American in the kinds of changes that we have to make. We've always been proud, through our history, of being efficient people. We've always been proud of our ingenuity, our skill at answering questions. Now we need efficiency and ingenuity more than ever.

We've always been proud of our leadership in the world. And now we have a chance again to give the world a positive example.

We've always been proud of our vision of the future. We've always wanted to give our children and our grandchildren a world richer in possibilities than we have had ourselves. They are the ones that we must provide for now. They are the ones who will suffer most if we don't act.

I've given you some of the principles of the plan. I'm sure that each of you will find something you don't like about the specifics of our proposal. It will demand that we make sacrifices and changes in every life. To some degree, the sacrifices will be painful—but so is any meaningful sacrifice. It will lead to some higher costs and to some greater inconvenience for everyone. But the sacrifices can be gradual, realistic, and they are necessary. Above all, they will be fair. No one will gain an unfair advantage through this plan. No one will be asked to bear an unfair burden.

We will monitor the accuracy of data from the oil and natural gas companies for the first time, so that we will always know their true production, supplies, reserves, and profits. Those citizens who insist on driving large, unnecessarily powerful cars must expect to pay more for that luxury.

We can be sure that all the special interest groups in the country will attack the part of this plan that affects them directly. They will say that sacrifice is fine as long as other people do it, but that their sacrifice is unreasonable or unfair or harmful to the country. If they succeed with this approach, then the burden on the ordinary citizen, who is not organized into an interest group, would be crushing.

There should be only one test for this program—whether it will help our country. Other generations of Americans have faced and mastered great challenges. I have faith that meeting this challenge will make our own lives even richer. If you will join me so that we can work together with patriotism and courage, we will again prove that our great Nation can lead the world into an age of peace, independence, and freedom.

Thank you very much, and good night.

2. The *Houston Chronicle* Blasts Carter's Energy Program (1977)

American oil producers and their spokespersons disliked Carter's energy program. In the editorial reproduced below, the *Houston Chronicle* finds much fault with the President's proposals. To what feature of Carter's policies does it most strenuously object? What alternative solution does it suggest?

The President's energy program is in our opinion wrong in its basic philosophy, potentially disastrous in economic impact and unworkable as a practical matter.

The most tragic thing about it is the sick smell of defeatism that permeates the whole approach.

The American people deserve better than to be told they must suffer with no end in sight because a few people in this administration have timidly decided the problem cannot be solved, that misery can only be rationed by an all-wise government.

That is the no-win philosophy of an energy plan that totally emphasizes conservation and pays only lip service to increasing the supply.

The failure of faith in the country's ability is the sad part. The most disturbing part of the approach is the assumption that the federal bureaucracy must take over detailed management of the country's energy life—which

2. *Houston Chronicle* (April 22, 1977). Reprinted by permission of the publisher.

means its economic and social life. The government is in no way wise enough to do this.

The administration is attempting an enormous, almost unprecedented federal power grab and is attempting to stampede the country and the Congress into acquiescence.

The economics of the Carter plan are dead wrong. An energy-restricted economy is an economy which cannot furnish the jobs for its people. That is the bottom line of a policy which emphasizes conservation rather than production of a sufficiency of supply. It is all well and good to preach about "waste." There is certainly some of that. But all too often in that elitist philosophy about waste what is being ignored is that one man's waste is another man's job.

To restrict the economy and then artificially inflate prices on top of that with taxes is outrageous. Recycling the people's money through Washington and back to them is something that never quite works out the way it is soothingly promoted.

The single most damning indictment of the administration's thinking is that it embraces a demonstrated failure while trying to kill a demonstrated success.

Two decades of federal interstate regulation have turned the East, Midwest and parts of the South into natural gas disaster areas. In the intrastate market free of regulation there is sufficient gas. Yet the President proposes to kill the free market and extend the disaster. This cannot be rationalized, but unfortunately symbolizes the administration's energy proposals.

We have no quarrel with energy conservation, have supported it and will continue to support any reasonable efforts. But to rely on conservation without an equal, even greater, all-out effort to increase supplies is committing economic and social folly.

We noted the other day where it was said "the President feels it is ridiculous to burn precious fuels so we can be nice and hot in the winter and nice and cold in the summer."

Well, we feel it is ridiculous for the President to ask the people to go cold in the winter and hot in the summer, have fewer jobs and a stagnating, no-growth type of economy, pay artificially higher taxes and prices and be smothered in federal controls—to put up with all this when he isn't moving heaven and Earth, and anything else in the way, to produce the energy that would make it unnecessary.

C. CARTER'S TROUBLED PRESIDENCY

1. Carter Diagnoses the National Mood (1979)

In July, 1979, Jimmy Carter unexpectedly cancelled a scheduled television address and retired to the presidential retreat at Camp David, Maryland. There for ten days he sought the advice of scores of Americans about the state of the nation's soul. Finally, he ended

1. *Public Papers of the Presidents of the United States: Jimmy Carter, 1979*, Book II (1980), pp. 1235–1241.

his period of contemplation and delivered the following remarkable address on network television. What exactly does Carter mean by a "crisis of confidence"? Where does he lay the blame for the crisis? What does this speech reveal about Carter's character?

Good evening.

This is a special night for me. Exactly 3 years ago, on July 15, 1976, I accepted the nomination of my party to run for President of the United States. I promised you a President who is not isolated from the people, who feels your pain, and who shares your dreams and who draws his strength and his wisdom from you.

During the past 3 years I've spoken to you on many occasions about national concerns, the energy crisis, reorganizing the Government, our Nation's economy, and issues of war and especially peace. But over those years the subjects of the speeches, the talks, and the press conferences have become increasingly narrow, focused more and more on what the isolated world of Washington thinks is important. Gradually, you've heard more and more about what the Government thinks or what the Government should be doing and less and less about our Nation's hopes, our dreams, and our vision of the future.

Ten days ago I had planned to speak to you again about a very important subject—energy. For the fifth time I would have described the urgency of the problem and laid out a series of legislative recommendations to the Congress. But as I was preparing to speak, I began to ask myself the same question that I now know has been troubling many of you. Why have we not been able to get together as a nation to resolve our serious energy problem?

It's clear that the true problems of our Nation are much deeper—deeper than gasoline lines or energy shortages, deeper even than inflation or recession. And I realize more than ever that as President I need your help. So, I decided to reach out and listen to the voices of America.

I invited to Camp David people from almost every segment of our society—business and labor, teachers and preachers, Governors, mayors, and private citizens. And then I left Camp David to listen to other Americans, men and women like you. It has been an extraordinary 10 days, and I want to share with you what I've heard.

First of all, I got a lot of personal advice. Let me quote a few of the typical comments that I wrote down.

This from a southern Governor: "Mr. President, you are not leading this Nation—you're just managing the Government."

"You don't see the people enough any more."

"Some of your Cabinet members don't seem loyal. There is not enough discipline among your disciples."

"Don't talk to us about politics or the mechanics of government, but about an understanding of our common good."

"Mr. President, we're in trouble. Talk to us about blood and sweat and tears."

"If you lead, Mr. President, we will follow."

Many people talked about themselves and about the condition of our Nation. This from a young woman in Pennsylvania: "I feel so far from government. I feel like ordinary people are excluded from political power."

And this from a young Chicano: "Some of us have suffered from recession all our lives."

"Some people have wasted energy, but others haven't had anything to waste."

And this from a religious leader: "No material shortage can touch the important things like God's love for us or our love for one another."

And I like this one particularly from a black woman who happens to be the mayor of a small Mississippi town: "The big-shots are not the only ones who are important. Remember, you can't sell anything on Wall Street unless someone digs it up somewhere else first."

This kind of summarized a lot of other statements: "Mr. President, we are confronted with a moral and a spiritual crisis."

Several of our discussions were on energy, and I have a notebook full of comments and advice. I'll read just a few.

"We can't go on consuming 40 percent more energy than we produce. When we import oil we are also importing inflation plus unemployment."

"We've got to use what we have. The Middle East has only 5 percent of the world's energy, but the United States has 24 percent."

And this is one of the most vivid statements: "Our neck is stretched over the fence and OPEC has a knife."

"There will be other cartels and other shortages. American wisdom and courage right now can set a path to follow in the future."

This was a good one: "Be bold, Mr. President. We may make mistakes, but we are ready to experiment."

And this one from a labor leader got to the heart of it: "The real issue is freedom. We must deal with the energy problem on a war footing."

And the last that I'll read: "When we enter the moral equivalent of war, Mr. President, don't issue us BB guns."

These 10 days confirmed my belief in the decency and the strength and the wisdom of the American people, but it also bore out some of my long-standing concerns about our Nation's underlying problems.

I know, of course, being President, that government actions and legislation can be very important. That's why I've worked hard to put my campaign promises into law—and I have to admit, with just mixed success. But after listening to the American people I have been reminded again that all the legislation in the world can't fix what's wrong with America. So, I want to speak to you first tonight about a subject even more serious than energy or inflation. I want to talk to you right now about a fundamental threat to American democracy.

I do not mean our political and civil liberties. They will endure. And I do not refer to the outward strength of America, a nation that is at peace tonight everywhere in the world, with unmatched economic power and military might.

The threat is nearly invisible in ordinary ways. It is a crisis of confidence. It is a crisis that strikes at the very heart and soul and spirit of our national will. We can see this crisis in the growing doubt about the meaning of our own lives and in the loss of a unity of purpose for our Nation.

The erosion of our confidence in the future is threatening to destroy the social and the political fabric of America.

The confidence that we have always had as a people is not simply some romantic dream or a proverb in a dusty book that we read just on the Fourth of July. It is the idea which founded our Nation and has guided our development as a people. Confidence in the future has supported everything else—public institutions and private enterprise, our own families, and the very Constitution of the United States. Confidence has defined our course and has served as a link between generations. We've always believed in something called progress. We've always had a faith that the days of our children would be better than our own.

Our people are losing that faith, not only in government itself but in the ability as citizens to serve as the ultimate rulers and shapers of our democracy. As a people we know our past and we are proud of it. Our progress has been part of the living history of America, even the world. We always believed that we were part of a great movement of humanity itself called democracy, involved in the search for freedom, and that belief has always strengthened us in our purpose. But just as we are losing our confidence in the future, we are also beginning to close the door on our past.

In a nation that was proud of hard work, strong families, close-knit communities, and our faith in God, too many of us now tend to worship self-indulgence and consumption. Human identity is no longer defined by what one does, but by what one owns. But we've discovered that owning things and consuming things does not satisfy our longing for meaning. We've learned that piling up material goods cannot fill the emptiness of lives which have no confidence or purpose.

The symptoms of this crisis of the American spirit are all around us. For the first time in the history of our country a majority of our people believe that the next 5 years will be worse than the past 5 years. Two-thirds of our people do not even vote. The productivity of American workers is actually dropping, and the willingness of Americans to save for the future has fallen below that of all other people in the Western world.

As you know, there is a growing disrespect for government and for churches and for schools, the news media, and other institutions. This is not a message of happiness or reassurance, but it is the truth and it is a warning.

These changes did not happen overnight. They've come upon us gradually over the last generation, years that were filled with shocks and tragedy.

We were sure that ours was a nation of the ballot, not the bullet, until the murders of John Kennedy and Robert Kennedy and Martin Luther King, Jr. We were taught that our armies were always invincible and our causes were always just, only to suffer the agony of Vietnam. We respected the Presidency as a place of honor until the shock of Watergate.

We remember when the phrase "sound as a dollar" was an expression of absolute dependability, until 10 years of inflation began to shrink our dollar and our savings. We believed that our Nation's resources were limitless until 1973, when we had to face a growing dependence on foreign oil.

These wounds are still very deep. They have never been healed.

Looking for a way out of this crisis, our people have turned to the Federal Government and found it isolated from the mainstream of our Nation's life. Washington, D.C., has become an island. The gap between our citizens and our Government has never been so wide. The people are looking for honest answers, not easy answers; clear leadership, not false claims and evasiveness and politics as usual.

What you see too often in Washington and elsewhere around the country is a system of government that seems incapable of action. You see a Congress twisted and pulled in every direction by hundreds of well-financed and powerful special interests. You see every extreme position defended to the last vote, almost to the last breath by one unyielding group or another. You often see a balanced and a fair approach that demands sacrifice, a little sacrifice from everyone, abandoned like an orphan without support and without friends.

Often you see paralysis and stagnation and drift. You don't like it, and neither do I. What can we do?

First of all, we must face the truth, and then we can change our course. We simply must have faith in each other, faith in our ability to govern ourselves, and faith in the future of this Nation. Restoring that faith and that confidence to America is now the most important task we face. It is a true challenge of this generation of Americans.

One of the visitors to Camp David last week put it this way: "We've got to stop crying and start sweating, stop talking and start walking, stop cursing and start praying. The strength we need will not come from the White House, but from every house in America."

We know the strength of America. We are strong. We can regain our unity. We can regain our confidence. We are the heirs of generations who survived threats much more powerful and awesome than those that challenge us now. Our fathers and mothers were strong men and women who shaped a new society during the Great Depression, who fought world wars, and who carved out a new charter of peace for the world.

We ourselves are the same Americans who just 10 years ago put a man on the Moon. We are the generation that dedicated our society to the pursuit of human rights and equality. And we are the generation that will win the war on the energy problem and in that process rebuild the unity and confidence of America.

We are at a turning point in our history. There are two paths to choose. One is a path I've warned about tonight, the path that leads to fragmentation and self-interest. Down that road lies a mistaken idea of freedom, the right to grasp for ourselves some advantage over others. That path would be one of constant conflict between narrow interests ending in chaos and immobility. It is a certain route to failure.

All the traditions of our past, all the lessons of our heritage, all the promises of our future point to another path, the path of common purpose and the restoration of American values. That path leads to true freedom for our Nation and ourselves. We can take the first steps down that path as we begin to solve our energy problem. . . .

2. Carter Agonizes Over the Iranian Hostages (1979–1980)

On November 4, 1979, militant Iranian revolutionaries over-ran the American embassy in Teheran, Iran, and took several dozen American diplomats hostage. For the remainder of Carter's term in office, the Iranian hostage issue clouded his presidency. In his memoirs, Carter dwells at length on his involvement with the Iranian episode, including the abortive rescue mission that he authorized in April, 1980. What does his account of the Iranian crisis suggest about Carter's qualities as a leader? As a human being? Was he a victim of events beyond his, or any president's, control?

Sunday, November 4, 1979, is a date I will never forget. Early in the morning I received a call from Brzezinski, who reported that our embassy in Tehran had been overrun by about 3,000 militants, and that 50 or 60 of our American staff had been captured. Immediately afterward, I talked to Secretary Vance, who reviewed with me again the precautionary measures that had been taken and the assurances of protection we had received from the Iranian officials. We were deeply disturbed, but reasonably confident that the Iranians would soon remove the attackers from the embassy compound and release our people. We and other nations had faced this kind of attack many times in the past, but never, so far as we knew, had a host government failed to attempt to protect threatened diplomats. We had a firm pledge from both the Iranian Prime Minister and the Foreign Minister to give our staff and property this protection. During the past week or two, even Khomeini's forces had helped to dispel crowds of demonstrators near the American Embassy.

Prime Minister Bazargan did his best to keep his word and to remove the militants, but after a few hours passed without forceful action we grew increasingly concerned. We began to contact any officials we knew in Iran, both in the Bazargan Cabinet and within the so-called Revolutionary Council, where government and religious leaders made the basic decisions about the nation's policies. All our efforts were fruitless. The militants had become overnight heroes in Iran. Khomeini praised their action, and no public offi-

2. *Keeping Faith: Memoirs Of A President*, pp. 457–58, 506–510, 518, 521, 594, by Jimmy Carter, published by Bantam Books. Reprinted by permission of International Creative Management. Copyright © 1982 by Jimmy Carter.

cial was willing to confront them. Bazargan and Yazdi resigned in disgust, but this did not help set the Americans free.

It was not at all clear what the militants wanted. My impression was that originally they had not intended to remain in the embassy or to hold the Americans captive beyond a few hours. However, when they received the adulation of many of their fellow revolutionaries and the support of Khomeini and other leaders, they prolonged their illegal act. As kidnappers, they seemed to have no clear ideas about ransom, except to repeat the cry we had been hearing ever since January 16 of the previous year—return the Shah and his money to Iran.

I spent most of the day, every spare moment, trying to decide what to do. . . . We began to assess punitive action that might be taken against Iran. We still have 570 Americans there. I directed that the companies who employ these people be informed to get them out of the country. We also asked the Algerians, Syrians, Turks, Pakistanis, Libyans, PLO, and others to intercede on behalf of the release of our hostages. It's almost impossible to deal with a crazy man, except that he does have religious beliefs, and the world of Islam will be damaged if a fanatic like him should commit murder in the name of religion against 60 innocent people. I believe that's our ultimate hope for a successful resolution of this problem. We will not release the Shah, of course, as they demand.

                                                            Diary, November 6, 1979

As soon as the embassy was seized, an Iran working group was formed in the State Department, headed by Henry Precht, Director for Iranian Affairs. Twenty-four hours a day, the work of this group never ceased; they were to continue their efforts until the crisis was over. None of us dreamed that we would wait more than fourteen months before our prayers were answered and our people were finally home. . . .

[*Diplomatic efforts to free the American hostages proved futile. In Iran, confusion reigned. When Iran's powerful religious leader, the Ayatollah Ruhollah Khomeini, blocked the transfer of the hostages from the "militants" who had stormed the embassy to the shaky revolutionary government of Iran, Carter despaired. Over the objections of his Secretary of State, Cyrus Vance, he ordered a daring military rescue mission to attempt to rescue the hostages in a surprise raid on the embassy compound.*]

My hope had been that the Iranian leaders would behave courageously. Now I realized this was not to be. Another serious development was that Iraq was threatening to invade Iran. We had no previous knowledge of nor influence over this move, but Iran was blaming us for it nevertheless.

The Iranian terrorists are making all kinds of crazy threats to kill the American hostages if they are invaded by Iraq—whom they identify as an American puppet.

                                                            Diary, April 10, 1980

We could no longer afford to depend on diplomacy. I decided to act. On April 11, I called together my top advisers, and we went over the rescue plans again. Because the militants in the compound had threatened to "destroy all the hostages immediately" if any additional moves against them should be launched, we had to plan any action with the utmost care. . . .

We had blueprints of our embassy buildings in Tehran, of course, and we had talked to the black and female hostages who had been released before Christmas, although they were unable to tell us much about the others. Much more important, we received information from someone (who cannot be identified) who was thoroughly familiar with the compound, knew where every American hostage was located, how many and what kind of guards were there at different times during the night, and the daily schedule of the hostages and their captors. This was the first time we knew the precise location of the Americans.

Our agents, who moved freely in and out of Tehran under the guise of business or media missions, had studied closely the degree of vigilance of the captors. They had grown lax, and security around the compound was no longer a serious obstacle to a surprise entry by force. Our satellite photographs of the embassy compound and the surrounding area kept us abreast of any changes in the general habits and overall composition of the terrorists' details. We could, for instance, identify individual cars and trucks that went inside the compound each day.

Life for the guards around the embassy grounds seemed to have settled into a relaxed and humdrum existence, perfectly designed for a lightning strike by a highly trained and well-equipped force which, with night-vision devices, could easily distinguish in the dark between our people and the Iranian captors. We would need six large helicopters to fly into the center of Tehran, pick up the three Americans in the foreign-ministry building and the other hostages in the embassy, and carry them and the rescue team to safety.

The biggest problem was how to travel the enormous distance from the sea or from other countries to extract the hostages from the center of Tehran. Our solution was to fly in seven helicopters (later changed to eight to provide two rather than one backup) from our aircraft carriers in the Gulf of Oman to the remote area—now known as Desert One—that had been surveyed earlier. The only drawback of this site was a seldom-used dirt country road going by it, but the team was prepared to hold any passers-by, hide their vehicles, and release them only when it was too late for the operation to be disrupted. Everyone was under strict orders from me not to harm any innocent bystanders and to avoid bloodshed whenever possible.

The helicopters were scheduled to take off on Thursday, April 24 at dusk (10:30 A.M. Washington time) and arrive about six hours later, at approximately 11:00 P.M. Iran time. This six-hundred-mile flight from the Gulf of Oman would push to the limit the capabilities of these aircraft. They would be joined at Desert One by six C-130's carrying the ninety members of the rescue team, plus fuel and supplies. After the team was transferred from the C-130's to the helicopters, the airplanes would leave Iran, and the helicopters with the rescue team would fly a short distance northward into the nearby mountains, where they would arrive at about 4:00 A.M. and be hidden from view during the following daylight hours. This place was remote and uninhabited, and detection would be highly unlikely. Communication between the Pentagon and the rescue team, using satellites and other relay facilities, would be instantaneous. I would receive telephone reports from David Jones and Harold Brown.

The next night, provided everything went well and I decided the rescue mission should proceed, the trucks our agents had purchased would be removed from a warehouse on the outskirts of Tehran, driven to a point near the mountain hiding place, and used to carry the rescue team into the city. At a prearranged time, the rescue team would simultaneously enter the foreign-ministry building and the compound, overpower the guards, and free the American hostages. Guided by radio communications and prearranged schedules, the helicopters would land at the sites, picking up our people and carrying them to an abandoned airstrip near the city. From there, two C-141's would fly all the Americans to safety across the desert area of Saudi Arabia. The helicopters would be left in Iran. I planned to notify the Saudis only after the rescue mission was completed. . . .

[*The rescue mission ended in disastrous and embarrassing failure. Mechanical problems plagued the rescue team's helicopters, and team leader Colonel Charles Beckwith was forced to scrap the mission at mid-point in the Iranian desert. During withdrawal, two aircraft collided, killing eight of the team members.*]

I am still haunted by memories of that day—our high hopes for success, the incredible series of mishaps, the bravery of our rescue team, the embarrassment of failure, and above all, the tragic deaths in the lonely desert. I actually slept a couple of hours, and then got up early to prepare my television breadcast, which would explain to the American people what had occurred.

In my brief statement, I took full responsibility for the mission, outlined what had happened, and gave my reasons for the effort. I reminded the world of the continuing Iranian crime and praised the courageous volunteers who had given their lives for the freedom of others. . . .

As soon as they returned home, I wanted to meet the members of the rescue team (known as "Delta"). Without any notice to the news media, I flew to see the team on Sunday, April 27. Their identities and location were confidential. When I stepped off the helicopter, Colonel Beckwith was waiting. He was really a tough guy, a former University of Georgia football player who had grown up a few miles from my hometown of Plains and had dedicated his life to self-sacrifice for our country in the most dangerous and personal kind of combat service. His chin was quivering and tears were running down his cheeks. I opened my arms, and we embraced and wept together. He said, "Mr. President, I'm sorry we let you down!" For a few moments he couldn't talk, while I expressed with all my heart my appreciation for what his men had done. Then he said, "Will you let us go back?" I told him we were in the struggle together, and that I would do everything possible to find freedom for our fellow Americans. I meant to bring them out, and I would certainly rely on the Delta team, as we had before, if I decided it was necessary. Although I did not say it at the time, I knew that the Iranians would be vigilant about detecting another intrusion into their country; the hostages were being dispersed to various locations then unknown to us. Furthermore, we had not been able to devise a significantly different rescue scheme that was feasible—and to repeat the first one might be suicidal.

Beckwith told me that after the last helicopter had failed in the desert, he had made an instant decision to recommend withdrawal, and that he had no doubt it was right. I asked why they had not destroyed the remaining helicopters before they left Iran, and he explained that the helicopters were loaded with ammunition; any fires or explosions would have endangered the C-130's on which their lives depended.

I also met with five Iranians who had helped us with the mission. They, too, were eager to return and assist us. Then I went around and talked to every one of the men individually, expressing to them again and again our nation's gratitude for their heroism. They were superb. I would not hesitate to put my own life into their hands. . . .

Secretary Brown wanted to let Beckwith answer some questions from the press, but Charlie had been trained to conceal his identity and was reluctant to do it. He insisted on coming by to explain to me why he was going public.

While he was in the Oval Office, he paid me a compliment that may never be exceeded. With some embarrassment, he said, "My men and I have decided that our boss, the President of the United States, is as tough as woodpecker lips." Before he left, we agreed that he and I would walk together behind a bird dog around the fields of our native south Georgia— some day when both of us had more time. . . .

[*The Iranian crisis haunted the remainder of Carter's presidency. Carter's inability to resolve it undoubtedly contributed to his defeat by Ronald Reagan in the election of 1980. In the closing days of Carter's term in office, he continued to work intensely on the Iranian problem. But the Iranians withheld from him the crown of success, and released the hostages on Ronald Reagan's inauguration day, January 20, 1981.*]

The release of the American hostages had almost become an obsession with me. Of course, their lives, safety, and freedom were the paramount considerations, but there was more to it. I wanted to have my decisions vindicated. It was very likely that I had been defeated and would soon leave office as President because I had kept these hostages and their fate at the forefront of the world's attention, and had clung to a cautious and prudent policy in order to protect their lives during the preceding fourteen months. Before God and my fellow citizens, I wanted to exert every ounce of my strength and ability during these last few days to achieve their liberation. I knew that if we failed, it might take many months to reweave the fabric of complex agreements that had been so laboriously created. . . .

3. Hugh Sidey Assesses the Carter Presidency (1980)

Veteran *Time* White House reporter Hugh Sidey wrote the following assessment of Carter's presidency on the eve of the Democratic presidential nominating convention in 1980. What does he find to be Carter's greatest weaknesses as president? his greatest strengths?

The stately old East Room of the White House, which has managed to maintain its dignity through the drying laundry of the John Adams family, the gallons of lemonade poured by the abstemious Lucy Hayes and the baleful exit of Richard Nixon, witnessed another extraordinary event last week in the long and colorful caravan of presidential history.

Jimmy Carter, the 38th man in this procession, went somberly and with weighted shoulders before the television cameras (nudging out *M*A*S*H*) to spend an hour attempting to untangle himself and his Administration from the clumsy conniving of his brother Billy for Libyan oil and a vision of millions in commissions.

It was the best of Carter, a profoundly caring man, loving his brother through stress, as honest as a political human knows how to be, skillfully projecting his concern from his electronic stage to an estimated 65 million Americans. He was forceful in his conviction of his own rectitude and a master of every detail in the intricate caper of Billy, the wily and greedy buffoon.

And it was the worst of Carter, the President. Rarely in the past 3½ years have we seen the President so focused and eloquent on a problem—a problem that never should have been, and even now should be relegated to the lawyers who love to niggle. In a world that is stalled and frightened, with only a handful of men and women wielding the power to address the malaise, Jimmy Carter, as so often in his stewardship, confused his personal and political concerns with his larger duties as President. While most Americans surely felt admiration for Carter the man, there hovered in the background those dark clouds of doubt about his leadership that were reflected in the question by CBS's Lesley Stahl, "How do you think you got into this big mess?" He never seemed to understand why this was the real question —and the implications of his failure to answer it.

West German Chancellor Helmut Schmidt once broke into tears in the presence of a friend, so distraught was he over his conviction that Carter did not grasp his true responsibility as leader of the U.S. The world drifts toward war, believes Schmidt, with Carter uncomprehending. The same sentiment echoes from Asia, where Singapore's Prime Minister Lee Kuan Yew finds Carter's vision "a sorry admission of the limits of America's power." An official of Moscow's Institute of the U.S.A. and Canada complains: "What drives us crazy about Carter is his capriciousness, his constant changing of the points of reference in our relationship." Following this summer's economic summit meeting in Venice, a participant observed: "Mr. Carter cannot merely keep declaring himself the leader of the free world; he must demonstrate that capacity."

When Jimmy Carter stood before the 1976 Democratic National Convention and pledged "new leadership," he had never met a Democratic President or slept in the White House. The presidency was a legend from books, the Federal Government a classroom exercise, and Washington was a distant citadel of power that somehow had been corrupted by its residents. "It's time for the people to run the Government," Carter told his audience in that moment of warm, rising hope that filled New York's Madison Square Garden.

After greeting a Democratic President in the bathroom mirror every one of 1,299 mornings and sleeping in the White House at least 700 nights, Carter has indeed brought the nation a new kind of leadership. It is at least one promise that he kept among the 600 that he made during his remarkable march to the Oval Office.

But if Carter's years have been a true return to Government by popular will, filtered through the mind and ear of this earnest troubadour of the town meetings and televised press conferences, therein lies a huge and unexpected irony. The people do not like their own political creation. . . .

Carter's record of achievement is not a bare cupboard. There is civil service reform, airline, trucking and financial institutions deregulation, the Panama Canal treaties, restored relations with China, the Egyptian-Israeli peace treaty, and a commendable energy program on the books. As a symbol of personal integrity and candor, he is undimmed. A majority of Americans probably would still endorse most of his ideas he set forth in his first euphoric weeks, ideas for tax reform, national health care and Government reorganization. For the most part, Carter's farm program was a wonder, expanding exports and raising prices and farm income. He has increased the military budget, put the new MX missile system in planning, leapfrogged a new manned bomber to develop the cruise missile and persuaded NATO to make significant increases in arms and readiness.

Yet Carter is today a political cripple both at home and abroad because the larger issues have swamped him. Inflation and interest rates have doubled in his time. The true anguish at home, as described by Patricia Harris, Secretary of Health and Human Services, is among members of the middle class, who are far from deprivation but find themselves losing ground economically. Their fear is directed at Carter. Overseas, Soviet influence massed and grew and almost everywhere shoved a clumsy and reluctant U.S. against the wall. "We feel," says Raymond Aron, the distinguished French student of *Realpolitik*, "that American power is in decline. It is that simple and that unfortunate." It is, for instance, one of Kissinger's views that Americans are beginning to reproach themselves and Carter because the U.S. did not take dramatic action to resolve the Iranian hostage crisis when it first occurred. The public wanted nothing done then, but now is blaming the President for failure to act against popular will. That may be another manifestation of what has gone wrong on Jimmy Carter's watch. In his own inexperience and uncertainty, the President could not define a mission for his Government, a purpose for the country and the means of getting there. Former Secretary of the Treasury W. Michael Blumenthal confided to friends after he was fired that at first he thought Carter's long pauses during economic discussions were periods of thought. Later he decided they came from Carter's inability to decide what to do or even what questions to ask. . . .

His civics-class approach to the world appeared again when the Shah of Iran fell. While cautious in public statements, Carter in private had nearly convinced himself that Iran would return to the constitution of 1906, that the legislature would reassemble, the military would hold order and a stable government take root. "It was preposterous," says one who helped plan the American response. "The President's thinking was not based on any actual experience of how governments really work in this world."

In trying to fathom the man and his times, almost every Carter analyst comes back, both in admiration and in doubt, to the President's religiosity. It bolsters him for the great waves of criticism that pound now at the White House. But it also seduces him and contributes to many of his falterings. He is a believer—in Bert Lance, his old friend and economic counselor whose banking improprieties forced him from the Office of Management and Budget; in Billy Carter, the kid brother with a good heart who must mean well; in Leonid Brezhnev, who pledged his hope for peace in the shadowy halls of Vienna's Hofburg Palace. Carter's matrix is that found in the Scriptures, where the rules of a just and loving life are laid out. He wants to prevail by purity. Applying those patterns of human concern and behavior to the world's masses is far more difficult.

When a close Carter aide found out that the President was going to Washington's National Cathedral to pray with the families of the hostages, he knew instinctively that the U.S. would not for the time being assert its power in any way that might jeopardize the hostages. For months Carter resisted using the rescue plan devised by his National Security experts. He was consumed by fear of losing individual lives in such an operation. The hostage crisis was incorporated into his political campaign, and from the Rose Garden he sounded the theme of peace, noting proudly that not a single American had died in combat during his presidency.

The wider interest of America's position in the world was only vaguely appreciated, if at all. Always Carter's mind fixed on the small parts of the effort and not the whole. At one stage in reviewing the attack plans on the embassy compound where the hostages were held, the President asked about the Iranian guards stationed inside the embassy, near the wall that the commandos intended to scale. Were they volunteers or conscripts? he wondered. If they were radicals, Carter explained, he could go along with killing them, but if they were only peasant conscripts, he wanted them knocked out temporarily. . . .

In almost every political arena that Carter has entered, his conviction that fervid good will would carry the day has proved false, and in many instances has worsened the problems. His belief that the Soviets would respond to dramatic overtures to scrap many of their nuclear missiles helped to fuel the continuation of arms competition. Carter's human rights campaign is now viewed as having often embarrassed U.S. allies and hardened the opposition of adversaries. His vague notion, preached mostly by his friend and onetime U.N. Ambassador Andrew Young, that the radical nations were our natural allies has been mocked in Viet Nam, Cambodia and Iran. "It is not that he does not mean well," says one thoughtful critic of Carter. "It is that almost everything he has touched he has made worse. He operated from the wrong concept of his job, the wrong theory of international affairs, and he uses administrative procedures that fail."

If there is a modern manual of leadership widely admired in the world today, it is the memoirs of France's Charles de Gaulle. His lessons are simple but rarely heeded in most White House proceedings. De Gaulle wrote of the need to concentrate on the questions of greatest national importance, of the necessity of delegating authority, of remaining at a distance but not in an ivory tower, of talking constantly to his people not about themselves but the greater interests of the nation.

In a peculiar way Jimmy Carter is consumed by himself. His world still resembles the small stretch of Plains, Ga. His goodness becomes an end in itself, defined in the Main Street encounters where the audiences are people with names and problems that are manageable. This does little, however, to define the tastes of the presidency, where decisions must have heroic dimensions, where leaders must balance their immense egos against a deeper understanding that they are but specks of dust in the ultimate sweep of history, where the future must be just as real as the present.

D. THE REAGAN "REVOLUTION"

1. President Reagan Asks for a Tax Cut (1981)

Ronald Reagan scored a stunning electoral victory over Jimmy Carter in 1980, and after his inauguration he set out energetically to cut the federal budget and reduce federal taxes. A former actor and television personality, Reagan used the electronic media with more effectiveness than almost any other modern president—earning for himself the title of "Great Communicator." In his nationally televised address of July 27, 1981,

1. *Weekly Compilation of Presidential Documents,* Vol. 17, no. 31 (August 3, 1981), pp. 814–820.

reproduced below, Reagan called upon Congress to grant a three-year, 25 percent personal income tax cut across the board to all American taxpayers. Why does he feel that such a cut is necessary?

It's been nearly 6 months since I first reported to you on the state of the Nation's economy. I'm afraid my message that night was grim and disturbing. I remember telling you we were in the worst economic mess since the Great Depression. Prices were continuing to spiral upward, unemployment was reaching intolerable levels, and all because government was too big and spent too much of our money.

We're still not out of the woods, but we've made a start. And we've certainly surprised those longtime and somewhat cynical observers of the Washington scene, who looked, listened, and said, "It can never be done; Washington will never change its spending habits." Well, something very exciting has been happening here in Washington, and you're responsible.

Your voices have been heard—millions of you, Democrats, Republicans, and independents, from every profession, trade and line of work, and from every part of this land. You sent a message that you wanted a new beginning. You wanted to change one little, two little word—two letter word, I should say. It doesn't sound like much, but it sure can make a difference changing "by government," "control *by* government" to "control *of* government."

In that earlier broadcast, you'll recall I proposed a program to drastically cut back government spending in the 1982 budget, which begins October 1st, and to continue cutting in the '83 and '84 budgets. Along with this I suggested an across-the-board tax cut, spread over those same 3 years, and the elimination of unnecessary regulations which were adding billions to the cost of things we buy.

All the lobbying, the organized demonstrations, and the cries of protest by those whose way of life depends on maintaining government's wasteful ways were no match for your voices, which were heard loud and clear in these marble halls of government. And you made history with your telegrams, your letters, your phone calls and, yes, personal visits to talk to your elected Representatives. You reaffirmed the mandate you delivered in the election last November—a mandate that called for an end to government policies that sent prices and mortgage rates skyrocketing while millions of Americans went jobless.

Because of what you did, Republicans and Democrats in the Congress came together and passed the most sweeping cutbacks in the history of the Federal budget. Right now, Members of the House and Senate are meeting in a conference committee to reconcile the differences between the two budget cutting bills passed by the House and Senate. When they finish, all Americans will benefit from savings of approximately $140 billion in reduced government costs over just the next 3 years. And that doesn't include the additional savings from the hundreds of burdensome regulations already cancelled or facing cancellation.

For 19 out of the last 20 years, the Federal Government has spent more than it took in. There will be another large deficit in this present year which ends September 30th, but with our program in place, it won't be quite as big as it might have been. And starting next year, the deficits will get smaller until in just a few years the budget can be balanced. And we hope we can begin whittling at that almost $1 trillion debt that hangs over the future of our children.

Now, so far, I've been talking about only one part of our program for economic recovery—the budget cutting part. I don't minimize its importance. Just the fact that Democrats and Republicans could work together as they have, proving the strength of our system, has created an optimism in our land. The rate of inflation is no longer in double-digit figures. The dollar has regained strength in the international money markets, and businessmen and investors are making decisions with regard to industrial development, modernization and expansion—all of this based on anticipation of our program being adopted and put into operation.

A recent poll shows that where a year and a half ago only 24 percent of our people believed things would get better, today 46 percent believe they will. To justify their faith, we must deliver the other part of our program. Our economic package is a closely knit, carefully constructed plan to restore America's economic strength and put our Nation back on the road to prosperity.

Each part of this package is vital. It cannot be considered piecemeal. It was proposed as a package, and it has been supported as such by the American people. Only if the Congress passes all of its major components does it have any real chance of success. This is absolutely essential if we are to provide incentives and make capital available for the increased productivity required to provide real, permanent jobs for our people.

And let us not forget that the rest of the world is watching America carefully to see how we'll act at this critical moment.

I have recently returned from a summit meeting with world leaders in Ottawa, Canada, and the message I heard from them was quite clear. Our allies depend on a strong and economically sound America. And they're watching events in this country, particularly those surrounding our program for economic recovery, with close attention and great hopes. In short, the best way to have a strong foreign policy abroad is to have a strong economy at home.

The day after tomorrow, Wednesday, the House of Representatives will begin debate on two tax bills. And once again, they need to hear from you. I know that doesn't give you much time, but a great deal is at stake. A few days ago I was visited here in the office by a Democratic Congressman from one of our Southern States. He'd been back in his district. And one day one of his constituents asked him where he stood on our economic recovery program—I outlined that program in an earlier broadcast—particularly the tax cut. Well, the Congressman, who happens to be a strong leader in support of our program, replied at some length with a discussion of the technical points involved, but he also mentioned a few reservations he had on certain points. The constituent, a farmer, listened politely until he'd finished, and then he said, "Don't give me an essay. What I want to know is are you for 'im or agin 'im?'"

Well, I appreciate the gentleman's support and suggest his question is a message your own Representatives should hear. Let me add, those Representatives honestly and sincerely want to know your feelings. They get plenty of input from the special interest groups. They'd like to hear from their home folks.

Now, let me explain what the situation is and what's at issue. With our budget cuts, we've presented a complete program of reduction in tax rates. Again, our purpose was to provide incentive for the individual, incentives for business to encourage production and hiring of the unemployed, and to free up money for investment. Our bill calls for a 5-percent reduction in the income tax rates by October 1st, a 10-percent reduction beginning July 1st, 1982, and another 10-percent cut a year later, a 25-percent total reduction over 3 years.

But then to ensure the tax cut is permanent, we call for indexing the tax rates in 1985, which means adjusting them for inflation. As it is now, if you get a cost-of-living raise that's intended to keep you even with inflation, you find that the increase in the number of dollars you get may very likely move you into a higher tax bracket, and you wind up poorer than you would. This is called bracket creep.

Bracket creep is an insidious tax. Let me give an example. If you earned $10,000 a year in 1972, by 1980 you had to earn $19,700 just to stay even with inflation. But that's before taxes. Come April 15th, you'll find your tax rates have increased 30 percent. Now, if you've been wondering why you don't seem as well-off as you were a few years back, it's because government makes a profit on inflation. It gets an automatic tax increase without having to vote on it. We intended to stop that.

Time won't allow me to explain every detail. But our bill includes just about everything to help the economy. We reduce the marriage penalty, that unfair tax that has a working husband and wife pay more tax than if they were single. We increase the exemption on the inheritance or estate tax to $600,000, so that farmers and family-owned businesses don't have to sell the farm or store in the event of death just to pay the taxes. Most important, we wipe out the tax entirely for a surviving spouse. No longer, for example, will a widow have to sell the family source of income to pay a tax on her husband's death.

There are deductions to encourage investment and savings. Business gets realistic depreciation on equipment and machinery. And there are tax breaks for small and independent businesses which create 80 percent of all our new jobs.

This bill also provides major credits to the research and development industry. These credits will help spark the high technology breakthroughs that are so critical to America's economic leadership in the world. There are also added incentives for small businesses, including a provision that will lift much of the burden of costly paperwork that government has imposed on small business.

In addition, there's short-term but substantial assistance for the hard pressed thrift industry, as well as reductions in oil taxes that will benefit new or independent oil producers and move our Nation a step closer to energy self-sufficiency. Our bill is, in short, the first real tax cut for everyone in almost 20 years. . . .

If I could paraphrase a well-known statement by Will Rogers that he had never met a man he didn't like, I'm afraid we have some people around here who never met a tax they didn't hike. . . .

In a few days the Congress will stand at the fork of two roads. One road is all too familiar to us. It leads ultimately to higher taxes. It merely brings us full circle back to the source of our economic problems, where the government decides that it knows better than you what should be done with your earnings and, in fact, how you should conduct your life. The other road promises to renew the American spirit. It's a road of hope and opportunity. It places the direction of your life back in your hands where it belongs.

I've not taken your time this evening merely to ask you to trust me. Instead, I ask you to trust yourselves. That's what America is all about. Our struggle for nationhood, our unrelenting fight for freedom, our very existence—these have all rested on the assurance that you must be free to shape your life as you are best able to, that no one can stop you from reaching higher or take from you the creativity that has made America the envy of mankind.

One road is timid and fearful; the other bold and hopeful.

In these 6 months, we've done so much and have come so far. It's been the power of millions of people like you who have determined that we will make America great again. You have made the difference up to now. You will make the difference again. Let us not stop now.

Thank you. God bless you, and good night.

2. The *New York Times* Attacks Reagan's Policies (1981)

Critics of President Reagan's budget-slashing and tax-cutting policies fumed furiously but ineffectively during Reagan's first year in office. The new president appeared to be a masterful politician whose will was impossible to thwart. But some observers worried about the real purposes behind Reagan's deft display of presidential leadership. In the following editorial from the *New York Times,* what are alleged to be Reagan's true intentions? What does the editorial mean when it states that Reagan "gathers power for the purpose of denigrating its value in shaping America"? Is this assessment fair?

One thing is surely settled: the Presidency is no feeble office. Let a shrewd President single-mindedly pursue a policy broadly grounded in his election mandate, and he can put it across.

It does not follow that Mr. Reagan's economic program is therefore wise or efficient, or that a different program, without tax cuts, could have fared so well. But conservatives did not invent the technique of buying votes with Federal monies; democracy tilts toward gratifying private wants. It is plainly untrue, however, as many have complained, that the democracy of Congress is bound to frustrate the democratic will that elects Presidents.

Nor is it true that Presidential power requires a telegenic face. Rest in peace, Lyndon Johnson. Power lies in circumstance and in the skill with which it is exploited. The Democrats who opposed Mr. Reagan's budget and tax bills played weak hands, but they played them badly. By turning for help to special-interest lobbies, they only challenged the President to outbid them. By forcing a showdown when they lacked decisive strength, they only magnified the drama of his victory.

But is this President's paradoxical triumph also the nation's? He gathers power for the purpose of denigrating its value in shaping America. He does not say the nation is overextended financially. He does not say guns are momentarily more important than butter. He does not rerank the nation's needs or argue against assorted remedies. He denounces all Federal government as oppressive, as the cause of economic distress and a threat to liberty.

So Mr. Reagan has arranged to shrink annual Federal spending by 1984 by about $150 billion and cut taxes to let individuals and businesses spend that sum instead. Economically, that is mostly a transfer of purchasing power which cannot much reduce inflation or unemployment, the Federal deficit or debt. On the contrary, a big increase in military spending will enlarge the deficit unless the President finds further huge savings in civilian programs. And the pressure to find them—wherever—is what he values most about his accomplishment.

But why does the President boast that he has thus improved economic prospects? Because he holds, as a matter of faith, that a dollar spent privately creates more wealth than a dollar spent by Government.

That is surely sometimes true: a Government-run railroad that is politically beholden to its unions will tolerate more waste than a private bus company. But it surely also is sometimes untrue: a Government investment in a student or road or depressed community can stimulate more productive activity than the same sum spent by private citizens on diamonds or cameras. Government may be incompetent to achieve some of its social goals. But uncoordinated private spending is notoriously inefficient in meeting large public needs.

Take the obvious, urgent need to cool inflation. Mr. Reagan's answer is a tortuous chain of incentives: cut a family's taxes by $500 and the money goes to banks and merchants who invest in more businesses and machines which will be more efficient and hold down prices. Also: reduce a citizen's tax on the *next* earned dollar from 29 to 25 cents and he'll work harder longer and thus reduce costs.

But if it were primarily interested in economic results, Government has surer ways to achieve those results—as even Mr. Reagan's plan recognizes. For it aims large tax reductions directly at businesses that buy cost-reducing machines or job-producing plants. A still more efficient plan would have aimed more precisely at the most wanted machines and at workers who hold down wages or communities that reduce sales taxes.

The unavoidable conclusion is that Mr. Reagan wants to use his power primarily to diminish Government—even where that dilutes economic recovery and prevents efficient allocation of resources.

That the President's plan will revive the economy remains to be proved. What is no longer in doubt is that his economic remedies mask an assault on the very idea that free people can solve their collective problems through representative Government. One day soon Americans will rediscover that their general welfare depends on national as well as parochial actions. And then they will want not just a powerful President but one who cherishes the power of Government to act for the common good.

THOUGHT PROVOKERS

1. Was the control of the Panama Canal by the United States "imperialistic"? Is a nation's control over foreign territory ever justified? Did the Panama Canal treaties improve the relations of the United States with Latin America—especially Central America?

2. How serious was the energy crisis of the 1970's? What were its causes? Is the crisis now over?

3. Was Jimmy Carter's presidency a failure? If so, why? What role did the Iranian hostage crisis play in Carter's political life? How might the hostage crisis have been handled differently? What successes did Carter have as President? What will be his historical reputation in another ten or twenty years?

4. Did the Reagan administration constitute a "revolution" in American politics? Did Reagan's electoral victory ring the death knell for the philosophy of the New Deal and the Great Society? How much difference can one president make, for good or ill?

48 · *The American People since World War II*

> *The challenge of the next half century is whether we have the wisdom to use (our) wealth to enrich and elevate our national life—and to advance the quality of American civilization.*
>
> PRESIDENT LYNDON BAINES JOHNSON, 1964

PROLOGUE: The United States stood triumphant at the end of World War II. Americans had been spared the worst ravages of the global conflict. In contrast to the plight of other combatants, their homeland had not been scorched by fighting, they had lost relatively few fighting men, and their economy was snapped out of depression and whipped into robust trim as a result of the war effort. Confident of the future, Americans immediately after the war launched a "baby boom" that added some 50 million persons to the nation's population over the next decade and a half.

Americans were also a people on the move in the post-war decades, as population shifted massively from the countryside to cities and suburbs, and from the north to the "sunbelt" states in the South and West. The civil rights movement scored dramatic gains, revolutionizing the status of blacks in American society. Other racial and ethnic groups, including native Americans and Hispanics, self-consciously asserted their claim to participate more centrally in the life of the larger society. The women's movement also forged ahead vigorously, bringing changes in the workplace and in family life. Prompted in part by the disillusionment spawned by the Vietnam War, a "counter-cultural" movement emerged in the 1960's. Its adherents sharply dissented from the traditional American values of self-discipline and upward social mobility. But as recession and inflation ravaged the economy in the 1970's and 1980's, many young people worried less about cultivating their "life-style," and more about the mundane necessity of securing a job. Whether the post-war period had truly witnessed a fundamental alteration of American values remained an open question as the century approached its end.

A. THE CHANGING AMERICAN FAMILY

1. Dr. Spock Advises Parents (1957)

The post-World War II "baby boom" exploded in an American society that was fast-moving and fragmented. Parents could no longer assume, as they once had, that their children would grow up to inhabit a world much like that which the older generation had known. Moreover, the remarkable geographical mobility of Americans in the post-war era meant that many families now faced the responsibilities of child-rearing without the traditional support and advice of grandparents and other relatives—who were now likely to live hundreds of miles away. Confronted with these uncertainties, Americans turned to books for guidance—especially to Dr. Benjamin Spock's *The Common Sense Book of Baby and Child Care*, first published in 1945, and possibly the most widely used advice book in American history. When the "youth movement" of the 1960's erupted, many critics blamed Dr. Spock's "permissive" philosophy of child-rearing for raising a generation of anti-authoritarian, undisciplined young Americans. Does the selection from his book given below support that charge? What does Spock mean by "permissiveness"? What historical factors does Spock see as unique to the modern era? He has also been accused of opposing the movement for women's liberation. What is his view of the mother's role?

I may as well let the cat out of the bag right away as far as my opinion goes and say that strictness or permissiveness is not the real issue. . . .

We've been through a big transition. It's hard to get any perspective on this topic without taking a historical view. Styles in strictness vary from one period to another. The Victorian Age was quite strict, for instance, about manners and modesty. In the twentieth century, especially after World War I, a reaction set in. Several factors pushed it along. The great American pioneers in educational research, like John Dewey and William Kilpatrick, showed that a child learns better and faster with a method of teaching that makes allowance for his particular readiness to progress and that recognizes his eagerness to learn if the subject matter is suitable. Freud and his followers showed that harsh toilet training or frightening a child about sex can distort his personality and lead to neurosis. Studies of delinquents and criminals revealed that most of them had suffered more from lack of love in childhood than from lack of punishment. These discoveries, among others, encouraged a general relaxation in child discipline and a greater effort to give children what they seemed to need as individuals. Several wise leaders in American pediatrics, Aldrich and Powers and Gesell, began to introduce a similar philosophy into the medical care of babies and children. But physicians remained strict about infant feeding right into the 1940's, because they still feared that irregular schedules and irregular amounts of formula might bring on the severe diarrheal diseases that used to cause so many infant deaths. Then the experiments of Dr. Preston McLendon and Mrs. Frances P. Simsarian with the "self-demand" schedule, published in 1942, helped to convince doctors that most babies can do very well choosing their own feeding times and will remain healthy. Since then, there has been a rapid and widespread shift in medical practice. Today a majority of American babies are being put on more or less flexible schedules at first.

Doctors who used to conscientiously warn young parents against spoiling are now encouraging them to meet their baby's needs, not only for food, but for comforting and loving.

These discoveries and these changes of attitudes and methods have benefited most children and parents. There are fewer tense ones, more happy ones.

But it's not possible for a civilization like ours to go through such a change of philosophy—it really amounts to a revolution—without raising doubts in many parents' minds and without getting some parents thoroughly mixed up. It's basic human nature to tend to bring up your children about as you were brought up. It's easy enough to pick up new ideas about vitamins and inoculations. But if your upbringing was fairly strict in regard to obedience, manners, sex, truthfulness, it's natural, it's almost inevitable, that you will feel strongly underneath about such matters when raising your own children. You may have changed your theories because of something you've studied or read or heard, but when your child does something that would have been considered bad in your own childhood, you'll probably find yourself becoming more tense, or anxious, or angry than you imagined possible. This is nothing to be ashamed of. This is the way Nature expects human beings to learn child care—from their own childhood. This is how different civilizations have managed to remain stable and carry on their ideals from generation to generation.

The reason that most parents have been able to a good job with their children during the past fifty years of changing theory is that they themselves had been brought up reasonably happily, were comfortable about raising their children the same way, and didn't follow any new theory to extremes. When doctors were emphasizing regularity, confident parents followed a regular schedule in general (and *most* babies adjusted to it *most* of the time), but they weren't afraid to make an occasional exception when the baby became painfully hungry ahead of time, because they felt in their bones that this was right. . . .

During the first half of this century in this country, babies were usually kept on very strict, regular schedules. A newborn 7-pounder would be fed at exactly 6 A.M., 10 A.M., 2 P.M., 6 P.M., 10 P.M. and 2 A.M.—no earlier, no later, regardless of when he seemed hungry.

Strictness was preached and practiced everywhere—on the dairy farm, in the commercial dairy, and in the home. Doctors and nurses feared irregular feeding so strongly that they came to disapprove of it psychologically, too, and taught mothers that it would lead to spoiling the child. In the general enthusiasm for strictness, mothers were usually advised to ignore their baby except at feeding time. Even kissing was frowned on by a few.

Strict regularity worked well enough with a majority of babies. When they took an ample feeding at breast or bottle, it lasted them for *about* 4 hours just because that is the way a young baby's digestive system usually works. But it's also a fact that we are creatures of habit at any age, and if we are always fed at exactly the same hour we soon learn, inside, to become suddenly hungry right at that moment.

But there were always a few babies who had trouble adjusting to regularity in the first month or two—babies whose stomachs couldn't seem to hold 4 hours' worth of milk, babies who went to sleep halfway through feedings, restless babies, colicky babies. They would cry miserably for shorter or longer periods each day, but their mothers and doctors dared not feed them (or even pick them up) off schedule. It was hard enough on the babies. I think it was harder still on the mothers, who had to sit listening, biting their nails, wanting to comfort their babies but not allowed to do so. You don't know how lucky you are to be able to be natural and flexible.

Anyway, the serious diarrheal diseases almost disappeared. The chief factor was the pasteurization of milk in the commercial dairy, but care in preparing the formula and better refrigeration helped, too. But it took many more years before doctors dared to begin experimenting with flexible schedules. When they did, they found that flexibility did *not* lead to diarrhea or indigestion, nor did it lead to spoiling, as many had feared. . . .

THE WORKING MOTHER

To work or not to work? Some mothers *have* to work to make a living. Usually their children turn out all right, because some reasonably good arrangement is made for their care. But others grow up neglected and maladjusted. It would save money in the end if the government paid a comfortable allowance to all mothers of young children who would otherwise be compelled to work. You can think of it this way: useful, well-adjusted citizens are the most valuable possessions a country has, and good mother care during early childhood is the surest way to produce them. It doesn't make sense to let mothers go to work making dresses in a factory or tapping typewriters in an office, and have them pay other people to do a poorer job of bringing up their children.

A few mothers, particularly those with professional training, feel that they must work because they wouldn't be happy otherwise. I wouldn't disagree if a mother felt strongly about it, provided she had an ideal arrangement for her children's care. After all, an unhappy mother can't bring up very happy children.

What about the mothers who don't absolutely have to work but would prefer to, either to supplement the family income or because they think they will be more satisfied and therefore get along better at home? That's harder to answer.

The important thing for a mother to realize is that the younger the child the more necessary it is for him to have a steady, loving person taking care of him. In most cases, the mother is the best one to give him this feeling of "belonging," safely and surely. She doesn't quit on the job, she doesn't turn against him, she isn't indifferent to him, she takes care of him always in the same familiar house. If a mother realizes clearly how vital this kind of care is to a small child, it may make it easier for her to decide that the extra money she might earn, or the satisfaction she might receive from an outside job, is not so important, after all.

What children need most from parents or substitutes. The things that are most vital in the care of a child are a little bit different at different age periods. During the first year, a baby needs a *lot* of motherly care. He has to be fed everything he eats, he eats often, and his food is usually different from the adults'. He makes a great deal of laundry work. In cities he usually has to be pushed in his carriage for outings. For his spirit to grow normally, he needs someone to dote on him, to think he's the most wonderful baby in the world, to make noises and baby talk at him, to hug him and smile at him, to keep him company during wakeful periods.

A day nursery or a "baby farm" is no good for an infant. There's nowhere near enough attention or affection to go around. In many cases, what care there is is matter-of-fact or mechanical rather than warm-hearted. Besides, there's too much risk of epidemics of colds and diarrhea.

Individual care at least until three. The infant whose mother can't take care of him during the daytime needs *individual* care, whether it's in his own home or someone else's. It may be a relative, neighbor, or friend whom the mother knows and has confidence in. If a new maid or nurse is to come into the home, the mother should know her well before she leaves the baby in her care. Or the mother may decide to leave him in a foster home for "foster day care," that is to say, in the care of a woman who makes a profession of caring for children. But the foster mother should be doing it more because she loves children than for the income it brings. The only safe way to choose a foster home is through a first-rate, conscientious child-placing agency that investigates and supervises the individual homes it recommends. But whoever the mother chooses should be a woman who is gentle and loving, and who is not trying to take care of more than two or, at the very most, three babies or small children.

Between the ages of 1 and 3, the care of a child requires a little less time but a lot more understanding. It's good for him to have other children around. He's a person now, with ideas of his own. He needs more and more opportunity to be independent, has to be steered tactfully. An adult who is too bossy makes him balky and frantic. One who lacks self-confidence may be helpless to control him. One who smothers him with too much attention hampers his development. Furthermore, this is the age when he comes to depend for security on one or two familiar, devoted people, and is upset if they disappear or keep changing. This is the least advisable period for the mother who has always taken care of him to go off to work for the first time, or to make changes in the person who takes her place. Many day nurseries do not have enough nurses or attendants to give each child the feeling of really belonging to someone. And the staff may not have had the expert training in understanding small children to be able to foster their fullest development, spiritually, socially, and physically.

So if you have to go off to work when your baby is about a year old, the best solution is individual care, just as it is for the younger infant. But for this age it is particularly important to find a person who has the ability to understand a child and get along with him easily, and who is not likely to quit the job in a few months.

2. Betty Friedan Strikes a Blow for Women's Freedom (1963)

By the early 1960's millions of American women were working for wages outside their homes. Yet cultural values had not kept pace with this change, and a woman's "proper" role was still considered to be in the kitchen and the nursery. In 1963 Betty Friedan published a remarkable book, *The Feminine Mystique*, vigorously attacking that traditional definition of women's place. Her book helped massively to launch the modern women's movement. How, exactly, does she define the "feminine mystique"? Why does she find it so objectionable? Is she speaking about all women, or about a particular class of women?

The problem lay buried, unspoken, for many years in the minds of American women. It was a strange stirring, a sense of dissatisfaction, a yearning that women suffered in the middle of the twentieth century in the United States. Each suburban wife struggled with it alone. As she made the beds, shopped for groceries, matched slipcover material, ate peanut butter sandwiches with her children, chauffeured Cub Scouts and Brownies, lay beside her husband at night—she was afraid to ask even of herself the silent question—"Is this all?"

For over fifteen years there was no word of this yearning in the millions of words written about women, for women, in all the columns, books and articles by experts telling women their role was to seek fulfillment as wives and mothers. Over and over women heard in voices of tradition and of Freudian sophistication that they could desire no greater destiny than to glory in their own femininity. Experts told them how to catch a man and keep him, how to breastfeed children and handle their toilet training, how to cope with sibling rivalry and adolescent rebellion; how to buy a dishwasher, bake bread, cook gourmet snails, and build a swimming pool with their own hands; how to dress, look, and act more feminine and make marriage more exciting; how to keep their husbands from dying young and their sons from growing into delinquents. They were taught to pity the neurotic, unfeminine, unhappy women who wanted to be poets or physicists or presidents. They learned that truly feminine women do not want careers, higher education, political rights—the independence and the opportunities that the old-fashioned feminists fought for. Some women, in their forties and fifties, still remembered painfully giving up those dreams, but more of the younger women no longer thought about them. A thousand expert voices applauded their femininity, their adjustment, their new maturity. All they had to do was devote their lives from earliest girlhood to finding a husband and bearing children.

By the end of the nineteen-fifties, the average marriage age of women in America dropped to 20, and was still dropping, into the teens. Fourteen million girls were engaged by 17. The proportion of women attending college in comparison with men dropping from 47 per cent in 1920 to 35 per

---

2. Reprinted from *The Feminine Mystique*, pp. 11–16, 22–27, by Betty Friedan, by permission of W. W. Norton & Company, Inc. Copyright © 1973, 1963 by Betty Friedan.

cent in 1958. A century earlier, women had fought for higher education; now girls went to college to get a husband. By the mid-fifties, 60 per cent dropped out of college to marry, or because they were afraid too much education would be a marriage bar. Colleges built dormitories for "married students," but the students were almost always the husbands. A new degree was instituted for the wives—"Ph.T." (Putting Husband Through). . . .

By the end of the fifties, the United States birthrate was overtaking India's. The birth-control movement, renamed Planned Parenthood, was asked to find a method whereby women who had been advised that a third or fourth baby would be born dead or defective might have it anyhow. Statisticians were especially astounded at the fantastic increase in the number of babies among college women. Where once they had two children, now they had four, five, six. Women who had once wanted careers were now making careers out of having babies. So rejoiced *Life* magazine in a 1956 paean to the movement of American women back to the home.

In a New York hospital, a woman had a nervous breakdown when she found she could not breastfeed her baby. In other hospitals, women dying of cancer refused a drug which research had proved might save their lives: its side effects were said to be unfeminine. "If I have only one life, let me live it as a blonde," a larger-than-life-sized picture of a pretty, vacuous woman proclaimed from newspaper, magazine, and drugstore ads. And across America, three out of every ten women dyed their hair blonde. They ate a chalk called Metrecal, instead of food, to shrink to the size of the thin young models. Department-store buyers reported that American women, since 1939, had become three and four sizes smaller. "Women are out to fit the clothes, instead of vice-versa," one buyer said.

Interior decorators were designing kitchens with mosaic murals and original paintings, for kitchens were once again the center of women's lives. Home sewing became a million-dollar industry. Many women no longer left their homes, except to shop, chauffeur their children, or attend a social engagement with their husbands. Girls were growing up in America without ever having jobs outside the home. In the late fifties, a sociological phenomenon was suddenly remarked: a third of American women now worked, but most were no longer young and very few were pursuing careers. They were married women who held part-time jobs, selling or secretarial, to put their husbands through school, their sons through college, or to help pay the mortgage. Or they were widows supporting families. Fewer and fewer women were entering professional work. The shortages in the nursing, social work, and teaching professions caused crises in almost every American city. Concerned over the Soviet Union's lead in the space race, scientists noted that America's greatest source of unused brain-power was women. But girls would not study physics: it was "unfeminine." A girl refused a science fellowship at Johns Hopkins to take a job in a real-estate office. All she wanted, she said, was what every other American girl wanted—to get married, have four children and live in a nice house in a nice suburb.

The suburban housewife—she was the dream image of the young American women and the envy, it was said, of women all over the world. The American housewife—freed by science and labor-saving appliances from the drudgery, the dangers of childbirth and the illnesses of her grandmother. She was healthy, beautiful, educated, concerned only about her husband, her children, her home. She had found true feminine fulfillment. As a housewife and mother, she was respected as a full and equal partner to man in his world. She was free to choose automobiles, clothes, appliances, supermarkets; she had everything that women ever dreamed of.

In the fifteen years after World War II, this mystique of feminine fulfillment became the cherished and self-perpetuating core of contemporary American culture. Millions of women lived their lives in the image of those pretty pictures of the American suburban housewife, kissing their husbands goodbye in front of the picture window, depositing their stationwagonsful of children at school, and smiling as they ran the new electric waxer over the spotless kitchen floor. They baked their own bread, sewed their own and their children's clothes, kept their new washing machines and dryers running all day. They changed the sheets on the beds twice a week instead of once, took the rug-hooking class in adult education, and pitied their poor frustrated mothers, who had dreamed of having a career. Their only dream was to be perfect wives and mothers; their highest ambition to have five children and a beautiful house, their only fight to get and keep their husbands. They had no thought for the unfeminine problems of the world outside the home; they wanted the men to make the major decisions. They gloried in their role as women, and wrote proudly on the census blank: "Occupation: housewife." . . .

If the woman had a problem in the 1950's and 1960's, she knew that something must be wrong with her marriage, or with herself. Other women were satisfied with their lives, she thought. What kind of a woman was she if she did not feel this mysterious fulfillment waxing the kitchen floor? She was so ashamed to admit her dissatisfaction that she never knew how many other women shared it. . . .

But on an April morning in 1959, I heard a mother of four, having coffee with four other mothers in a suburban development fifteen miles from New York, say in a tone of quiet desperation, "the problem." And the others knew, without words, that she was not talking about a problem with her husband, or her children, or her home. Suddenly they realized they all shared the same problem, the problem that has no name. They began, hesitantly, to talk about it. Later, after they had picked up their children at nursery school and taken them home to nap, two of the women cried, in sheer relief, just to know they were not alone.

Gradually I came to realize that the problem that has no name was shared by countless women in America. As a magazine writer I often interviewed women about problems with their children, or their marriages, or their houses, or their communities. But after a while I began to recognize the telltale signs of this other problem. I saw the same signs in suburban ranch houses and split-levels on Long Island and in New Jersey and Westchester County; in colonial houses in a small Massáchusetts town; on patios in Memphis; in surburban and city apartments; in living rooms in the Midwest. Sometimes I sensed the problem, not as a reporter, but as a suburban housewife, for during this time I was also bringing up my own three children in Rockland County, New York. I heard echoes of the problem in college dormitories and semi-private maternity wards, at PTA meetings and luncheons of the League of Women Voters, at suburban cocktail parties, in station wagons waiting for trains, and in snatches of conversation overheard at Schrafft's. The groping words I heard from other women, on quiet afternoons when children were at school or on quiet evenings when husbands worked late, I think I understood first as a woman long before I understood their larger social and psychological implications.

Just what was this problem that has no name? What were the words women used when they tried to express it? Sometimes a woman would say "I feel empty somehow . . . incomplete." Or she would say, "I feel as if I don't exist." Sometimes she blotted out the feeling with a tranquilizer. . . .

It is no longer possible to ignore that voice, to dismiss the desperation of so many American women. This is not what being a woman means, no matter what the experts say. For human suffering there is a reason; perhaps the reason has not been found because the right questions have not been asked, or pressed far enough. I do not accept the answer that there is no problem because American women have luxuries that women in other times and lands never dreamed of; part of the strange newness of the problem is that it cannot be understood in terms of the age-old material problems of man: poverty, sickness, hunger, cold. The women who suffer this problem have a hunger that food cannot fill. It persists in women whose husbands are struggling interns and law clerks, or prosperous doctors and lawyers; in wives of workers and executives who make $5,000 a year or $50,000. It is not caused by lack of material advantages; it may not even be felt by women preoccupied with desperate problems of hunger, poverty or illness. And women who think it will be solved by more money, a bigger house, a second car, moving to a better suburb, often discover it gets worse.

It is no longer possible today to blame the problem on loss of femininity: to say that education and independence and equality with men have made American women unfeminine. I have heard so many women try to deny this dissatisfied voice within themselves because it does not fit the pretty picture of femininity the experts have given them. I think, in fact, that this is the first clue to the mystery: the problem cannot be understood in the generally accepted terms by which scientists have studied women, doctors have treated them, counselors have advised them, and writers have written about them. Women who suffer this problem, in whom this voice is stirring, have lived their whole lives in the pursuit of feminine fulfillment. They are not career women (although career women may have other problems); they are women whose greatest ambition has been marriage and children. For the oldest of these women, these daughters of the American middle class, no other dream was possible. The ones in their forties and fifties who once had other dreams gave them up and threw themselves joyously into life as housewives. For the youngest, the new wives and mothers, this was the only dream. They are the ones who quit high school and college to marry, or marked time in some job in which they had no real interest until they married. These women are very "feminine" in the usual sense, and yet they still suffer the problem. . . .

If I am right, the problem that has no name stirring in the minds of so many American women today is not a matter of loss of femininity or too much education, or the demands of domesticity. It is far more important than anyone recognizes. It is the key to these other new and old problems which have been torturing women and their husbands and children, and puzzling their doctors and educators for years. It may well be the key to our future as a nation and a culture. We can no longer ignore that voice within women that says: "I want something more than my husband and my children and my home."

3. Margaret Mead Assesses the Modern Family (1971)

In the 1960's, many young people, disenchanted with "middle American" values, sought "alternative" life styles—sometimes in "communes" designed to replace the traditional structure. Some alarmists saw in such developments the end of civilization as they had known it. The noted anthropologist Margaret Mead, in the selection below, offers a balanced historical perspective. What features of conventional family life does she criticize? What is her prediction for the future of the family? How does she judge the changing role of women in the post–World War II era? How do her views of women's role compare with those of Dr. Spock? with those of Betty Friedan?

Whenever there is a period of upheaval in the world, somebody's going to do something to the family. If the family's being very rigorous and puritanical, you loosen it up. And if it's being very loose, you tighten it up. But you have to change it to really feel you're accomplishing something. If we go back into history we find over and over again, in moments of revolutionary change, that people start talking about the family, and what they're doing to it, and what's wrong with it. They even predict it's going to disappear altogether. It is in fact the only institution we have that doesn't have a hope of disappearing.

No matter how many communes anybody invents, the family always creeps back. You can get rid of it if you live in an enclave and keep everybody else out, and bring the children up to be unfit to live anywhere else. They can go on ignoring the family for several generations. But such communities are not part of the main world. . . .

3. Published by permission of Transaction, Inc. from *Transaction*, pp. 52–53, Vol. 8, no. 11. Copyright © 1971 by Transaction, Inc.

It's very, very difficult to lead a life unless you're married. So everybody gets married—and unmarried—and married, but they're all married to somebody most of the time. And so that we have, in a sense, overdepended on marriage in this country. We've vastly overdone it. . . .

The Nuclear Family is a family consisting of one adult man and one adult woman, married to each other, and minor children. The presence of any other person in the household is an insult. The only people that can come in are cleaning women and sitters. In-laws become sitters—which means that when they come in, you go out, and you never have to see them. Furthermore, today, mothers are very uncomfortable with adolescent daughters in the house. So they push them out as rapidly as possible. If they're rich, they send them to Barnard, and if they're poor, they get them married, and they work at it, very hard, because there isn't room in the kind of kitchens we've had since 1945 for two women.

We have put on the Nuclear Family an appalling burden, because young couples were expected to move as far from both sets of relatives as they could, and they had to move, a great deal of the time.

Millions and millions of Americans move every year, moving miles from relatives or anybody that they know. We know now that the chances of a post-partum depression for a woman are directly proportional to the distance she is from any female relative or friend. When we put her in a new suburb all by herself, her chances of getting a post-partum depression go way up. There are millions of young families living in such suburbs, knowing nobody, with no friends, no support of any kind.

Furthermore, each spouse is supposed to be all things to the other. They're supposed to be good in bed, and good out of it. Women are supposed to be good cooks, good mothers, good wives, good skiers, good conversationalists, good accountants. Neither person is supposed to find any sustenance from anybody else. . . .

So it's a good style of family for change, but it's a hazardous kind of family, nonetheless. And if it is hazardous enough in the city, it's a hundred percent more hazardous in the suburbs. There's a special kind of isolation that occurs in the suburbs. So the attack on the Nuclear Family is, I think, thoroughly justified.

There is a need to have more people around: more people to hold the baby, more people to pitch in in emergencies, more people to help when the child is sick, when the mother is sick, more children for other children to play with so you don't have to spend a thousand dollars sending them to nursery school, more kinds of adults around for the children to pick models from in case father or mother can't do the things they want to do. . . .

We've been cheating women when, in the last ten years, we wanted women to work. We were very short of cheap labor so we told them they needed to be fulfilled. The last source of educated cheap labor was women. So finally everybody discovered that it is very unfulfilling to stay at home, and a woman, of course, when she had her children, maybe she would stay at home for a few years and then she'd leave to be fulfilled. And the foundations gave money, centers were established to lure her out and get her re-educated.

But of course they weren't going to pay her like men, because after all she was more interested in her home, she wouldn't want to leave her children, and you know art lessons sometimes take up more time than little babies—and so she'd want a job from which she could get home early like being a clerk in a team-teaching outfit, instead of a teacher. Something like that—so she could go home when her children did. And of course she wouldn't want to be very ambitious, because all the strain would be bad; she'd want to keep something for home.

In the last ten years, women have been pretty well beguiled and bedazzled into becoming self-fulfilling, educated cheap labor. And I think it's not surprising if some of them are saying that they think they are exploited, and they don't want to be exploited any more.

At the end of World War II, when they wanted all the women that held jobs to go home so the men could get them back, women who'd done well in Washington were told they were overmature, overexperienced:—"Please go home."

I think we'll be bringing girls up with more sense of themselves as people, and that they're going to be people all the way through. If they choose parenthood, they'll choose it much more as they've chosen vocations, and much less as if it were just something the neighbors are doing.

4. A Bill of Rights for Modern Women (1967)

The National Organization for Women (NOW), which Betty Friedan helped to found, emerged in the 1960's as one of the foremost champions of women's rights. At its first national conference in 1967, NOW adopted the following resolution. What does it reveal about the nature of the modern women's movement? How does it compare with the Seneca Falls Declaration of 1848? (See p. 327) What aspects of women's situation changed the most between 1848 and 1967? What caused those changes?

WE DEMAND:

I. That the U.S. Congress immediately pass the Equal Rights Amendment to the Constitution to provide that "Equality of rights under the law shall not be denied or abridged by the United States or by any State on account of sex," and that such then be immediately ratified by the several States.
II. That equal employment opportunity be guaranteed to all women, as well as men, by insisting that the Equal Employment Opportunity Commission enforces the prohibitions against racial discrimination.
III. That women be protected by law to ensure their rights to return to their jobs within a reasonable time after childbirth without loss of seniority or other accrued benefits, and be paid maternity leave as a form of social security and/or employee benefit.

---

4. Reprinted by permission, National Organization for Women.

IV. Immediate revision of tax laws to permit the deduction of home and child-care expenses for working parents.

V. That child-care facilities be established by law on the same basis as parks, libraries, and public schools, adequate to the needs of children from the pre-school years through adolescence, as a community resource to be used by all citizens from all income levels.

VI. That the right of women to be educated to their full potential equally with men be secured by Federal and State legislation, eliminating all discrimination and segregation by sex, written and unwritten, at all levels of education, including colleges, graduate and professional schools, loans and fellowships, and Federal and State training programs such as the Job Corps.

VII. The right of women in poverty to secure job training, housing, and family allowances on equal terms with men, but without prejudice to a parent's right to remain at home to care for his or her children; revision of welfare legislation and poverty programs which deny women dignity, privacy, and self-respect.

VIII. The right of women to control their own reproductive lives by removing from the penal code laws limiting access to contraceptive information and devices, and by repealing penal laws governing abortion.

B. ECONOMIC CONTRADICTIONS

1. John Kenneth Galbraith Criticizes the Affluent Society (1958)

America knew fabulous prosperity in the post-war era—or did it? In an influential book first published in the late 1950's, Harvard economist John Kenneth Galbraith probingly questioned the implications of America's apparent affluence. His ideas contributed significantly to discussion among policy-makers about the kinds of social reforms that later were enacted as the "Great Society" programs. What is the distinction that Galbraith draws between the private and the public realms? How convincing is his argument? What does the relationship between private and public goods suggest about the character of American values?

The final problem of the productive society is what it produces. This manifests itself in an implacable tendency to provide an opulent supply of some things and a niggardly yield of others. This disparity carries to the point where it is a cause of social discomfort and social unhealth. The line which divides our area of wealth from our area of poverty is roughly that which divides privately produced and marketed goods and services from publicly rendered services. Our wealth in the first is not only in startling contrast with the meagerness of the latter, but our wealth in privately produced goods is, to a marked degree, the cause of crisis in the supply of public services. For we have failed to see the importance, indeed the urgent need, of maintaining a balance between the two.

1. From *The Affluent Society*, pp. 221–223, 236–238, by John Kenneth Galbraith. Copyright © 1958, 1969, 1976 by John Kenneth Galbraith. Reprinted by permission of Houghton Mifflin Company.

This disparity between our flow of private and public goods and services is no matter of subjective judgment. On the contrary, it is the source of the most extensive comment which only stops short of the direct contrast being made here. In the years following World War II, the papers of any major city—those of New York were an excellent example—told daily of the shortages and shortcomings in the elementary municipal and metropolitan services. The school were old and overcrowded. The police force was under strength and underpaid. The parks and playgrounds were insufficient. Streets and empty lots were filthy, and the sanitation staff was underequipped and in need of men. Access to the city by those who work there was uncertain and painful and becoming more so. Internal transportation was overcrowded, unhealthful and dirty. So was the air. Parking on the streets should have been prohibited, but there was no space elsewhere. These deficiencies were not in new and novel services but in old and established ones. Cities have long swept their streets, helped their people move around, educated them, kept order, and provided horse rails for equipages which sought to pause. That their residents should have a nontoxic supply of air suggests no revolutionary dalliance with socialism.

The discussion of this public poverty competed, on the whole successfully, with the stories of ever-increasing opulence in privately produced goods. The Gross National Product was rising. So were retail sales. So was personal income. Labor productivity had also advanced. The automobiles that could not be parked were being produced at an expanded rate. The children, though without schools, subject in the playgrounds to the affectionate interest of adults with odd tastes, and disposed to increasingly imaginative forms of delinquency, were admirably equipped with television sets. We had difficulty finding storage space for the great surpluses of food despite a national disposition to obesity. Food was grown and packaged under private auspices. The care and refreshment of the mind, in contrast with the stomach, was principally in the public domain. Our colleges and universities were often severely overcrowded and underprovided, and the same was even more often true of the mental hospitals.

The contrast was and remains evident not alone to those who read. The family which takes its mauve and cerise, airconditioned, power-steered and power-braked automobile out for a tour passes through cities that are badly paved, made hideous by litter, blighted buildings, billboards and posts for wires that should long since have been put underground. They pass on into a countryside that has been rendered largely invisible by commercial art. (The goods which the latter advertise have an absolute priority in our value system. Such aesthetic considerations as a view of the countryside accordingly come second. On such matters, we are consistent.) They picnic on exquisitely packaged food from a portable icebox by a polluted stream and go on to spend the night at a park which is a menace to public health and morals. Just before dozing off on an air mattress, beneath a nylon tent, amid the stench of decaying refuse, they may reflect vaguely on the curious unevenness of their blessings. Is this, indeed, the American genius? . . .

A feature of the years immediately following World War II was a remarkable attack on the notion of expanding and improving public services. During the depression years, such services had been elaborated and improved partly in order to fill some small part of the vacuum left by the shrinkage of private production. During the war years, the role of government was vastly expanded. After that came the reaction. Much of it, unquestionably, was motivated by a desire to rehabilitate the prestige of private production and therewith of producers. No doubt some who joined the attack hoped, at least tacitly, that it might be possible to sidestep the truce on taxation vis-à-vis equality by having less taxation of all kinds. For a time, the notion that our public services had somehow become inflated and excessive was all but axiomatic. Even liberal politicians did not seriously protest. They found it necessary to aver that they were in favor of public economy too.

In this discussion, a certain mystique was attributed to the satisfaction of privately supplied wants. A community decision to have a new school means that the individual surrenders the necessary amount, willy-nilly, in his taxes. But if he is left with that income, he is a free man. He can decide between a better car or a television set. This was advanced with some solemnity as an argument for the TV set. The difficulty is that this argument leaves the community with no way of preferring the school. All private wants, where the individual can choose, are inherently superior to all public desires which must be paid for by taxation and with an inevitable component of compulsion.

The cost of public services was also held to be a desolating burden on private production, although this was at a time when the private production was burgeoning. Urgent warnings were issued of the unfavorable effects of taxation on investment. . . .

Finally, it was argued, with no little vigor, that expanding government posed a grave threat to individual liberties. . . .

With time, this attack on public services has subsided. The disorder associated with social imbalance has become visible even if the need for balance between private and public services is still imperfectly appreciated. . . .

Nonetheless, the postwar onslaught on the public services left a lasting imprint. To suggest that we canvass our public wants to see where happiness can be improved by more and better services has a sharply radical tone. Even public services to avoid disorder must be defended. By contrast, the man who devises a nostrum for a nonexistent need and then successfully promotes both remains one of nature's noblemen.

2. Michael Harrington Discovers Another America (1962)

Some books shape the course of history. Michael Harrington's *The Other America*, published in 1962, was such a book. It shook middle-class Americans out of their com-

2. Reprinted with permission of Macmillan Publishing Company from *The Other America* by Michael Harrington. © Michael Harrington, 1962.

placent assumption that the problem of poverty had been solved in their country. With
reasoned yet passionate argument, Harrington forcefully documented the existence of
an "invisible" America populated by hopelessly impoverished people. The book's millions
of readers—many of them idealistic young people—helped form the political constituency that made possible the Johnson administration's "War on Poverty" in the late
1960's. Who are the poor people Harrington describes? Why are they "invisible"? What
does Harrington identify as historically "new" about their condition? Are the problems
he describes now resolved?

There is a familiar America. It is celebrated in speeches and advertised
on television and in the magazines. It has the highest mass standard of living
the world has ever known.

In the 1950's this America worried about itself, yet even its anxieties were
products of abundance. The title of a brilliant book was widely misinterpreted, and the familiar America began to call itself "the affluent society."
There was introspection about Madison Avenue and tail fins; there was discussion of the emotional suffering taking place in the suburbs. In all this,
there was an implicit assumption that the basic grinding economic problems
had been solved in the United States. In this theory the nation's problems
were no longer a matter of basic human needs, of food, shelter, and clothing.
Now they were seen as qualitative, a question of learning to live decently
amid luxury.

While this discussion was carried on, there existed another America. In it
dwelt somewhere between 40,000,000 and 50,000,000 citizens of this land.
They were poor. They still are.

To be sure, the other America is not impoverished in the same sense as
those poor nations where millions cling to hunger as a defense against starvation. This country has escaped such extremes. That does not change the
fact that tens of millions of Americans are, at this very moment, maimed
in body and spirit, existing at levels beneath those necessary for human
decency. If these people are not starving, they are hungry, and sometimes
fat with hunger, for that is what cheap foods do. They are without adequate housing and education and medical care. . . .

This book is a description of the world in which these people live; it is
about the other America. Here are the unskilled workers, the migrant farm
workers, the aged, the minorities, and all the others who live in the economic underworld of American life. . . .

The millions who are poor in the United States tend to become increasingly invisible. Here is a great mass of people, yet it takes an effort of the
intellect and will even to see them.

I discovered this personally in a curious way. After I wrote my first article on poverty in America, I had all the statistics down on paper. I had
proved to my satisfaction that there were around 50,000,000 poor in this
country. Yet, I realized I did not believe my own figures. The poor existed
in the Government reports; they were percentages and numbers in long,

close columns, but they were not part of my experience. I could prove that the other America existed, but I had never been there.

My response was not accidental. It was typical of what is happening to an entire society, and it reflects profound social changes in this nation. The other America, the America of poverty, is hidden today in a way that it never was before. Its millions are socially invisible to the rest of us. No wonder that so many misinterpreted Galbraith's title and assumed that "the affluent society" meant that everyone had a decent standard of life. The misinterpretation was true as far as the actual day-to-day lives of two-thirds of the nation were concerned. Thus, one must begin a description of the other America by understanding why we do not see it.

There are perennial reasons that make the other America an invisible land.

Poverty is often off the beaten track. It always has been. The ordinary tourist never left the main highway, and today he rides interstate turnpikes. He does not go into the valleys of Pennsylvania where the towns look like movie sets of Wales in the thirties. He does not see the company houses in rows, the rutted roads (the poor always have bad roads whether they live in the city, in towns, or on farms), and everything is black and dirty. And even if he were to pass through such a place by accident, the tourist would not meet the unemployed men in the bar or the women coming home from a runaway sweatshop.

Then, too, beauty and myths are perennial masks of poverty. The traveler comes to the Appalachians in the lovely season. He sees the hills, the streams, the foliage—but not the poor. Or perhaps he looks at a run-down mountain house and, remembering Rousseau rather than seeing with his eyes, decides that "those people" are truly fortunate to be living the way they are and that they are lucky to be exempt from the strains and tensions of the middle class. The only problem is that "those people," the quaint inhabitants of those hills, are undereducated, underprivileged, lack medical care, and are in the process of being forced from the land into a life in the cities, where they are misfits.

These are normal and obvious causes of the invisibility of the poor. They operated a generation ago; they will be functioning a generation hence. It is more important to understand that the very development of American society is creating a new kind of blindness about poverty. The poor are increasingly slipping out of the very experience and consciousness of the nation.

If the middle class never did like ugliness and poverty, it was at least aware of them. "Across the tracks" was not a very long way to go. There were forays into the slums at Christmas time; there were charitable organizations that brought contact with the poor. Occasionally, almost everyone passed through the Negro ghetto or the blocks of tenements, if only to get downtown to work or to entertainment.

Now the American city has been transformed. The poor still inhabit the miserable housing in the central area, but they are increasingly isolated from contact with, or sight of, anybody else. Middle-class women coming in from Suburbia on a rare trip may catch the merest glimpse of the other America on the way to an evening at the theater, but their children are segregated in suburban schools. The business or professional man may drive along the fringes of slums in a car or bus, but it is not an important experience to him. The failures, the unskilled, the disabled, the aged, and the minorities are right there, across the tracks, where they have always been. But hardly anyone else is.

In short, the very development of the American city has removed poverty from the living, emotional experience of millions upon millions of middle-class Americans. Living out in the suburbs, it is easy to assume that ours is, indeed, an affluent society. . . .

It is a blow to reform and the political hopes of the poor that the middle class no longer understands that poverty exists. But, perhaps more important, the poor are losing their links with the great world. If statistics and sociology can measure a feeling as delicate as loneliness (and some of the attempts to do so will be cited later on), the other America is becoming increasingly populated by those who do not belong to anybody or anything. They are no longer participants in an ethnic culture from the old country; they are less and less religious; they do not belong to unions or clubs. They are not seen, and because of that they themselves cannot see. Their horizon has become more and more restricted; they see one another, and that means they see little reason to hope. . . .

There are mighty historical and economic forces that keep the poor down; and there are human beings who help out in this grim business, many of them unwittingly. There are sociological and political reasons why poverty is not seen; and there are misconceptions and prejudices that literally blind the eyes. The latter must be understood if anyone is to make the necessary act of intellect and will so that the poor can be noticed.

Here is the most familiar version of social blindness: "The poor are that way because they are afraid of work. And anyway they all have big cars. If they were like me (or my father or my grandfather), they could pay their own way. But they prefer to live on the dole and cheat the taxpayers."

This theory, usually thought of as a virtuous and moral statement, is one of the means of making it impossible for the poor ever to pay their way. There are, one must assume, citizens of the other America who choose impoverishment out of fear of work (though, writing it down, I really do not believe it). But the real explanation of why the poor are where they are is that they made the mistake of being born to the wrong parents, in the wrong section of the country, in the wrong industry, or in the wrong racial or ethnic group. Once that mistake has been made, they could have been paragons of will and morality, but most of them would never even have had a chance to get out of the other America.

There are two important ways of saying this: The poor are caught in a vicious circle; or, The poor live in a culture of poverty.

In a sense, one might define the contemporary poor in the United States as those who, for reasons beyond their control, cannot help themselves. All the most decisive factors making for opportunity and advance are against them. They are born going downward, and most of them stay down. They are victims whose lives are endlessly blown round and round the other America.

Here is one of the most familiar forms of the vicious circle of poverty. The poor get sick more than anyone else in the society. That is because they live in slums, jammed together under unhygienic conditions; they have inadequate diets, and cannot get decent medical care. When they become sick, they are sick longer than any other group in society. Because they are sick more often and longer than anyone else, they lose wages and work, and find it difficult to hold a steady job. And because of this, they cannot pay for good housing, for a nutritious diet, for doctors. At any given point in the circle, particularly when there is a major illness, their prospect is to move to an even lower level and to begin the cycle, round and round, toward even more suffering. . . .

Throughout, I work on an assumption that cannot be proved by Government figures or even documented by impressions of the other America. It is an ethical proposition, and it can be simply stated: In a nation with a technology that could provide every citizen with a decent life, it is an outrage and a scandal that there should be such social misery. Only if one begins with this assumption is it possible to pierce through the invisibility of 40,000,000 to 50,000,000 human beings and to see the other America. We must perceive passionately, if this blindness is to be lifted from us. A fact can be rationalized and explained away; an indignity cannot.

What shall we tell the American poor, once we have seen them? Shall we say to them that they are better off than the Indian poor, the Italian poor, the Russian poor? That is one answer, but it is heartless. I should put it another way. I want to tell every well-fed and optimistic American that it is intolerable that so many millions should be maimed in body and in spirit when it is not necessary that they should be. My standard of comparison is not how much worse things used to be. It is how much better they could be if only we were stirred. . . .

These, then, are the strangest poor in the history of mankind.

They exist within the most powerful and rich society the world has ever known. Their misery has continued while the majority of the nation talked of itself as being "affluent" and worried about neuroses in the suburbs. In this way tens of millions of human beings became invisible. They dropped out of sight and out of mind; they were without their own political voice.

Yet this need not be. The means are at hand to fulfill the age-old dream: poverty can now be abolished. How long shall we ignore this underdeveloped nation in our midst? How long shall we look the other way while our fellow human beings suffer? How long?

3. Working for a Living (1971)

Most Americans are neither very rich nor very poor—they are the "Middle Americans" who rarely become the objects of government economic policy, yet do not truly qualify as "affluent." Their lives are so "ordinary" that they tend not to get the attention of the media, which is devoted to reporting dramatic and extraordinary material. In the unusual selection below, one such typical family's life-style in the late 1960's is described. What is the attitude of the Capellis toward work? toward welfare? What are their greatest concerns in life? How do they view the government?

Eugene Cappelli, Jr., is driving home from work in the well-kept, second-hand Chevy II (a '63 with about 41,000 miles) that his parents gave him as a present last Christmas to replace a tottering '60 Studebaker. He is a pleasant-faced young man in a white shirt, tie and slacks and he still has on the white-lettered red badge that says "Gene—Psychiatric Asst." It's his badge of employment, and the salary that goes with it signifies his membership in the great army of the struggling class.

Cappelli works the 7:30 a.m. to 4 p.m. shift as an attendant at New York's Pilgrim State Hospital in Brentwood; he received a small raise recently and earns $200.75 every two weeks. That means he takes home $174.60, or about $87 a week. One reason he likes the job is that "it has satisfactions; you see results in people." And another reason is economic. "The idea is that the money's steady, even though it's low," he says. At twenty-nine, Cappelli, a high-school graduate and one-time Air Force jet mechanic, is intensely concerned with job security.

He has a variety of reasons for his concern. He has a special checking account that rarely has more than $200 in it, and he has no savings account. He has a wife and two children, a $26-a-month life insurance policy, a $24-a-month oil bill and a home in Ronkonkoma with a thirty-year mortgage. It's a six-room ranch with a full cellar, and it cost $13,990 when he bought it new five years ago with a down payment of $650. The monthly carrying charges were originally quoted at $104 but they were $118 by the time the family moved in four months later, and now they are $141. It's a sizable chunk for Cappelli and his wife, Andrea, who is twenty-six and works part time as a teacher's aide at a grade school just off her backyard for $2.10 an hour. Last year, she made about $550, and their combined income was $5,378. About $217 of that went for income taxes. (This year they expect their income to be $5,500.)

With Andrea's average take-home pay added to her husband's the couple has a weekly cash income of $101, or $404 a month for themselves and their children, Debbie, six, and Sandy, five. Andrea says that after they take out for the mortgage, life insurance, oil, electricity, phone and car expenses, they have about $150 a month left for food, clothing, incidentals and medical care (they had been entitled to Medicaid for the children, but won't be

3. Harvey Aronson, "Life with Cappelli on $101 a Week," *Newsday* (May 1969), pp. 25–34.

after June 1). "The way I figure it," she says, "that is about a dollar twenty-five per day a person, which is less than the amount some poor people on welfare receive." In understanding the Cappellis' situation, it is important to know that if they wanted to earn a few hundred dollars less a year and to pay rent instead of having a mortgage, they could probably qualify for welfare. However, what is important is this: it wouldn't be part of their life style.

They consider themselves working-class people but not needy people, and it is a distinction that has to do with pride. "It's the way I brought him up," says Cappelli's mother, who works as an attendant with him at the new Hempstead Psychiatric Division in Pilgrim State, and that's part of the sociology. His mother also says that "you help your children," and that, too, is part of the sociology—Eugene and Andrea get help in the form of gifts from their parents. The car and their bedroom set from his parents, for example, and the refrigerator and the wallpaper and linoleum in Debbie's room from Andrea's parents. And their living-room furniture, which is twenty years old, once belonged to Andrea's grandmother. But they would break their backs before they asked the government to support them.

"Welfare?" says Gene Cappelli. "No, I can't sit back and try to get money. I can't see that it's mine. I went through that a little when I got out of the service and collected some unemployment insurance. People acted like they were doing you a big favor. I figured the hell with this. I like to feel self-sustaining.". . .

The day starts at about 7 a.m. for Eugene and Andrea Cappelli, who have been married for eight years, and are young enough to dig rock 'n' roll, and old enough to be mystified by the disorder in the schools. "I think all those kids on those college campuses should be put over somebody's knee and spanked," says Andrea, who took a secretarial course at the Long Island Agricultural and Technical Institute for nine months after graduating from Newfield High School in Centereach. Gene, who put in a four-year Air Force hitch after graduating from Smithtown High, says, "They're holding back the ones who want to learn." It is relevant that the Cappellis compare student troubles to race problems. "I think there are a few militants who are making it bad for the rest of the people," says Andrea in discussing black unrest. "It's the same as with the students." She and Gene preface this by denying bias. "In the service," says Gene, "I had some very close friends who are colored people.". . .

Cappelli says he has aspirations for the future. "But it's hard to say how right now. I would like to try to better myself, but it's a little hazy right now."

Eugene and Andrea Cappelli are Lutheran, and their children attend Sunday School. For the most part, they vote Republican—they voted for Richard Nixon last year, but not with any wild enthusiasm. Gene feels that unions are good and bad ("Working people have a right to ask for more money," he says, "but sometimes the unions are atrocious in their demands"), and he and his wife are as confused about the war as most Americans. "We can't walk out, but we have to do something else," says Andrea. And Gene says, "I don't have anything against these kids who don't want to get shot . . . And I don't think half the boys over there know what it's about. You don't know what's right and what's wrong.

They don't have it easy, but they get by. As Andrea says, they have healthy kids and they own their own home. Their house is on a 50-by-150 plot on Louis Kossuth Avenue in a comparatively uncrowded neighborhood of homes that range from small bungalows to large split-levels, and there are still a good many wooded areas around. E. J. CAPPELLI, JR., it says in large black letters on the mailbox, and that means something.

At least to Gene Cappelli, it means something. Whether it means anything to the people who run the government is something he's not sure about. "It's hard to say whether the higher-ups care about us," he says. "They say so, but sometimes I don't really believe it. Unless they come down to the little guy's level, they don't really know how it is."

C. HEATING UP THE MELTING POT

1. *Black Enterprise* Champions Affirmative Action (1978)

Black Americans scored dramatic social and economic gains in the 1960's and 1970's —thanks largely to the leadership of Martin Luther King, Jr., and the vigorous commitment of the federal government, especially in the Johnson administration, to making black civil rights a reality, not just a dream. "Affirmative action" programs, designed to redress historical injustices by giving women and members of minority groups preference in hiring and admission to educational institutions, were one vehicle by which blacks speeded their progress into the mainstream of American society. Then in 1978 the United States Supreme Court cast a cloud over affirmative action programs in the case of *University of California Regents* v. *Bakke.* Allan Bakke, a white candidate for admission to the Medical School of the University of California at Davis, claimed that he was denied admission because of the school's policy of reserving several places in the entering class for minority students. The Court held that it was unlawful to take minority status so explicitly into account in admissions decisions, and ordered the school to admit Bakke. (However, in its complex and confusing opinion, the Court did not altogether rule out reliance on ethnic or racial criteria in the admissions process.) *Black Enterprise,* a magazine aimed primarily at black readers, criticizes the *Bakke* decision in the following editorial. The magazine endorses the dissenting opinion of the Court's only black Justice, Thurgood Marshall. What does the editorial especially admire about Marshall's position? How sound is the argument that "in order to treat some persons equally, we must treat them differently"?

There are moments in your life when you feel you've reached a turning point; when you stop, make an assessment of your situation and feel good, knowing that hard work, effort and imagination have paid off. These moments are all too few and, invariably, before they can be fully appreciated they are shattered by the naked reality of the daily struggle. Last June was such a time.

In that month, the President of the United States, for the first time in the nation's history, invited the leading black executives in the country to the White House so that he could personally inform them of the policies and directions of his administration, especially as they affect black economic well-being.

The assemblage was historic: a gathering of men—and one woman—linked not only by race but by success, not only by ideology or civil rights but by their proven ability to run businesses, employ people, meet payrolls. When one considers that over one hundred years ago their ancestors could own nothing—not even themselves; that fifty years ago their fathers could probably not borrow money from the local bank or be insured; that fifteen years ago the very meeting they attended at the White House could not have been held, the significance of that moment at the White House brightens. Here were over one hundred black executives who had started out with little more than hope, now standing at the symbolic seat of power. Through their companies they represented an aggregate wealth of almost nine hundred million dollars. It was a moment to remember, to savor.

But not for long. A little over two weeks after this gathering came the stinging reality of the racial struggle these businessmen face—the *Bakke* decision.

On June 28, the Supreme Court of the United States rendered its much awaited decision on the *Bakke* case. Suddenly, affirmative action was out and, incredibly, blacks could be charged with discriminating against whites. There is much discussion concerning the *Bakke* decision. Some claim the case was interpreted "narrowly" and that blacks, if not achieving a total victory, at least were not subjected to a total loss.

I am not a lawyer but a businessman. As I go about the task of keeping my organization going I encounter many whites and know that for some of them the *Bakke* decision means that affirmative action is over. Many companies were faint of heart when they began their programs. This decision will encourage them to stop their efforts altogether. However, we must insist that those firms that have programs continue them; we must insist that those firms doing business with black entrepreneurs continue doing so; we must lobby for the continuation of set asides and we must hold the administration to its commitment to triple federal contract procurement no matter what was decided in *Bakke*.

The fact that the Court seems to have sanctioned the use of race as a factor in determining admissions should not lull us into inaction. *Bakke* means that blacks are in trouble. This was nowhere stated more clearly or succinctly than in Justice Marshall's dissent. Marshall said:

> I agree with the judgment of the Court only insofar as it permits a university to consider the race of an applicant in making admissions decisions. I do not agree that the petitioner's admissions program violated the Constitution. For it

must be remembered that during most of the past 200 years, the Constitution as interpreted by this Court, did not prohibit the most ingenious and pervasive forms of discrimination against the Negro. Now, when a State acts to remedy the effects of the legacy of discrimination, I cannot believe that this same Constitution stands as a barrier.

The position of the Negro today in America is the tragic but inevitable consequence of centuries of unequal treatment. Measured by any benchmark of conduct or achievement, meaningful equality remains a distant dream for the Negro.

It is because of a legacy of unequal treatment that we now must permit the institutions of this society to give consideration to race in making decisions about who will hold the position of influence, affluence and prestige in America. For far too long, the doors to those positions have been shut to Negroes. If we are ever to become a fully integrated society, one in which the color of a person's skin will not determine the opportunities available to him or her, we must be willing to take steps to open those doors. I do not believe that anyone can truly look into America's past and still find that a remedy for the effects of the past is impermissible . . .

I fear that we have come full circle. After the Civil War our government started several "affirmative action" programs. This Court in the Civil Rights cases and Plessy v. Ferguson destroyed the movement toward complete equality. For almost a century no action was taken and this nonaction was with the tacit approval of the Courts. Then we had Brown v. Board of Education and the Civil Rights Acts of Congress followed by numerous affirmative action programs. Now, we have this Court again stepping in, this time time to stop affirmative action programs of the type used by the University of California.

Marshall's eloquence in defense of the admission's policy was matched by that of Justice Blackmun who observed that "In order to treat some persons equally, we must treat them differently." . . .

2. George Will Blasts Reverse Discrimination (1978)

Conservative columnist George Will also disliked the *Bakke* decision—because it failed to put an end, once and for all, to the "reverse discrimination" of affirmative-action programs. How does his argument fit with that of *Black Enterprise* magazine, given above? What are the American values that Will believes are being betrayed by "reverse discrimination"? Is he right?

You cannot spill a drop of American blood without spilling the blood of the whole world," Herman Melville wrote in 1849. ". . . Our blood is as the flood of the Amazon, made up of a thousand noble currents all pouring into one. We are not a nation, so much as a world." But government policy has been, increasingly, to divide the majestic national river into little racial and ethnic creeks. If that policy succeeds, the United States will be less a nation than an angry menagerie of factions scrambling for preference in the government's allocation of entitlements.

That policy was endorsed by the Administration's brief against Allan Bakke, a brief which urged that the nation should cultivate "race consciousness." The brief did not suggest how the government will decide, someday, that persons who have been "victims," personally or through "their forebears," have been "restored"—a strange choice of verb—"to the position they would have occupied" but for discrimination. The Bakke decision pleases the Administration.

Bakke won because a medical school, with no record of discrimination to rectify, adopted a numerical quota for certain minorities, and admitted some who were dramatically less qualified than he was. The Bakke decision has made little law. Therefore, most existing policies will continue, so the law can be riddled with racial considerations. With regard to higher education, the decision suggests broad tolerance for reverse-discrimination policies that are less raw than that which excluded Bakke. And Justice Powell's opinion for the Court can be read plausibly as somewhat permissive regarding considerations of race and ancestry in the allocation of other government benefits generally.

'SUSPECT' DISTINCTIONS

The opinion says racial and ethnic distinctions are "suspect" and require "exacting judicial examination." But when state distribution of benefits "hinges" on race or ethnicity, the racial and ethnic classifications are acceptable if they are "necessary" to promote a "substantial" state interest, such as diversity in enrollments. Four Justices even assert the constitutionality of programs like the one that excluded Bakke, programs that do not just use "minority status as a positive factor," but that "set aside a predetermined number of places" for minorities. These Justices say, not groundlessly: "For purposes of constitutional adjudication, there is no difference between the two approaches."

Powell says that the "equal protection" clause precludes "recognition of special wards entitled to a degree of protection greater than that accorded others"; he rejects a "two-class theory" of equal protection. But then he says there can be compelling state interests served by constitutional forms of discrimination which disadvantage whites for the benefit of preferred minorities. This necessarily means distinguishing two classes of citizens.

Powell says there is a distinction of constitutional dimension between an "explicit racial classification" that "totally" excludes members of some groups from full participation in a program, and "properly devised" racial considerations that are "flexible" in treating race or ancestry as a "plus." But this can be a distinction without a significant difference. For most professional schools, the pool of qualified minority applicants is shallow. Schools that dip too deeply will produce striking disparities between the test scores and academic records of minorities and whites they accept. At some point such disparities must be *prima facie* evidence of a quota, whether it is acknowledged or surreptitious.

'STATISTICAL PARITY'

The Bakke decision does not necessarily mean the Court will say that reverse discrimination in employment and awarding contracts is "necessary" to a "substantial" state interest. But the Court may not seriously impede the bureaucratic drive to transform the core concept of American justice from "equal opportunity for individuals" to "statistical parity for government-approved groups." There is, indeed, a substantial state interest in broadening membership in the middle class, and especially in professions. But the Fourteenth Amendment guarantees equal protection to "persons," and any reverse discrimination grants special entitlements to preferred groups. Nevertheless, the Bakke decision will leave unscathed an array of programs by which the government encourages or compels public and private institutions to consider ethnic quantities more, and individual qualities less, when conferring benefits.

In 1954, the Court seemed on the way to saying what Congress subsequently seemed to say in the 1964 Civil Rights Act: race is an inherently unacceptable basis for state action. But now, in the Bakke case, the Court has refused to find that principle in the 1964 act, and the Court rejected that principle in cases before Bakke. For example, it held that states can tailor redistricting plans racially to create or preserve legislative districts that enhance the electoral power of preferred minorities (in the particular case, blacks and Puerto Ricans). The plan in question diluted the electoral strength of Hassidic Jews who do not enjoy government preference.

WARDS OF THE STATE

Reverse discrimination began as a means of ameliorating the condition of blacks, but it was quickly claimed as a "right" by groups defined by race, ancestry or sex. It is demanded in spite of the fact that it devalues the achievements of its beneficiaries and stigmatizes them as wards of the state, unable to compete. This taint is not disguised by tactical euphemisms, such as saying that employers must "differentially validate" employment tests when they are required to set lower passing scores for preferred minorities than for whites. Whether called "affirmative action" or (as in the 1976 Democratic platform) "compensatory opportunity," reverse discrimination, and the quest for statistical parity for "underrepresented" groups, involve what Prof. Ben L. Martin calls the "sensory" theory of representation: "only personal qualities crude enough to be obvious to sense perception, such as skin color, language, or sex, are acceptable bases of representation." Martin explains reverse discrimination in terms of "the foot-race analogy":

"In a fair race, none is disadvantaged at the starting line. But if all begin with equal advantage, then all should finish together, because contemporary liberalism leaves virtually no personal quality—not character, personality, motivation, self-discipline, or any other personal trait—as the responsibility of the individual."

The premise behind reverse discrimination is this: an unfair start can be inferred from an unequal outcome. The traditional American premise is this: the equal status of citizenship is the basis on which a structure of inequality *should* be built by a population in which talents are neither equally distributed nor equally rewarded. Reverse discrimination is a betrayal, not a fulfillment, of American values.

3. Robert Coles Examines the White American Mind (1966)

The racial upheavals of the post-war era unsettled many white Americans. White northerners, long smug about their moral superiority to white southerners in racial matters, suddenly realized in the 1960's that they, too, had to confront America's historic racial problems at first hand. Robert Coles, a psychiatrist with a deep interest in the psychological effects of changing racial relationships, interviewed several northern white families while preparing the article below. How do these white people view themselves? What is their attitude toward blacks? Are they bigots, pure and simple?

Recently in Boston some Negro children were bused into neighborhood schools serving white children, not by the city, but upon the initiative of individual Negro parents. Indignation spread through the area. The people became aroused, and in unusually large numbers registered their sentiments at the polls. There is uneasy talk about a so-called "white backlash vote," waiting in the wings to single out and dismiss summarily anyone trying to give special favor to Negroes, most particularly by encouraging them to live and go to school in white neighborhoods.

Here are the words of a thirty-year-old woman, the mother of six. She is Irish. Her husband works in the repair shop of a utility company. They live in a mixed Irish and Italian neighborhood in Boston where homes vary, some modestly comfortable and well kept, others in obvious decline. Her young children now have several Negro children in classes with them, and though the two young boys and the little girl do not seem to mind, their mother is quite upset.

Why do they do it? I don't understand them at all. They have their own people, just as we do, but suddenly they're not happy together. They want to go here and there, and send their children everywhere. All you hear these days is news about them. You'd think Negroes were the only people in America that have a tough time. What about the rest of us? Who comes here asking us how we get by, or how we feel about what *we* had to go through?

My father couldn't find a job either, not a steady one, anyway. I remember my mother telling us how he walked and walked, practically begging for work. She said he would almost offer to work for nothing rather than sit around home doing nothing. The day he applied for relief was the saddest day of his life. It broke him. He hated himself ever after. He was always against taking charity, and to have to ask for it was too much for him. When the war came he got steady work again, but my mother said he never was the same. He was always

3. Robert Coles, "The White Northerner: Pride and Prejudice," *Atlantic Monthly*, Vol. 217 (June, 1966), pp. 53–57. Reprinted by permission of the author.

nervous, worried about losing his job, like in the thirties. He became very tight with his money; he even hoarded pennies in a bank. . . . He was plain scared for the rest of his life. To be truthful, I think he died happy. It was like a relief for him. He was very religious. He went to Mass every morning. He died with a smile on his face, and our mother, she said he had been waiting for that day for a long time. He used to say to her that whether it was heaven or hell the good Lord chose for him, it would be better than the worry and the trying to make ends meet of this world.

That's the trouble, though, with Negroes. They're a superstitious lot. They have no real faith, except all that shouting they do, and they only know how to ask, not go out and earn. I know they had it bad here, but so did we all, my father and everyone else practically, except for the rich. And it's the rich, out there in the suburbs, who keep on telling us what we should do. They preach at us to take them here and let them live there, and act this way to them, and that, and so on until you get sick hearing it all. Suddenly they're so kind, the suburban crowd. They stepped all over us, and kept us out of everything, the Yankees and the college people over there at Harvard did. Now they're so good. They're all excited and worried about people, but only the Negroes get their sympathy, only them. Talking about prejudice, that's what we face, prejudice against *us*. I think we should start suing in all the courts, and marching down those streets, like the Negroes. Maybe if we had done that a long time ago, we wouldn't still be so up against now.

In nearly every interview, I hear in one way or another certain common themes: we all have it rough, the Negro being only one of many in that regard; what the Negro calls the civil rights movement in the North is in fact an attempt to crowd out others, from schools, jobs, and opportunities of one sort or another; no one is entitled to anything "special," not when others have to sit by and get little or nothing; somehow the Negro is rather devious and clever, as well as half-witted and immoral, because he has managed to exact both sympathy and consistent help from people—the well born, the well educated—who have ignored the misery of other people for decades.

In the South the Negro can be lived with by the white man, at very close quarters, too. Even the poorest white man can keep company with Negroes, share jokes and general talk with them. The white child can play with negroes; while growing up he can eat from their hands; as an adult he works with them every day. The Negro's general position helps the white man feel on sure ground, above the uncertain social and economic waters that threaten most of us at one time or another with feelings of worthlessness or insecurity. In the particular situations of daily life, however, a given Negro can be depended upon, even though, as a race, they can be excluded or looked down upon.

In the North, for many white people the Negro, perhaps pitied in the past, is now a constant topic of news and conversation. He comes upon a scene where his presence is new. He comes upon a region with its own history of religious prejudices and racial antagonisms, at times cloaked perhaps, but no less grim and brutal than those the South has lived with so defiantly. While he has aroused the concern, even the devotion, of many, to others his arrival and the widespread solicitous response to his arrival only confirm a number of existing fears and suspicions. Life is indeed harshly competitive; another group is coming, and at a time when jobs may be scarce. Moreover, those who favor the Negro and want so earnestly to aid him are the very people who care not at all about the poor (and white) people who have been living in the cities and towns of the North for generations, or at the least before the Negro came to stake out his claim. . . .

In many ways the poor and lower-middle-class white people in our Northern cities are going through a kind of experience precisely opposite to that of Negroes. At this time in history Negroes are being affirmed, while these white people feel increasingly deserted and alone. The Negro's excuse for his present condition is everywhere made known: it was not his fault, but ours. We carried him here by force and kept him in bondage for three centuries. He was not simply poor, but singled out for a very particular form of exploitation. The brutality and exclusion that he experienced have now become our national problem, because the price once exacted for the Negro's compliance lives on in the illiteracy and fearfulness we encouraged in him for so long.

In the Northern cities a white man who is poor has no such past history to justify his condition. He is poor, or uneasily not-poor, but no more than that. Even our expanding middle class has its definite limitations. Those limitations are now shifting in character, but by no means disappearing. While it is true that educational opportunity and the money to secure it are much more available than ever before, we are also facing severe technological problems, as machines replace not only men but other machines. It no longer is fatuous to predict an astonishing productivity harnessed to a relative handful of workers.

Meanwhile, we stubbornly cling to an ethic that prefers to reward only those who can find work, while consigning all the rest to charity, and not a little contempt. Through no fault of their own, not improvidence, not ignorance, not apathy, many people simply cannot obtain the regular work they want and need. Others may have reasonably secure jobs, but they are jobs that hardly pay enough to guarantee much security against an inflationary economy. "Who can keep up with it?" a mother who was barely able to make ends meet said to me in an aside during a talk we were having on racial tensions in Boston.

The Negroes say they have nothing. Well, we have more, that's true. My husband works, and it's a steady job. We're Irish, so in this city there's no trouble there, I'll have to admit. But it's as hard as can be just living and staying even with everything. My husband has to work extra just to pay the bills. We don't have any money put away. The kids always want something. All the television does is tell you to buy, buy, buy. A few years ago my husband didn't have a job, and we didn't know where our next penny was coming from. Now he has the job all right, but it's even harder in a way. Any raise he gets means nothing compared to what happens to the cost of everything. You have to be an owner of something or a professional man to have an easy mind today.

On another occasion I found her directly envious of Negroes. They were on the bottom, and at least had somewhere to go. She didn't think there was much room "up there" for her family. Moreover, the Negro gets an enormous amount of sympathy and attention, and from people and institutions she feels possessive about. As a matter of fact, in one of the bluntest conversations I have had, she said to me:

They may be poorer than a lot of white people, but not by very much. Anyway, what they don't get in money they more than gain in popularity these days. The papers have suddenly decided that the Negro is teacher's pet. Whatever he does good is wonderful, and we should clap. But if he does anything bad, it's our fault. I can't read the papers anymore when they talk about the race thing. I'm sick of their editorials. All of a sudden they start giving us a lecture every day on how bad we are. They never used to care about anything, the Negro or anything else. Now they're so worried. And the same goes with the Church. I'm as devout a Catholic as you'll find around. My brother is a priest, and I do more than go to Church once a week. But I just can't take what some of our priests are saying these days. They're talking as if we did something wrong for being white. I don't understand it at all. Priests never used to talk about the Negro when I was a child. Now they talk to my kids about them all the time. I thought the Church is supposed to stand for religion, and eternal things. They shouldn't get themselves into every little fight that comes along. The same goes with the schools. I went to school here in Boston, and nobody was talking about Negroes and busing us around. The Negroes were there in Roxbury and we were here.

Everybody can't live with you, can they? Everybody likes his own. But now even the school people tell us we have to have our kids with this kind and that kind of person, or else they will be hurt, or something. Now how am I supposed to believe everything all these people say? They weren't talking that way a few years ago. The governor wasn't either. Nor the mayor. They're all just like cattle stampeding to sound like one another. The same with those people out in the suburbs. Suddenly they're interested in the Negro. They worked and worked to get away from him, of course, and get away from us, too. That's why they moved so far, instead of staying here, where they *can* do something, if they mean so well. But no. They moved and now they're all ready to come back—but only to drive a few Negro kids out for a Sunday picnic. Who has to live with all this, and pay for it in taxes and everything? Whose kids are pushed around? And who gets called "prejudiced" and all the other sneery words? I've had enough of it. It's hypocrisy, right down the line. And we're the ones who get it; the final buck gets passed to us.

Can we really solve the racial problem in this country without coming to terms with the worries and fears of this woman? There is an unnerving thread of truth that runs through her remarks. She and her husband do indeed have cause to worry about jobs and money, even as Negroes do. It is quite true that our newspapers, our churches, our political leaders have changed recently. Because they have learned new social concerns does not mean that the people who for years followed their leadership can fall in line easily, particularly when there are no concrete, persuasive reasons for them to do so. Moreover, the rivalrous and envious observations made by the people I have quoted ring sadly and ironically true: there is a certain snobbish and faddish "interest" in Negroes from people who would not think of concerning themselves with those many white families who share with Negroes slums, poor schools, uncertain employment—the parade of crippling events that make up what "we" so easily call "poverty" or "cultural disadvantages." . . .

If such people are frustrated, then so are we—the comfortable, well-educated, and secure. This nation has yet to settle upon a policy that would aim to distribute fairly our astonishing wealth, including all its surpluses and potential productive capacities. Do we need wars and military spending to keep our economy going, or can it be harnessed to provide the schools, houses, hospitals, and just plain food and clothing that millions of us need and don't have? Until such problems are solved, the bitterness and resentment we see between whites and Negroes will continue, and perhaps increase—a reminder of man's devious ability to conceal his real struggles, and thus remain at their mercy.

4. Chicanos on the Move (1979)

As the twentieth century neared its close, Hispanic-Americans began to emerge as America's most numerous ethnic minority. They were predicted to outnumber blacks by the 1990's. Within that group, which included many Puerto Ricans, Cubans, and other Latin Americans, the largest single element was made up of Chicanos, or Mexican-Americans. *Newsweek* magazine painted the following profile of the burgeoning Chicano community in 1979. In what ways are Chicanos similar to other ethnic minorities in American history? What, if anything, is different about their situation?

They are neither here nor there exactly—both immigrant and indigenous, tenaciously Mexican yet indisputably American. They have been part of this country as long as the Southwest that bears so much of their imprint, but they have been invisible to most of their countrymen, shrouded by their own language and culture. Now, they are growing and flexing, solving the riddle of their dual identity and marching into the American consciousness—on their own terms. "We are just beginning to become aware of ourselves and the power we represent," says Houston community leader Héctor García. The result of these stirrings may well be a phenomenon unique in the American experience—a vast Mexican-American population that is, in effect, a nation within a nation.

The single most compelling fact about chicanos is that there are a lot of them—officially 7.2 million, a 60 per cent increase since eight years ago. They are concentrated in the five-state "Tamale Belt" of California, Arizona, New

4. *Newsweek,* Vol. 93 (1), January 1, 1979, pp. 22–26. Copyright 1979 by Newsweek, Inc. All rights reserved. Reprinted by permission.

Mexico, Colorado and Texas, near the Mexican border that yields a fresh flow of about 1 million immigrants, legal and illegal, every year. One in four Texans is Mexican, and one in five Californians. Los Angeles, already the second largest Mexican metropolitan area in the world, will probably have a chicano majority within twenty years, and California, the nation's largest state, will have a chicano-dominated "majority of minorities" at about the same time. By then, too, the entire Hispanic-American population, three-fifths of it Mexican-American, will surge past black Americans to become the biggest U.S. minority.

INFLUENCE AND ANXIETY

The Mexican presence permeates the Southwest, in place-names, architecture, food and, increasingly, the arts. The hundreds of huge, colorful murals in East Los Angeles have become a tourist attraction . . . while "Zoot Suit," a play by Luis Valdez based on a Los Angeles race riot, is headed for Broadway. Individuals are making their mark in business and entertainment, and, over-all, their numbers are large enough to command the interest of politicians like Jimmy Carter and Jerry Brown. But their growing presence in the Southwest is also stirring anglo anxiety about an alien tide pouring into the country, competing for jobs and straining public services. "Anglos are afraid," says California Assemblyman Richard Alatorre. "They think they will get to be the minorities and we'll be opposing them."

The Mexican emergence is marked by a determination to enter mainstream America without becoming assimilated by the anglo culture. Theirs is a special situation among American immigrants, nearly all of whom crossed an ocean to get here and rarely looked back. But Mexico is a familiar reality for chicanos, and the constant border traffic reinforces their ties to the homeland. As a result, it has taken until now for many chicanos to decide that this is their country, too. "What we are saying is that we want to be here, but without losing our language and our culture," says news executive Daniel Villanueva of KMEX-TV in Los Angeles. "They are a richness, a treasure that we don't care to lose."

A LACK OF CLOUT

For now, Mexican-Americans must overcome a slew of other problems: poverty, poor education, urban gang warfare, police brutality and discrimination. The problems seem all the more intractable because chicanos have remarkably little political clout and few political leaders. No chicanos hold statewide elective office in California, and there have been no Mexican city councilmen in Los Angeles since Rep. Edward Roybal (one of four chicanos in Congress) left for Washington in 1963. Mexican-American Governors Raúl Castro of Arizona and Jerry Apodaca of New Mexico, both elected in 1974, are no longer in office. Perhaps the best-known chicano, labor leader César Chávez, has shunned urban politics, preferring to organize migrant farm workers.

There has been a growth of grass-roots political groups like COPS in San Antonio and UNO in Los Angeles that combine the organizing tactics of the late Saul Alinsky with the influence of the Roman Catholic Church. In San Antonio, the result has been a substantial boost in chicano political power. But elsewhere, turnout at the polls has been dismal. "You go to a black community and you get a strong bloc vote," says Los Angeles political activist Frank Casado. "You go to East L.A. and you get nothing. Half are illegal and the other half don't vote."

Contrary to popular perception, only 8.5 per cent of chicanos are farm workers. Four out of five live in cities, and many of them are poor. The median family income for Mexican-Americans is $11,421, as opposed to $16,284 for non-Hispanic families. Nearly 19 per cent live below the poverty line. Much of their potential lies in their youth. Close to half are under 18 and the median age is 21.3, compared with 29.5 for the total population. But only 34 per cent of Mexican-Americans over 25 have completed four years of high school and about a quarter of them have less than five years of schooling.

The statistics tell only part of the story of La Raza, a people who are basically conservative, hardworking, religious and family-oriented. They live largely in barrios—Mexican neighborhoods—and seem to like it that way. "The country is a melting pot, but you see blacks, Italians, Hispanics wanting to stay together," says David Lizárraga, executive director of The East Los Angeles Community Union. "That pluralism is the strength of our nation. It isn't racist. It's just comfortable." Even well-to-do chicanos are often reluctant to leave the barrio. Cecilia Castañeda, 29, a painter whose father moved the family to the suburbs when she was a child, recently moved back to the barrio. "I want my children to have pride and a sense of who they are," she explains. María Franco, a 45-year resident of Los Angeles, found she also missed the warm communion of the barrio. " 'Good morning' just doesn't sound as good as 'Buenos días'," she says.

East Los Angeles is the nation's biggest barrio. It is a community of 700,000, where a full third of the people speak only Spanish. It is a pleasant collection of pastel-colored stucco rental homes with trimmed hedges and bright splashes of color from the murals. And it remains a vital, coherent community even though it is riven by freeways, split by the city-county line and ruled by a hodgepodge of government bodies. Except for gang violence, crime is not a major problem, and drug-related arrests are below the county rate. "The barrio is not a ghetto," says Los Angeles school-board member Julián Nava. "It is a haven."

BAJA HOLLYWOOD

On any weekend at El Mercado, a large marketplace, patrons go up to the microphone and sing songs from their Mexican hometowns, while whole families, including old folks and young children, listen. In downtown Los Angeles, a few miles away, the sounds of Armando Manzanero and Lucha

Villa flow from music shops along Broadway, also known as Spanish Broadway or Baja Hollywood. Signs are in Spanish, peddlers hawk in Spanish and the Librería México offers fourteen Spanish-language newspapers and dozens of magazines. The Million Dollar Theater, opened in 1918 by Sid Grauman of Chinese Theater fame, now features movies like "Adán y Eva."

In a city so enamored of cars, chicano youth have turned to an unusual form of hot rodding known as "low riding." The ritual begins just before sunset on a weekend evening, when members of groups like the New Trend Car Club gather at an appointed corner to fork over their $1 weekly dues and have their cars inspected. The owner of a dirty car is fined $1, as is anyone who uses bad language. The cars themselves—a candy-apple red Caprice here, a midnight blue Thunderbird there—are mostly coated with metal-flake and acrylic paint, loaded with gleaming chrome and finished with velour interiors. And they are all set low to the ground, sometimes so low as to generate sparks as the front end scrapes the pavement. Some low riders invest $500 in driver-operated hydraulic lifts, so the car can clear obstacles or simply hop up and down in the parking lot like a grasshopper. Out on the street, the object is to cruise as slowly as possible; 5 mph is cool. The low-riding clubs also sponsor dances, picnics and softball games for members.

THE CRAZY LIFE

The disturbing flip side of barrio culture is gang warfare. Young men with short, slicked-back hair and wearing khaki pants and white T shirts collect into gangs with names like El Hoyo, La Arizona, La Rock and Varrio Nuevo and engage in bloody battles over barrio turf. There were 67 gang-related killings in the city of Los Angeles alone last year and 90 so far this year. In addition, there have been 258 attempted murders and 835 felonious assaults so far this year. "A lot of my friends are dead now," says Jaime García, 21, a former "cholo" (gang member) who bears the tattoo "mi vida loca" (my crazy life) as a constant reminder of his past. Like the middle-class car-clubbers, the gang members are mostly second-generation Americans, the products of strained family relationships and culture clash. They rarely terrorize barrio residents who are not gang members, but they are seen as a sobering example of what can go wrong when the old ways are abandoned.

Those old ways are treasured by Mexican-Americans, and they are rooted in the family and the Catholic Church. Nearly two-thirds of all Catholics in the Southwest are Hispanic, and the church's teachings reinforce the Mexican bent toward large families and rigid sex roles. It is a male-dominated society; fathers are stern and aloof autocrats and boys are taught early to protect their sisters. Women have tended to be self-sacrificing nurturers. "Chicanas are quite indoctrinated in the essential role of motherhood," says Faustina Solís, deputy director of the California state public-health division. "This is maximum fulfillment, and any action which would deviate from her

role is not easily accepted." Family values include strong ties to the com-
padres—each child's own set of godparents. "The old-age home is a no-no
for Mexicans," says Raúl Arreola of the Los Angeles Mexican-American
Education Commission. "We always have brothers and uncles and cousins
we can turn to for emotional support," says José Ortega, director of the
Hispanic Urban Center in East Los Angeles.

Some of the Mexican's cultural strengths, however, are seen as weaknesses in American society. "We tend to be unaggressive—submissive, almost—in a competitive culture where those are the losing qualities," says
Ortega. "Our people don't compete on an equal footing with the general
society." Some of that chicano passivity can be laid to the strict, sheltering
home environment, but it is also to some extent the legacy of a race that
has never quite shaken off the stigma of being a conquered people.

The anglo domination of Mexicans began in the 1820s when Mexico invited American settlers to Texas. The settlers stayed and pushed the Mexicans south of the Rio Grande. After the U.S. annexed Texas and won the
Mexican War, Mexico ceded what is now California, Arizona, New Mexico,
Utah, Nevada, and parts of Colorado to the U.S. for $15 million in 1848.
Nearly all of the 75,000 Mexican nationals living in the ceded territory
elected to stay, but they did not fare well. In Texas, Mexicans were lynched
and their land was stolen. In California, 200 Mexican families were forced
from the 14 million acres of land they owned. By the 1880s, the Mexicans
were largely landless and powerless. An 1894 law that required English
literacy for voter registration was not struck down until 1970.

'WE ARE NOT FOREIGNERS'

Now, there is a reaffirmation of chicano feeling for what scholar Rodolfo
Acuña calls Mexico's Northwest Territory. "We are not foreigners in this
land," says Los Angeles political leader Lucy Casado. "The Southwest is a
Spanish place. Here, this is our climate. Here is what God endowed us with.
Here is where he planted us." Another indication of newfound pride is simply identification with the term Mexican, which once had disparaging overtones and was thus replaced by "chicano." Like Ed Muskie saying he's Polish
or Tip O'Neill saying he's Irish, many chicano politicians now stress their
heritage. "I'm not an Hispano," says Denver City Councilman Sam Sandos,
51. "I'm a Mexican."

By far the most controversial issue involving Mexican-Americans in the
influx of "illegal aliens"—or "undocumented workers," as chicano leaders
prefer to call them. Around the turn of the century, thousands of Mexicans
were imported to build U.S. railroads, work the fruit groves and dig in the
desert mines. More came to do industrial work during the First World War
—but were deported during the Depression. In the mid-'60s, immigration
began to soar as poverty and population pressures in Mexico encouraged
people to leave. The population of Mexico has soared from 25 million in
1950 to 65 million today and is projected to reach 130 million by 2000.

Nearly one-fifth of all Mexicans earn less than $75 a year, and even the most menial migrant laborer can increase his wages tenfold in the U.S. "If I were in Mexico now, I'd be running across that wire as fast as I could," says David Lizárraga. "This is the land of opportunity."

Getting here is relatively easy. The Immigration and Naturalization Service's Border Patrol caught more than 860,000 would-be immigrants at the 2,000-mile Mexican border last year—but a bigger number got through. They run across bridges, slip through drainage tunnels, scramble over fences or simply wade across the Rio Grande, which is only a foot deep in spots between Juárez and El Paso. Some are commuters who sneak across each day to regular jobs as construction workers or domestics. The odds against the Border Patrol are enormous. "Some days we stop catching them because we just don't have any more room to hold them," says El Paso supervisor Mike Williams. Many Mexicans pay "coyotes" hundreds of dollars to smuggle them across the border in vans or trucks. The Border Patrol has been planting electronic sensors on mountainsides and testing a helicopter equipped with infra-red scanners, but so far the new technology hasn't helped much.

Once illegals cross the border, they tend to melt into the great barrios of the Southwest, filling low-wage jobs in restaurants and hotels, car washes and parking lots and the L.A. garment industry. "You couldn't eat at a hotel in this town if a vacuum cleaner scooped up all the illegal aliens," says Julián Nava of Los Angeles. Because they are desperate for work and unable to complain to authorities, they are vulnerable to exploitation; by one account, a quarter of them are paid less than the minimum wage. "I wanted a job and didn't ask how much they paid," says Pedro, a 23-year-old illegal in Los Angeles. "For three weeks I didn't get a check. When I got the first check it was for $12."

QUOTAS AND RESIDENCY

They are also sometimes a burden for native chicanos (derisively known as "pochos" in Mexico), who must often compete for the same jobs. And largely because of their clandestine presence, nobody really knows just how many Mexicans are in the U.S. Illegals also require public services—though they often don't seek welfare or medical help because they fear they will be detected by the government. Since the immigrant population is so young, the biggest public cost is education. Most schools around the country simply absorb illegal-alien children without asking many questions. In Texas, however, many school districts charge tuition for such children to attend public schools; a group of Mexican families in Tyler, Texas, won a court injunction against the tuition requirement this year.

The situation is so chaotic that everyone agrees something ought to be done—either to let more Mexicans in legally or keep them out more effectively. "I think the necessity for legislative action grows every day," says INS Commissioner Leonel Castillo, one of the highest-ranking chicanos in the Carter Administration. But Carter's plan—which would, among other things, have given permanent residency to illegals who were here before 1970 and fined employers who knowingly hired illegals—was killed in Congress. Last week, the House population committee announced its recommendations for restricting immigration, including increased aid to Mexico for jobs and family planning and more funds for tighter border enforcement.

Castillo has his own priorities, however. The permanent-residency aspect of Carter's program should be enacted separately, he says, along with a provision allowing illegals already in the U.S. to stay and work for five years as legal temporary residents. He also advocates doubling the Mexican immigration quota to 40,000 and taking steps internally to make INS more efficient. But Castillo himself is somewhat controversial—even among chicanos. Last October, the INS announced it would spend $3.5 million on three fences, 6 miles long and 10 feet high, along the Mexican border. Castillo was promptly picketed—by chicano groups who likened the fence to the Berlin Wall and by labor groups who thought the fences weren't enough of a barrier.

If immigration laws are changed the way Carter and Castillo want, hundreds of thousands of Mexicans would remain in this country legally—their sheer numbers adding to a formidable new power base. But it would still require massive voter-registration and citizenship drives among those who are eligible to overcome the apathy and suspicion so prevalent in the barrio. To many chicanos, American politicians are "Olympians"—because they sprint through the barrio every four years. Chicanos generally are not very savvy about the nuances of the game. "We didn't understand power, clout, trade-offs," says Alatorre. "We are just beginning to understand what the process is all about."

A SPANISH BOBBY KENNEDY?

One example of that awareness is the push for more civil-service jobs, to get chicanos into the bureaucracy where bread-and-butter decisions are made. Now, only 3.4 per cent of Federal civil servants are Hispanic, most concentrated in the lower grades. In the past year, there have also been some tentative first steps toward a chicano coalition with blacks—who have done far better at building power bases and getting the government's attention.

In addition to learning the political fundamentals, Mexican-Americans also see a pressing need to produce political personalities. Ben Fernández, a chicano businessman in Los Angeles, recently announced his candidacy for the Republican Presidential nomination; either Alatorre or Art Torres, both assemblymen, may run for governor in California in 1982; and Vilma Martínez of the Mexican-American Legal Defense and Educational Fund has gained a reputation as a spokeswoman. But that's not enough. "We need a Spanish Bobby Kennedy or Martin Luther King," says television executive Villanueva. "Right now he's just not there."

What chicanos do have now is a small but growing middle class deter-mined to bring its resources, skills and optimism back to the barrio and start the long process of community development. Perhaps the best example of what can result from that ambition is TELACU (The East Los Angeles Community Union), a community-development corporation funded with both government and private money. TELACU has launched several banks, is building a $22 million industrial park that could generate 2,000 jobs and is planning a hotel complex.

Many more such economic initiatives will be needed, combined with po-litical advances, if Mexican-Americans are to succeed in synthesizing their two cultures. The potential is there and, increasingly, so is the will. As Arizona gubernatorial aide Ronnie López puts it: "We're hungry for the future."

D. ASSESSING MODERN AMERICA

1. A Russian Journalist Looks at American Violence (1981)

America has not lost its fascination for foreign observers—including those from the Soviet Union. In the following article from the Russian newspaper *Izvestia,* a Soviet journalist offers his opinions on the frequently remarked high level of violence in modern American society. (His observations were occasioned by the assassination attempt against President Reagan in March, 1981.) What implications does he draw from the facts of American violence? How convincing is his argument? In what ways is he biased?

New York—The six shots that rang out on March 30 at the entrance to the Hilton Hotel in Washington were heard all over America. The country also saw how it happened. But no matter how important the details are, Americans are interested in something else, too: what made this possible. After the shock of the assassination attempt wore off, people began to think about a typical American phenomenon—the violence that has swept the United States.

Violence has become so common in this country that it arouses little emo-tion in daily life. But when its victim is a well-known person, especially the US president, violence becomes sensational. Along with the questions of what is happening to America and Americans, there are answers. Politicians and the mass media are trying to convince the public that political assassi-nation attempts have little to do with ordinary violence, so to speak, and that they are an entirely different matter. They also maintain that such crimes are only committed by loners and failures.

Finally, it is alleged that the increase in violence in the US has no con-nection with the socioeconomic system and with the activities of state in-stitutions. . . .

In the past few years, however, many crimes of an obviously political

1. Translation copyright 1981 by *The Current Digest of the Soviet Press,* published weekly at the Ohio State University by the American Association for the Advancement of Slavic Studies; reprinted by permission of *The Digest.*

nature have been committed in the United States. Martin Luther King and Malcolm X were murdered because their political activities bothered right-wing circles. The racists feared these people and wanted to intimidate the Negro population and deprive it of prestigious leaders. The recent attempt to kill prominent Negro figure Vernon Jordan was made for the same reasons.

The American press is currently writing a great deal about the fact that J. Hinckley, the man who shot President R. Reagan, is undergoing psychiatric examination. Judging from preliminary data, he is in good mental health. But for some reason, little attention is being paid to another fact: Hinckley belonged to the American Nazi Party, and his former colleagues say that he had "a penchant for killing."

Violence is violence, no matter who its target—the man in the street or the statesman. There has to be a certain political and moral climate in society for violence to become a typical phenomenon and affect its morals. This is precisely the situation that exists in the United States.

Violence is above all connected with society's social structure. Extremes of wealth and poverty always arouse antagonism that is especially aggravated during times of economic hardship. And this is typical of modern-day America. . . .

In its three months in power, the Republican administration has done much to reinforce class inequality in the country. Its first move in domestic policy was to cut the budget for the next fiscal year by $49 billion, above all in the sphere of social services, with even greater cuts in the future. The administration's proposal to reduce income tax is meant to increase the incomes of the wealthy strata of society. Even the American bourgeois press was forced to admit recently that the White House's policy is arousing resentment among people with low incomes and resulting in the greater impoverishment of hundreds of thousands of poor people. . . .

Various scientific studies and police statistics show that Americans' growing feelings of alienation from and lack of faith in state and social institutions often lead to so-called motiveless murders. . . .

Many crimes are committed under the influence of drugs. The addict will do anything to get money to buy drugs. . . .

American television and movies play a considerable role in the forming of morals. . . .

In the majority of films, violence is shown to be the only means of achieving vital success and resolving business and family conflicts. It is not surprising that a 9-year-old imitates his screen heroes by showing up at a bank with a toy pistol and demanding money. The tellers don't argue with him: After all, the gun could be real and what's more, they have grown accustomed to violence. In the US, a serious crime is committed every 2.6 seconds and someone is murdered every 24 minutes.

In the US, it is very easy to buy or order through the mail a handgun or rifle of any caliber in one of 177,000 gun stores. . . . During the recent presidential campaign, the Republican candidate derided those who were demanding that steps be taken to restrict the sale of firearms or at least make gun registration mandatory. The candidate assured them that he himself would never resort to such measures if he were elected President.

Just recently, after winning the election, he reaffirmed his intention. "The lowest level of crime in the United States," he said in a speech to some newspaper editors, "is found in areas where you can walk around with a gun in your pocket." American daily life, full of violence, refutes this idea.

2. A Frenchman Praises the American Example (1971)

In the midst of the upheaval and self-criticism of the late 1960's and early 1970's, French journalist Jean-Francois Revel published an extraordinary book, *Without Marx or Jesus: The New American Revolution Has Begun.* The book shocked many foreign observers of the American scene, who had become exceptionally critical of American society, largely due to their disenchantment with the Vietnam War. Even American commentators were surprised at Revel's perspective on the American character. What does he find most remarkable about America? What is his prediction about America's future, and especially its future role in the world? How convincing is he?

The revolution of the twentieth century will take place in the United States. It is only there that it can happen. And it has already begun. Whether or not that revolution spreads to the rest of the world depends on whether or not it succeeds first in America.

I am not unaware of the shock and incredulity such statements may cause at every level of the European Left and among the nations of the Third World. I know it is difficult to believe that America—the fatherland of imperialism, the power responsible for the war in Vietnam, the nation of Joe McCarthy's witch hunts, the exploiter of the world's natural resources—is, or could become, the cradle of revolution. . . .

On the other hand, one of the most striking features of the past decade is that the only new revolutionary stirrings in the world have had their origin in the United States. From America has come the sole revolutionary invention which can be described as truly original. I mean the complex of new oppositional phenomena designated by the term "dissent." Similar movements have agitated western—and eastern—Europe, but these are imitations of the American prototype, or extensions of it, and subsequent to it. In 1964–65, at Berkeley, occurred the first of those student revolts which are a wholly new phenomenon, and which spread rapidly over the country, and then to Europe and the Third World. Even before that, in 1960, there were student strikes, and the first sit-ins in Southern universities protesting racial discrimination and supporting the nonviolent action of Martin Luther King. Dissent, whether it spread by contagion or sprang up simultaneously in different parts of the world, was nonetheless conceived and perfected in the

2. Excerpts from *Without Marx or Jesus: The New American Revolution Has Begun* by Jean-Francois Revel, translated by Jack Bernard. Translation copyright © 1971 by Doubleday & Company, Inc. Used by permission of the publisher.

United States. This unprecedented exercise in revolutionary activity, this ubiquitous radicalism, this all-encompassing sedition, has left governments virtually helpless, for the usual methods of repression are practically useless against it. And European dissenters, who represent the only force which has been able to rouse both the Left and the Right, the East and the West, from their academic torpor, are the disciples of the American movement.

Student dissenters are not, of course, the only group who refuse to compromise in their attitude of rejection and of attack. There are also the black revolutionary movement, and the women's liberation movement, among others." . . .

It is difficult to say whether or not dissent will succeed or fail; whether it will presevere until it results in the building of a new society, or serve only to facilitate the triumph of an authoritarian reaction. It is possible, too, that the movement of dissent will become bogged down in intellectual mediocrity and, instead of leading to a real transformation of society, will wander off onto the path of persecutor-persecuted narcissism, and degenerate into a marginal movement so ineffectual that it will come to be tolerated in the industrial states of the world. In other words, it can become either the fulcrum of a new social contract—or a refuge for social deviants. Which of these things it becomes will determine, to a large extent, the answer to the question of whether the second American Revolution will be the beginning of a second world revolution. It will also decide whether or not, even in America, dissent will attain its positive goal. . . .

It is highly significant that the movement of dissent—the only original contribution to the technique of sedition to appear in the past decade, and perhaps since World War II—has originated in the United States. Still, taken by itself, that fact is not enough to warrant our speaking of a New American Revolution, let alone of a subsequent world revolution. But there are other signs. In the midst of dissent in America, certain of the fundamental conditions for revolution have either been fulfilled, or are well on the way to being fulfilled. . . .

My thesis is that, if a second world revolution is to take place, it can have its beginning only in the United States. And I base that thesis on the following conclusions:

(a) This revolution has not taken place in the communist countries, nor can it take place there, either in the U.S.S.R. or in China.

(b) It cannot take place in western Europe; or, at least, not unless the American Revolution takes place first—or, more accurately, continues to take place. (The same holds true for Japan, which will be discussed separately.)

(c) It cannot take place in the so-called developing countries, or in the Third World. On the contrary, the revolution must occur in the United States before it can happen elsewhere. . . .

The United States is the country most eligible for the role of prototype-nation for the following reasons: it enjoys continuing economic prosperity and rate of growth, without which no revolutionary project can succeed;

it has technological competence and a high level of basic research; culturally it is oriented toward the future rather than toward the past, and it is undergoing a revolution in behavioral standards, and in the affirmation of individual freedom and equality; it rejects authoritarian control, and multiplies creative initiative in all domains—especially in art, life style, and sense experience—and allows the coexistence of a diversity of mutually complementary, alternative subcultures. . . .

The "hot" issues in America's insurrection against itself, numerous as they are, form a cohesive and coherent whole within which no one issue can be separated from the others. These issues are as follows: a radically new approach to moral values; the black revolt; the feminist attack on masculine domination; the rejection by young people of exclusively economic and technical social goals; the general adoption of noncoercive methods in education; the acceptance of the guilt for poverty; the growing demand for equality; the rejection of an authoritarian culture in favor of a critical and diversified culture that is basically new, rather than adopted from the old cultural stockpile; the rejection both of the spread of American power abroad and of foreign policy; and a determination that the natural environment is more important than commercial profit. None of the groups concerned with any one of these points, and none of the points themselves, would have been able to gain as much strength and attention as they have if they had been isolated from other groups and other points. The blacks and the feminists—one a racial group and the other a sexual group, both of which comprise several socioeconomic levels—are two categories of Americans which (along with students, of course) have always been most strongly opposed to the Vietnam war. . . .

Today in America—the child of European imperialism—a new revolution is rising. It is *the* revolution of our time. It is the only revolution that involves radical, moral, and practical opposition to the spirit of nationalism. It is the only revolution that, to that opposition, joins culture, economic and technological power, and a total affirmation of liberty for all in place of archaic prohibitions. It therefore offers the only possible escape for mankind today: the acceptance of technological civilization as a means and not as an end, and—since we cannot be saved either by the destruction of the civilization or by its continuation—the development of the ability to reshape that civilization without annihilating it.

THOUGHT PROVOKERS

1. Did the "baby boom" generation have a unique up-bringing, on the average, and thus a historically unique set of values? In what ways has the environment of the modern family changed in the last half-century? Have those changes been for better or worse? What forces have most dramatically affected the status of women in post–World War II America?

2. What obligations does a rich society have to its least fortunate citizens? What accounts for the persistent strength of the American belief that the government

should restrict its economic and social role to a necessary minimum? Are there different social classes in modern America? How are they defined?

3. Is affirmative action justified? Are its beneficiaries more deserving, or simply more lucky, than earlier minority groups (such as immigrants) that had to make their way in American society without the assistance of such positive supports? Should any white (European-derived) minority groups today have a claim on affirmative action preferences? What might be the social and political implications of the rise of Hispanic-Americans to the status of the nation's largest minority group?

4. What features of American society continue to attract the attention of foreign commentators? Why? Is America still, in the words of Abraham Lincoln, "the last best hope of earth"?

CONSTITUTION OF
THE UNITED STATES OF AMERICA

[Boldface headings and bracketed explanatory matter have been inserted for the reader's convenience. Passages which are no longer operative are printed in italic type.]

PREAMBLE

We the people of the United States, in order to form a more perfect union, establish justice, insure domestic tranquillity, provide for the common defense, promote the general welfare, and secure the blessings of liberty to ourselves and our posterity, do ordain and establish this CONSTITUTION for the United States of America.

Article I. Legislative Department

Section I. CONGRESS

Legislative power vested in a two-house Congress. All legislative powers herein granted shall be vested in a Congress of the United States, which shall consist of a Senate and a House of Representatives.

Section II. HOUSE OF REPRESENTATIVES

1. The people to elect representatives biennially. The House of Representatives shall be composed of members chosen every second year by the people of the several States, and the electors [voters] in each State shall have the qualifications requisite for electors of the most numerous branch of the State Legislature.

2. Who may be representatives. No person shall be a Representative who shall not have attained to the age of twenty-five years, and been seven years a citizen of the United States, and who shall not, when elected, be an inhabitant of that State in which he shall be chosen.

3. Representation in the House based on population; census. Representatives and direct taxes[1] shall be apportioned among the several States which may be included within this Union, according to their respective numbers, *which shall be determined by adding to the whole number of free persons, including those bound to service for a term of years* [apprentices and indentured servants], *and excluding Indians not taxed, three-fifths of all other persons* [slaves].[2] The actual enumeration [census] shall be made within three years after the first meeting of the Congress of the United States, and within every subsequent term of ten years, in such manner as they shall by law direct. The number of Representatives shall not exceed one for every thirty thousand, but each State shall have at least one Representative; *and until such enumeration shall be made, the State of New Hampshire shall be entitled to choose three, Massachusettes eight, Rhode Island and Providence Plantations one, Connecticut five, New York six, New Jersey four, Pennsylvania eight, Delaware one, Maryland six, Virginia ten, North Carolina five, South Carolina five, and Georgia three.*

4. Vacancies in the House to be filled by election. When vacancies happen in the representation from any State, the Executive authority [governor] thereof shall issue writs of election [call a special election] to fill such vacancies.

1. Modified in 1913 by the 16th Amendment authorizing income taxes.
2. The word "slave" appears nowhere in the Constitution; "slavery" appears in the 13th Amendment. The three-fifths rule ceased to be in force when the 13th Amendment was adopted in 1865.

5. The House to select its officers; to vote impeachment charges (i.e., indictments). The House of Representatives shall choose their Speaker and other officers; and shall have the sole power of impeachment.

Section III. SENATE

1. Senators to represent the states. The Senate of the United States shall be composed of two Senators from each State, *chosen by the legislature thereof,*[1] for six years; and each Senator shall have one vote.

2. One-third of Senators to be chosen every two years; vacancies. *Immediately after they shall be assembled in consequence of the first election, they shall be divided as equally as may be into three classes. The seats of the Senators of the first class shall be vacated at the expiration of the second year, of the second class at the expiration of the fourth year, and of the third class at the expiration of the sixth year,* so that one-third may be chosen every second year; *and if vacancies happen by resignation or otherwise, during the recess of the legislature of any State, the Executive* [governor] *thereof may make temporary appointments until the next meeting of the legislature, which shall then fill such vacancies.*[2]

3. Who may be Senators. No person shall be a Senator who shall not have attained to the age of thirty years, and been nine years a citizen of the United States, and who shall not, when elected, be an inhabitant of that State for which he shall be chosen.

4. The Vice-President to preside over the Senate. The Vice-President of the United States shall be President of the Senate, but shall have no vote, unless they be equally divided [tied].

5. The Senate to choose its other officers. The Senate shall choose their other officers, and also a President pro tempore, in the absence of the Vice-President, or when he shall exercise the office of President of the United States.

6. The Senate to try impeachments. The Senate shall have the sole power to try all impeachments. When sitting for that purpose, they shall be on oath or affirmation. When the President of the United States is tried, the Chief Justice shall preside:[3] and no person shall be convicted without the concurrence of two-thirds of the members present.

7. Penalties for impeachment conviction. Judgment in cases of impeachment shall not extend further than to removal from office, and disqualification to hold and enjoy any office of honor, trust or profit under the United States: but the party convicted shall nevertheless be liable and subject to indictment, trial, judgment and punishment, according to law.

Section IV. ELECTION AND MEETINGS OF CONGRESS

1. Regulation of elections. The times, places and manner of holding elections for Senators and Representatives shall be prescribed in each State by the legislature thereof; but the Congress may at any time by law make or alter such regulations, except as to the places of choosing Senators.

2. Congress to meet once a year. The Congress shall assemble at least once in every year, and such meeting *shall be on the first Monday in December, unless they shall by law appoint a different day.*[4]

1. Repealed in favor of popular election in 1913 by the 17th Amendment.
2. Changed in 1913 by the 17th Amendment.
3. The Vice-President, as next in line, would be an interested party.
4. Changed in 1933 to January 3 by the 20th Amendment.

Section V. ORGANIZATION AND RULES OF THE HOUSES

1. Each House may reject members; quorums. Each house shall be the judge of the elections, returns and qualifications of its own members, and a majority of each shall constitute a quorum to do business; but a smaller number may adjourn from day to day, and may be authorized to compel the attendance of absent members, in such manner, and under such penalties, as each house may provide.

2. Each House to make its own rules. Each house may determine the rules of its proceedings, punish its members for disorderly behavior, and with the concurrence of two-thirds, expel a member.

3. Each House to publish a record of its proceedings. Each house shall keep a journal of its proceedings, and from time to time publish the same, excepting such parts as may in their judgment require secrecy; and the yeas and nays of the members of either house on any question shall, at the desire of one-fifth of those present, be entered on the journal.

4. Both Houses required to agree on adjournment. Neither house, during the session of Congress, shall, without the consent of the other, adjourn for more than three days, nor to any other place than that in which the two houses shall be sitting.

Section VI. PRIVILEGES OF AND PROHIBITIONS UPON CONGRESSMEN

1. Congressional salaries; immunities. The Senators and Representatives shall receive a compensation for their services, to be ascertained by law and paid out of the treasury of the United States. They shall in all cases except treason, felony and breach of the peace, be privileged from arrest during their attendance at the session of their respective houses, and in going to and returning from the same; and for any speech or debate in either house, they shall not be questioned in any other place [i.e., they shall be immune from libel suits].[1]

2. Congressmen not to hold incompatible federal civil offices. No Senator or Representative shall, during the time for which he was elected, be appointed to any civil office under the authority of the United States, which shall have been created, or the emoluments whereof shall have been increased, during such time; and no person holding any office under the United States shall be a member of either house during his continuance in office.

Section VII. METHOD OF MAKING LAWS

1. Money bills to originate in the House. All bills for raising revenue shall originate in the House of Representatives; but the Senate may propose or concur with amendments as on other bills.

2. The President's veto power; Congress may override. Every bill which shall have passed the House of Representatives and the Senate, shall, before it become a law, be presented to the President of the United States; if he approve he shall sign it, but if not he shall return it with his objections to that house in which it shall have originated, who shall enter the objections at large on their journal, and proceed to reconsider it. If after such reconsideration two-thirds of that house shall agree to pass the bill, it shall be sent, together with the objections, to the other house, by which it shall likewise be reconsidered, and, if approved by two-thirds of that house, it shall become a law. But in all such cases the votes of both houses shall be determined by yeas and nays, and the names of the persons voting for and against the bill shall be entered on the journal of each house respectively. If any bill shall not be returned by the President within ten days (Sundays

---

1. Senator Joseph R. McCarthy in the 1950's was accused of abusing this privilege.

excepted) after it shall have been presented to him, the same shall be a law, in like manner as if he had signed it, unless the Congress by their adjournment prevent its return, in which case it shall not be a law [this is the so-called pocket veto].

3. All measures requiring the agreement of both Houses to go to the President for approval. Every order, resolution, or vote to which the concurrence of the Senate and House of Representatives may be necessary (except on a question of adjournment) shall be presented to the President of the United States; and before the same shall take effect, shall be approved by him, or being disapproved by him, shall be repassed by two-thirds of the Senate and House of Representatives, according to the rules and limitations prescribed in the case of a bill.

Section VIII. Powers Granted to Congress

Congress possesses certain enumerated powers:

1. Congress may lay and collect taxes. The Congress shall have power to lay and collect taxes, duties, imposts, and excises, to pay the debts and provide for the common defense and general welfare of the United States; but all duties, imposts and excises shall be uniform throughout the United States;

2. Congress may borrow money. To borrow money on the credit of the United States;

3. Congress may regulate foreign and interstate trade. To regulate commerce with foreign nations, and among the several States, and with the Indian tribes;

4. Congress may pass naturalization and bankruptcy laws. To establish an uniform rule of naturalization, and uniform laws on the subject of bankruptcies throughout the United States;

5. Congress may coin money and regulate weights and measures. To coin money, regulate the value thereof, and of foreign coin, and fix the standard of weights and measures;

6. Congress may punish counterfeiters. To provide for the punishment of counterfeiting the securities and current coin of the United States;

7. Congress may establish a postal service. To establish post offices and post roads;

8. Congress may issue patents and copyrights. To promote the progress of science and useful arts by securing for limited times to authors and inventors the exclusive right to their respective writings and discoveries;

9. Congress may establish inferior courts. To constitute tribunals inferior to the Supreme Court;

10. Congress may punish crimes committed on the high seas. To define and punish piracies and felonies committed on the high seas [i.e., outside the three-mile limit] and offenses against the law of nations [international law];

11. Congress may declare war, may authorize privateering. To declare war,[1] grant letters of marque and reprisal,[2] and make rules concerning captures on land and water;

12. Congress may maintain an army. To raise and support armies, but no appropriation of money to that use shall be for a longer term than two years;[3]

1. Note that the President, though he can provoke war or wage it after it is declared, cannot declare it.
2. Papers issued to private citizens in time of war authorizing them to capture enemy ships.
3. A reflection of fear of standing armies earlier expressed in the Declaration of Independence.

13. Congress may maintain a navy. To provide and maintain a navy;

14. Congress may regulate the army and navy. To make rules for the government and regulation of the land and naval forces;

15. Congress may call out the state militia. To provide for calling forth the militia to execute the laws of the Union, suppress insurrections, and repel invasions;

16. Congress shares with the states control of militia. To provide for organizing, arming, and disciplining the militia, and for governing such part of them as may be employed in the service of the United States, reserving to the States respectively the appointment of the officers, and the authority of training the militia according to the discipline prescribed by Congress;

17. Congress makes laws for the District of Columbia and other federal areas. To exercise exclusive legislation in all cases whatsoever, over such district (not exceeding ten miles square) as may, by cession of particular States, and the acceptance of Congress, become the seat of government of the United States,[1] and to exercise like authority over all places purchased by the consent of the legislature of the State, in which the same shall be, for the erection of forts, magazines, arsenals, dock-yards, and other needful buildings;—and

Congress has certain implied powers:

18. Congress may enact laws necessary to enforce the Constitution. To make all laws which shall be necessary and proper for carrying into execution the foregoing powers, and all other powers vested by this Constitution in the government of the United States, or in any department or officer thereof.

Section IX. Powers Denied to the Federal Government

1. Congressional control of slave trade postponed until 1808. *The migration or importation of such persons as any of the States now existing shall think proper to admit shall not be prohibited by the Congress prior to the year 1808; but a tax or duty may be imposed on such importation, not exceeding $10 for each person.*

2. The writ of habeas corpus[2] not to be suspended; exception. The privilege of the writ of habeas corpus shall not be suspended, unless when in cases of rebellion or invasion the public safety may require it.

3. Attainders[3] and ex post facto laws[4] forbidden. No bill of attainder or ex post facto law shall be passed.

4. Direct taxes to be apportioned according to population. No capitation [head or poll tax], or other direct, tax shall be laid, unless in proportion to the census or enumeration herein before directed to be taken.[5]

5. Export taxes forbidden. No tax or duty shall be laid on articles exported from any State.

6. Congress not to discriminate among states in regulating commerce; interstate shipping. No preference shall be given by any regulation of commerce or revenue to the ports of one State over those of another; nor shall vessels bound to, or from, one State, be obliged to enter, clear, or pay duties in another.

1. The District of Columbia, ten miles square, was established in 1791.
2. A writ of habeas corpus is a document which enables a person under arrest to obtain an immediate examination in court to ascertain whether he is being legally held.
3. A bill of attainder is a special legislative act condemning and punishing an individual without a judicial trial.
4. An ex post facto law is one that fixes punishment for acts committed before the law was passed.
5. Modified in 1913 by the 16th Amendment.

7. Public money not to be spent without Congressional appropriation; accounting. No money shall be drawn from the treasury, but in consequence of appropriations made by law; and a regular statement and account of the receipts and expenditures of all public money shall be published from time to time.

8. Titles of nobility prohibited; foreign gifts. No title of nobility shall be granted by the United States: and no person holding any office of profit or trust under them, shall, without the consent of the Congress, accept of any present, emolument, office, or title, of any kind whatever, from any king, prince, or foreign state.

Section X. POWERS DENIED TO THE STATES

Absolute prohibitions on the states:

1. The states forbidden certain powers. No State shall enter into any treaty, alliance, or confederation; grant letters of marque and reprisal [i.e., authorize privateers], coin money; emit bills of credit [issue paper money]; make anything but gold and silver coin a [legal] tender in payment of debts; pass any bill of attainder, ex post facto law,[1] or law impairing the obligation of contracts, or grant any title of nobility.

Conditional prohibitions on the states:

2. The states not to levy duties without the consent of Congress. No State shall, without the consent of the Congress, lay any imposts or duties on imports or exports, except what may be absolutely necessary for executing its inspection laws: and the net produce of all duties and imposts, laid by any State on imports or exports, shall be for the use of the treasury of the United States; and all such laws shall be subject to the revision and control of the Congress.

3. Other federal powers forbidden the states. No State shall, without the consent of Congress, lay any duty of tonnage [i.e., duty on ship tonnage], keep [non-militia] troops or ships of war in time of peace, enter into any agreement or compact with another State, or with a foreign power, or engage in war, unless actually invaded, or in such imminent danger as will not admit of delay.

Article II. Executive Department

Section I. PRESIDENT AND VICE-PRESIDENT

1. The President the chief executive; his term. The executive power shall be vested in a President of the United States of America. He shall hold his office during the term of four years,[2] and, together with the Vice-President, chosen for the same term, be elected as follows:

2. The President to be chosen by state electors. Each State shall appoint, in such manner as the legislature thereof may direct, a number of electors, equal to the whole number of Senators and Representatives to which the State may be entitled in the Congress; but no Senator or Representative, or person holding an office of trust or profit under the United States, shall be appointed an elector.

A majority of the electoral votes needed to elect a President. *The electors shall meet in their respective States, and vote by ballot for two persons, of whom one at least shall not be an inhabitant of the same State with themselves. And they shall make a list of all the persons voted for, and of the number of votes for each; which list they shall sign and certify, and transmit sealed to the seat of govern-*

1. For definitions see footnotes 3 and 4 on preceding page.
2. No reference to re-election; clarified by the anti-third term 22nd Amendment.

ment of the United States, directed to the President of the Senate. The President of the Senate shall, in the presence of the Senate and House of Representatives, open |all the certificates, and the votes shall then be counted. The person having the greatest number of votes shall be the President, if such number be a majority of the whole number of electors appointed; and if there be more than one who have such majority, and have an equal number of votes, then the House of Representatives shall immediately choose by ballot one of them for President; and if no person have a majority, then from the five highest on the list the said house shall in like manner choose the President. But in choosing the President the votes shall be taken by States, the representation from each State having one vote; a quorum for this purpose shall consist of a member or members from two-thirds of the States, and a majority of all the States shall be necessary to a choice. In every case, after the choice of the President, the person having the greatest number of votes of the electors shall be the Vice-President. But if there should remain two or more who have equal votes, the Senate shall choose from them by ballot the Vice-President.[1]

3. Congress to decide time of meeting of Electoral College. The Congress may determine the time of choosing the electors and the day on which they shall give their votes; which day shall be the same throughout the United States.

4. Who may be President. No person except a natural-born citizen, or a citizen of the United States at the time of the adoption of this Constitution, shall be eligible to the office of President; neither shall any person be eligible to that office who shall not have attained to the age of thirty-five years, and been fourteen years a resident within the United States [i.e., a legal resident].

5. Replacements for President. In case of the removal of the President from office or of his death, resignation, or inability to discharge the powers and duties of the said office, the same shall devolve on the Vice-President, and the Congress may by law provide for the case of removal, death, resignation, or inability, both of the President and Vice-President, declaring what officer shall then act as President, and such officer shall act accordingly, until the disability be removed, or a President shall be elected.

6. The President's salary. The President shall, at stated times, receive for his services a compensation, which shall neither be increased nor diminished during the period for which he shall have been elected, and he shall not receive within that period any other emolument from the United States, or any of them.

7. The President's oath of office. Before he enter on the execution of his office, he shall take the following oath or affirmation:—"I do solemnly swear (or affirm) that I will faithfully execute the office of President of the United States, and will to the best of my ability preserve, protect and defend the Constitution of the United States."

Section II. POWERS OF THE PRESIDENT

1. The President has important military and civil powers, The President shall be commander in chief of the army and navy of the United States, and of the militia of the several States, when called into the actual service of the United States; he may require the opinion, in writing, of the principal officer in each of the executive departments, upon any subject relating to the duties of their respective

1. Repealed in 1804 by the 12th Amendment.

offices, and he shall have power to grant reprieves and pardons for offenses against the United States, except in cases of impeachment.[1]

2. The President may negotiate treaties and nominate federal officials. He shall have power, by and with the advice and consent of the Senate, to make treaties, provided two-thirds of the Senators present concur; and he shall nominate, and by and with the advice and consent of the Senate, shall appoint ambassadors, other public ministers and consuls, judges of the Supreme Court, and all other officers of the United States, whose appointments are not herein otherwise provided for, and which shall be established by law: but the Congress may by law vest the appointment of such inferior officers, as they think proper, in the President alone, in the courts of law, or in the heads of departments.

3. The President may fill vacancies during Senate recess. The President shall have power to fill up all vacancies that may happen during the recess of the Senate, by granting commissions which shall expire at the end of their next session.

Section III. OTHER POWERS AND DUTIES OF THE PRESIDENT

Submitting messages; calling extra sessions; receiving ambassadors; executing the laws; commissioning officers. He shall from time to time give to the Congress information of the state of the Union, and recommend to their consideration such measures as he shall judge necessary and expedient; he may, on extraordinary occasions, convene both houses, or either of them, and in case of disagreement between them, with respect to the time of adjournment, he may adjourn them to such time as he shall think proper; he shall receive ambassadors and other public ministers; he shall take care that the laws be faithfully executed, and shall commission all the officers of the United States.

Section IV. IMPEACHMENT

Civil officers may be removed by impeachment. The President, Vice-President, and all civil officers[2] of the United States shall be removed from office on impeachment for, and on conviction of, treason, bribery, or other high crimes and misdemeanors.

Article III. Judicial Department

Section I. THE FEDERAL COURTS

The judicial power lodged in the federal courts. The judicial power of the United States shall be vested in one Supreme Court, and in such inferior courts as the Congress may from time to time ordain and establish. The judges, both of the Supreme and inferior courts, shall hold their offices during good behavior, and shall, at stated times, receive for their services a compensation which shall not be diminished during their continuance in office.

Section II. JURISDICTION OF FEDERAL COURTS

1. Kinds of cases that may be heard. The judicial power shall extend to all cases, in law and equity, arising under this Constitution, the laws of the United States, and treaties made, or which shall be made, under their authority;—to all cases affecting ambassadors, other

---

1. To prevent the President's pardoning himself or his close associates.
2. I.e., all federal executive and judicial officers, but not members of Congress or military personnel.

public ministers and consuls;—to all cases of admiralty and maritime jurisdiction;—to controversies to which the United States shall be a party;—to controversies between two or more States;—*between a State and citizens of another State;*[1]—between citizens of different States;—between citizens of the same State claiming lands under grants of different States, and between a State, or the citizens thereof, and foreign states, citizens or subjects.

2. Jurisdiction of the Supreme Court. In all cases affecting ambassadors, other public ministers and consuls, and those in which a State shall be party, the Supreme Court shall have original jurisdiction.[2] In all the other cases before mentioned, the Supreme Court shall have appellate jurisdiction,[3] both as to law and fact, with such exceptions, and under such regulations, as the Congress shall make.

3. Trial for federal crime to be by jury. The trial of all crimes, except in cases of impeachment, shall be by jury; and such trial shall be held in the State where the said crimes shall have been committed; but when not committed within any State, the trial shall be at such place or places as the Congress may by law have directed.

Section III. TREASON

1. Treason defined; necessary evidence. Treason against the United States shall consist only in levying war against them, or in adhering to their enemies, giving them aid and comfort. No person shall be convicted of treason unless on the testimony of two witnesses to the same overt act, or on confession in open court.

2. Congress to fix punishment for treason. The Congress shall have power to declare the punishment of treason, but no attainder of treason shall work corruption of blood, or forfeiture except during the life of the person attainted.[4]

Article IV. Relations of the States to One Another

Section I. CREDIT TO ACTS, RECORDS, AND COURT PROCEEDINGS

Each state to respect the public acts of the others. Full faith and credit shall be given in each State to the public acts, records, and judicial proceedings of every other State.[5] And the Congress may by general laws prescribe the manner in which such acts, records, and proceedings shall be proved [attested], and the effect thereof.

Section II. DUTIES OF STATES TO STATES

1. Citizenship in one state valid in all. The citizens of each State shall be entitled to all privileges and immunities of citizens in the several States.

2. Fugitives from justice to be surrendered by the states. A person charged in any State with treason, felony, or other crime, who shall flee from justice, and be found in another State, shall on demand of the executive authority [governor] of the State from which he fled, be delivered up, to be removed to the State having jurisdiction of the crime.

3. Slaves and apprentices to be returned. *No person held to service or labor in one State, under the laws thereof, escaping into another,*

1. The 11th Amendment restricts this to suits by a state against citizens of another state.
2. I.e., such cases must originate in the Supreme Court.
3. I.e., it hears other cases only when they are appealed to it from a lower federal court or a state court.
4. I.e., punishment only for the offender; none for his heirs.
5. E.g., a marriage valid in one is valid in all.

shall, in consequence of any law or regulation therein, be discharged from such service or labor, but shall be delivered up on claim of the party to whom such service or labor may be due.[1]

Section III. NEW STATES AND TERRITORIES

1. Congress to admit new states. New States may be admitted by the Congress into this Union; but no new State shall be formed or erected within the jurisdiction of any other State; nor any State be formed by the junction of two or more States, or parts of States, without the consent of the legislatures of the States concerned as well as of the Congress.

2. Congress to regulate federal territory and property. The Congress shall have power to dispose of and make all needful rules and regulations respecting the territory or other property belonging to the United States; and nothing in this Constitution shall be so construed as to prejudice any claims of the United States, or of any particular State.

Section IV. PROTECTION TO THE STATES

Republican form of government guaranteed; also protection against invasion and rebellion. The United States shall guarantee to every State in this Union a republican form of government, and shall protect each of them against invasion; and on application of the legislature, or of the executive [governor] (when the legislature cannot be convened), against domestic violence.

Article V. The Process of Amendment

The Constitution may be amended in one of four ways. The Congress, whenever two-thirds of both houses shall deem it necessary, shall propose amendments to this Constitution, or, on the application of the legislatures of two-thirds of the several States, shall call a convention for proposing amendments, which, in either case, shall be valid to all intents and purposes, as part of this Constitution, when ratified by the legislatures of three-fourths of the several States, or by conventions in three-fourths thereof, as the one or the other mode of ratification may be proposed by the Congress; provided *that no amendments which may be made prior to the year one thousand eight hundred and eight shall in any manner affect the first and fourth clauses in the ninth section of the first article;*[2] and that no State, without its consent, shall be deprived of its equal suffrage in the Senate.

Article VI. General Provisions

1. The debts of the Confederation secured. All debts contracted and engagements entered into, before the adoption of this Constitution, shall be as valid against the United States under this Constitution, as under the Confederation.

2. The Constitution, federal laws, and treaties the supreme law of the land. This Constitution, and the laws of the United States which shall be made in pursuance thereof; and all treaties made, or which shall be made, under the authority of the United States, shall be the supreme law of the land; and the judges in every State shall be bound thereby, anything in the Constitution or laws of any State to the contrary notwithstanding.

1. Invalidated in 1865 by the 13th Amendment.
2. This clause, relating to slave trade and direct taxes, became inoperative in 1808.

3. Federal and state officers bound by oath to support the Constitution; religious tests forbidden. The Senators and Representatives before mentioned, and the members of the several State legislatures, and all executive and judicial officers, both of the United States and of the several States, shall be bound by oath or affirmation to support this Constitution; but no religious test shall ever be required as a qualification to any office or public trust under the United States.

Article VII. Ratification of the Constitution

The Constitution to become effective when ratified by nine states. The ratification of the conventions of nine States shall be sufficient for the establishment of this Constitution between the States so ratifying the same.

Done in Convention by the unanimous consent of the States present, the seventeenth day of September in the year of our Lord one thousand seven hundred and eighty-seven and of the Independence of the United States of America the twelfth. In witness whereof we have hereunto subscribed our names.

[Signed by]   G⁰ WASHINGTON
                                         Presidt and Deputy from Virginia
                                         [and thirty-eight others]

AMENDMENTS TO THE CONSTITUTION

Article I. Religious and Political Freedom (1791)

Congress not to interfere with freedom of religion, speech or press, assembly, and petition. Congress shall make no law respecting an establishment of religion, or prohibiting the free exercise thereof; or abridging the freedom of speech, or of the press; or the right of the people peaceably to assemble, and to petition the government for a redress of grievances.

Article II. Right to Bear Arms (1791)

The people secured in their right to bear arms. A well-regulated militia being necessary to the security of a free State, the right of the people to keep and bear arms [i.e., for military purposes] shall not be infringed.

Article III. Quartering of Troops (1791)

Quartering of soldiers on the people restricted. No soldier shall, in time of peace, be quartered in any house without the consent of the owner, nor in time of war, but in a manner to be prescribed by law.

Article IV. Searches and Seizures (1791)

Unreasonable searches forbidden. The right of the people to be secure in their persons, houses, papers, and effects, against unreasonable searches and seizures, shall not be violated, and no [search] warrants shall issue but upon probable cause, supported by oath or affirmation, and particularly describing the place to be searched, and the persons or things to be seized.

Article V. Right to Life, Liberty, and Property (1791)

Individuals guaranteed certain rights when on trial and the right to life, liberty, and property. No person shall be held to answer for a capital, or otherwise infamous, crime, unless on a presentment [formal charge] or indictment of a grand jury, except in cases arising in the land or naval forces, or in the militia, when in actual service in time of war or public danger; nor shall any person be subject for the same offense to be twice put in jeopardy of life or limb; nor shall be compelled in any criminal case to be a witness against himself, nor be deprived of life, liberty, or property, without due process of law; nor shall private property be taken for public use [i.e., by eminent domain] without just compensation.

Article VI. Protection in Criminal Trials (1791)

Accused persons assured of important rights. In all criminal prosecutions, the accused shall enjoy the right to a speedy and public trial, by an impartial jury of the State and district wherein the crime shall have been committed, which district shall have been previously ascertained by law, and to be informed of the nature and cause of the accusation; to be confronted with the witnesses against him; to have compulsory process [subpoena] for obtaining witnesses in his favor, and to have the assistance of counsel for his defense.

Article VII. Suits at Common Law (1791)

The rules of common law recognized. In suits at common law, where the value in controversy shall exceed twenty dollars, the right of trial by jury shall be preserved, and no fact tried by a jury shall be otherwise re-examined in any court of the United States, than according to the rules of the common law.

Article VIII. Bail and Punishments (1791)

Excessive bail, fines, and punishments forbidden. Excessive bail shall not be required, nor excessive fines imposed, nor cruel and unusual punishments inflicted.

Article IX. Concerning Rights Not Enumerated (1791)

The people to retain rights not here enumerated. The enumeration in the Constitution, of certain rights, shall not be construed to deny or disparage others retained by the people.

Article X. Powers Reserved to the States and to the People (1791)

Powers not delegated to the federal government reserved to the states and the people. The powers not delegated to the United States by the Constitution, nor prohibited by it to the States, are reserved to the States respectively, or to the people.

Article XI. Suits against a State (1798)

The federal courts denied authority in suits by citizens against a state. The judicial power of the United States shall not be construed to extend to any suit in law or equity, commenced or prosecuted against one of the United States by citizens of another State, or by citizens or subjects of any foreign state.

Article XII. Election of President and Vice-President (1804)

1. Changes in manner of electing President and Vice-President; procedure when no presidential candidate receives electoral majority. The electors shall meet in their respective States, and vote by ballot for President and Vice-President, one of whom, at least, shall not be an inhabitant of the same State with themselves; they shall name in their ballots the person voted for as President, and in distinct ballots the person voted for as Vice-President, and they shall make distinct lists of all persons voted for as President, and of all persons voted for as Vice-President, and of the number of votes for each, which lists they shall sign and certify, and transmit sealed to the seat of government of the United States, directed to the President of the Senate;—the President of the Senate shall, in the presence of the Senate and House of Representatives, open all the certificates and the votes shall then be counted;—the person having the greatest number of votes for President shall be the President, if such number be a majority of the whole number of electors appointed; and if no person have such majority, then from the persons having the highest numbers not exceeding three on the list of those voted for as President, the House of Representatives shall choose immediately, by ballot, the President. But in choosing the President, the votes shall be taken by States, the representation from each State having one vote; a quorum for this purpose shall consist of a member or members from two-thirds of the States, and a majority of all the States shall be necessary to a choice. And if the House of Representatives shall not choose a President whenever the right of choice shall devolve upon them, before *the fourth day of March*[1] next following, then the Vice-President shall act as President, as in the case of the death or other constitutional disability of the President.

2. Procedure when no vice-presidential candidate receives electoral majority. The person having the greatest number of votes as Vice-President shall be the Vice-President, if such number be a majority of the whole number of electors appointed; and if no person have a majority, then from the two highest numbers on the list the Senate shall choose the Vice-President; a quorum for the purpose shall consist of two-thirds of the whole number of Senators, and a majority of the whole number shall be necessary to a choice. But no person constitutionally ineligible to the office of President shall be eligible to that of Vice-President of the United States.

Article XIII. Slavery Prohibited (1865)

Slavery forbidden. 1. Neither slavery[2] nor involuntary servitude, except as a punishment for crime whereof the party shall have been duly convicted, shall exist within the United States, or any place subject to their jurisdiction.

2. Congress shall have power to enforce this article by appropriate legislation.

Article XIV. Civil Rights for Negroes, etc. (1868)

1. Citizenship defined; rights of citizens. All persons born or naturalized in the United States, and subject to the jurisdiction thereof, are citizens of the United States and of the State wherein they reside. No State shall make or enforce any law which shall abridge the privileges or immunities of citizens of the United States; nor shall

---

1. Changed to January 20 by the 20th Amendment.
2. The only explicit mention of slavery in the Constitution.

any State deprive any person of life, liberty, or property, without due process of law; nor deny to any person within its jurisdiction the equal protection of the laws.

2. When a state denies [Negroes] the vote, its representation shall be reduced. Representatives shall be apportioned among the several States according to their respective numbers, counting the whole number of persons in each State, excluding Indians not taxed. But when the right to vote at any election for the choice of Electors for President and Vice-President of the United States, Representatives in Congress, the executive and judicial officers of a State, or the members of the legislature thereof, is denied to any of the male inhabitants of such State, being twenty-one years of age and citizens of the United States, or in any way abridged, except for participation in rebellion, or other crime, the basis of representation therein shall be reduced in the proportion which the number of such male citizens shall bear to the whole number of male citizens twenty-one years of age in such State.

3. Certain ex-Confederates ineligible for federal and state office; removal of disability. No person shall be a Senator or Representative in Congress, or Elector of President and Vice-President, or hold any office, civil or military, under the United States, or under any State, who, having previously taken an oath, as a member of Congress, or as an officer of the United States, or as a member of any State legislature, or as an executive or judicial officer of any State, to support the Constitution of the United States, shall have engaged in insurrection or rebellion against the same, or given aid or comfort to the enemies thereof. But Congress may, by a vote of two-thirds of each house, remove such disability.

4. Public debt valid; debt of rebels void. The validity of the public debt of the United States, authorized by law, including debts incurred for payment of pensions and bounties for services in suppressing insurrection or rebellion, shall not be questioned. But neither the United States nor any State shall assume or pay any debt or obligation incurred in aid of insurrection or rebellion against the United States, or any claim for the loss or emancipation of any slave; but all such debts, obligations, and claims shall be held illegal and void.

5. Enforcement. The Congress shall have power to enforce, by appropriate legislation, the provisions of this article.

Article XV. Negro Suffrage (1870)

Restrictions on denial of vote. 1. The right of citizens of the United States to vote shall not be denied or abridged by the United States or by any State on account of race, color, or previous condition of servitude.

2. The Congress shall have power to enforce this article by appropriate legislation.

Article XVI. Income Taxes (1913)

Congress empowered to lay and collect income taxes. The Congress shall have power to lay and collect taxes on incomes, from whatever source derived, without apportionment among the several States, and without regard to any census or enumeration.

Article XVII. Direct Election of Senators (1913)

Senators to be elected by popular vote. 1. The Senate of the United States shall be composed of two Senators from each State, elected by the people thereof, for six years; and each Senator shall have one vote. The electors in each State shall have the qualifications requisite for electors of [voters for] the most numerous branch of the State legislatures.

2. When vacancies happen in the representation of any State in the Senate, the executive authority of such State shall issue writs of election to fill such vacancies: Provided, that the Legislature of any State may empower the executive thereof to make temporary appointments until the people fill the vacancies by election as the Legislature may direct.

3. This amendment shall not be so construed as to affect the election or term of any Senator chosen before it becomes valid as part of the Constitution.

Article XVIII. National Prohibition (1919)

The manufacture, sale, or transportation of intoxicating liquors forbidden. 1. *After one year from the ratification of this article the manufacture, sale, or transportation of intoxicating liquors within, the importation thereof into, or the exportation thereof from the United States and all territory subject to the jurisdiction thereof, for beverage purposes, is hereby prohibited.*

2. *The Congress and the several States shall have concurrent power to enforce this article by appropriate legislation.*

3. *This article shall be inoperative unless it shall have been ratified as an amendment to the Constitution by the legislatures of the several States, as provided by the Constitution, within seven years from the date of the submission thereof to the States by the Congress.* [Repealed 1933 by 21st Amendment.]

Article XIX. Woman Suffrage (1920)

Women permitted to vote. 1. The right of citizens of the United States to vote shall not be denied or abridged by the United States or by any State on account of sex.

2. Congress shall have power to enforce this article by appropriate legislation.

Article XX. Presidential and Congressional Terms (1933)

1. **Presidential, vice-presidential, and Congressional terms of office to begin in January.** The terms of the President and Vice-President shall end at noon on the 20th day of January, and the terms of Senators and Representatives at noon on the 3rd day of January, of the years in which such terms would have ended if this article had not been ratified; and the terms of their successors shall then begin.

2. **New meeting date for Congress.** The Congress shall assemble at least once in every year, and such meeting shall begin at noon on the 3rd day of January, unless they shall by law appoint a different day.

3. **Emergency presidential and vice-presidential succession.** If, at the time fixed for the beginning of the term of the President, the President-elect shall have died, the Vice-President-elect shall become President. If a President shall not have been chosen before the time fixed for the beginning of his term, or if the President-elect shall have failed to qualify, then the Vice-President-elect shall act as President until a President shall have qualified; and the Congress may

by law provide for the case wherein neither a President-elect nor a Vice-President-elect shall have qualified, declaring who shall then act as President, or the manner in which one who is to act shall be selected, and such persons shall act accordingly until a President or Vice-President shall have qualified.

4. The Congress may by law provide for the case of the death of any of the persons from whom the House of Representatives may choose a President whenever the right of choice shall have devolved upon them, and for the case of the death of any of the persons from whom the Senate may choose a Vice-President whenever the right of choice shall have devolved upon them.

5. Sections 1 and 2 shall take effect on the 15th day of October following the ratification of this article.

6. This article shall be inoperative unless it shall have been ratified as an amendment to the Constitution by the legislatures of three-fourths of the several States within seven years from the date of its submission.

Article XXI. Prohibition Repealed (1933)

1. **18th Amendment repealed.** The eighteenth article of amendment to the Constitution of the United States is hereby repealed.

2. **Local laws honored.** The transportation or importation into any State, Territory, or Possession of the United States for delivery or use therein of intoxicating liquors, in violation of the laws thereof, is hereby prohibited.

3. This article shall be inoperative unless it shall have been ratified as an amendment to the Constitution by conventions in the several States, as provided in the Constitution, within seven years from the date of the submission thereof to the States by the Congress.

Article XXII. Anti-Third Term Amendment (1951)

The President limited to two terms. 1. No person shall be elected to the office of President more than twice, and no person who has held the office of President, or acted as President, for more than two years of a term to which some other person was elected President shall be elected to the office of President more than once. But this article shall not apply to any person holding the office of President when this article was proposed by the Congress [i.e., Truman], and shall not prevent any person who may be holding the office of President, or acting as President, during the term within which this article becomes operative [i.e., Truman] from holding the office of President or acting as President during the remainder of such term.

2. This article shall be inoperative unless it shall have been ratified as an amendment to the Constitution by the legislatures of three-fourths of the several States within seven years from the date of its submission to the States by the Congress.

Article XXIII. District of Columbia Vote (1961)

1. **Presidential Electors for the District of Columbia.** The District constituting the seat of Government of the United States shall appoint in such manner as the Congress may direct:

A number of electors of President and Vice-President equal to the whole number of Senators and Representatives in Congress to which the District would be entitled if it were a State, but in no

event more than the least populous State; they shall be in addition to those appointed by the States, but they shall be considered for the purposes of the election of President and Vice-President, to be electors appointed by a State; and they shall meet in the District and perform such duties as provided by the twelfth article of amendment.
2. Enforcement. The Congress shall have the power to enforce this article by appropriate legislation. [Adopted 1961.]

Article XXIV. Poll Tax (1964)

1. Payment of poll tax or other taxes not to be prerequisite for voting in federal elections. The right of citizens of the United States to vote in any primary or other election for President or Vice-President, for electors for President or Vice-President, or for Senator or Representative in Congress, shall not be denied or abridged by the United States or any State by reason of failure to pay any poll tax or other tax.
2. Enforcement. The Congress shall have the power to enforce this article by appropriate legislation. [Adopted 1964.]

Article XXV. Presidential Succession and Disability [2] (1967)

1. Vice President to become President. In case of the removal of the President from office or of his death or resignation, the Vice President shall become President.[3]
2. Successor to Vice President provided. Whenever there is a vacancy in the office of the Vice President, the President shall nominate a Vice President who shall take office upon confirmation by a majority vote of both Houses of Congress.
3. Vice President to serve for disabled President. Whenever the President transmits to the President pro tempore of the Senate and the Speaker of the House of Representatives his written declaration that he is unable to discharge the powers and duties of his office, and until he transmits to them a written declaration to the contrary, such powers and duties shall be discharged by the Vice President as Acting President.
4. Procedure for disqualifying or requalifying President. Whenever the Vice President and a majority of either the principal officers of the executive departments or of such other body as Congress may by law provide, transmit to the President pro tempore of the Senate and the Speaker of the House of Representatives their written declaration that the President is unable to discharge the powers and duties of his office, the Vice President shall immediately assume the powers and duties of the office as Acting President.

Thereafter, when the President transmits to the President pro tempore of the Senate and the Speaker of the House of Representatives his written declaration that no inability exists, he shall resume the powers and duties of his office unless the Vice President and a majority of either the principal officers of the executive department[s] or of such other body as Congress may by law provide, transmit within four days to the President pro tempore of the Senate and the Speaker of the House of Representatives their written declaration

2. Passed by a two-thirds vote of both houses of Congress in July, 1965; ratified by the requisite three-fourths of the state legislatures, February, 1967, or well within the seven-year limit.
3. The original Constitution (Art. II, Sec. I, para. 5) was vague on this point, stipulating that "the powers and duties" of the President, but not necessarily the title, should "devolve" on the Vice President. President Tyler, the first "accidental President," assumed not only the power and duties but the title as well.

that the President is unable to discharge the powers and duties of his office. Thereupon Congress shall decide the issue, assembling within forty-eight hours for that purpose if not in session. If the Congress, within twenty-one days after receipt of the latter written declaration, or, if Congress is not in session, within twenty-one days after Congress is required to assemble, determines by two-thirds vote of both Houses that the President is unable to discharge the powers and duties of his office, the Vice President shall continue to discharge the same as Acting President; otherwise, the President shall resume the powers and duties of his office.

Article XXVI. Lowering Voting Age (1971)

1. Ballot for eighteen-year-olds. The right of citizens of the United States, who are eighteen years of age or older, to vote shall not be denied or abridged by the United States or by any State on account of age.

2. Enforcement. The Congress shall have power to enforce this article by appropriate legislation.

Article XXVII. Sex Equality (Sent to states, 1972)

1. Women's rights guaranteed. Equality of rights under the law shall not be denied or abridged by the United States or by any State on account of sex.

2. Enforcement. The Congress shall have the power to enforce, by appropriate legislation, the provisions of this article.

3. Timing. This amendment shall take effect two years after the date of ratification.

Index

Acres of Diamonds, 519-20
Acheson, Sec'y. Dean, 830-31 ff.,
    834-35
Affirmative action, 991-93
Affluent Society, The, 982-84
Agricultural Adjustment Act (1933),
    754
Aguinaldo, Emilio, 584, 586
Allied war debts, 731-35
Altgeld, John P., 557, 565
American Federation of Labor, 501,
    505
American Protective Association, 509-10
Ameringer, Oscar, 735-37, 739-40
Anarchists, 503-4, 565-66, 700-704
Anglo-Japanese Alliance, 730-31
Anti-foreignism, 700-704
Anti-imperialism, 580-81, 583
Antin, Mary, 506-7
Anti-war protesters, 912-15
Arizona, recall of judges, 627
Arms embargo (1930's), 770-73
Article X, 687-90 ff.
Ashurst, Sen. H. G., 696
Atlantic Charter (1941), 781-83
Atomic bomb, 803-7
Automobile, 711-21

Baer, George F., 606
Baker, Newton D., 665-66, 733-34
Bakers, hours of, 608-10
Bakke decision, 991-93
Banking reform, 637-39
Beecher, Catherine, 523-24
Beecher, Rev. Henry Ward, 514-16, 524
Belgium, atrocities, 645-46
Beveridge, Albert J., 581-83, 584-86
Birth control, 721-23
Bitter Cry of the Children, The, 606-8
Blacks, 447-68, 737-38, 846-52, 864-
    77, 991-1000
Blaine, James G., 483 ff.
Bonsal, Stephen, 692-94
Bonus marchers (1932), 752
Boole, Mrs. Ella A., 710-11
Brandeis, Louis D., 634-35
Brown *vs.* Board of Education of
    Topeka (1954), 846-48

Bryan, William Jennings, 562-68, 586-
    87; Sec'y., 649-50, 652-54
Bryce, James, 645-46
Buchanan, James, 540-42
Budget, balanced, 744-45

Cambodia, 907-15
Canada, 921-22, 932-33
Cappelli family, 989-91
Carnegie, Andrew, 516-19
Carter, Jimmy, 944-63
Casablanca Conference (1943), 800-801
Catholicism, 509-10, 704-7, 780
Cavalleri, Rosa, 529-31
Chafee, Zechariah, Jr., 668-69
Chandler, Zachariah, 476-78
Chiang Kai-shek, 830-33
Chicanos, 1000-1007
Chief Joseph, 535-36
Child labor, 606-8
China, and U.S., 808 ff., 830-33
Church. *See* Religion
Churchill, Winston, 781-83, 796 ff.,
    808-10
Cisneros, Evangelina, 570-71
Cities, corruption in, 601-5
Civil rights, 868-74
Civil service, 478-83. *See also* Spoils
    system
Clayton Anti-Trust Act (1914), 639
Cleveland, Grover, 483-89, 511-12,
    554, 560-61
Coal strike (1902), 606
Coin's Financial School, 557-59
Coles, Robert, 996-1000
Colombia, 589-92
Committee on Public Information, 670
Communism, 700-704, 762-65, 795 ff.,
    820 ff., 831-33, 841-45. *See also*
    Russia
Concentration camps, Cuban, 569 ff.
Congress of Industrial Organizations,
    761-65. *See also* Labor; Unions
Connally, Sen. Tom, 770-71, 827-29,
    834-35
Conscription (1917-18), 661-62
Conservation, 613-15
Conwell, Rev. Russell H., 519-20

Coolidge, Calvin, 728
Creel, George, 670
Criminals, 900–907
"Cross of Gold" speech, Bryan's, 562–65
Cuba, 569 ff.
Cuban missile crisis, 857–61
Cummins, Sen. Albert B., 633–34
Curtis, George W., 480–81
Custer, Gen. George, 533–35

Darwinian Theory. *See* Evolution
Dawes, Charles G., 743
Day, Rev. James R., 663
Deane, Gen. John R., 795–96
Depression, 1930's, 734–49
Dillon, Sidney, 491–93
Disarmament, 729–30
Discrimination, reverse, 993–96
Dooley, Mr., 506, 518, 557, 582
Doughboys, 678–80
Douglass, Frederick, 465–66
Draft: (1917–18), 661–62; Vietnam,
    894–96
Du Bois, Dr. W. E. B., 460–61
Dunne, F. P., 506, 518, 557, 582
Dust Bowl, 545

Economy, 982–91
Education, 596, 846–52
Eisenhower, Dwight D., 848–55
Elections (Presidential): 1872, 470–71;
    1876, 472–73, 475–76; 1884, 483–
    86; 1888, 489; 1920, 696–99; 1932,
    740–49; 1940, 768–69
Emancipation, 451–54
Embargo, 770–73
Energy crisis, 944–50
England, 559–60, 567–68, 645–49,
    781–85
Espionage Act (1917), 664, 668–69
Evans, George H., 538–39
Evolution, 513–16

Family, changing American, 970–82
Farmers' Alliance, 545, 547
Farmers' protest movement, 545–49
Federal Reserve Act (1913), 637–39
Feminine Mystique, The, 975–79
Ford, G. R., 933–34
Ford, Henry, 711–16
Ford Motor Company, 716–21
Forest Reserve Act (1891), 613
Forests, and T. Roosevelt, 613–15
Fourteen Points, 671–75, 683 ff., 781
Fourteenth Amendment, 846–47
Freedom of the seas, 1914–17, 646–49,
    652–60
Free enterprise, 740–41

"Free love," 523–26
Free silver, 557–68
Free Speech (1917–18), 666–69. *See
    also* Civil rights
Friedan, Betty, 975–79, 981
Fundamentalists. *See* Evolution; Religion

Galbraith, John Kenneth, 982–84
Gentlemen's Agreement (1908), 596–97
Germany: World War I, 645 ff., 650–51,
    654–55, 661–80; World War II, 770 ff.
Girdler, Tom, 761–65
Godkin, E. L., 463–65, 548–49
Gompers, Samuel, 501–3, 522–23
"Gospel of Wealth," 516–19
Grady, Henry W., 498–99
Grant, Ulysses S., 469, 472–75
Great Britain. *See* England
Great Society, 862–64
Greece, 820 ff.
Greeley, Horace, 470–71, 523
Greer, 784
Grey, Sir Edward, 647

Haines, H. S., 490–91
Haldeman, H. R., 927–31
Harding, Warren G., 689, 697–98,
    728–29
Harlan, Justice J. M., 903
Harrington, Michael, 984–88
Harris, David, 894–96
Harvard College, 844–45
Harvey, George, 687–88
Harvey, William H., 558–59
Havemeyer, Henry O., 553–54
Hawaii, Pearl Harbor, 791–95
Hay, John, 589–90, 595
Hayes, Rutherford, B., 475–76
Haymarket Riot, 504, 565
Hearst, William R., 569–71, 729–30,
    780–81
Herberg, Will, 874–75
Hill, David B., 561–62
Hiss, Alger, 814, 832, 842, 844
Hitchcock, Sen. Gilbert M., 690, 694
Hitler, Adolf, 770 ff.
Hoar, Sen. George F., 583
Ho Chi Minh, 877
Holmes, Justice Oliver W., 610
Homestead Act (1862), 542–44
Homesteads, 538–43
Hoover, Herbert, 731–32, 735, 737–38,
    740–49
Hostages, American, in Iran, 955–60
House, Col. E. M., 685–86, 692, 694
Houston, D. F., 631–32, 661–62
Howard, Rep. V. E., 539–40
Huddleston, George, 738

Huerta, Gen. Victoriano, 639 ff.
Hull, Cordell, 787–90, 797, 801–2
Humphrey, William E., 641–44

Ickes, Sec'y. Harold L., 765–67, 785–86
Impeachment, Johnson's, 454, 456–57
Immigration, 506–12
Imperialism, 569–89
Indians, 533–38
Initiative, 624–26
Integration. *See* Segregation
Interlocking directorates, 634–35
Interstate Commerce Act (1887), 494, 545
Iran, hostage crisis in, 955–60
Isolationism, 1939–41, 773–77, 779–80

Japan, 595–97, 730–31, 785–90, 791–807 *passim*, 808 ff.
Johnson, Pres. Andrew, 447 ff., 454–57
Johnson, Pres. Lyndon B., 862–64, 868–74, 880–81
Jones, Mrs. Gilbert E., 618–20
Joseph, Chief, 535–36
Judges, recall of, 626–28
Judicial decisions, recall of, 628–30
Jungle, The, 598, 599

Kansas, 544, 547–48
Kennan, George F., 814–20, 896–99
Kennedy, John F., 857–61
Kent State University, 896
Khrushchev, Nikita S., 857 ff.
Kimmel, Admiral H. E., 792–93
King, Rev. Martin Luther, Jr., 864–68, 874–75, 991
Kissinger, Henry, 912–15
Kitchin, Rep. Claude, 658–60
Knights of Labor, 501–5. *See also* Labor; Unions
Korean crisis, 834–40
Ku Klux Klan, 704–7

Labor, 554–57, 606–10, 716–21, 761–65
La Follette, Robert M., 611–13, 666–68
La Guardia, Fiorello, 708–9
Lansing, Robert, 647–49
League of Nations, 681 ff.
Lease, Mary E., 547–48
Leigh, J. W., 458–59
Lend-Lease Act, 775, 777–81, 784
Lewis, John L., 764–65
Liberal Republican Party, 469–75
Libraries, public, 518
Lindbergh, Charles A., 773–75
Lippmann, Walter, 703–4, 734–35
Literacy test, 510–12
Little Rock crisis, 848–52

Lobbying, 633–34
Lochner *vs.* New York (1905), 609–10
Lodge, Sen. H. C., 510–11; and League, 688–96
Luckner, Felix von, 707–8
Lusitania, 652–56
Lynd, Helen Merrell, 723–26
Lynd, Robert S., 723–26
Lyttleton, Capt. Oliver, 788

McAdoo, William G., 637–39
MacArthur, Gen. Douglas, 791, 836–40
McCarthy, Sen. J. R., 831–33, 841–45
McKinley, William, 550–51, 565–68, 573–76, 579–80, 586
McNamara, Robert S., 882–89
Maine, 572–75
Marshall, Gen. G. C., 823–24, 830
Marshall, Thurgood, 991–93
Marshall Plan, 823–27
Martin, Joseph W., 838
Mayo, Admiral Henry T., 639
Mead, Margaret, 979–81
Meat packers, 598–99
Mexico, 639–44
Middletown, 723–26
Mills, Rep. Roger Q., 551–52
Miranda case, 900 ff.
Monetary reform, 634–39
Money trust, 634–39
Monopoly, trusts and, 494–98
Monroe Doctrine, 593–95
Morgan, J. Pierpont, 634–37
Morton, Oliver P., 478–80
Muckraking, 598–601
Mugwumps, 484–86
Munitions, 649–51, 770–73
Muscle Shoals Bill, 740. *See also* TVA

National Organization for Women (NOW), 981
N.A.T.O., 827–30
Negro. *See* Blacks
Neutrality: 1914–17, 645–60; 1930's, 770–90
New Deal, 739, 751–69 *passim*
Nez Percés, 535–36
Nixon, Pres. R. M., 906–10, 916–23; move to impeach, 924–34
Norris, Sen. G. W., 757–59
North Atlantic Pact, 827–30
Norton, Charles E., 576
Nye, Sen. Gerald P., 770

October appeal (1918), 681–83
"Open Door Policy," 595
Organization of Petroleum Exporting Countries (OPEC), 944

Other America, The, 984–88
Owen, Robert L., 616–18

Page, Walter H., 646–47
Panama Canal, 589–92, 935–44
Panama Revolution (1903), 589–92
Paris Peace Conference, 681–87 ff.
Pearl Harbor, attacked, 791–95
Peckham, Justice Rufus W., 609–10
Peffer, Sen. William A., 554–55
Pendleton Civil Service Reform Act,
    480–81. *See also* Civil service
Perkins, Frances, 752, 798–99
Pershing, Gen. J. J., 675–78
Philadelphia, corruption in, 601–4
Philippines, 579–83, 584–89
Philippine Insurrection, 584–89
Platt Amendment (1901), 578
Plessy *vs.* Ferguson (1896), 846–47
Plunkitt, George W., 604–5
Poland, 810 ff.
Populists, 547–49
Porter, Stephen G., 651
Poverty program, 862–64
Powderly, Terence V., 501, 504–5
Powell, Lewis F., Jr., 906
Power, electric, 740–42. *See also* TVA
Prager, Robert Paul, 665
Pre-emption, 542–43
Preparedness (1917), 662–63
Progressives, 598 ff., 616 ff.
Prohibition, 707–11. *See also* Temperance
Propaganda (1914–18), 645–46 ff.,
    670–75
Protest, politics of (1960's), 891–99
Pujo Committee, 634–37
Pulitzer, Joseph, 569–70
Pullman, George M., 554–57

Quay, Sen. Matthew S., 554
Quayle, Dr. William A., 663–65
Quintanilla, Luis, 594–95

Railroads, 490–96
Reagan, Ronald, 939–44, 963–69, 1007
Recall of judges, 626–28
Recall of judicial decisions, 628–30
Reconstruction, 447–68
Reconstruction Finance Corporation,
    743
Red scare (1920's), 700–704
Referendum, 624–26
Reform movements, 598–613
Rehnquist, Justice W. H., 906
Religion, 513–16, 663–65, 705–7
Revel, Jean-François, 1009–11
Rice, George, 496–97
Richardson, A. D., 542–43
Richardson, Dorothy, 526–28

Richardson, J. C. Peter, 844–45
Riis, Jacob A., 507–8
Rockefeller, John D., 494–97
Roosevelt, Eleanor, 751–52
Roosevelt, Franklin D., 595; and Depres-
    sion, 739, 740–46, 749; and New
    Deal, 751–69 *passim;* and threat of
    war, 770–90 *passim;* and World War
    II, 791–801, 808–10
Roosevelt, James, 783
Roosevelt, Theodore, 537–38, 577–78;
    post-1903, 590–91, 593–97, 599–
    601, 610–13, 628–30; post-1917,
    662–63, 671–75, 682–83
Roosevelt Corollary, 593–95
Root, Sen. Elihu, 622–23
Rotation in office. *See* Civil service;
    Spoils system
Rough Riders, 577–78
Russia, 780–81, 795–99; post-1945,
    808–33 *passim,* 857–61. *See also*
    Communism

Sacco, Nicola, 701–4
Sackville-West, Sir Lionel, 489
Safety-valve theory, 539–40
Saloon, 522–23. *See also* Prohibition;
    Temperance
San Francisco, and Japanese, 596
Sanger, Margaret, 721–23
Santo Domingo, and T. R., 594–95
Schulz, Commander Lester, 794–95
Schurz, Carl, 447–50, 469–70, 481–83
Second front, 797–98
Segregation, 846–52
Senators, popular election of, 621–23
Shafter, Gen. William, 577
Shame of the Cities, The, 601–4
Sherman Anti-Trust Act, 610–12
Sherwood, Robert E., 753–54, 799–801
Short, Gen. W. C., 792, 794
Shuler, Rev. Bob, 705–7
Sidey, Hugh, 960–63
Sinclair, Upton, 598, 599
Slums, 507–8
Smith, Sen. Margaret C., 842–44
Smuts, Gen. Jan C., 683–85
South, 475–78, 498–500. *See also*
    Blacks; Segregation
Spanish-American War, 569–79
Spargo, John, 606–8
Spies, August, 503–4
Spock, Benjamin, 970–74
Spoils system, 469–70, 478–80. *See also*
    Civil service
Stalin, Joseph, 796–99, 808–10
Standard Oil Co., 494–97
Steel, Little, 761–65
Steffens, Lincoln, 601–4

Stettinius, Sec'y. E. R., Jr., 812–14
Stevens, Rep. Thaddeus, 457–58
Stimson, Sec'y. Henry L., 793–94
Stock watering, railroads, 491–93
Stokes, Mrs. Rose Pastor, 668
Student left, 896–99
Students for a Democratic Society, 891–94
Submarines, German, 652–54, 656–57, 784–85
Suffrage: Black, 457–63; woman, 616–21
Sugar Trust, 552–54
Sumner, William G., 580–81
Supreme Court, 765–68, 846–48, 900–907
Sussex, 656

Taft, Sen. Robert A., 829–30
Taft, William H., 616 ff., 625–28
Tammany Hall, 604–5
Tampico incident, 639
Tariff, 486–89, 550–54, 631–33
Tatlock, Prof. J. S. P., 670–71
Tax cut, Reagan's, 963–69
Taylor, Maxwell D., 877–80
Teller Amendment (1898), 578
Temperance, 521–23. *See also* Prohibition
Tennessee Valley Authority (TVA), 740, 757–61
Tenure of Office Act (1867), 456
Thayer, Judge Webster, 701–2
Thomas, Norman, 754–55
Thompson, Dorothy, 767–68
Tillman, Sen. B. R., 461–63, 560–61
Tōgō Shigenori, 787–88
Tonkin Gulf, 880
Treaty of Paris (1899), 583
Truman, Pres. Harry S., 803–33 *passim*, 835–40
Truman Doctrine, 814–23
Trumbull, Sen. Lyman, 456–57
Trusts, 494–98, 552–54, 610–13, 634–39
Turkey, and U.S. aid, 820 ff.
TVA, 740, 757–61

Unconditional surrender, W.W. II, 799–803
Underwood-Simmons Tariff, 633–34
Unions, labor, 501–5. *See also* Labor
United Nations, 810, 834 ff.
Urbanization, 506–12

Vance, Cyrus, 935–39
Vandenberg, Sen. Arthur H., 772–73, 788, 824–26

Vanzetti, Bartolomeo, 701–4
Vera Cruz incident (1914), 641
Versailles, Treaty of (1919), 683–87
Viereck, George S., 655–56
Viet Cong, 880
Vietnam War, 877–91, 916–24
Villard, Oswald G., 686–87
Voting Rights Act (1965), 874

Wagner Act (1935), 761
Wallace, Henry A., 755–57
War debts, Allied, 731–35
Warner, Charles D., 499–500
Warren, Justice Earl, 847, 900 ff.
Washington, Booker T., 451–53, 466–68
Washington Naval Conference (1922), 728–31
Watergate, 924 ff.
Watts, 874–77
Weaver, Gen. J. B., 493, 497–98, 548–49
West, 533–45, 614–15, 625
Weyler, Gen. Valeriano, 569 ff.
Wheeler, Sen. B. K., 779–80
Wheeler, Everett P., 559–60
White, Andrew D., 513–14
White, William A., 544, 700–701, 728–29
Will, George, 993–96
Willard, Frances, 521–22
Willkie, Wendell, 759–61, 777
Wilson, Edith B., 690–92, 694–95
Wilson, Harold, 881–82
Wilson, Sec'y. William L., 565
Wilson, Woodrow: belligerent, 661–80 *passim;* domestic problems, 631–44 *passim;* neutrality, 645–60 *passim;* peacemaker, 681–99 *passim;* reformer, 621–22, 624–25
Without Marx or Jesus, 1009–11
Woman suffrage, 616–21
Woman's Christian Temperance Union, 521–22, 710–11
Women: Bill of Rights for, 981–82; changing role of, 523–31; freedom for, 975–79; new goals for, 721–26
Wood, Gen. Leonard, 662
Woodford, Gen. Stewart L., 571–72, 576
Woodhull, Victoria, 523–26
World War I, 661 ff.
World War II, 791–807

Yalta Conference (1945), 808–14
Yellow journalism, 569 ff.
Yezierska, Anzia, 507